C. H. Marshall

Western Reserve and Northern Ohio Historical Society

PAMPHLETS.

Nos 1 to 22.

List of Books and Bound Pamphlets,

PRINCIPALLY HISTORICAL, ON DEPOSIT IN THE ROOM OF

WESTERN RESERVE & NORTHERN OHIO HISTORICAL SOCIETY,

CLEVELAND, OHIO,

BY CHARLES WHITTLESEY,

SUBJECT TO BE WITHDRAWN ON DEMAND.

JANUARY 1, 1872.

A.

No.
3. Adams, Rev. S. W., Biography. Cleveland, 1867.
63. American Local History. New York, 1846.
64. Alsop's Maryland. New York, 1869.
85. American Revolution. Columbus, O., 1834.
109. Arctic Journal. New York, 1852.
128. American Antiquities. Priest. Albany, 1835.
129. American Letters (in French,) 2 vols. Paris, 1788.
167. Art of War in Europe, 1854 to 1856. McClellan and Mordecai. Washington, 1860.
175. Annual Report Adj. Gen. Ohio, 1863-5.
176. do do do
179. Army Register, (U. S. A.) Washington, 1866.
186. Army Register, (Alphabetical.) New York, 1863.
202. Army Register, (Ohio Vols.) Columbus, 1862.
216. Army Regulations. New York, 1857.
6. Andrews, Rev. Alfred. History of New Britain, Conn. Chicago, 1867.

No.
240. American Review. New York, 1849.
120. Atwater. Caleb. Tour to the West. Columbus, 1850.
166. Army Medical Statistics. Washington, 1839, 1854 and 1856.
165. Agriculturist, bound vol. Columbus, 1851.
174. Army Officers, U. S. M. A. Graduates, Biographical notice, 2 vols. Cullum. New York, 1868.
73. American Revolution of 1776. Botta. Buffalo, 1854.
245. Artillery Field Instruction, U. S. A. Philadelphia, 1869.
246. Army Regulations. New York, 1857.
247. Army Dictionary. Gardner. New York, 1853.
260. Army and Navy Journal, 2 vols., 1863 to 1865. New York.
99. Agricultural Society, Hamilton Co., O. 1844. Bound pamphlets No. 12.
American Biographical Dictionary. Drake. Boston, 1872.
Army of the Cumberland. Reports of Meetings to 1871.
Army of the Potomac, Swinton. 1866.

B.

6. Badger, Rev. Joseph. Biography. Hudson, Ohio, 1851.
10 & 11. Baylies, Francis. History of New Plymouth, Mass. Boston, 1866.
92. Black Hawk. Biography. Cin'ti, 1847.
41. Beltrami, Constantino Bergamo. Biography. Italy, 1865.
46. Bouquet's Expedition against the Ohio Indians. Reprint Rob't Clarke, Cincinnati, 1868. (Duplicate.)
54. Burgoyne, Lieut. Gen. Expedition from Canada. London, 1780.
96. Bound Pamphlet. Battle of Lake Erie, by J. F. Cooper. Cooperstown, 1843.
102. Blannerhasset, Herman. Biography. Cincinnati, 1853.
119. Blue Laws of Connecticut, 1685. Hartford, 1838.
141. Bushnell's Historical Discourse. Hartford, 1851. (Bound pamphlets.)
147. Buckeye Celebration. Cincinnati, 1835. (Bound pamphlets.)
149. Boonesborough, Ky., Celebration, 1840. Moorehead.

No.
184. Battle of Pittsburgh Landing.
187. Battle of Pittsburgh Landing. Letter of Lt. Gov. Stanton. Columbus, 1862.
188. Battle of Pittsburgh Landing. Letter of Hon. Thos. Ewing. Columbus, 1862.
202. Buffalo Academy of Fine Arts, 1866.
203. Blue Book, United States. Washington, 1860.
94. Boone, Daniel. Biography. Cincinnati, 1849.
21. Bradford. Notes on the North-West. New York, 1846.

No.
201. Bross, J. A., Memorial of. Chicago, 1865.
258. Burke's European Settlements in America, 2 vols. London, 1768.
267. Boone, Daniel. Bryant. Harrisonburgh, Ky., 1813.
270. Barnard, Maj. J. G. Tehuantepec Survey. New York, 1852.
279. Bell's History of Canada, 2 vols. Montreal, 1862.
94. Boone, Daniel. Timothy Flint. Cincinnati, 1847.

C.

2. Congregational Council of the United States. Boston, 1865.
7. Champlain Valley, New York, History of. Watson. Albany, 1863.
19. Cincinnati, 1859. By Cist. (Duplicates.)
21. Church Union, Plan of. Kennedy. Hudson, Ohio, 1856.
70. Chase, Rev. Philander. Autobiography. 2 vols. Boston, 1848.
91. Canadian Insurrection, 1837. McLeod. Cleveland, 1846.
115. Coal Bank Disaster, near Zanesville, Ohio. Malta, Ohio, 1856.
161. Census U. States, 1860. (Duplicates.)
139. Cincinnati Water Works Report. Cincinnati, 1852.
163. Civil Service United States. Washington, 1868.
189. Comments on Gen. McClellan in Western Virginia. Col. Hill. Toledo, 1864.
225. Chicago Directories, 1851-2-3-4-5-6-7-8-9.
232. Census of United States, 1850. Washington, 1854.
253. Coast Survey U. S. Washington, 1867.
256. Construction cours de. Paris, 1821. Cæsar, Life of. Louis Napoleon. 2 vols. New York, 1865.

D.

61. Davis, W. H. H. Conquest of New Mexico. Doylestown, Penn., 1869.
110. Dakota, History and Resources. Yankton, Dakota, 1866.
121. Darnell, Captivity of. Philadelphia, 1854. (Duplicates.)
228. Documents, Executive U. S. A. 1840, 1848, 1860. Washington.
229. Documents, Executive U. S. A. 1845. Washington.
230. Documents, Executive U. S. A. General Land Office, 1861.
241. Documents, Executive U. S. A. and Message, 1851-2.
242. Documents, Executive U. S. A. and Message, 1846.
118. Das leben des Geo. Washington, Baltimore, 1817.
159. Documents, U. S. General Land Office. Washington, 1866.
20. Drakes, S.G. Indian Biography. Boston.
260. Davenport, Iowa. Wilkie. Davenport, 1858.
278. Denny, Maj. Ebenezer. Military Journal. Philadelphia, 1859.

E.

169, 170, 171, 172, & 173. Elements of Mammology, Herpetology, Ichthyology, Botany, and Concology. Ruschenberger. Philadelphia, 1844.
238. Eclectic Magazine. New York, 1849.
280. Eminent Mechanics. New York, 1842.
235. England, History of. Macauley. Vol. 1. New York, 1849.
283. Edwards. History of Illinois prior to 1833. Springfield, 1870.

F.

26 & 27. Fire Lands, Pioneer. Sandusky, 1859 and 1860.
43. Fire Lands. Pioneer, Sandusky, 1858.
98. Fitch, John. Biography. Wescott. Philadelphia, 1857.
236. Fremont's Report of Explorations. Washington, 1845.
218. Field Fortifications. Mahan. New York, 1861.
164. Family Magazine. Cincinnati, 1836.
286. Fathers of New England, 6 vols. Boston, 1870.
248. Fitch, John. Petition to Kentucky Legislature relating to a Monument, 1843.

G.

207. Grant, Lieut. Gen. Army Report, 1864-1865.
277. Gordon's History of Pennsylvania prior to 1776. Philadelphia, 1829.

H.

24. Hull, Gen. William. His defence. Hartford, 1814.
48. Hunter's Indian Captivity. London, 1823.
51. Henry, Alexander. Travels in Canada. New York, 1809.
66. Huntington Family Genealogy. Stamford, Conn., 1863.
67. Holt Family Genealogy. Albany, 1864.
69. Historical Tracts. Peter Force. 4 vols. Washington, 1838.
101. Harrison, Gen. W. H. Biography. Montgomery. Cleveland, 1852.
117. Harrison, W. H. Biography. Cincinnati, 1845.
144. Herald of Truth, 1 bound vol. Cincinnati, 1847.
142. Hesperian, vol. No. 3, bound. Cincinnati, 1839.
158. Heckewelder, John. Nations Indienne. Paris, 1822.
259. Histoire Philosophique, (without name or date.)
262. Hazard's Annals of Pennsylvania, 1609 to 1682. Philadelphia, 1850.
285. Hotchkiss' Western New York. New York, 1848.

I. & J.

No.
36. Jones, David. Journal Northwest of the Ohio River, 1772-3, Reprint. New York, 1865.
83. Illinois, History of. Reynolds. Bellville, Ill., 1852.
88. Illinois, History of. Brown. New York 1844.
123. Indian Narratives. Claremont, N. H., 1854.
182. Jackson, Gen. Andrew. Sword of, &c. Washington, 1855.
15. Iowa, Hand-book of. Parker. Boston, 1856.

No.
75. Jesuits in North America. Parkman. Boston, 1867.
226. Illinois, Directory of, 1860.
1. India, Ancient and Modern. Allen. Boston and Cleveland, 1856.
217. Infantry Tactics. Hardee. 2 vols.
266. Johnston. Captivity, Narrative, &c., 1790. New York, 1837.
275. a,b&c. Jesuits. Relations. French. 3 vols. Reprint. Quebec, 1858.
280. Iowa. Annals complete, 1863 to 1870.
281. Indian Treaties and Laws, from 1633 to 1831. Washington City, 1832.

K.

50. Kentucke, Histoire de. Paris, 1785.
32. Keating's Expedition to the Mississippi River, 2 vols. London, 1825.
114. Knight & Slover's Narrative. Reprint. Cincinnati, 1867.

L.

37. Lake Champlain, History of. Albany, 1866.
56. Logan and Cresap. Albany, 1861.
84. Letters from the West. London, 1828.
113. Lewis and Clark's Narrative. Dayton, 1847.
206. Lucknow. India, Defence of. Cleveland, 1858.
223. Lallemande's Artillery. NewYork, 1820.
49. La Salle's Last Voyage. Joutel. London, 1714.
249. Land Office Report. Washington, 1853.
274. Lossing. Pictorial History of the U. S. New York, 1857. (Duplicates.)
279. Lossing. War of Independence. New York, 1849.

M.

28. Minnesota. its place among the States. Hartford, 1860.
29. Minnesota Historical Soc'y Collections. St. Paul, 1867.
30. Minnesota Historical Soc'y Collections. St. Paul, 1865.
47. Morse's Report on the Indians. New Haven, 1822.
60. Maine Historical Society Collections. Portland, 1869.
77. Minnesota, History of. Neill. Philadelphia, 1858.
122. Medina County, Ohio, History of. Northrop. Medina, 1861.
168. Military Commission to Europe, 1855. 2 vols. Washington, 1860.
220. Manual of the Bayonet. New York, 1860.
225. Manual of Artillery. Gibbon. New York, 1860.
71. Mississippi, Discovery of. Schoolcraft. Philadelphia, 1855.
82. Marshall and Putnam counties, Illinois, History of. Dillon. 1860.
152. Mackenzie's Voyages to the Arctic Sea. 2 vols. New York, 1814.
154. Michigan, Early History of. Sheldon. New York, 1856.
243. Merchants Magazine, vol. 20. New York, 1847.
138. McKenney's Tour to the Lakes. Baltimore, 1827.
146. Mississippi Valley Directory. Cincinnati, 1848.
178. Military Academy U. S. Register of Graduates. New York, 1850.
250. Merchants Magazine. New York, 1847.
254. Medical Statistics U. S. A. Washington, 1856.
258. Meteorological Report. Espy. Washington, 1857.
259. Meteorology. New York. Hough. Albany, 1855.
269. McDonald. Sketches. Cincinnati, 1838.
272. Michaux. Travels in the West. London, 1805.

MILITARY PAMPHLETS, CASE NO. 1.

Orders Adjutant General Ohio, 1861.
Orders Department of Missouri, 1861.
Orders Department of Mississippi, 1861.
U. S. Military Academy. Services of graduates. (Mansfield,) 1847.
Army Register, 1861. Do. 1862.

MILITARY PAMPHLETS, CASE NO. 2.

Ohio Volunteers Register, 1862; Ohio Adj't General's Report, 1861-2-3 ; Ohio Q. M. General's Report, 1861; Ohio Militia Laws, 1861; Ohio Volunteers at battle of Shiloh Church; Lt. Gov. B. F. Stanton and Hon. Thos. Ewing on same; Report of Military Commission Cincinnati 1865.

MILITARY PAMPHLETS, CASE NO. 3.

Army Register, 1863; Campaign Shenandoah, Gen'l Patterson, 1861; Report on the Navy Yards, 1862; Colonel Worthington's Court Martial, Memphis, 1862: Col. Hill on the West Virginia Campaign, 1864; Ohio Report on Clothing of Troops, 1861; Report on Military Arrests, 1864; Report on the assault at Petersburg, 1864; Report on battle of Shiloh Church, 1862; do. battle of Fredericksburgh, 1864; Ages of U. S. Volunteers, 1866; Military Rambles, (Turchin); Outpost and patrol duty; Gen. Grant's Report, 1865.

N.

8. New York, History of. Howe & Barber. 1841.
35. Native Races of the Indian Archipelago, or Papuans. New York, 1853.
39. Niagara Frontier. O. H. Marshall. Buffalo, 1865.
53. North America. Concise Account of. Rob't Rogers. London, 1764.

No.
55. New Gate, Conn., History of. Albany, 1860.
93. Napoleonic Ideas. Louis Napoleon, New York, 1859.
130. New York Historical Soc'y Collections, New York, 1849.

No.
89. New York Canal Papers, and Public Documents. New York, 1825.
252. New York. Documentary History. Albany, 1849.
261. Norfolk, Va. Forest. Philada., 1853.

O.

34. Ohio. History and Antiquities. Howe. Cincinnati, 1847.
78. Ohio Gazetteer. Columbus, 1837.
106. Ohio Legislative Reports. Columbus, 1840-1844.
108. Ohio Gazetteer. Columbus, 1833.
127. Ohio Gazetteer. Columbus, 1841.
153. Ohio, History of. Taylor. Cincinnati, 1854.
155. Olden Time Magazine. Craig. 2 vols. Pittsburgh, 1848.
160. Ohio Statistics. Report of Commissioners. Mansfield. Columbus, 1857, 1858, 1859 and 1861.
177. Ohio Military Regulations. Col., 1854.
185. Ohio. Report of Quartermaster General. Columbus, 1862.
191. Ohio. Acts Relating to the Militia. Columbus, 1864.
192, Ohio. Acts Relating to the Militia.
202. Ohio Volunteers, Register of. Columbus, 1862.
215. Our Battery. Cutter. Cleveland, 1864.
58. Ohio Historical Society's Transactions. Part 1 and 2. Columbus and Cincinnati, 1838-39, and Whittlesey's Address, 1842.
106. Ohio. Reports of Public Officers, 1840-44. (Bound Pamphlets.)

P.

20. Pioneer Women of the West. Mrs. Ellett. New York, 1852.
44 Pre-Columbian Discovery of America. De Costa. Albany, 1868.
72. Pioneer History of Ohio. Cincinnati, 1848.
76. Pontiac, Conspiracy of. Parkman. Boston, 1855.
90. Pittsburgh, History of. Craig. Pittsburgh, 1851.
156. Pioneer Magazine. 2 vols. Williams. Cincinnati, 1842-3.
205. Patrol Duty, Instructions on. Mahan.
224. Prisoners in Mexico.
271. Pennsylvania Historical Soc'y Memoirs. Vol. 6. Philadelphia, 1858.

PAMPHLETS BOUND.

22. Fremont's Report, 1839.
Mythology of the Algonquins. Squier.
Western Farmer and Gardener. Cincinnati, 1844. 3 numbers.
Ohio. Report on Public Lands, 1847.
Michigan. Report on Mineral Rights, 1846.
Farmington, Conn., Historical Discourse. Porter. Hartford, 1841,
Adams, John Quincy, Biography of. Parker. Hartford, 1848.

PAMPHLETS BOUND.

42. Pittsburgh last hundred years. Upfold. Pittsburgh, 1845.
Military Academy U. S. Graduates to 1845.
Oregon Question, British view of. 1845.
Cleveland & Warren Railroad Report, 1838.
Ohio Railroad Report, 1837.
Hanging Rock Railroad Report, 1837.

PAMPHLETS BOUND.

96. Battle of Lake Erie. Cooper. Cooperstown, 1843.
Isle Royale Mining Company, Report of. Cassells. 1843.
Hamilton County Agricultural Society, Report of, 1844.
Cleveland & Columbus Railroad Report, 1846.
Pacific Railroad, Petition for, by A. Whitney, 1843.
Army Uniform.

PAMPHLETS BOUND.

99. Tallmadge, History of. 1842.
West Point Merit Roll, 1844.
Hamilton Co. Agricultural Soc'y, 1844.
Cleveland, History of, 1842.

PAMPHLETS BOUND.

105. Kirtland's Horticultural Address, Oberlin, 1845.
Cleveland & Columbus Railroad Report, 1846.
Northern Lakes and Southern Invalids. Drake. Louisville, 1842.
National Magazine, vol. 2, No. 7, 1845.
Journal and Review, vol. 1, No. 1. Cincinnati, 1846.

PAMPHLETS BOUND.

105. Commercial Review, vol. 1, No. 2. Cincinnati, 1846.
Cleveland Mining Company. Articles of Association, 1846.
Superior Copper Co., Report of, 1846.
Oneota or Red Race of America, 1844.
Military Resources of the West. Washington, 1845.
Lake Superior Copper Company, Report, 1845. Jackson.

PAMPHLETS BOUND.

106. Ohio Legislature, Reports 1840-44.
Ohio. Common Schools Report, Jan. 1842.
Ohio, Deaf and Dumb Asylum Report, 1840.
Ohio. Blind Asylum Report, Jan., 1840.
Ohio. Deaf and Dumb Asylum Report, 1841.
Ohio. State Prison Report, Dec., 1841.
Ohio. Public Works Report, Jan., 1842.
Ohio. State Auditor Report, Dec., 1844.
Ohio. Public Works Report, Dec., 1844.

PAMPHLETS BOUND.

107. Smithsonian Report, 1869.
Pension Laws U. S., 1869.
Patent Office Instructions. Squier.
Volcanos, Central America.
Interoceanic Canal, Central America.
Drift Deposits, Milwaukee, Wis. Lapham.
The Ocean. Desor.

No.
107. Ohio. Governor's Message, 1850. Ford.
Mercantile Library, Cincinnati, 1850.
Austrio-Hungarian Question. Daniel Webster.
Historical Discourse. W. D. Gallagher, 1850.
Lake Shore Railroad Report, 1850.
Ohio. Report on Banks, 1850.
Algonquin, Condition of. Squier.

PAMPHLETS BOUND.

139. Cincinnati Water Works Report, 1852.
Penn'a & Ohio Railroad Report, 1850.
Marietta & Cin'ti Railroad Report, 1851.
Erie & Franklin, Penn., Railroad and Canal Report, 1850.
Lake Shore Railroad Report, 1850.
Lake Shore Railroad Report, 1852.
Clevel'd & Pitts. Railroad Report, 1846.
Western Reserve College, 1851.
Mercantile Library, Cincinnati, 1851.
Mercantile Library, Cincinnati, 1852.
Gold Mines, Sonora, 1852.
Patent Office Forms.
Supreme Court Report. Irwin's Heirs against Nicholas Longworth.

PAMPHLETS BOUND.

140. Railroad Convention, St. Louis, Mo., Nov., 1852.
North Mo. Railroad Convention, Nov., 1852.
Zanesville & Coshocton Railroad Report, 1853.
Bellefontaine & Indiana Railroad Reports, 1853 and 1856.
Akron Branch Railroad Reports Nos. 1 and 2, 1853.

PAMPHLETS BOUND.

141. Ohio. Board of Public Works Report, 1852.
Ohio. Deaf and Dumb Asylum Report, 1852.
Ohio. Auditor of State's Report, 1852.
Jared Sparks and Lord Mahon, Historical.
Hartford, Conn., Historical. Bushnell.
Shields, Hon. James. Speech on Ireland.
Ohio. Governor's Address. Wood. 1852.
Charles Sumner. Address to Kossuth.
William Johnson Slave Case, Kentucky, April, 1846.

No.
141. Cass, Lewis. Welcome to Kossuth, Dec. 1851.
Smithsonian Institute Report, 1850.
Hygrometric Tables. Report. Bache. 1857.

PAMPHLETS BOUND.

147. Buckeye Celebration, Forty-seventh Anniversary, 1835.
Morehead. Speech on Colonization.
Adams, John Quincy. Address. Cincinnati, 1843.
Pennsylvania and Virginia Boundary Question. Craig. 1843.
Fitch, John. Watson. 1843.
Cincinnati Report of Common Schools, 1843.
147. Memorial on the Tariff, Cincinnati, 1842.
Cass, Lewis and Dan. Webster. Correspondence on the English Treaty, 1842.
Cincinnari Astronomical Society Address. Burnett. 1844.
Cincinnati Memorial, Ohio and Mississippi Rivers, 1844.

PAMPHLETS BOUND.

148. Railroad Convention at Harrisburg, 1838
Northmen. Discoveries of North America, A. D. 900.
Military Memorial. Gen. Gaines. 1840.
Ohio. State Auditor's Report, 1840.
Ohio. Governor's Address. Lucas. 1836.
Ohio, Report on Public Instruction in Europe, 1837, Stow.
Kentucky Internal Improvement Report, 1837.
Webster, Daniel. Speech on Finances. 1840.

PAMPHLETS, BOUND.

244. Canfield, Rev. S. B. Sermon. Cleveland, 1852.
British Free Trade.
Homeopathic College, 1853. Brainerd.
Natural Science. California Academy, 1853.
Cincinnati Mercantile Library Report, 1853.
Daniel Webster, Life of. 1852.
Chicago, Trade and Commerce of. 1856.
Niagara Ship Canal, and Illinois River and Canal Report, 1834. Roberts.

287. Lake Superior Railroads, 1854--1856.

R.

74. Rhode Island Colonial Records, 1780 to 1783. Vol. 9. Providence, 1864.
81. Richardson's, Sir John, Arctic Expeditions. New York, 1852.
192. Reply to H. L. Burnett, Judge Advocate, (Suratt case.) Cincinnati, 1865.
227. Railroad Journal, 1843.
273. A & B } Rhode Island Historical Soc. Providence, 1835. 2 vols., 2 and 3.
288. Ruggles' History of Suffield, Conn. Springfield, Mass., 1859.

S.

4. Salem Witchcraft. Upham. 2 vols. Boston, 1867.
11. Sons and Daughters of Newport, R. I. Mason. 1867.
20. Statistics, &c. Bartlett. Rochester, 1857.
23. Schoolcraft, Henry R. The Indian in his Wigwam. New York, 1848.
45. Sexagenary. Bloodgood. Albany, 1866.
79. Sparks' American Biography. Vol. 6. Boston, 1845.
100. Sketches of Western Methodism. Finley. Cincinnati, 1856.
104. Stone, William L. History of Wyoming. Albany, 1864.
127. Stobo, Capt. Robert, Memoirs of. Pittsburg, 1854. (Duplicates.)
197. Smithsonian Institute, Guide to. Washington, 1861.
180. Shenandoah Valley Expedition. Patterson. Philadelphia, 1865.

No.
95. Summit County, History of. Bierce. Akron, 1854.
251. Smithsonian Reports, 1857, '59, '61, '62, 63 (dup.,) '67, '68.
255. Stone Cutting, Minutes on. 1831.
268. Spencer, O. M. Indian Captivity. 1834. Cincinnati; reprint New York.
276. Sabin's Bibliotheca Americana.
284. Sergeant Winthrop. Braddock's Expedition. Philadelphia, 1855.

T.

13. Toledo War. W. V. Way. Perrysburg, 1869. (Duplicate.)
25. Tallmadge Semi-Centennial Celebration. Akron, 1857.
59. Tennessee, History of. Putnam. Nashville, 1859.
125. Tecumseh, Life of. Drake Cincinnati, 1852.
99. Tallmadge, Ohio, History of. Whittlesey. Cleveland, 1842. (Bound pamphlets No. 12.) Hamilton Agricultural Society, 1844. West Point Merit Roll, 1844.

V.

52. Virginia, Notes on. Jefferson. Baltimore, 1800.

W.

10. Winthrop, Mass., History of. Thruston. Portland, 1855.
14. Western Reserve Register. Hudson, 1852.
33. Western Annals. Albach. Pittsburg, 1856.
40. Washington's Journal, 1754. London, 1754.
68. Winchell, Family Genealogy of. Winchell. Ann Arbor, 1869.
87. Whittlesey, Charles. Fugitive Essays. Hudson, 1852.
103. Western Adventures. McClung. Dayton, 1854.
112. West, a New Guide to. Cincinnati, 1848.
113. Wisconsin, History of. Lapham. Milwaukee, 1844.
124. Wallace, Poems of. Cincinnati, 1837.
131. Wisconsin, its Resources, &c. Philadelphia, 1857.
132. Wisconsin Gazetteer. Madison, 1853.
133. Wisconsin Historical Society. Madison, 1855.
134, 135, and 136. Wisconsin Historical Collections; vols. 1, 2, 3 and 4.
137. Western Monthly Magazine, 2 volumes. Cincinnati, 1833 to 1837.
145. Western Journal. St. Louis, 1848.
150. Western Magazine. Bound Pamphlets. Cincinnati.
173. War of the Rebellion, Report on the Conduct of. 3 Parts. Washington, 1863.
173 *a*. Ditto. Washington, 1865.
181. War. Report of General McClellan.
190. War of the Rebellion. Report of McCook and Brown. Columbus, 1861.
195. War of the Rebellion. Evidence in the Memphis Cases, Tenn.
198. War of the Rebellion. U. S. Service Magazine, Vol. 1, No. 6. N. York, 1864.
199. War of the Rebellion. Report of Committee on Military Arrests.
213. War of the Rebellion. U. S. Soldiers, Ages of. New York, 1866.
221. War of the Rebellion. General Orders. Washington, 1861.
222. War, Science of. 2 vols. New York, 1817.
234. Western Law Journal, Vol. 10. Cincinnati, 1853.
239. Whig Review. New York, 1845 to 1846.
219. West Point, History of, and Merit Rolls. Philadelphia, 1840.
264. Wayne, Gen. Anthony. New York, 1860.
265. Winchester's (Gen.) Campaign of 1812. Darnell. Philadelphia, 1854.
War of the Rebellion, Twelve decisive Battles of. Swinton. New York, 1867.

MISCELLANEOUS.

57. History of the Line, &c., 1728. Byrd. 2 vols. Richmond, 1866.
86. Essays and Reports. Cleveland, 1842.
116. Pennsylvania and Virginia Boundary. Pittsburg, 1843.
162. U. S. Official Register. New York, 1863.
194. Female Seminary, Cleveland. Eleventh Annual Report.
204. Army Register, U. S. A. New York, 1862.
208. State Law College, Catalogue of. Cleveland, 1865.
209 & 210. Pennsylvania Academy of Fine Arts. Thirty-ninth Catalogue, 1862.
211. Cleveland Medical College, 1864 & 1865.
231. Bound Volume of Pamphlets, Ohio 1838 to 1839.
237. Lincoln and Douglas' Political Debate.

SCRAP AND MEMORANDA BOOKS.—War of the Rebellion, 1861-2. 3 vols.—General Scrap Books, 1840 to 1860. 4 vols.—General Memoranda Books, 1830 to 1865. 5 vols.—Antiquities of the West, 1838 to 1872. 3 vols.—Field Notes, 1838 to 1872. 32 vols.—Historical Letters, 1800 to 1825. 3 vols.—Pamphlets in pamphlet cases. Vols. 1 to 14 inclusive.—Maps in pamphlet cases. Vols. 15 to 21 inclusive.

LIST OF PAMPHLETS.

No. 1.—Battle of Frenchtown, Michigan, Jan., 1813.
Rev. Thomas P. Dudley.

No. 2.—Judges of Supreme Court of Ohio, 1803–1854.
Alfred T. Goodman.

No. 3.—War of 1812. *Papers of Elisha Whittlesey.*

No. 4.—First White Child in Ohio. *A. T. Goodman.*

No. 5.—Ancient Earth Works of the Cuyahoga Valley.
Col. Charles Whittlesey.

No. 6.—First White Settlers in Ohio. *A. T. Goodman.*

No. 7.—War of 1812, Selection No. 2.

No. 8.—Indian Affairs, Detroit, 1706. *Papers of Gen. Cass.*

No. 9.—Archæological Frauds. *Col. Charles Whittlesey.*

No. 10.—Annual Meeting, May, 1872—Death of Mr. Goodman.

No. 11.—Ancient Rock Sculptures, Barnesville, Belmont Co., O.
Ancient Mound, Hardin Co., O.

No. 12.—War of 1812, Selection No. 3.

No. 13.—Col. Bradstreet's Expedition, 1764, Selection No. 1

No. 14.—Same, Selection No. 2.

No. 15.—War of 1812. *Papers of Major George Tod.*

No. 16.—Annual Meeting, May, 1873—Origin of the State of Ohio.

No. 17.—War of 1812, Selection No. 5.

No. 18.—War of 1812, Selection No. 6.
Papers of Maj. Tod and Gen. S. Perkins.

No. 19.—War of 1812, Selection No. 7.

No. 20.—Northwest Territory, Discovery and Ownership.
Hon. Jas. A. Garfield.

No. 21.—Annual Meeting, May, 1874.

No. 22.—Battle of Frenchtown. *Rev. Thos. P. Dudley.*
Major Isaac Craig on Lake Erie, 1782.
White Men as Scalpers.
Thos. Hutchins, Geographer General United States, 1779–1788.

Western Reserve Historical Society,

CLEVELAND, O., AUGUST, 1870.

HISTORICAL AND ARCHÆLOGICAL TRACTS.

NUMBER ONE.

BATTLE AND MASSACRE AT FRENCHTOWN, MICHIGAN,

JANUARY, 1813

BY REV. THOMAS. P. DUDLEY,

ONE OF THE SURVIVORS.

The following incidents relating to the march of a detachment of Kentucky troops under Colonel Lewis to Frenchtown, on the River Raisin, Michigan, January, 1813; the battles of the 18th and 22d; the massacre of the prisoners, and the march to Fort George, on the Niagara river, were written by the Rev Thomas P. Dudley, of Lexington, Kentucky, May 26, 1870, and indorsed as follows:

A. T. Goodman, Esq., Secretary Western Reserve Historical Society:

DEAR SIR: I take pleasure in forwarding to your society an interesting and *reliable* narrative, by the Rev. Thomas P. Dudley, of this city. Very truly yours,

LESLIE COOMBS.

LEXINGTON, June 1st, 1870.

On the seventeenth day of January, 1813, a detachment of five hundred and fifty men, under command of Colonel William Lewis, with Colonel John Allen, and Majors Ben. Graves and George Madison, from the left wing of the Northwest Army, was ordered to Frenchtown, on the River Raisin, where it was understood a large nnmber of British had collected, and were committing depredations on the inhabitants of that village. On the 17th, at night, the detachment encamped at the mouth of Swan Creek, on the Maumee of the lake. On the 18th, they took up the line of march, meeting a number of the inhabitants retreating to the American camp, opposite to where Fort Meigs was subsequently built. Our troops inquired whether the British had any artillery, to which the reply was, "They have two pieces about large enough to kill a mouse." They reached the River Raisin about three o'clock in the afternoon, and while crossing the river on the ice the British began firing their swivels, when the American troops were ordered to drop their knapsacks on the ice. Reaching the opposite shore, they raised a yell, some crowing like chicken cocks, some barking like dogs, and others calling, "Fire away with your mouse cannon again." The troops were disposed as follows: The right battalion commanded by Colonel Allen, the center by Major Madison, the left by Major Graves. The latter battalion was ordered to dislodge the enemy from the position occupied by them, "being the same occupied by the American troops in the battle of the twenty-second," during which the right and center were ordered to remain where they were, in the open field, until Major Graves's command should force the enemy to the woods. While Graves was driving the enemy occasional balls from the woods, opposite Colonel Allen's command, wounded some of his men. Hence Colonel Allen ordered a partial retreat of some forty or fifty yards, so as to place his men out of reach of the Indian guns. Just as this order was accomplished, we discovered, from the firing, that Major Graves had driven the enemy to the woods, when he was ordered to advance the right and center. Up to this time the fighting was done bv Major Graves's battalion. So soon as the right and center reached the woods the fighting became general and most obstinate, the enemy resisting every inch of ground as they were compelled to fall back. During three hours the battle raged, the American detachment lost eleven killed and fifty-four wounded. About dusk Major Graves was sent by Colonel Lewis to stop the pursuit of the enemy, and direct the officers commanding the right and center, who had been hotly engaged in the conflict, and had killed many of the enemy, to return to Frenchtown, bearing the killed for interment, and the wounded for treatment. Nothing of importance occurred until the morning of the 20th, when General Winchester, with a command of two hundred men, under Colonel Wells, reached Frenchtown. Wells's command was ordered to encamp on the right of the detachment, who fought the battle of the 18th, and to fortify. The spies were out continually, and brought word on the 21st that the enemy were advancing in considerable force to make battle. On the 21st morning Wells asked leave to return to the camp, which he had recently left, for his baggage. General Winchester declined giving leave, informing Wells that we would certainly and very soon be attacked. In the afternoon Wells again applied for leave to return for his baggage. General Winchester again replied, "The spies bring intelligence that the enemy have reached Stony Creek, five miles from here. If you are disposed to leave your command in the immediate vicinity of the enemy, when a battle is certain, you can go." Wells left and went back.

On the 22d, just as the reveille was arousing the troops, (about daybreak,) the first gun was fired. Major Graves had been up some hours, and had gone to the several companies of his battalion, and roused them. Upon the firing of the first gun he immediately left his quarters and ordered his men to stand to their arms. Very many bombs were discharged by the enemy, doing, however, very little execution, most of them bursting in the air, and the fighting became general along the line, the artillery of the enemy being directed mainly to the right of our lines, where Wells's command had no protection but a common rail fence, four or five rails high. Several of the Americans on that part of the line were killed and their fence knocked down by the cannon balls, when General Winchester ordered the right to fall back a few steps and reform on the bank of the river, where they would have been protected from the enemy's guns. Unfortunately, however, that part of the line commenced retreating, and reaching Hull's old trace along the lane, on either side of which the grass was so high as to conceal the Indians. At this time, Colonels Lewis and Allen, with a view of rallying the retreating party, took one hundred men from the stockade and endeavored to arrest their flight. Very many were killed and wounded, and others made prisoners, among the former, Colonel Allen, Captains Simpson, Price, Edmundson, Mead, Dr. Irwin, Montgomery, Davis, McIlvain and Patrick, and of the latter, General Winchester, Colonel Lewis, Major Overton, &c. The firing was still kept up by the enemy on those within the pickets and returned with deadly effect. The Indians, after the retreat of the right wing, got around in the rear of the picketing, under the bank, and on the same side of the river, where the battle was raging, and killed and wounded several of our men. It is believed that the entire number of killed and wounded within the pickets did not exceed one dozen, and the writer doubts very much whether, if the reinforcements had not come, those who fought the first battle, although their number had been depleted by sixty-five, would not have held their ground, at least until reinforcements could have come to their relief. Indeed, it was very evident the British very much feared a reinforcement, from their hurry in removing the prisoners they had taken, from the south to the west of the battle ground, and in the direction of Fort Malden, from which they sent a flag, accompanied by Dr. Overton, aid to General Winchester, demanding the surrender of the detachment, informing they had Generals Winchester and Lewis, and in the event of refusal to surrender, would not restrain their Indians. Major Graves being wounded, Major Madison was now left in command, who, when the summons to surrender came, repaired to the room in which Major Graves and several other wounded officers were, to consult with them as to the propriety of surrendering. It is proper here to state that our ammunition was nearly exhausted. It was finally determined to surrender, requiring of the enemy a solemn pledge for the security of the wounded. If this was not unhesitatingly given, determined to fight it out, but O, the scene which now took place! The mortification at the thought of surrendering the Spartan band who had fought like heroes, the tears shed, the wringing of hands, the swelling of hearts, indeed, the scene beggars description. Life seemed valueless. Our Madison replied to the summons, in substance, "We will not surrender without a guarantee for the safety of the wounded, and the return of side-arms to the officers." (We did not intend to be dishonored.) The British officer haughtily responded: "Do you, sir, claim the right to dictate what terms I am to offer?" Major Madison replied: "No, but I intend to be understood as regards the only terms on which we will agree to surrender." Captain William Elliott, who had charge of the Indians, it was agreed should be left with some men, whom it was said would afford ample protection until carryalls could be brought from Malden to transport the prisoners there, but the sequel proved they were a faithless, cowardly set. The British were in quite a hurry, as were their Indian allies, to leave after the surrender. Pretty soon Captain Elliott came into the room where Major Graves, Captain Hickman, Captain Hart, and the writer of this (all wounded) were quartered. He recognized Captain Hart, with whom he had been a *room-mate*, at Hart's father's in Lexington, Kentucky. Hart introduced him to the other officers, and after a short conversation, in which he (Elliott) seemed quite restless and a good deal agitated, (he, I apprehend, could have readily told why,) as he could not have forgotten the humiliation he had contracted in deceiving Hart's family, pecuniarily. He proposed borrowing a horse, saddle and bridle for the purpose of going immediately to Malden, and hurrying on sleighs to remove the wounded. Thence assuring Captain Hart especially of the hospitality of his house, and begging us not to feel uneasy; that we were in no danger; that he would leave three interpreters, who would be an ample protection to us. He obtained Major Graves's horse, saddle and bridle, and left, which was the last we saw of Captain Elliott. We shall presently see how Elliott's pledges were fulfilled. On the next morning, the morning of the massacre, between daybreak and sunrise, the Indians were seen approaching the houses sheltering the wounded. The house in which Major Graves, Captains Hart and Hickman and the writer were, had been occupied as a tavern The Indians went into the cellar and rolled out many barrels, forced in their heads and began drinking and yelling. Pretty soon they came crowding into the room where we were, and in which there was a bureau, two beds, a chair or two and perhaps a small table. They forced the drawers of the bureau, which were filled with towels, table cloths, shirts, pillow slips, &c. About this time Major Graves and Captain Hart left the room. The Indians took the bed clothing, ripped open the bed tick, threw out the feathers, and apportioned the ticks to themselves. They took the overcoat, close bodied coat, hat and shoes from the writer. When they turned to leave the room, just as he turned, the Indians tomahawked Captain Hickman in less than six feet from me. I went out on to a porch, next the street, when I heard voices in a room at a short distance, went into the room where Captain Hart was engaged in conversation with the interpreter. He asked: "What do the Indians intend to do with us." The reply was: "They intend to kill you." Hart rejoined: "Ask liberty of them for me to make a speech to them before they kill us." The interpreters replied: "They can't understand." "But," said Hart, "you can interpret for me." The interpreters replied: "If we undertook to interpret for you, they will as soon kill us as you." It was said, and I suppose truly, that Captain Hart subsequently contracted with an Indian warrior to take him to Amherstburg, giving him $600. The *brave* placed him on a horse and started. After going a short distance they met another company of Indians, when the one having charge of Hart spoke of his receiving the $600 to take Hart to Malden. The other Indians insisted on sharing the money, which was refused, when some altercation took place, resulting in the shooting of Hart off the horse by the Indian who received the money. A few minutes after leaving the room, where I had met Hart and the interpreters, and while standing in the snow eighteen inches deep, the Indians brought Captain Hickman out on the porch, stripped of clothing except a flannel shirt, and tossed him out on the snow within a few feet of him, after which he breathed once or twice and expired. While still standing in the yard, without coat, hat or shoes, Major Graves approached me in charge of an Indian, and asked if I had been taken. I answered no. He proposed that I should go along with the Indian who had taken him. I replied "No, if you are safe I am satisfied." He passed on and I never saw him afterward. While standing in the snow two or three Indians approached me at different times, and I made signs that the ball I received was still in my shoulder. They shook their heads, leaving the impression that theydesigned a more horrid death for me. I felt that it would be a mercy to me if they would shoot me down at once, and put me out of my misery. About this time I placed my hand under my vest, and over the severe wound I had received, induced thereto by the cold, which increased my suffering. Another young warrior passed on and made signs that the ball had hardly struck and passed on, to which I nodded assent. He immediately took off a blanket capot (having two) and tied the sleeves around my shoulders, and gave me a large red apple. The work of death on the prisoners being well nigh done and the houses fired, he started with me toward Detroit. After going a short distance he discovered my feet were suffering, being without shoes, and he having on two pair of moccasins, pulled off the outer pair, and put them on my feet. Having reached Stony Creek, five miles from the battle ground, where the British and Indians camped the night before the battle of the 22d of January. Their camp fires were still burning, and many had stopped with their prisoners to warm. In a short time I discovered some commotion among them. An Indian tomahawked Ebenezer Blythe, of Lexington. Immediately the Indian who had taken me resumed his march, and soon overtook his father, whom I understood to be an old chief. They stopped by the roadside, and directed me to a seat on a log and proceeded to *paint me*. We reached Brownstown about sundown in the evening, when having a small ear of corn we placed it in the fire for a short time, and then made our supper on it. A blanket was spread on bark in front of the fire, and I pointed to lie down. My captor finding my neck and shoulder so stiff that I could not get my head back, immediately took some of his plunder and placed under my head and covered me with a blanket. Many Indians, with several prisoners, came into the council house afterward, and they employed themselves dressing, in hoops, the scalps of our troops. There was the severest thunder storm that night witnessed at that time of the year. The water ran under the blanket, and the ground being lower in the centre around the fire, I awoke some time before day and found myself lying in the water, possibly two inches deep, got up and dried myself as well as I could. About daybreak, they resumed their march toward Detroit, stopping on the way and painting me again. We reached Detroit about three o'clock in the afternoon, and as we passed along the street, a number of women approached us, and entreated the Indians not to kill me. Passing on, we met two British officers on horseback, and stopped and chatted with the Indians, exulting with them in the victory, to whom the women appealed in my behalf, but they paid no more regard to me than if I had been a dog. I passed the night with the Indians at the house of a white woman in the city, who the next morning asked liberty to give me a cup of tea, with a loaf of bread and butter. In the afternoon the Indians paraded with their prisoners and the trophies, *scalps*, and marched to the fort. After remaining some time in the guard-house, where all the prisoners were surrendered but myself, my captors arose to leave with me. When we reached the door the guard stopped me, which seemed to excite the Indians considerably. Major Muir, commanding the fort, was immediately called for, and entered into a treaty for my release. It was said he gave as a ransom for me an old broken down pack horse and a keg of whisky. My Indian captor took affectionate leave of me, with a promise to see me again. Let me here say my Indian captor exhibited more the principle of the man and the soldier than all the British I had been brought in contact with up to the time I met Major Muir. The next day the British officers, Hale and Watson, invited me to mess with them so long as I remained in the fort. Three or four days afterward, and the day before our officers, Winchester, Madison and Lewis, were to leave for the Niagara river, one of these officers accompanied me across the Detroit river to Sandwich. When passing to the hotel where they were, when I became opposite the dining room door, I saw Major Madison sitting down to supper, The temptation was so strong I entered the door, to the astonishment of the Major and other officers, who supposed I had been murdered with many other prisoners. I am constrained to acknowledge the great mercy of God in my preservation thus far. On the following morning, when arrangements were being made for transportation of officers to Fort George, but none for me, my heart felt like sinking within me at the thought of being left to the care of those I had no confidence whatever in. Providentially a Canadian Lieutenant was listening and so soon as all, both British and American officers, left the room, nobly came to me and said: "I have a good span of horses and a good carryall. You are welcome to a seat with me." I joyfully accepted his offer, and I hereby acknowledge that I met in his person a whole souled man and a soldier, through whose kindness, mainly, I reached Niagara river. When I was once more permitted to look on the much loved flag of my country, and paroled and put across the Niagara river on American soil, then, with all my suffering, I felt that I could once more breathe freely. I have again to acknowledge the goodness of God, in providing for reaching my home and friends, after traveling more than one thousand miles, badly wounded, a half ounce ball buried in my shoulder. But I lived to be fully avenged upon the enemies of my country in the battle of the 8th of January, 1815, below New Orleans. I have omitted many minor incidents that were in this communication, the writing of which has given great pain in my wounded shoulder.

THOMAS P. DUDLEY.

Lexington, Ky., May 26, 1870.

Western Reserve and Northern Ohio HISTORICAL SOCIETY.

NUMBER TWO.

JUDGES OF THE SUPREME COURT OF OHIO, UNDER THE FIRST CONSTITUTION, 1803—1852.

BY THE LATE A. T. GOODMAN—1871.

1787—1803.

Upon the establishment of the Northwest Territory in 1787, by ordinance of the Continental Congress, provision was made for the government of the same by an executive officer, and three judges. The Governor with the judges had supreme power; made the laws, created counties; in fact, had almost the prerogatives possessed by the autocrats of Europe. Under the ordinance it became the duty of Congress to choose the officers above mentioned. On the 16th of October, 1787, they selected and appointed Arthur St. Clair, Governor, James M. Varnum, Samuel H. Parsons, and James Armstrong, judges. St. Clair was from Pennsylvania, Varnum from Rhode Island, Parsons from Connecticut, and Armstrong from Pennsylvania. Each of the appointees had been Generals in the Army of the Revolution, and were known to their fellow-citizens as men of good judgment and sound common sense, which in those days were the best recommendations one man could furnish for another. The commission of Parsons found him in the enjoyment of the peaceful pursuits of a private citizen, while St. Clair, Varnum, and Armstrong were members of the body that appointed them.

After much hesitation General Armstrong declined accepting the position tendered him. The other two Judges with the Governor accepted. In place of Armstrong, Congress on February 19th, 1788, chose John Cleve Symmes, of New Jersey, a very prominent lawyer of that State, who had been a member of Congress in 1785-6. Thus began the government of the Northwest Territory; the officers being acceptable to the people everywhere. They had the full confidence of Congress, and though the task they were required to perform was arduous and difficult, they began the work with a zeal and energy that augured well for success.

In the fall of 1788, the governor and the judges commenced the performance of their duties, with headquarters at "Campus Martius," Marietta. Their first act created the county of Washington, in honor of General Washington, and sundry laws were framed for the government of the people. But the bench of the territory did not long remain as Congress had formed it.

Judge Varnum died of consumption at Marietta, January 10th, 1789, aged forty years.

To fill the vacancy thus created, President Washington, August 20th, 1789, appointed William Barton, of Philadelphia, Pa., a prominent lawyer and gallant soldier in the recent war. Mr. Barton declined the position, and on the 12th of September, 1789, George Turner, of Virginia, was appointed. He was a man of considerable talent, but extremely "old fogyish" in his notions of what was best for the settlements, and the result was a number of quarrels between the bench and populace.

Judge Parsons was drowned while descending the Big Beaver river, November 17th, 1789, aged fifty-two years. He was succeeded March 31st, 1790, by Rufus Putnam, one of the pioneers and founders of

Marietta, who had served as a Brigadier General of Massachusetts troops in the Continental service. He made a good judge and was popular with all classes. Governor St. Clair and himself were fast friends.

From 1790 to 1796, the government of the Territory was in the hands of Arthur St. Clair, Governor, John Cleve Symmes, George Turner, and Rufus Putnam, Judges. During that period the Territory prospered, and began to assume the position and appearance of a civilized State, instead of a wilderness, the habitation of prowling Indians and wild beasts.

In 1796, Judge Putnam resigned his commission, to accept that of Surveyor General, and Joseph Gillman, a resident of Hamilton county, was appointed Judge (December 22d, 1796). The following year (1797) Judge Turner, having purchased largely of lands near Kaskaskia, removed to the then far West, and resigned his judgeship. He was succeeded, February 12th, 1798, by Return Jonathan Meigs, of Marietta, a pioneer settler of that place, and one of the ablest men in the Territory. He afterwards was Governor of Ohio, U. S. Senator, and Postmaster General, U. S. As then constituted, the Supreme Court continued until the admission of Ohio into the Union as a State. Judge Symmes had served from 1788 to 1803, Judge Gilman seven years, and Judge Meigs five years. A short time previous to the formation of our State Government, President Jefferson, for partisan reasons, removed (fall, 1802) Arthur St. Clair from the position of Governor of the Territory. From that time until the spring of 1803, the time the new Constitution went into effect, Charles Willing Byrd, Secretary, was Acting Governor of the Territory.

It is proper here to state that the Ordinance of 1787 provided that when the Territory should contain a population of 5,000 free white males, a change in its government should take place. In 1798 it contained the required number, when a Territorial Legislature was chosen by the people, and a Council of ten citizens appointed by the President. These two bodies framed the laws, while the Governor possessed the veto power. Thus from 1798 until 1803, the judges were restricted in their duties, so far as the making of laws was concerned.

1803—1852.

It is a proud satisfaction for the people of the Buckeye State to know that Ohio has furnished the country with many of the most distinguished names which adorn its history. Whether in the field or the Cabinet, on the bench or in the forum, Ohio has no mean or scanty record. Her statesmen have ranked high in the councils of the Nation, while her sons who have been called to command on the field of battle have had no superiors as military leaders. Her judiciary is known wherever the law governs, and forms a record of which the State may well be proud.

Our Supreme Judges under the old Constitution were not always the ablest lawyers in the State, but generally speaking were men of sound judgment, good understanding, fair and impartial in their judicial relations. The lives of Meigs, McLean, Wright, Lane, Hitchcock, and such men will form an important chapter in the civil and judical history of Ohio. They were great lawyers, men of character and wisdom, who made the judiciary of Ohio the pride of its bar, and the envy of tribunals abroad.

The early admitted attorneys—as connected with the judiciary—who practiced at the Bar of Ohio deserve mention. They were intelligent, industrious, and zealous in the interests of their clients. Some of them attained national fame, others local distinction; all were known to the public.

T e first admitted attorney within the limits of the present State of Ohio was Paul Fearing. His certificate was granted in September, 1788, at "Campus Martius," Marietta, by Judges Varnum and Parsons. Of those who soon followed him were Dudley Odlin, Matthew Backus, William Littel, Solomon Sibley, David Putnam, Willis Silliman and Philemon Beecher. The first attorney admitted under the Constitution of 1802 was Lewis Cass, whose certificate bore date 1803. The honored name of Lewis Cass is known to all Americans. Of later names we might mention Charles Hammond, William Woodbridge, since Senator from Michigan, Thomas Ewing, Judge Francis Dunlavy, Arthur St. Clair, Jr., son of the Governor, Judge Luke Foster, Robert B. Parkman, D. K. Este, Elisha Whittlesey, Robert F. Slaughter, Judge John W. Willey, Judge John W. Campbell, William Creighton, Joseph H. Crane, Benjamin Ruggles, John Woods, Robert T. Lytle, Eleutheros Cooke, Alfred Kelley, Sherlock J. Andrews, Henry Stanberry, Thomas L. Hamer, Samson Mason, Judge B. S. Cowan, A. W. Loomis, Salmon P. Chase, Samuel F. Vinton, Simon Nash, Eben Newton, Henry B. Payne, Hiram V. Willson, and Humphrey H. Leavitt. Among the above names I have not mentioned any of the judges of the Supreme Court from 1803 to 1852.

Under the Constitution framed at Chillicothe, November 29th, 1802, the judicial power of the State, both as to matters of law and equity, was vested in a Supreme Court, in Courts of Common Pleas, in justices of the peace, and in such other courts as the Legislature from time to time established. The Supreme Court was to consist of three judges, any two of which to constitute a quorum. They were given original and appellate jurisdiction, both in common law and chancery, in such cases as directed by law, and the Legislature was authorized, after a lapse of five years, to elect an additional judge. This power was afterward exercised, and the number of judges increased to four. They were to be elected by the Legislature for a term of seven years, if so long they behaved themselves well, and were obliged to hold a session in each county at least once a year. From time to time the Legislature enacted laws regulating the Supreme Court, and on the 20th of January, 1823, passed an act requiring the judges to hold a Court in Bank annually, at the seat of Government, and provided for reporting and publishing the decisions of the Court in Bank, and such other decisions as the judges might desire published. Agreeably to this resolution, the judges held a session at Columbus in December, 1823. This was their first sitting under the new law. Rules of practice, etc., were made and adopted, and Hon. Charles Hammond appointed reporter. The Supreme Court in Bank continued until the adoption of the new Constitution in 1852.

The following is a correct list of those who served on the Supreme Bench under the old Constitution, ending in 1852. They are given in the order of their election or appointment:

Samuel Huntington, Return J. Meigs, William Sprigg, George Tod, Daniel Symmes, Thomas Scott, Thomas Morris, William W. Irvin, Ethan Allen Brown, Calvin Pease, John McLean, Jessup N. Couch, Jacob Burnet, Charles R. Sherman, Peter Hitchcock, Elijah Hayward, John M. Goodenow, Reuben Wood, John C. Wright, Joshua Collett, Ebenezer Lane, Frederick Grimke, Matthew Birchard, Nathaniel C. Read, Edward Avery, Rufus P. Spalding, William B. Caldwell, and Rufus P. Ranney.

Twenty-eight judges in a period of half a century! How illustrious the list! The twenty volumes of Ohio reports bear ample testimony to their ability, industry and correctness of judgement. But few remain among the living. We believe that Judges Birchard, Spalding, Caldwell, and Ranney alone survive. Of the number, four, Meigs, Huntington, Brown and Wood were Governors of the State; four, Meigs, Morris, Brown and Burnet were United States Senators; seven, Irwin, McLean, Hitchcock, Hayward, Goodenow, Wright and Spalding were members of Congress, and two, Meigs and McLean, were Cabinet officers.

The first commissioned official under the constitution of 1802 was Samuel Huntington. He was elected Judge of the Supreme Court on the 2d of April, 1803. Governor Tiffin, in his letter to Judge Huntington, enclosing his commission, refers to it as the first one issued "in the name of and by the authority of the State of Ohio." Judge Huntington was born at Norwich, Conn., in 1765. He removed to Cleveland in 1801. In 1802 he was a member of the Constitutional Convention of Ohio; in 1808 elected Governor, serving one term; was District Paymaster in the war of 1812, and died at his residence near Painesville in February, 1817. Judge Meigs was born at Middletown, Conn., in 1765. He became famous as a lawyer, and served as Judge of Michigan, Louisiana, and Northwest territories. He was United States Senator from Ohio 1809-10, Governor 1810-14, and Postmaster General of the United States from 1814 till he resigned in June, 1823. He died at Marietta, O., March 29th, 1825.

Judge Sprigg was a native of Maryland, and early settled at Steubenville. He was a brother of Samuel Sprigg, Governor of Maryland, 1819-22. He was a well educated man, a fine writer, and a sound lawyer. He resigned his judgship in May, 1806, and resumed practice at Steubenville. He was again chosen to the bench, and was removed from office in 1809, with Judge Tod. He afterward returned to Maryland, where he died at an advanced age.

George Tod was born at Suffield, Conn., December 11th, 1773, graduated at Yale in 1795, and in 1800 settled at Youngstown. He was State Senator in 1804-5, and was elected Judge of the Supreme Court in 1806. In 1808, the Legislature impeached Judges Tod, Sprigg, and Huntington for declaring a law of the Legislature unconstitutional. They escaped by *one vote*, but in 1809 the Legislature passed an act declaring their offices vacant. In the meantime, Huntington had been elected Governor of Ohio. To show the feeling on this subject we give below a letter to Judge Tod, from David Abbot, a member of the Legislature, and one of the framers of the Constituttion of 1802.

HON. GEORGE TOD—Sir: If the judges have a right to set aside laws, because they deem them unconstitutional, the people have no security, except the infallibility of the judges.

If the judges have a right to set aside laws, because they are unconstitutional, they cannot be removed from office, because it would be hard indeed to remove a judge for error in judgment.

If the judges have a right to set laws

aside, then the people have no power left them, except choosing their representatives, for the representatives may enact laws, the judges set them aside, and thus Government would be at an end.

But, saith the judges, if we have not a right to judge of the constitutionality of the laws, the Legislature have no check; they might enact that there should be an equal distribution of property, which is unconstitutional. It is a true a Legislature might be so corrupt as to pass such a law, but if the people allow the judges the right to set aside laws, does it not make the judiciary a complete aristocratic branch by setting the judges over the heads of the Legislature?

Nothing, I think, could have originated the idea, except it is the Scripture account of God and the devil—one to create, the other to destroy.

Please explain how the above mentioned evils can be avoided.

Very respectfully your humble servant,

DAVID ABBOT.

Judge Tod served as Major and Lieutenant Colonel in the regular army in the war of 1812, acquitting himself with great credit. In 1815, he was chosen President Judge of the Court of Common Pleas, Third Judicial District, serving until 1834. He then retired to private life, and died at Brier Hill, O., April 11th, 1841. His second son was the late Governor David Tod.

Judge Daniel Symmes was appointed from Hamilton county, in place of R. J. Meigs, resigned. He was born in New Jersey, graduated at Princeton College, and was an early settler in Southwestern Ohio. John Cleve Symmes was his uncle. Probably his influence secured the appointment of his nephew to the Supreme Bench, as Daniel Symmes never ranked high, either as a lawyer or judge. He died in 1810.

Thomas Scott was a native of Maryland, born in 1762. From 1789 until 1796, he was an itinerant minister of the Methodist Episcopal Church. In 1798 he commenced the study of law, and soon after located in Chillicothe, O. He was secretary of the Convention that framed the Constitution of Ohio, in 1802, and it is thought was the last survivor of that body. He was for a time clerk of the courts, and Secretary of the State Senate, from 1803 to 1809, when he was chosen Judge of the Supreme Court, in place of Judge Tod, removed. He was Chief Justice from 1810 until 1815, when he resigned, the salary being insufficient. From that time almost until his decease, Judge Scott was engaged in the practice of his profession. He did did not rank high as a judge, though in Southern Ohio he acquired a good reputation as a lawyer. He died in Chilicothe, O., February 25th, 1856, aged eighty-four years.

Thomas Morris was elected a Supreme Judge in 1809, in place of William Sprigg, legislated out of office, He was born in Virginia, January 3d, 1776. In 1795 he settled in Hamilton county, O. He afterward removed to Clermont county, and in 1806 was elected to the Legislature, and served twenty-four years in the Senate and House of Ohio. He was a Senator in Congress from 1833 to 1839, and died December 7th, 1844. He was more of a politician than lawyer.

Judge Irvin was frequently in the Legislature of Ohio, from Fairfield county. He was born in Albemarle county, Va., in 1778. He was a Judge of the Supreme Court from 1809 until 1815, when he resigned. He was a member of Congress from 1829 to 1833, and died at Lancaster, O., in April, 1842. Judge Irvin was a very able jurist, and as an advocate had a widespread reputation.

Judge Brown was born at Darien, Conn., July 4th, 1776. He studied law with Alexander Hamilton in New York City. In 1804, he located at Cincinnati for the practice of the law. In 1810, he was chosen a Supreme Judge, and held the position until 1818, when he was elected Governor. He served as Governor four years, and in 1822 was sent to the United States Senate, where he remained until 1825. In 1830, President Jackson appointed him Minister to Brazil. In 1835, he became Commissioner of the General Land Office. In 1836, he changed his residence to Rising Sun, Indiana, where he afterward lived. He died while on a visit to Indianapolis, February 24th, 1852. Judge Brown was one of the most honest, upright and incorruptible judges that ever sat upon the Supreme Bench. He was not as learned as some, but he was very popular with the Bar and people.

Calvin Pease was born at Suffield, Conn., September 9th, 1776. He graduated at Yale, and read law with Hon. Gideon Granger, afterward Postmaster General. After admission to the bar, Mr. Pease emigrated (1800) to Warren, O., where he engaged in practice. The same year he was appointed Prothonotary for the Court of Common Pleas for Trumbull county, and in 1803 was elected judge of the same court. This position he held until 1810, when he resigned. In 1812 he was elected State Senator. In 1816 the Legislature chose him Judge of the Supreme Court. Re-elected in 1823, he served until 1830, when he retired from judicial life. In 1831 Judge Pease was elected to the Legislature from Trumbull county, serving one term, after which he declined accepting office. He died at Warren, September 17th, 1839. Judge Pease was a man of talents, and was greatly respected for his private virtues and public usefulness.

John McLean was born in Morris county New Jersey, in 1785. When four years of age, his father emigrated to Virginia, thence to Kentucky, finally locating in Warren county, Ohio. In 1807, John McLean was admitted to the bar, and at once began practice at Lebanon, O. From 1812 to 1816, he was a member of Congress. In the latter year he was chosen a Judge of the Supreme Court, and remained upon the bench until 1822, when President Monroe appointed him Commissioner of the General Land Office. The following year (1823) he was made Post-master General. In 1829, President Jackson appointed him a Judge of the Supreme Court of the United States, which position he held until his death at Cincinnati, O, April 4th, 1861. Judge McLean was a man of commanding talents, of great learning and extended research. He was often spoken of as a candidate for the Presidency.

Jessup N. Couch resided in Cincinnati. He was a pioneer settler of Hamilton county, a man of weak intellect, who never stood high either as a lawyer or judge. As a politician, however, he had no equal. He could tell a good story, and make stump speeches, which never failed to please the backwoodsmen of early days. He was justice of the peace for several years, and served in the State Legislature, where he was very popular. He was chosen a Judge of the Supreme Court in 1818, and died while on the bench, in 1821. Judge Couch was probably the weakest of all the lawyers who have occupied a place upon the Supreme Bench of Ohio.

Judge Burnet was born in Newark, N. J., February 22d, 1770. He came from a distinguished family. In 1796 he located at Cincinnati. In 1799 he was a member of the Territorial Council, in 1812 a member of the Legislature, and in 1821 was chosen a Judge of the Supreme Court, serving until 1828. He was a Senator in Congress from 1828 to 1831. He died at Cincinnati in 1853. Judge Burnet was an eminent lawyer and reflected honor on the Supreme Bench.

Judge Sherman was a lawyer of fine talent. He was a native of Connecticut, born in 1787, removed to Ohio in 1810, and at once acquired a large practice. He was revenue collector and held other local offices of trust and profit. In 1825 he was chosen Judge of the Supreme Court, and held that position at the time of his death, which occurred at Lebanon, Warren county, while on the circuit, in 1829. His remains repose in the cemetery at Lancaster, O. Judge Sherman was a man of genial temperament, kind, social and agreeable, very popular with members of the bar. He is the father of Senator Sherman, General W. T. Sherman, and Charles T. Sherman, United States District Judge, Northern District of Ohio.

Peter Hitchcock served as a Judge of the Supreme Court for twenty-eight years. Born in Cheshire, Conn., October 19th, 1780, he graduated at Yale College in 1801. In 1806 he removed to Burton, Geauga county, O. In 1810 he was a member of the House of Representatives of Ohio, and from 1812 to 1816 was in the State Senate. He was member of Congress from 1817 to 1819, and from 1819 till 1852, with the exception of five years, was on the Supreme bench. From 1833 to 1835 he was in the State Senate, and in 1850 a delegate to the State Constitutional Convention. He died at Painesville, O., May 11th, 1853. Judge Hitchcock ranks as one of the purest and ablest jurists this State has produced.

Elijah Hayward was appointed Judge of the Supreme Court on the 15th of February, 1830. He was born at Bridgewater, Mass., November 17th, 1786. His education was limited, and he began life as a merchant. In 1811 he went to England and was in the House of Commons, May 11th, 1812, when Bellingham shot the Right Honorable Spencer Percival, Prime Minister of Great Britain. In 1818 he again visited England. In 1820, after studying eighteen months, Mr. Hayward was admitted to practice law, and immediately removed to Hamilton county, O., where he opened an office. In October, 1830, while Judge of the Supreme Court, he was appointed by President Jackson Commissioner of the General Land Office. This position he held until 1835, when he resigned and returned to Ohio. Judge Hayward afterward served as State Librarian, and held several local offices of trust and profit. He died at Connellsville, O, September 22d, 1864. He was a plain, practical man, but never took rank as a leading lawyer.

John M. Goodenow was a native of Massachusetts, and early settled in Jefferson county, O. He served in the Legislature, and held other offices of trust and honor before his election to Congress in 1829. While in Congress, 1831, he was chosen a Judge of the Supreme Court, holding the position until 1832, when he resigned. He was a man of fine abilities, and enjoyed a large practice at the bar. He resided at Steubenville, where in 1819 he published a work entitled "American Jurisprudence in Contrast with the Doctrine of English Common Law." This work is now very rare, less than fifty copies having been printed. Judge Goodenow died several years since.

Reuben Wood was an excellent judge, and highly respected by the bar and the people. He was born in Rutland county, Vt., in 1792, served in the war of 1812 as captain of Vermont volunteers, studied law with Hon. Barnabus Bidwell, was admitted to the bar, and in 1818 removed to Cleveland, O. In 1825 he was elected to the Senate and was twice re-elected, In 1830 he was chosen President Judge of the Third Judicial District, and in in 1833 was transferred to the Supreme Bench. He retired from his judicial service in 1845, and in 1850 was elected Governor of Ohio. In 1851 he was re-elected, serving until 1853, when he resigned to accept the Consulship to Valparaiso, tendered him by President Pierce. For nearly three years he was acting Minister to Chili. He died at Rockport, near Cleveland, October 2d, 1864.

John C. Wright is known in the judicial annals of Ohio as an able, industrious, and incorruptible judge. He was born in 1783, and at an early age settled at Steubenville, O. He soon attained eminence in his profession. He was a member of Congress from 1823 to 1829, and for many years served on the Supreme Bench. His law reports are in high estimation throughout the West. After retiring from the bench, Judge Wright removed to Cincinnati, where for a long period of time he was owner and editor of the Cincinnati Gazette. In 1861 he was appointed a delegate to the Peace Convention, which met at Washington City, and he died during its session, February 13th, 1861.

Joshua Collett was born in Virginia in 1781. He received a common school education, and was early admitted to practice law. In 1801 he located at Lebanon, O., and the following year opened a law office, being the first lawyer in Warren county. From 1802 to 1817 he practiced at the bar, and was everywhere known as "the honest lawyer." During the year 1817 he was elected Common Pleas Judge, and served several years. In 1828, he was chosen a Judge of the Supreme Court, which position he held until 1842. Though not a brilliant lawyer, Judge Collett was an able and industrious one. He died in 1855, aged seventy-three years and six months. The inscription on his tombstone says, "As a man and as a Christian he maintained a character for piety, simplicity, righteousness, and love of truth, such as only the fear of God and faith in the gospel of Jesus Christ can impart."

Ebenezer Lane was born at Northampton, Mass., September 17th, 1793. He studied at Leicester, and at the at the age of fourteen entered Harvard College, graduating with high honors in 1811. He then entered the office of Judge Matthew Griswold at Lyme, Conn., where he studied law, and was admitted to practice in 1814. In September of that year he located at Norwich and practised there and other small places until his removal to Ohio in 1817. In 1818 Mr. Lane married Frances Ann, daughter of Governor Roger Griswold, of Connecticut. The same year he located at Elyria. In 1819 he removed to Norwalk, and was almost immediately chosen Prosecuting Attorney of Huron county. In 1824, Mr. Lane was chosen Judge of the Court of Common Pleas of the Second Judicial Circuit. Six years later he was chosen Judge of the Supreme Court, occupying a seat upon the bench of that Court until his resignation in February, 1845 In 1842, he changed his residence to Sandusky. Judge Lane was a remarkable man. He was a diligent student, not only of the law, but of history and science. His opinions have given him a national reputation. He died of cancer in the throat, at Sandusky, June 18th, 1866.

Frederick Grimke was born in Charleston, S. C., September 1st, 1791. He graduated at Yale, studied law, and at an early age removed to Ross county, O., where he was a protege of Governor Worthington. He practiced law at Chillicothe with marked success until his elevation to the Supreme Bench, in February, 1836. He served as Judge of the Supreme Court until 1841, when he resigned, and retired from practice. He died in 1863, aged seventy-two years. Judge Grimke was an author of considerable repute. He published a work on the "Nature and Tendency of Free Institutions," and an essay, entitled "Ancient and Modern Literature." His brother was the celebrated Thomas S. Grimke, of South Carolina. Judge Grimke died a bachelor. He was a very retired, urbane man, and mingled little in society. As a lawyer, he was not widely known.

Matthew Birchard is well known to the bar of Ohio. He was born at Becket, Mass., January 19th, 1804. In 1812, his parents, with their family of seven children, removed to Windham, Portage county. Judge Birchard's education was principally received at schools and academies on the Reserve. At an early age he determined to follow the medical profession, but after a year's study abandoned it for the law. In 1824 he became a student in the office of the late General Roswell Stone, at Warren, and was occupied there four months in the year—the other eight being employed in alternately teaching at Braceville and Nelson. In August, 1827, he was admitted to the bar, and began practice at Warren with the late Governor Tod. The Legislature, in 1833, chose him a Judge of the Court of Common Pleas, to succeed Judge Wood, transferred to the Supreme Bench. In December, 1836, President Jackson appointed him Solicitor of the General Land Office at Washington. Three years later, President Van Buren appointed him Solicitor of the United States Treasury, in place of Hon. Henry D. Gilpin, promoted to Attorney General. This office Judge Birchard held until March, 1841, when he returned to Ohio, and resumed practice at Warren with his old partner, Governor Tod. In December of the same year the Legislature elected him a Judge of the Supreme Court, which position he held until 1849. Since that time Judge Birchard has not held office, with the exception of serving a term of two years in the State House of Representatives, 1854-5. He was a candidate for Congress in 1856, against the late Mr. Giddings, but failed of an election. As a lawyer, Judge Birchard has always held a place in the front ranks of the profession. As a judge he was deservedly popular. His opinions are noted for their clear, concise language, strong reasoning, and good sense.

Judge N. C. Read was a native of Champaign county, Ohio, born on the Mac-Jack, about the year 1810. He was educated at Athens College, Athens, O., and studied law with the Hon. Israel Hamilton at Urbana. After admission to the bar he removed to Cincinnati, where he early displayed great talent as an advocate, especially in criminal cases. So great was his popularity that at the age of twenty-six he was made Prosecuting Attorney for Hamilton county, and before his thirtieth year was elected President Judge of the Court of Common Pleas. In 1841 the Legislature chose him Judge of the Supreme Court, in place of Judge Grimke, resigned. This position he held until February, 1849. Upon leaving the bench Judge Read returned to Cincinnati, but left shortly afterward for California. He practiced two or three years in San Francisco, but soon fell a victim to that vice which has proved the destroyer of so many of our distinguished men. He died in 1853, at the early age of forty-three years.

Judge Read was a man of elegant scholarship, an erratic genius, whose whole-souled liberality and generous hospitality proved his ruin. Whatever his faults, he was a genial companion, and we can but pity the weakness that proved his downfall.

Judge Edward Avery was a native of Connecticut, born in the year 1790. His primary education was received in Fairfield county, after which he entered Yale, graduating in 1810. He studied law and was admitted to the bar in 1813. In 1816 he made a tour of Europe. In 1817 he located at Wooster, O., where he afterward resided. Judge Avery early secured an extensive practice at the bar. He grew up with the community in which he lived, and though often urged, seldom accepted office. He served two years in the State Senate, and in 1847 was chosen a Judge of the Supreme Court. This position he held until March, 1851, when he resigned. From that time until his decease he remained in private life. He died at Wooster, June 27th, 1866. Judge Avery was an exemplary Christian and a good citizen. He was a fair lawyer, but never ranked high upon the bench.

Rufus Paine Spalding was born in West Tisbury, Martha's Vineyard, Mass., May 3d, 1798, and removed with his parents to Connecticut when very young. He received a good academical education, and graduated at Yale in 1817. He married a daughter of Judge Zephaniah Swift, with whom he studied law. In 1821 Judge Spalding located in Trumbull county, O. In 1829 he was elected to the House of Representatives of Ohio, and being re-elected in 1841, was chosen Speaker. In February, 1849, he was elected a Judge of the Supreme Court, and continued in that office until February, 1852, when the new Constitution went into effect. Soon afterward he located in Cleveland, and continued in practice until 1862, when he was elected to Congress. Judge Spalding continued a member of the National House until 1869, when he declined a re-election. He is a lawyer of marked ability, and as a Judge of the Supreme Court gave general satisfaction.

William B. Caldwell was born June 23d, 1808, in Butler county, O. He was educated at Miama University, Oxford, O., graduating in 1835,—and studied law with Hon. John Woods, of Hamilton, O. He was admitted to the bar in 1837 at Chillicothe and commenced practice at Xenia. The following year he removed to Cincinnati, where he has resided ever since. In 1841 he was elected Prosecuting Attorney for Hamilton county, and in 1842, President Judge of the Court of Common Pleas. This position he held until 1849, when the Legislature chose him a Judge of the Supreme Court. In 1853 he resigned judical honors and returned to practice in Cincinnati. Judge Caldwell has always ranked high as a lawyer and judge.

Rufus Percival Ranney was born at Blandford, Mass., October 30th, 1813. In 1822 his parents removed to Ohio, locating first at Fairpoint and shortly afterward at Freedom, Portage county. Judge Ranney's early education was limited. He worked on his father's farm in summer, and attended village school in winter. At a later day, by his own industry, he managed to attend college at Hudson for a short period. In college at Hudson for a short period. In 1836 he entered the law office of Wade & Giddings at Jefferson, O., and after two years study was admitted to practice. In 1839 he became the partner of Hon. Benjamin F. Wade, one of his preceptors. In 1846 and 1848, Judge Ranney was a candidate for Congress against General John Crowell, but failed of an election, though he ran largely ahead of the Democratic State and county tickets. In 1850 he was chosen to represent the counties of Trumbull and Geauga in the Constitutional Convention. In the debates of that body he took a prominent part. On the 17th of March, 1851, he was chosen by the Legislature a Judge of the Supreme Court, in place of Edward Avery, resigned. This was the last election of Supreme Judge under the old Constitution. In October, 1851, Judge Ranney was re-elected by the people. He resigned in 1856, and in 1857 was appointed by President Buchanan United States District Attorney for Northern Ohio. This position he held two months and resigned. The same year he removed from Warren to Cleveland. In 1859 Governor Chase appointed him one of the Commisioners to examine into the condition of the State Treasury, but the appointment was declined. In the fall of 1859 he was the Democratic candidate for Governor against William Dennison, but failed of an election. In 1862 he was again elected Judge of the Supreme Court, which he resigned in 1864. From 1864 to 1868 he served upon the Democratic National Committee. Since 1864, he has held no official position, but has been engaged in the practice of his profession at Cleveland. As a lawyer and jurist, Judge Ranney has no superior in the State.

As before remarked, Judge Ranney was the last Judge of the Supreme Court, chosen under the old Constitution. The new Constitution, framed by a convention chosen by the people, was submitted to for ratification or rejection at the fall election of 1851. The result was its adoption by a large majority. In February, 1852, it went into operation. Under its provisions the powers and privileges of the court were largely extended, and the number of Judges increased to five, one to be chosen by the people annually, after the first election of the whole number. At some future time we may notice the Supreme Court as it has existed since the adoption of the present Constitution.

Western Reserve Historical Society.

CLEVELAND, O., NOVEMBER, 1870.

HISTORICAL AND ARCHÆOLOGICAL TRACTS,

NUMBER THREE.

PAPERS RELATING TO THE WAR OF 1812.

Among the voluminous papers of the late Elisha Whittlesey, of Canfield, Ohio, are many which relate to the war on the frontier in 1812. By the provisions of his will, a fire-proof room has been built for their preservation on the old homestead. Some of them are being transcribed for the use of the Western Reserve Historical Society, from which the following extracts are taken:

There had been but four divisions of Ohio militia. Major General Elijah Wadsworth, of Canfield, was in command of the Fourth division, composed of three brigades, which embraced the northeastern portion of Ohio. He had been a Captain in Colonel Benjamin Tallmadge's regiment of the Connecticut line during the war for independence, having removed to Ohio in 1802. The first brigade was to the south of the Reserve, commanded by Brigadier General Reasin Beall; the second brigade, to the southwest, by Brigadier General Miller; and the third on the Reserve by Brigadier General Simon Perkins. As war had been anticipated, the Legislature of Ohio made provision for a draft, and on the 27th of April, 1812, orders were received from Governor Meigs to raise one company in each brigade. In case a sufficient number to form a company should volunteer from one regiment, or battalion, they were to elect their own officers.

Mr. Whittlesey was aide to General Wadsworth, performing the duty of Adjutant, and afterwards brigade inspector to General Perkins, and thus came into possession of a large part of the papers and correspondence relating to the war in this quarter. On receiving news of Hull's surrender at Detroit, of the 15th of August, General Wadsworth instantly gave orders, which bear date August 22d, for each brigade to rendezvous at Cleveland, without delay. A second draft was at once ordered by the government for one hundred thousand men, of which the quota for the Fourth division was five hundred to each brigade.

President Madison was a man of great personal rectitude, and a statesman of the first rank; but lacked the personal independence, promptness and energy for a war executive.

Dr. William Eustis of Virginia was Secretary of War, whose administration of that department in this critical moment rose but little above imbecility. The declaration of war was sent to General Hull by *mail* through Cleveland, and did not reach him at Maumee until several days after the British had it at Malden. He lost a vessel with stores, and his papers, by this culpable neglect Although the war had been clearly foreseen for at least two years, supplies for the western troops were almost wholly wanting. As late as the 3d of October, while a part of the levies of the Fourth division were lying on the Cuyahoga, at old Portage, near Akron, General Wadsworth was obliged to send a horse express to Pittsburg for gun flints, without which muskets were of little value. When the levies of this division were well in the field under the command of General Perkins, General Wadsworth was relieved at his own request.

Colonel John Campbell, of Ravenna had command as Captain of the company raised under the draft of April 27th, in which John Harmon of that place, who is yet living, was a volunteer. He has recently written a minute history of the services of this company for this society.

Campbell was Colonel of the Second Regiment, Third Brigade. Calling his regiment together at Ravenna, on the 23d of May, fifty men enrolled themselves as volunteers, and thus were enabled to choose their officers. On the first of July they were called into service, and reached Cleveland on the 10th. Here they took boats and proceeded to Sandusky, where his letter is dated on the 17th. In giving the papers and correspondence below, it cannot always be produced in the order of dates, and at the same time have relation to one subject or expedition.

ANTICIPATIONS OF THE WAR—MAJOR GENERAL WADSWORTH TO THE BRIGADE COMMANDERS.

CANFIELD, Sept. 14, 1811.

I am directed by the commandant of the Fourth Division of the Militia of this State to call your attention to the subject of making returns of the brigade under your command. It is important that the government of this State and that of the United States should know at a time *when war almost appears inevitable*, their actual strength. There is little or no doubt but that "the weighty and important matters" which the President has to lay before Congress, by reason of which it is called to meet earlier, than usual, relate to our differences with foreign powers.

Should Congress deem it expedient to declare war against one or both of the belligerents, its attention must necessarily be drawn to ascertain the force they could compel to take the field. This information cannot be derived from any other quarter than the returns made from the several States, and their neglecting o make returns at the Adjutant General's ffice dries up the source of information on this subject. The Adjutant General has heretofore complained of the remissness of this department, and it has been impossible for the commandant of this division to be more punctual in the discharge of the duties assigned to him, as the returns from the brigades under his command have in some instances been partially, and in others wholly withholden from him, and they have been made months after; it was his duty to have forwarded them. The general expects from your attention and exertions, that a return of your brigade will be duly made and transmitted to him, agreeable to the 27th section of the militia law of this State.

With esteem and regard I am your obedient and humble servant,

ELISHA WHITTLESEY, Aide-de-Camp.

GENERAL PERKINS TO GENERAL WADSWORTH.

WARREN, April 29, 1812.

DEAR SIR: Your order of the 27th inst., was received that day, and I have issued orders for raising the quota assigned to my brigade.

SIMON PERKINS, Brig. General,
3d Brigade, 4th Division, Ohio Militia.

GENERAL PERKINS TO GENERAL WADSWORTH.

WARREN, May 11, 1812.

DEAR SIR: On the 9th inst. I received returns from the several colonels, complying with my order of April 28th. From two regiments volunteers were returned, and in one a draft was made. The volunteers returned here have been sufficient in this regiment to form a company, but they were from two regiments. I have issued an order for drafts to those regiments which returned volunteers, and my return will no doubt be complete in the course of the present week. SIMON PERKINS.

SIMON PERKINS TO ELIJAH WADSWORTH.

WARREN, June 12, 1812.

SIR:—In compliance with your order of the 27th day of April last I have caused to be drafted and who now hold themselves in readines for your further order the following list of cers and men:

John W. Seely, Captain; James Kerr, Ensign; Samuel Bill, 1st Sergeant; Zadock Bowell, 3d Sergeant; John Cherry, 1st Corporal.

PRIVATES.

Asa Lane, Peter Lanterman, Miller Blackley, Wm. Strader, Joseph Netterfield, Wm. Crawford, James Chalpin, Robert Brewer, Nathaniel Stanley, Alexander Hayes, David Kiddle, Wm. Martin. Conrad Knafe, James Anderson, John Strain, Matthew Dobbins, Ezra Buell, Solomon Wartrous, Peter Yatman, Urial Burnett, Hugh Markee, Amos Rathburn, David Fitch, Joseph Walker, Michael Crumrine, Barnabas Slavin, Martin Tid, Jr., Justin Fobes, William Meeker, James Mears, Aaron Scroggs, Andrew Markee, Jr., Eathen Newman, Daniel Fowler, SIMON PERKINS,
Brigadier General Third Brigade, Fourth Division, Ohio Militia.

COLONEL JOHN CAMPBELL TO ELISHA WHITTLESEY.

LOWER SANDUSKY, July 17th, 1812.

Dear Sir: We arrived here on the morning of the 14th. From Cleveland we came by water. We found the fortifications here in considerable forwardness. The stockade is nearly completed; we are progressing in the work. It is difficult to say to whom the command of this post belongs. A man who bears the title of Major Butler has instructions from the Governor relating to the fortifying of this place somewhat similar to mine, but cannot ascertain that he has, or ever has had, a commission either under this State or the UnitedStates. Captain Norton from Delaware is here with about thirty men, he continues to command his company and I mine, and intend so to do until the pleasure of the commander-in-chief is known. Harmony prevails among us, and our men are in good spirits. A gentleman arrived here this morning from Detroit. He confirms the report that Gen. Hall has crossed into Canada, and that he is now fortifying Sandwich. No opposition was made to his landing. Col. Munson, aid to Governor Meigs, has received a mortal wound by an accidental shot from one of his party. The ball passed through his left arm and lodged in his body. The ball has not been extracted. To the politeness of this gentleman we are indebted for the perusal of Gen. Hull's proclamation of the inhabitants of Canada. He invites them to accept the friendship and protection of the United States, and promises security and protection to their property and possessions, but threatens extermination of those who unite wi h the merciless savages to murder our unoffending citizens. The Indians here appear perfectly friendly, Some of them brought here an Indian who had stolen horses from General Hull's army. He is still a prisoner here. The Detroit mail has arrived. It informs us that General Munson is dead. With due respect, Sir,

JOHN CAMPBELL.

SIMON PERKINS TO MAJOR GENERAL WADSWORTH.

August 15th, 1812.

SIR: Inclosed are my returns for this division, which would have been forwarded sooner if the returns had been received from the commandants of regiments. Colonel Rayen delayed his, expecting to have completed his return of the artillery company, but finding it impossible, his, and of course my return, is made without it. My return to the Adjutant General was made by the last mail. I have ordered a muster of officers to be held at the house of Asahel Adams, in Liberty, on the 2d and 3d days of September next, and should be very happy to wait on you at that time and place.

I am, Sir, most respectfully, your humble servant. SIMON PERKINS.

GENERAL WADSWORTH TO SECRETARY OF WAR

Headquarters, Camp at Cleveland, O., August 26, 1812.

SIR:—On the instant I received information that General Hull had capitulated with the British commander for the surrender of Detroit; that our army were prisoners, and the British and Indians in possession of the Michigan territory, and on their march to this State. I immediately ordered out all the militia under my command, consisting of the First brigade, commanded by Brigadier General Beall; the Second brigade, commanded by Brigadier General Miller; the Third brigade, commanded by Brigadier General Perkins, to repair immediately to Cleveland with their arms and —— days provisions. My orders have been promptly complied with, about ——— troops have already arrived, and others are continually coming in from all quarters. I expect in a few days to have a sufficient force to repel any force that the enemy can at present bring against us, but I am destitute of everything needful for the use and support of an army. The troops are badly armed and clothed, with no provisions or camp equipage, or the means of procuring any. But the dangerous situation of the country obliges me to face every difficulty, since my command arrived at this place, on the —instant, and established my headquarters. Since my arrival at this place about ——— prisoners have been landed here by the British. Yours with respect,

ELIJAH WADSWORTH.

Extract from the "*Trump of Fame*" newspaper, Warren. Trumbull county, Ohio, Sept. 2d, 1812—T. D. Webb, editor.

"Major General Wadsworth has established his headquarters at Cleveland, and pushed forward a body of troops under the command of Brigadier General Perkins to Huron. The detachment, from the brigade under the command of General Beall has been ordered to Mansfield. The unfortunate prisoners belonging to this State, who surrendered at Detroit, are daily coming into Cleveland. All accounts concur in the establishment of the treachery of General Hull. But we trust if the government of the United States will put arms in our hands that the patriotic militia of Ohio will soon take abundant satisfaction. As soon as the news of the fall of Detroit was confirmed, every man ran to arms, old and young without distinction of politics, repaired to the post of danger, no man waited for the cold formality of the reception of orders, but every one, exempt or not from military duty put on his armour.

W. EUSTIS, SECRETARY OF WAR, TO GENERAL WADSWORTH.

WAR DEPARTMENT, Sept. 5, 1812.

Sir: It has been determined by the President to repair the disaster at Detroit, and to prosecute with increased vigor the important objects of the campaign, for which an adequate force will be provided. The Governor of Ohio will furnish reinforcements on the requisition of General Winchester or officer commanding the northwestern army, and as the troops in your vicinity, and those of your division, are near the frontier, it is requested that you will order fifteen hundred to march to the frontier with as little delay as may be, and with directions to report to General Winchester or officer commanding on the frontier. Fifteen hundred stands of arms, equipments, ammunition, and such camp equipage as the public stores can supply will be forwarded from Pittsburgh, as you will be more particularly informed by the return of Mr. Huntington. You are requested to inform Governor Meigs and the commanding officer of this arrangement.

Very respectfully, I have the honor to be, Sir, your obedient servant. W. Eustis.

ELIJAH WADSWORTH TO GENERAL PERKINS

Headquarters,
Cleveland, Sept 6th, 1812.

Sir: Orders have been issued to General Beall to march the troops from the First and Second brigades to Mansfield in Richland county. That force is more than six hundred men. To them will be joined the force from Virginia under Colonel Connell, amounting to two hundred men. General Beall is ordered to keep open a communication with you, and to consult and arrange with you on a line of defense from Mansfield to Huron. Until the army under my command is provided with munitions of war we shall not extend ourselves far into the enemy's country, but arrange the defense of the frontier in the best manner. Several good blockhouses should be erected at convenient distances on the road from Huron to Mansfield. The positions you and General Beall will fix on, and if from either of your detachments a party may be prudently advanced to a point nearer the Sandusky bay, say to somewhere near where the Maumee road strikes the west line of the Fire Land, it would be advisable. Much must be left to your direction, as particular instructions cannot be given without a better knowledge of the country. Your troops will be better contented if you keep them employed.

General Beall marches for Mansfield on the 8th or 9th inst., and in five days will reach that place. The utmost confidence is placed in your skill and vigilance, and it is expected that you send to headquarters and to General Beall (when he informs you of his arrival at Mansfield) every occurrence of interest to the service.

Yours, Elijah Wadsworth,
Maj. Gen. Fourth Division.

N. B.—Forward a weekly report of your strength, and also a weekly return of the Quartermaster's stores.

WAR OF 1812.

From the Papers of Hon. C. Whittlesey.

SELECTION No. 2.

PETITION OF CITIZENS IN THE WEST PART OF PORTAGE COUNTY, RELATING TO THEIR EXPOSED CONDITION.

To GEN. ELIJAH WADSWORTH, Canfield, Ohio :

We, the subscribers, citizens and committee of the towns of Stoe, Franklin, Northhamton and Harmansburgh, do Humbly show that the inhabitants of said towns are entirely destitute of ammunition such as powder, lead or flints, and a very great number destitute of arms. We, the said committee, petition to your Honour to forward on as many arms as can be spared, about one hundred pounds of powder, five hundred flints, and lead in proportion. Our present defenceless situation is well Known to your Honour, and no doubt will give such relief as may be in your power. We do not consider the number of men in this part of our frontier sufficient to protect it. We therefore pray that you may send on such a number of men as you may think sufficient for that purpose.

FRED'K HAYMAKER,
WM. WETMORE,
SAMUEL KING,
JOHN HAYMAKER,
STEPHEN BUTLER.

STOE, 22nd August, 1812.

N. B. It is reported and generally believed that Gen. Hull has surrendered to the British.

PETITION OF THE OFFICERS OF THE ODD BATTALION.

HUDSON, August 22, 1812.

To ELIJAH WADSWORTH, ESQ., Major General of Division:

We, the undersigned officers of the Odd Battalion, in the Fourth Brigade and Fourth Division of Ohio Militia, do humbly state that a part of the soldiers in said Battalion are destitute of arms; and the situation of the country generally, and our particular situation, is well known to your Honour as being a frontier. We do, therefore, petition that fifty stands of arms be sent to the Battallion for the use of such soldiers as are destitute who may be called to do duty in actual service. And likewise that a proportion of powder be sent; which articles will be placed under such directions as your Honor shall think proper.

GEORGE DARROW, Major.,
AMOS LUSK, Capt.,
GEORGE W. HOLCOMB, Lieut.,
CHARLES POWERS, Ensign,
THOMAS RICE, Capt.,
THOMAS VANHYNING, Lieut.

RETURN OF DRAFTS FROM 1ST REGIMENT, 3RD BRIGADE, 4TH DIVISION, MADE 5TH SEPTEMBER, 1812.

I do certify this to be a true Return of Drafts from 1st Regiment, 3rd Brigade, 4th Division Ohio Militia as made to me.

WILLIAM RAYEN, Lt. Col.

A RETURN OF NAMES OF THE COMMISSIONED AND NON-COMMISSIONED OFFICERS AND PRIVATES.

First Company.

Captain—JOSHUA T. COTTON.
Lieutenant—GEORGE MONTIETH.
Ensign—JACOB IRWIN.

Sergeants.

John Cotton, John Myres,
George Wintermute, Ab'hm. Wintermute.

Corporals.

John Carlton, Boardwin Robins,
John Russell, Jesse Graham.

Privates,

Henry Peter, John Truesdale,
Daniel Shatto, Francis Harvey,
James Crooks, Anthony Whitterstay,
Matthew Guy, Thomas Cummons,
John McCollum, Jacob Parkust,
Henry Bronstetter, Isaac Parkust,
Robert Kerr, Samuel Calhoun,
Henry Crum, George Gilbert,
Nicholas Vinnemons, Abraham Simons,
William McCrery, Thomas Craft,
Joseph Osburn, Archibald Maurace,

Adam Swazer, James Fitch,
Henry Thom, Henry Foose,
John Parkust, Abraham Leach,
Samuel White, Daniel Stewart,
Senaca Carver, Joseph Carter,
Jacob Hull, Isaac Fisher,
John White, Jacob Powers,
John Muskgrove, Thomas Irwin,
George Smith, William Munn,
John Hayes, Nathan Angue,
Thomas McCrery, Philip Kimmel,
John McGlaughlin, Abraham Hoover,
Michael Storm, Benjamin Roll,
John McMahon.

Second Company.

Captain—Samuel Denison.
Lieutenant—David A. Adams.
Ensign—William Swan.

Sergeants.

Amos Gray, William Carlton.

Corporals.

James Walton, Mathew I. Scott,
Robert Stewart, David Ramsey.

Privates.

John Dunwoody, David McClelland,
Ephrahim Armitage, Isaac Lyon,
Samuel Ferguson, Samuel Mann,
Conrad Miller, John McMurry,
Jacob Fight, Senr., William McMurry,
Jacob Oswalt, William Bell,
James Eckman, John Nelson,
Andrew Boyd, Peter Carlton,
John Moore, Jacob Fight, Jr.,
David Kays, David Stewart,
John Day, Joseph Baggs,
Robert Walker, William McNight,
Thomas Wilson, Thomas Fowler,
John Tulley, Sampson Moore,
James Lynn, John Poynes,
William Crawford, John Bradon,
David Willson, Daniel Augustine,
David McConnell, John Polly,
John Yast.

Third Company.

Captain—Warren Bissell.
Lieutenant—Alexander Rayne.
Ensign—Nicholas McConnell

Sergeants.

A. Stilson, Parkus Woodrough,
Asa Baldwin, Simon Stall,

Corporals.

William Hamilton, Amanuel Hull
Jacob Dice. Isaac Blackman,

Privates.

David Noble, Alexander Craze,
Aaron Dawson, David McCombs,
David Conizer, George Mockerman,
Henry Rumble, John Dowler,
John Riddle, Josiah Bearsley,
James Moody, John Murphy,
Joseph Mearchant, Josiah Walker,
John Bucannon, John Earl.
John Dickson, John Ross,
John Moore, John Cowdan,
Joseph McGill, John Brothers,
Phillip McConnell, Robert McGill,
Richard McConnell, Renalds Cowdan,
Robert Goucher, Samuel Love,
Thomas McCombs, William McGill,
William Bucannon, Walter Bucannon,
William Reed, William Cowdan,
William Shield, John Zedager,
William Frankle.

A RETURN OF CAPTAIN HINES' COMPANY.

Lieut.—Edmund P. Tanner.
Ensign—Thomas McCane.

Sergeants.

Julius Tanner, Daniel Fitch,
Silas Johnson, John Hutson.

Corporals.

Christopher Rasor, Joseph Bruce,
John McMullen.

Privates.

Henry McKinney, George Leonard,
John Turner, Robert Cain,
John Young, Henry Boyd,
John Chub, William McKinnie,
James McDonald, George Heater,
Jacob Shook, Henry Houck,
Samuel Green, James Saseton,
Conrad Osburn, James Polluck,
Benj. Manchester, John McConnell,
William Thomas, Arthur Anderson,
William Leonard, Elijah Stevenson,
John Hill, Henry Stump,
William Steel, John McCully,
Robert McCrary, Frances Henry,
Nicholas Leonard, John McKey,
Henry Ripley, James Jack,
James Moore, Garret Peckard.

Colonel Richard Hays to the commanding officer at Fort Wayne or Urbana, September 7, 1812. Sent by Lieut. Pomeroy and his party of scouts.

Camp at Pipe Creek.
September 7, 1812.

To the commanding officer at Fort Wayne or Urbana.

Sir.—We are encamped at this place and at Huron with four hundred militia of Ohio. The inhabitants are in a state of consternation at this place. Most part fled at news of our Northwestern Army surrendering. We should esteem it a great favour to receive some infor mation from you by the bearer of this, so far as would not be detrimental, if it should be taken from the bearer by the Indians. Lieut. Pomeroy commands the scouting party sent out. Accept my respects.

Richard Hayes.

Lieut. Col. Command't 3d Regiment, 3d Brigade, 4th Divison Ohio Militia at this place.

GEN. SIMON PERKINS TO GEN. WADSWORTH, CLEVELAND.

Camp at Huron, Sept. 8, 1812.

Dear Sir: I wrote you this morning by a sick man going home on furlough, since which our scouts have come in and inform that there is or was last night, at Sandusky, a number of Indians and British who have burned the public store. The spies saw the enemy and fire but could not determine their numbers.

My present arrangements are to march my whole force to Pipe Creek, except one company, who will be left at this station to compete this encampment and guard the provisions, from Pipe Creek send a force to Sandusky, the amount of which will be determined on the return of some spies now out, which will be in this afternoon. As occurrences present themselves I will inform you, and am sir, yours,

SIMON PERKINS.

MAJOR GENERAL WADSWORTH.

GENERAL PERKINS TO GENERAL WADSWORTH.

CAMP AT HURON Sept. 9, 1812, 4 P. M.

Major General WADSWORTH, Cleveland, Ohio.

SIR :—Yours by the express came to hand last evening which I should have answered and have returned the messenger immediately, but thinking it important to detain him until this morning I presume you will pardon the proceeding. I had as I wrote you yesterday made arrangements to send a company to Sandusky, but in consequence of the information in your letter of the 8th I have thought it prudent to order the companies of Dull and Murray to fall back on the east side Huron, and Parker with his company to return to his former station in the town of Avery to complete his Block house there, then he will be ordered to join the camp at Huron. Two boats that went lately to the Peninsula returned last evening with the loss of two men killed; one private from Col. Rayens' Regiment and the other an inhabitant of this part of the country. One of those boats, commanded by Lieutenant Benj. Allen, of Col. Hayes' Regiment, found a British schooner aground on Cunningham's Island, which, after dismantling and loading the boat with the most valuable part of the rigging, set fire to and burned her.

I wrote yesterday to Col. Williams and Maj. Krutzer, a copy of which is enclosed. I have also this day received a message from Maj. Krutzer, informing me that he has commenced his march, and is building a Block house at what they (the messenger) call the Black Fork; they are in doubt whether he will march faster than can be done with the erection of Block houses at suitable distances for protection. I wrote him and solicited of him information as to his determination on that subject.

If I could receive a few more arms for my detachment they would be very acceptable.

Utensils for cooking and camp equipage generally is very much wanted; we have not so much as one kettle to a mess and no teakettle in the camp.

Returns as required shall be made out and forwarded.

All occurrences of note shall be communicated, and, Sir, I shall ever be happy to be instructed by you, and believe me very respectfully your most humble Servant,

SIMON PERKINS.

Krutzer has with him about (80) eighty men.

Western Reserve Historical Society,

CLEVELAND, O., JANUARY, 1871.

HISTORICAL AND ARCHÆLOGICAL TRACTS.

NUMBER FOUR.

First White Children Born on Ohio Soil.

BY ALFRED T. GOODMAN,

SECRETARY OF THE SOCIETY.

The earliest known occupation of the territory now embraced within the limits of the State of Ohio, by any collective body of white men, was by the French in 16 0. From that time until the conquest of Canada by the English, French traders were scattered throughout the territory, having a post, station or "store" at almost every Indian town.

English traders first made their appearance in the Ohio country in 1699—1700. From that time until 1745, we frequently hear of them at various towns and stations. In 1745 they built a small fort or block house among the Hurons on the north side of Sandusky bay. In 1748, they were driven off by a party of French soldiers from Detroit. Prior to to 1763, the English in Ohio were very few in comparison to the numbers of the French. Up to the period of the American revolution, thousands of French and English traders had passed into the Ohio country. It is impossible to determine how many lived there at any one time. At some villages there was but one or two traders, at others ten, twenty and sometimes as many as fifty. For the most part the traders were married to squaws, and had children by them. In rare cases, white women accompanied their husbands on trading excursions, which generally lasted for months. This was probably because the savages always preferred to trade and barter with those connected with their people by marriage. We have never heard of but two instances where traders had white wives living with them in Indian villages. (*) We have no information that would throw light upon the object of this paper, (which is to ascertain if possible the date of birth of the first white child born in Ohio) from any of the French and English occupants of Ohio prior to the peace of 1763. White children were doubtless born unto some of the many traders in Ohio before 1763, and yet there is no evidence whatever, that such was the fact. It is possible that among the French, English or Canadian archives there may be records that would enlighten us upon the subject, but nothing has appeared thus far.

The information we possess is so meagre and perhaps unsatisfactory, that the object of

(*) These were a man named —— Henry, (brother of Judge Henry, of Lancaster, Pennsylvania), who was domiciled on the Scioto, at a Shawnese village called "Chelokraty," and Richard Conner, a Maryland trader, who lived on the Scioto at Pickaway. Both these men exercised great influence among the Shawnese. Mr. Henry was living among them as early as 1768, and married a white woman, who when a child, had been taken captive. We do not know whether they had children born in Ohio, but it is likely they did, for Henry continued on the Scioto for many years, and amassed a fortune there.

In 177[illegible] Mr. Conner, who had lived among the Western Indians as a trader for years, married a oung white woman, cap ive among the Shawnese at Pickaway. In 1771 a male child he query, "who was the first white child orn in Ohio?" may still remain as hereto-ore, "a simple matter of conjecture," but we ope that this paper will be the "opening wedge" or others on the subject more clear, compre-ensive and decisive.

For many years, indeed, until recently it has een generally stated and believed, that Miss ohanna Maria Heckewelder was the first vhite child who saw the light of Heaven in Dhio. That belief made Miss H. the object f unusual attentions; visitors from all parts f the country resorted to her residence, to see nd converse with the *first* white child born n the wilderness of Ohio. Historians sought er acquaintance, antiquarians her photo-raph and autograph; learned societies her orrespondence through complimentary mem-erships, in fact everybody who knew her his-ory, honored and respected "Aunt Polly Ieckewelder," as she was familiarly called at Bethlehem where she lived and died. Until he year 1848 Miss Heckewelder's claim re-nained undisturbed, that is to say, no one ublicly denied her right to appear in the ole of the "first white child." Mr. Howe, in is "Historical Collections of Ohio," first put doubt on her claim, in a brief statement of he birth of a Frenchman, named Mille-omme, which we shall notice hereafter. At latter period the investigations of Judge Blickensderfer, of Tuscarawas county, Ohio, nd Rev. Edmund De Schweinitz, Bishop of he Moravian church, among the achives of he early mission station at Gnadenhutten, evealed the interesting fact that a white hild named Roth, son of a missionary, had een born there nearly eight years before Miss Heckewelder's birth at Salem.

The birth of Roth occurred one year before hat of the Frenchman, Millehomme, men-ioned by Howe. Here, therefore, are two nstances of the birth of white children prior o Miss Heckewelder. These are all the cases we have, except one occuring in 1764, which is deserving of attention and investigation.

We have already stated that no *known* white child was born in Ohio before the close of the French and English War, (1763). The information we have of the birth of one dur-ing the year 1764, is perhaps not definite enough for acceptance by the historical reader and critic, but we have gathered in the facts, such as they are, and place them upon record in connection with the other statements on the subject. But we think there is *reasonable* ground for asserting that the first known birth of a white child, occurring within the limits of Ohio, was that belonging to a white woman from Virginia, who had been taken prisoner by the Delawares in April, 1764. This woman was, at the time of her capture, far advanced in pregnancy, and during the month of July, 1764, gave birth to a child at or near the In-dian town of Wakatomaka, near the the pres-ent site of Dresden, Muskingum county, Ohio. Let us examine into the matter:

When Colonel Bouquet advanced with his army into the Ohio country in October, 1764, he was met by the principal chieftains of the Senecas, Delawares and Shawnese, who sued for peace. In answer to their overtures, Bouquet, who was a stern, fearless and resolute man, made a dignified reply. He said: "I give you twelve days from this date to deliver into my hands at Wakatomaka all the prison-ers in your possession, without any exception —Englishmen, Frenchmen, women and children, whether adopted in your tribes, mar-ried or living amongst you under any denomi-nation and pretence whatsoever; together with all negroes. And you are to furnish the said prisoners with clothing, provisions and horses to carry them to Fort Pitt. When you have fully complied with these conditions, you shall then know on what terms you may obtain the peace you sue for."

This bold answer made a profound impres-sion upon the savages. An only alternative was left them—peace upon these conditions or war. They judiciously resolved to give up the white and black captives under their con-trol, and on the 9th of November, brought to Bouquet's camp all the prisoners within the Ohio country, except a few held by a Shaw-anse tribe, who were absent hunting. Those delivered numbered 206: Virginians—males, 32, females and children, 58. Pennsylvani-ans—males, 49, females and children, 67.

Among the Virginians was the white wo-man and her child heretofore alluded to. Her situation is thus noticed in the history of "Bouquet's Expedition," page 79.

was born unto them. It is impossible to state at what place, though in all probability the birth occurred at Pickaway on the Scioto. In 774, agreeably to the treaty of Fort Pitt, all whites residing among the Shawnese were de-ivered up at that post. Among these were Mr. Conner and wife, but the Shawnese held back their son. The same year Mr. and Mrs Conner went to reside with the Moravians at Shoenbrun, Ohio, Mr. Conner having obtained permission from the American Commandant at Pittsburg, went to the Scioto in search of his on. He left Mrs. Conner at Shoenbrun. In the pring he returned without his child, having nade a fruitless search at all the Shawnese owns. During the year 1776, Mr. Conner made a second search after his boy and finally found him, and succeeded in purchasing his ransom. Mrs. Conner afterwards had children at Shoen-brun, though we are without dates.

"Among the captives, a woman was brought into the camp at Muskingum, with a babe about three months old at her breast. One of the Virginia volunteers soon knew her to be his wife who had been taken by the Indians six months before. She was immediately delivered to her overjoyed husband, who flew with her to his tent, and clothed her and his child in proper apparel. But their joy, after the first transports, was soon damped by the reflection that another dear child of about two years old, captured with the mother and separated from her was still missing, although many children had been brought in.

"A few days afterwards, a number of other prisoners were brought to the camp, among whom were several more children. The woman was sent for and one supposed to be hers was produced for her. At first sight she was uncertain, but viewing the child with great earnestness, she soon recollected its features; and was so overcome with joy, that literally forgetting her sucking child she dropped it from her arms, and catching up the new found child in an ecstacy, pressed it to her breast, and bursting into tears, carried it off unable to speak for joy, The father seizing up the babe she had let fall, followed her in no less transport and affection."

But it may be said, "the Moravians had settled at Bolivar in 1761, and children may have been born unto them!" This inquiry is easily answered and correctly so. Prior to 1764 there were but two white Moravians in Ohio, Heckewelder and Post. Heckewelder did not marry until 1780, and Post was married to an Indian Squaw. Add to this, the fact that there were no white women in the Moravian settlements, prior to the year 1764, and we think the answer is complete. If any white children either French, English or American, were born within the limits of Ohio before the year 1764, we have been unable to find evidences of the fact. We think therefore that we are safe in stating that the child of the Virginia captive, born in 1764, was the first *known* white child born in Ohio.

In 1772, John George Jungmann and wife arrived at Shoenbrun, Ohio, from Bethlehem, Pa. Jungmann was a Moravian Missionary, and his wife was the first married white woman who came west among the Christian Indians.

In April 1773, John Roth and wife reached Gnadenhutten, Ohio. Roth was also a missionary, sent out by the Moravian Church. Nearly three months after her arrival, Mrs. Roth gave birth to a son at Gnadenhutten, who was named John Lewis Roth. His birth occurred on the 4th of July, 1773, and he was baptised on the 5th, by the Rev. David Zeisberger.

In the life of Zeisberger, by Bishop De Schweinitz, will be found an interesting biographical notice of John Lewis Roth, as well as sketches of his father and mother.

When John Lewis was one month old, August 1773, his parents removed from Gnadenhutten to Shoenbrun. At that place Mr. Roth labored for nearly a year, with marked success. His converts were many, which filled his heart with great joy and gratitude to God. It was at this time that Dunmore's war broke out. The Christian Indians were threatened, the missionaries' lives were despared of, and the entire destruction of all the Moravian towns daily looked for. In this trying moment Zeisberger recommended Roth to return to Pennsylvania with his family. This advice was followed. Mr. and Mrs. Roth reached Bethlehem in June, 1774, when their infant son, John Lewis, was less than a year old. Mr. Roth continued in the service of the Moravian Church many years, being successively employed at Mount Joy, York, Emmans, and Hebron, Pennsylvania. He died at York, July 22, 1790. Mrs. Roth died at Nazareth, February 25, 1805.

John Lewis Roth, whom Bishop DeSchweinitz and Judge Blickensderfer claim to have been the first white child born in Ohio, was educated at Nazareth Hall, Bethlehem, Pennsylvania. At an early age he married and settled on a farm near Nazareth, Pennsylvania, where he lived until his 63d year. In 1836, he removed to Bath, Pennsylvania, and while residing there joined the Lutheran Church, of which the Rev. A. Fuchs was pastor. Mr. Roth was an exemplary christian, and brought up his children in the love and fear of God. He died September 25th, 1841, and is buried in the cemetery at Bath, where a small marble tombstone bears this inscription:

"Zum Andenken an Ludwig Roth, geboren 4th. Juli, 1773. Gestorben, 25th, September 1841, Alter 68 Jahre, 2, M, 21 Tage."

The village of Gnadenhutten where Mr. Roth was born, was situated on the Tuscarawas river, in Clay township, Tuscarawas county, Ohio, not far from the outskirts of the present town of Gnadenhutten. It was there that the horrible massacre of Christian Indians took place in March, 1782.

The next white birth in Ohio, is founded upon the assertion made by Mr. Henry Howe, in his "Ohio Historical Collections," page 437. He says, "Mr. Dinsmoore, a planter of Boone county, Ky., orally informed us that in the year 1835, when residing in the parish of

Terre-Bonne, La., he became acquainted with a planter name Millehomme, who informed him that he was born in the forest, on the head waters of the Miami, on or near the Loramie Portage, about the year 1774. His parents were Canadian French, then on their route to Louisiana."

We know nothing of the facts in this case other than as given by Mr. Howe. We presume he considered the statement of Mr. Dinsmoore perfectly reliable, or it would not have found a place in his valuable work.

Early in the year 1780, the Moravian Church at Bethleham sent to the Ohio Missions as teacher, Miss Sarah Ohneberg. She was a young woman of fine education, amiable disposition and unaffected Christian piety. Soon after her arrival at Shoenbrun, she was the recipient of marked attentions from Rev. John Heckewelder, then in his 38th year. Friendship soon ripened into firmer attachment, and in July 1780, they were united in marriage in the Chapel at Salem, by the Rev. Adam Grube. All the Mission familes and the converted Indians witnessed the interesting ceremony. This was the first wedding of a white couple ever held in Ohio.

During the following year, Mrs. Heckewelder gave birth to a female child at Salem. It was baptized and named Johanna Maria Heckewelder. We have already introduced this child to the reader. Her claim, (for she always asserted it,) to have been the first white child born in Ohio, has been shown to be unsustainable. Her history, however, is very interesting. A short time before her father's death, at her request, he wrote out a statement regarding her birth and the events of her early childhood. This manuscript she sacredly retained until her death, and it has never been published, with the exception of a portion, which appeared in the *Moravian*, the Church paper published at Bethlehem. The writer has been favored with a copy, through the politeness of Charles Brodhead, Esq. The original manuscript was written in the German language, and was translated with great care by the editor of the newspaper referred to. The translation is as follows:

"Johanna Maria Heckewelder was born on Easter Monday, April 16th, 1781, at Salem, a village of Christian Indians on the Muskingum River. She was baptized on the day following by Rev. William Edwards, minister at Gnadenhutten. A few days after her birth the Indians in that region were thrown into a state of great alarm by the sudden attack of an American army upon a town of the savages, named "Goschachking," and a number of the latter were killed. About eighty warriors came to our settlements, determined to break up the Indian congregations of Shoenbrun, Gnadenhutten and Salem, or at least to remove them about one hundred miles further westward; but during their stay amongst us they changed their minds, and the majority of them, especially the chief, said they considered us a happy people, to injure whom would be a great sin, and that they wished that they themselves were partakers of the same happiness. Amongst them, however, was one evil disposed man, who had resolved to murder me (your father) and for two days he waited eagerly for an opportunity to carry out his purpose, but the Lord watched over and saved me from this danger in a very striking way.

"After this event the three Indian congregations continued for some time to live in peace, and increased in spiritual knowledge and grace, so that we were filled with great joy. But in the beginning of the month of August we heard that there was a new movement amongst the Indians to drive us away, some even being in favor of destroying our settlements, but as they failed to find amongst their own number any who were ready to undertake this, certain wicked white persons joined them, and on the 12th of August they arrived at Salem with the advance-guard. The others arrived during the following days numbering in all 300 warriors, who camped in the square at Gnadenhutten. They endeavored by all sorts of promises to entice our Indian brethren and sisters to leave our stations and to come and live with them. After spending three weeks in these efforts, which were entirely unsuccessful, and being in the end disposed to leave the matter drop, they found that they had compromised themselves to such an extent that they were compelled to use force.

"They accordingly set apart the 2d of September for a general council, and all the Brethren at the three stations were summoned to be in attendance. Bro. David Zeisberger repaired to Shoenbrun, eight miles above, I to Salem about six miles below Gnadenhutten, and the Brethren Edwards and Senseman to the latter place. Bro. Jungmann and his wife remained at Shoenbru with Sisters Zeisberger and Senseman, the latter of whom had an infant at the breast, and Bro. Michal Jung remained at Salem with you and your mother. We passed the night in much sorrow, but without fear. Finally on the 3d of September, as we were walking up and down on a level spot behind the gardens, several warriors of the Wyandotte nation came up and took us prisoners to their camp. Here we were stripped of our best clothes, and one of them, who probably did not know what he was about, seized us by the head and shook us, saying in a scornful tone, 'Welcome, my friends.'"

"After a while we were placed in charge of a guard. When we were taken prisoners the appearance of the Indians was indeed terrible, as they all grasped their arms and we thought we should be dispatched on the spot, but our grief at the thought of your mother and yourself and the others, was more terrible than everything else, for just as we were led into the camp, about twenty warriors, brandishing their arms and with terrible cries, galloped off on their horses towards Salem and Shoenbrun. When he saw them coming at a distance, Brother Jung locked the door of the house. You were lying in your cradle asleep. Finding the outer door locked, they burst it open by force and would have killed Brother Jung on the spot, but a white man who was with them prevented them. Your mother snatched you from the cradle and was told that she was a prisoner and must accompany them to Gnadenhutten. The house was then plundered from top to bottom. In the meanwhile it had commenced to rain, and some of the Indian sisters begged very urgently that you and your mother might remain with them over night, promising to bring you to Gnadenhutten the next day. Bro. Jung they took with them, arriving at the camp at about midnight. We had heard their scalp-cries all the while as we sat on the banks of the river, and the night was thereby made all the more horrible to us.

"We were all prisoners together. Our houses had been plundered, and we had nothing to cover our bodies but what our Indian brothers and sisters brought us. After several days, we received permission to be with our Indians, but together with them were conducted through the wilderness to Upper Sandusky. On this journey the mothers and children suffered much, as the warriors would grant no halts. In the beginning of October we arrived at Upper Sandusky. We were entirely destitute, and yet were quite happy. We cared not for the morrow, and yet we were provided with our daily bread. We commenced to build little huts for ourselves, but before they were completed we received orders from the Commandant at Detroit to repair to that place. This was a new and severe trial. Winter was at hand, and we were to leave our wives and children behind without any provisions. In addition, the savages daily threatened to kill us. The day of our departure was fixed, and the Brethren Zeisberger, Edwards, Senseman and myself set out on the long journey. Bro. Schebosch promised to provide our families with provisions brought from our deserted village.

"We had not proceeded more than sixty miles on our journey before a messenger caught up with us, bringing the news that Bro. Schebosch and his company had been seized and carried off by a party of militia. Other messengers arrived bringing the same inteligence, so that our anxiety for our wives and children became intense. At the Iowa (?) river we encountered endless difficulties in continuing our journey. We could not proceed alone, even if we had had permision to do so. The Captain who had charge of us, procured a keg of rum and all his men became drunk, and a number of evil-disposed people gathered at our halting-place. At last, since we had some of our Indian brethren with us, we received permission from a white man to proceed. After several days' journey we came within four miles of Detroit, but for want of a boat to cross a deep river that lay right before us, we were compelled to spend the night, which was intensely cold and stormy, on the open plain, without any protection whatever, so that we were quite stiff and almost frozen by morning.

"The next morning, at about eight o'clock, without having had anything to eat, we were ferried across in a hay boat, and by ten o'clock we made our appearance before the Commandant at the fort, who received us with many harsh words. Finally, as we remained perfectly composed, he seemed to have changed his mind somewhat and dismissed us in a much pleasanter manner. For a week we remained in a state of great uncertainty as to what was to become of us. We were not permitted to appear before the Commandant to make any statements, nor were we permitted to address any written communications to him. At last, our accusers being all assembled, we were summoned to attend, and after a thorough examination into the accusations brought against us, the result was that two of our accusers were completely silenced, and the third became our defender. The council, which consisted of the military officers and other officials at this post and of a number of Indian chiefs, decided that we had been falsely accused and had innocently been compelled to endure many hardships. Thus even here, the glory of God's name was promoted.

"From this time forth, the Commandant became our warm friend, and from other gentlemen at the post we received many kindnesses.

Provided with some needful clothing and provisions by order of the former, we set out on our return. Our Heavenly Father granted us, at this late season, the most pleasant weather, and by the end of November we rejoined our families once more [at Sandusky.] On the very day of our return, the winter set in, a great deal of snow fell and the cold became intense. The distress of our Indians became terrible. In a short time they lost one hundred and fifty head of cattle, which were their main dependence for food. The wild Indians again threatened to stop the preaching of the Gospel, and the power of the prince of darkness seemed almost supreme. The scarcity of food became so great that we began to fear that some, especially the little children, would perish from hunger.

"A number of Indian brethren and sisters accordingly resolved to return with their families to their deserted villages and gather in the harvest, which was yet standing in the fields, and little by little to forward the proceeds to this place. They had almost finished this work and were preparing to return to us, when they were attacked by a party of American militia, taken prisoners, and butchered in cold blood. These dear martyrs, 96 in number, resigned themselves cheerfully to God's will. They united together in prayer to the Savior, begged each other's forgiveness for past offences, sang hymns of faith and trust, and testified that they died as Christians. The many little children in this company shared the same fate as their parents. Thus a whole Indian congregation was in one night 7th—8th of March, 1782, translated from earth to heaven.

"In the meanwhile we who remained at Upper Sandusky were suddenly summoned to appear at Detroit, whilst our Christian Indians were to unite themselves to some of the wild tribes in the vicinity. Our poor Indian brethren could not understand nor reconcile themselves to these orders. Many of them accompanied us as far as our first camping-place, weeping as they walked beside us. Some went with us the whole way to Lower Sandusky, a five days' journey, amongst whom were two Indian sisters, one of whom carried you in a blanket the whole way, and the other Sister Senseman's child. Here we waited three weeks for further orders, receiving during our stay the certain intelligence of the murder of our beloved Indians at Gnadenhutten.

Those were days of bitter suffering and most distressing doubts, but the Savior comforted and strengthened us. As we were sitting in a friendly trader's house, a wicked man, an English officer, made his appearance and threatened to kill us on the spot. We knew that he could readily summon confederates to carry out his purpose, and committed ourselves to the protection of Him whose own we were. And wonderfully did He interpose in our behalf, for just then two boats arrived to fetch us away, and brought besides an order from Major Arent De Peyster at Detroit, in which he threatened to punish severely any persons who should, in any way, molest us. April 14th, 1782, we set out in the boats, descending Sandusky River for 30 miles and then crossing Lake Erie to Detroit. On the 16th, your first birthday anniversary, we were compelled at four different times to draw our boat to the shore during a storm, once at great risk to us all. As I was afflicted with rheumatism and could not help myself, Bro. Edwards built a shelter against the wind for your mother and you out of cedar boughs. April 29th, we crossed Miami Bay, not without considerable danger, and the next day we arrived at Detroit.

"Here our whole company remained until August. Our Indians, who had been scattered in many different places, received permission to assemble here, and after several families of them had come, we commenced a settlement on Huron River, which empties into Lake St. Clair. Many of our Indians joined us here, and the Commandant, now Colonel De Peyster, provided us with provisions. As the Brethren Jungmann and Senseman were in the year 1785 to return to Bethlehem your parents concluded to send you with them to the school at Bethlehem. After a farewell lovefeast, these Brethren set out, May 16th, your father accompanying you as far as Detroit. The journey was made by boat across Lake Erie, and after being detained at Niagara for two weeks, in the same way across Lake Ontario to Wood's Creek, and thence by way of Schennectady and Albany to Bethlehem, at which place you arrived July 8th."

To the above account, Miss Heckewelder a number of years before her death, added the following:

"On this journey we were often compelled to spend the night in the woods in tents. We heard the wolves howling about our camp, and built large fires to keep them away. As we were often compelled to go on foot, I became very tired, and old Father Jungmann used to carry me for miles on his back. Arrived at Bethlehem, I was placed in the Children's Institute, being then only five years old. There was at that time no boarding school. This was only instituted the following year. I look back upon the years spent at this institution with the greatest pleasure. We received the most affectionate and tender treatment, and the exemplary Christian demeanor of our teachers has made an abiding impression upon my heart. My school days being ended, I entered the Sisters' House. Having been received into the Church a short time before, I partook of my first communion on August 13th, 1795.

"In my twentieth year I received a call as teacher in the recently established boarding-school at Litiz. Here I remained for five years, until the impaired state of my hearing compelled me to resign, and I returned to Bethlehem. At Litiz I had many severe experiences; many, too, which were very beneficial to me. The Holy Spirit wrought powerfully upon my heart, and the sinful state of my heart was revealed to me. I spent many sad and troubled hours, trying to build up a righteousness of my own, and yet never discerning what a Redeemer I had. On the occasion of a choir communion, September 10, 1803, I had a peculiarly deep feeling of my own poverty and sinfulness, and yet I experienced the peace of God in my soul in a way which I cannot in words describe. An ineffable feeling of love and gratitude to Him who could bless and forgive one so unworthy as myself, filled my soul. Now, everything was bright within me; I had passed from death to life. In this blessed frame of mind I remained for a long time, but I had yet many things to learn, and in spite of many alternations in my spiritual life, the Savior was ever my helper and consoler. The total loss of my hearing occasioned me much pain, and I had a severe struggle before I could resign myself implicity to this deprivation. The thought that this trial came from the Lord and was intended for my advancement in the heavenly life, has now entirely reconciled me to it.

"A review of my experience fills me with grateful love to Him, whose leadings have been so gracious and wise. I know myself to be nothing. Through grace alone I am what I am."

The loss of her hearing prevented Miss Heckewelder from devoting her future to the object chosen—the education of young women for useful occupations in life. From 1806 she resided at Bethlehem; up to 1823 in the family of her father, and afterwards with the Sisters of the Church. She was obliged to use a slate in conversation. Her habits were those of a pious, industrious woman. Her acts of benevolence and charity were frequent and disinterested. She abounded in good works. Old age curtailed her deeds of kindness and her "missions of love." Her latter days were spent in meekness and quietness—waiting the coming of her time. Her last illness was short, and her end was peace. She died in the assurance of a blessed immortality, September 19, 1868, aged 87 years, 5 months and 2 days. Her remains were deposited by those of her father, in the Moravian Cemetery at Bethlehem.

We here leave our first inquiry, and give the reader a brief sketch of the first white person born in Ohio, after the settlement made at Marietta, on the Ohio, in 1788. That person was Leicester G. Converse. He was born at Marietta, February 7, 1789, and resided there for many years. In 1834 he located in Morgan county, engaging in mercantile operations, from which, in 1846, he retired to his farm, situated on the west bank of the Muskingum, about five miles above McConnelsville. There he continued to reside until his death, which occurred February 14, 1859. Mr. Converse was a man of character and ability; an exemplary christian, and a citizen of great usefulness. He was passionately fond of farming, and for several years before his death was interested in the operations of the Ohio State Board of Agriculture.

CLEVELAND, O. Dec. 23, 1870.

ANCIENT EARTH FORTS

OF THE

Cuyahoga Valley, Ohio,

BY

COL. CHAS. WHITTLESEY,

PRESIDENT OF THE WESTERN RESERVE AND NORTHERN OHIO HISTORICAL SOCIETY.

PUBLISHED FOR THE SOCIETY BY A GENTLEMAN OF CLEVELAND.

CLEVELAND, OHIO:

FAIRBANKS, BENEDICT & CO., PRINTERS.

1871.

Ancient Earth Works of Ohio.

HISTORY OF THE SURVEYS.

The existence of ancient earth works in Ohio was first brought to notice by the Rev. David Jones, in 1772–3; by Arthur Lee, in 1784; and in 1785, through a plan and description of those at Marietta, by Capt. JONATHAN HEART, of Colonel Harmar's battalion.

Capt. Heart assisted in building Fort Harmar, at the mouth of the Muskingum river. He was evidently a man of education, and had served in the Revolutionary army. His survey was made while the ground was yet covered with a heavy growth of forest trees.

In 1801, the Rev. Mr. Harris, while on a tour through the Ohio country, resurveyed them and inserted an engraved plan in his published Journal.

Caleb Atwater, Esq., of Circleville, Ohio, made the first general survey of the Ohio Earth Works in 1819, under the auspices and at the expense of the American Archæological Society, at Worcester, Mass.

His plans and descriptions fill an important portion of the first volume of their transactions, published in 1820. When the first Geological Survey of Ohio was in progress, I continued the survey of the newly discovered works, intending to make the subject of our antiquities a part of the final report.

This survey came to an end in 1839, without a final report. J. H. SULLIVANT, Esq., of Columbus, requested me to continue this part of the survey at his expense, with a view to publication by himself.

My plans included all the ancient works then known, but Mr. Sullivant's health failing, they were not published, and many of them were lost.

In 1845, the Hon. E. George Squier, who has since done so much to develop the Archæology of the United States, commenced a resurvey of them in connection with Dr. E. H. Davis, both of Chillicothe, Ohio.

These gentlemen made the first systematic descriptions with figures, of the numerous relics of the Mound Builders. They operated under the auspices of the Smithsonian Institute at Washington. The results of their labors, fully illustrated, constitute the first volume of its Contributions.

Their surveys in this State were confined to the works on waters of the Ohio. A part of my plans were published with theirs, and a part in May, 1850, as Article 7, Vol. 3, of the Contributions, which relate principally to the works on the waters of Lake Erie.

Ancient Inhabitants

OF THE

MISSISSIPPI VALLEY AND THE LAKE REGIONS.

Ruins of ancient earth works are plainly to be seen throughout a large part of the United States, constructed by a people who preceded the race first encountered here by the whites. These works are numerous on the Ohio river and on the streams which discharge into it. They are also found, but of a quite different character, on the streams which empty into Lakes Erie and Ontario from the South. Here, all or nearly all of them have a military purpose, and are less imposing than those on the waters of the Ohio.

In Wisconsin is another and quite a different type of ancient earth works, which are principally mounds, in the form of effigies of animals.

It does not follow that the builders of these different styles of works were one nation or were cotemporary. They had, however, traits enough in common to be ranked as a *race*, under the denomination of "*Earth Builders*." These differences were also sufficiently marked to require a separation into nations or tribes; occupying territories easily defined. The people who inhabited Central and Southern Ohio, also covered an extensive country farther to the southward and westward; down the great valley of the Mississippi to the Gulf of Mexico. They are already known by the name of "*Mound Builders*."

To distinguish the three peoples by their most marked characters, I designate those on the Ohio as the *Agricultural nation;* the Fort Builders on the lakes as the *Military nation*, and those between the Mississippi and Lake Michigan as the *Effigy nation.* Those who wish to study the works of the "Mound Builders" are referred to the elaborate descriptions of Messrs. Squier and Davis. The remains of the "Fort Builders" in New York have been surveyed and described by Mr. Squier, in the year 1849. The Effigy mounds of Wisconsin were surveyed by Dr. I. A. Lapham, of Milwaukee. The results of his work are to be found in the Contributions for 1855.

From the water-shed of the rivers that discharge southerly into the Ohio and the Mississippi, near the 40th parallel of north latitude, southerly to the Gulf of Mexico, including Arkansas and Texas, there is a similarity in the style of the ancient works, indicating that they are the work of one people.

Their leading pursuit was agriculture, having little use for military defences. Their most striking works are burial mounds of earth or loose stone, and altar pyramids, showing a large religious development.

In the effigy region, west of Lake Michigan, it is less easy to devine the leading characteristics of their builders. In the third division of this ancient population, occupying the lake country, in Ohio and New York, military defences take the lead, but their works are far less prominent.

There are certain things which all these people had in common, though they possessed very different degrees of advancement. They all erected earth monuments over the remains of some of their dead, while the bodies of the many were consumed by fire. They had native copper as their only metal, obtained from the mines of Lake Superior, which were extensively wrought

All of them used implements of flint and other stones in a great variety of forms, which are similar, though not identical with those of the red man of our times. Their copper tools, spear heads, spades and knives, were numerous and superior in form and finish to the few and rude copper knives of Indians, which were made from stray nuggets, found in the glacial drift.

It would seem that their dwellings and their weapons of war were principally of wood; but we are as yet in comparative ignor ance in regard to both.

Comparison of the Pre-Historic Races

IN EUROPE AND AMERICA.

EUROPE.

PRIMITIVE MAN.

Cave dwellers cotemporary with the elephant, mastodon, rhinoceros, cave bear, cave lion, cave hyena, and the great stag, all now extinct; and with the closing out of the glacial or drift era, there known as diluvium—they were hunters, dressed in skins—had stone and flint implements, without polish—and pottery. Antiquity exceeding fifteen thousand years.

SECOND ERA.

Polished implements of stone and flint; domestic animals, with pottery, but no pipes, no tools of metal—not cultivators of the soil—hunters with the bow and spear—dress in skins.

AMERICA.

PRIMITIVE MAN.

In South and Central America cotemporary with the elephant, mastodon and extinct horse, dwellers in caves. In North America, evidence, though not as yet conclusive, to show him here as early as the diluvium or later drift; with the elephant, mastodon, extinct horse and megalonyx. Implements, dress and antiquity not known.

SECOND ERA.

In the Mississippi Valley copper cutting tools, beads, daggers, spears, ornaments and spades—cultivated the soil—built earth forts and mounds: polished stone axes and implements, rare. No beasts of burden—flint knives, arrow heads and other implements and weapons of stone, rare; stone calls or whistles and spindle whorls; beads made of bone and shells—domicils not known—had burial mounds for the dead—pipes of stone and clay—coarse cloth of hemp or nettles—miners of copper—cotemporary with the beaver and bear. Antiquity four to five thousand years. Slight evidence of an intervening race between the mound builder and the primitive man.

AGE OF BRONZE.

THIRD ERA.

Lake dwellings of wood; domestic animals; cultivate the soil; nets and cloth of flax; flint implements; cutting tools of bronze (alloy of copper and tin), with handles of bone and wood; pottery; dress in skins. Antiquity six thousand to seven thousand years; calls or whistles of bone; earth forts with ditches.

RED MEN AS THEY WERE BEFORE THE DISCOVERY OF AMERICA.

Hunters with spears and arrow heads; knives and daggers of flint, with stone mauls or axes; and flesh or skin scrapers—very little cultivation of the soil—mats and nets made of bark; a few and rude tools, gorgets and ornaments of copper; not workers of copper mines; not builders of earth forts with ditches; their forts made of wood and stones—dress in skins—no metal axes—no horses—domicils of bark and skins, or wooden frames covered with brush and earth—used rock shelters, and made inscriptions on trees, clay banks and rocks.

This comparison indicates on this continent quite a diversity from the old; in the progress of the early races towards civilization. Here the metal age preceded that of stone, corresponding better with the age of bronze, or of alloys in Europe. We have no certain representative of the rough or unpolished stone period, which there preceded the age of polished stone implements. Our "Mound Builders" were as far advanced, as their fabricators of bronze. From them there was a relapse towards a barbarism nearly entire, in their successors, the red Indian of the North. Of the diluvial man in America we know as yet almost nothing.

SURVEYS ON THE CUYAHOGA.

Since 1850 works have been reported that were not then known to me. Such of them as lie on or near the Cuyahoga river, I have since then, from time to time, examined, and now give a condensed description of them with illustrations. To make the subject complete, it is necessary to republish in this connection those heretofore described. In 1869, some of the members of the Western Reserve Historical and Archæological Society, located at Cleveland, gave me their assistance on those surveys and excavations, particularly, Dr. J. H. Salisbury, Vice-President; Dr. E. Sterling and C. C. Baldwin, Esq.

About this time the Society was enabled, through the liberality of a gentleman of Cleveland, to make more extended and systematic researches, and to publish the results.

It is possible that all the old earth works of this valley are not yet discovered. They are even in an undisturbed condition, not very prominent, the embankments seldom exceeding three feet in height, with a ditch of equal depth. In old fields that have been under cultivation twenty-five to forty years, none but a practiced eye would detect them. Fifty years since this country was but little settled; most of it being then covered with a heavy forest. When the old forts were from time to time discovered they attracted little attention.

The soil within them is invariably rich, owing to prolonged occupation in ancient times by human beings. This fact the early settlers soon discovered, and for this reason these grounds have been cropped closer than those of poorer soil. The plow, the drag, and the cultivator, have thus done extra work in leveling the parapets and filling the ditches of fort builders.

The earth works of the Cuyahoga are a fair representative of the military nation, extending from the west end of Lake Erie, north-eastwardly along the southern shore of Lake Ontario and the river St. Lawrence to Lake Champlain. There are very few on the immediate bank of the lakes. None are reported north of the lakes. They were built on bluffs and bends of the rivers, in strong defensive positions, near springs and small streams of water, not far from batteau navigation, and in the vicinity of rich bottom lands.

The territory of this people in Ohio may be seen by reference to the miniature outline map of the State, presented on Plate III. Those represented by a circular blot, belong to them. Those represented by a square or rectangle, are works of the "Mound Builders." Between them is a wide space of neutral or unoccupied country, on the head waters of the streams which flow in opposite directions, through the State. In this space there are no earth forts, or they have not yet fallen under my observation. I shall refer hereafter to the differences between these ancient nations, as shown in their implements and their works, the only records of their pursuits and their character, which are accessible to us.

Fort No. 1—Newburg.

The topographical surroundings of this fort are seen at once on the engraving, Plate II. It occupies one of the numerous headlands that project from a gravelly plain towards the rivulets which have, in the progress of ages, excavated these deep and nearly impassible ravines. The sides of the adjacent gullies are as steep as the earth will lie, and are wet and slippery from springs. Probably there was some defence of pickets or brush in the form of abattis, around the crest of the space within the double wall. Through the outer one, no gateway or open passage was left. This is not uncommon in the old earth forts. There must have been some mode of entering them, over the walls by stairs or ladders that could easily be removed.

Like most of those on the Cuyahoga and on the waters of Lake Erie, this was evidently a fortified village; like those of the Colorado Indians, in New Mexico, and the strong holds of the ancient Canaanites in Palestine, into which the inhabitants entered at night. The banks are now from one and a half to two feet above the natural surface, and the ditches two feet below. About one-fourth of a mile south-east, on the same level plain, is a mound which was ten feet high in 1847, but has since been much reduced by the plow.

Fort No. 2—Newburg.

This is smaller in size than any of those which stud the river bluffs. It is simply a projecting point, rendered more defensible by a bank of earth and a moat. The view from it is quite commanding and picturesque. Its position is about midway between Nos. 1 and 3, about one and a half miles below Lock No. 8, on the right bank of the river. At the middle, the ditch was never excavated, but there is no opening in the wall at this point. There is a narrow passage around the south end of the embankment along the edge of the ravine, by which the work may be entered. The soil is dry and sandy. In 1850 it had not been long in cultivation, and the elevation of the wall above the bottom of the ditch varied from four to six feet.

FORT NO. 3—INDEPENDENCE.

There is little difference between this and No. 1, except in size. The interior wall is now wholly obliterated—the outer one with its ditch nearly so. A resurvey in 1870 disclosed a slight bank at *a a*, parallel with the bluff, for which there is no apparent object, nor for the horse-shoe outwork, *c c*.

As the soil within the lines is very rich it has been mercilessly cropped during one generation, and is still not exhausted. A rank growth of corn was waving over the entire enclosure in August last. About one-fourth of a mile southerly along the bluff, Mr. Henry Tuttle, the owner of the land, has found numerous relics and bones of the Indian race, indicating the site of a village. Among them is a small neatly carved pipe from the famous red pipe-stone quarry on the Coteau de Missouri, in Dakota. It is in the form of the head of a bird, and is among the collections of the Society, donated by Mr. Chas. Tuttle.

FORT NO. 4—SOUTH-EAST PART OF INDEPENDENCE—PLATE II.

Mr. Dickson, whose daughter, Mrs. Roreback, still resides on the premises, cleared the enclosed space *A*, in the year 1810. The embankment, *b*, was then three or four feet high. A house and barn were built upon it, which are there now, and little can be seen of its primitive condition. It is not certain there was a ditch.

There are springs of perpetual flow in the river bluff and in the adjacent ravines. Within the space *A*, near the mound, great numbers of human bones have been plowed up, so many that they were collected and reburied. The position is beautiful and commanding. On the same farm now owned by Messrs. DAVID L. and N. A. PHILIPS, about half a mile east there are four small mounds, nearly levelled by long cultivation. Near the township corners, about one-third of a mile south of these, is another mound which was five feet high when the early settlers first saw it. Polished stone implements were once common in this vicinity. One presented by Mr. Philips is in the Society's Cabinet, which is different from anything hitherto described. It is a soft crystalline coarse grained sienite, cut into the form of an acorn, with a flat base and a groove around it. Its length is two and a half inches, and its base an inch and eight-tenths.

FORT NO. 5 AND CACHÈS—PLATE III.

When this fort was surveyed in 1847, the ancient pits across the ravine on the east were not known. Mr. L. Austin, of this city, first apprised me of their existence and went with me to the spot. I cannot say that there is any connection or relation between them and the fort. There are similar pits but more regular and circular in and around the space A, which were regarded by the early settlers as wells, because most of them contained water.

The hard-pan of this level space, only a part of which is enclosed, is not favorable for cachè pits, but the appearance of those on the crest of the bluff is the same as at C. For a time I regarded them as the remains of pit dwellings, both at the fort and and at B, C. With the assistance of Messrs. A. B. and Lorin Bliss, of Northfield, I made trenches through some of those in the group B. No relics, ashes or charcoal was discovered in them, such as are invariably found in the ancient pit dwellings of England. My present conviction is that they are cachès, and the work of the red men. A further notice of them will be found below.

It is necessary to add little to the exhibit given in the plate in respect to this fort. The engineers who selected the site understood its natural advantages, but it is not apparent why they left a part of the plateau without their lines, or why the wall is single on that side and the ditch is within it.

The earth of the bluffs is as steep as it will stand, and the ravines as well as the river, furnish abundance of water. Before the ground was cultivated, a man standing in the ditches could not look over the embankment. Along the sharp ridge or "hogs back," *e e*, there is barely room for a single team to pass. On this side there was no gateway or entrance, but at the west end of the inner parapet, there was a very narrow passage around it. The main entrance was evidently from the river side, near where the present road ascends the hill. Inside the lines the ground was much richer than without them. The mounds are small, and have not been explored. Pieces of flint, pottery and wrought stone implements, are numerous in the space A. They are of the Indian type. The cachès at B C, are on a level with the fort, and the ravine between them is sixty and seventy feet deep. As their strongest apprehensions of attack were from the country side, it is not probable that the fortress would have its magazines so far away, more than fifty rods distant, in an exposed position, beyond a very difficult gulf. As the present red race have made similar pits for storing their corn, and wild rice, it is reasonable to attribute all works of that kind to them. But in no instance, have the northern tribes been known to have occupied earth forts at, the period when they were first known to the whites, and rarely if ever since. We must therefore regard the forts, as the work of a different and an older race.

FORT NO. 6—BOSTON.

This work is situated on the land of WILLIAM and RANDOLPH ROBINSON, on an elevated point of the river bluffs, near the east bank of the Cuyahoga, and near the south line of the township. It is upon ground very inaccessible, elevated about one hundred feet above the river. Its general topography, extent and form are fully shown on Plate V. As the ground has not been cultivated, and is now covered with full-grown oaks, the work is as near its first condition, as is possible after the lapse of centuries. The walls are low—seldom more than a foot above the natural surface, and two to two and one-half feet above the bottom of the ditches, which are double. At *a* is an opening only a few feet wide, and at *b* a broader one of twenty-one feet.

Very likely the slides at C have carried down a part of the wall on that side. Outside the work, the unenclosed space A A, is on a level with the terreplein B. Why, in this and several other of the Cuyahoga forts, there should have been left around the parapets, a level place above the bluff, for the convenience of the assailants, can not easily be explained.

From the center of one ditch to the center of the other is ten to fourteen feet. C. C. Baldwin, Esq., of the Society, and the Messrs. Robinson assisted at the survey.

About a mile up the valley to the south, on the same or eastern bank, is a mound which has been much lowered by long cultivation. It is situated on NATHAN POINT'S land, upon the second terrace, about fifty feet above the river, and one-fourth of a mile from it. The brothers O. K. and W. K. Brooks, of Cleveland, and Mr. Baldwin volunteered to employ what remained of the day in opening this mound. It was then three feet above the natural surface, which is a dry, sandy plain. At two and one-half feet below the natural surface, they found parts of two human skeletons, with charcoal and ashes, showing that they had been burned. Only a few and small portions of the skull were sound enough to be raised or handled, and these soon fell to pieces. Even the teeth were soft and rotten, except their enameled crowns.

With the remains were two flint arrow points, without notches at the base, one of which is represented on Plate VIII. There was also a small thumb and finger stone, such as are common on the surface along the valley, and a portion of a call or whistle, fabricated from a piece of iron ore. It is nearly the same in size and figure, with the one from a mound in Cleveland, as figured on the same plate.

Another and larger one was found on the surface in Northfield. The arrow points, thumb stones and whistles were evidently articles highly prized by, and therefore necessary to the parties buried there.

At first we supposed that this arrow head, without a neck, was typical of the Mound Builder, and would serve to separate those of the red men, from those of his predecessor. On this account it was accurately sketched by Mr. W. J. Rattle, and engraved for this pamphlet. But flint arrow points have since been found on the surface, without the usual notchings at the base; and which may have been wrought and used by the recent Indians.

On the plains it is reported that arrows provided with poison, for use in war, are not securely fastened to the shaft. They are intended to remain in the wound. Those designed for killing game are notched, and firmly tied in a slit at the end of the shaft.

Mr. Austin and other gentlemen of the Society have seen some relics procured in the southerly part of this township, on the west side of the river. They were found, in excavating a cellar, within a small circle or hexagon of earth, about thirty-five feet in diameter. Among them was a copper knife about twelve inches long, very perfect, a copper awl or bodkin, four or five inches in length, and a copper chisel. These tools evidently belonged to the Mound Builders. There were several stone implements, and large pieces of mica; also, a piece of galena or lead ore. Most of the stone implements are scattered and probably lost. One of them had a figure, not heretofore observed in this region. It was made of the fine-grained, striped, greenish gray metamorphic slate of Lake Superior, and highly polished. Its length is four inches, the cross section everywhere a circle in form, like a short rolling pin, with a bilge in the middle. The diameter at each end is about an inch, at the middle an inch and a half, tapering from the center to the ends in a curve, everywhere symmetrical. Dr. Sterling says the Indians of the Pacific Coast have similar stones, by means of which they play games of chance.

Fort No. 7—Plate V.

Across the valley from the mound which was opened, is the stronghold No. 7, on the west side of the river, in a south-west direction, about a mile and a half distant.

Its position and general characteristics can be readily ascertained from the sketch, and the notes attached to it. It is neither very extensive nor imposing. The plateau A is not strictly inaccessible, but may easily be defended. Not more than one mounted man, could ride at once along the narrow ridge *h h*, which connects this tongue of land with the country in the rear. About one hundred and fifty feet beyond this narrow pass, is a broad bank and ditch, extending partly across the space between the bluffs. It has passages at the ends forty-four and twenty-one feet wide. The pits *c c* have precisely the aspect of modern cachès of the northern Indians, and were doubtless made by them.

It is less than half a mile in a south-west direction to the enclosed cachès represented on Plate VII. The village of Niles is about half a mile to the north. In this vicinity, in the townships of North Hampton and Bath, is a numerous group of mounds, cachès and embankments, which are shown on the map, Plate I.

Earthwork No. 8, Plate VI, belongs to this cluster of ancient remains. It is a low bank, without a ditch, situated near the river, on the second terrace, which is about thirty feet above the channel.

In the rear, and overlooking it, is higher land in the form of a terrace, and drift knolls. This is on the land of Mr. Richard Howe, between the road and the river. Near the house of Mr. P. W. Osborne, adjoining it on the north, on the ridge, *b*, is a mound which is now four and one-half feet high, after being plowed over many years. Across the road to the north-west, half a mile distant, is another, in which a human skull was found seventeen years ago, reputed to be that of a Mound Builder.

With the assistance of Mr. Andrew Hale and his son, we made an open cut through this mound, without discovering anything but a few human bones near the top, evidently a burial much more recent than the erection of the mound; a stone chisel and a flint arrow point. It is composed of rich surface soil of a dark color. Originally it was seven feet high, now five feet, one diameter being forty-nine and the other forty-seven and one-half feet. Mr. Waggoner saw the skull plowed out of the mound, and is satisfied it lay near the surface. It is evidently more modern than the Mound Builders.

Between this mound and the cachès on Hale's Brook, Plate VII, are six small mounds, which Mr. Osborne and others have opened at different times, and in which are human bones and charcoal.

EARTHWORKS NOS. 8 AND 10—PLATE VI.

No. 8 is a low bank of earth, generally less than a foot in height, with an average breadth at base of nine feet. It has no ditch, and its situation precludes the idea of a design for a fort. The ground is yet a forest of venerable oaks, one of which stands on the embankment in full vigor, having a diameter of three feet.

If we had proof that the Indians or the Mound Builders had domestic animals, this work and the one in Granger, (No. 10,) not represented among the plates, might be taken for permanent corrals, surrounded with pickets as a protection against wild animals.

No. 10 is nearly a circle, eighteen rods in diameter, with a wall two feet high (1850) and ten feet broad, having one opening. The ditch is about equal in dimensions to the bank. It is situated upon ground lower than the general level of the country, except on the north-west, where there is a large swamp. Near it on the west is a terrace several feet higher. On each side are two small rivulets of permanent water. The road running east from the center, passes through it at about half a mile, but the owner had, twenty years since, nearly leveled it with the natural surface, for the accommodation of his house, barn and outhouses.

FORT NO. 9—PLATE VI.

This work is situated on a high and very precipitous bluff, on the land of JOHN HOVEY. He has been laboring during many years to obliterate it, by turning the furrows always towards the ditch, which has now nearly disappeared. Originally the bank was more bold than is usual in the Cuyahoga forts, being full six feet above the bottom of the moat.

In its general characters and position it resembles No. 6, on Robinson's land, in Boston. In both of them only a part of the plateau is included within the work, and the surrounding bluffs are very high and steep. Within No. 9, stone implements, pottery and flint arrow points were very numerous, and the soil rich. If there were entrances or gate-ways, they have been wholly obscured by long cultivation.

Neither here nor in any of the forts on this river, are the lines so constructed as to give mutual support to their several parts. The positions are well chosen for natural strength, but each part of the defense, relied upon its own power of resistance. Here, as usual, there are convenient springs, a rivulet, and the river itself, for supplying water.

Fort No. 11—Plate VII.

The east branch of Rocky river, at Weymouth, rushes through a narrow channel, with vertical walls of rock, seldom more than fifty feet wide, which it has excavated for itself, to a depth about equal to its width. It has assumed the figure of a peninsula, in the form of an ox-bow, about four hundred feet long from base to point. The stream is so rapid, that it has an estimated fall of one hundred and twenty-five feet in a mile and a half, furnishing valuable water power, which the inhabitants have turned to good account.

It would, in this region, be difficult to find a position more inaccessible to an assaulting party, than the water sides of this peninsula. About three hundred feet from its point, the ancient engineers made a triple wall of earth, with exterior ditches, as shown on the plate. From the outer wall to the middle one, is forty-two, and from this to the inner one thirty-eight feet. All the ditches are yet (1850) three feet in depth, and the banks two to three feet high, as represented on the profile *a b*. If there were entrances or gate-ways on the land front, they are not now visible. Probably the entrance was effected by wooden steps, that could be easily drawn within the work.

Inside the fort is a low mound, *m*, and near the road, at the edge of the village, a group of six still smaller and lower ones, which contain human bones. This enclosed space was selected by the early white settlers for a cemetery. As the soil is a stiff clay, and but a few feet in depth, resting upon layers of sandstone flags, it has been abandoned as a place of burial. The crevices of the river ledges were, in the pioneer times, infested with yellow rattle-snakes, from whence in spring they spread themselves over the adjacent country. There is no higher land within arrow shot. This must be regarded as a very secure position, both artificially and by nature.

The Domiciles of the Mound Builders.

The archæologists of Europe have discovered three styles of domicile, which were occupied by pre-historic races. In France and England there are remains of "pit dwellings," probably made with wood, the lower parts sunk several feet into the earth. In Switzerland there are still visible, in the waters of shallow lakes, the foundations of habitations set on piles, which were also places of defence.

An earlier and ruder race in Belgium, and Eastern France occupied natural caves; which are no doubt the primitive domiciles of men.

The caves of the United States, also exhibit evidences of occupation; but the explorations do not yet show, how many races have made use of them. As at present known the relics of red men predominate.

Over a vast field, extending from the Gulf of Mexico to Lake Superior; the indications of a dense ancient population are conclusive, but we have no certain evidences of the character of their habitations. The temporary shelters of the red races of the north, usually made of boughs, poles and bark, disappear in a few years. In the few cases where they construct cabins, they are wholly of wood, or of wood covered with earth. They are without the cellars of the ancient pit dwellers of Salisbury in England.

The Mandans of the Upper Missouri, and the Digger Indians of the Pacific Coast; have in some cases however put earth on their lodges, making a slight excavation beneath them; which faintly shows the site of their villages. We should expect a people like the Mound Builders who had the intelligence, and the industry; to construct so many, and so extensive earth works; over a territory so broad; would have built for themselves comfortable and permanent dwellings, of which the remains would now be visible.

I wish to call attention to this subject by referring to pits, and artificial cavities; which still exist in the vicinity of ancient earth works in Ohio. In those which I have examined the evidence is by no means conclusive, as to their age or their purposes. The style of the earth works, in different parts of the Mound country, is by no means the same. The differences are such, as to indicate at least three races or nations, as already stated; but they may not have occupied their respective territories at the same time.

Ancient Pits or Cachès.

On the farm of Mr. Andrew Hale at the northeast corner of Bath, in Summit county, are the remains of two very remarkable groups of pits. Fifty years since when Mr. Hale commenced clearing away the heavy forest, which then covered this country; they were quite conspicuous, and were covered with trees of the largest size.

The largest group, was near the south line of lot 11, on a small branch running east into the Cuyahoga river, near where it crosses the north and south lines, between Bath and North Hampton. It consisted of an enclosure or bank of earth of an irregular figure, approaching a pentagon; with the corners rounded off. It was situated at the crest of a terrace, but a few feet above the branch; and was about one hundred and twenty feet across. Nothing but a dim outline is now visible, the ground having been plowed many times over. On the north and west sides at a distance of fifty to sixty rods is a high drift ridge, overlooking the valley of the brook. The soil is dry and gravelly. At present it has the appearance of a broad cavity, with a slightly raised rim. When Mr. Hale first saw it, there was a series of cavities like those hereafter described.

About half a mile north-west of this spot, on a part of the drift ridge just referred to, and at a much greater elevation, there was another but smaller group of pits. Here the embankment was only about thirty feet across. It stood on the edge of a dry gravelly terrace, and overlooked towards the north-west; the valley of Hale's brook. This is also obliterated by the plow.

Less than half a mile down the brook on the south bank stands a similar work, represented in Plate VII. This is still covered with growing trees, one of which is an oak, two and a half feet in diameter. Mr. Hale says it is in all respects like the others except the size. The largest diameter of this is sixty feet, the shorter one thirty. A man standing in the deepest pits can with difficulty look over the highest part of the bank, which encloses them. It is two to four feet high, and the pits two to six feet long, somewhat oblong, and irregular. The breadth of the bank is five to sixteen feet, the soil dry and gravelly, forming part of a plain about twenty feet above the creek. An open cut was made by us, at the south-east corner through the bank, and the pits; and no relics, coals or ashes were found. The bottom of the cavities is clean sand and gravel, and somewhat dish shaped.

On the stream above these remains there had evidently been a village or camp. Old hearths of stone, charcoal and ashes; cover a large space on its northern bank. A large Indian trail passed near this old camp, and thence over the hills to the west; along which there were very old hacks or blazes, upon the trees. In one of them, Mr. H. found a leaden bullet forty years since; which then had sixty annual layers of growth over it. Over one of the axe marks, there was a growth of one hundred and sixty layers. Near by on the hills, was an old and extensive sugar camp of the Indians.

The only other work of this character in this vicinity, is represented on Plate IV., upper corner at the right. It has the same ear like outline, with a narrow entrance; is situated on the edge of a terrace near water like the others, and has eight oblong pits in the interior. It is eighty-two feet in length, thirty feet broad at the narrowest part, and forty-five at the widest. A part of the timber had been cut away but the stumps remained, and the work was not injured by the hand of man. Outside of this group however, were a large number of pits at C; not quite as deep or as regular as those within, which are also represented. On the east are the remains of a slight bank at B, inclosing a space one hundred and sixty feet long by one hundred feet broad; which is in an old field. Mr. George McKisson on whose land it is found, says that in a state of nature, the pits within this embankment, were like those on the other side of the enclosure, at C. Here the soil is dry and gravelly requiring no draining. Some of the pits at C are partly down the side of the bluff; which led me to regard them as remains of cave dwellings, but on cleaning out some of them, and especially after making an open cut across B, it appeared necessary to abandon this conjecture. In one of them was nearly half a cart load of the blue hard pan or clay, which lies twelve to fifteen feet below the surface, and which crops out on the side of the gullies. Numerous springs of water issue at the top of this blue impervious clay.

There is no rim of earth around the edges of these, or of any of the pits. The earth from the enclosed ones at B, is about equal to that of the embankment. It is the same for the one on Plate VII. The earth taken from those which are outside the enclosures, must have been carried away. They appear to have been sunk from two to four feet, with perpendicular sides; probably sustained with wood, and the whole covered with wood or bark, of which nothing remains.

Such cavities are found in many other places in Ohio and the north-west, generally near the old earth works. They are quite numerous on Kelly's Island, opposite Sandusky; where they are regarded as the old cachès of the red man. There is a group of them on the land of Mr. Edmund Ward, partly demolished by the east and west road past his house, which is almost identical with those on the Cuyahoga. In the vicinity implements of polished stone are abundant; such as axes or mauls, chisels, fleshers, and arrow points of flint. There are also on the Island small mounds and enclosures of earth, but as yet no implements of copper have been found there; or any of stone, that may not be of recent Indian make. No certain traces of the Mound Builders are known on this Island.

Around some of the ancient works in the south part of Ohio, there are old pits of irregular form, without borders. They are generally made in dry gravelly soil, and are both within and without the embankments. I have long regarded some of them as the remains of domiciles. If they are not, we have nothing which indicates what shelters were in use, by those old inhabitants.

On the river bluff, above Piketon, in Pike county, there is one which was, in 1839, thirty feet across and twelve feet deep; its outline being a perfect circle. This cavity is precisely what would result from a circular pit, twenty feet across, with upright sides, and about fifteen feet deep. It has not, to my knowledge, been cleared out. If it is an ancient habitation, there must be at the bottom, charcoal and domestic implements of stone.

According to Squier and Davis, at Dunlop's earth work, in Ross county, there are *five;* at another in Liberty township, same county, *twenty*, partly within and partly without the walls; and at "Mound City" there are *twenty* mounds and *seven* pits.

The works represented in Plates XVI and XVII, of the same book; show respectively five and six, large exterior pits. In the southern part of the State there are frequently, large and irregular depressions that hold water, from which part of the earth of the banks was no doubt taken; but most of them are too small in comparison with the embankments, to furnish a material part of the earth for them. They are not as regular or circular as those on the Cuyahoga.

In article 155 of the Smithsonian Contributions (1852), I have described a remarkable series of ancient pits, on the north shore of Portage Lake, in Houghton county, Michigan. These have raised rims or banks, and are large and deep; but are not circular. They have not been opened in such a manner, as to decide for what purpose they were made; and are now in part covered by the village of Hancock. There are in these works features, which indicate more of the domicile than the cachè.

In Montcalm county, Michigan, there is a collection of pits, described by Mr. Steele, which he regards as Indian cachès. Near them are old corn hills, on which are growing pine trees of the usual size for that region. They are two and three feet deep, and there are pine trees in them, the same as those among the ancient hills of corn. There are also relics of the red man in the vicinity.

Mr. Alf D. Jones, of Omaha, has described the earth covered lodges of the Omahas, or Eromahas of the plains. They are twenty feet in diameter and ten feet high, with a long low entrance, like the snow-house of the Eskimos. The weight is sustained by posts and rafters, covered with brush. Over this they lay earth, which is taken in part from within; and in part from an exterior trench. The sites of these abandoned villages, are plainly visible; long after the woody parts of their lodges have disappeared, but the remains are in the form of low mounds, and not of depressions. There are other northern tribes who cover the base of their skin or bark lodges, with earth. Where earth is thrown up around the base of a wigwam, it leaves a low rim or bank generally in the form of a circle.

Major Kennon, of the Russian Telegraph Exploring Company, states that the permanent Kowaks of Siberia, have their lodges partly sunk into the soil. They enter their lodges, through the smoke hole in the top. Such domiciles, when abandoned, would leave circular pits, provided they are sunk so deep, that the earth covering is not sufficient to fill the cavity. At the bottom there is always a pile of ashes and charcoal, mingled with bones and broken utensils. These relics would remain immensely long periods of time; and if our old pits were ever put to the same use, we should find the same evidence of it.

Near Salisbury, in England, there are old pits, usually circular, in all of which remains of fires and of stone implements, are found. I expect that farther examinations in our ancient pits, will show that some of them were sunk as a part of a lodge; but in all that I have opened this evidence is wanting.

Isolated Mounds.

The largest artificial mound of the Cuyahoga Valley, is on the land and near the residence of Col. John Schoonova, in North Hampton. It is now eighteen feet high, and its base is three hundred feet in circumference. Except for the purpose of making a milk house, it has not been opened. A short distance west of it, on a gravel ridge, which corresponds to the second terrace of the valley, is an Indian burial ground; and some irregular cavities, probably cachès. Excavations among the group of mounds, at the corners of Bath, Boston, Richfield and North Hampton townships, have disclosed very little of interest. The contents of one further down the river, in Boston, and of a small work in the same vicinity, have already been noticed. There must have been a time, when this neighborhood was very populous.

Most of the mounds in and near the city of Cleveland have been destroyed. About the year 1820, one which stood on the lot of the Methodist Church, at the corner of Euclid and Erie streets, was partially opened by Dr. T. Garlick and his brother Abel. Two implements were found, one of which was a bodkin or piercing instrument, made of green siliceous slate, very hard, and well polished; its upper or dull end is flattened, to make it more effectual in boring. The other was a piece of the same material, about six and one-half inches long, three wide, and at the middle three-eighths of an inch thick, made thinner towards the ends. Flatwise near the middle, an inch and one-half apart, were two holes, about the size of a rye straw; which tapered towards the center both ways.

This class of stones is very common in Ohio. They are presumed to have been used in sizing, and perhaps in twisting their coarse thread. The size of the holes is quite uniform, and the circular marks of a boring tool are plain. From the mound on Sawtell avenue, opposite the Water Cure, Mr. Goodman and myself took an artificially wrought sphere, made of the iron stone of the coal series, two inches in diameter. It was perforated to the center by two tapering holes, at right angles to each other, by which it was probably suspended, as an ornament. Near it, and about three feet below the top, were four small copper rings or beads. Several feet away, and a little deeper, a stone whistle or call was found, which is figured on Plate VIII. Such whistles, flutes or calls, as they are variously named; are common in the Ohio mounds. Some of them are flattened at the upper end like a bark whistle, and some have holes at the side like a flute. In this the bore is perfectly circular and straight, but tapers slightly towards the mouth hole. The material is fire clay rock of the coal series, polished without and within; the spiral marks of a revolving boring tool, being yet visible.

As this mound forms one of the ornaments of his grounds, Mr. Freese did not wish to have it demolished. Only a small part of it was opened, consisting of a cut from the east side to the center, where it was enlarged several feet in a circular form. At the base was a large bed of rammed gravel and clay, which was followed two and one-half feet below the natural surface; without reaching undisturbed earth. The human skeleton, which almost every mound contains, was not found. To make such examinations complete, the tumulus must be entirely shoveled over, and also all puddled layers that may be noticed beneath it.

The mounds of the lake country, are like the other earth works; much smaller than those on the waters of the Ohio, but there is a close resemblance in the relics, throughout both regions. Their weapons of war are so imperfectly known, that they can neither be said to have been similar or dissimilar.

There is no evidence that either of these ancient nations, made general war upon each other. Their fortified camps and villages, were more likely intended for the security of clans and tribes of the same people, against each other; like the feudal castles with which Europe is thickly dotted over.

Among the works of the lake folk, are none which have a religious aspect. There are no "altar mounds," truncated pyramids, or raised platforms; such as are common farther south.

Our aborigines have been seen to erect mounds of stone over their dead, and very rarely mounds of earth. But in all cases theirs are small and low, and the bodies were not burned. There is little difficulty in distinguishing the Indian, from the Mound Builder tumulus, by its external aspects, but if there are doubts on this point, they are always put to rest when the relics are exhumed.

Rock Inscriptions.

As yet it is not known of what substance, or in what form the ancient inhabitants fashioned their picks. It is evident they must have had an instrument for this purpose, not only hard enough to work up earth, clay and hard pan; but to cut sand stone, lime rock, and granite boulders.

The rock inscriptions at Independence, Plate IX, were made upon a very hard surface of grindstone grit, in which the marks of a sharp pick, are too plain to be mistaken. Those described by Mr. Squier, on the Guyandotte river, in West Virginia, are worked out in the same way. On a flat grit of the coal series, a mile above Wellsville, on the north shore of the Ohio, is a large group of uncouth effigies, sunk into the rock by means of a pick. These are the work of the Indians. Those figured by Mr. Jas. W. Ward on boulders of sandstone, near Barnesville, Belmont Co., O., are in a less hard material, and the points of the tool are not as plain, but are visible.

There is reason to believe that the Independence and the Belmont County inscriptions, are more ancient than the others, and perhaps they are of the age of the Mound Builders.

This people certainly wrought the copper mines of Point Kewenaw, on Lake Superior. On the walls of copper veins worked by them, I have seen marks of a pick; but no copper tool has been found, or at least not described; which would answer this purpose.

During the bronze period in Europe, people had such a tool made of metal; and those made of horn, bone or wood were common in the stone period.

The Winnebagoes who mined lead at Dubuque, in Iowa; nearly a century since, had a pick made of the horn of a deer, with a handle of wood. This evidently would not cut away the grits of Ohio, or the trap and granite boulders, on which we see the marks of a sharp and hard point. It might have been done by a point of flint or quartz, inserted in a stock of horn or bone; but as yet no such points have been described.

The ancients also needed something resembling a pick, to work the flint quarries, of which there are many in Ohio. In working up ordinary earth, hoes, spades and picks of bone, could easily be made; but none of them have been found in the mounds. Spades, and probably hoes, of native copper have been found.

The Independence Stone.

Great care has been taken to obtain a correct sketch, of what remains of this inscription. A very rude drawing of it was published in Schoolcraft's great work upon the Indian tribes, in 1854. He probably regarded it as the work of the red man. In 1869, Dr. J. H. Salisbury, of this city, who has long been engaged in the investigation of rock inscriptions at the West, in company with Dr. Lewis, of the Asylum at Newburg, made a copy by means of full and exact measurements.

As no sketch is of equal authenticity with a photograph, Mr. Thos. T. Sweeny, an artist of Cleveland, at our request went to Independence, and took a copy with his instrument. The light on that day was not favorable, but the outlines of all the artificial work upon the stone, were thus secured with exactness. For the purposes of the engraver, the figures were filled in by Dr. Salisbury from his sketch. The engravers, Messrs. Morgan & Vallendar, have made of this perfected copy a faithful transcript.

Without expressing an opinion as to the authors of these inscriptions, I present, in connection with the engraving, the details furnished by Dr. Salisbury:

"Description of Sculptured Rocks at Independence, Cuyahoga Co., O.

"by J. H. Salisbury, M. D.

"*History.*—Mr. W. F. Bushnell, who resides at Independence, and M. B. Wood, of Cleveland, state that these markings were discovered about 1853, while stripping the earth from the surface of a quarry, on the north brow of the hill on which the village of Independence stands. Here the rocks projected in the form of a perpendicular cliff, from twenty to forty feet in height. On the top of this cliff, and near its edge, the markings were discovered. The soil over the markings was from five to eight inches in depth, and was black, having been formed from decaying vegetation. A tree was growing directly over the markings, that was one foot or more in diameter. Within a few feet of the spot there was an oak tree, over four feet in diameter. This tree—some years previous to the discovery of the sculptured rock—had fallen nearly across the markings, and in 1853 was much decayed. Besides the markings represented in Plate IX, there were others adjacent, belonging to the same group; which had been destroyed by the quarry men, before Messrs. Bushnell and Wood were aware of it. Among the markings destroyed were the outline figures of a male and female, very well executed. There were also the representations of the wolf's foot, and figures of the feet of other animals.

"At the time of the discovery the stone church at Independence was being built; and, at the suggestion of Deacon Bushnell and others, all the markings not previously destroyed, were carefully cut out and the block placed in the rear wall of the church, about eight feet above the ground. It was prudently placed at this height to prevent its being defaced.

"In company with Dr. Lewis, Superintendent of the Northern Ohio Lunatic Asylum, I visited the locality on the 5th day of June, 1869, and made careful drawings of all the markings visible on the block, in the rear wall of the church. These with accurate measurements, are represented in Plate IX, made more perfect by the use of Mr. Sweeney's photography.

"*Description.*—The rock here described only contains a portion of the inscription. The balance was destroyed in quarrying. The markings on the portion of the rock preserved, consist of the human foot clothed with something like a moccasin or stocking; of the naked foot; of the open hand; of round markings, one in front of the great toe of each representation of the clothed foot; the figure of a serpent; and a peculiar character *w*, which might be taken for a rude representation of a crab or crawfish, but which bears a closer resemblance to an old-fashioned spear head, used in capturing fish.

"The clothed feet are of five different sizes. There are eighteen impressions of this kind, arranged in nine pairs. Of the largest size, there are five pairs, *a, c, g, l, m.* Of the next size smaller, there is only one pair, *o.* Of the next smaller size, one pair, *q.* Of the next smaller size, one pair, *e*; and of the smallest size, one pair. Of the naked foot there is only a single figure, which is rudely carved, and which is much longer than the clothed representations. There are two figures of the open hand—one with a large palm and short fingers—the other smaller, with the fingers long and slender.

"The sculptures have all been made with a sharp pointed instrument, by the process of *pecking,* and sunk in throughout, instead of being mere outlines. The cuttings are from one-eighth to half an inch deep. The two hands are sculptured the deepest. In the illustrations, I have endeavored to give an idea of the markings left by the tool used; though these are less evident than the representations.

"The length of the largest feet in figures *a, c, g, l, m,* from the extremity of the great toe to the heel is six and three-fourths inches, and the width at the widest place two and three-fourths inches. The length of the next in size *o,* is five inches and width two and one-eighth inches, and of *q* five inches by two inches. Length of next smaller size *e,* three and a half inches and width one and three-fourth inches, and three and three-fourth inches by one and a half inches. The length of the naked foot *s,* is nine inches, and greatest width four and three-fourths inches. The great toe is one inch long, the second toe one and one-fourth inches long,—the third toe one and a half inches long; the fourth toe one and a fourth inches in length, and the little toe one inch long.

"In the large hand *t,* the palm is five and a half inches long and three and a half inches wide. The length of the thumb is one and a half inches,—the index finger one and three-fourths inches,—the middle finger two inches,—the ring finger one and three-fourths inches, and the little finger one and a half inches. In the other hand *u*,— the palm is three and a half inches long and two and a half inches wide. The length of the thumb is two and one-fourth inches,— the index finger two and a half inches;— the middle finger two and three-fourths inches; the ring finger two and one-fourth inches; and the little finger two inches.

The diameter of the circular markings,— invariably found in front of the clothed feet, are as follows :—*b*, one and one-eighth inches; *d*, one and three-fourths inches; *f*, three-fourths inch; *h*, one inch; *k*, half inch; *n*, one and a half inches; *p*, one and one-fourth inches; *p*, one inch.

"The diameter of the serpent's head is two and three-fourths inches. Length of body ninety-four inches,— making the entire length of the figure about eight feet.

"In the sculptured figure *w*, the measurements are omitted.

"It is evident this slab does not contain the entire inscription. The tracks *l*, are only partially present; while it is very probable that more tracks occurred in the direction *a b*, arranged in a line as those are from *c* to *l*, where there are ten tracks and eight round characters, and which are probably not all that were orginally in this line, previous to the stones being quarried. The round markings in front of the clothed tracks, may have been intended to represent the tracks of dogs or cats; but at present they are so smoothed by time, that it is impossible to make out anything but simple irregular circular depressions.

"The rock on which the inscription occurs, is the grindstone grit of the Ohio Reports, an extensive stratum in Northern Ohio, about one hundred and fifty feet below the conglomerate. It is almost pure silex, and possesses the property of resisting atmospheric changes to a remarkable degree. Boulders and projecting portions of the formation, from which this block was obtained,— that have been exposed to the weather for ages,— preserve perfectly their sharp angular projections. As a building stone, it is superior, on account of its extreme durability. This durability of the rock, and the fact that these markings were covered with earth, explains why they have been so finely preserved.

"The markings *a*, *c*, *e*, *g*, *l*, *m*, *o* and *q*, have been supposed by some to represent the tracks of the buffalo. After carefully measuring and drawing them, however, I have come to the conclusion that they were designed to represent tracks of the clothed human foot, and as such have described them.

"The so called bird tracks which are few and faint on this slab, are numerous and bold on most of the rock inscriptions of Ohio."

Serpent Effigies.

The serpent or snake in some of its varieties, has had much to do with the symbolic worship of nations, especially the rude and ancient nations. This is shown not only in history, and as far back as we get information from this source; but from inscriptions and effigies, that extend to still more ancient periods.

In the third chapter of Genesis it is referred to as an example of subtlety, and is made the representative of evil or satanic power. By the oriental nations it is regarded as the embodiment of sagacity and cunning, allied to wisdom. Our Saviour desired his disciples to be as "wise as serpents," which in their circumstances inculcated a high form of prudence.

Dr. Kalisch an eminent student of the Asiatic people, says it is generally represented as the emblem of evil, disobedience, and contumely; but the Phœnicians and Chinese use it as a symbol of wisdom and power. The last named people imagine that the kings of heaven, have the bodies of serpents. It appears with great frequency among their pictorial representations.

In Egypt this reptile was worshiped, as a symbol of health and life. It was probably in this aspect, that the Children of Israel regarded the brazen serpent, set up by Moses.

The early inhabitants of our continent, placed the snake foremost among their sculptures and their effigies. Among the North American Indians the evil principle is worshiped, or if not adored, is the object of supplication, as much as the good. The Ojibwas have their good and their bad Manitous, to both of whom they offer sacrifice and prayer. As a living creature they respect the snake, and treat it kindly. In ancient Mexico it was an object of worship.

It is not therefore strange, that we find among the earth mounds of Ohio and Wisconsin; some which are in the form of a serpent. It was here as in Asia and probably in all parts of the world, an animal which symbolized something, which was held sacred. The sculptured effigies at Independence in this county and near Barnesville in Belmont county, O., with their surroundings, are no doubt records of religious sentiments or formulas, the meaning of which remains a mystery.

Those made upon the sand rock near Wellsville, on the Ohio, are evidently the work of the red man, and among many animals and human beings grotesquely cut, is a rude rattlesnake with a fancy head.

Serpent worship being as it were inherent with the barbarous and semi-barbarous races in all countries, there is nothing marvelous in finding evidences of it here.

Spindle Socket Stones.

On Plate No. VIII is a Photographic copy, of one of hundreds of stones; found in this valley and throughout Northern Ohio. On one side, and sometimes on both, are circular cup-shaped cavities, from a mere point to a diameter of an inch and a half. They are nearly half the diameter in depth, and are perfectly symmetrical, forming nearly a hemisphere a little flattened. I have seen none that exceed an inch and a half across, and none that are deeper than the semi-diameter. They are evidently formed by revolution, for they are smooth and the section is a true circle. They are so numerous that they must have been in general use for domestic purposes. I have never seen them described among the relics of the mounds, or the implements of the savage races now in existence.

From accounts that have reached us, of the mode of spinning among the Aztecs, and also the modern Mexicans; they used an upright wooden spindle like the stem of a top, on which was a stone collar to act as a balance wheel. The Romans, Greeks and Egyptians had something similar to this. The Puebla Indians have been seen spinning cotton, on such a spindle fifteen and eighteen inches long, the foot of which rested in a bowl. None of the descriptions are very minute, as to the mode of twirling this primitive spindle. It could be done by hand, or by a cord, wound several times around it, and pulled back and forth; or by a bow-string, worked each way, as the Iroquois did when they got fire by friction. The most primitive way of making twine is by twisting it between the thumb and forefinger, which is nearly as rapid as with a spindle worked by hand; but with a spindle the thread can be wound, as fast as it is made, into a bunch by reversing the motion.

In France and Italy there are peasants, who made thread recently on a wooden spindle with a stone whorl, or balance, twirled by hand; and in the island of Islay, an old woman was seen spinning with a stick, on which she had impaled a potatoe to give it a steadier motion.

It was not till the eighteenth century, that spindles were propelled by wheels, which did not change the principle; but only increased the speed and steadiness.

We know the Mound Builders had a very coarse fabric like hemp, the threads of which resembled in size those of the gunny bags, made by an equally rude people in India. They may have cultivated some plant for its fiber, or they may have appropriated that of the nettle, as the first settlers of the Miami valley did, who found it very durable.

If a small socket was made in a stone, or a piece of wood for the foot of a spindle, which also passed through a hole or a forked stick, to steady it above; a very rapid motion could be got up, by the bow-string; and the process of spinning carried on by one person. The foot of the spindle would wear a smooth round cavity, precisely such as we see on these stones. When it became deep the friction would increase, and its foot would be changed to another place on the same stone. Some of them are so near each other, that the rim between them is cut away.

In the Ohio mounds, and on the surface, there is found flat circular stones, with a hole in the center, such as are found in England, and in the Swiss lake dwellings, where they are called "spindle whorls."

There is found also among the remains of the pile dwellings of the European lakes, a coarse cloth made of flax.

These facts induce me to regard these cavities, as part of the spinning apparatus of the fort builders. The northern Indians were dressed in skins, when they were first encountered by the whites, and did not know the use of cloth. Their nets were made of coarse twine from the prepared bark of trees, and their mats from flat strips of bark or of rushes.

In lower latitudes, on the waters of the Gulf of Mexico and California, the Indians had cloth made of cotton, as they make it now.

The stone represented here is one of six specimens in the museum of the Western Reserve Historical Society.

Thumb and Finger Stones.

There is in our collection a large representation of water worn pebbles and other stones, which have on each side an artificial cavity, which is not as large, as deep, or smooth; as the spindle socket. These stones are generally elongated and flattened pebbles, not trimmed or altered except as to the artificial depression, or thumb place. Many of them are not of hard material, and the sunken places are often rough, as though they were sunk with a pick, not bored out by a revolving tool. The size of the depressions is about that of the end of a thumb, and they are exactly opposite each other. Some of them would not weigh more than a quarter of a pound, rising to a weight of two pounds. They are found on the surface and in the mounds. We have one which a party from our society took, from a depth of three feet below the natural surface, beneath a mound five feet in height, in North Hampton, Summit county, Ohio, about a year since. It lay among the remains of a charred skeleton, and with it were two flint arrow points, one of which is figured in Plate VIII.

Most of those I have examined have their ends bruised and fractured, as though they were used as a light hammer. Mr. Wilson, in his work on the ancient stone implements of Scandinavia, refers to hammers which he considers were flint breakers. Mr. Evans describes similar stones, and both of these authors made flints with pebbles, used as hammers. With those in our collection, even where the pebble is soft, I can easily chip fragments of the hornstones or flint, from the Ohio pits.

Savage nations the world over have modes of manufacturing flint implements. After the block or piece is rudely trimmed by blows from a stone maul, flakes are split off by quick strokes with a small stone hammer. These splinters are fashioned by light blows of bone or horn chisels, or by a slight of hand pressure with a wooden implement; throwing off light flakes. Obsidian quartz and glassy lava are wrought in the same way.

Ancient Flint Quarries.

Arrow points of flint or chert are so common in Ohio, that the sources of supply must have been large. Among the strata of our coal series are numerous bands of limestone, that frequently pass into chert, hornstone and flint. The famous "buhrstone," in Jackson and Vinton counties, is one of those strata; which, like all others of the coal-bearing rocks of Ohio, are very irregular in thickness, quality and extent.

It has long been known that a flint bed existed in Licking county, near Newark; and that it had been extensively quarried in ancient times. The old pits are now visible, covering more than a hundred acres. They are partially filled with water, and are surrounded by piles of broken and rejected fragments; for it is only clear homogenous pieces, that can be wrought into arrow and spear points. With what tools and appliances the ancients wrought such extensive quarries, has not yet been settled. This flint is of a grayish white color, with cavities of brilliant quartz crystals. It appears the stones were sorted, and partially chipped into shape, on the ground; after which they were carried great distances over the country as an article of traffic; arrow points from these quarries having been found in Michigan. Many acres of ground are now covered with flint chips—the result of this trimming process. The business of manufacturing arrows, knives, spears and scrapers, no doubt became a trade among the Mound Builders, as it is known to have been among the Indians. What tools they used for this work is not known, although I conjecture that this was the use of the thumb stones.

Flint arrow heads and implements, are not plenty among the relics of the mounds; but on the surface they are found on nearly every cultivated farm in Northern Ohio. They were in general use among the red men, when the whites first came into their country.

The Indians must therefore have worked the flint quarries, more extensively than the prior race. Several other places are now known besides "Flint Ridge," where old quarries are visible.

There are some on the land of James Hoile, two miles south of Alliance, in Stark county, near the C. & P. Railroad. Here the color of the flint is red, white and mottled.

Flint beds are also known in Tuscarawas county, west of the Muskingum River.

The color in some localities is black. There are ancient excavations in Coshocton county, two miles south of Warsaw, which were doubtless made to procure the dark colored, impure chert, which here sometimes overlies a bed of cannel coal.

On the Great Kanawha, in West Virginia, above Charleston, is a heavy chert bed, on the outcrop of which probably such quarries will be found.

There is another on the Alleghany river, above Freeport, in Pennsylvania.

It is on and near to rivers capable of canoe navigation, that the flint beds should be most extensively wrought, because the product could be more easily transported.

Every Indian hunter required a large number of arrow points, and scarcely a day would pass, without losing some of them. As the Mound Builders were more of agriculturists, and less of hunters, they would require and would consequently scatter fewer of them over the country. Those which are found so profusely on the surface, must have belonged principally to the red race.

It was easier to fabricate knives, cutting edges, and warlike instruments, to be fastened in wooden handles, than the common arrow point; and yet very few flint implements are found, which were designed for such uses. In other countries, in early times, flint cutters were very abundant. They seem to have been among all people, the first invention to answer the purposes of modern cutlery. The Jews used flint knives upon their sacrifices. They have also been found in the Egyptian pyramids.

As late as the battle of Hastings, the English are supposed to have used flint pointed arrows, against William of Normandy. Several thousand flakes, knives and arrows, have been taken out of the later quaternary or drift deposits, in England and France; of the era of the cave man, made from flint nodules of the chalk.

The Digger Indians of California, who represent the diluvial cave dwellers, in their mental and moral developments; manufacture flint knives and arrows at this time.

In Mexico the lowest order of natives do the same, with obsidian—a volcanic glass thrown out of volcanoes.

A general prevalence of these simple cutting implements, among the relics of a lost people, is quite conclusive proof that they were very near to their primitive condition.

Relics of the Mound Builders

IN THE MUSEUM OF THE SOCIETY, JAN., 1871.

Charred cloth from an ancient mound in Butler county, Ohio; procured by Hon. JOHN WOODS.

Bone beads, and red flint arrow point from a mound in Lawrenceburg, Indiana.

Small earthen kettle, from same mound. A. G. GAGE, Esq.

These may be relics of the red man.

Fac-similes in wood, of two stone implements from an ancient mound, corner of Euclid and Erie streets, Cleveland; taken out by Dr. T. GARLICK, in 1820.

They were made of a fine grained greenish striped metamorphic slate found on Lake Superior. One is a bodkin five inches long; the other a flat thin polished stone, six inches long, three wide, and three-eighths thick in the middle, handsomely thining towards the ends. There are two holes through it at the center, made flatwise, one and a half inches apart, which taper towards the middle. This is a common relic of the mounds, and appears to have been used in spinning the coarse netting or cloth made by that people.

Portion of a human jaw and teeth, three feet below a mound on NATHANIEL POINTS' land, Boston, Summit county, Ohio; also a thumb and finger stone; part of a call or whistle made of clay iron stone, and two flint arrow heads, without necks. (Plate VIII.)

Portion of an Oak Post, forming part of a row around a human skeleton, from a mound of loose stone forty feet high, near Jacktown, Licking county, Ohio. I. N. WILSON, Newark, Ohio.

Plates of silvery Mica, from an ancient work near Portsmouth, O.

A sphere of Iron Ore, two inches in diameter, with holes for suspending it, made at right angles to each other. Four copper beads or rings. A stone call or whistle of fire clay rock. (See Plate VIII.) From a mound on the homestead of A. FREESE, Esq., Sawtell avenue, Cleveland, Ohio.

Fac-simile in wood of a large copper dagger or dirk, wrought from a nugget, found seven feet below the surface at Ontonagon, Lake Superior. A. W. ECKHART.

Numerous other copper tools calculated for cutting wood, for mining, and for weapons, have been found near the mouth of the Ontonagon river, and at the ancient copper mines ten to twelve miles up the river. The Mound Builders worked these mines probably two thousand years or more ago.

SPINDLE SOCKET STONES.

1. Kelly's Island, engraved Plate VIII, from a Photograph of the original. Dr. E. STERLING.

2. Independence, Cuyahoga co., Ohio. W. H. KNAPP.

3. East Cleveland. P. H. BABCOCK.

4. Chattanooga, Tenn. Dr. J. S. NEWBERRY.

5. Northfield, Cuyahoga county, Ohio. A. and L. BLISS.

Fac-simile in copper of a spear head, from an ancient mound near Sterling Illinois. *Chicago Academy of Natural Science.*

Pieces of skids and shovels of wood, and mauls of stone; from the ancient copper mines of Lake Superior, ten to twenty feet below the surface.

Among the numerous relics of the aborigines or red men, are some that probably belong to the Mound Builders, but in separating them we place nothing to the credit of this race, where there is doubt in regard to its origin.

They had some stone implements in common; and they have been left by both races in the same mounds.

I.

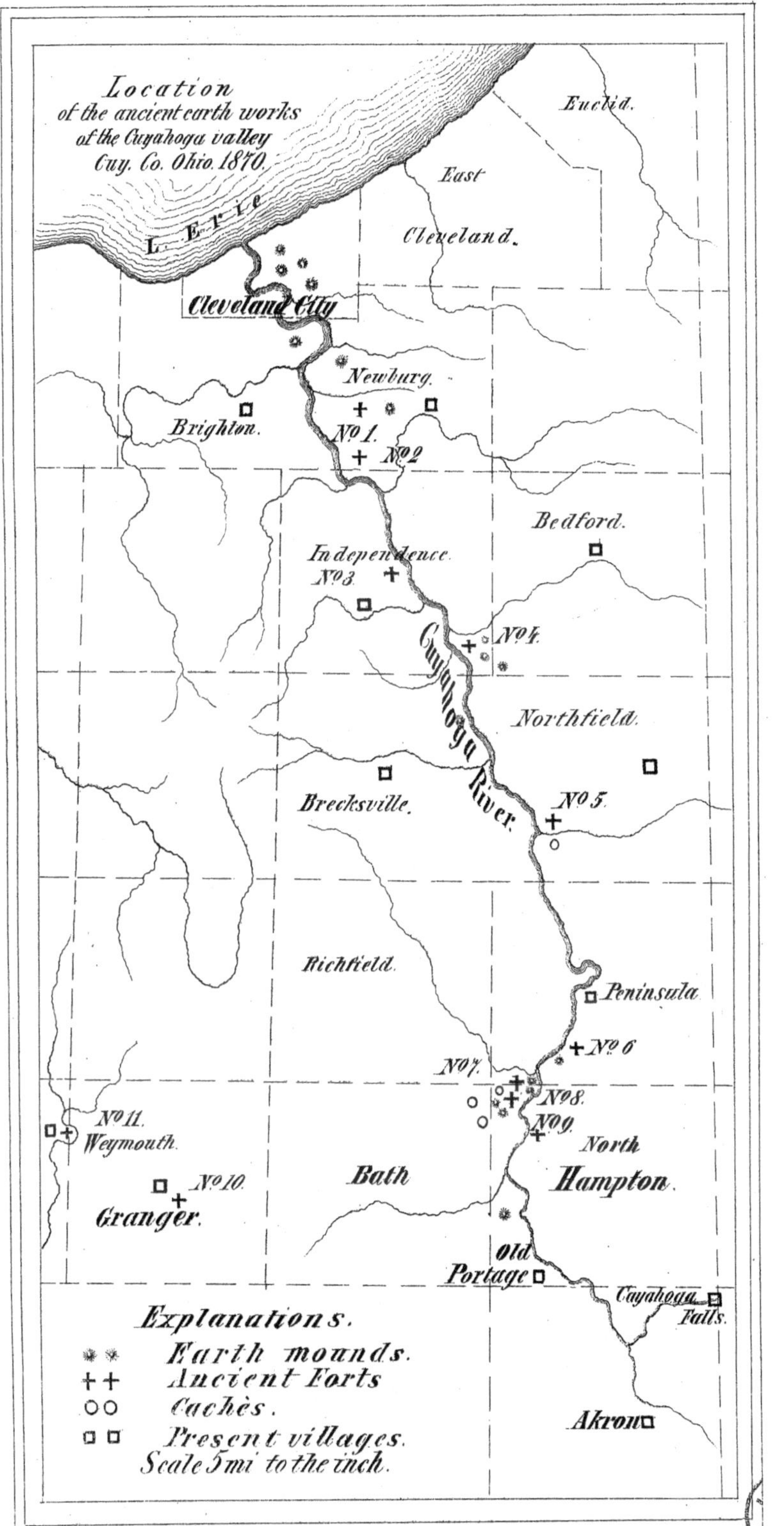

Morgan & Vallondar Lith. Cleveland, O.

II.

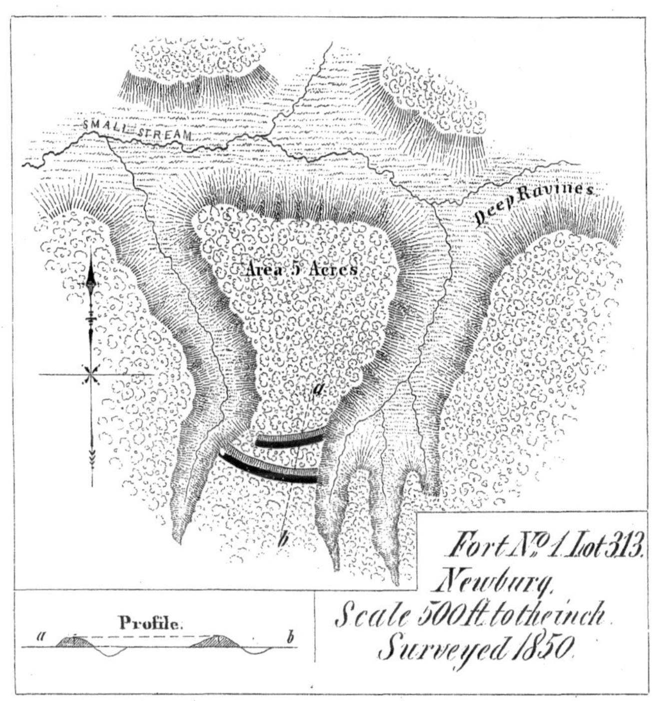

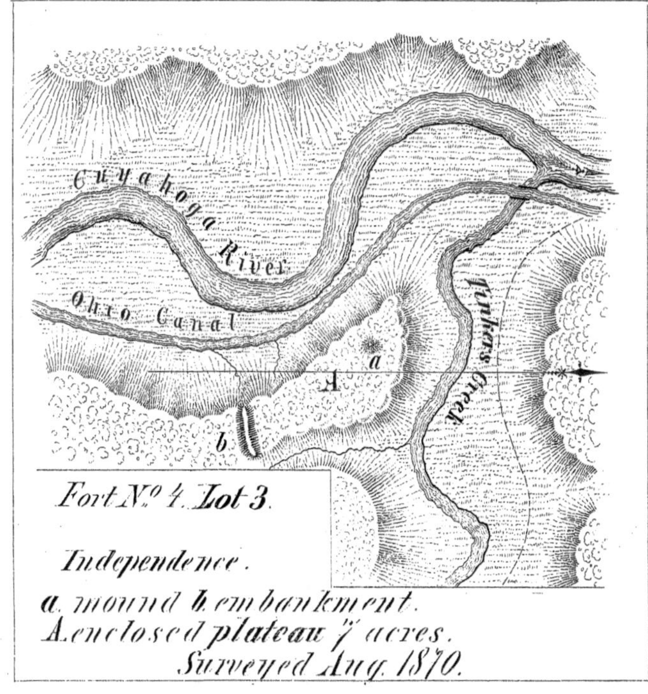

Morgan & Vallendar Lith. Cleveland, O.

Fort No. 3. Lot 1. Tract 3.

Independence.

Surveyed 1847.-1870.

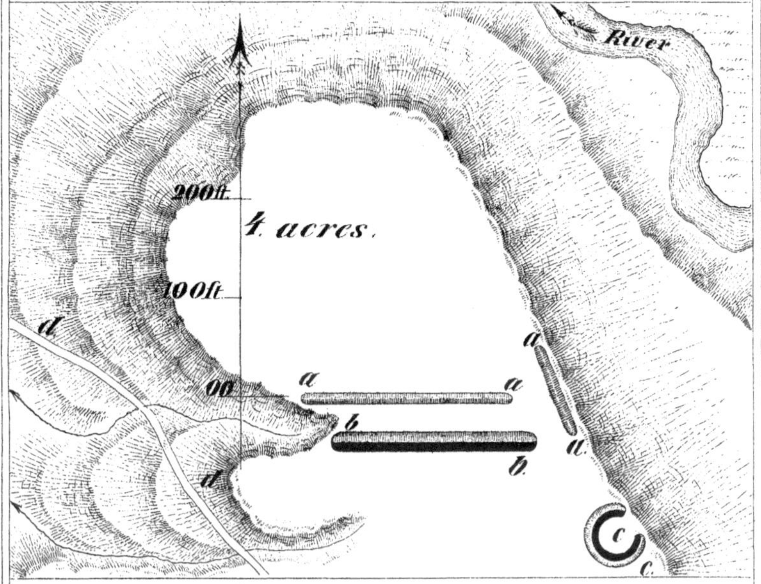

a. a. embankments now obliterated.

b. b. embankment & ditch – c. c. out work.

d. d. road Newburg to Independence.

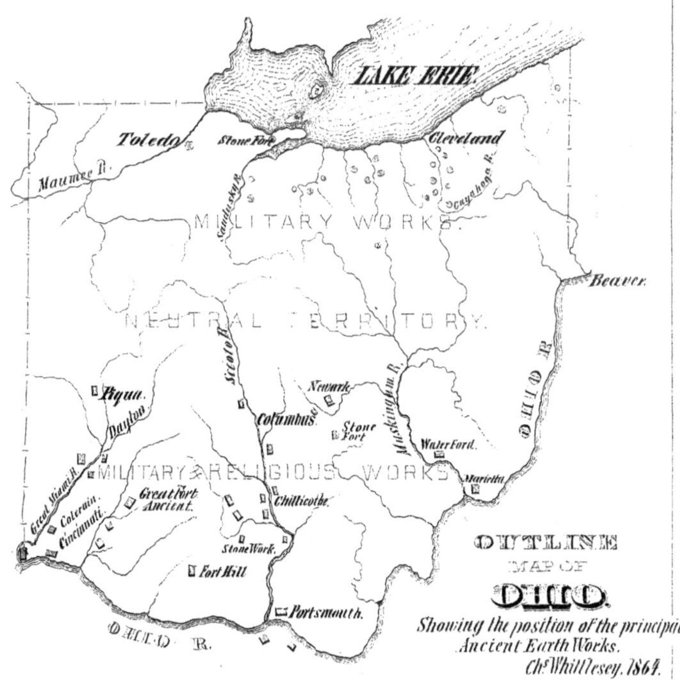

IIII.

Ancient Fort and cachès No. 5_ Lot 79.
Northfield.
Surveyed 1850 & 1870.
A. Old Fort. 2 acres.
B. Cachès enclosed.
C. Cachès not enclosed.
D. Enclosed cachès obliterated.
○○ Pits 1. to 2½ ft. deep.
⊗ Mounds. e. e. hogs back
+ Large oak stump.
Profile a.-b.
32 ft.
loam.
gravel.
Profile c.-d.
drift clay.
Plateau 2 acres.
Road
Ohio Canal
Cuyahoga R.
A.
B.
C.
D.
a
b.
c
d
e
Morgan & Vallender, Lith. Cleveland, O.

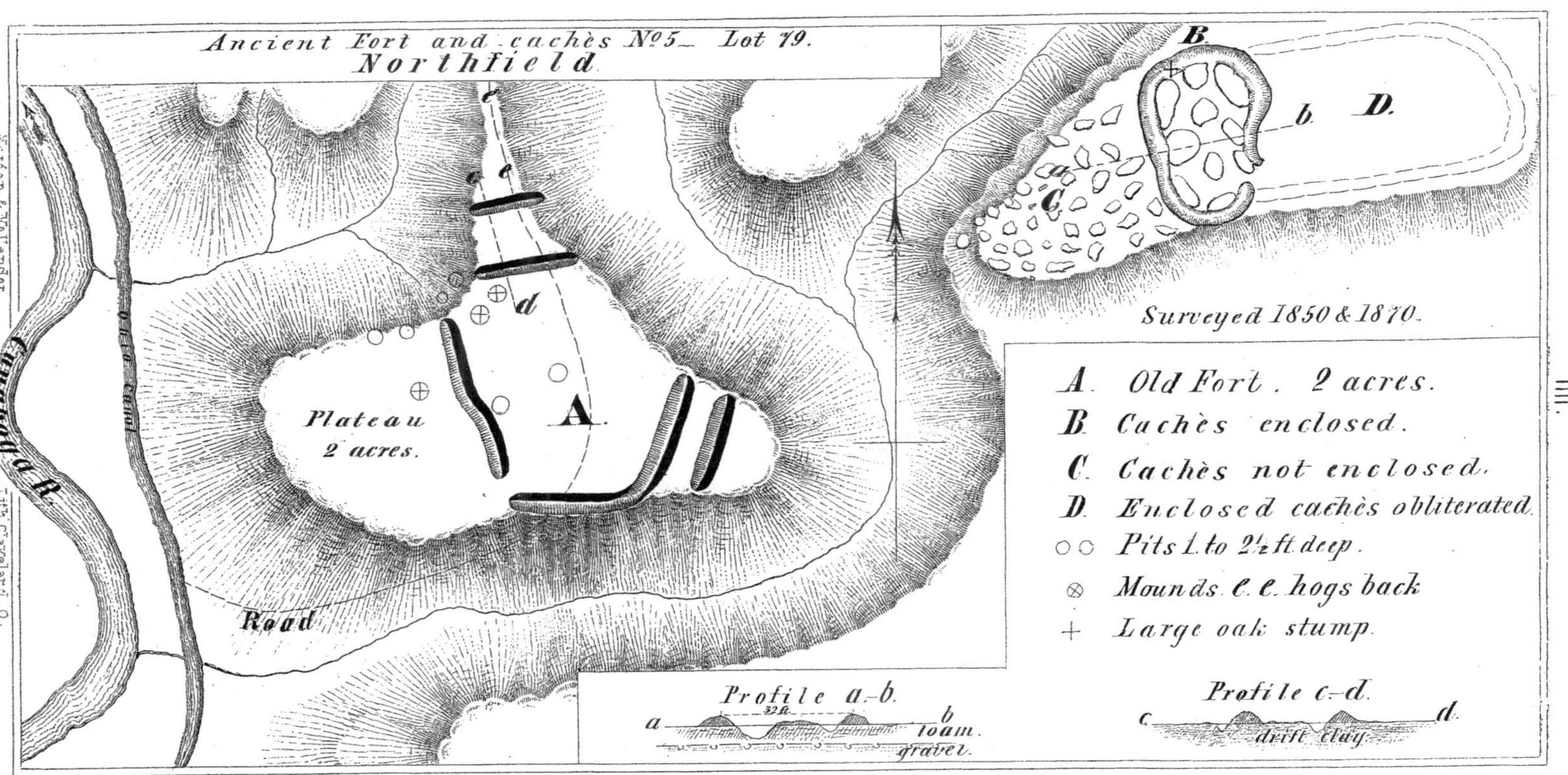

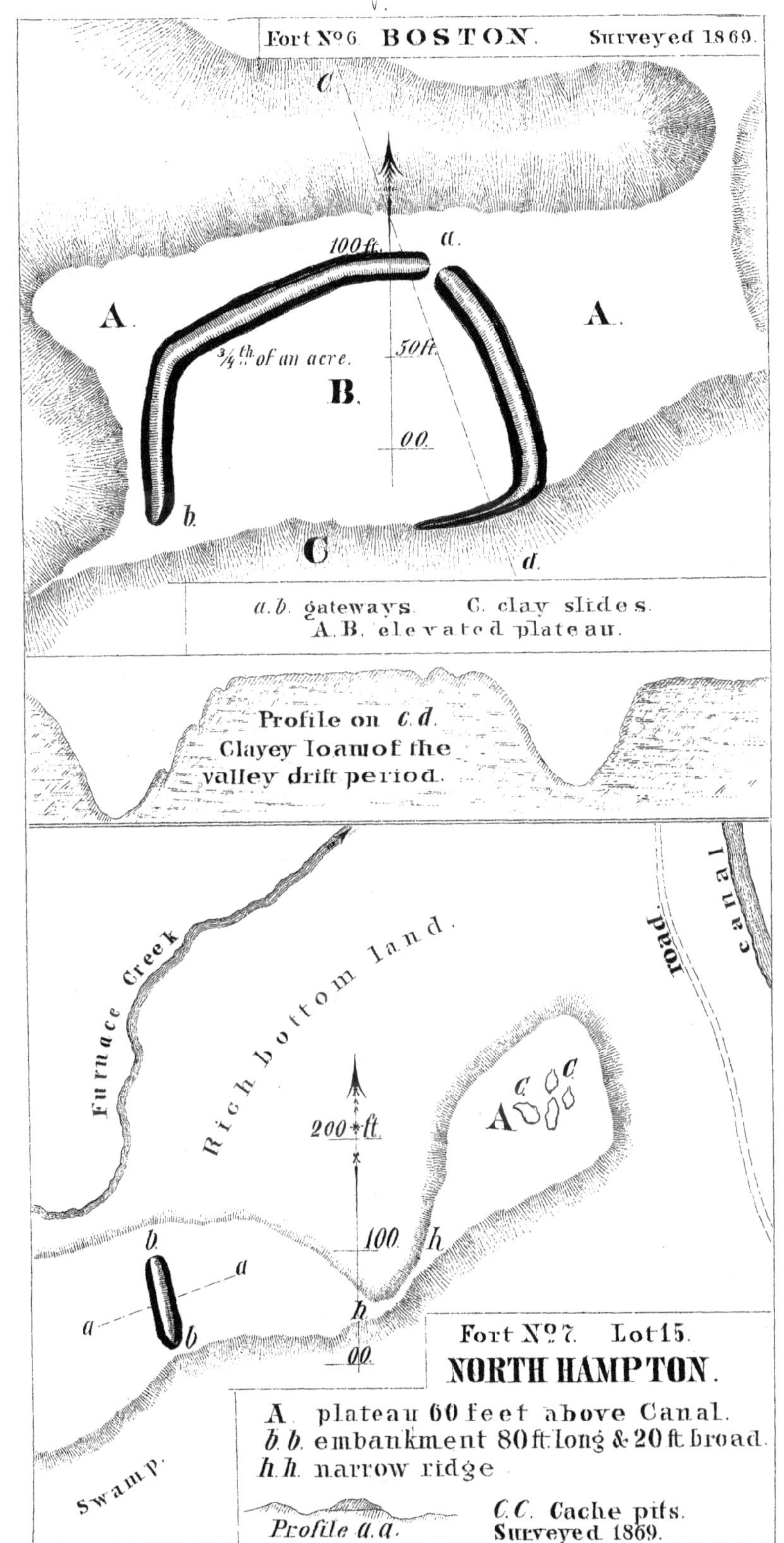

Morgan & Vallendar Lith. Cleveland O.

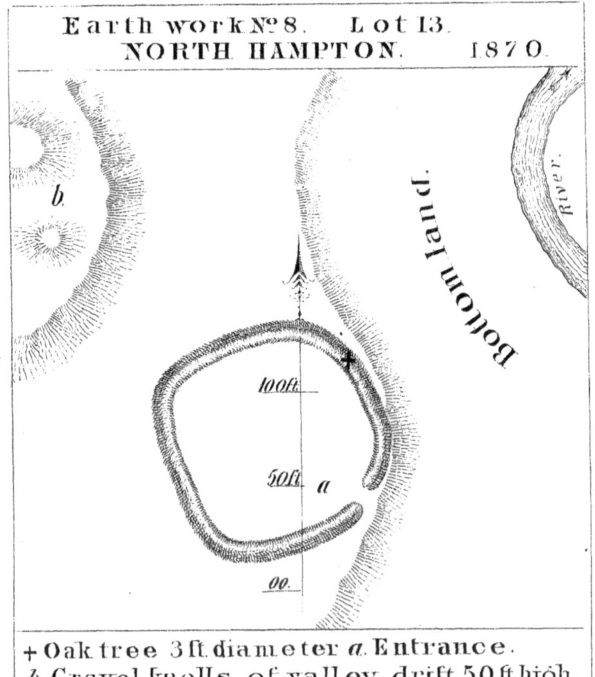
Earth work No. 8. Lot 13.
NORTH HAMPTON. 1870.
b.
Bottom land.
River.
100ft.
50ft.
a
00.
+ Oak tree 3 ft. diameter a. Entrance.
b. Gravel knolls of valley drift 50 ft. high.

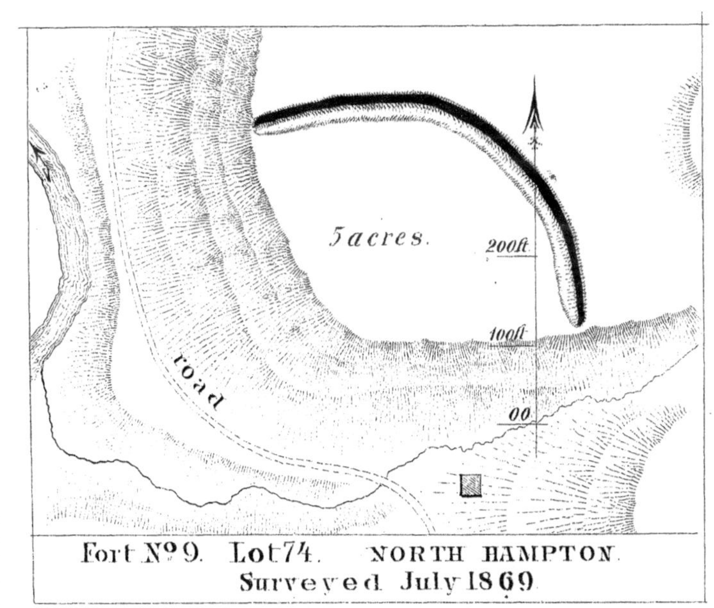
5 acres.
200ft.
100ft.
00.
road
Fort No. 9. Lot 74. NORTH HAMPTON.
Surveyed July 1869.

VII.

Enclosed cachès, Lot. 13
N. HAMPTON. O. 1870
Hales Brook.
b
c
c
c
c
c
c
d.
a.
Dry gravelly plain.
ccc. pits
1 to 2 feet deep.
d. entrance.
Profile b. a.
a
b
Sand & gravel.
creek.
Fort No 11.
WEYMOUTH.
MEDINA CO.
March 1850.
Village of
Weymouth
m
b.
200 ft.
100 ft.
00.
m
a.
ROCKY RIVER E. Branch
Enlarged profile a. b.
Morgan & Vallendar Lith. Cleveland O

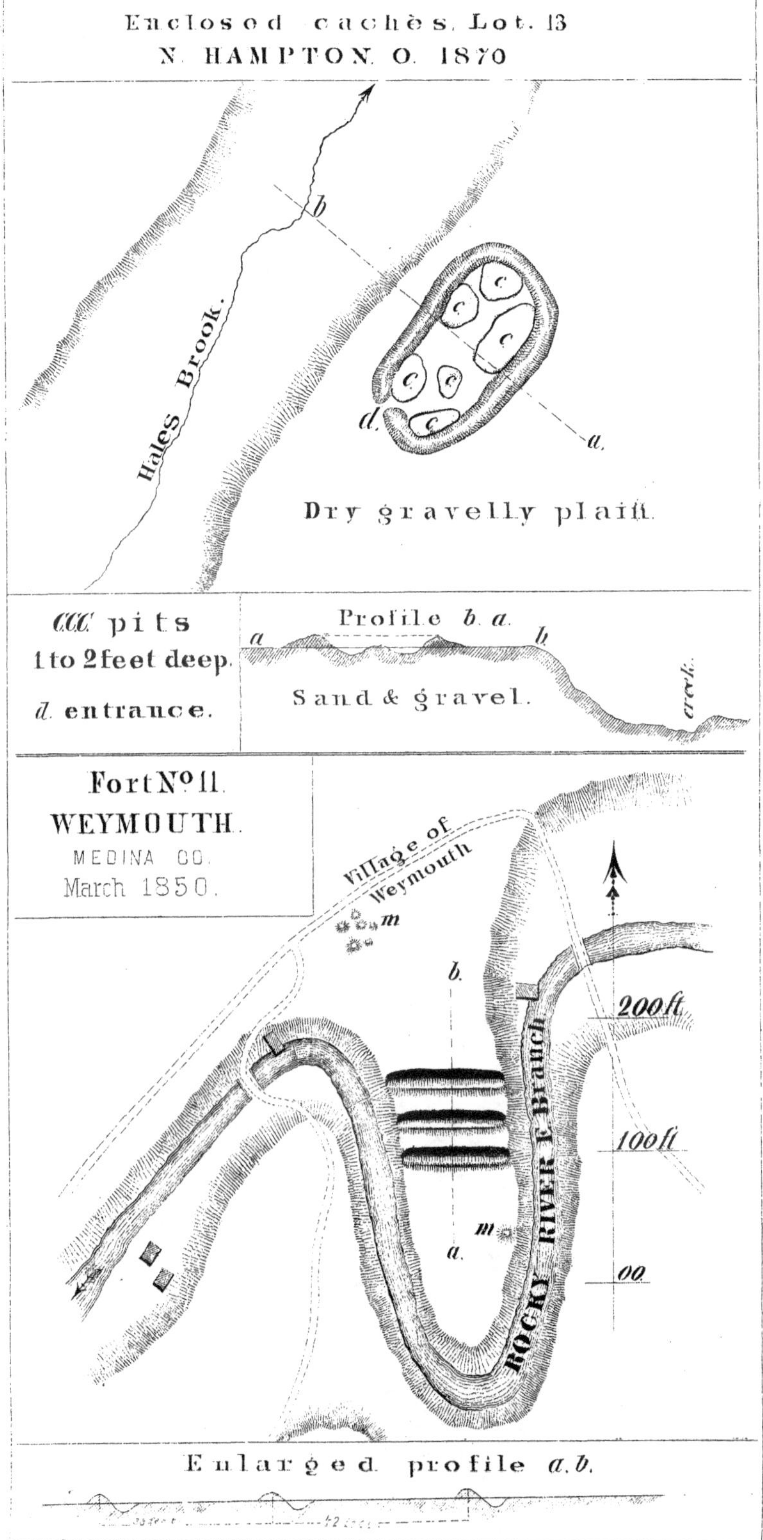

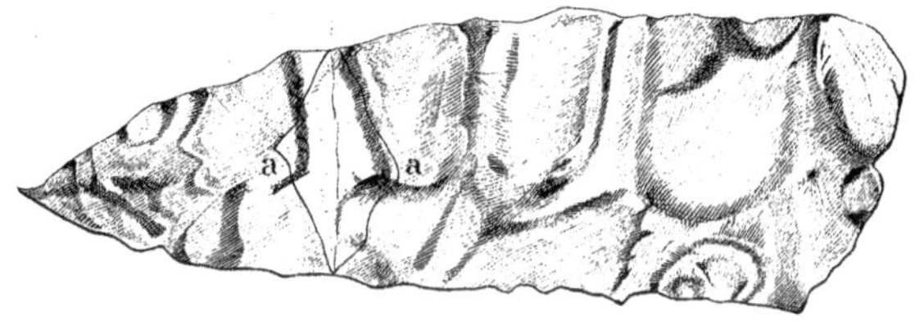

Outline of an ARROW POINT of whitish gray flint from an ancient grave beneath a mound North Hampton, Summit Co. Ohio.
a. a. cross Section. Size of nature.

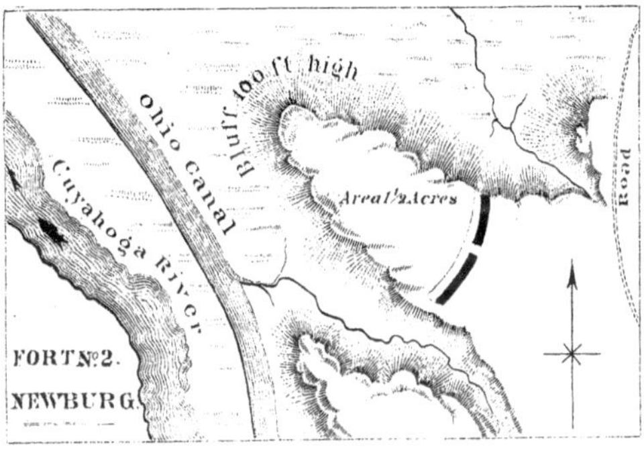

Ohio Canal
Bluff 100 ft. high
Cuyahoga River
Area 1½ Acres
Road
FORT No. 2.
NEWBURG.

Spindle Sockets.

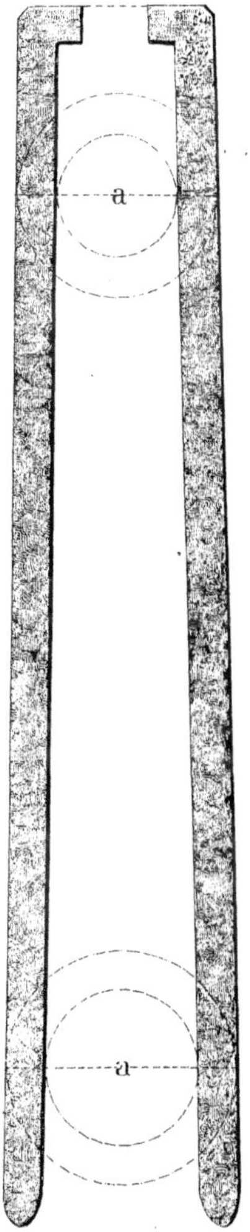

Section of a Stone whistle from a mound on Sawtell Avenue Cleveland. Fire clay rock. Size of nature a. a cross section

Slab of coarse grained Sandstone 6½ ft. by 4, in the west wall of the Stone Church at Independence, Cuyahoga Co. O.

Morgan & Vallendar Lith. Cleveland. O.

Western Reserve Historical Society.

CLEVELAND, O., JULY, 1871.

HISTORICAL AND ARCHÆOLOGICAL TRACTS,

NUMBER SIX.

PAPERS RELATING TO THE

FIRST WHITE SETTLERS IN OHIO.

An article appeared in the Cleveland HERALD in the spring ot 1871 announcing the receipt by the Historical Society from the Department of State at Washington of valuable transcripts of letters and documents. They have now been examined and are highly interesting, relating as most of them do, to settlements and attempted settlements northwest of the Ohio River prior to that of Marietta in the spring of 1788.

The announcement of this discovery has attracted the attention of students in history, particularly of those who reside in the States formed out of that vast region, the old Northwestern Territory as defined by the ordinance of 1787. These disclosures have nowhere excited more attention than at Marietta, so long regarded as the first formed, first named, and first peopled settlement by the English race in Ohio.

It has hitherto been supposed that with the exception of traders and missionaries and the occupation by the military under Colonel Harmar during the existence of the Confederation no attempts had been made prior to 1788 at permanent occupation for the purpose of cultivating the soil. I do not here propose to enter into a discussion of this point, preferring first to present the material in our possession.

A brief reference to some of the early occupants both French and English will not however be out of place. As early as the year 1745 English traders penetrated as far as Sandusky or "St. Dusky" and established a post on the North side of the Bay near the carrying place or portage from the Portage River across the Peninsula. They were driven away by the French probably in 1748 or 1749. During this period a celebrated Indian trader from Pennsylvania by the well known name of George Croghan had a station at or near the mouth of the Cuyahoga then known as the Cayahaga, and sometimes as Hioga. In 1750 or 1751 the English Post at Pickawillany was established at a town of the Miamies or Tawixtawes near the mouth of Loramie's Creek, in Shelby county Ohio. The French and Indians destroyed this post in June 1752. In 1761 Frederick Post, a Moravian missionary established a mission on the Tuscarawas near Bolivar on the line between Stark and Tuscarawas counties, Ohio. Until the cession made to the United States by Virginia of her claims on the northern bank of the Ohio river, her citizens regarded Ohio as a part of the old Dominion and undertook to locate their land certificates here. Before the war of the revolution Great Britain had great difficulty in confining her adventurous colonists to the southern side of the Ohio. At a Congress of the Colonies held at Albany in 1754, Benjamin Franklin presented the draft of an English Confederation very much like the one now adopted for Canada. The plan was adopted by the Congress but declined by England. A part of this scheme was the establishment of a colony at the mouth of the Cuyahoga protected by a fort and another on the Ohio river. Colonel Brodhead, was the military commander at Pittsburg during the early part of the war of the Revolution whose letters we now proceed to give so far as they relate to the settlers north of the Ohio. The salt spring in Weathersfield, Trumbull county, was well known to the English in 1754, and also the existence of bituminous coal and petroleum springs in Ohio. The correspondence which is quite fragmentary is presented in the order of dates as near as practicable.

COL. BRODHEAD TO JOHN JAY, 1779.

PITTSBURG, OCT. 26, 1779.

SIR—Since I did myself the honor to address you by a former letter, some of the inhabitants from Youghaginia and Ohio counties have been hardy enough to cross the Ohio River and make small improvements on the Indian lands from the river Muskingum to Fort McIntosh and thirty miles up some of the branches of the Ohio River, As soon as I received information of the trespass, I detached a party of sixty men under command of Capt. Clarke, to apprehend the trespassers and destroy their huts, which they have in a great measure effected, and likewise dispatched a runner to the Chiefs of the Delawares at Cooshoeking to prevent their attacking the innocent inhabitants, but as yet have received no answer from them. Capt. Clarke informs me that the tresspassers had returned and that the trespass appeared to have been committed upwards of a month ago. It is hard to determine what effect this impudent conduct may have on the minds of the Delaware chiefs and warriors, but I hope a favorable answer to the speech I sent them. I presume a line from your Excellency to the Governor and Council of Virginia will tend to prevent a future trespass and the murder of many innocent families on this frontier.

I have the honor to be with perfect respect
Your Excellency's most obt. and most
H'ble Serv't
D. BRODHEAD,
Col. Command'g W. D.

His Excellency JNO. JAY, Esq.

BRODHEAD TO WASHINGTON.

PITTSBURGH, OCT. 26, 1779.

DEAR GEN'L—Immediately after I had closed my last (of the 9th of this instant) I rec'd a letter from Col. Shepherd, Lieut. of Ohio County, informing me that a certain Decker, Cox & Comp'y with others had crossed the Ohio River, and committed trespasses on Indian lands wherefore I ordered sixty rank and file to be equipped, and Capt. Clarke of the 8th Penn. reg't proceeded with this party to Wheeling with orders to cross the river at that p s, and to apprehend some of the principal tresspassers and destroy their hutts. He returned without finding any of the tresspassers, but destroyed some huts. He writes me the inhabitants have made small improvements all the way from the Muskingum River to Fort McIntosh and thirty miles up some of the Branches. I sent a runner to the Delaware Council at Coohoching to inform them of the trespass, and assure them it was committed by some foolish people, and requested them to rely on my doing them justice and punishing the offenders, but as yet have not received an answer.

* * * * *

I have the honer to be with perfect regard and esteem, your Excellency's most
Ob't H'ble Serv't
D. BRODHEAD.

His Excellency GEN. WASHINGTON.

BRODHEAD TO MAJOR TAYLOR.

HEADQUARTERS, PITTSBURGH,
Nov. 21, 1779.

DEAR SIR— * * * I am glad to hear of Capt. Vance's return, but I sincerely wish he had taken under guard some of those fellows who, by their unlicensed encroachments on the Indian's Hunting grounds, seem determined to provoke new calamities to the already much distressed inhabitants of the frontier; and as I consider it a duty not to be dispensed with, I desire you will send a party equal to that under the command of Captain Vance, to go in search of those disturbers of the general tranquility, and give them orders to apprehend any white man who may be found hunting or encamped on the Indians' lands, and use all possible means for that purpose

The party cannot render more essential services to the country, than by apprehending silly people in order that proper examples may be made, and the effusion of blood (consequent) be prevented.

* * * * *

I am with great regard
Your Most Humble Servant
DAN'L BRODHEAD,
Col. Commading W. D.

Major RICHARD TAYLOR.

SETTLEMENT AT THE SALT SPRINGS, TRUMBULL COUNTY.

During the revolutionary war a party of settlers from Fort Pitt built a number of cabins at the Salt Springs, in what is now the township of Weathersfield, Trumbull county. Here they lived in peace and security, tilled the land, and made salt which they sold to the Moravian Indians. How many congregated there is not known, but from the reports of Colonel Harmar it is judged there were ten or more families. These had been located at the springs by Pennsylvania traders, who claimed the land by reason of purchases from the Indians. Harmar sent Ensign Armstrong in May 1785, and after dispossessing the inhabitants, burnt their cabins and destroyed all improvements about the Springs. The land was afterwards purchased by General Samuel H. Parsons and Jonathan Heart of Connecticut.

On the 30th of November, 1782, a preliminary treaty of peace between the United States and Great Britain was signed at Paris, and a definitive treaty was signed at the same place by American and English Commissioners, on the 3d of September 1783. By that treaty the United States became a free and independent nation. Under its provisions the English evacuated New York on the 25th of November 1783, when the acknowledgement of our sovereignty as a nation became a reality, for no foreign soldier was from that day in power on the territory of the thirteen colonies. The government of the United States claimed that by the terms of the treaty of Paris, all the territory Northwest of the Ohio to the Mississippi, was surrendered to the United States, but Great Britain refused to acknowledge this claim until 1796, when all their posts within the tract referred to were delivered to the United States.

On the 21st of January, 1785, a treaty was concluded at Fort McIntosh, between George Rogers Clarke, Richard Butler and Arthur Lee as Commissioners for the United States, and the representatives of the Wyandot, Delaware, Chippewa and Ottawa Nations, with this clause:

"If any citizen of the United States, or other person, not being an Indian, shall attempt to settle on any of the lands allotted to the Wyandot and Delaware Nations in this Treaty, excepting the lands reserved to the United States in the preceding article, such person shall forfeit the protection of the United States, and the Indians may punish him as they please."

The treaty made at Fort Finney, at the mouth of the Great Miami, January 31, 1786, between George Rogers Clarke, Richard Butler, and Samuel H. Parsons, Commissioners on the part of the United States, and the chiefs and warriors of the Shawanees, provided in article VII:

"If any citizen or citizens of the United States shall presume to settle upon the lands allotted to the Shawanees by this Treaty, he or they shall be put out of the protection of the United States."

THE INDIAN COMMISSIONERS TO COL. HARMAR, 1785

"Surveying or settling the lands not within the limits of any particular State being forbid by the United States in Congress assembled, the commandant will employ such force as he may deem necessary in driving off persons attempting to settle on the lands of the United States."

Given at Fort McIntosh, this 24th day of January, 1785.

G. R. CLARK,
RICHARD BUTLER,
ARTHUR LEE.

Owing to the small force under his command, it was impossible at that time for Colonel Harmar to carry into effect the orders of thé Commissioners. Even had the number of troops been sufficient, Colonel Harmar, in his discretion as commander, would have long hesitated before driving from their houses in midwinter in a wilderness, those who had settled on the public lands. As it was, he waited until he obtained further instructions from the government, then vested in Congress. In a note to Harmar the Hon. Richard Henry Lee, President of Congress, approved of the orders of the Commissioners, and directed them to be carried into execution. This was in March. Toward the latter end of the month, the following instructions were given to Ensign John Armstrong.

FORT MCINTOSH, March 29, 1785.

To Ensign John Armstrong,

SIR:—Having received intelligence that several persons in defiance of the orders of Congress, have presumed, to settle on the lands of the United States, on the western side of the Ohio, about forty or fifty miles from hence, you are hereby ordered to proceed with your party as far down as opposite Wheeling, and dispossess the said settlers. At Wheeling you will leave copies of the above instructions which I received from the honorable. the Commissioners for Indian Affairs, and of these your orders, in order that all persons may be fully acquainted therewith.

I am Sir, your humble servt,
JOS. HARMAR,
Lt. Col. Comd.

Ensign Armstrong left on his mission on the 31st of March. His operations are fully detailed in the following official reports.

FORT MCINTOSH, 12th April, 1785.

SIR:

Agreeable to your orders, I proceeded with my party early on the 31st of March down the river Ohio. On the 1st instant, we crossed little Beaver and dispossessed one family. Four miles from there we found three families living in sheds, but they having no raft to transport their effects, I thought proper to give till the 12th inst., at which time they promised to demolish their sheds and move to the east side of the river.

At Yellow Creek I dispossessed two families and destroyed their buildings. The 2d being stormy, no business could be done. The 3d we dispossessed eight families. The 4th we arrived at Mingo Bottom, or Old Town. I read my instructions to the prisoner Ross, who declared they never came from Congress, for he had late accounts from that Honorable body, who he was well convinced gave no such instructions to the Commissioners. Neither did he care from whom they came, for he was determined to hold his possession, and if I should destroy his house he would build six more in the course of a week. He also cast many reflections on the Honorable, the Congress, the Commissioners, and the commanding officer. I conceived him to be a dangerous man, and sent him under guard to Wheeling. Finding most of the settlers in this place were tenants under the prisoner; I gave them a few days at which time they promised to move to the eastern side of the Ohio, and that they would demolish their buildings. On the evening of the 4th, Charles Norris, with a party of armed men, came to my quarters in a hostile manner and demanded my instructions. After conversing with them for some time and showing my instructions, the warmth with which they first expressed themelves appeared to abate, and from some motive lodged their arms with me till morning.

I learnt from the conversation of the party that at NorrisesTown (by them so called) eleven miles further down the river a party of seventy or eighty men were assembled with a determination to oppose me.

Finding Norris to be a man of influence in that country I conceived it to my interest to make use of him as an instrument which I effected by informing him it was my intention to treat any armed party I saw as enemies to my country, and would fire on them if they did not disperse.

On the 5th when I arrived within two miles of the town or place where I expected to meet with opposition, I ordered my men to load their arms in presence of Norris and then desired him to go to the party and inform them of my instructions.

I then proceeded on with caution but had not got far before the paper No. 1 was handed me by one of the party, to which I replied I should treat with no party, but intended to execute my orders.

When I arrived at the town there were about forty men assembled who had deposited their arms. After I had read to them my instructions they agreed to move off by the 19th inst. This indulgence I thoughtproper to grant, the weather being too severe to turn them out of doors. The 6th I proceeded to Haglins' or Mercer's Town, where I was presented with paper No. 2, and from the humble and peaceable disposition of the people, and the impossibility of their moving off immediately, I gave them to the 19th, and believe they will generally leave the settlement at that time.

At that place I was informed that Charles Norris and John Carpenter had been by the people elected Justices of the Peace, that they had, I found, precepts, and decided thereon.

I then proceeded on till opposite Wheeling, where I dispossessed one family, and destroyed their buildings.

I hope, Sir, the indulgence granted to some of the inhabitants will meet your approbation. The paper No. 3 is an advertisement, a copy of which is posted up in almost every settlement on the western side of the Ohio.

Three of my party being lamed, I left them about forty miles from this place, under the care of a Corporal. The remainder I have ordered to gain their respective companies, and the prisoner I haye delivered to the care of the garrison guard.

I am sir with every respect,
Your obedient servt,
JOHN ARMSTRONG,
Ensign.

To Colonel Harmar, or the chiefest in command at Fort McIntosh.

SIR:—Agreeably to the order we have Received for Removing off the Lands to the West of the Ohio, we are preparing to execute the utmost dilligence but find it will be impracticable to entirely clear off the place. According to our engagements with Ensign Armstrong when we received the orders, which, if you will condescend to take under your consideration, we make no doubt you will Readily Grant, for we have neither houses nor lands to move too; have every Necessary to Procure by our Labour, for the Support of our families and stocks, for we have no money. Therefore if you Can Consistant with your Honor allow us a few Weeks more to move off and prepare Dwellings to move to, we shall Greatly Acknowledge the favour.

We have sent a full Representation of our distressed circumstances by way of Petition to Congress, and whatever Orders and Regulations they in their wisdom may think proper to prescribe we shall as in duty bound obey.

Therefore the furtherest time we request is till we know the resolutions of Congress in regard to our petition, which if you grant, we request the favour of you to send us your pleasure and directions by the Bearer, Mr. James Cochran, which will be gratefully acknowledged by your humble Serv'ts, the Subscribers :

Thomas Tilton,	James Clark,
John Nixon,	his
Henry Cassill,	Adam [A H] house,
John Nowles,	mark
John Tilton,	Thomas Johnson,
John Fizpatrick,	Hunamet Davis,
Daniel Menser,	William Wallace,
Zephenia Dunn,	Jos. Reburn,
John McDonald,	Jon. Mapies,
Henry Froggs,	William Mann,
Wiland hoagland,	William Kerr,
Michael Rawlings,	Daniel Duff,
Thomas Dawsson,	Joseph Ross,
William Shiff,	James Watson,
Solomon Delong,	Abertions Bailey,
Charles Ward,	Charles Chambers,
Fred'k Lamb,	Robert Hill,
John Rigdon,	James Pauf,
George Atchinson,	William McNees
Hanes Pliey	Archibald harbson,
Walter Cain,	William Bailey,
Jacob Light,	Jonas Amspoker,
James Weleams,	Nicholas Decker,
Jesse Edgerton,	John Platt,
Nathanial Parremore,	Benjamin Reed,
Jesse Parremore,	Joseph Godard,
Jacob Clark,	Henry Conrod,
John Custer,	William Carpenter,
Thomas McDonald,	John Godard,
James Noyes,	George Reno,
John Casstleman	John Buchanan,

Daniel Mathews.

FORT McINTOSH, 13th April 1785.

Sir:

As the following information through you, to the honorable the Congress, may be of some service, I trust you'd not be displeased therewith. It is the opinion of many honorable men (with whom I conversed on my return from Wheeling) that if the Honorable the Congress don't fall on some speedy method to prevent people from settling on the Lands of the United States, west of the Ohio, that country will soon be inhabited by bandits whose actions are a disgrace to human nature.

You will in a few days receive an address from the Magistracy of Ohio County through which most of those people pass; many of whom are flying from justice.

I have Sir taken some pains to distribute copies of your instructions, with those from the Honorable, the Commissioners for Indian Affairs, into almost every settlement west of the Ohio, and had them posted up at most public places on the east side of the river, in the neighborhood through which those people pass. Notwithstanding they have saw and read those Instructions they are moving to the unsettled country by forties and fifties.

From the best information I could receive there are at the falls of Hawk Hawkins [Hockhocking], upwards of three hundred families. At Muskingum a number equal.

At the [word illegible] Towns there are several families and more than fifteen hundred on the rivers Miame & Siota. From Wheeling to that place there is scarcely one Bottom on the river but has one or more families living thereon.

In consequence of the Advertisement by John Amberson I am aprised meetings will be held at the times therein mentioned.

That at mengons and Haglins Town mentioned in my report of yesterday, the Inhabitants had come to a resolution to comply with the requisition of the Advertisement.

The supposed distance from this place to Wheeling pursuing the river, is seventy miles.

I am Sir with due respect.

Your most Obedient Servant.

John Armstrong

Ensign.

To Col. Harmar.

FORT McINTOSH, April 2, 1785.

To all those persons who have settled on the Lands of the United States, westward of the Ohio River contrary to the Orders of Congress.

I have received your Representation by James Cochran, and must inform you that my instructions are positive in driving off by force all persons who presume to settle upon or survey the Lands of the United States.

As you inform me that you have sent on a petition to Congress upon the subject, and upon a consideration of your present distressed circumstances, according to your own account, I am induced to forbear sending any troops for one month from this date to dispossess you, or until further orders from authority.

At the same time you must be as expeditious as possible in preparing to remove yourselves, as I am very confident that the Honorable body the Congress, will not grant the prayer of your petition, in which case I shall be under the necessity of executing my orders.

JOS. HARMAR,

Lt. Col. Comd.

The Indian commissioners were men of character and distinction, in whom the public had full confidence. Arthur Lee was a native of Virginia and a man of fine talents. During the revolution he represented this country at the Court of Versailles, and in 1784 was selected by Congress to treat with Western Indians. Mr. Lee died December 14, 1792, aged 52 years.

George Rogers Clark has been called "*the Washington of the West.*" A Virginian by birth he rendered invaluable services to America during the War for Independence. His appointment as Indian Commissioner was a happy selection, for he was a man of great nerve, indomitable will and energy, whose voice was potential among the Savage nations.

FORT McINTOSH,

May 1st, 1785.

Sir:—

In obedience to the instructions received from the honorable, the Commissioners for Indian Affairs, upon their departure from this post, I have to inform your Excellency, that I detached Ensign Armstrong "with a party of twenty men" furnished with fifteen days provisions, on the 31st of March last, to dispossess sundry persons who had presumed to settle on the lands of the United States on the Western side of the Ohio River.

The enclosed copy of the instructions together with his orders were posted up at Wheeling and distributed throughout the different parts of the country, in order that all persons might be fully acquainted therewith.

Ensign Armstrong having marched with his party as far down as opposite Wheeling, which is about seventy from hence, pursueing the course of the river, and executing his orders (except in a few indulgencies granted on account of the weather), returned on the 12th ulto.

I have the honor of enclosing to your Excellency, his report with sundry petitions, handed him by the settlers, likewise the opinion of some reputable inhabitants on the Eastern side of the river, with respect to them.

On the 20th ult. I received the inclosed representation signed by 66 of them praying for a further indulgence of time, and informing me that they had sent on a petition to Congress upon the subject.

In answer to which I thought it most expedient to grant them one month from the 21st ulto. to remove themselves, at the expiration of which time, parties will be detached to drive off all settlers within the distance of one hundred and fifty miles from the garrison, which in my present situation is all that is practicable. The number of settlers lower down the river is very considerable, and from all accounts daily increasing.

I would therefore (before I proceed farther in the business) beg to know the pleasure of your Excellency, and your particular order upon the subject.

I have the honor to be with the highest esteem and respect,

Your Excellency's
Most humble and obt. servant,
JOS. HARMAR,
Lt. Col. Comd. 1st Amer. Regt.

His Excellency
Richard Henry Lee,
President of Congress.

It is possible that papers exist which will determine the exact location of the various settlements mentioned in Ensign Armstrong's report. From the distances given by him, we are enabled to fix the localities as follows:—

1st. The settlers on or near the Little Beaver were in what is now Columbiana county, Ohio.

2d. Those four miles from the Little Beaver were also in Columbiana county.

3d. That at Yellow Creek was near Wellsville, Columbiana county.

4th. The eight families between Yellow Creek and Mingo Bottom were in Jefferson county.

5th. The settlement at Mingo Bottom was in Jefferson county, three miles below Steubenville on farms formerly belonging to J. H. Hallock and Daniel Potter.

6th. The place called Norris' Town, was in Jefferson county, fourteen miles below Steubenville.

7th. Haglin's or Mercer's Town, between Norris' Town and opposite Wheeling, was in Belmont county.

8th. The settlement opposite Wheeling was in what is now Pease Township, Belmont county.

In many parts of the State after the permanent settlers became located, tracts were found which had been partially cleared and a new growth of timber formed. Especially was this the case along the Ohio, on the same ground passed over by Ensign Armstrong.

The Congressional Committee, consisting of Mr. Howell, Mr. Grayson, Mr. McHenry, Mr. Pettit and Mr. King, to whom was referred a letter of the first of May, 1785, from Col. J. Harmar,—Report

That Congress approve of the conduct of Colonel Harmar in carrying into execution the order given him by the Commissioners for removing intruders from the lands of the United States.

That he be authorized to remove the troops under his command, and to take post at any place on or near the River Ohio, between Muskingum and the great Miami, which he shall conceive most advisable for farther carrying into effect the before mentioned order.

That the Board of Treasury advance Colonel Harmar six hundred dollars on account and for the purpose of transporting the said troops and their baggage to such place as he shall deem proper for the advance of the public service.

June 24, 1785.

Ordered. That the first and second paragraphs be referred to the Secretaries at War to take order. That the third paragraph be referred to the Board of Treasury to take order.

FORT MCINTOSH, June 15, 1785.

SIR: * * * * *

I have already sent you a copy of Ensign Armstrong's report, from which you will have learned the extent and character of the settlements west of the river. Most of those engaged in this business are shiftless fellows from Pennsylvania and Virginia, though I have seen and conversed with a few who appear to be intelligent and honest in their purposes. A few days after Ensign Armstrong returned, I dispatched him with a small force to Salt Springs towards the Lakes, to dispossess a number of adventurers who had located there. This he accomplished without serious difficulty. * * * * *

* * * * * * *

The force under my command, would not warrant the sending a detachment to the Scioto or Miami, but I have sent written notices by trustworthy Indians to all who have settled there. Be assured Sir, I shall make every effort within my means, for carrying out your orders, and those of the honorable, the Congress.

I am, your very obedient servant,
JOS HARMAR.

Hon'able
Major General Knox.

FORT MCINTOSH, June 21. 1785.

DEAR JOHNSTON:

* * * * * * * *

The nations down the river have killed and scalped several adventurers who have settled on their lands.

* * * * * * * *

JOSIAH HARMAR.

COL. FRANCIS JOHNSTON.

FORT MCINTOSH, June 1. 1785.

SIR:

* * * * * * * *

The Shawanese make great professions of peace. The Cherokees are hostile, and have killed and scalped seven people near the mouth of the Scioto, about three hundred and seventy miles from hence.

* * * * * * * *

Your most obt servt,
JOSIAH HARMAR.

MAJ. GENL. KNOX, Sec. at War.

FORT MCINTOSH, June 25, 1785.

Dear General:

* * * * *

The Indians down the river, viz.: the Shawanese, Miamis, Cherokees and Kickapoos have killed and scalped several adventurers—settlers on their lands.

* * * * *

JOSIAH HARMAR.

Gen. THOS. MIFFLIN.

The following extracts from letters written by Jonathan Heart, a captain in Harmar's corps, relate to the subject under consideration. Heart afterward became Major and was killed at St. Clair's defeat, November 4, 1791.

FORT HARMAR, 8th January, 1786.

MAJOR WILLIAM JUDD,

Farmington, Conn.

DEAR SIR :

* * * * * * *

Agreeable to established customs in this country, cutting down a few trees, planting three hills of corn and fencing them, gives a right of soil to 400 acres and a pre-emption to 400 more; conformable to this custom every valuable situation on the grant is located. Congress in their wisdom to prevent this improper mode of possession have forbid such locations and we have actually burnt, destroyed and turned off great numbers of inhabitants holding under this tenure, and unless Congress put a full and final stop to this mode of settlement the whole Federal territory will not raise one thousand pounds. * * *

Your most obedient humble servt,

JONATHAN HEART.

FORT HARMAR, 7th February, 1786.

MAJOR WILLIAM JUDD.

Farmington, Conn.

Sir:

* * * * * * * * * * *

The extent of the territory proposed will furnish lands for all people wishing to remove into new countries for five years, and some of the conditions as to mode and manner of settlement are very exceptionable, particularly that allowing a pre-emption to all persons claiming lands by possession or improvements, for custom in the country has established the rule, that cutting a few trees and fencing in as much land as your length of rails will encompass and planting the hills of corn, gives possession to 400 acres and a right to purchase 400 more. In conformity to this idea possession has been taken of every extensive bottom, beautiful situation, or advantageous place over the whole extent, and little more than broken ground, narrow strips of such lands as from situation or some circumstance are of little value, will be left for the petitioners. Congress acquainted with this circumstance as to mode of settlement have positively forbid all such settlements and ordered off such settlers holding lands on that tenure; this was absolutely necessary, for while this mode was admitted, no man would give 400 dollars for a farm which one day's work would secure,

* * * * * * * * * *

Your most obt. And humble serv't,

JONA. HEART.

SETTLEMENT AT THE MOUTH OF THE SCIOTO RIVER, 1785.

In the first volume of William's *American Pioneer*, page 56, the late George Corwin of Portsmouth (1842) gave his recollections of the first attempt to settle there. It was probably not on the present site of the town but on the west side of the old mouth of the River Scioto near where the village of Alexandria is located.

Until the Ohio canal was constructed and an artificial cut made at Portsmouth no water discharged there from the Scioto at its ordinary stage. The site of Alexandria was very attractive, but the ground between it and Portsmouth is most of it subject to inundation. The late Robert B. McAfee of Kentucky stated to F. C. Cleveland of Alexandria, who was an engineer on the Ohio canal forty years since that there were whites on the Kentucky side of the Ohio opposite Scioto in 1773. Mr. Cleveland said there was a space of about forty acres at Alexandria which had been chopped, and when the early settlers came this space was covered with a second growth of trees, standing among the stumps.

This was probably the work of the parties referred to by Mr. Corwin. The four families who attempted to settle at the mouth of the Sciota in 1785, came from Redstone, Pa. "They commenced clearing the ground to plant seeds for a crop to support their families, hoping that the red men of the forest would suffer them to remain and improve the soil."

The four heads of the families,—only one of whose names has been preserved went up the Sciota on a tour of exploration as far as Pee Pee Creek and encamped. Peter Patrick, one of the party, cut his initials upon a beech tree. Here they were surprised by Indians and two of them killed. Two of them escaped across the country to the mouth of the Little Sciota, just in time to meet a boat descending the Ohio for Post Vincent. This boat took the survivors from their intended home to Maysville, where the settlement was large enough to protect itself against their red enemies.

From a letter dated Fort McIntosh, June 1st, 1785, written by General Josiah Harmar to General Knox, Secretary at War, we take it there must have been another settlement on the Scioto, other than that referred to by Mr. Corwin. General Harmar says: "The Shawanese make great professions of peace. The Cherokees are hostile, and have killed and scalped seven people near the mouth of the Scioto, about three hundred and seventy miles from hence."

In a letter to Col. Francis Johnston of Philadelphia, dated Fort McIntosh, June 21, 1785, General Harmar refers to the same event in these words: "The nations down the river have killed and scalped several adventurers who have settled on their lands."

SETTLEMENTS ON THE MIAMI.

While the number of inhabitants on the Miami is no doubt extravagantly estimated, there were operations going on along that river by white adventurers at the time mentioned. Four years prior to the landing of John Cleves Symmes at the Miami, almost the whole bottom of that river as far north as the site of Hamilton, in Butler county, had been explored, and openings made with a view to pre-empting the best localities under the laws of Congress. This was by a party from Washington county, Pennsylvania, one of whom named Hindman was living as late as 1846, a few miles from Hillsborough Highland county. In the Cincinnati *Miscellany*, edited by Charles Cist, we find a short narrative of Mr. Hindman relating to the subject He says:

"My father, John Hindman was a native and resident of Lancaster county, Pennsylvania, where I was born in 1760, and at the age of twenty left that neighborhood for Washington county, where I remained four years. In the month of March, 1785, I left the state of Pennsylvania, taking water at the mouth of Buffalo creek with a party consisting of Wm. West, John Simons, John Sept, and old Mr. Carlin and their families.

We reached Limestone point, now Maysville, in safety, where we laid by two weeks. The next landing we made was at the mouth of the Big Miami. We were the first company that had landed at that place. The Indians had left two or three days before we landed. We found two Indians buried as they were laid on the ground, a pen of poles built around them, and a new blanket spread over each one. The first we found was near the bank of the Ohio, and the second near the mouth of White Water.

Soon after we landed, the Ohio raised so as to overflow all the bottoms at the mouth of the Big Miami. We went over therefore to the Kentucky side, and cleared thirty of forty acres on a claim of a man by the name of Tanner, whose son was killed by the Indians some time afterward on a creek which now bears his name. Some time in May or June we started to go up the Big Miami, to make what we called improvements, so as to secure a portion of the lands which we selected out of the best and broadest bottoms between the mouth of the river and where Hamilton now stands.

We started a north course to White Water, supposing it to be the Miami; we proceed up the creek, but Joseph Robinson who started from the mouth of the Miami with our party, and who knew something of the country from having been taken prisoner with Col. Langhery and carried through it, giving it as his opinion, that we were not at the main river, we made a raft and crossed the stream, having the misfortune to lose all our guns in the passage. We proceeded up where Hamilton now is, and made improvements wherever we found bottoms firmer than the rest, all the way down to the mouth of the Miami. I then went up the Ohio again to Buffalo, but returned the same fall, and found Gens. Clarke, Butler and Parsons at the mouth of the Big Miami, as Commissioners to treat with the Indians. Major Finney was there also. I was in company with Symmes when he was engaged in taking the meanders of the Miami river at the time John Filson was killed by the Indians."

There is one mistake in Mr. Hindman's statement; that referring to the murder of young Tanner by the Indians. He was not killed, but taken prisoner, and afterwards published an interesting narrative of his captivity.

WAR OF 1812.

From the Papers of Hon. E. Whittlesey.

SELECTION No. 2.

PETITION OF CITIZENS IN THE WEST PART OF PORTAGE COUNTY, RELATING TO THEIR EXPOSED CONDITION.

To GEN. ELIJAH WADSWORTH, Canfield, Ohio:

We, the subscribers, citizens and committee of the towns of Stoe, Franklin, Northhamton and Harmansburgh, do Humbly show that the inhabitants of said towns are entirely destitute of ammunition such as powder, lead or flints, and a very great number destitute of arms. We, the said committee, petition to your Honour to forward on as many arms as can be spared, about one hundred pounds of powder, five hundred flints, and lead in proportion. Our present defenceless situation is well Known to your Honour, and no doubt will give such relief as may be in your power. We do not consider the number of men in this part of our frontier sufficient to protect it. We therefore pray that you may send on such a number of men as you may think sufficient for that purpose.

FRED'K HAYMAKER,
WM. WETMORE,
SAMUEL KING,
JOHN HAYMAKER,
STEPHEN BUTLER.

STOE, 22nd August, 1812.

N. B. It is reported and generally believed that Gen. Hull has surrendered to the British.

PETITION OF THE OFFICERS OF THE ODD BATTALION.

HUDSON, August 22, 1812.

To ELIJAH WADSWORTH, ESQ., Major General of Division:

We, the undersigned officers of the Odd Battalion, in the Fourth Brigade and Fourth Division of Ohio Militia, do humbly state that a part of the soldiers in said Battalion are destitute of arms; and the situation of the country generally, and our particular situation, is well known to your Honour as being a frontier. We do, therefore, petition that fifty stands of arms be sent to the Battallion for the use of such soldiers as are destitute who may be called to do duty in actual service. And likewise that a proportion of powder be sent; which articles will be placed under such directions as your Honor shall think proper.

GEORGE DARROW, Major,
AMOS LUSK, Capt.,
GEORGE W. HOLCOMB, Lieut.,
CHARLES POWERS, Ensign,
THOMAS RICE, Capt.,
THOMAS VANHYNING, Lieut.

RETURN OF DRAFTS FROM 1ST REGIMENT, 3RD BRIGADE, 4TH DIVISION, MADE 5TH SEPTEMBER, 1812.

I do certify this to be a true Return of Drafts from 1st Regiment, 3rd Brigade, 4th Division Ohio Militia as made to me.

WILLIAM RAYEN, Lt. Col.

A RETURN OF NAMES OF THE COMMISSIONED AND NON-COMMISSIONED OFFICERS AND PRIVATES.

First Company.

Captain—JOSHUA T. COTTON.
Lieutenant—GEORGE MONTIETH.
Ensign—JACOB IRWIN.

Sergeants.

John Cotton, John Myres,
George Wintermute, Ab'hm. Wintermute.

Corporals.

John Carlton, Boardwin Robins,
John Russell, Jesse Graham.

Privates,

Henry Peter, John Truesdale,
Daniel Shatto, Francis Harvey,
James Crooks, Anthony Whitterstay,
Matthew Guy, Thomas Cummons,
John McCollum, Jacob Parkust,
Henry Bronstetter, Isaac Parkust,
Robert Kerr, Samuel Calhoun,
Henry Crum, George Gilbert,
Nicholas Vinnemons, Abraham Simons,
William McCrery, Thomas Craft,
Joseph Osburn, Archibald Maurace,

Adam Swazer, James Fitch,
Henry Thom, Henry Foose,
John Parkust, Abraham Leach,
Samuel White, Daniel Stewart,
Senaca Carver, Joseph Carter,
Jacob Hull, Isaac Fisher,
John White, Jacob Powers,
John Muskgrove, Thomas Irwin,
George Smith, William Munn,
John Hayes, Nathan Angue,
Thomas McCrery, Philip Kimmel,
John McGlaughlin, Abraham Hoover,
Michael Storm, Benjamin Roll,
John McMahon.

Second Company.

Captain—SAMUEL DENISON.
Lieutenant—DAVID A. ADAMS.
Ensign—WILLIAM SWAN.

Sergeants.

Amos Gray, William Carlton.

Corporals.

James Walton, Mathew I. Scott,
Robert Stewart, David Ramsey.

Privates.

John Dunwoody, David McClelland,
Ephrahim Armitage, Isaac Lyon,
Samuel Ferguson, Samuel Mann,
Conrad Miller, John McMurry,
Jacob Fight, Senr., William McMurry,
Jacob Oswalt, William Bell,
James Eckman, John Nelson,
Andrew Boyd, Peter Carlton,
John Moore, Jacob Fight, Jr.,
David Kays, David Stewart,
John Day, Joseph Baggs,
Robert Walker, William McNight,
Thomas Wilson, Thomas Fowler,
John Tulley, Sampson Moore,
James Lynn, John Poynes,
William Crawford, John Bradon,
David Willson, Daniel Augustine,
David McConnell, John Polly,
John Yast.

Third Company.

Captain—WARREN BISSELL.
Lieutenant—ALEXANDER RAYNE.
Ensign—NICHOLAS McCONNELL

Sergeants.

A. Stilson, Parkus Woodrough,
Asa Baldwin, Simon Stall,

Corporals.

William Hamilton, Amanuel Hull
Jacob Dice. Isaac Blackman,

Privates.

David Noble, Alexander Craze,
Aaron Dawson, David McCombs,
David Conizer, George Mockerman,
Henry Rumble, John Dowler,
John Riddle, Josiah Bearsley,
James Moody, John Murphy,
Joseph Mearchant, Josiah Walker,
John Bucannon, John Earl.
John Dickson, John Ross,
John Moore, John Cowdan,
Joseph McGill, John Brothers,
Phillip McConnell, Robert McGill,
Richard McConnell, Renalds Cowdan,
Robert Goucher, Samuel Love,
Thomas McCombs, William McGill,
William Bucannon, Walter Bucannon,
William Reed, William Cowdan,
William Shield, John Zedager,
William Frankle.

A RETURN OF CAPTAIN HINES' COMPANY.

Lieut.—EDMUND P. TANNER.
Ensign—THOMAS McCANE.

Sergeants.

Jullus Tanner, Daniel Fitch,
Silas Johnson, John Hutson.

Corporals.

Christopher Rasor, Joseph Bruce,
John McMullen.

Privates.

Henry McKinney, George Leonard,
John Turner, Robert Cain,
John Young, Henry Boyd,
John Chub, William McKinnie,
James McDonald, George Heater,
Jacob Shook, Henry Houck,
Samuel Green, James Saseton,
Conrad Osburn. James Polluck,
Benj. Manchester, John McConnell.
William Thomas, Arthur Anderson,
William Leonard, Elijah Stevenson,
John Hill, Henry Stump,
William Steel, John McCully,
Robert McCrary, Frances Henry,
Nicholas Leonard, John McKey,
Henry Ripley, James Jack,
James Moore, Garret Peckard.

Colonel Richard Hays to the commanding officer at Fort Wayne or Urbana, September 7, 1812. Sent by Lieut. Pomeroy and his party of scouts.

CAMP AT PIPE CREEK.
September 7, 1812.

To the commanding officer at Fort Wayne or Urbana.

SIR.—We are encamped at this place and at Huron with four hundred militia of Ohio. The inhabitants are in a state of consternation at this place. Most part fled at news of our Northwestern Army surrendering. We should esteem it a great favour to receive some infor mation from you by the bearer of this, so far as would not be detrimental, if it should be taken from the bearer by the Indians. Lieut. Pomeroy commands the scouting party sent out. Accept my respects.

RICHARD HAYES.

Lieut. Col. Command't 3d Regiment, 3d Brigade, 4th Division Ohio Militia at this place.

GEN. SIMON PERKINS TO GEN. WADSWORTH, CLEVELAND.

CAMP AT HURON, Sept. 8, 1812.

DEAR SIR: I wrote you this morning by a sick man going home on furlough, since which our scouts have come in and inform that there is or was last night, at Sandusky, a number of Indians and British who have burned the public store. The spies saw the enemy and fire but could not determine their numbers.

My present arrangements are to march my whole force to Pipe Creek, except one company, who will be left at this station to compete this encampment and guard the provisions, from Pipe Creek send a force to Sandusky, the amount of which will be determined on the return of some spies now out, which will be in this afternoon. As occurrences present themselves I will inform you, and am sir, yours, SIMON PERKINS.

MAJOR GENERAL WADSWORTH.

GENERAL PERKINS TO GENERAL WADSWORTH.

CAMP AT HURON Sept. 9, 1812, 4 P. M.

Major General WADSWORTH, Cleveland, Ohio.

SIR :—Yours by the express came to hand last evening which I should have answered and have returned the messenger immediately, but thinking it important to detain him until this morning I presume you will pardon the proceeding. I had as I wrote you yesterday made arrangements to send a company to Sandusky, but in consequence of the information in your letter of the 8th I have thought it prudent to order the companies of Dull and Murray to fall back on the east side, Huron, and Parker with his company to return to his former station in the town of Avery to complete his Block house there, then he will be ordered to join the camp at Huron. Two boats that went lately to the Peninsula returned last evening with the loss of two men killed; one private from Col. Rayens' Regiment and the other an inhabitant of this part of the country. One of those boats, commanded by Lieutenant Benj. Allen, of Col. Hayes' Regiment, found a British schooner aground on Cunningham's Island, which, after dismantling and loading the boat with the most valuable part of the rigging, set fire to and burned her.

I wrote yesterday to Col. Williams and Maj. Krutzer, a copy of which is enclosed. I have also this day received a message from Maj. Krutzer, informing me that he has commenced his march, and is building a Block house at what they (the messenger) call the Black Fork; they are in doubt whether he will march faster than can be done with the erection of Block houses at suitable distances for protection. I wrote him and solicited of him information as to his determination on that subject.

If I could receive a few more arms for my detachment they would be very acceptable.

Utensils for cooking and camp equipage generally is very much wanted; we have not so much as one kettle to a mess and no teakettle in the camp

Returns as required shall be made out and forwarded.

All occurrences of note shall be communicated, and, Sir, I shall ever be happy to be instructed by you, and believe me very respectfully your most humble Servant,

SIMON PERKINS.

Krutzer has with him about (80) eighty men.

Western Reserve Historical Society.

CLEVELAND, O., DEC., 1871.

HISTORICAL AND ARCHÆOLOGICAL TRACTS,

NUMBER EIGHT.

INDIAN AFFAIRS AROUND DETROIT IN 1706.

Speech of Miskouaki, an Ottawa Chief to the Marquis Vaudreiul, Governor General of Canada and his reply, September 1706. Translated by Col. Charles Whittlesey from a manuscript brought with other historical papers, from Paris by Gen. Lewis Cass.

These transcripts are so negligently made, on poor paper and in a hurried chirography; that it is frequently difficult to read them. They give a vivid idea of Indian ferocity, duplicity and cruelty, depicted by one of their own number; from personal observation. It is not known that this remarkable speech; or the reply of Vaudreiul have before this appeared in print. Miskouaki certainly appears well as a narator and a speaker. The Manoir Menard is presumed to be near Quebec.

Speech of Miskouaki, Brother of Jean Le Blanc an Ottawa of Detroit, who came from Mackinaw to the Manoir Menard to Monsieur the Marquis De Vaudreiul, September 26th, 1706.

My father you will be surprised by the bad affairs that I am about to inform you of on the part of Pesant, and of Jean Le Blanc touching what has passed at Detroit. I desire you my father to open to me your door, as to one of your children, and listen to what I have to say.

When I left Mackinaw, my father, our old men did not expect me to come so far as this place, hoping you would be still at Montreal. The time is short for me to return. I desire you to be willing to listen to me.

Listen—The Ottawa nations who were at Detroit the Kikakous the Sinagoes and the nation DuSables have been killed, and such as have returned to Mackinaw, came in the greatest distress. It is the Miamis, my father, who have killed us.

The reason we were obliged to fight the Miamis is, that having gone to war against the Sioux, as we have said to Sieur

Bourmont, we had been informed by a Potawatomie encamped near the fort of the Hurons, that the Miamis, who were at Detroit, had resolved to allow us to depart and march three days, after which they would attack our village and eat our women and children. My father, we were unable to comprehend, and you yourself will be surprised, as well as we, when you know that Quarante Sous, who was employed by Le Sieur La Mothe to bring all the nations to Detroit, made use of this pretext, to give them wampum privately, to engage them to destroy us. I have not come, my father, to lie to you, I have come to speak the truth. You will do after this what shall please you.

We have learned by a Pottowatomie named ——, who married a Miami, that the Miamis would eat our villagers. Upon this news, my father, the war chiefs of three nations of Ottawas with whom we had set out, held a council, and concluded that we should not deliberate upon an affair of this consequence without the consent of Pesant and of Jean Le Blanc, who are their principal chiefs, and who were sent for at once. Le Pesant and Jean Le Blanc, after having heard the news told us by the ——, concluded by stamping his foot, that since the Miamis had resolved to kill and boil us, it was necessary to forestall them.

When Pesant had said it was necessary to strike, we soon saw, and Jean Le Blanc first of us all, that he was going to do a wicked thing, but no person dared contradict him, on account of his influence and because we should then have made ourselves contemptible, in the eyes of the young men. My father; my brother and myself inquired what Pesant thought, of striking while our people were divided. Some were at war with the Hurons, some at Montreal, and what would the commandant at Detroit say if we struck at his gate.

We said thus to Pesant, but he would not listen. It is he, my father, who has caused all the misfortunes that have happened.

Jean Le Blanc, my father, would have come with me but being stripped of everything, and not daring to come as a malefactor he told me to come, and know your mind. He would have come, my father, but according to our custom during all the time we were at war, being at Detroit; he had given the Sieur Bourmont all that we had, thinking it more safe there, than in our fort, and in consequence of the misfortunes that have happened, since our departure to war with the Sioux, it remains there, and all I can do is to offer you this wampum, on the part of my nation, which is all I have, and have taken this from my pouch.

According to our resolution, we resumed the way to our fort, and as we approached the fort of the Hurons, we found eight Miami Chiefs, who were going there to a feast.

As we met them Pesant said, behold our enemies. These are the men which wish to kill us. Since there are the leaders, it is necessary to rid ourselves of them, and thereupon made a cry as a signal, encouraging us to let none of them escape. At the first cry no person moved, but Pesant having made a second, as we marched along on each side of the way, and as we were in the midst, we fired; and none of them saved themselves but Pamakona, who escaped to the French fort.

I dare tell you one thing, that I have never said before, and it is, that he is a strong friend of mine. I made a signal to him before the discharge to withdraw, and it is thus he was saved.

After those were killed, our young men rose to take such as might remain in the lodges, and as LePesant and Jean LeBlanc could not go as fast as the others, I was one of the first to reach there, but to prevent this some one forced me between the French and our people.

The Miamis being camped near their fort when I arrived I found the Miamis had withdrawn into the fort of the French, and one of our young men, a chief, had been killed, and that our youth in despair on account of his death, resolved to burn the Fort. I threw myself in the midst of them, and many times snatched the burning arrows repeatedly imploring them with vehemence, not to do the French any injury, for they were not connected with the quarrel we had with the Miamis.

I heard during this time a voice cried there is a Black Robe (a priest) and I saw my brother sending the PereRecolet into the Fort, having not harmed him, and having desired him to say to Sieur Bourmont, that he should not fire upon us, nor give any ammunition to the Miamis, but put them out of the fort and leave us alone.

We had not known, my father, that a Pere Recolet and the French soldiers, had been killed, but the next day those who had fired upon them, not being (illegible) then I blamed my brother very much, that he had not detained the Recolet father and the soldiers; who replied that he thought they would be more safe there than in our fort, on account of the irritation among our young men, for the death of two chiefs that we had lost.

The next day, my father, my brother took a flag that you had given him, and insisted on speaking to Monsieur Bourmont, desiring him, our arms reversed all around, to give us Missionaries, an opportunity to explain. He said he had no reply for us, but that the Sieur De La Foret, whom he had expected early in the spring, would soon arrive with five canoes when we could give our reasons. Seeing he did not wish to listen to us, we were obliged to return ; and that night our young men determined to burn the fort. Our old men were embarrassed, and to prevent them passed three entire days in council.

After having been three days in council Jean Blanc rose and said to Pesant, "since it is you who has caused all this difficulty what do you say ? what do you think ?" As for me I say we are dead, and that we have killed ourselves by striking the Miamis at the French stockade. In turn the Miskowakies and the Sinagoes will say the same thing.

As soon as the Sieur De Tonty was gone, we were well agreed that affairs were becoming embroiled, of which there were sure signs in this last matter ; since the Sieur De Bourmont being able to arrange everything did not wish to listen to us, referring us always to the arrival of the Sieur De La Foret.

However we had certain signs that he wished to fight (illegible) for he put swords at the end of his pike staves. We continued some time to have parleys with him, and went without fear to the fort of the Hurons, believing that they were our allies, but for fear of the Miamis we always went in canoes.

My father, the Hurcns called the Ottawa Sinago, and said to him, "my brothers it is a long time that we have been brothers, and that together we have fought the Iroquois." When we speak to you we speak to all the nations, "Outawase," (Ottawas,) Sacs, Sauteurs, Poutawatamies, Saukies, Chippeways and Mississaugies.

"Look at this string of beads, my brothers, I take it out for you to look at. It is a long time our old men have preserved it. Upon this string there is seen the figures of men. This string (or belt) signifies much. It is never shown unless we give life or death to those to whom we speak. I return it, and say to you on the part of the French, that he wishes you to meet him at the feast. It will not be in the lodges, for you might thus have apprehensions, but it will be near this spot, on the prairie, where the French flag will be planted, and there you will come to the feast."

On the morrow the day of the feast, we were to have, Jean Le Blanc having his garden, near the place where the French flag was planted, was walking there and saw a number of the French bring wheat and throw it upon a sail cloth, spread out upon the prairie. The Huron women did the same, and brought the wheat and poured it upon the cloth. Then my brother thought the Hurons had spoken truly, and that we should have a good time, nevertheless being with Pesant they reflected, that the French had never been willing to speak to them.

It might be that under the name of this feast, the Hurons would betray them, and give the Miamis the opportunity of attacking them, while their women and children were gone to fetch the wheat. They resolved to send out scouts for discovery in the woods, and four young men departed, who returned and said, they saw many ways which led into the depths of the forest, and seemed to encircle those which led to the wheat. As some of our people had already departed we caused them to be recalled, seeing clearly it was a bait which they had spread for us. We then knew it was a design of the French, of the Miamis, as also of the Hurons, as soon as we should leave our Fort to go to the wheat which was intended for us ; and when they thought as we were very hungry, we should enjoy ourselves very much, the greater part of the Miamis and the Hurons, who were in the thick woods, were to come to take the fort, and the other portion, composed of French, Hurons and Miamis, were concealed in the glades opposite the flag, and from thence would fall on us. As we had recalled all of our people, and no one went for the wheat, they were much deceived on their part, and the Miamis who were in the thick wood, thinking that we had gone out of our fort, or at least a great part of us, rushed forward with great shouts to take it. Our young men who were in the bastion, having discovered them afar off, we fought them all day with guns, and lost one of our men, who was killed by a woman. In the evening the Miamis returned, without our being able to determine how many of their people were killed. In returning they met Katalibou and his brother, whom they killed and scalped.

The Miamis in attacking our fort took the precaution to form two companies, and one of them came along the water, where they threw away such of our canoes as they found, for the purpose of depriving us of the means of escape.

The next day, my father, we were convinced that the Hurons had joined the Miamis. They came together to attack us at our fort, and this day more of the Miamis were killed, than the day before. They returned again the next day. We attacked the Hurons, who undertook to overwhelm us with injuries. We had so little powder we dare not fire, though we had some. They took new life since Onontio had abandoned (MSS. not legible here).

Cletart, the brother of Quarante Sous, said then that our young men, indignant at the injuries that the Hurons had done us, should make a sortie, and we fought against them and the Miamis, a long time out of the fort The Hurons held their ground, but the Miamis fled, although there were 400 of them.

On this day one of our people who had been at war with the Hurons at the (not legible), arrived at our fort, and said that all the others who had started with him and had returned, were bound in the French fort; that the Hurons had bound them, and that they had sent him to let us know of it; that two of our war allies of the Hurons were prisoners in their fort, and that the rest had been taken to the French fort, for what reason we did not know.

The next day the Hurons and Miamis came again and attacked our fort. They had apparently lost some person of consideration among them. They shot before they left one of their prisoners, who was one of our allies.

Some time after the Hurons (Wyandots) sent for the relatives of those who were confined in the French fort, saying that they well remembered what we had done to them, and that it was by way of reprisal that they had bound our people, but that they did not wish to kill them. We had but to come and cover them according to custom. We caused some to carry blankets thither, and they told us to come and cover them to-morrow (MSS. defective,) we observing a place at the gate of the French fort where the cannon was, and where they placed poles.

They ordered us to bring presents then, according to the favors they were granting us. Our people, believing them to act in good faith, returned, and each one exhausted their goods and carried them, even to the beads of our children.

Scarcely had we put on the poles (or pickets) ten pieces of porcelain beads, twenty kettles, two packs of Beaver, and all that we had brought, when Quarante Sous gave his hand to Jean Blanc. At this moment Jean Blanc received a shot, and at the same time a discharge was made from the fort, upon us, who being there in good faith, were without arms, relying upon the sincerity of the French, and were obliged to fly. The Hurons and the Miamis having made a sortie, those of our people who remained in the fort came to the assistance of those who fled, and the remainder of the day was passed in fighting on both sides. We lost in this treachery, two men, killed at the discharge from the French fort, and five wounded. The last stroke which the Miamies have given us, my father, was done at our homes by their young men. There they killed a woman and took another prisoner, and as we sent after them to know what they would do with her, our people heard cries in the French Fort where they were burning her.

The exhaustion of war and hunger, obliged our people to send (not legible) one of our chiefs to speak to the Ouyatanons. Heretofore the Ouyatanons (a tribe on the waters of the Wabash, a Miami tribe) had danced with him the calumet of peace. Our people employed this man to speak to the Miamis. He said, my father, the Ouyatanons had treated us as sons in dancing this calumet, and also "I am astonished that you remain so long to kill us at our palisades. Art thou not wrong in killing us, and dost not thou kill thyself also, hast thou no pity on thy young men."

An Ouyatanon replied "that it was not his tribe who had done that, but it was the Hurons and the French who wished to oblige them to remain until the Ottawas should perish in their fort by hunger," and the Ouyatanons ceased to speak. Having determined to return the slaves, we separated. Two of our people were given to the Ouyatanons, two were given to the nation of the Crane, Miamis, who are of the river St. Josephs; one was burnt in the French Fort, another shot, and the son of Aiontache a Mississauga saved from death by the commandant of a French Fort. There was one of our men married to a woman of whom we have no news. The two others, Sieur De La Mothe has restored to the Mississaugas. Behold my father all which I know, and the old men have requested me to say to you, that on account of all the treachery that the Hurons have done them, it is with difficulty they can restrain their young men from going against him, so long as he remains at Detroit, from whence we have withdrawn only to be less exposed.

The two Ottowas, my father, who were given to the Ouyatannos saved themselves on the way and came to rejoin us. They say they were not misused by the Ouyatanons. They report that the Miamis have in killed and wounded fifty persons; and we have lost twenty-six, including those who were returned from the war, and those the Hurons bound through treachery.

My father, I speak in the name of all nations, Ottowas, Poutawotomies, Saukis, Outagamies, Kickapous, Quinepigs, Matamini, Sauters and Mississaugas, all the people of the county bordering upon the Lakes, in short of all our allies, and of their indignation against the Hurons for the treachery they have done us. They desire you through me to allow us to fight him. I desire you, my father, to tell me your thoughts, so that I may report the same to our people, and that we may fully know each other's wishes.

REPLY OF MONSIEUR DE VAUDREUIL TO MISKOUAKI, BROTHER OF JEAN LE BLANC, AN OTTOWA CHIEF OF THOSE WHO WERE AT DETROIT, SEPTEMBER 28, 1706.

I have listened quietly Miskouaki to all you have said, and although I am already informed of what has passed at Detroit, could not fail to be greatly surprised by your recital. I do not reply, because it does not appear to me that you are sent by all the nations, as you say: but only by your brother, Jean Le Blanc to pre-occupy my mind, and for this purpose you left Mackinaw, intending to remain here. It is only the arrival of your brother that has given you a desire to return.

However that may be, I am not sorry to have seen you, and am glad to hear what you have said, touching the conduct of your brother.

You wish to know my thoughts Miskuouaki, you desire me to give them to you. Listen to me well, I am a good father, and so long as my children listen to my voice, no evil will happen to them. You have proofs of this in what happened at Detroit, and if Le Pesant and Jean Le Blanc, had not undertaken anything without knowing my wishes, you would not have attacked the Miamis. You would not have killed of mine, and you would not have been in the distress and misery where you are now.

We have been killed Miskouaki, and until I see all the nations whom I have always regarded as my children, come here, recognize their fault and ask pardon, I cannot forget that I have lost at Detroit a missionary and a soldier, who are of value among us.

This is what you can say to your brother and to all the nations, when you arrive there. I have seen and examined the speech you have delivered. As you have yourself said that the belt you drew from your pouch, was not given you by your people when you departed, I return it to you, and do not receive it, not because I despise it as coming from you, but because I cannot reply to it, since it does not come directly from them, and I am pleased to return it to you as a thing that belongs to you, that you may use it to accommodate the bad affairs which might happen.

In regard to what has passed at Detroit, I say to all your people that I stop the tomahawk, and prohibit them from going to war, either with the Hurons or Miamis, or any one else, and order them to remain strictly on the defensive, until I am better informed, As to other matters, I expect news daily from M. De La Mothe, and during the winter I shall examine all you have said, and that which he shall advise, in order to be able to regulate affairs.

If the recital you have made us is true, as a consequence of the present state of things, you cannot move aside very far in hunting this winter. Your people will be able to come here early in the spring, with the Frenchmen I leave above; to know my thoughts.

This is what they should have done this year, and not to have sent you alone, and without belts on the part of all the nations. It is not beads, Miskoukai, that I demand, neither presents where my children have disobeyed, and done such wrongs as you have. The blood of Frenchmen is not paid by beaver skins.

It is constant reliance in my goodness that I demand, a real repentance of faults they have committed, and entire resignation to my will. When your people shall be in this state of mind, I will accommodate everything as before; but for this it is necessary to come early in the coming spring, or at least a part of the chiefs. It is necessary that they lead here all the French, and that your young men assist them to bring down their furs.

It is necessary also that they remain quietly upon their mats, without going to war, either with the Hurons or the Miamis or others, that they remain entirely on the defensive, and even if they are attacked at home, to be content until the coming year to defend themselves, and to come here and make their complaints to me.

These, Miskouaki, are my thoughts and it is thus you can speak to all the nations on my part. I do not make you presents for your brothers nor the other chiefs, it not being natural to recompense children when in a state of disobedience like you. I take pity however on you on account of the trouble you have been at, and the confidence you have shown in me. I give you a blanket, a shirt, some trinkets, powder lead and tobacco, to excite you to diligence on your return and in the expectation you will behave yourself, in the upper country and also that the father Marest, will report to me in such a manner that I shall have consideration for you and it will be for you to conduct yourself, so as to receive evidences of my goodness, when you shall return here with the others.

Western Reserve Historical Society.

CLEVELAND, O., FEBRUARY, 1872.

HISTORICAL AND ARCHÆOLOGICAL TRACTS,

NUMBER NINE.

ARCHÆOLOGICAL FRAUDS.—Inscriptions attributed to the Mound Builders—Three Remarkable Forgeries.

BY COL. CHAS. WHITTLESEY,

PRESIDENT OF THE WESTERN RESERVE AND NORTHERN OHIO HISTORICAL SOCIETY.

During the past thirty-five years, three artificially wrought stones have been produced, purporting to have been found in ancient mounds on the waters of the Ohio, on which were inscribed characters, letters or hieroglyphics, supposed to have the force of written records capable of interpretation. As there has long been an expectation that among the relics of the mound-builders such inscriptions would be found, these were seized upon by antiquarians with great eagerness. I know of only three such stones purporting to be from the mounds of the Mississippi valley, all of which are now regarded as spurious. We are, therefore, now as far as ever from the settlement of the question whether the mound-builders had a written language. I shall notice them in the order of their appearance.

THE GRAVE CREEK MOUND.

In 1838, Mr. A. B. Tomlinson, the owner of the great mound at Grave Creek, West Virginia, constructed an adit or gallery along the natural surface of the ground to the center of the mound, which is an artificial truncated cone of earth, about seventy feet high, with a flat place fifty feet in diameter on the top. At the base it is 900 feet in circumference. White men examined it as early as 1734. From the top he sunk a shaft to the adit, and made other excavations and improvements, with a view to render this remarkable burial monument of an ancient people, and his collection of ancient implements of copper, bone and stone, attractive to visitors. He produced among other articles purporting to have been found in the excavations a small flat stone, nearly circular in form, about half an inch thick, and an inch and a half in diameter. On one of the flat surfaces there were engraved characters, concerning which many conjectures were formed. A fac simile, or an attempted fac simile, was published in the Cincinnati *Chronicle*, Feb. 2d, 1839, and in the *American Pioneer* for May, 1843.

The antiquarian, Henry R. Colcraft, having examined the stone in August, 1843, published the following opinion upon the characters and their interpretation:

"The most interesting object of antiquarian inquiry is a small flat stone, inscribed with antique alphabetical characters, which was disclosed on opening this mound. These characters are in the ancient rock alphabet, of sixteen right and acute angled strokes; used by the Pelasgi and other early Mediterranean nations, and which is the parent of the modern *Runic*, as well as the *Bardic*." * * "Several copies of it soon got abroad which differ from each other and from the original."

Mr. Tomlinson says, "We commenced on the north side, and excavated towards the center, an adit ten feet high, and seven feet wide, along the natural surface. At the distance of one hundred and eleven feet we came to a vault that had been excavated in the earth before the mound was commenced; 8 feet by 12 square and seven in depth. Along each side and across the ends upright timbers had been placed which supported timbers thrown across the vault, as a ceiling. These timbers were covered with loose unhewn stone, common in the neighborhood. The timbers had rotted and the stone tumbled into the vault." "In this vault were two human skeletons, one of which had no ornaments. The other was surrounded by 650 ivory beads and an ivory (probably bone) ornament about six inches long, see figure herewith." (A similar stone may be seen in the Museum of the Historical Society.) * * * In sinking the shaft from the top, at 34 feet above the first or bottom vault, Mr. Tomlinson found a second or upper one, similar to the first, with 1,700 beads of ivory (bone?) 500 small shells perforated and worn as beads, and five copper rings, or bracelets, on the wrists of the skeleton, in all weighing 17 ounces. There were also 150 pieces of mica, and about two feet from the skeleton, *this stone*, with the supposed Runic characters.

Mr. Levering, of Lancaster, Ohio, commenting upon the stone in 1843, (American Pioneer vol. 2, p. 406.) says: "In examining a work relating to the chirography of the ancient Britons, I was astonished and gratified to discover a striking similarily between the fac simile of their style of writing and that found in the mound at Grave Creek." * * *

"The ancient Britons cut their alphabet upon a stick with a knife, which thus inscribed, they call 'Billet of signs of the Bards" or the "Bardic alphabet," Compositions and memorials were registered in this way, on long narrow boards, several of these being united together in the following manner: (here an engraving of a stick book and its letters was inserted) form a connected composition. Although there are but few characters, on the flat stone of Grave creek, several of that few exactly resemble those of the stick book of the ancient Britons."

This stone thus verified and commented upon with so much learning, is now universally regarded by archæologists as a fraud. Probably Mr. Tomlinson himself was imposed upon by some one who secreted it there, whose genius and ambition took that direction, and who had seen the Bardic characters of the ancient Britons. As late as 1866 a clerk at Washington City went through the labor of cutting an Icelandic or Runic inscription upon a rock at the Falls of the Potomac, which purported to record the death and mark the grave of Syuso or Suaue aged 25 years, widow of Kjoldr one of the Icelandic explorers in America, A. D. 1051. Having posted himself on the history of the Northmen of this continent, he prepared a learned article for the New York *Tribune* which appeared January 31, 1867.

The examination purported to have been made in company of Professor Lesquereux of Columbus, Ohio, Professor Brand of Washington City and Dr. Boyce of Boston.

CINCINNATI STONE.

In the Cincinnati *Gazette* of Dec. 24, 1842, a communication is printed from Erasmus Gest, a well known citizen of Cincinnati, relating to an engraved stone, purporting to have been found in removing an ancient mound, about twenty feet high, at the north-west corner of Fifth and Mound streets. He says, "this hieroglyph was found with a skeleton, together with two bones taken from the same grave, each about seven inches in length; nicely rounded and pointed at one end. In the excavation several skeletons were disinterred in a good state of preservation, but so near the surface, as to give rise to the inference, that they were deposited since the mound was erected."

(NOTE. It was a common practice for Indians, and also with the early white settlers, to bury their dead on the top and sides of ancient artificial mounds of the west.)

"But the one found with the pointed bones and hieroglyphic, was in a decayed state, in the center of the mound and somewhat below the natural surface, and was no doubt the object for which it was erected."

"I think there is little doubt about its being a hieroglyph, and is probably the history of a great chief who once swayed the destinies of a powerful nation."

This stone is four and one half inches long, two and one fourth inches broad at the ends, and is in the form of a rectangle with its longest sides curved gracefully inward. Its upper and lower faces are flat and parallel, and its thickness is three-eighths of an inch. The material is fine grained sandstone. The supposed hieroglyphics on the upper face resemble the ornamentation of sculptured stones in Central America, figured by Catherwood. On the other face, there are only some longitudinal furrows, such as might be made by sharpening a pointed tool of metal upon the stone. The publishers had a fac simile tracing of the ornamented side, taken and engraved on wood, which accompanied the description of Mr. Gest. The editors appended a column of remarks. Plaster models were made and distributed among antiquarians. The engraving which is a very faithful representation of the stone, has been reproduced in many books subsequently published, from one of which I make some extracts.

Professor Daniel Wilson, L. L. D., of Toronto Canada, in his learned work entitled Pre-Historic Man; London, 1865, refers at length to the "Cincinnati Stone," after having discarded the "Holy Stone," of Newark as a forgery.

"Upon its smooth surface, an elaborate figure is represented, as shown in the accompanying illustration; by grinding the interspaces within a rectangular border, so as to produce what has been regarded as a hireoglyphic inscription. But a remarkable feature of its graven device is the series of lines, by which the plain surface at each end is divided. The ends of the stone form arcs of different dimensions. The greater arc is divided by a series of lines, twenty-seven, into equal spaces, and within this is another series of seven oblique lines. The lesser arc, at the opposite end, is divided in like manner, by the series of lines twenty-five, and eight in number, similarly arranged. This tablet has not failed to receive due attention. It has been noted that it bears a singular resemblance to the Egyptian Cartouch. The series of lines were discovered to yield, in the form of the products of the longer and shorter ones, a near approximation to the number of days in the year, a result which furnished the requisite grounds for ascribing to the tablet an astronomical origin, and so constituting it an ancient calender, recording the approximation of the Mound Builders to the true length of the solar year. Mr. Squier perhaps runs to the opposite extreme, in suggesting that it is probably nothing but a stamp, such as have been found made of clay in Mexico and the Mississippi Mounds, used in impressing ornamental patterns on cloth or prepared skins. Such clay stamps always betray their purpose, by a handle attached to them, as in the corresponding bronze stamp of the Romans."

"Another hypothesis may be admissible, that is a record of a certain scale of measurement."

"If so, the discovery of a record pertaining to the standards of measurement of the Mound Builders, is calculated to add new and more definite interest to our study of their geometrical constructions."

Thus for, near thirty years, this ornamented stone was received as genuine, though its hieroglyphic character was not generally admitted. All illusions and all speculations on this relic are now dissipated. Recently looking over Professor Wilson's work in our library, I perceived a written leaf pasted into the book, at the place where it is noticed by the author, which proved to be the following statement. It wipes out the last supposed record of the race of the Mounds.

COMMENTS OF DR. JARED P. KIRTLAND, CLEVELAND, OHIO, DECEMBER 1871, ON FIGURE 17, PAGE, 221 WILSON'S PRE-HISTORIC MAN "CINCINNATI TABLET."

In early days a high and regular formed mound was located in the western part of Cincinnati. General Wilkinson at an early time placed upon it an observatory and sentries for watching the Indians. In the year 1841 the corporation established a street through this mound and its destruction rapidly progressed.

One morning while I was in the Chemical Laboratory of my colleague in the Ohio Geological Survey and in the Medical College of Ohio, Professor John Locke, in the Spring of that year, an artful and sinister looking man rushed into the room and assuming a high degree of excitement, stated that while excavating the centre of the mound he had dug out a curiously engraved stone, which he could sell to us for $40 or $50, and handed out the Tablet figured on page 221. Prof. Locke took it, and calmly examined the engraving through a magnifier. He, in a sarcastic manner, said to the stranger, "I would advise you, before you attempt to palm this off as a piece of antiquity, to carefully brush from the excavations in the stone the fine grains of sand formed by the cutting instrument." I then examined it in a similar manner, and plainly detected the imposition. The fellow hastily seized the stone and made his exit without a reply.

The next year a figure and description of this stone appeared in the *American Pioneer*.

I afterwards learned that this stone was cut and engraved in a marble shop in that city and was carefully buried the night previous, in the mound, where it would be reached by the excavators in the next day's labors. J. P. KIRTLAND.

THE NEWARK HOLY STONE.

Near Newark, Licking county, is a series of ancient earth-works, more extensive than any that have hitherto been described on the waters of the Mississippi. When I made the first detailed survey of these works, in February, 1838, they were little injured by cultivation, most of the ground being then in its original condition of thick forest. They occupy in all their ramifications more than a thousand acres. A plan with full descriptive maps may be seen in the "Monuments of the Mississippi Valley," by Squier & Davis, published by the Smithsonian Institute in 1847. A portion of the less conspicuous works are now obliterated, but they are still an object of wonder to all tourists, and of still deeper interest to all students of American antiquity.

Near the close of the month of June, 1860, I was at Newark on business having no connection with the old earth-works, for which this place has now become celebrated

About 4 o'clock in the afternoon the late David Wyrick, an old resident of the town, was seen in a very excited manner, hurrying along the main street, from the direction of the canal. He was regarded there as an eccentric character, an uneducated man, but on some subjects, particularly mathematics, as possessed of decided ability. He had held the office of county surveyor until long continued attacks of acute rheumatism rendered him physically incompetent. With his limbs and joints so swollen by elephantisis, attended by intense suffering, his feet and hands so disfigured as scarcely to retain their human aspect, he was everywhere regarded with commiseration. For some years he had adopted the theory that the Hebrews were the builders of the earth works of the West, and when his physical condition would allow it, sought dilligently among them for proofs to sustain this hobby. He was certainly an enthusiast, his mind somewhat distorted, in sympathy with his body, but no one of his neighbors thought him capable of deliberate deception.

As he passed rapidly from shop to shop, and store to store, on this hot afternoon of June, he exhibited with exultation the stone, afterwards known as the "Holy Stone," as a triumphant proof and settlement of his Jewish theory. General Israel Dille, who had known Wyrick since he was a young man and had full confidence in him proposed that we should take him in a buggy, and at once proceed to the spot where it was found. A lad of his, about 14 years of age, helped to make the excavation, and he was taken with us. We drove immediately to the spot, about a mile southwest of the town, where the earth they had thrown out was still fresh and moist. The hole they had made was near the center of an artificial circular depression, common among the earth works, about twenty feet in diameter and three feet deep at the middle, with a low rim or bank around it. He said he and his son were searching for human bones, and, at a depth of 12 or 14 inches, about an hour previous, had thrown out the inscribed stone. It had been only partially cleaned, and the dirt being a fine yellow loam, which filled the sunken spaces, corresponded fully with that of the pit. The lad confirmed what his father said, and added that as soon as the characters on the stone were discovered he ran away to town with it like a crazy man.

The stone had not the appearance of great antiquity, but suggested that it might have been buried fifty years. The Free Masons of Newark at once recognized it as one of their emblems, representing the "Key Stone" of an arch which Master Masons wore in early times as an insignia of their rank. On these "Key Stones" and on their modern substitutes the owner was priviledged to engrave mottos according to his taste. There were modes enough to account for such a stone being found in this depression, without giving it any connection with the Mound Builders. It might have been dropped there since the advent of the present race of white men and covered by the accumulations of loam and vegetation continually washed towards the center of the cavity. It was secured by the Ethnological Society of New York and commented upon fully by the members, but with a general doubt of its genuineness

Mr. Wyrick's account, which he published soon after in pamphlet, reads thus:

"The following is a representation of the four sides of the supposed keystone that was found on the 29th of June, 1860, in a sink or depression, commonly called a "well hole," whilst looking for bones that said holes were said to contain. The object of looking for human bones was to ascertain the truth of such assertion. This stone is in the size and shape represented by the cuts, and has upon each of the four sides a Hebrew inscription, in the Hebrew character, which, when translated, reads, "The King of the Earth," "The Word of the Lord," "The Laws of Jehovah," "The Holy of Holies."

The letters are nearly an inch long, and well sunk into the stone. Taken in the same order as Mr. Wyrick has recited them, the Hebrew sentences are "Torah Adonai," "Dabbah Adonai," "Kadosh Kadosheem," "Malach Aratz," and with a free reading give a consecutive sentence thus, according to three Hebrew scholars acting independently: "The law of God, the word of God, the King of the earth is most holy." While this stone was being discussed Wyrick went on digging, and his discoveries were much more startling and doubtful than those already given, but much more appropos of Moses and the Jews. On page 8 of his illustrated pamphlet, the results are thus described:

"The following four cuts are those of four sides of a very singular stone, found enclosed in a stone box buried twenty feet in the earth, or in the earth of a tremendous stone mound. This stone was found on the first of November, 1861, in company with five others (persons). In the first place, on removing this stone pile (several years before), which was said (truly) to have been forty feet high, rising from a base 182 feet in diameter, some of the workhands came to a mound of pure clay, of which they say there was or is quite a number within the periphery of this stone base, entirely around it, but covered by this enormous stone stack." * * * "In one of these, in the clay, they found the shell of an old log, on which lay seven copper rings, with the appearance of some extremely coarse cloth. * * Removing the old shell, they found it to be the cover to another piece of timber, resembling a trough, in which was coarse cloth (very rotten), human bones, hair, and ten copper rings, which they took, and covered up the trough and its contents.

"In July, 1860, I happened to see a piece of the wood and four of the rings (now in possession of Dr. Wilson, of Newark), and repaired to the place—(two miles east of Jacktown and south of the National Road) —with some work hands, and sacrilegiously took it up." In November, 1861, Wyrick and three others, one of whom is said to have been Dr. Nichols, again attacked the wooden sarcophag s, which had by that time been so much covered by falling earth, that they labored, from morning till three P. M. uncovering the pile of clay. It was the usual fire clay of the coal series, about two feet thick, evidently brought there. In this the wooden trough was firmly imbedded, and in this manner it had been preserved.

"Near the under surface, imbedded in the clay, was taken the stone box (engraved size of nature in the pamphlet) whilst digging in the hole in the clay, in which (the box) was enclosed a black stone, as is shown by the four following cuts of it, with the characters on each side, the English of which appears to be an abridgement of the Ten Commandments."

On one of the sides of the blackstone, is a likeness of Moses with his name in Hebrew over his head. He is represented as a very savage and pugnacious individual. The Hebrew letters were like those of the Holy Stone readily translated by Hebrew scholars. Wyrick closes his pamphlet in in these words: "Would it not require a very profound scholar in Hebrew to make such an abridgement of the Hebrew decalogue with foreign characters as is made above." * * * "Bacon's arrant school boy borrowing a Hebrew Bible even in Ohio of some minister and whittling hone stones into gin bottles (Bacon's Life Elexir) forever with all the jack knives in Christendom could produce even in Ohio such an outrage or piece of scholarship."

This somewhat blind and sarcastic allusion was intended for those who questioned the genuineness of these inscribed stones. Experienced archeologists had never much faith in the Holy stone. When Moses and the ten commandments appeared, Wyrick's character as an impostor was soon established.

Not long after this he died, and in his private room among the valuable relics he had so zealously collected, a Hebrew Bible was found, which fully cleared up the mystery of Hebrew inscriptions "even in Ohio." This had been the secret and study of years, by a poverty stricken and suffering man, who in some respects was almost a genius. His case presents the human mind in one of its most mysterious phases, partly aberation and partly fraud. When the Arabs who are employed to explore ruins on the Nile and the Euphrates, discover what relics their employers are in pursuit of, they generally produce them. Here the motive is plain, it is money. Perhaps this was the case with the "sinister" individual, who presented himself to Professors Locke and Kirtland with the Cincinnati stone. The Grave Creek inscription if it was gotten up by the proprietor Mr. Tomlinson, might be placed in the same catagory If, as is more probable, it was the work of another party, who must have industriously studied the Runic or Bardic alphabet, it can only be attributed to an innate pleasure in the practice of deception amounting to monomania. We have frequent exhibitions of this disease in the case of articles presented to our museum, in some instances by persons who profess to be respectable and conscientious.

Western Reserve Historical Society.

CLEVELAND, O., MAY, 1872.

HISTORICAL AND ARCHÆOLOGICAL TRACTS,

NUMBER TEN.

ANNUAL MEETING AT THE MUSEUM, MAY 13th, 1872.

OFFICERS OF THE ASSOCIATION.

Col. Chas. Whittlesey, President and curator.

Dr. J. H. Salisbury, Vice President.

Secretary, (vacant.)

Hon. S. Williamson, Treasurer and curator.

Mrs. M. Milford, Librarian.

CURATORS ELECTED.

Joseph Perkins, C. T. Sherman, J. H. A. Bone, C. C. Baldwin, Mrs. J. H. Sargent, John W. Allen, Miss Mary C. Brayton.

CURATORS EX-OFFICIO.

Wm. Bingham, Benj. A. Stanard, H. M. Chapin, James Barnet.

LIFE MEMRERS.

Leonard Case, H. M. Chapin, Joseph Perkins, H. A. Harvey.

General Statement by the President.

—Memorial Notice of Alfred T. Goodman.

Our collection of books, maps, manuscripts, pamphlets, relics and general curiosities continues to increase as heretofore with a rapidity greater than we had anticipated, almost entirely the result of voluntary donations. We have no systematic catalogue of relics, pioneer or war implements, and other articles of general interest, constituting our museum; but our efficient and systematic librarian, Mrs. Milford, reports the relative number of books, pamphlets and registered visitors for 1871 and 1872 to be as follows:

	1871	1872	Increase during the year.
No. of Books........	1181	2002	321
No. of Pamphlets...	2529	3000	411
No. of Visitors......	625	1024	409

It is not our purpose to collect a large library. The designs of the institution in this respect are special; to procure as far as possible, and to preserve for reference all the matter within our reach, whether books, pamphlets, maps or manuscripts, which has a bearing upon the early history of Ohio, in particular, and of the Northwestern States in general.

The printed books on this subject are few in number, not exceeding four or five hundred, but most of them are so rare as not to be found in ordinary book stores. I think when our catalogue is made out we shall find that we are now in possession of three-fourths of them, and that there is not a more complete collection on early history, to be found west of the Alleghany Mountains. It has already become a place much frequented by persons who are working up the local and general history of Ohio. Our historical maps and manuscripts are not as complete as the books and pamphlets, but are highly valuable. Among the old maps in our collection are the following:

A general atlas of the world, very full as to Europe, containing with illustrations 95 sheets folio bound, of date 1701 to 1720 by John Baptiste Homan Nuremberg. Deposited by Breno Nicolais, Cleveland.

Map of "Caroiana and the River Meschacebe," by Daniel Coxe, 1727.

British North America, with the French and Spanish settlements adjacent, by Henry Popple, London, 1733.

"Possessions Anglaise et Francaise," by I. Rotter, Amsterdam, 1752.

"British and French Dominions in North America," eight large sheets, bound by John Mitchel, Amsterdam, 1755. Presented by Rev. E. A. Dalrymple, Secretary Maryland Historical Society.

"Middle British Colonies in America," by Lewis Evans, with Pownall's topographical descriptions, London and Philadelphia, 1755; same second edition, with descriptions by Evans, Philadelphia, 1760. Printed by B. Franklin and D. Hall.

"Atlas of British Colonies in North America." including admiralty surveys, twenty-five large sheets, by William Fadden, London, 1777.

Charts and illustrations of Captain Cook's voyages around the world, 1772 to 1780, thick volume folio, on deposit by C. C. Baldwin, Esq.

Large map of Pennsylvania, on cloth, by R. Howell, 1792.

Large bound volume of manuscript maps, from the papers of the Connecticut Land Company, 1796-7.

Map of Ohio, 1806, by John F. Mansfield. Presented by Joseph Sullivant.

Map of Ohio, 1815, by Hough & Bourne, Chillicothe, 1816.

Manuscript map of the west end of Lake Erie, apparently for the use of the army in 1813, from the papers of John Walworth.

Manuscript plat of a State road from the forks of Muskingum (Coshocton) to Painesville, by Abram Tappen, 1805.

General Atlas of the World: Dublin, 1800. Presented by Hon. S. Williamson.

General Atlas, by Matthew Carey & Son, Philadelphia, 1818. Presented by J. P. Kirtland, L. L. D.

Maps of northern boundary, commission of 1820. Presented by the late M. B. Scott, Esq.

Map of Paris and its fortifications. Presented by N. C. Winslow, Esq.

Maps of twenty counties in Ohio.

We have been presented during the year with a series of works relating to the antiquities of North and Central America, embraceing everything on that subject which we find in the market. This munificent donation includes the great work of Lord Kingsborough in nine folio volumes, reproducing the picture writings of Mexico, in fac simile, with translations, so far as they are accessible in America or Europe. Few libraries in the United States possess these rare and splendid volumes. Next to what relates to general history and antiquities, we desire to have in our library works of a local and statistical character, such as official reports of Legislatures, municipal corporations and public institutions of all kinds, whether new or old; city and county maps of Ohio, and sketches of the settlements of townships, including the earliest settlers.

Public feeling in this community is so favorable to this institution that our donations of articles for the museum, come in more rapidly than we can provide cases to arrange and display them. I believe that an equally liberal feeling exists in regard to money contributions, and that it is only necessary to make an effort in the way of solicitation to put ourselves in a good condition financially. At present the annual subscriptions, for membership do not meet current expenses, without an occasional resort to the legacy of the late Mr. Warner. Something more than a year since we had a special contribution in money for the purpose of developing the antiquities of the State, an investigation which should have attracted the attention of the State geologists. Surveys of the aneient works in the Cuyhoga valley have been made by the help of this fund; of which the members have evidence in pamphlet No. 5, of our series. Examinations have been made, and fac simile copies of several ancient inscriptions upon rocks, within this State, have been procured. These tracings now on exhibition in this room, are taken full natural size, and then photographed to a scale convenient for engraving. In this way they will be made available for antiquarians; by a process, the accuracy of which no one can call in question.

Since the last annual meeting the society has sustained an irreparable loss in the death of our Secretary, Mr. Alfred T. Goodman. The committee appointed by the curators to prepare a notice of his short but busy life, and his ever zealous services in the cause of history, have not fully completed their work. It will soon be ready, and will appear as part of the proceedings of this meeting. The mortality of our officers and members during the year has been unusually great. Besides our lamented Secretary, our First Vice President, M. B. Scott, Esq., an original member and substantial friend of the society, died suddenly on the 2d of February last. The venerable John Harmon of Ravenna, Ohio, an honorary member, who has contributed many valuable papers on the history of the Reserve, died at the ripe age of eighty-two years on the 29th of August, 1871. The Hon. W. B. Castle, one of our active members, and formerly Mayor of Cleveland, departed this life on the 28th of February, and Dr. E. W. Sackrider, one of the original members, on the 12th of April, 1872.

An experiment was tried during the past winter to revive the public interest which existed before the war in useful and scientific lectures. The old Library room in the Case Block was handsomely fitted up for that purpose, and a course of six lectures delivered for the joint benefit of the members of the Library Association, the Kirtland Society of Natural Science, and the Historical Society. The subjects and lectures were, On the Structure of Sponges, by Prof. A. H. Tuttle, of Cambridge, Mass.; The Scenery and Resources of Colorado, by Geo. H. Ely, Esq., of Cleveland; on the Motive Power of Animals, by Prof. E. S. Morse, of Salem, Mass; two on the Extinct Saurian Reptiles, by Prof. S. G. Williams, Superintendent Cleveland High School; The Teachings of Nature, by Hon. H. Rice, Cleveland. The audiences were not large but appreciative, and the lectures were throughout both interesting and highly instructive.

I conclude by urging on the curators the adoption and the energetic execution of some plan to secure a permanent income for this association. The amount required is not large, but it should be certain and permanent.

MEMOIR OF ALFRED THOMAS GOODMAN, LATE SECRETARY OF THE SOCIETY.

The committee appointed by the curators to prepare a memorial notice of our late Secretary, believe that nothing can be more proper and acceptable than the spontaneous expressions of his friends, and of the press at the time of his decease. We can add nothing to the earnestness and the tenderness of these expressions, but will give in addition thereto, something more of his personal history. For one who died so young he had already accomplished much.

[From the Cleveland Plain Dealer, Dec. 21 1871]

The late Alfred T. Goodman was a young man of unusual promise, mentally. His mind ran to specialties. He had a mania for gathering autographs, and his collection was one of the finest in the country, containing the signatures of all the American Presidents, and of many crowned heads and literary and other celebrities of Europe. Very few young men were so deeply read in the political and general history of this country, particularly in the early history of the West. The Western Reserve Historical Society owes its present flourishing condition more to his efforts than those of any other man. The historical papers which he contributed to the press of this city attracted general attention.

When quite young he was connected with the Harrisburg *Patriot*. After his return to Cleveland, he studied law for some time in Judge Ranney's office, but had abandoned the idea of completing his studies and permanently entering the profession, owing to ill health. His education was entirely obtained in the schools of this city, and what accrued through self-government. Mr. Goodman was but twenty-six years of age at the time of his death. It seems lamentable that this young man, apparently moulded for a career of mark, should be taken so early; but "man proposes and God disposes."

[From the Cleveland Herald Dec. 21, 1871.]

We have just learned of the decease of Mr Goodman, late Secretary to the Historical Society, which occurred in this city, Wednesday evening, December 20th. Those who have taken an interest in the work of the Historical Society know how much of his short life has been devoted to historical researches. In 1868 he was elected Secretary and has given since then, without pecuniary compensation, at least half his time and labor to its affairs, besides numerous and valuale donations of coins, autograqhs, maps, pamphlets and books. He was attacked with hemorrhage of the lungs about two years since, and has been constantly sinking until the fatal hour arrived. It is a disease which entails incessant physical suffering under which he has borne up heroically, even after all hope of recovery had been abandoned. His brilliant mind was clear throughout the depressing influences of a malady known to be fatal. We have recently made note of his edition of the journal of Captain Wm. Trent, through Ohio in 1752 with copious and learned notes. Gen. Arthur St. Clair, first Governor of the Northwest Territory, was a favorite of his, and for several years with great assiduity, he had labored upon a biography, which is nearly complete, calculated to do justice to that unfortunate public man. To one so young his acquaintance with the scources of history, especially in manuscript, was probably without a parallel. The pamphlets and tracts published by the Society are largely original historical matter, prepared by him. In the pursuit of valuable manuscripts he perserved until every chance of recovery was gone. Mr. Goodman is an example of the value of our High Schools, and the completeness of home education. He had no other training to literary life, and probably had all that was necessary to success. As a penman he was not only plain and elegant, but very rapid. His most hasty composition left no excuse for errors of the compositors.

Why one so promising, and apparently destined to be honored and useful, should so soon be removed from life and his beloved pursuits, is one of the inscrutable acts of that Supreme Providence, who, to use his own words: "doeth all things well."

REMARKS OE THE REV. W. H. GOODRICH AT THE FUNERAL, DEC. 24th, 1871.

It was one of the last requests of our young friend and brother, whose remains we are now to lay in the grave, that I should assist at his funeral, and speak some words of remembrance and of sympathy. I have known him for many years, since he was about fourteen years old, and have held him from that time in peculiar esteem. No one could become acquainted with him even as a boy, without being struck by his marked traits of character, and unusual tokens of promise. Though my meetings with him have not been frequent, they have always been warm and interesting. I recall especially an hour spent with him in Harrisburg some years ago which heightened my regard for him, and impressed me with his development and worth. He always seemed to seek and value the society of older men. He had his own young friends and associates as others have, but he sought every opportunity to gain knowledge from those who could impart it, and was always aspiring after some new acquisition. He had great capacity for gathering facts and reasoning about them. How far he cultivated recondite science, I do not know, but for the broader and commoner sciences he had peculiar aptitude, and was making steady attainment. He was already of value in our community. He was unconsciously making a place for himself which no one is at hand to fill; and had he lived, would have occupied an honorable position, as a man of high self culture, and of authority in certain branches of knowledge. Meanwhile he neglected no duty to the household, which in its trials and amenities, relied much on his counsel and care. How faithful a son and brother he has been these mourning hearts could testify. His memory will remain fresh and precious in all this circle of kindred.

It is these remembrances of his worth and promise which makes this affliction bitter. Death does sometimes seem, to our reason, without order. It has no respect of persons, and takes away the very one we least could spare. It regards no seasons or circumstances, but breaks with its summons upon the gladdest holiday of the year. It is blessed to know that strange as it may seem to us, it never is without order in God's sight. Our times are in His hands. The number of our months is with Him, and He hath appointed our bound that we shsll not pass. Nothing passes unpermitted by His wisdom. And all the circumstances of trial, the attendant pains and weariness that accompany a death like this, are fully comprehended in the thoughts of our Heavenly Father. Our friend and brother submitted to disease and death patiently as to the will of God. He was comforted by a child-like trust in His gracious love. He rested, yes he rejoiced in the knowledge of a Savior on whom he laid his sins, and to whom he committed the keeping of his soul till the day of God.

EXTRACT FROM A PRIVATE LETTER.

CINCINNATI, Dec. 29th, 1871.

"I have just learned with great regret of the death of our young friend, Alfred T. Goodman. Though I have not had the pleasure of a personal acquaintance with him, my correspondence for the last two years has been so frequent, so profitable, and so pleasant to me, that I esteemed him very highly as a personal friend. His death is a great loss, not only to his family and your society; but to the State of Ohio, as I know of no one whose knowledge, taste and perseverance in historical matters, presented the prospect of so important and profitable a future; especially valuable to this State, where that particular talent is rare." R. C.

L. C. Draper, the veteran historian of the West, wrote to us "that among the promising young men of this new country, it is rare to find one of historical talent, such as our young friend possessed, and who may take the place of the fathers who are so rapidly passing away."

His parents, John Goodman and Ann Goodman (*nee* George) are natives of Warwickshire, England, near Leamington and Warwick Castle. They emigrated to Washington, Washington county, Pennsylvania, where Alfred was born December 15th, 1845. The family removed to Cleveland just in time to give him the benefit of the public schools in this city. A fixed number of the scholars of the primary schools who stands highest are selected for the high school, which is practically a college. Young Goodman took the lead in his classes throughout. The Superintendent of the High School says his capacity to acquire knowledge was remarkable, and that his industry kept pace with his capacity.

In 1864, soon after graduating, he joined the 150th regiment of Ohio National Guards, and served at Washington, D. C., in the defence of that place against the attack on Fort Saunders under General Breckenridge. Soon after the discharge of those regiments, he became assistant editor and Legislative Reporter to the *Daily Patriot and Union*, at Harrisburg, Pa., a connection which lasted until 1868. He was attracted to Harrisburg more by his historical than by his political bias. The State papers, the archives of the State Historical Society, and especially the collection of the late General Wm. H. Miller, presented irresistable attractions to him. His remarkably rapid use of his pen, coupled with—what is so unusual—a clear and plain chirography, enabled him to report speeches and take notes, which were ready for the press without revision. Old and indistinct manuscripts were deciphered by him as it were by instinct. He was never happier than while engaged picking out, here and there, an historical fact, from a pile of old letters —an occupation that to most men is tiresome, if not disgusting.

As Secretary, of this Society he was engaged in collecting historical letters and manuscripts. His fondness for correspondence enabled him to trace out and recover valuable papers or copies of them from the most distant and obscure places."

He had a capacious memory, without which no one can gather up and marshal the detached facts which constitute history. From 1868 to 1870 his health was apparently robust, and his promise of life uncommonly good. In stature he was small, but compact and active, with a fair and fresh complection, dark hair and eyes; well represented in the photograph which is placed over his desk in our hall.

During these two years of perfect health, he wrote and published in different newspapers a brief notice of the Governors of Ohio, of William Crawford, who perished on the Sandusky plains, tortured to death by fire, in 1782; and a history of the campaign of General Harmar to the Maumee River in 1790. Of our historical tracts, he wrote those entitled "First White Child in Ohio," "First White Settlers in Ohio," and "Judges of the Supreme Court of Ohio." He had labored assiduously upon a biography of General St. Clair, which is nearly completed, but is not in proper shape for publication. In 1871 after his health became visibly impaired; and by frequent hemorrhages of the lungs; be became conscious of his doom; the "Journal of Captain Wm. Trent" in 1752, was prepared fer publication, and issued by Wm. Dodge of Cincinnati, only a few weeks prior to his death.

More than an hundred of the sketches, in Drakes American Dictionary of Biography, were furnished by Mr. Goodman, but the work itself, he was not permitted to see. Before the fatal disease assumed such proportions, as to take away the hope of prolonged life, he was looking forward to the composition of a history of Ohio, for which a large part of the materials are already collected in our library. His last days were characterised by intense physical suffering, which he bore without complaint, looking forward to the hour of death, with resignation and hope, and not with dread.

WESTERN RESERVE

AND

NORTHERN OHIO

HISTORICAL SOCIETY.

HISTORICAL AND ARCHÆOLOGICAL TRACT No. 11.

ANCIENT ROCK INSCRIPTIONS IN OHIO,

AN

Ancient Burial Mound, Hardin County, O.,

AND A

Notice of some Rare Polished Stone Ornaments.

EDITED BY THE PRESIDENT OF THE SOCIETY AND PUBLISHED
BY A GENTLEMAN OF CLEVELAND.
AUGUST, 1872.

CLEVELAND:
FAIRBANKS, BENEDICT & CO., PRINTERS.
1872.

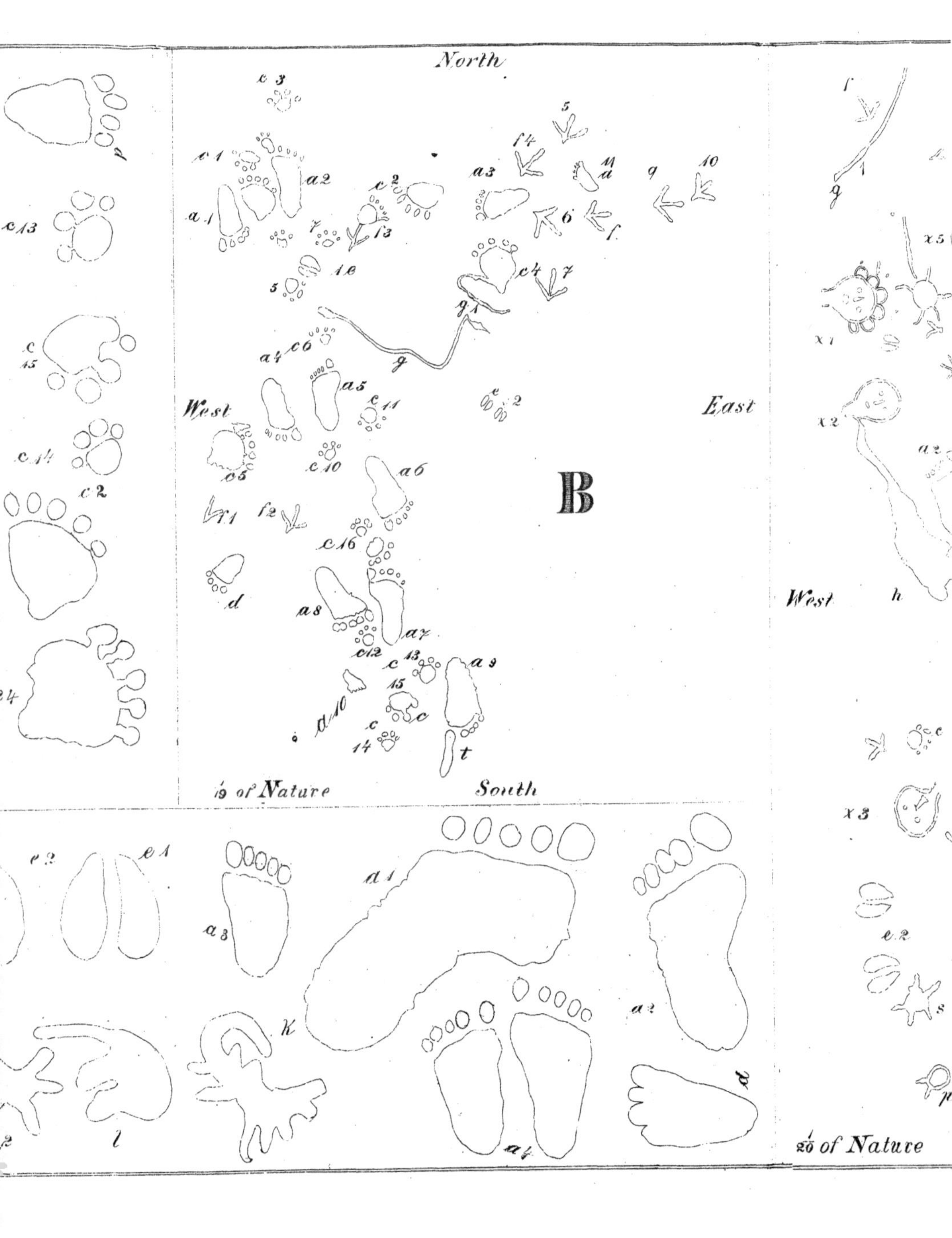
North
West
East
South
B
1/9 of Nature
West
1/20 of Nature

PLATE NO. 2.

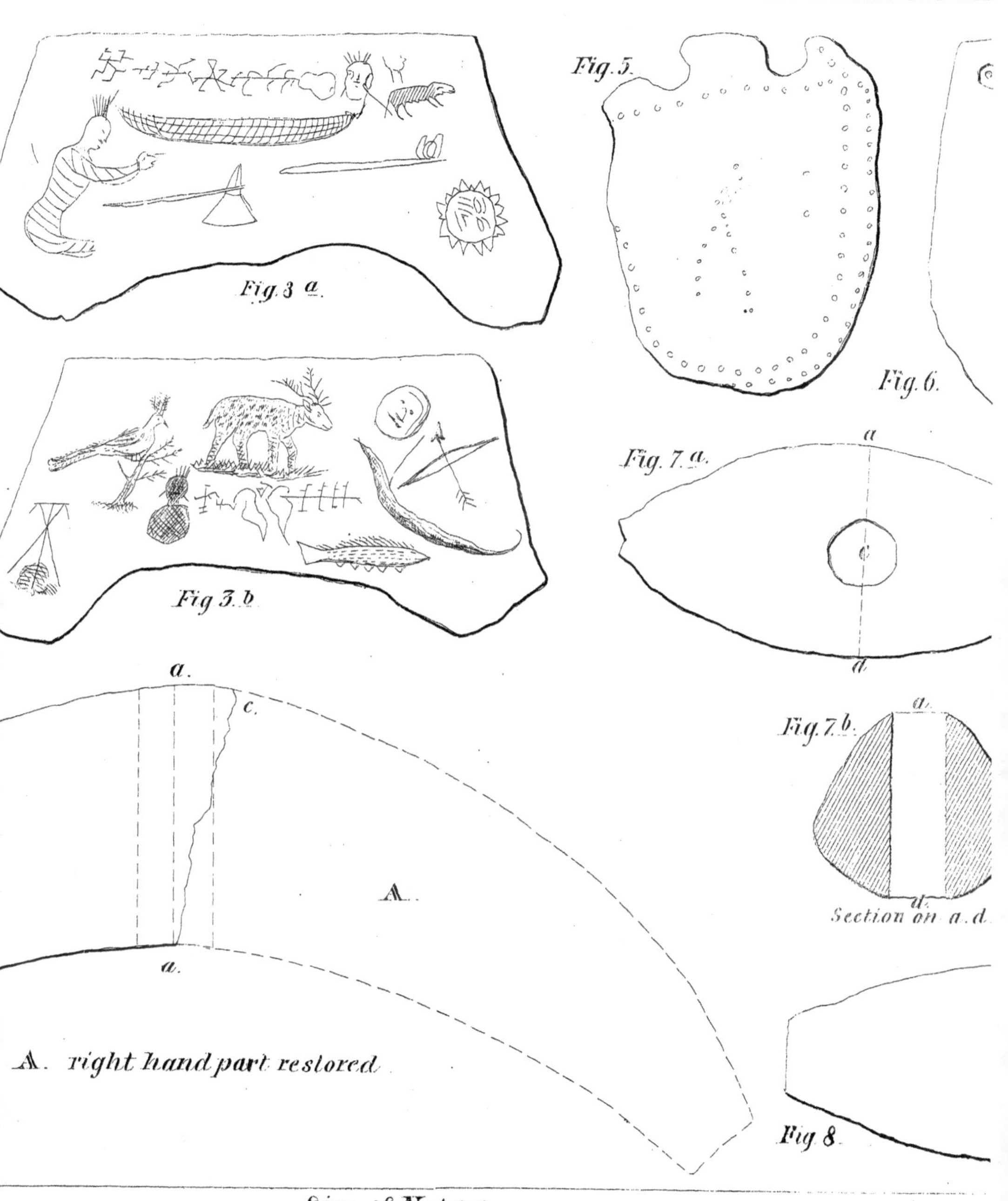

Size of Nature

ROCK SCULPTURES NEAR BARNESVILLE,

BELMONT COUNTY, OHIO.

In 1857 or '58 Mr. Thomas Kite of Cincinnati examined the "track rocks" near Barnesville, and took casts of some of the sculptured figures. Jas. W. Ward, Esq., of the same city, soon afterward, made a detailed sketch, which he caused to be engraved and circulated. In 1869 Dr. J. H. Salisbury and myself made a visit to the place, with a view to get a tracing on cloth, but were compelled to give it up for want of time. An arrangement was made with Dr. Jas. W. Walton of Barnesville to take a tracing for this Society, which, however, was not received until the fall of 1871. The discussion which took place at the Indianapolis meeting of the American Association, in August, 1871, was based upon Mr. Ward's sketch, which had been made with much care, he being not only an artist, but an antiquarian.

This was reproduced, with a detailed description, by Mr. Ward, in the first number of the *American Anthropological Journal*, issued in January, 1872, at New York. When Dr. Walton's *fac simile* tracings, size of nature, were received it was evident that notwithstanding the care exercised by Mr. Ward, there were important omissions, which destroyed the value of the discussions at Indianapolis, based upon his sketch. It is now conceded that copies of such sculptures must be made by casts, squeezes, or tracings, in order to be reliable. In the different representations that have appeared of the "Dighton Rock," the supposed Grave Creek stone, the "Big Indian Rock," on the Susquehanna, and the "Independence Stone," of this County, something material is omitted, or palpably distorted. Mere sketches are of little or no ethnological value. I think the mode adopted by us, leaves little room for errors, either in size or proportion, but there may be in the manner or aspect that belongs to every object, and which is known by the plain but forcible expression, "life like." The rock was first thoroughly cleaned of the moss and dirt, as Dr. Walton explains in his letter accompanying the tracings. All of the artificial depressions were then filled with paint, and a sheet of muslin covering the entire block, pressed into the sculptured figures. This coarse grit is so nearly imperishable, that whatever distinct markings were originally cut upon it, are doubtless there now, and are not perceptibly injured by exposure. These groups present the first instance among the rock inscriptions of Ohio, where it can be said that we now have complete and entire, in their primitive condition, all the figures that are capable of being traced, not mutilated by man, or obliterated by the elements. Dr. Walton's description will now be both intelligible and interesting.

"The copies I send you exhibit every definite figure those rocks contain, and indeed many more than will be noticed by a casual observer of them.

"Some of them were discovered only after removing the lichens of ages; others after glancing the eye along the surface of the rocks from every point of the compass; and others after the sun had declined low in the west, casting dim shadows over depressions too shallow to be seen before. And there are many indistinct impressions on each of the rocks that could not be copied—these resemble the indefinite remains of innumerable tracks of men and animals overlying each other, as may be seen on our highways, after a rain has effaced almost every outline.

"Upon examining the point of the smaller rock it will appear that two men, each accompanied by a dog, seem to have passed over it in opposite directions. This idea has never, so far as I have learned, occurred to any person who has heretofore examined the rocks; the figures being regarded as distinct and disconnected, as they appear on the larger stone. I did not catch the idea, until after I had painted all the distinct figures on this stone, and had impressed the cloth on the paint, when upon removing and examining the print I found, say, first a right foot print, then a left one at its appropriate position, then a right foot where it should be, but the succeeding left one wanting.

"This set me on a more careful examination of the motley indentations covering this part of the rock for traces of the lost feet, and it was not a great while before I found sufficient remains of just what was wanting, and at their appropriate places, but in exceedingly indistinct impressions.

"The rude cuts of human faces, part of the human feet, the rings, stars, serpents, and some others, are evidently works of art, as in the best of them the marks of the engraving instrument are to be seen; and it is barely possible that the residue of those figures were carved by the hands of men; however, I must say that the works of the best sculptors, do not surpass the exquisite finish of most of the tracks on those rocks."

DESCRIPTION OF MR. WARD.

CINCINNATI, August 24, 1858.

CHARLES WHITTLESEY:

My Dear Sir: I went to the "track rocks," as I found the neighbors had already christened them, in pursuance of the intention I intimated to you, wishing very much you could have gone with me. You would have been pleased with the trip, and interested in the sculptures, which these so called tracks undoubtedly are. They are *perfect* enough to deceive any one who does not critically examine them. There are two main tables—though a few scattering sculptures are found upon other stones in the vicinity. I have made pretty accurate drawings of the two tables, omitting, however, in the one represented by the left hand cut, a few "tracks" removed from the main group, that I could not get in. The magnified, though still much reduced, figures on the sheet are taken from *casts* of some of the most conspicuous objects, made by Mr. Kite. These rocks are the sandstone grit of the coal series, and have the appearance of being boulders. They stand about three feet above the surface of the ground, and are surrounded by large trees of oak, walnut, poplar and locust. The markings until lately were quite concealed by a heavy growth of moss.

The two figures upon the small fragment lying upon the left hand tablet are upon another stone not many feet distant from the one upon which I have placed it. [NOTE.—These are not on our copy.] These sculptures, as you may judge from the casts, are remarkably well made. It is difficult not to believe the birds' feet natural. An examination of the rock will convince any one, however, that the whole is the work of art. Historically these tables must be regarded as very interesting. I design making a little paper on the subject, and have therefore got the drawings engraved.

I should say further that these tables are about ten to twelve feet long, and six to eight broad. The bear's foot is eight inches long; the large human foot on the right hand drawing, marked "ax," is fifteen inches in length. In the rest I have preserved the relative proportion as to distance and magnitude. One interesting question is as to their probable age.

Very truly, your friend,

J. W. WARD.

PLATE No. 1.

GROUP A. 1-20TH OF NATURE.

In all cases, whether single or in groups, the relative dimensions of the figures are preserved. The surface of this block is eight by eleven feet. An error has crept into the engraving of this group, in regard to the east and west sides, which should be reversed: for east read west, and for west east.

a^1—human foot, greatest length 15 inches.

a^2 " " " " 10 "

a^6 " " " " 3½ "

b—Nos. 1 and 2, apparently the fore foot of a bear, 5½ to 9 inches long.

c—hind foot of wolf or dog, breadth across the toes 3½ inches.

c^1—hind foot of a wolf or dog, breadth across the toes 2½ inches.

d—probably the hind foot of a bear, length 5½ inches.

e—Nos. 1 to 5, buffalo tracks, length 2 to 5 inches.

f—Nos. 1 to 13, so called "bird tracks," 3½ to 5 inches in length.

g—Nos. 1 to 4, snakes, or portions of them, 13 to 21 inches in length.

h—effigy of a bird, greatest length 22 inches.

i—Nos. 1 to 9, resembles the spread out skin of an animal, 3 to 8 inches greatest diameter.

k—not recognized as an animal form, length 6 inches.

l—an imperfect figure.

n—probably a variation of *i*, with a groove that may have been part of the figure.

o—apparently incomplete.

p—greatest length 6 inches.

q—spirit circle, diameter 7½ inches.

x—Nos. 1 to 3, outlines of the human face, breadth 3½ to 6 inches.

There is a rock in Georgia, described by the antiquarian, C. C. Jones, of that State, on which are a number of circles like "g," a sign used by the Chippeways to represent a spirit.

GROUP B. BLOCK 7 FEET BY 8, LYING 20 FEET SOUTH OF A.

a—Nos. 2, 6, 7 and 8, human foot 9 inches long.

a^{10} " " 3½ " "

c—Nos. 1 and 10 to 16, hind foot of a dog or wolf, 2½ to 4 inches broad across the toes.

c—Nos. 2, 3, 4 and 5, five toes, greatest breadth 4 to 5½ inches across the toes, (the animal not recognized.)

d—hind foot of a bear.

e^1—buffalo track, 3 inches long.

e^2 " " 1½ " " a pair.

f—so called "bird tracks," 3½ to 5 inches long.

g—snake, 21 inches long. g^1—part of same.

t—groove 5 inches long.

GROUP C. "TURKEY FOOT ROCK."

Opposite Fort Meigs, at the foot of the rapids of Maumee river, north shore, on a limestone boulder.

a—an eliptical depression, 6½ inches long and 1 inch deep.

b b—shallow grooves, 5 to 9 inches long.

c c c—"bird tracks," 2½ to 6 inches long.

The cross under the word "north" is 2½ inches long.

We have here as good representations as it is possible to procure, of two of the rock inscriptions of Ohio. The copy of the Independence stone, which was published in our Tract No. 5 (1870), embraces only a fragment of the original, not exceeding one-fourth of the surface; once covered with sculptured effigies. If the figures had a general relation to each other, it could not be determined by an inspection of only a portion of them. In 1842, when I first saw the "Turkey foot rock," at the rapids of the Maumee, it had many more characters on it than are represented on group C; but even at that time it was evident the group was not complete. The inscriptions near Newark, in Licking Co., O., originally covered a vertical face of conglomerate rock, fifty or sixty feet in length, by six and eight feet in height. This rock is soft, and therefore the figures are easily erased. As the place was partially sheltered from the weather by overhangs, the injury done to them by exposure was not much; but from the earliest settlement of the country, about the year 1800; it became a place where white men, sought to immortalize themselves by cutting their names across the old inscriptions. When Dr. Salisbury in 1864 undertook to rescue what remained of them, it was only possible to trace the ancient figures over a space about seven feet by thirteen, and here many of them were restored with difficulty, by great patience and labor.

His copy is in the hands of the American Antiquarian Society, and is in the course of publication. It is therefore like the Independence stone, only a fragment. On the rock faces and detached sandstone blocks of the banks of the Ohio river, there are numerous groups of intaglios, but in them the style is quite different from those to which I have referred, and which are located in the interior. Those on the Ohio river, resemble the symbolical records of the North American Indians—such as the Kelley Island stone, described in Schoolcraft, by Capt. Eastman—the Dighton Rock—the Big Indian Rock of the Susquehanna and the "God Rock" of the Alleghany river.

In those the supposed bird track is generally wanting. The large sculptured rock near Wellsville, which is only visible at low water of the Ohio; has among the figures one that is prominent on the Barnesville stones. This is the fore-foot of the bear, with the outside toe distorted and set outward at right angles.

Dr. Salisbury has analyzed the characters of the Newark group, and finds that there are (22) twenty-two of them. He is comparing them with the alphabets or syllable characters of Asia; but as yet without a satisfactory result. About eight (8) centuries before Christ, the bird track, formed a part of the Chinese syllable alphabet, which led him to give them a more ancient date here, than the advent of the red race. Some of the earth mounds of Ohio have the same form, as for instance, the one at the center of the Newark circle; but no connection has yet been established between the "mound builders," and these rock inscriptions. The mound builders did not, as the proofs now stand, make engraved figures on stone. The bird track character, partakes of the arrow-head type, which pervades the records of many eastern nations. Here there are sometimes one of the toes or prongs wanting, but sometimes there is a center line, inserted like an arrow stem, or at right angles, transforming it into a cross. In no case, are the supposed bird tracks, as they appear on the canvass, placed in the order of walking, alternately right and left; in fact none of the tracks whether of buffalo, bear, wolf or the human foot, are in the order of walking. They are single or in pairs. The Mexican picture writings, frequently have the human foot, and the remarkable projections of the great toe joint, which these sculptures present, but they are the tracks of walkers, and are a symbol; intended to show the direction in which the parties were moving.

The pair of carved feet, on the lime rock at St. Louis, referred to by Schoolcraft, are in the position of a man standing upright. Dr. Owen, late of N. Harmony, Indiana, procured the slab for his cabinet, where I have seen it. It is now in the State collection at Bloomington, from whence, through Prof. Richard Owen, we expect to have casts. The feet are fifteen inches in length, the heels six inches apart, and the toes thirteen, with enlarged joints. In the Mexican writings the feet are single, and placed opposite the spaces as in walking. On our stones they must have had a different meaning.

I do not purpose to dwell here on the general subject of Western antiquities, but will present in addition to Plate 1, some sketches of wrought stones which I have not seen described, and which are principally designed for ornament or badges. These are represented in Plate No. 2. But before describing them, I insert a very full and clear account of the excavation of a large burial mound in Hardin Co., Ohio, by Dr. Matson, of Shelby, Ohio. The cold-wrought copper tool, fig. 1, Plate 2, is inserted as the only one yet found, either of stone or metal; which might have been used as a pick, to do the stone engravings. It was found at the Bohemian mine, Flint Steel river, near Ontonagon, Michigan, and near to ancient mine pits. I have seen on the walls of those old mines, one or two marks, which might have been made with such a point. By inserting it in a prong of the horn of a deer, or of the branch of a tree, standing at right angles to a helve; it could perform the office of a pick. This is merely a surmise, but it is the nearest approach now known, to a pick for working in rock—a tool which the ancient miners, and also whoever made these stone cuttings, must have had. The effigies on the north side of Cunningham's island, Lake Erie, are cut on a boulder of very hard quartzose granite, requiring a hard and tough corner or point, for the work.

ANCIENT BURIAL MOUND AND ITS CONTENTS,

HARDIN CO., OHIO,

BY JOHN S. B. MATSON, M. D.

SHELBY, OHIO, December 10, 1869.

JUDGE JOHN BARR, CLEVELAND:

Dear Sir:—In the fall of 1856, in Hardin County, Ohio, near the Bellefontaine and Indiana Railway, between Mt. Victory and Ridgeway, I commenced removing a gravel bank for the purpose of ballasting a part of the above named railroad. I learned shortly after my arrival there, that the bank was an ancient burial-ground. This information caused me to examine the ground, and note discoveries.

Before I came on the ground there had been a track graded and laid. This track separated a short distance east of the mound, one track on the south, the other on the north. The men who graded the track, had taken the loam off where the track ran, and cast it out from the mound. We removed the gravel from both sides, moving the track up to the bank, when it became difficult to load. The loading was done by men with shovels into gravel cars, and hauled out with an engine. The average amount removed was about two hundred and twenty cubic yards per day. About six weeks in the winter we had to suspend operations, on account of freezing. The mound covered an area of *one and a half acres;* being covered with an orchard of apple trees, then in bearing. Several stumps and a few trees of the original forest still remained; on the mound. I was informed by citizens of the vicinity that there had been a remarkably heavy growth of timber on the mound. The stumps remaining were large. The mound was what I would call double; the larger and higher part to the west. About two-thirds of the mound was embraced in this part. The eastern part, presenting the appearance of a smaller hill having been pressed against the other; leaving a depression between them of three or four feet, below the highest point of the smaller and five or six feet below a corresponding point of the larger. Both parts had the appearance of having had surface work done, to give them a beautiful oval shape. The loam I found deepest on the highest points, where it is generally of less depth. The interior was composed of a clean limestone gravel, and sand; evidently formed by decomposition of the strata and very plainly marked. In the eastern or smaller part of the mound, was an excavation that had been made by citizens of the vicinity for sand for building purposes, in which excavation, I learned a number of skeletons had been exhumed, having beads and trinkets on which were reported as being similar to those I afterwards found. I was unable to obtain any of them. A little south of the highest point of the western mound, was an excavation made by the railroad company, for the purpose of ascertaining the amount of gravel. No remains were found in that excavation. Shortly after commencing to load gravel, indications of graves were visible in three places, on both sides of the eastern part, and nearly north of the center of the larger or western part. At the last named place, two skeletons side by side were found in a horizontal position; the feet pointing east, which had been deposited there without their heads; there being no evidences of skulls. With them I found a stone axe or celt of granite, two flint arrow points, and an implement made of blue stone resembling slate, but much harder the outlines of which I give full size; also a large fresh water clam, filled with red paint, in good preservation.* The flint implements had the appearance of never having been used being very sharp pointed. The bones crumbled on exposure to the atmosphere. These graves were about four feet deep. The first skeletons taken out of the eastern part of the mound were in better preservation, especially those on the south side. Several skulls were sound and the other bones of some were so well preserved that by applying sole leather for ribs they were wired together. With the first skeleton taken out of this part of the mound I found a thin piece of ivory (Fig. 6, plate 2) with two small holes, evidently an ear ornament. Next was the skeleton of a little girl who may have been eight or ten years old. Skull in good preservation, which remains in my cabinet. She had a string of beads, so made as to be larger in the center of the neck in front, tapering almost to a point at the back of the neck; she also had a plate of copper (Fig. 5 plate 2) on her neck. The lower maxilary and upper joints of the vertebra, are yet green from its oxidation. The plate had two rows of dents a part of the way around. The dents look like an impression made on a board with the heel of a boot, with tacks. The two last skeletons had been buried in a sitting posture. On the north side nearly opposite the last named skeletons, was a grave about four feet deep, in which the remains had been deposited and apparently burned. There were ashes and charcoal with pieces of charred bones, one or two of the hands being entire.

In the progress of removal, I found the eastern or smaller part of the mound, to be literally filled with graves. The modes of burial had been various; the depth of remains varying from two to nine feet; while there was a difference of posture in nearly every skeleton. I found that not less than ten or twelve dogs had also been buried; the human and canine side by side. One group of nine graves, I was so impressed with, I will endeavor to be particularly explicit. The first had two skeletons, that of a male and female, side by side, there not being more than four inches of sand between them. Both had evidently been buried in one grave. The female was buried on her knees, both hands spread over the face, which was downwards, and a string of conch shell beads around her neck. I found inside of her ribs the remains of a fœtus. Her partner was buried horizontal, with face down; both hands had been placed with their palms on the face, their heads towards the east. After tracing the bones with particular reference to their positions, and to save these skeletons which were best preserved, I took down the disturbed strata with my hands; and at the head of the grave, I found above the remains, and pointing down, the bones of the index finger, while at the foot of the grave, and at a corresponding height, the bones of a great toe, pointing in a similar manner. The balance of the group were some buried with face down, both hands over the face, others with one hand, some with face up and both hands over the face; while another had one hand over the breast, the other over the face. All this group had the heads to the east. On one of this group, I found a string of copper beads, of which the metal had never been smelted, but evidently been flaked from the native metal, and rolled around a twisted string, evidence of which was still visible, in the beads which were rude. On the north side of the eastern portion, under an oak tree stump (150 years old by growths), was the remains of the largest human

---

* The celt is eight inches long, and the blue slate stone two and three-fourths. It is of a common form flat with two tapering holes near the middle.

bones I have ever seen. The joints of the vertebra seemed as large as those of a horse. I think they did not indicate a taller frame than some others; but the bones were heavier than any in the mound. I have its inferior maxillary broken, but glued together, in my cabinet. The other bones were so decomposed, that they were useless. I could not say as to his posture, as the stump brought down the grave, rendering it out of the question to note the position. Near the last named skeleton, perhaps ten feet from it, we came upon a grave, that had been dug oblong almost six feet deep, three feet wide, and over seven feet long, which they had filled with human bones promiscuously, without regard to order, to the depth of four feet; on these, in regular order, were placed twenty-seven skulls, with the top of skulls up. They were about two feet below the surface; the bones so much broken, and I regret to say I did not examine them as particular as I should have done. One of the skulls had a small hole broken in, and I learned afterward that a piece of the femur was found where they were dumped on the road, having a flint dart fast in the bone. There was an implement or ornament found, having one part like the head of a bird's neck, and shoulders like a horse, cut off back of the shoulders, and turned up like the back part of a saddle seat; the lower part being flat, with a hole drilled diagonally, from the lower part of the neck to the base, with a corresponding hole in the back part. This implement was manufactured of a blue stone resembling slate, but extremely hard.* It is probable they had had a battle, and after the flesh had decomposed, they collected the bones and brought them to the mound for burial. I am sure from the positions of the bones, they had not been interred with the flesh on. I found in this part of the mound the remains of at least fifty children, under the age of eight years; some with two, others with four incisors; some with eight, and others with no teeth. On the neck of one infant having two incisors, there was a string of conch shell beads of the largest size, one hundred and forty in number; four of these beads were black, and were about three-fourths of an inch in diameter. The string would weigh one pound or more. Some of the graves had trinkets and beads made of clam shell; some had bones of the deer sharp pointed, others had pieces of deer horns; some had long shaped beads around the wrists, I think of ivory. One had a conch shell plate, round, about five inches in diameter, with a hole in the center, half an inch diameter, with two holes near the edge, for suspension with a string from the neck, like a breast-plate. Some had birds buried with them. One skeleton taken out of this part of the mound, had the appearance of a very aged man; the point of the inferior maxillary was almost in two parts, while the trachea was bone all around. Quite a number showed indications of extreme age; seven or eight that I observed had bone tracheas.

I now return to the western or larger portion of the mound. This part was removed as fast as the former. I soon discovered there were two rows of graves, leading direct from the *two first mentioned*, containing the flint implements, paint, etc., towards the center, each pair having been dug deeper as they approached the center of the mound. Those with the stone axe, paint and flint implements were four feet deep, the depth of each pair increasing about a foot in regular gradation till the last pair, which was as near the center and highest point of the mound as I could calculate, the last pair being *eighteen feet* below the surface. The pair next to those with the axe, paint and flint implements were in a sitting posture, as were all in these two files except the first two. On the head of one of the second

* This is the saddle-shaped stone figured on page 239 of Squier and Davis' "Monuments of the Mississippi Valley." It is either an ornament or a badge, which was suspended, and is frequently found on the surface.

pair was a conch shell plate, resembling in shape the sole of a moccasin, nine inches in length and three and a half inches greatest breadth. This plate has three holes in it towards the wider end, and it was placed on the top of the head, with the larger end back. Two other skeletons of these two files had similar plates, differing only in size, the smaller being about half the size of the larger. Several implements of stone were found, all differing in shape. They were made of stone resembling slate, but much harder. One of them is three inches long by one and a half broad, in form of a shield, with two holes through it flatwise. Farmers picked up some implements in the field adjoining the mound. One given me by Judge Baldwin is a flat stone of slate, with one transverse hole, that I supposed belonged to the same race. As we approached the center of the mound, the graves getting deeper, the bones were much better preserved. Several bodies in decomposition had formed a cement that would have preserved them an almost incalculable length of time. In fact, when first taken out of the cement they had the appearance of bones just dissected, being nearly one-third heavier than those without cement. The four last and deepest skeletons *all* had beads on, some of them quite small, the smallest not as large as a pea. Some were made of clam shells, but mostly of conch or sea shells. Those of clam were so decomposed that they fell to pieces. Three of these skeletons had beads only around the neck, the fourth, being the last one taken out, and the file leader (as he ought to be called) of the two deepest, had I should think nearly thirty yards of beads, having four wraps around the neck crossed over the breast and back, passing down between his legs; strings down his legs to the feet; also strings along his arms and around his wrists. This remains presented the appearance of being decorated all over. He had no other ornaments or implements that I could find. Near the south side of the western part of the mound, near one of the forest trees, I found the remains of a human being that seemed to be detached from all the rest. I thought perhaps he was an Indian of some of the late tribes, who had been buried perhaps on some hunting expedition. There was a piece of deer horn with him that had the appearance of having been the handle of a butcher knife. I could not detect any evidence of rust, however.

On the highest part of the mound, and about twelve or fifteen feet from the two deepest graves, was evidence of fire. The loam had been burned till it had a brick color. I have seen it look very much so where a large log heap had been burned, and would have thought such was the cause, had it not been that it was below the surface about three feet. The whole number of skeletons exhumed by me was *three hundred and eight.* I could not ascertain how many had been taken out by diggers of sand. The citizens of the vicinity informed me that there was a very heavy forest on the mound at the time of clearing it. They also stated that the Indians who were there with the first settlers knew nothing of the race who interred their dead there. I have very little doubt they belonged to the age of Stone. There was no evidence that they ever had any communication with the age of Iron, or Bronze. They must have had some commercial arrangements for getting conch shells and copper. The copper has the appearance of the Lake Superior copper, and the conch shells must have come from the Atlantic, Pacific or Gulf of Mexico. There was no evidence of pottery that I was able to discover. I have visited as many as twenty in the Mississippi Valley, on nearly every one of which were pieces of broken pottery, literally covering the mounds. East of Vicksburg, near Black River, we turned a mound into a redoubt. In excavating, there were layers of charcoal of about two inches in depth in the mound. I found a small stone ax or celt, also a stone shaped like the knob of a bureau. There was a circle hollowed out in the center of the raised part; within the circle was a depression as if the stone had been turned in a lathe on a pivot. This mound was small in area and not over six feet high. In a southwest direction, and not further than twelve rods, was a smaller mound four feet in height, and southeast from this was a large belt of gravel in the shape of a horse shoe, that had been strewn with shells in sufficient quantities to whiten the ground. About a mile from this, in a northeast direction, across Clear Creek, I visited a mound on which the plough had turned up human bones. But I will not weary you further with Mississippi mounds.

About three-fourths of a mile from where I now reside, on a farm owned by a Mr. Stump, is a very beautiful little mound about thirty feet across and six feet high. Some years ago Dr. Craig, of Ontario, Richland, County, made an excavation in which he discovered charcoal, ashes, and a flint knife five inches long. It is my impression that no signs of human bones were discovered by him. There has been a large number of stone axes (or celts) of all sizes between two and seven inches in length found on the surface, some of them finely made, mostly of granite. Various other implements have from time to time been picked up, and I have made a practice of preserving the flint implements on my farm and vicinity, until I have over two hundred specimens of various shapes and sizes.

Another mound in Shelby County lies about a mile north of Sidney, north of the Blue Cut, as it is called on the railroad. This mound seems to me to indicate that it had been made by carrying gravel from Musquito Creek, which is near it. It is long-shaped and as near as I can judge, about eight or ten feet high. I had a desire to excavate it, but had no opportunity.

Yours, truly,

JOHN S. B. MATSON,
Shelby, Richland County, Ohio.

The articles found, and the leading features of the burials, which Dr. Matson has so thoroughly described, are principally Indian. Adair, a century since, saw the Creeks of central Georgia, wearing oval plates on their heads and breasts; made from large shells. The stone chisel, the ornamental stones, and the arrow points are Indian relics, but it is very rare to find copper, in the graves of red men. Evidently the mound had been trimmed, rounded and raised, since the bodies of the central part were deposited; a work which the red race has never been known to do.

The large number of bones, of which Dr. Matson speaks, not buried with the flesh on, forms no doubt one of those ossuaries which the early Jesuits saw the Hurons make, on the shores of the Georgian Bay. Every few years they exhumed the remains of their dead relatives, and bore them to a central point, where a funeral feast was held, and the collection tumbled into a pit, amid the most dismal cries of grief. In the ancient burial mounds, no bones of domestic animals have been found. In this a number of dogs were buried with their masters. With the Indians, it is, and has been, not only a common, but an almost universal rule; to place with the dead body a good supply of food. The dog is not only his choicest meat, but his dearest companion. This mound presents features not fully consistent with the sepulture of the red man, or of the mound builders, but the predominent ones, are characteristic of the Indian of our day. If all the circumstances surrounding each skeleton could have been determined; the two races, could probably have been separated.

Plate No. 2.

Figure 1.

A pointed tool of cold wrought copper, with a socket to receive a haft, indicated by the dotted lines.

It is introduced here as the only implement yet known, that may have served the purpose of a pick—not only the stone inscriptions, but most of the stone chisels, axes, and hammers, show that they were first wrought into shape by means of a sharp pointed tool; and it must have been very common. This was found at the Bohemian Mine, Flint Steel River, near Ontonagon, Lake Superior, in 1865. I saw it in possession of General Walbridge of Detroit.

Figure 2.

One half of an egg shaped ornament of polished iron ore, (limonite) split through the middle, and the other part lost; represented by an outline of the stone, flat side downwards, and a cross section at the middle, "a. b." It is one of the so called "plumb bobs", which are very common; but in this the hole for suspension is wanting. It is a very perfect ellipsoid, and highly polished. In possession of Herman Bliss, Northfield, Cuyahoga County, Ohio, where it was found by him on the surface.

Figures 3^a and 3^b.

This stone was found near Columbus, Ohio, by Mr. Grover, and appears to be but one-half of the original, broken through the middle. Its thickness is about two-fifths of an inch, polished on both sides, perfectly flat, and parallel. The material is the universal greenish gray, striped, fine grained, silicious slate; existing in place on Lake Superior, in great abundance and from thence transported, with the northern drift; to the Ohio country. Fragments, with the edges worn by attrition, are easily found in our gravel banks. This stone is hard, tough, fine grained, capable of a polish, and is ornamental. A large part of the tubes, gorgets, flat pendants, and other ornaments, scattered so profusely over the northwest, are of this material. Most of them are of Indian origin, but some have been found in such close connection with acknowledged mound builder relics; as to show that they used and prized the same stone. It is not so near a precious stone as the "chalcihuites" of Mexico, Central America and Peru; on which the ancient inhabitants engraved their most perfect cameos. The chalcihuites were not precious stones, according to Mr. Squier; but a superior quality of jade and quartz. They are however an approach to emeralds and turquoises, and had the practical value of precious stones. The northern nations, whether mound builders or Indians, had the same passion as the southern for green colored stones; and these striped slates, principally silicious, in alternate lamina of gray quartz, tinged with a dull green silicate of iron, answered their purpose.

The engraved figures occupy both sides of this stone. They are evidently Indian, and might be read by Indians. This man with his scalp lock, the canoe, the tomahawk and the pipe, are precisely in the style of the records of the northern tribes, being made every day on trees, clay banks and rocks. On the other side (3^b) is the fish, bird and arrow, (the point broken), pointing to a human face; the moose, a bird; another decorated head, and a kettle on a rude tripod over a fire.

The photograph for the engraving was furnished by Mr. O. Gates, of Columbus, Ohio, who has the stone in his very valuable cabinet of relics. On both sides are characters that bear some resemblance to hieroglyphics, but are probably rude signs, drawn from natural objects. That on the right hand of the line (3^a) may represent a plant lying flat, with its bulb or root. In Indian picture writings the human face has a great many meanings.

Figure 4.

This belongs to a series of finely wrought stones of striped slate, that appear to have been emblems or wands, used by medicine men or officials. They have a counterpart in the fiduceus of Mercury, and are numerous and various in form. However, the Indian medicine man has not, to my knowledge, been known to use them since the advent of the white man.

Some of them are like a slight thin double-edged axe, or mace, as may be seen in Squier's Ancient Monuments of the Mississippi Valley, pages 218-19. The small size of the perforation for a handle, and their light ornamental figure, precludes the inference that they were used as implements. This one is of a fine grained slate, clouded with red. It was broken near the edge at "a. c.," the right hand part A being lost, and put in as a restoration.

The hole "a. a." is bored perfectly true with a drill, but tapers slightly towards the upper side, as they usually do. It was found on the surface in Northfield, Summit County, Ohio, by Mr. George McKissan, who presented it to the Society.

Figures 5 and 6 have already been noticed in notes to the paper of Dr. Matson.

FIGURE 7.

This is an oval of green slate, but is not an ellipsoid, like the pendants, and the perforation is through the middle, as shown in the section "a. d." Like the eye or handle hole of figure 4, this is bored by a circular revolving drill, the spiral stria, being very distinct. The bore is true, but tapers slightly from d to a, and is a little to the right of the middle. Like figure 4, it is doubtless a badge. Among the collections of this Society, there are none of the heavy stone implements pierced for handles, nor have I seen any such in other collections.

FIGURE 8

is the outline, flatwise, of a thin miniature chisel of red limonite, the edge of which has been nicked since it was found. The polish consists of a series of plane faces, as though it had been rubbed on a flat stone. Locality not known. A donation from Mrs. Chas. H. Norton, of Cleveland. Its appearance is that of a child's plaything, in the form of a chisel.

FIGURE 9.

In none of the western collections have I seen anything resembling this cup of red limonite, which has been called a "paint muller." If anything like a pestle or grinder had been observed, which would fit such a tray, this would be a reasonable conjecture, especially if the pestle was of the same material. Two such stones rubbed together would produce an inferior paint, like Spanish brown. This was not formed by a revolving tool, for it is not strictly circular, within or without. As a muller it would have been much more convenient with a flat instead of a pointed base. It was found on the surface, in East Cleveland, and presented to us by T. R. Chase, Esq.

FIGURE 10.

This is another of the series of iron ornaments, fashioned from a piece of shell ore into a rude sphere, with two holes, "*a a*," for suspension. They extend at right angles to each other to the center, tapering to a point, where they intersect. The tool with which such perforations were made has not yet been discovered. The stone must have been firmly held while it was being bored, and the same with the drill or borer, or the holes and tubes would not be true, as they all are. In general the spiral stria made by the borer are in one direction, as though it was not worked back and forth, like a spindle. Sometimes the holes are scratched longitudinally by scouring, after the boring. All of them have more or less taper, as though the drill became smaller as it descended into the stone.

The ball which is outlined here was taken by Mr. Goodman, our late secretary, and myself, from near the base of a mound on Sawtell Avenue in this city. It was in ground apparently not disturbed since the erection of the mound, and near by the tube and the copper beads, described in tract No. 5, but not in connection with the human skeleton, which we did not find. It must be regarded as a relic of the mound builders.

A similar globe, an inch and one-tenth in diameter, is described by Mr. Squier, from Ocosingo, in Guatemala, the material of which is the green chalcihuite stone, and on which are ancient Mexican inscriptions, having a straight hole bored through its center.

Western Reserve and Northern Ohio
HISTORICAL SOCIETY.

CLEVELAND, O., NOV., 1872.

HISTORICAL AND ARCHÆOLOGICAL TRACTS.

NUMBER TWELVE.

Selection No. 3. WAR OF 1812, from the Papers of the late ELISHA WHITTLESEY.

We now present our third selection from the papers of the late Elisha Whittlesey relating to the war of 1812, on this frontier.

ELIJAH WADSWORTH TO JOHN WALWORTH.

CANFIELD, June 10, 1812.

DEAR SIR: There are rumors afloat in this quarter, which I deem not altogether groundless, that the citizens to the westward are not perfectly secure from the Indian depredations, particularly at this time, and that threats have been made to rescue the Indian in confinement. Should there be any probability of a rescue, you will deliver without delay, if you please, the enclosed order to Major Jones, and I shall order two or more companies, if you should deem it expedient, to act in concert with Major Jones' battalion. I should place much reliance on your opinion and those with whom you shall confer on the subject. Should the men be raised I should also crave your assistance in procuring provisions. Maj. Whittlesey will attend if the men should be embodied on the fifteenth, and probably I shall attend at that time myself. Please insert Maj. Jones's christian name previous to delivering the orders. Your obed't servant,

ELIJAH WADSWORTH.

John Walworth, Esq.

ELIJAH WADSWORTH TO MAJOR SAMUEL JONES.

CLEVELAND, June, 1812.

SIR:—You will, without delay, order the battalion under your command to be embodied at the City of Cleveland on the 15th day of this June, armed and equipped agreeable to the laws of the State. You will see that your men are each provided with half a pound of powder and two pounds of lead run into balls, suited to the calibre of their rifles, if armed with rifles, or if armed with muskets, that they be each provided with forty-eight cartridges and forty-eight balls. In execution of this order I depend upon your vigilance and activity. Your men will also be provided with carts.

ELIJAH WADSWORTH,
Major General 4th Division.

SIMON PERKINS TO MAJ. GEN. WADSWORTH.

WARREN, June 21st, 1812.

SIR: Yours of this instant is received. The rank roll which you require shall be immediately made out and forwarded as soon as it can be procured. The returns as you ordered for the draft are not yet prepared. Maj. Cotgreave, who is the bearer of this, will be so good as to inform you the cause of the delay, but as soon as it is in my power it shall be completed and forwarded.

I am, sir, your most humble servant,

SIMON PERKINS.

Judge Tod of Youngstown, was commissioned a Major of the Nineteenth regiment of United States Infantry (Colonel John Miller), July 6, 1812. He performed a gallant and important part in the sortie from Fort Meigs, in May, 1813, in which the British were driven from their guns in a position across the ravine, near the fort, on the south-east. On the 1st of January, 1815, he was promoted to be Lieutenant-Colonel of the Seventeenth United States Infantry. The Nineteenth regiment was raised in Ohio. After the evacuation of Malden by the British, on the approach of General Harrison in September, 1813, Major Tod was left in command of that post. He was the father of Governor David Tod, late of Briar Hill, and a very prominent character in Northeastern Ohio during the first thirty years of the present century. Before the war he held the position of Justice of the Supreme Court.

MAJOR TOD TO ELISHA WHITTLESEY.

[Extracts.]

HEAD QUARTERS, CAMP LOWER SENECA, August 19th, 1813,

ELISHA WHITLLESEY, Esq., Canfield, Ohio.

"Generals Harrison, Cass and McArthur, their suits &c., have left this morning for the mouth of Sandusky Bay, off which lies Commodore Perry with his Erie fleet. We expect much from him, and I am deceived if the country may not expect success to follow Gen. Harrison's movements. We have about one thousand effective men here, two thousand militia (Ohio), under the command of Gov. Meigs in person, at Upper Sandusky, ready to advance at the word. I am for the present attached to the 27 Reg't, U. S. Inf. How long I shall continue to fill my present station I know not. Sitting on courts martial and superintending the drill service, constitute my essential duty.

GEORGE TOD.

TRUMP OF FAME PRINT,
WARREN, OHIO, Sept. 16, 1812.

"A detachment under the command of Major Austin, of this town, was sent a few days since on to the Peninsula between Lake Erie and Sandusky Bay, for the purpose of procuring refreshment for the troops under the command of Gen. Perkins. They passed over to Cunningham's Island, where they discovered a British schooner on shore, and abandoned by her crew; they set fire to her. On their return they discovered the dead body of Mathew Guy of this neighborhood. Returning from that place one of their own number was shot through the head and fell dead. This is the first blood shed since the declaration of war at Sandusky Bay.

We are told the President has ordered on to Gen. Wadsworth 1500 muskets."

BRIG.-GEN. REASIN BEALL TO MAJ.-GEN. WADSWORTH.

CAMP NEAR WOOSTER, OHIO, Sept. 13, 1812.

DEAR GENERAL:—Enclosed is the strength of the detachment under my command. I do not see that it will be in my power to erect block-houses on the route contemplated, owing to the want of forage and provision. I believe a sufficient quantity could be had, providing we had money. The day before yesterday the Indians killed and scalped four persons on the Black Fork of Mohican, about twenty-five miles west of this, and eight miles east of Mansfield. At Mansfield there are upwards of two hundred men stationed, from the counties of Muskingum and Knox. I have last night and to-day detached three companies to range north-west of the place about twenty miles, and in case they should discover any sign of the enemy making toward the settlements to pursue and destroy them. I shall attend to the detaching the number required from my brigade, but I can assure you that I almost despair of getting them to camp. The unparalleled number of deserters are truly astonishing to me. I feel quite weak in consequence of my late spell of sickness, and at times feel strong symptoms of relapse. I do not believe that I shall be able long to perform the duties required in camp, much less the fatigues of a campaign. I am very desirous to return home in order to regain my health. I find it impracticable to keep up a line of communication with Gen. Perkins, owing (as I before observed) to the want of provisions and forage, which prevents my moving farther west, I hope the enclosed returns will be satisfactory, my forwarding the strength of the detachment and return of camp equipage, etc., shows there is a deficiency, and it will remain with the government to make it up. I know not what articles the government intend furnishing. I, however, have stated such as I know will be wanted. In case I should continue in my present state of health, I believe I shall be under the necessity of returning home, which I hope will meet with your approbation. Pray sir, signify your approbation relative thereto by next opportunity.

Sincerely, General, I am your friend,

REASIN BEALL.

HON. WM. EUSTIS TO GEN. WADSWWORTH.

WAR DEPARTMENT, Oct. 3, 1812.

SIR:—Your letter of Sept. 27th is received. Mr. Huntington is appointed paymaster to the troops in your vicinity. Major Stoddard will continue to forward supplies. The Pennsylvania detachment is assembling at Pittsburgh, and it is hoped the judicious arrangements of General Harrison will soon quiet the Indians on the frontier, and at least restore our possessions on the Upper Lakes. A train of artillery will immediately leave Pittsburgh, subject to the order of General Harrison, and every exertion is making for the comfort and convenience of the troops on the frontier.

Very respectfully, sir,
Your ob't servant, W. EUSTIS.

HON. WM. EUSTIS TO MAJ. GEN. WADSWORTH.

WAR DEPARTMENT,
Oct. 10th, 1812.

SIR: You will organize the detachment requested by my letter of Sept. 5th, put them under the command of a Brigade General and report them to Gen. Harrison for such disposition as he may think proper. Blankets, stockings, shoes and other clothing, with medicines and hospital stores are on the way, and will be distributed by General Harrison according to the wants of the army. Very Respectfully, Sir, Your Obedient Servant.

W. EUSTIS.

GENERAL WADSWORTH TO SECRETARY OF WAR.

HEADQUARTERS, HURON,
Oct. 24th, 1812.

HON. WM. EUSTIS, Secretary of War, Washington, D. C.

SIR: Your letter of the 10th instant was received by express last evening. I shall, without a moment's delay, comply with the requisition therein contained. I feel it a duty incumbent on me to make you acquainted in some measure with the situation of my detachment. The extent of line which required guards from my detachment exceeded 150 miles. At this place between four and five hundred men have been placed. Of those a very considerable part, by sickness and death, have been discharged and new drafts ordered. You may be acquainted with the extent of my division—more than 110 miles square. Almost the whole of this extent is uninhabited. My detachment takes from the draft of 100,000 ordered by the President.

After my detachment is completed, I must ask the question how and in what manner are the heavy bills accrued in this business to be defrayed? I have spared no pains to effect the object, and involved myself and may be my ruin, should the Government neglect me. I have, and still continue to place, the greatest confidence in the present Administration; have had the strongest assurance verbally from Mr. Huntington for my support.

Your obt. servant,
ELIJAH WADSWORTH,
Maj. Gen. 4th Division Ohio Militia.

GEN. WADSWORTH TO WM. EUSTIS.

HEADQUARTERS,
HURON, Nov. 20th, 1812.

SIR: I have, in obedience to your directions of Sept. 5th, called out fifteen hundred men from my Division, most of them have now been in the service on the frontier nearly three months, one Regiment is organized and marched to the Lower Sandusky, the residue are in this camp; they also would be at Sandusky if we had any provisions for them, but the contractor after some time dealing out damaged flour, is now entirely out of corn. When to this is added that since the troops were first called out they have received no pay I trust you will appreciate the difficulty of keeping them together, and the delay (incident to such a situation of things) in completing the arrangements you have directed. I trust, however, that within a week I shall be able to cause the residue of the troops from my division to join their brethren at Sandusky, and give up the command of them to General Harrison.

Very respectfully,
Sir, I am your obedient,
ELIJAH WADSWORTH.

GENERAL WADSWORTH TO SEC. OF WAR.

HURON, Nov. 28th, 1872.

SIR:—I have organized three Regiments from the Division under my command, comprising the number of men you required me to order to take the field, and have placed them under the command of *Brig. Gen. Simon Perkins*, agreeable, to instructions from *Gen. Harrison*. One Regiment has advanced to the Sandusky Bay, where they occupy the Fort, Parties are detached daily, to gather corn and other Forage, and every means are made use of to prepare for a continuous campaign. I trust Sir that the men will signalize themselves when they engage with the enemy. I have drawn three several Bills of Exchange on you to defray a part of the expenses incurred in organizing this detachment and keeping it in the field. The draft that I mentioned in my letter of Nov. 8th was not forwarded by Lieut. Church from Pittsburg, owing to his having been informed by Major Stoddard that the subsistence of the provisions from Detroit was improperly embraced in his estimate on which my draft was predicated. It would accommodate the public creditors if some person in the Western Country should be authorized to purchase bills on the War Office.

GEN. WADSWORTH TO WM. EUSTIS, ESQ., SECRETARY OF WAR.

CANFIELD, Dec. 20th, 1812.

SIR: Having on the 29th ult. completed the force ordered by you from my division by your letter of Sept. 5th, and placed them under the immediate command of General Harrison, reporting to him the whole force, it seemed that my service was no longer necessary or required by Government, and accordingly on the 30th I left the head quarters of the right wing of the Northwestern army at Huron and returned home.

Various causes combined, which were altogether beyond my control, has in some measure lengthened the time in completing the organization of the detachment. However, no time has been lost. The extensive new settlements have been saved from savage barbarity, and the detachment equally ready to go forward with the main army. Doubtless you are sensible of the great disadvantages I have labored under to equip, support, and march into the field such a detachment of men without money. Although the credit of the United States may be good, there are a class of citizens that will not lend any assistance or support to the war. Of course it is more difficult to procure supplies for a military force, and in the present case has fallen heavy on the real friends of the Government. You will see I am placed in a critical situation. By my orders great expenditures have accrued. I am daily called on for payment and several suits have been actually commenced, although I do not conceive myself personally holden, yet it will make extra expense and, Sir, I do conceive it necessary as well for the honor of the Government as the good of the creditors, that some effectual measures be immediately adopted to save expense, would it not be advisable to appoint some person within the limits of my Division to audit and pay off those demands?

I can assure you, Sir, that many of the creditors are much embarrassed for want of their just dues.

Yours very respectfully,
ELIJAH WADSWORTH.

WESTERN RESERVE AND NORTHERN OHIO

HISTORICAL SOCIETY.

TRACT No. 13—FEBRUARY, 1873.

PAPERS RELATING TO THE EXPEDITIONS OF COLONEL BRADSTREET AND COLONEL BOUQUET, IN OHIO, A. D., 1764.

SELECTION NO. 1.

It is our first duty to acknowledge the cordial assistance we have received in collecting these papers, extending through many years, from Messrs. Motley and Schenck, American plenipotentiaries at London, Mr. Moran, their Secretary and the British Premiers Lord Clarendon and Earl Granville; also to James W. Ward, Esq., of New York, Dr. F. B. Hough, of Lowville, New York, Rev. H. A. Homes, Librarian of the State Library at Albany, New York, George H. Moore, L. L. D., of the New York State Historical Society, A. K. Spofford, Esq., Librarian of the United States Library at Washington, William M. Darlington, Esq., of Pittsburg, and J. P. Kirtland, L. L. D., Rockport, Ohio.

In 1764 the British government sent two military expeditions into the Ohio country to chastise the western Indians. One of them had its rendezvous at Fort Niagara, commanded by Colonel John Bradstreet, quartermaster general for the colonies. It came from Albany in boats, by way of the Mohawk, to Fort Stanwix, now Rome, New York; crossing the portage to Oneida Lake, down the river to Oswego, and along the south shore of Lake Ontario to Fort Niagara.

The other had its rendezvous at Fort Pitt, now Pittsburgh, Pennsylvania, under Colonel Henry Bouquet, of the Royal Americans, or Sixtieth Regiment of Foot. This expedition marched by land in October, down the north bank of the Ohio to the mouth of Beaver; thence along an Indian trail, passing near New Lisbon, Columbiana county, Ohio, to the heads of Yellow Creek, and down the Big Sandy to its mouth at Bolivar.

Colonel Bradstreet crossed the old portage at Lewiston, on the east side of the Niagara river, to Fort Schlosser, early in August, carrying his boats on wagons. Launching them on the waters of Lake Erie, he followed the south shore to Detroit, where he arrived on the 25th of that month. Some chiefs of the threatened bands met him on his way up at "L'Ance aux Feuilles," or Leaf Bay, probably the Bay of Erie, in Pennsylvania, and on the 14th of August he entered into stipulations with them. Returning from Detroit, he reached Sandusky Bay, with a part of his command, in September. He sent out messengers to the tribes represented at Presque Isle, as Erie was then called and remained until the 18th of October, when, with about 1,100 men, he proceeded in boats down the Lake.

On the night of the 19th and 20th, a severe disaster overtook the expedition at or near Rocky River, Cuyahoga county, Ohio. After many years of diligent research in every quarter where authentic accounts might be expected, no detailed description of the event has been found. A number of papers, however, have been collected, which are here produced for the first time. Probably they contain the substance of all existing records, and all that may be expected relating to the expedition, relics of which the citizens of Rockport have discovered in great numbers, evidently belonging to this command. These are fully described in Whittlesey's "Early History of Cleveland," by Dr. Jared P. Kirtland.

When Bradstreet was leaving Sandusky to return, Bouquet was pushing on to the Indian towns near Coshocton, Ohio, where he thoroughly humbled the tribes residing on the Muskingum and the Scioto.

On his return, Bouquet was promoted and Bradstreet received official censure. This may have been the reason why there is now so little to be found concerning the homeward bound march of Bradstreet's troops. His brigade inspector, Major Thomas Mante, published a book on the French war, in which he defends Bradstreet's policy with the Indians, giving some information in regard to the disaster, an abstract of which, by Mr. Darlington, is inserted below. In Captain Degarimo's diary, of which we give a part, the days of the wreck and the stay at Rocky River are a blank.

MINUTES FROM MAJOR MANTE, BY WILLIAM M. DARLINGTON.

PITTSBURG, Dec. 6th, 1870.

Col. C. Whittlesey:

DEAR SIR:—The best account of General Bradstreet's expedition in 1764 is that of Mante, Major of Brigade in the campaign of that year; indeed it is the only narrative of that expedition yet published, giving a detailed account from its inception to its close, although it is not as minute as is now desirable.

He notes that the boats were "forty-six feet in keel, to carry 27 men and three weeks' provisions."

Now, as the army numbered 1,180 men, exclusive of 300 Indians in their own boats and canoes, *at least* 44 boats formed the fleet. As to the shipwreck, the main point of your inquiry, he states, "in the "evening as he (Bradstreet) was going to "land the troops, a hidden swell of the "lake without any visible cause, destroyed "several of his boats; *but no lives were lost.* "This surprising phenomenon proved to "be the forerunner of a storm, which con-"tinued several days, whereupon it be-"came necessary to detach part of the "army by land to Niagara."

The letters of Sir William Johnson, cited in your history, and also in the New York Colonial History, vol. 7th, confirm the statements of Mante, if any were needed, that no lives were lost. Sir William Johnson was very inimical to Bradstreet, and prejudiced the weak General Gage against him. See Bancroft's U. S., vol. 5th, p. 210, note.

The last paragraph in the "Diary of the Siege of Detroit," p. 119, notes that the schooner Victory was sent (in May, 1765,) to take up the cannon left by Colonel Bradstreet, last fall, near the "Riviere aux Roches." The bad weather, however, defeated the object. This is all that I have yet seen that clearly defines the place of the shipwreck. Wilkins's disaster undoubtedly took place at Point aux Pins—on the north shore of the lake, in Kent District, Canada—so marked on "Maps in Bell's Canada." (See Rocques's Map, 1761; Mitchell's Map, 1755; Pownall's Map, 1777; Charleviox's Map, 1734; Bellin's Map, 1754.)

In the journal of Sir William Johnson's journey to Detroit he says he dined there on the 28th of August, 1761. (Stone's Life, vol. 2, page 455.)

While no other point on the lakes is so named, on any map that I have examined, in truth the north shore of the lake was oftener traveled than the south, by voyageurs on their way to and from Detroit, being shorter.

Yours truly, WM. M. DARLINGTON.

THE DEPARTURE FROM OSWEGO—EXTRACTS FURNISHED BY THE NEW YORK HISTORICAL SOCIETY FROM UPCOTT, VOL. 2, PAGE 167.

NEW YORK, July 19, 1764.

Our last advices from the lakes are that on the 3rd instant, Sir William Johnson and Colonel Bradstreet, with the forces under their commands, set out from Fort Ontario at Oswego, for Niagara Colonel Bradstreet was so ill that he was obliged to be carried to the vessel. The forces consisted of the following men, viz:

Of the 17th Regiment	243	
" 55th Regiment	98	
" New York Regiment	344	
" New Jersey Regiment	209	
" Connecticut Regiment	219	
" Battoe Men	74	
" Carpenters	9	
		1,196
INDIANS.		
Mohawks	74	
Cocknawagas	106	
Oneidas	70	
Onondagas	68	
Senecas	60	
Cayugas	45	
Tuscaroras	37	
Ockwagoes	31	
Nanticokes	28	
Stockbridge	17	
Ossiningoes	31	
Ottawas from Meckillimackin	41	
	608	
Cocknawagas and other Indians at Niagara	120	
		728
		1,924

THE FORTS AT SANDUSKY.

It is not easy to determine the precise location of the early French and English forts or trading posts on Sandusky Bay. The earliest map which has on it the name of this bay is that of Henry Popple, London, 1733, where it is called "Lake Sandoski." Indian traders from Pennsylvania were there in 1748, but probably had not then a permanent post or fort. On Mitchell's Map, London, 1755, and on that of Evans, Philadelphia, same date, there is a "fort" laid down on the north side of the bay, near the mouth. It is much more probable that this fort, house, or post, was situated where the trail or portage path came out on the bay, across the neck from the Portage or Carrying River, at Ottawa. The English government had no fortifications there at that time. Mitchell states that the fort on the north side, meaning post, was "usurped by the French in 1751." Fort "Junendat," on Evans's map, is placed south of the bay and east of Sandusky river, "built in 1754." This was a French establishment for trade, perhaps with a stockade for defense against the English, and their Indian allies. When the English got possession of Lake Erie and its tributaries in 1760, a military post was planted somewhere on Sandusky Bay.

Ensign Paully and a squad were captured there in 1763, at the uprising of Pontiac's conspiracy, and most of them murdered on the spot. One of the letters which we give, dated October, 1765, refers to a block house a short distance out, on the trail to Fort Pitt. The natural point for a fort or a trading post, is on the north side of the bay, west of the plaster beds, where the trail from Portage River touched the shore. This was the route from Detroit into the Ohio country, and commanded the mouth of Sandusky River. Bradstreet's camp was here. It is also probable that Ensign Paully's block house, or stockade, was at the same place. It was only about two miles along the trail northward to Lake Erie, from where all parties moving in canoes could be observed, and intercepted at the mouth of the Bay. To the west, around the Bay, the ground is a low, swampy, and very difficult of passage, even by Indians, in its primitive condition, which gave importance to the carrying place in a military point of view. It would add much to the historical interest of the region if we could determine the blood stained point where Paully's little command was butchered.

JOURNAL OF CAPTAIN DEGARIMO.

Among transcripts with which we have been courteously furnished by the New York Historical Society, is the military record of Captain Degarimo, from Sandusky to Niagara on the return of the expedition, commencing at the "Camp at St. Dusky Lake, Oct. 3d, 1764." It is merely an abstract of the order book, or the order book itself. At some future time we hope to be able to put it in print. A part of the 46th, 55th, 60th and 80th Regiments were then with the detachment, also Lieutenant-Colonel Putnam and his provincials.

On the morning of the 14th a detachment of two lieutenants, three sergeants and eighty privates, were ordered out, destination not given. A detachment from the 46th and 55th regiments is directed to embark on the evening of the 15th. October 17th, "the boats to be loaded by the dawn of day, the troops to be in readiness at the shortest notice. It is Col. Bradstreet's orders that no huts be burned when we leave the camp."

"19th of October, camp at ——" no name given, but somewhere on the beach east of Sandusky Bay. Here there is a blank in the journal to the 22d at the "Camp at Grand Riviere" where they remained to the 29th. On the 22d the "army was ordered to receive two days provisions immediately. Each corps to give the same number to march as this morning to parade at 4 o'clock this afternoon in front of Major Dayly's Light Infantry, Major Hagan to command the detachment." Col. Putnam was with the command on the 29th, which is the last entry until November 14th, when they were at Fort Ontario, Oswego, New York. The expectations of a detailed description of the Rocky River disaster, excited by the discovery of this journal were entirely dissipated when it came to hand. Capt. Degarimo was no doubt too much occupied on the night of the 19th and 20th to make memoranda.

EXTRACTS FROM NEWSPAPERS OF 1764-5.

From the Newport *Mercury*—Files in Congressional Library Washington, D. C., date of July 30th, 1764, a letter from Niagara, of June 19th.

"Two new vessels are got on Lake Erie and another expected."

May 28th—From Detroit March 25th. "Scalping parties of Potawattamies are around Detroit, killing cattle and killing and scalping white men."

Pennsylvania *Gazette*—B. Franklin and D. Hall publishers, Philadelphia, May 3d, 1764.

"Advices from Detroit to Gen. Gage state that the Indians, 2,000 in number, have burned their huts, and departed suddenly, probably for Niagara."

"Aug. 23d—Col. Bradstreet and his army left Niagara for Detroit on the 6th of Aug.

Aug. 30—By advices from Fort Schlosser of the 12th of August, the army left Erie on the 8th, and went up the lake.

Waited on the 9th for some men of the 17th Regiment, who had lost some of their boats in the rapids—on the 10th crossed to the South shore."

Newport *Mercury*, Nov. 8th, 1764—"Col. Bradstreet was at St. Dusky on the 28th of September, waiting for the Indians to come in according to terms. The faithless and malicious creatures are seeking pretexts for delay"—same paper Nov. 19th—letter from an officer, dated Oct. 5th, given below. Same paper, Dec. 10th—A letter from Lt. Col. Israel Putnam to Maj, Durkee, of date October 7th. [See below].

Annual *Register* 1764, page 181—"Col. Bradstreet made a treaty at Presque Isle, (Erie, Pa.), in August. He made another at Tuscaroras, (Sandusky), with the Shawnese and Delawares in October. [This is probably an error, and confounded with the operations of Col. Bouquet]. The substance of both of them was, that war was to cease, and all prisoners be delivered up, and ten (10) hostages left as guarantees.

EXTRACT OF A LETTER FROM NIAGARA, DATED JULY 15, 1764.

Last Sunday afternoon, the snow Johnson, arrived here from Ontario, with Sir William on board; who, since his arrival, has been much busied in holding council with the Indians, of whom there are now at this place. above 1,000 of different nations, some to join and proceed with the army; some for peltry, expecting trade to be opened, and others to treat of peace. This morning, 105 men of the Follies Avoines. (Menomonies) arrived here, and are now in Council in the Fort. The Senecas have been expected for several days past, but are not yet come in. We are informed that there are about 900 of them, and the Delawares assembled together. It is whispered about, that if they don't come in in a few days, the army will march against them. The army in the boats was eight days in the passage from Fort Ontario hither, having met with some violent storms, in which four of the largest boats were cast away and wrecked to pieces; the men's lives were all saved, and most of the provisions and baggage.

"About two-thirds of the army, with their boats &c., are got over the carrying place, and the remainder will be over in two or three days. We have now four vessels on Lake Erie, the last of which set out for Detroit yesterday. A few days ago, a soldier was fired at by an Indian on the Carrying Place; the ball struck the haversack on his back; the things therein prevented its entering his body; he returned the fire, and made his escape to one of the little forts. If Sir William's indefatigable diligence and influence over the Indians does not prevent it, we will be at loggerheads in a few days."—Newport *Mercury*. Aug. 27, 1764.

EXTRACT OF A LETTER FROM NIAGARA, AUG. 2, 1764.

"We are here attending Congress day after day, with about 1300 Indians of different nations, some of whom have come 600 miles. They have concluded a peace with Sir William Johnson, except the Delawares and Shawnese, whom we have near a month waited for, as they are to bring their prisoners, in order to be delivered up. We expect to set off for Detroit in a few days, having everything ready for that purpose.—Newport *Mercury*, Aug. 27, 1764.

EXTRACT OF A LETTER FROM FORT SCHLOSSER, AUG. 27, 1764.

"The morning of the 8th instant the army went off from hence, and in the evening arrived at Fort Erie, which is on the north shore, about two miles above the rapids, at the entrance of the lake. The 9th they set out about ten o'clock, and proceeded along the north shore about six miles, where they remained all night, waiting for the 17th regiment, which was detained by having lost some of their boats in going up the rapids. Early on the morning of the 10th they stood across the lake to the south shore. I left Fort Erie the same day at 10 o'clock, since which time have heard nothing from them, though we have reason to think they are a considerable way on their journey, the weather having been pretty favorable since they went off.

The schooners Victory and Boston sailed from Fort Erie for Detroit on the 9th, in the night. I propose to proceed with them to Detroit, and hope to arrive there as soon as the army,"—Newport *Mercury*, *Sept.* 3, 1764.

LETTER FROM AN OFFICER AT BRADSTREET'S CAMP, NEAR THE CARRYING PLACE, SANDUSKY LAKE, OCT. 5, 1764.

"We all expected we came here to finish the peace with the Shawnese and Delawares, which our colonel began at L'Anceaux Feuilles. Instead of that, in consequence of orders just come, we are to attack them and destroy them root and branch, or they must give us ten men to be put to death."

* * * They were bringing in 200 prisoners would have ratified the peace, and we should have jogged home, etc.

"The impractibility of a march into that country, 300 miles from home, without any horses, is well known, and the incapacity of the troops to attempt it too evident if you but look at them. More than half of them are in the condition of Fallstaff's. Our boats are the most excellent that were ever formed for the service of this country; from hence, I believe you think below, we have some contrivance to make them sail upon *dry ground*, for the rivers which we were ordered to go up, in order to get to the Shawnese and Delawares, have no water in them. I saw it myself, there is not water for an Indian canoe; and I assure you, as yet we have no intention, altho' I think it should be considered, as it is the only improvement they want to make them quite perfect. The service then would never suffer for want of geographical knowledge of the country.

For my part, I never think myself in danger in one of these boats, led by our colonel, who has been all along as careful of the army on these lakes, as though we had been his children.

"You know we brought from Niagara Indians of the Five Nations; we expected great things of them. They were ordered to go with the army to attack the Miamis. "No, they say they would not; they were now desired to go against the Shawnese, etc. They stand like stocks, the devil of one will budge. You see what our dependence ought to be on these dear friends of ours, but no more of that.

* * * I hear we are to stay till November, God forbid. If we are, I shall wish for some of that courage-inspiring wine you have so plentifully at York.

My heart already akes at the aprehension of snow and ice, as my poor kegg is almost out; so it is with us all. * * * *

EXTRACTS FROM A LETTER OF LIEUT. COL. ISRAEL PUTNAM TO MAJOR DURKEE, NORWICH, CONN., "CAMP SANDUSKY" NEAR THE CARRYING PLACE, OCT. 7TH, 1764.

"We sent an officer and three Indians to the Delawares and Shawnese from Preiskeal, (Presque Isle) and Captain Peter from Moammee, (Maumee). We also sent Capt. Morris of the 17th, and one Thomas King, with three Indians. Capt. Morris returned some time ago, and was much abused and stripped, whipt, and threatened to be tomahawked, but had his life spared in case he would return."

"Captain Thomas King and three of the Conawawas proceeded. This Captain King is one of the chiefs of the Oneida Castle."

"About ten days ago, King came into Detroit, and had left all the Conawawas, who gave out for want of provision, and could not travel. He supposes they are perished in the wood. Three days ago he arrived here and yesterday had a conference with the Indians. He expresses himself in this manner."

SPEECH OF CAPTAIN KING.

"Friends and brothers, I am now to acquaint you with facts too obvious to deny. I have been since I left you to Monsieur Pontuck's (Pontiacs) camp, and waited on him to see if he was willing to come and make peace with our brothers the English.

He asked me what I meant by all that, saying you have always encouraged me to the war against the English, and said the only reason you did not join me last year was for want of ammunition, and as soon as you could get ammnnition you would join me."

"King replied that there was nothing in it. At this Pontuck produced six belts of wampum, that he had last year from the Six nations, to join with them in carrying on the war against the English."

"King said he did not know what to say about that, but he knew nothing of it.

Pontuck said "that the Six nations said that the English were so exhausted they could do no more, and that one years war well pushed, would drive them into the sea,"—a pause.—King. "Brothers you know this to be true, and you have always deceived me." At this the Six nations were all angry, and to-day are packing up to go off. What will be the event I don't know nor don't care; for I have no faith in the Indian peace, patched up by presents."

"Yesterday Captain Peters arrived which is the last party we have out. He says the Wyandots are all coming in, but the Delawares and Shawanees are not, nor durst they come, for they are afraid if they do Colonel Bouquet will be on their towns and castles."

He has sent to them to come to him and make peace. On the contrary if they go to him, we should be on them, and they intend to lie still until Bouquet comes to them, then send out and make peace if possible; if not, to fight him as long as they have a man left.

We believe they wait to get some advantage of us before they try peace. Captain Peters says Bouquet is within thirty miles of their towns and believes it to be best for him to make peace with them, for Colonel Bradstreet had orders from General Gage eight days ago, to make no peace with them and to march to meet Bouquet.

On a council of war being called, and examining the Indians and Frenchmen that were acquainted with the road, found it to be thirty leagues to travel by land and nothing to carry provisions but on men's backs; which after allowing for hindrances must take forty days to go and come; with four large rivers to pass; two of which with rafts and that very difficult, considering the season of the year, it was judged impracticable. Here we are, for what, I know not, nor when we are to leave it.

"I suppose you will think it strange that in many places in this country there are 10,000 to 20,000 acres of land without a bush or a twig, all covered with grass so big and high that it is very difficult to travel; and all as good plow land as you ever saw, any of it fit for hemp.

ISRAEL PUTNAM.

New Port *Mercury*, Dec. 10, 1764.

WESTERN RESERVE AND NORTHERN OHIO
HISTORICAL SOCIETY.

TRACT No. 14—FEBRUARY, 1873.

PAPERS RELATING TO THE EXPEDITIONS OF COLONEL BRADSTREET AND COLONEL BOUQUET, IN OHIO, A. D., 1764.

SELECTION NO. 2.

[TRANSCRIBED BY DR. F. B. HOUGH.]

From the Connecticut *Courant*. Oct. 29, 1764, and Newport *Mercury*, Nov. 8, 1764.

* * * * * Our last advices from the army under Colonel Bouquet are dated the 28th of September, when they had crossed the Ohio and were encamped on the other side near Pittsburg.

Col. Bradstreet with the army under his command, was still at St. Duskey, waiting for the arrival of the Indians, to execute the articles of accommodation according to the stipulated terms.

The Indians had been for some time past very quiet in those parts. Yet many people doubt their sincerity, and think if they can gain time to get in their winter stores, and find pretenses to delay the operations against them till the season is past, and all our expensive preparations, and the difficult and painful services of the year rendered entirely useless, that they will show themselves as inveterate and destructive enemies as ever; and that our easiness in admitting a reconciliation after suffering the most provoking and cruel expressions of their implacable malice that they could possibly invent, will probably give them reason to suppose that they may treat us in the same manner again with impunity."

From the Newport *Mercury*, (Rhode Island,) Dec. 19, 1764.

"Pondiac finding the other Indians had made peace, sent a message and a string of wampum, desiring to be included in the treaty. Colonel Bradstreet broke the wampum and sent back the messenger to acquaint him that he must come himself or send his son. But he found pretences to decline both, and the peace was concluded without him."

From the New York *Mercury*, Nov. 26, 1764.

Monday night last an officer arrived express from the army to the northward, from whence we have received advices that Colonel Bradstreet had broke up his camp at Sandusky, on the 18th of October; having first engaged many of the Upper nations, with whom peace had been concluded, to declare against the Shawanese and Delawares, and to send parties out to war against them. That about seventy miles from Sandusky the lake rose in the night on a sudden, and the surf beat with such violence on the shore where the army had landed that betwixt twenty and thirty boats were beat to pieces, notwithstanding the efforts made to save them. The night was very dark, and little else than the small quantities of provisions that was in them could be saved. The army proceeded to the Grand river, about seventy miles farther, which they entered in a storm. The tempestuous weather having the appearance of continuing, and the boats being deeply laden, by receiving the additional men from the boats which were lost, a number of the best marchers marched along the lake side and the Indians took to the woods. The men who marched were for a time relieved by other men from the boats; but provisions being out, and a snow storm upon the lake, about two hundred men pushed on for Fort Erie, in which they suffered greatly, and would have suffered more, had not the most advanced been relieved with provisions and boats, from Fort Erie in consequence of Col. Bradstreet's directions, sent by express. The remainder, except a few missing, were taken up by the boats on the 2d instant, and the army arrived at Niagara; from whence the regular troops, and some Provincials, sailed in vessels on the 9th instant; the rest of the army being left to follow in boats, under Lieut. Colonel Putnam. The vessels arrived at Oswego on the 11th instant, in a great storm, in which the Snow Johnson was lost, going into the Oswego River; by this accident, some baggage and arms were lost, but the men are happily saved."

[NOTE.—This letter may be found in the Newport *Mercury* (Rhode Island) of Dec. 2d, 1764, Pennsylvanian *Gazette*, Nov. 29th, and in the Boston *Gazette*, Dec. 3d, copies of which have been presented us by E. M. Barton, Esq., of the American Antiquarian Society, Worcester, Mass., and George H. Moore, LL. D. of the New York Historical Society.]

SUFFERINGS OF THE TROOPS.

From the Newport *Mercury*, Dec. 31, 1764.

"By a letter dated the 8th instant from the Mohawk river, of the best assurance, we are informed that, by the strange conduct of some, Sir William Johnson will have infinite work to do with the Indians. The distressed, struggling army are now daily crawling homeward. Many left their carcasses in the woods and along the lake, a prey to the wolves and other vermin, through mere fatigue and *want*. Some Indians and a few of the Indian officers are arrived in a shocking condition, having been in the woods twenty-six days without a morsel but what they killed, which was a trifle for this number. The main body, with Captains Montour and Johnson, Lieutenant Preston, &c., are expected in a few days at Sir William Johnson's. They are detained carrying *some sick* Indians on their backs thro' the woods."

[If the advice of Sir William had been attended to, near three years past, in all probability we should have had no Indian war; for at that time it was demonstrable that he could have formed upon the surest basis such a construction of amity with the far nations as would no doubt have been productive of the most sensible advantage to the inhabitants here as well as to those at home. But he was abridged by a poor £7,000, which, if properly applied then, would have prevented all the calamities of a scalping war.]

LETTER OF JAMES W. WARD, ESQ., RELATING TO HIS RESEARCHES IN THE BRITISH MUSEUM.

NEW YORK, Jan. 6, 1873.

MY DEAR COLONEL: I returned home in November last, and should have written you before in relation to the request you made me while in London, if I had not been in daily expectation of a mislaid package containing the papers I now send you, which only arrived from London yesterday. I am apprehensive after all that the documents I have copied may not interest you, or that you may already be familiar with them. However, these are all the papers I was able to find relating to the expedition of 1764, about which you are making inquiries. In the whole collection of manuscripts relating to this period, now in the British Museum, there is none in the form of a report by Colonel or General Bradstreet. This I ascertained by looking through the entire file, and by inquiry of the very thoroughly informed and polite custodian of the MSS. department. The only letter of Bradstreet in the collection relating to the expedition, I have copied for you and enclose, adding a couple of letters of Bouquet relating to matters covered by Bradstreet's quasi "report;" one of them being an answer to it. The papers are interesting, certainly *per se*, but you may already have had printed copies of them, though I am ignorant if any such exist. One thing would seem to be certain, there is no such report as the one you refer to among the British Museum MSS. If there is, those who *should* know do *not* know where to look for it; and I was allowed access to every MS. book and portfolio in the establishment. * * *

Hoping my very pleasant labor has not been altogether in vain,

I am yours, very sincerely,
J. W. WARD.

LETTER FROM COL. BRADSTREET—THE ONLY THING LIKE A "REPORT" AMONG THE BRITISH MUSEUM MSS.—COPIED BY MR. WARD.

SANDUSKY, LAKE, Oct, 17, 1764.

To Col. HENRY BOUQUET:

Your packet was delivered to me by the two Indians, who spoke to you in favor of the Shawanese and Delawares. They say that one of the Englishmen you sent with them was for coming on, but the other one would not; saying they must return to you, with the chiefs of the Delawares. They also say that some of the Shawanese chiefs were gone to you to ask peace. I have not settled anything with, or received any prisoners from the Shawanese or Delawares. I have sent to "All Nations of Savages" as far as "Illinois the Bay," (quotation marks original) letting them know what Genl. Gage desired, in his first letter to me, respecting the peace I had made, agreeably to his instructions, and indeed have taken every step in my power to prevent a storm. I hope all may go well on that score. *The savages have understanding.* I have been on this lake and up the river (Sandusky) as far as it is navigable for Indian canoes, for nearly a month, and am extremely sorry to tell you, it was impossible for me to put General Gage's orders into execution. It is necessity, absolute necessity, that obliges me to turn the other way. By my long stay here, and keeping of chiefs of such nations as could give assistance to those against whom you act, the two nations are left to defend themselves; and should they stand out, I am hopeful their efforts will be feeble. We keep them in constant alarm, that the safety of their families may prevent their collecting in a body. Part of our scouts have returned, in which were Ottawas, Chippewas and Hurons; four more go out this day and to-morrow, and I am not without hope, those people will continue the war. If they do not, it must be from bad management in us.

This letter is sent by two Indians of Cocknawaga, Canada; in company with twenty-three men for service.

Not a man of the Five Nations will act. The "faithful persons" you want, it is not in my power to send, though not for want of numbers of Indians.

Were I sure you would get this letter I should be more plain. The enemy have prisoners who read English. I wish you success; I have done all in my power to contribute to it, and have the honor to be.

Your most obedient Servant,

JNO. BRADSTREET.

REPLY OF COLONEL BOUQUET TO COLONEL BRADSTREET'S LETTER OF THE 17TH OF OCTOBER.

CAMP AT THE FORKS OF THE MUSKINGUM, Nov. 16, 1764.

Colonel BRADSTREET:

Sir:—I received on the 28th of October, by Capt. Artel and twenty Cocknawaga Indians, the favor of your letter of the 17th. The Senecas and the Delawares had at that time submitted to the terms I had prescribed to them; but the Shawnees had stood out to the last. However, seeing us at their towns and determined to carry our point, they accepted, two days ago, the same conditions as the other Nations, viz: to deliver immediately all their prisoners, to give hostages of their principal people, and to send deputies to make peace with Sir Wm. Johnson. I have received already upwards of 200 prisoners, including their own children born of white women, which I have obliged them to give up; and I expect more yet from the Shawnees, having sent parties to collect them at their towns. I have besides two hostages from the Senecas and six from the Delawares. I join entirely with you, that the peace will last, provided the savages are properly managed. It is now Sir William's business. I hope you and I have done with them. I wrote to Col. Campbell (commanding at Detroit) to acquaint the Nations with him that matters were settled in this way; though I believe they will never hurt one another much. I enclose you the speech I made at Tuscarawas, when I broke, by the General's orders, the peace they pretended to claim, after they had infringed it in every particular. The Wyandotts have sent me four prisoners, and promise to deliver fourteen more in the spring.

HENRY BOUQUET.

COL. BOUQUET TO GOVERNOR FAUQUIER OF VIRGINIA,

From the collection of General Haldeman's MSS.

CAMP AT THE FORKS OF MUSKINGUM, NEAR WACKATUMICA, THE MOST CONSIDERABLE SHAWNEE TOWN, November 15, 1764.

To Governor FAUQUIER:

I was favored the 4th inst. with your letter of 13th Sept., and I have now the pleasure to inform you that the Mingoes, the Delawares and the Shawnees, after numberless difficulties, have, at last, submitted to the terms prescribed to them, and without being allowed to stipulate any conditions on their behalf, they have delivered all the prisoners that could be collected, and even their own children born of white women, and given fourteen hostages to deliver the rest, and, as security that they shall commit no hostilities, or violence against His Majesty's subjects. On these conditions they are permitted to send deputies to make their peace with Sir Wm. Johnson. I am only to request you will publish a suspension of arms with the said Nations, and I may presume to assure you from their present disposition, that the militia on your Frontiers may be discharged; and the inhabitants return with safety to their abandoned settlements. Several of the captives have remained so long among the savages, that they leave them with the utmost reluctance; and we are obliged to keep guard upon them to prevent their escape. In my opinion these unfortunate people ought to be treated by their relatives with tenderness and humanity, till time and reason make them forget their unnatural attachments; but unless they are closely watched, they will certainly return to the barbarians.

I am now to return my thanks for the two distinguished corps of volunteers who have joined me from your government; one commanded by Colonel McNeil and

Captain Lewis, and the other by Major Field.

They have been of great service in enabling me to penetrate into this country with a sufficient force to compel these haughty savages to submit on our own terms. I flatter myself that the success of this expedition, so interesting to your province in particular, will recommend them to your notice, and that of your government. I promised you that they should create no expense to your province, as I intended to have mustered them in the Pennsylvania regiment, and to have made up to them the difference from that pay to that of your militia. But this method is so disagreeable to them, that I shall proceed no further in it till I know your intentions, and then of the House of Burgesses in that respect, as I can make no doubt that upon your recommendation the House will not leave it to another government to pay their own troops, who have exerted themselves with so commendable a spirit for the defense of their country, and whose behavior does so much honor to Virginia.

I have the honor to be, with great respect, etc. HENRY BOUQUET.

LEGATION OF THE UNITED STATES,
LONDON, 12th of August, 1869,

SIR: In reply to your letter of the 19th, I have great pleasure in forwarding to you herewith, extracts from such letters* in the Public Record Office of Great Britain as have reference to Col. Bradstreet's expedition to Rocky River on Lake Erie in 1764. It appears, from a letter of the Master of the rolls, that the public records contain no report of Col. Bradstreet to Gen. Amherst, the documents of which you required a transcript.

I have only to add the expression of my hope that these papers will be satisfactory to you, and to state that I have already expressed my thanks to Her Majesty's principle Secretary of State for Foreign Affairs, for the promptness and courtesy, with which your request on behalf of the Cleveland Historical Society has been complied with, so far as was possible.

I have the honor to be, sir,
Your obedient servant,
JOHN LOTHROP MOTLEY.

COL. CHARLES WHITTLESEY, Historical Society, Cleveland, Ohio.

LEGATION OF THE UNITED STATES,
LONDON, 11th January, 1872.

SIR:—By direction of his Excellency, General Schenck, I have the honor to say, that immediately on the receipt of your letter of the 13th of last October, he had much pleasure in forwarding a copy to Lord Granville, and in requesting his Lordship to favor him if possible, with a copy of the official report of Col. John Bradstreet, on his expedition along the southern shore of Lake Erie in 1764. That request has been fully considered, and I now forward to you herewith, copies of two notes in reply, from Lord Granville. From the last of these, it appears, that after a further careful search in the Public Record Office, no other document on the subject can be found there, but the one, a copy of which was communicated to Mr. Motley, on the 11th of August 1869, and which he sent to you in his letter of the next day.

General Schenck regrets that his efforts to serve you have been unsuccessful, and he is reluctantly compelled to come to the conclusion that Colonel Bradstreet's report has either been mislaid or lost.

I am, sir, your obedient servant,
BENJAMIN MORAN,
Secretary of Legation.

Charles Whittlesey, Esq., President Western Reserve Historical Society, Cleveland, Ohio.

GENERAL GAGE TO LORD HALIFAX—MILITARY CORRESPONDENCE 1763, 1764, 1765—AMERICA AND WEST INDIES, NO. 121.

NEW YORK, December 13, 1764.

MY LORD:—I have had the honor to receive your Lordship's letter of the 13th of October, and am to acquaint you, there is reason to believe that the report of the Cherokees killing five Frenchmen on the Mississippi is a mistake. When the last accounts left Carolina, all the Cherokees were returned from war against the Indians of the Ouabache, Twightwees or Miamis, Shawnese and Delawares; but are not accused of making any incursions on the Mississippi. One of the parties reported that they had seen some canoes, laden with skins going down the Ohio, and that four of the men in the canoes looked like Frenchmen. They fired upon them killed several of the people, and took four scalps. I conceive that the first report took rise from this circumstance, it is not mentioned whether the scalps are Indian or French. Some of them may possibly be French, as it is past a doubt that the inhabitants of Illinois have supplied the Shawneese and Delawares with ammunition by the way of the Ohio, and it is likely might be returning with the skins they had received in exchange for their merchandise. This affair was inquired into upon the first report, and if it shall be discovered that the Cherokees have attacked any settlement belonging to the French, I shall not fail to do everything that can tend to pacify the commandant of the district where the accident happened. The

*These are two letters from General Gage to the Earl of Halifax. One from New York Sept. 24, 1764, and another Dec. 13, 1764. That of Sept. 21st has been published in the New York Colonial History, vol. 7, page 655. The other which we give below is thought not to have been before in print.

Cherokees have had men killed and taken prisoners in these excursions; some of the latter were carried to the Illinois, from whence one of them has made his escape, and reports that last spring a French officer of rank, and others of less note under him were very assiduous in sending for the different tribes of Indians in their alliance, to whom they gave ammunition and arms of all kinds; that they made them speeches, in which they desired the Indians to go to war against the English and their allies: that they would kill all and not trouble them with prisoners. The accounts given by the Indians can rarely be relied upon, and it is to be hoped that this is nothing more than what is generally termed an Indian report.

Your Lordship will perceive from my former dispatches that the perfidy of the Shawnees and Delawares, the contempt they showed for us, and their having broke the ties which even the savage nations hold sacred amongst each other, required vigorous measures to reduce them.

I determined to make no peace with them but in the heart of their country, and upon such terms as should make it as secure as possible. I have now the pleasure and satisfaction to acquaint your Lordship that this conduct has produced all the good effects which could be wished or expected from it. Those Indians have been humbled and reduced to accept of peace, upon the terms prescribed to them, in a manner as will give reputation to His Majesty's arms amongst the several nations. The regular and provincial troops under Col. Bouquet, having been joined by a good body of volunteers from Virginia, and others from Maryland and Pennsylvania, marched from Fort Pitt the beginning of October, and got to Tuscarawas about the 15th. The march of the troops into their country threw the savages into the greatest consternation, as they had hoped their woods would protect them, and had boasted of the security of their situation from our attacks. The enemy hovered round the troops during their march, but despairing of success in an action, had recourse to negociations. They were told that they might have peace, but every prisoner in their possession must first be delivered up. They brought in near twenty, and promised to deliver the rest. But as their promises were not regarded, they engaged to deliver the whole on the first of November, at the Forks of the Muskingum, about 150 miles from Fort Pitt, the center of the Delaware towns, and near the most considerable settlement of the Shawnees. Colonel Bouquet kept them in sight, and moved his camp to that place. He soon obliged the Delawares and some broken tribes of Mohicans, Wyandotts and Mingoes to bring all their prisoners, even to children born of white women, and to tie those who were grown as savage as themselves, and unwilling to leave them, and bring them bound to the camp. They were then told that they must appoint deputies to go to Sir William Johnson, to receive such terms as should be imposed upon them, which the Nations should agree to ratify; and for the security of their performance of this, and that no further hostilities should be committed, a number of their chiefs must remain in our hands. The above Nations subscribed to these terms, but the Shawnees were more obstinate. They did not approve of the conditions, and were particularly averse to giving of hostages. But finding their obstinacy had no effect, and would only tend to their destruction, the troops having penetrated into the heart of their country, they at length became sensible that there was no safety but in submission, and were obliged to stoop to the same conditions as the other Nations. They immediately gave up forty prisoners, being the *sine qua non* of peace. It was agreed that parties should be sent from the army into their towns to collect the prisoners and conduct them to Fort Pitt.

They delivered six of their principal chiefs as hostages into our hands, and appointed their Deputy's to go to Sir William Johnson, in the same manner as the rest.

The number of prisoners already delivered exceeds two hundred and it was expected that our party would bring in near one hundred more from the Shawnese towns. These concessions seem sufficient proof of the sincerity and humiliation of those nations,—and in justice to Colonel Bouquet, I must testify to your Lordship, the obligation I have to him; and that nothing but the firm and steady conduct which he has observed in all his transactions with those treacherous savages, would ever have brought them to a serious peace.

Col. Bradstreet not finding the troops under his command in a condition to march to the plains of Scioto, kept the enemy in awe by remaining at Sandusky as long as the season would permit, and spiriting up the Indians with whom he had lately made peace to declare war and send out parties against them. He had regulated affairs at Detroit, got a vessel into Lake Huron, and re established the post Missilimakinak, which he has garrisoned with a detachment from the 17th regiment. He broke up his camp at Sandusky on the 18th of October, and had the misfortune to lose twenty-five of his boats from the violence of the surf of Lake Erie. This accident obliged part of the troops to march along the shore, who were for a time relieved by others from the boats. But the weather being very tempestuous, and continuing so a number of days, and provisions growing short, part of the troops pushed for Niagara, and suffered greatly in their march. Col, Bradstreet arrived at Niagara the beginning of November and embarking the regular troops, and some Provincials in the vessels, leaving the remainder to follow in Boats, sailed on the 9th for Oswego, where he arrived in a very great storm on the 11th. One of the vessels named Johnson Snow was drove upon the Bar of Oswego, where she was wrecked, and some Baggage and Arms lost, but the men were happily saved. Another vessel called the Mohock was lost on the same Lake some time before, so that the Marine has suffered this year a good deal.

I now flatter myself to be able to inform your Lordship. that the country is restored to its former tranquility: and that a general, and it is hoped a lasting Peace is concluded with all the Indian Nations, who have taken up arms against His Majesty The possessing of the Illinois is yet a difficulty which we have to encounter, though this last Peace with the Shawnese and Delawares may facilitate our designs in that quarter.

It seems to have opened a door to that country, and that nothing might be left undone which could be attempted, Colonel Bouquet has received directions in case a Peace should be concluded with the Shawnese and Delawares to try their influence to get an Officer if not a Detachment to the Illinois. The late season of the year is against us, but I have not as yet received any answer upon those points. The affections of several Nations are to be conciliated. particularly those inhabiting the Auabache and the District of the Illinois. And we must reckon that the French will privately give us all the obstruction in this that they can. We may accuse the French in general terms, tho' we cannot fix the blame on any one particular commander. The enclosed copy of a letter from Colonel Bradstreet to Mons. de St. Ange, who now commands at Fort Chartres with the enclosed copy of a letter to Colonel Bouquet, from Mr. Smallman, a Major of Militia who has been a long time prisoner amongst the Delawares, will shew your Lordship that there is reason to accuse them of doing us ill offices. Captain Morris's journal which I had the honor to transmit your Lordship in my last, is a further proof of this, and its apprehended that the bad reception that gentleman met with from the savages was in great measure owing to the management of the French. I have wrote to Monsieur d'Abbadie on this subject, and shewed him it was not without justice, that the English had accused the French of animating and supporting the Indians against them; and shall take the first opportunity to transmit him copy's of the enclosed letters, if he still remains at New Orleans.

The 80th Regiment has been disbanded agreeable to His Majesty's Orders and the 55th regiment is marching to this place by detachments as fast as they can be relieved in the posts they occupy by the other troops. All that regiment, except a small part, are expected to assemble here in a few days, and no time will be lost in embarking them for Ireland.

I trust this letter to the care of Major Small, an officer on half pay, who is returning to England. This gentleman having served the campaign under Colonel Bouquet, I take the liberty to refer your Lordship to him, for any particulars which you would choose to be informed of.

I have the honor to be, with the greatest regard, respect and esteem,

My Lord, your Lordship's most obedient, and most humble servant,

THOS GAGE.

[Endorsed]

NEW YORK, Dec. 13, 1764.

Major General Gage, by Major Small. R. 16th January, 1765.

Extract sent to the Board of Trade the 16th January 1765, informing of the Military Operations against the Indians —The Delawares and Shawnese reduced and brought to submission—Peace established—That five Frenchmen were killed, a mistake—The French continue to animate the Indians against us.] With two enclosures. Bundle B—No. 12.

The proceedings of the Colonial Legislature of New York have been examined by Rev. H. A. Homes, Librarian for the State Library at Albany, and by Dr. F. B. Hough, of Lowville, New York. Mr. Homes says "In looking over the Journals of the Assembly I find that it was prorogued from October 1764 to November 1765, partly in consequence of there being no Governor."

Dr. Hough has examined the printed Journals (Gaines' Edition, vol. 2, page 186), where the following entry has been found. No further Legislative proceedings or reports have been discovered:

"NOVEMBER 27, 1765.

"A petition of several officers late in the pay of this Colony, and on the expedition with Col. Bradstreet, in behalf of themselves and soldiers enlisted under them, was presented to the House and read, setting forth, that they have suffered great loss in their baggage and effects in a storm on Lake Erie, when on the expedition aforesaid. That there are sundry sums due them for billetting money; that they were upwards of forty days longer in the said service, than the time they were enlisted for, for neither of which they have received any satisfaction; and therefore humbly pray their case may be taken into consideration, and provision made for their payment.

"Referred to committee on Governor's speech."

Western Reserve and Northern Ohio
HISTORICAL SOCIETY.

TRACT No. 15, APRIL, 1873.

Correspondence of Major Tod, War of 1812.—History of Northfield.

The heirs of the late Governor Tod some time since placed the public and historical papers of his father, Judge Tod, on deposit at the Historical Rooms.

Judge Tod's life was an active and eventful one, a sketch of which will probably appear in due time. He had been a Judge of the Supreme Court of Ohio, and on the expectation of a war with England received an appointment as Major in the regular army. At that time he was Brigade Inspector to General Simon Perkins, the brigade including the entire Western Reserve. The first paper here given is the order to secure and organize the quota of the brigade, which had three regiments and a battalion. When the United States raised their first regiment, on the new establishment after the Revolution, it was commanded by a Lieutenant-Colonel. Following this example, the Ohio militia, under the Territorial government and of the State, pror to the war of 1812, had no Colonels'. The companies were small and they were very much scattered through the new settlements. This explains why this order was issued to the Lieutenant-Colonels of the regiments, which seldom numbered more than 500 men of the line.

Hayes, Rayen and Edwards entered the service at once, where Edwards soon fell a victim to the malaria of the waters of Sandusky Bay, where the Ohio troops were stationed, in 1812. Tod was soon commissioned a Major in the Seventeenth United States Regiment. to be raised in Ohio and Kentucky. Its Colonel was Samuel Wells of Kentucky, and its Lieutenant-Colonel, John Miller of Steubenville, Ohio.

GENERAL PERKINS TO MAJOR TOD.

WARREN, TRUMBULL CO., OHIO,
April 27, 1812.

SIR: The enclosed order from the Major-General, bearing date April 27, 1812, has just come to hand; and in order that it may be promptly executed, you are hereby requested to issue an order to the present commandants of regiments within this brigade to furnish with the least possible delay their proportion of the detachment called for; and if the corps should be raised by volunteer enrollment, the number assigned to the first regiment is thirty-three, to the second regiment twenty, and to the third regiment twenty-three. But if contrary to expectation a draft should be found necessary, then the number to be raised in the first regiment is sixteen, in the second regiment, eleven, and in the third, thirteen. The officers to command the detachment will be appointed as selected by law. You will strictly enjoin it on the said commandants that they make returns of the men thus raised by the 9th day of May next, and also that they order those volunteered or drafted within their home regiment to rendezvous at some convenient place in said regiment, on Wednesday, the 14th day of May next, for the purpose of receiving such orders as the exigencies of the case and circumstances may then require.

For information you will refer the proper commandant to a statute of the United States, passed the 6th day of February, 1812, entitled "An act authorizing the President of the United States to accept and organize certain volunteer militia corps." Likewise to the statute of the State of Ohio, regulating the militia thereof.

SIMON PERKINS,
Brigadier General 3d Bridade,
4th Division.

GEORGE TOD, ESQ., Brigade Major and Inspector.

BRIGADE ORDERS, 3D BRIGADE, 4TH DIVISION, OHIO MILITIA, ISSUED 28TH OF APRIL, 1812, TO LIEUT. COLONELS WILLIAM RAYEN, RICHARD HAYES AND JOHN S. EDWARDS.

SIR: You are hereby required to cause to be raised within the regiment over which you have command, if they can be raised by voluntary enlistment, twenty-three good and able-bodied men, to serve in the service of the United States as a detachment from the militia of this State. If that number of men cannot be attained by voluntary enrollment, you are required to cause to be raised by draft and on your regiment thirteen men of the above description, to be taken from the respective companies composing the same, in proportion to the numbers in each. In whatever way the detachment from the 3d Brigade, 4th Division, Ohio Militia, may be raised, it is to be officered in the manner as the law directs. On the execution of this order, you are to make the Brigadier of the aforesaid brigade a return of the men enrolled or drafted by the 9th day of May next. The above order is issued in consequence of recent and pressing orders from the President of the United States through the Major General of 4th Division of Ohio Militia. The detachment from your regiment shall rendezvous at some convenient place in your regiment, as you shall order, on the 14th of May next, when it will receive further orders.

The above orders are to be executed with the greatest possible promptitude and dispatch.

For information you are referred to a statute of the United States passed the 6th day of February, 1812, entitled "An act authorizing the President of the United States to accept and organize certain volunteer Military corps;" likewise to the statute of the State of Ohio regulating the Militia thereof April 27, 1812.

By order of SIMON PERKINS, Brigadier
GEORGE TOD, Brigade Major and Inspector.

HON. GIDEON GRANGER, WASHINGTON, D. C. TO EBENEZER GRANGER, ZANESVILLE.

WASHINGTON, Feb. 15, 1812.

EBEN'R GRANGER ESQ.:

The Ohio Delegation have recommended Gen'l Miller for Colonel, and George Tod for Major. I am astonished at Tod's entering the army. If I could see him I could change his mind.

Yr. friend,
G. GRANGER.

GENERAL WINCHESTER TO MAJOR TOD.

LEXINGTON, KY., 28th Apr. 1812.

MAJOR GEORGE TOD:

SIR:—On the receipt of this you will repair to this place for the purpose of receiving money and the necessary documents to place you on recruiting service in the State of Ohio. Its desirable that no time should be lost. The Secretary of War expects expedition in raising the quota of troops in Department No. 1, of which your State forms a part.

I am respectfully, Sir,
Your Obedient Servant,
J. WINCHESTER, B. Gen'l U. S. Army.

JAMES R. MUNSON, CINCINNATI, TO MAJOR TOD.

CINCINNATI, April 26, 1812.

My Dear Major:—The question and preparation for war engrosses the time and cares of all here. The requisition made by His Excellency has been punctually and gallantly met and completed. Cincinnatl hill is covered with tents, etc., and troops who were yesterday received by His Excellency, and will in the course of a few days be in a condition to move with security to the place of destination. Governor Meigs will advance in person at the head of the forces—Generals Gano and Cass in command. Governor Meigs has signified to me his pleasure that I should accompany him and make one of his military family, and also directs me to assure you of his high esteem, and that from present appearances a call on your section of the State for draft, will not be made.

JAS. R. MUNSON.

RENDEZVOUS, ZANESVILLE, OHIO,
June 17th, 1812.

I am ordered by Brigadier Generel Winchester to cause "recruits" to be taught the *soldiers' drill*, comformably to the rules and directions laid down in the book entitled "Instructions to Infantry," and prescribed by the Secretary of War for the discipline of the troops of the United States.

It is submitted, Sir, if a copy of that work should not be forwarded to this rendezvous. It would oblige the officers of this district could we be furnished with the pamphlet prescribing the uniform dress of the army of the United States. (Neither of these publications can be found in this country.)

I am, Sir, very respectfully,
Your obedient servant,
GEORGE TOD,
Major United States Army.

ALEXANDER SMYTH, Inspector General of Army of United States.

MAJOR TOD TO GENERAL WINCHESTER.

ZANESVILLE, OHIO, June 29, 1812.

DEAR SIR:—I have just received a file of newspapers from Washington City giving inteligence of a declaration of war, by the Congress of the United States against Great Britain.

This event will give a new aspect to affairs; and it is really to be hoped that it will produce a union of sentiment and action. I have commenced the recruiting service in the different parts of the District—so recently, however, has that work been commenced, that I have received no report from any of the recruiting officers, excepting the one at this place. He has reported to me six, which I have mustered. I indulge myself in the belief that from the arrangements which have been made for the recruiting service in this District, that service will go on prosperously.

You will, I trust, excuse me in the course which I have proposed to myself to pursue in regard to my returns, which is to make my first returns up to, and including the first Monday of July next, so that my weekly and monthly reports will be made with some regard to system.

I have made a contract for the necessary supplies at the rendezvous: rations at 16 cents each; have procured barracks sufficiently capicious for the accommodation of one hundred men, at six dollars per man; have employed a physician; vaccination will be strictly attended to. The pressure of the recruiting service has left me not a single subaltern officer for Drafting, Assistant Quartermaster or Acting Adjutant. The duties of these officers I must necessarily discharge at least for the present. I do not find them very burdensome.

There is here sufficiency of summer clothing for 200 men; kettles for the number; tin pans are, not however, furnished. It would help, I think, sir, the service we are engaged in had we even a small supply of muskets. The clothing I have compared with the invoices, and have forwarded to the United States Military Agent, Philadelphia, duplicate receipts for the same.

I am, very respectfully, sir,
Your obedient servant,
GEORGE TOD, Major.

RECRUITING RENDEZVOUS, Zanesville.

LIEUTENANT BOOKER, RECRUITING OFFICER, TO MAJOR TOD.

ST. CLAIRSVILLE, 9th July, 1812.

DEAR SIR: Since my last of the 6th inst., I have enlisted four fine able bodied fellows, and am much at a loss for blankets; and in fact I don't see how we can manage well without some, particularly * * * Would wish to go to some of the small * * * are near this place in order to pick up recruits * * * A sargeant's sword and six or eight suits of uniform clothing * * * be forwarded here, I think it would be attended with a beneficient effect, as it would charm our country buck, and put them in a greater spirit of being soldiers. If there should be no opportunity of any waggon starting from or coming through Zanesville to this place so as to have them sent, probably it would be as well for me to hire a horse and send out there and they could be * * * last in. I expect to get two or three more before the week is out. With due defference and respect, I remain your humble servant.
SAMUEL P. BOOKER.

Major GEORGE TOD.

CAPTAIN ELLIOTT TO MAJOR TOD.

WARREN, July 13th, 1812.

MAJOR GEORGE TOD:

SIR;—Enclosed you have my weekly return for the rendezvous at Warren. Should there be any inaccuracy in my return as to method, be so good as to inform me in your next communication. Lieut. Fredericks has obtained two recruits, when enlisted, or anything more on the subject I have not learned. Ensign Milligan has been here, and returned to commence * * * in Jefferson county.

It is reported and generally believed that the British have lately captured two of our vessels on Lake Erie. One loaded with provisions for the army at Detroit. The other had on some of Gen'l Hull's officers, destined for the same place. I am apprehensive from the number of the volunteers from this State, and the proceeding to a second draft of the Militia, that the recruiting service will progress but slowly. Yours Respectfully,
WILLSON ELLIOTT, Capt. United States Army.

GOVERNOR MEIGS TO MAJOR TOD.

CHILLICOTHE, July 27, 1812.

DEAR MAJOR—I am fairly fatigued with forming the new brigade. Boller went, long since, with McArthur, to Philadelphia. I know not what to advise you respecting your running for Congress. I certainly wish you to take that course you would best profit by, and be most agreeable. My wishes are that you was in Congress. I will duly apprise you of the time of election. 'Tis mail day, and I am in great haste, having come from Franklinton last evening.
Your friend, R. J. MEIGS.

LIEUT. COL. JOHN MILLER, (17TH REG'T U. S. INFANTRY), TO MAJOR TOD.

RENDEZVOUS,
CHILLICOTHE, July 29, 1812.

MAJOR GEORGE TOD:

SIR—I have this moment received orders from General Winchester to organize immediately one company of regulars in this State to consist of one hundred men, including non-commissioned officers, and to hold them in readiness to march at a moment's notice. He has ordered that the troops from your district be immediately marched to this place, or at least as many as will complete the company with what are here. You will therefore order all the recruits within your district to repair to Zanesville without delay, and detach and march to this place one 1st lieutenant, one 2d lieutenant and forty privates, should you have that number; if not you will march what you have. I wish you, if possible, to have your detachment at this place against the 10th or 12th of August. Every reliance is placed on your exertion on this important occasion.

General Winchester informs me that the object in calling the company out is to join a detachment from Kentucky to march immediately to Detroit. You will please forward by the detachment a muster roll of its strength. As neither of you have included New Lancaster in your recruiting district, you are at liberty to send a recruiting officer there, as soon as you see proper.

I have not as yet received any answer from General Winchester to the several inquiries I made him, concerning reports, returns, &c., &c. As soon as I do, I will inform you of it.

I am, very respectfully,
Your obedient servant,
JOHN MILLER,
Lieut. Col. U. S. Army.

NORTHFIELD.

BY IRVING A. SEARLES.

History of the Settlement of the Township—Reminiscences of Early Times.

In the spring of 1807, Isaac Bacon moved into Northfield, now in Summit county, and making a small clearing, erected a log house on the location where Francis Waite now lives. He had to raise his house without assistance, which he succeeded in doing in about five days. Here this family lived for three years before another white settler came. Their nearest neighbors were ten miles distant. Indians were numerous until the war of 1812, when they left to join the Britsh. There were, for some time, several wigwams on the farm of Bacon. The red men caused no trouble except in their attempts to secure all the whisky about Bacon's premises. One day a number of them came into the house and called for fire-water. Mr. Bacon was not at home and Mrs. Bacon told them they could not have any. They then drew their tomahawks, walked quietly up to the cupboard, found the whisky bottle, drank all they wanted and went away. David C. Bacon, then a small lad, tells us that he well remembers playing with the Indian children. In fact he had no other playmates. The favorite sports with the Indian boys were throwing the hatchet and shooting with the bow and arrow. He who could stand the farthest from a tree or stump and throw the hatchet so as to make it stick fast in the object at which it was aimed, was the best fellow. Mr. Bacon maintains that he could do quite as well at this as his playmates. In shooting with the bow and arrow, however, they could excel him. They had a tact in that which the white boy could never learn. From 1812 dates the last of the Indian race on the Reserve. Those who were once here, and survived the war, never returned, for they inwardly felt that they had forfeited all just claim to there former homes.

At the breaking out of the war there were only three families of whites in the township: Noble, Cramer and Bacon. They gave themselves no special uneasiness about the conflict until Hull's disgraceful surrender at Detroit. News then came that the British were coming to Cleveland by the way of Lake Erie and thence were to march directly through this section of the country This rumor sent the greatest consternation throughout all this region. It was well known that the enemy in its marches was accompanied by the merciless Indians, who refrained not from murdering all ages, sexes and conditions. Dwellings wrapped in flames, and shrieks of butchered innocents followed in the wake of the English soldiery. Our three Northfield friends therefore determined to move to Hudson, and thus augment the numbers which must repel the invading army. While Mr. Bacon went to Cleveland to ascertain the truth of the rumor, the others loaded the wagons with what furniture they could and buried the remainder. They had got about three miles out of town when Bacon returned and told them the report was false. The American prisoners taken from Hull were in Cleveland but no British force was there. The party then returned to their homes. One day shortly after this, several white men, including a number of non-residents of the township, were at the house of Bacon, and while conversing upon the prospects of a favorable or unfavorable termination of the war, they saw an Indian standing in the woods near the edge of the clearing. Mr. Cramer went out and kindly told him that if he wanted to save his life he had better leave that town, and then re-entered the house. From the appearance of the Indian it was conjectured that he was a member of a tribe that once lived in Northfield, and that he had in some way become separated from his people. There was in the company of whites one who was known to be an inveterate hater of the red men, and this man shouldered his rifle, left the house and walked slowly into the woods. He returned in about two hours, and when questioned as to where he had been, replied that "he guessed that Indian would never find his tribe." Nothing further would he tell about the matter, but it is the general opinion of those conversant with the circumstance that a rifle ball closed the earthly career of the savage long ere he passed the limits of Northfield township.

The women of the pioneer days had many experiences which ought not to go unrecorded. While the husband with stalwart arm felled the trees and reduced the wilderness to productive fields, the wife had no small task to perform. No one felt the hardships and privations of pioneer life more than she. In coming to the frontier she exchanged her comfortable dwelling house for the rude log cabin. In the place of the society which she once enjoyed she was almost isolated from all intercourse with the world. Oft times the husband must be absent from home for days at a time, and then the women were left all alone, miles from any neighbors, in the heart of a vast wilderness. The wife of Isaac Bacon was frequently thus situated. Mrs. Bacon was a brave woman, and the experiences through which she passed seem to us of this day almost incredible. We give but one instance illustrative of the statement just made. Our informant is David C. Bacon, oldest son of the woman of whom we are speaking. This son still resides in Northfield, near where his parents lived at the time. Mr. Bacon was frequently absent from home, and on one of these occasions a very suspicious looking man came to the cabin and asked admittance, which of course Mrs. Bacon granted. He seated himself and inquired the time of day, when Mr. Bacon would be at home, how far it was to the nearest neighbor, and, if she was not afraid to stay alone! From the first Mrs. Bacon did by no means like the appearance of the man, and every moment only strengthened her impression of him. She was undoubtedly as courageous as any woman; but there she was, so far from any neighbor that no assistance from that quarter, in case of emergency, could be expected. But she had one hope, and that was in the assistance of a powerful dog, which stood by her side. From the time that the man entered the house the knowing animal eyed him, as if to say: "You are here for no good purpose." It was now most dark, and Mrs. Bacon very politely told the man that she could not keep him over night and he had better be going. The man said nothing, but from his actions seemed to think otherwise. He stood and pondered a few minutes, and then called to one of the children to come and turn a grindstone which stood a short distance from the house. He accompanied this request by producing a large, ugly-looking knife. The child obeyed and he proceeded to sharpen the instrument. Mrs. Bacon expected the crisis was now at hand and began to prepare for the worst. She took her station in one corner of the room and called the dog to her side. The man soon came into the house and sat down at the opposite side of the room. They thus remained until midnight, neither speaking a word. The man then began to manifest considerable uneasiness. He finally asked the woman why she did not turn that dog out of doors. She replied that she always allowed the animal to remain in the house at night. He then advised her to turn the animal out of the house. She, knowing that her orders to the faithful creature would be disobeyed, opened the door and told the dog to go out. The animal growled and looked fiercely at the stranger, but would not move. The man then told the woman to sit down and he would see that the dog left the house. He then opened the door and told the dog to leave, but the creature, now aroused, again growled and exhibited a set of teeth which had the immediate tendency to cause the man to take his seat and desist from all further attempts to disturb the dog. The man made no further demonstrations, but went away about daylight, leaving Mrs. Bacon to thank her dog for the preservation of her life.

In the summer of 1826 there occurred one of the most singular affairs of which we have any knowledge. The parties immediately interested in the transaction were Dorsey W. Viers, then a citizen of Northfield, and now a resident of Norton township, and one Rubert Charlesworth. This last named individual was about thirty years of age, an Englishman and unmarried. For some time he had made it his home at Viers', and worked whenever he could, as a day laborer. Sometime in the month of July Charlesworth suddenly disappeared. At first but little was thought of his mysterious departure, but after a time an effort was made to discover his whereabouts. The most dilligent search after the missing man was, however, unavailing. Suspicion that he had been foully dealt with began to develop itself, and to make the matter still more posisive, it was whispered among the neighbors that Viers knew more about Charlesworth's disappearance than he was willing to confess. A hint of this kind was sufficient to lead many to at once pronounce Viers the murderer. But notwithstanding this strong suspicion no decisive legal action was taken until five years after Charlesworth left. During these years the excitement, instead of abating had become more intense, until popular clamor demanded a full investigation. Accordingly, G. N. Wallace, Justice of the Peace in Northfield, arrested Viers January 8, 1831. A trial of eight days ensued, and we wish the reader to carefully note the testimony elicited. It was said that parties going to the house of Viers the next morning after Charlesworth's disappearance, found Mrs. Viers hurriedly mopping up the floor. Viers himself appeared greatly agitated and was much confused in his statements about the missing man. He once said that he saw Charlesworth go, and then, soon after, said that he was sound asleep when the man left. These contradictory stories had only served to heighten the suspicion of Viers' guilt. Viers' hired girl also testified that a bed blanket which had been on Charlesworth's bed for a few weeks prior to his disappearance was missing, and that it was afterwards found with clots of blood on it, under a hay stack. It was also suddenly discovered that Charlesworth was immensely rich, that Viers was poor until after the murder when he became all at once flush of money. The reader may here conclude that testimony sufficient has already been adduced to hang any man, but the evidence of Viers' terrible crime did not cease here. When witches were believed in, every man, woman and child saw them. So it was in this case. That Viers had murdered that man was believed, and the public could see in everything the evidence of hir guilt. The body of a murdered man was found in every nook and corner in Northfield. One man at the trial swore point blank that he went one morning to Viers' door yard, and passing by a meadow containing about twenty acres of grass, yet uncut, he saw plainly the trail where some heavy body had been dragged through the grass. Here now is the key to the whole mystery! "Murder will out," and the heart of our searcher after truth is made to rejoice that he is to be no small instrumentality in giving to justice what had long been her due. He accordingly followed the trail through the meadow to a piece of woods adjacent. Ever and anon as he passed along he found spots of clotted blood, and his tender heart went out in loving sympathy for the departed Charlesworth. Coming to the fence separating the meadow from the woods he lost the trail, and therefore conjectured that the murderer had here taken the body of his victim in his arms and carried it to the place of burial. The avenger of blood entered the woods, and while searching for further trace of the trail he saw a chipmunk dart into a pile of leaves. He instantly conceived the idea of killing the poor creature, and going to the leaves began poking them about with his cane—and what a sight met his eyes! There lay the body of the long lost Charlesworth. T'is true but little beside the skeleton was left, but those were the remains of the missing man. Thus the witness in substance testified. The lawyers defending Viers asked how he knew it was Charlesworth's body, and he replied that one of the front teeth was broken, as he had often observed in Charlesworth. The court, of course, sent a committee to visit the place where the corpse lay. They came back and reported that while the remains of the departed were there visible they were the remains of an old dog and not those of Charlesworth. The witness would have been put under arrest on the charge of perjury had he not left town. He soon went away from Northfield and never returned.

In the midst of the trial two men from Sandusky came to Northfield and swore that they had seen Charlesworth but a short time before. On this testimony Viers was acquitted, although the public was firm in its belief that he had murdered Charlesworth.

A person, in his right mind, will do a good deal to preserve his reputation, and especially when it is assailed by so serious a charge as that of murder, and Viers resolved that the remainder of his days, if necessary, should be spent in search of Charlesworth. He opened correspondence with proper authorities, both of this country and Europe. He also visited in person many of the more prominent cities of the United States. Years rolled on and the search was unsuccessful. One day Viers went into a tavern in Detroit, and to the crowd in the bar room he propounded the oft-repeated query: "Is there any one here who knows a man by the name of Charlesworth?" To this he received the heart-sickening reply—"No." But as he left the room and stepped out into the street a man confronted him and said, "My name is Charlesworth and yours is Viers, and you are from Northfield, Ohio." Viers recognized the long lost man and the meeting was, indeed, most cordial. Viers told Charlesworth that he must immediately return with him to Northfield. The latter for a time refused, saying that he had important business which must be attended to at once. Viers would accept no excuse, and the two came direct to Northfield. Hand-bills were posted up all over the country announcing that on such a day Charlesworth would be at the church, and earnestly requesting all interested to call and satisfy themselves as to the identity of the supposed murdered man. This was a great day in Northfield. The church was crowded. Individuals who used to know Charlesworth would give him some hint in reference to some old transaction, and then he would go on and fill out the details. They would ask him, for instance, if he once kept company with such and such a girl; and when he answered "Yes," they would tell him to go on and describe her. In this way, after a long examination, the public were fully satisfied that the murdered man stood in their midst. Mr. Viers was fully cleared of all part or lot in the matter, and we presume he never regretted the efforts he made to find his alleged victim. The only reason Charlesworth assigned for his strange conduct was that he had passed a counterfeit ten dollar bill, and fearing an arrest he fled the township.

The first school building erected in Northfield stood where Mr. Rianier now lives. The children from miles around assembled at this house of learning, until the number of scholars exceeded a dozen. The first winter that school was taught here was a very severe one. There was no chimney to the house. Cracks between the logs freely admitted the wintry wind, and the building in all respects come far short of the modern idea of a public school edifice. Teachers then were not paid so much as they are now. A lady, for teaching in the summer, received, perhaps, a dollar a week and board around. In the winter a man was paid from eight to ten dollars per month and board. While wages were less than those paid now, the teacher's qualifications were correspondingly low. Reading, spelling, writing and arithmetic, to the "Rule of

Three," were about all that were taught in the backwood's school. The teacher did not have to bother about "certificates." No public money was available for school purposes, and employing a teacher was simply a matter of agreement between a few of the neighbors and any man or woman whom they might thus constitute "teacher." Private parties paid the bill, and private parties said to whom it should be paid.

The first white person who died in the township was an infant daughter of Isaac Bacon. The child died in 1808.

In September, 1813, occurred the first wedding. It was the marriage of Henry Wood to Esther Cranmer. Father Wood, "Uncle Harry Wood" as he is familiarly called by his friends, is still living in Northfield. There is but one other person now living who attended this wedding, and that is Miss Lucy Wood, maiden sister of Henry. The brother and sister are both residing with Mr. C. S. Bates, son-in-law of Father Wood. The Justice who performed the ceremony came all the way from Hudson, and received for his services the then large sum of one dollar and a half. Father Wood humorously remarked that he did not do as it is said one young couple in Northfield did a few years later. Rumor has it that a young gentleman and lady, bent on uniting their fortunes and going hand in hand down life's rugged pathway started through the woods to have the marriage rite consummated by a Justice who lived several miles distant. They, in some way or other, had procured a license, which then only cost one dollar and a quarter, but neither of them had the wherewith to pay the Justice. Here was a dilemma, but they would trust in Providence and all things would be for the best. Fortune is said to favor the brave, and these persons must have been very brave, for they were exceedingly lucky While the face of the young man had become nearly as long as that of a horse, and his eyes wore a look of melting and yet wonderful tenderness, as he thought of the solemnity of a circumstance which bid fair to prevent the legal union of two loving hearts, and while his dear companion, mild and gentle in all her movements, with a voice modulated after the sweetest cadences of the screech owl, was about to whisper in the large ears of her lover some fond word of encouragement and cheer, a "coon" sprang from a small sappling which stood near them and ran toward a large white oak tree. The young man seemed to be moved by some invisible power, and giving a yell, which would have done honor to the greatest Mohawk chieftain, started off in a brisk canter after the fugitive animal. Here history is blank as to details, but, at all events, the man caught the coon, skinned it, and took the hide to the justice and paid the marriage fee with it.

Mr. Wood and his wife did not have a vast deal of furniture with which to begin house keeping, for their whole stock was one chair with a broken round, three table knives, three forks, three tea cups, three saucers and three plates. They sent to Pittsburgh for these articles. The reader will see that it would not do to break more than a dozen cups and saucers every time they washed dishes. We apprehend that house-wifes were then a little more careful in this matter than some are now-a-days. As already stated they had but one chair. When Mrs. Wood wanted to sit in the chair the husband would sit on the floor, and likewise, when Mr. Wood wanted to occupy the chair, his wife would occupy the floor, or a part of it at least. And yet, at what time since have people enjoyed life more than did these good old pioneers, if we were only a mind to think so? How true it is, that "Man wants but little here below, nor wants little long."

Bears and wolves were numerous in those early days. The bears committed no further depredations than carrying off the hogs of the settlers; but this act of robbery was enough to bring down bitter curses upon the shaggy criminals. Mr. Bacon, one night, heard one of his hogs squeal, and going out he saw a large bear, walking on its hind legs and carrying a good sized hog in its fore paws. The hog, perhaps, knew that Bruin was simply caressing him, but he, nevertheless, did not appreciate such outbursts of affection, and he made the forest vocal with his squealing. Before Bacon could get his gun the bear had killed his victim, and laying it down beside a log had run off, his pursuer knew not where. Bacon made a pen of logs and left a door at one side just large enough for the bear to enter, and placed the hog in this pen. He then arranged his gun, with the aid of a string, so that the contents of the weapon would be discharged at the bear the moment he should attempt to enter the enclosure. Bacon returned to his house, and in about two hours, hearing the report of the gun and going back, he found the bear stark dead, with a rifle ball through his heart.

Mr. Wood had a dog which seems to have been about as remarkable as any animal of that or later times. He bought the dog of an Indian squaw and paid a dollar for it. When we say that this dog was a strange animal we feel as if we were but very faintly expressing the idea which we would like to convey. In fact we have not the right kind of language at our command to speak in fit terms of that dog. If Mark Twain were here we would give him the job of describing him. The animal had no color to which any name has ever been given. He was of medium size and his head, in proportion to his body, was very large. His large eyes were overhung by a profusion of eyelashes which ta times rendered the gaze of the animal very repulsive. He did not possess a diversity of gifts. He was not a five talented nor yet a three talented dog. He had but one talent, that of barking. He would bark all day and he would bark all night. There was not an animal in Northfield, from a bear down to a chipmuck, at which this dog had not poured forth volumes of howls. But this was all the harm the dog would do to any creature,—just stand and bark until the animal left in disgust. Mr. Wood was one day out in the field at work when as usual he heard the dog bark. He noticed that the sound was constantly receding, and thinking that there might be some large game, and wishing to rest a little from his work, he started off in the direction of the sound. Presently he saw the dog barking at a large, long-legged, white-faced bear. The two animals were about a rod apart and each seemed to enjoy the other's company very much. As soon as the bear saw Wood it ran off, and the dog, barking of course followed at a safe distance behind. Mr. Wood, having no gun, returned to his work. Soon the dog came back and trotted up to his master, and in about ten minutes along came the bear, returning to see what had become of the dog. The dog's greatest delight was to remain somewhat quiet at night until Mr. Wood and his family were all nicely asleep, and then to go out two or three rods from the house and mounting a stump, send into heaven and into the woods and into the house some of the finest specimens of his yelps. He had to bark only for a short time before he could call up all the wolves within a circuit of five or ten miles. As soon as he was fully satisfied that he had got a sufficient number of these howling creatures started to take his place at barking for the remainder of the night, he would run under the house and remain silent and secreted until daylight. The wolves, in the meantime, would surround the house, and yelp, to the by no means infinite amusement of the occupants of the building. The dog seemed to have the idea that there must be barking of some kind all the time, and if he could get the wolves to take his place once in a while it was nobody's business. We have not heard that this dog was ever either killed or died a natural death. We are of the opinion that the dog never did die,—he just passed away. If he is yet living, either in this world or any other, he is probably still barking. We hope the people of Northfield will remember this dog. Not every township can boast of such an animal. You may forget the writer, but don't forget the dog.

Western Reserve and Northern Ohio
HISTORICAL SOCIETY.

TRACT No. 16—MAY, 1873.

List of Publications.—Annual Report, 1873.—Origin of the State of Ohio.

LIST OF PUBLICATIONS.

1870.

Tract No. 1.—Battle and massacre at River Raisin, Michigan, January 18 and 21, 1813. By Rev. Thos. P. Dudley, of Lexington, Ky., one of the survivors, 4 pages.

No. 2.—Notices of the Judges of the Supreme Court of the Territory and State of Ohio, 1788 to 1851. By Alfred T. Goodman, late Secretary, 8 pages.

No. 3.—Papers relating to the war of 1812. From the collection of the late Elisha Whittlesey, Canfield, Ohio, 4 pages.

1871.

No. 4.—First white child born in the Ohio territory. By A. T. Goodman, Secretary, 8 pages.

No. 5.—Ancient earth forts of the valley of the Cuyahoga. By Chas. Whittlesey, 40 pages illustrated by nine plates.

No. 6.—First white settlers in Ohio, and original documents from the war office. By A. T. Goodman, Secretary, 8 pages.

No 7.—Selection No. 2, from papers of Elisha Whittlesey, relating to the war of 1812, 4 pages.

No. 8.—Indian affairs around Detroit in 1706, from French archives, procured by General Cass, 6 pages.

1872-73.

No. 9.—Archeological frauds. Three remarkable forgeries, by Charles Whittlesey. 4 pages.

No. 10.—Annual meeting of the Society, Memorial notices of the late secretary, A. T. Goodman, 4 pages.

No. 11.—Rock inscriptions in Ohio, Ancient Mound, Hardin county, Ohio, Polished stone ornaments, 16 pages, illustrated by two plates.

No. 12.—Selection No. 3, papers of E. Whittlesey, war of 1812, 4 pages.

No. 13.—Papers relating to the expeditions of Colonel John Bradstreet and Colonel Henry Bouquet into Ohio in 1764. Selection No. 1, 6 pages.

No 14.—Same, selection No. 2, 6 pages.

No. 15.—Correspondence relating to the war of 1812, papers of Major George Tod, U. S. A., History of Northfield, Summit county, Ohio, by I. W. Searles.

Annual Meeting.

The annual meeting of the members of the Western Reserve and Northern Ohio Historical Society, was held in the room of the Society, in the Savings Bank building, Tuesday evening, May 13th.

OFFICERS OF THE SOCIETY.

President—Charles Whittlesey.
First Vice President—J. H. Salisbury.
Second Vice President—Vacant.
Secretary—Vacant.
Treasurer—S. Williamson.
Librarian—Mrs. M. Milford.

CURATORS ELECTIVE.

For one year—J. H. A. Bone, Samuel Williamson, Mrs. J. H. Sargent.

For two years—C. C. Baldwin, C. T. Sherman, Miss Mary C. Brayton.

For three years—Joseph Perkins, Charles Whittlesey, John W. Allen.

Ex-officio as Trustees of the Library Association—W. J. Boardman, William Bingham, James Barnett, H. M. Chapin, B. A. Stannard.

LIFE MEMBERS.

Horace Kelley,	C. F. Glaser,
T. M. Kelley,	Leonard Case,
Colgate Hoyt,	C. C. Baldwin,
Joseph Perkins,	H. B. Tuttle,
A. W. Fairbanks,	P. H. Babcock,

R. C. Parsons,	E. Cushing,
L. E. Holden,	S. V. Harkness,
A. Cobb,	A. Bradley,
George Willey,	T. S. Beckwith,
William Chisholm,	S. L. Mather,
O. A. Childs,	H. C. Blossom,
H. P. Weddell,	H. M. Chapin,
George Mygatt,	N. C. Baldwin,
A. G. Colwell,	J. H. Salisbury,
R. P. Ranney,	William Edwards,
J. P. Bishop,	William Collins,
James J. Tracy,	Amos Townsend,
W. S. Streator,	T. P. Handy,
J. H. Wade,	R. P. Wade,
J. H. Devereux,	Alfred E. Buell,
Joseph Perkins, Jr.	L. Lewis Perkins,
Douglas Perkins,	Jacob B. Perkins,
E. P. Morgan,	Miss L. T. Guilford,

Miss Mary E. Ingersoll,
Miss Sarah L. Andrews.
Eben Newton, Canfield.
Kent Jarvis, Massillon.
Wm. G. Lane, Sandusky.
George T. Perkins, Akron.

Annual Report on the Condition of the Society, May 13th, 1873.

During the past year the general progress of the Society has been satisfactory. The donations of flags, relics, maps, pamphlets, manuscripts, and articles of interest, have continued to increase as usual.

As our library is special, and intended particularly to include works relating to the early history, antiquities, and statistics of Ohio, and the Northwest, it would not be large, if it was complete. We have already on history and antiquities about two-thirds of the published works, and not having money to purchase the remainder, which are both few and scarce, we have not during the year added many to our shelves. The increase of current pamphlets has been large.

The number of visitors to the museum has at least doubled, but during a portion of the year our prospects, in a financial point of view, were quite discouraging. Our old members were more and more remiss in the payment of their annual dues, and new ones were obtained with difficulty. Our current expenses are light, but the annual receipts, are lighter still. It became evident that the museum could not be kept open to the public, on the income from memberships alone. The curators determined to advance personally what might be necessary, until the time of the annual meeting, and to appeal to our citizens to provide an irreducible endowment fund. With the annual dues of members, who are prompt in their payments, and the permanent income on $10,000, we can make the museum free to the public, and accomplish most of the leading objects of the institution. The plan of solicitation adopted, was to rely hereafter on life memberships more than upon the uncertain one of annual members. Certificates of life memberships, are issued for each sum of one hundred dollars, paid to the endowment fund; the principal of which is to be invested, by Messrs. Bingham, Bishop and Willey, as trustees. The subscribers were not to be called upon, unless $5,000 should be secured. A thorough canvass of the city has not been made, but this sum has been subscribed, and a portion of it collected. If each curator will pledge himself to secure one such membership annually, we shall soon have a sufficient and perpetual income.

This spacious fire-proof room is substantially a donation from the Society for Savings and the Cleveland Library Association.

Since the origin of the society, in the year 1867, our expenditures have not been large, as the following statement will show:

GENERAL FINANCIAL STATEMENT FROM 1867 TO DATE.

Donations from a number of gentlemen (beyond their annual dues), towards furnishing the rooms.........	$662 00
For cases for the war relics, by the Cuyahoga Co. Military Committee...	198 12
For procuring papers of the Connecticut Land Company by the County Commissioners......	200 00
For exploring the antiquities of Ohio, and publications relating to them (Tracts 5 and 11), a special donation,	1,000 00
For books, binding, and transcribing, a special donation..	963 67
Legacy of the late John F. Warner.....	500 00
Received from memberships..........	888 90
Total.......................... ...	$4 412 69

All of which has been expended. Without the endowment fund the year would have closed without debts, but also without resources, sufficient to maintain the museum as a public institution.

BIOGRAPHICAL NOTICES.

It is a part of our plan to give, from year to year, biographical notices of our members and patrons.

During the year 1871-2, an unusually large number of members were removed by death. In the current year we are advised of the loss of D. H. Pease, Esq., of Norwalk, Ohio, a valuable corresponding member, but have not the materials for a proper notice of his life. He was for many years the secretary and moving spirit of the "Fire Lands Pioneer Association."

THE MARGRY PAPERS.

For some years a correspondence has been going on by us, in connection with other societies to secure a collection of manuscripts, which are at Paris, relating to French explorations on the St. Lawrence and Mississippi, between 1680 and 1750.

Monsieur Pierre Margry has spent a long life in one of the bureaus of the French Government, and has been engaged more than twenty years in making transcripts of official reports, letters, maps and documents sent from Canada to France during that early period. They embrace all that remains, or that can be hoped for, to complete the history of those interesting times in North America. The manuscripts fill nine volumes of nine hundred pages each, which he was unable to publish, or to find a publisher. A petition originated here, suggesting to Congress the propriety of purchasing those papers. Other societies and individuals interested in historical matters, readily circulated and signed the petition, and an appropriation of $10,000 was secured.

The Hon. James Monroe, of Oberlin, gave it his active support, in which he had the assistance of many other members of Congress, in this, and in the Eastern States.

A WAR TROPHY AND OTHER RELICS.

Messrs. Foote, Moore & Co., of Detroit, in June last, signified a willingness to donate to the Society one of the large iron guns captured by Commodore Perry, in the naval action on Lake Erie, Sept. 10, 1813. On the application of Dr. E. Sterling, the Commissioners of Public Grounds advanced the expenses of transportation to Cleveland, on condition that this trophy of war be deposited on Monument Square at the base of Perry's statue, where it now lies. It is soon to be placed in a more conspicuous position. This gun, which is a 32-pounder, had been mounted on the works at Amherstburg, and was put hastily on board the British fleet, with others, to complete its armament.

A. M. Burke, Esq., of Newburg, donated to us, and delivered at his own expense, the first mill stone used in Cuyahoga county, in 1799, which the Park Commissioners have placed on the north side of the arcade, on the Square.

We shall continue to place bulky articles which are of general public interest at the disposal of the managers of the public grounds, hoping that the time may come when they will assume somewhat the character of a museum.

The Hon. George Willey has lately placed in our collection a large and convenient writing desk or secretary with numerous drawers, now in good condition, which was once the property of the famous English statesman, Edmund Burke.

The tattered battle flag of the 124th Ohio, Colonel Payne, and the flag of the 103d, with the battles through which they went have recently been deposited here.

METEORITE.

A very interesting and valuable specimen of an Ohio meteorite has been obtained, which fell in the county of Muskingum, near the village of Concord, about noon, on the 1st of May, 1860. It weighs 11 pounds, and was secured by Mr. J. Grummen, immediately after its fall. It is the fourth fragment of that meteorite, in the order of weight; the other large ones having been purchased, one by the Marietta College, Ohio, another by Yale, and a third by the Medical College at Louisville, Ky. As it approached the earth its brilliancy was almost equal to that of the sun. As usual it broke into numerous fragments, weighing from a few ounces to 130 pounds. Some of them were seen to fall, and were dug out of the ground, while they were yet warm. This is the only instance in America where a meteorite has been observed to strike the earth, and the fragments secured at once.

ROCK INSCRIPTIONS.

Our mode of copying rock inscriptions leaves no room to question their correctness hereafter, in case the originals are obliterated. It is effected by tracings on cloth full size; copied from the cloth by photograph; reduced to the exact size used by the engraver.

This subject is now engaging the attention of antiquarians in all parts of the world.

EXCHANGES AND DISTRIBUTION.

We have frequent calls for exchanges with other societies, and with individuals, which gives a money value to our duplicates. In September last, we received through the Smithsonian Institute, at Washington, a request to do something toward filling up the large and ancient Library at Strasburg, in Alsace, which was nearly destroyed during the siege. A box of surplus copies was sent there through Mr. Muckle, their agent at Philadelphia, for which a cordial acknowledgment has been received.

As the vacancy caused by the death of Mr. Goodman in the office of secretary has not been filled, Mrs. Milford has performed its duties in addition to her regular and efficient care of the room and the library, on a salary so small that I prefer not to mention the amount. Most of the lads who visit the rooms do so for good purposes and behave with propriety. We made an effort to secure for her some authority from the Board of Education, analogous to that of a teacher, which might be exercised over those who shall misbehave themselves while in the building; but in this we did not succeed. It was necessary several times to call in the aid of the police. Finally the curators were compelled to adopt a rule requiring lads under 18 years whose parents are not members or donors, to procure certificates of admission from one of the curators on request of the parents, who are held responsible for their good conduct.

Mrs. Milford has nearly completed a catalogue of our purely historical works. Our collection of articles of general interest, such as relics, coins, autographs and manuscript letters, has continued to grow steadily in size and value. It will be catalogued as soon as we have cases in which to arrange them.

THE PRESS OF THE CITY.

It is our pleasure and our duty to acknowledge our obligations to the press of this city, particularly to the Cleveland HERALD, for many favorable notices, which have been of substantial value to us.

Under our by-laws it is made the duty of the President to deliver an address at each annual meeting. I have prepared for this occasion a short article relating to an historical error as to the date from which the political existence of this State should be reckoned.

Respectfully submitted,

CHAS. WHITTLESEY, Pres't, &c.

ORIGIN OF THE STATE OF OHIO—DATE OF ITS LEGAL EXISTENCE.

It has been the practice for at least half a century to date the existence of the the State of Ohio from November 29th 1802. On that day the convention which met at Chillicothe on the first of that month, to form a State Constitution, finished its work. It had, or assumed to have, final power over the adoption of a Constitution, without the consent of the people. This made the establishment of an organic law a very speedy and very simple affair.

A large number of aspiring young men were elected to the convention, who controlled its action, and soon assumed the management of the new state. At that time there had been little experience in the formation of States. Even the Democratic element in politics, under the name of the Republican party, was strongly tinctured with British ideas of the prerogatives of office. Governor St. Clair, who was of the Federal party, differed from his opponents in the Territorial legislature, and in the convention, not so much in principle as in degree, and in the objects they wished to secure.

At present, however, we are dealing with dates, in order to correct an error which has become respectable by lapse of time, and by usage. While the Territorial government existed, it is plain the government of the State of Ohio did not exist.

No official act of the newly-organized State had any legal force until sanctioned by Congress, and until the officers of the prior government had surrendered their functions.

The breach between the last Territorial Legislature, which met at Chillicothe, Nov. 23, 1801, and Governor St. Clair, was open, bitter and personal. A majority of the members, however, were not then in favor of the project for a new State. The minority was more in earnest, as oppositions usually are, and therefore more active. They elected the Hon. Thomas Worthington to represent their views at Washington, who succeeded in committing the President and Congress to the organization of a State.

Congress, on the 30th of April, 1802, passed an act for that purpose. The delegates to form a Constitution were elected on the 12th of October following, and this being the second Tuesday of the month has permanently fixed the time for holding our Fall elections.

When they had framed and adopted a Constitution, they provided for the election of State officers and members of both Houses of the Legislature, to be held in January, 1803. Edward Tiffin was President of the Convention, which adjourned on the 29th of November.

LETTER OF THOMAS WORTHINGTON.

CITY OF WASHINGTON, Jan. 5th, 1803,

To the Honorable the President of the Senate of the United States:

SIR:—I have the honor to enclose to you herewith the Constitution of the State of Ohio, and request you will do me the favor to lay the same before the Senate of the United States.

Very Resp'y, I have the honor to be
Sir, your Ob't. Serv't,
T. WORTHINGTON,
Agent from the State of Ohio.

Jan. 5th.—Senate Journal p. 251, presented to the Senate by Vice President Burr, and a motion made for a special committee.

Jan. 6.—Committee, Messrs. Breckenridge, Anderson and Morris.

Jan. 7th.—Amended and ordered to be printed.

LETTER OF EDWARD TIFFIN.

CHILLICOTHE, Dec. 6, 1802.

To the Vice President of the United States:

Honored Sir—Enclosed you will receive an address from the Convention lately convened at this place, for the purpose of forming a constitution and State government, and which it has been made my duty to enclose to you, to be presented to the honorable body over which you preside.

With every sentiment of respect I have the honor to be your obedient servant.

EDWARD TIFFIN.

With Mr. Tiffin's letter, there was laid before the Senate an address to Congress, and the Administration which had been adopted by the Convention.

ADDRESS OF THE CONVENTION.

To the President and both Houses of Congress of the United States.

The Convention of the State of Ohio duly appreciating the importance of a free and independant State government, and impressed with sentiments of gratitude to the Congress of the United States, for the prompt and decisive measures taken, at their last session, to enable the people of the North Western Territory to immerge from their Colonial government, and to assume a rank among the sister States, beg leave to take the earliest opportunity of announcing to you this important event.

On this occasion the Convention cannot help expressing their unequivocal approbation of the measures pursued by the present administration of the General Government, and both houses of Congress in diminishing the public debt, cultivating peace with all nations, and promoting the happiness and prosperity of our country.

Resolved, That the President of the Convention do inclose to the President of the United States, to the President of the Senate, and to the Speaker of the House of Representatives of the United States, a copy of this address.

Done in Convention, November 27, 1802.

EDWARD TIFFIN, President.

THOMAS SCOTT, Sec'y. of Convention.

Received February 2, 1803, and ordered to lie on the table.

These papers are among the files of the Senate, but the files of the House of that date are not to be found. In volume 2 of the "Miscellaneous American State Papers," page 340, is a report on the same subject from Mr. Randolph, of the House, made February 3d, 1803. It apparently came up in both Houses simultaneously. In the Senate on the 27th of January, Mr. Breckinridge, from the special Committee, made the following report:

The committee to whom was referred the resolution of the 7th inst. to "inquire whether any, and if any, what legislative measures may be necessary for admitting the State of Ohio into the Union, and extending to that State the laws of the United States," report that the people of the eastern division of the territory northwest of the River Ohio, in pursuance of an act of Congress passed on the 30th day of April, 1802, entitled an act to enable the people of the eastern division of the territory northwest of the River Ohio, to form a constitution and State government and for the admission of said State into the Union on an equal footing with the original States, and for other purposes did on the 29th day of November, 1802, form for themselves a Constitution and State government; that the said Constitution and government, so formed, is Republican and in conformity with the principles contained in the articles of the ordinance, made on the 13th day of July, 1787, for the government of said territory; and that it is now necessary to establish a District Court within the said State, to carry into complete effect the laws of the United States within the same.

Passed to second reading, January 27. Senate Journal, p. 257. Read second time, January 28, 1803. Second reading resumed, January 31, and amendments offered. Ordered to be further considered February 3.

Feb. 3rd, letter of Edward Tiffin communicated and the address of the Convention received on the 5th of January, 1803, and refered to the special committee, composed of Breckinridge, Morris and Anderson.

Feb. 4, amendment withdrawn and bill passed to the third reading; February 7th, ordered to be engrossed; February 14th, message from the House that they had passed the bill.

The bill (House?) in relation to the disposition of the Public Lands in Ohio, etc. Received February 22d. Referred to a committee composed of Messrs. Breckenridge, Stone and Baldwin. Passed without amendment March 1st, 1803.

The intensity of party rancor in those days has not been exceeded in subsequent times. It was alleged that Governor St. Clair not only resisted the Administration by whom he had been appointed, and opposed its favorite project of a new State northwest of the Ohio, but that he had spoken disrespectfully of the President.

Mr. Jefferson was not inclined to deal severely with General St. Clair, but his friends in Ohio were so persistent that he yielded on the score of policy.

After the enabling act was passed and the delegates to establish a constitution had assembled at Chillicothe, St Clair was removed from office on the 22d of November, 1802. His secretary, Charles Willing Byrd, a member of the Convention, thus became the acting Governor, who performed the functions of a territorial executive until the first Legislature of Ohio assembled at Chillicothe March 3d, 1803. He then surrendered the office to Edward Tiffin, the first elective Governor. Until this act was performed there was no vitality in the State authority. Mr. Byrd was at once commissioned by President Jefferson as Judge of the United States District Court.

Thirteen other delegates to the Convention, nearly one-half of its members, received appointments or were soon elected to office under the new government.

Western Reserve and Northern Ohio
HISTORICAL SOCIETY.

CLEVELAND, O., NOV., 1873.

NUMBER SEVENTEEN.

CORRESPONDENCE OF MAJOR GEORGE TOD.
Selection No. 2—WAR OF 1812.

EBENEZER GRANGER TO MAJOR TOD.

ZANESVILLE, Feb, 27, 1812.

DEAR SIR:—I yesterday received this letter from Mr. Gideon Granger at Washington. I find that the information it contains was known in town by the Tammanies before the rising of the Legislature. I trust you will not accept a command under a trifling editor of a trifling newspaper.* If the appoinment is made agreeably to the nomination, I should not hesitate to tell Mr. President that I considered it an insult.

The Governor leaves town to-day. He says he trusts when you receive your appointment as Major you will protest it, and send it back to them. Nothing has occurred here since you left us. Your friend,

EBENEZER GRANGER.

*This refers to his appointment as Major in the Nineteenth Regiment, under John Miller, as Lieutenant Colonel.

HEADQUARTERS, LEXINGTON, KY., May 9, 1812.

SIR:—You will please to repair to this place without loss of time, to receive instructions, to enable you to commence the recruiting service in the State of Ohio.

I have written to you twice before on this subject, but not knowing the place of your residence, I fear my letters may not have reached you, I have therefore deemed it expedient to repeat my orders, and address them to you at Youngstown, where, I am since informed, that you reside. I am respectfully, sir, your obedient servant.

J. WINCHESTER,
B. Gen'l., United States Army.

Major George Tod, Youngstown, Ohio,
United States Army.

WARREN, July 28, 1812.

Major George Tod, Zanesville, O.:

SIR—Within I have returned you the number of recruits, since my last weekly report. The progress of recruiting in the State, I am apprehensive, moves slowly; arising in a great measure, I presume, from the number of volunteers furnished by the State of Ohio. I have not heard from Lieut. Fredericks or Milligan for sometime. I concluded it would be most advisable for Ensign Milligan to recruit in Jefferson county, and establish his rendezvous at Cadiz, from which place I directed him to report to you at Zanesville weekly. I also gave the same directions to Lieut. Fredericks, of Lisbon, to report weekly, and furnished them with blank forms.

Y'rs respectfully,
WILSON ELLIOTT,
Capt. U. S. Army.

CHILICOTHE, July 30, 1812.

Major Geo. Tod, Zanesville, O.:

DEAR SIR—I do myself the pleasure of enclosing you forms of subsistance and pay accounts. My motive in so doing is, that I expect that they will be both acceptable and serviceable to you, as you probably will not be able to procure forms of the kind in Zanesville.

I am with much respect,
Your ob't servant,
JOHN MILLER.

CINCINNATI, July 31, 1812.

MAJOR TOD—Dear Sir: Enclosed is $400 in Chilicothe and Marietta bank, notes which I received for the Kentucky notes and checks that you gave me to exchange. Please acknowledge the receipt of them. Our little town has a hundred and thirty-six men now, with General Hull, besides contractors, sutlers, wagoners, quartermasters, &c., &c., followers of the army. We are now called on for 114 more, to be drafted and held in readiness to march at a moment's notice. This will make 250 men from Cincinnati, exclusive of the followers of our little army. Our last returns of the militia of this place was 526 privates, and 593 including officers. These were no doubt some invalids and some transient people, of course. Our present call, including what is on duty now, takes every other man in town on the rolls. So much for *correct heads*. It is certainly a great hardship, and a very great injury to our place; more so than all those *heads* will be worth if they live to be old as Methusalah.

I am respectfully, dear sir,
Your friend and most ob't serv't,
WM. STANLEY.

RENDEZVOUS ORDERS.

ZANESVILLE, August 1, 1812.

The non-commissioned officers and privates at the barracks are required, when not on parade to salute all commissioned officers whenever they meet them by raising the right hand as high as the eyes, with palm of the hand turned toward the officer. They are never to come into a room where there are any commissoned officers but with hats off. Soldiers on duty, when having arms in their hands, without any command, on the approach of a commissioned officer, will carry their arms. Any soldier or other person belonging to the barracks, who shall be found drunk or intoxicated with liquor, when called on parade shall be immediately arrested by the officer or non-com missioned officer commanding on parade and put in confinement, and as soon as the parade has been dismissed, such offenders shall forthwith be reported to the Major or other commanding officer at the rendezvous.

The Major hopes these orders will be attended to with cheerfulness. If not, offenders will be punished.

GEORGE TOD,
Major U. S. Army.

RENDEZVOUS ORDERS.

Zanesville, Aug. 1st, 1812

On Sunday August 2d the non-commissioned officers and privates at the barracks will repar to the court house at 11 o'clock in the morning, for the purpose of attending divine worship, clothes clean, and heads powdered—without arms, but attended with drum and fife. The conduct of *all* must be decent and orderly.

GEORGE TOD,
Major U. S. Army.

CADIZ 2d, August 1812.

Major Tod, U. S. Army, Zanesville, O.

HONORED SIR—These few lines are to inform you that I this day received a letter from Captain Elliott, directing me to send on what recruits I had with Lieut. Booker to Zanesville, but Mr. Booker has gone on, and I am at a loss to know what to do. I have seven with my sergeant, but I should be glad for him to stay with me. You will please to send me some instructions by the bearer. He tells me he is going on for clothing, and if I am to keep my recruits any length of time, I should be glad if I could get a suit apiece for them. I think I could make much better progress recruiting. With respect, I am,

Your obedient servant,
JAMES MILLIGAN,
Ensign U.S. Army.

RENDEZVOUS CHILLICOTHE,
August 4th, 1812.

Major G. Tod, U.S. Army, Zanesville, Ohio:

SIR: Since my last letter to you of the 28th ult. I have received a second order from General Winchester to name and organize officers sufficient for two companies, in addition to those already called for, and to forward him a list of their names without delay. You will therefore please to name in addition to the first and second Lieutenants already ordered, one captain, one second Lieutenant and one ensign in your district, and forward their names to me by return of mail. You will hold them in readiness to march as soon as men enough are recruited to form a second company.

General Winchester urges the immediate organization of the company already called for. You will therefore make every exertion to have your detachment here as soon as possible. The Kentucky troops are expected to be at Urbanna about the 10th or 12th of this month, and I have wrote General Winchester that I expect to be ready to march the company ordered from this State about that time.

I am, very respectfully,
Your obedient servant,
JOHN MILLER,
Lieutenant Colonel U. S. Army.

RENDEZVOUS, CHILLICOTHE,
August 5, 1812.

Major Tod, U. S. A., Zanesville, O.:

SIR: I have this moment received yours of the 4th inst., and am glad to learn that you will be able to march the detachment required from your district, to this place, against Sunday next. I received a letter from General Winchester this day, in which he urges me to have the company ready to march immediately. If the number of recruits at your rendezvous should not exceed 35 on Sunday morning next, you need not wait longer for others to come in; but should you have 40, the number before asked for, you will please to send them on. Lieut. Van Horn, the bearer of this, arrived here last evening (express) from our army in Upper Canada. He will give you an account of what is going on in that quarter.

I am, very respectfully yours,
JOHN MILLER,
Lieut. Col. U. S. Army.

HEADQUARTERS,
LEXINGTON, KY., Aug. 8, 1812.

SIR: Your communications of the 29th of June and of the 29th of July are before me. The first came to this place in due time, in my absence though; and was mislaid, or it would have been sooner replied to. The order in which you propose to make your reports and returns meets my approbation—so does your contract for barracks, and the employment of a physician. The price of rations I think high, but if they could not be had for less it is justifiable. Is there is no agent for the contractor in your district? If there is he ought to be called on to supply the rations.

The course you have taken with the clothing is correct, and according to usage in such cases.

The latter covering a weekly report which exhibits honorable progress in the recruiting service; I rejoice to learn your recruits in point of discipline, are in your opinion equal to any under my command. Discipline and subordination are essentials not to be dispensed with in an efficient army.

Arms you shall be supplied with soon after the detachment for Detroit marches, which is to rendezvous at Newport, on the 20th inst., and will march as soon as equipped. When I can ascertain precisely the time that the line of march will commence at Cincinnati, I shall order Col. Miller to march the Ohio company from from Chilicothe, so as to fall in with the main detachment at Urbanna.

The application of, and expense for powder, on the occasion you mention was entirely proper andjustifiable in my opinion.

I some time ago wrote to Colonel Miller for a list of the names and grades of the officers of three companies, which is the proportion for the State of Ohio, for the first regiments to be formed and marched to Detroit. He informed me the list was delayed for the officers from your district. I hope it is on its way before now.

I am, with high respect,
Your ob't servant.
J. WINCHESTER,
Brig. Gen. U. S. Army.

P. S. You will herewith receive a form for a monthly return, which you will adopt instead of that received at this place. By order of the General.

J. OVERTON, A. D. C.

Major George Tod, U. S. Army, Zanesville, State of Ohio.

CANTON, STARK CO., O.,
Aug. 9th, 1812.

SIR:—Agreeable to your orders of 2nd inst., I have sent all the recruits I have, which are four, with the Sergt. Jere. Mead, viz: Saml. Sheller, Frederick Swaney. Robert Hannah, Artillerists, and James McMahon, who is intended for Infantry. He has been unwell with a wound received on his leg but has recovered. Since last return one has died Hezekiah Dodge. I will now repair to Steubenville, and prepare for recruiting there. I hope you will send the Serg't there. I would have started prior to this, but the men was unwell (two of them) which prevented me. If I had some uniform clothing to dress the Sergt. in, and one or two suits, I could come more speed recruiting.

I will forward an account of each man by next mail. I am in want of money.

I am Sir, Respectfully your
Ob't Serv't JAS. H. LARWILL,
1st Lieut. U. S. Army.

Major Geo. Tod, Zanesville.

Per Sergt. JERE. MEAD.

RENDEZVOUS, CHILLICOTHE,
August 27, 1812.

Major G. Tod, U. S. Army, Zanesville, O.

SIR—You will as soon as possible, order Captain Wilson Elliott on to this place with all the recruits belonging to the infantry in your district. It is the wish of General Winchester, to have the second company ordered from the State, organized, and march immediately. If you can send forty or fifty recruits from your district, I presume the balance can be made up in this without any difficulty.

I presume you have heard ere now of the dastardly conduct of Hull in delivering up our whole army to the British, without even firing a gun, to a very inferior force. It is certainly one of the most disgraceful transactions that ever fell to the lot of this or any other country.

You will also send on with Capt. Elliott, a 2d Lieutenant and Ensign. If you have clothing to spare I would be glad you would send on in the baggage wagon twenty privates' hats, forty shirts, and forty pairs of overalls, as we are entirely out of those articles here. I am, very respectfully, your obedient servant,

JOHN MILLER,
Lieut. Col. U. S. Army.

ZANESVILLE, September 2nd, 1812.

Major Tod, U. S. Army;

SIR: General Winchester has wrote you another letter, in answer I suppose to the last communications before you left this place, particularly calling your attention to recruiting officers with respect to their returns, accounts and reports. And also another letter by last mail from Col. Miller, ordering the second detachment, under the command of Capt. Wilson Elliott, to march as soon as possible. I have wrote to Captain Elliott by this mail. I know nothing as to his subalterns, what their names are, or where they live. Col. Miller requests to send him, with the party, a quantity of clothing. Sir, if it suited you I would be glad if you could be here before the detachment marched. I am entirely out of money, and have been for some time. I have enlisted one since I wrote. The strength of the party at present is thirty-two. Ensign Harrison is at Chillicothe at present, and will continue there, until the men march. This two weeks and some better, there has been great stir among the people in this place, in consequence of the disgraceful conduct of General Hull. Col. McArthur, with a number of soldiers and officers, has arrived at this place. In the course of last week, there marched from this place, about three hundred militia, and about double that number marches this day.

With due respect,
Your humble servant,
JAMES HERRON,
Captain U. S. Army.

RENDEZVOUS, CHILICOTHE,
Sept. 11, 1812.

MAJOR G. TOD—Sir: I had the pleasure to receive yours of the 6th inst. last evening. I wish you to cause all the troops that are at Zanesville, to be marched to this place against the 18th or 20th of the month at fartherest. If you can possibly send 40 or 60 men against that time, I shall be glad, as I believe there will be some difficulty in making up the 2nd company.

You will place 2nd Lieut. David Morris on the recruiting service in your district and I expect to be under the necessity of ordering several other officers to report themselves to you in a short time for that purpose. As all the officers belonging to the 19th regiment, who have resided in other States, have been ordered by Gen'l Winchester to report to me.

I am with much respect,
Your ob't serv't,
JOHN MILLER,
Col. 19th Reg't U. S. Infantry.

RENDEZVOUS, CHILLICOTHE,
Sept. 25, 1812.

DEAR SIR: I have the satisfaction to inform you that the detachment sent on from Zanesville by you, under the care of Capt. Elliott, arrived here in good health, on Monday last. They are a fine looking set of men, and for the time well disciplined.

I had the pleasure of receiving your letter of the 21st inst. by last mail; also the return of the troops.

Since my letter to you of the —— inst., directing you, by order of Genl. Winchester, to transmit your weekly reports, monthly returns, &c., &c., to the Adjutant Genl's office, I have been informed by the Adjutant Genl, that the recruiting service in future is to be conducted by the Colonel or a field officer of each regiment. You will therefore, in consequence of this arrangement, transmit me a weekly report, agreeably to the form enclosed, and monthly returns, agreeably to the form furnished by Genl Winchester—noting on the return, the men belonging to or * * by each Capt. and his subalterns. My understanding of the Adjutant Genl's instructions is, that the field officers who superintend the principal recruiting districts, are to advance money to none but Captains and Lieutenants, who are charged with the inferior recruiting districts, who will advance to their subaltern officers—consequently field officers will not receive weekly reports, monthly returns, &c., recruiting officers' accounts, from none but those they * * money to, leaving the subaltern officers to report to the Capts. or Lieutenants who are charged with recruiting. This appears to me to be the proper mode of doing business, as it leaves to each grade of officers their proportionate share.

I am desired by the Adjutant Genl to forward him complete returns of all the troops that have been enlisted in this State, I am therefore under the necessity of requesting you to furnish me with copies of all your monthly returns, since the commencement of the recruiting service. I wish you to do so as soon as circumstances will permit.

In obedience to orders, also from the Adjutant Genl, the troops here will not be marched until further orders. Capt. Elliott and Ensign Harrison will return to Zanesville in a few days to resume the recruiting service, but I have every reason to believe that it will not be long before they are ordered out, as very active preparations are now making to push on the second campaign with vigor.

I wish you to forward me the recruiting officers' accounts, as you receive them so that I may forward them to the Adjutant Genl, as requested.

You will in future draw money of me to carry on the recruiting service, but I am unfortunately entirely destitute of funds at present. I have sent Capt. Moore to Genl Winchester, now at Piqua, for the purpose of drawing money; should he succeed I will forward you some by Capt. Elliott. If you nor Capt. Herron have not drawn you will please to forward your accounts to me, and I will endeavor to obtain it for you, as I have frequent opportunities of sending to Cincinnati.

I should be very glad to have an opportunity of conversing with you, and hope soon to have the pleasure of seeing you either in this place or Zanesville. Our officers at this time wear a very gloomy aspect indeed, but I trust that the patriotism and bravery of our countrymen and the Congress of the Government when brought properly into action, will soon regain what we have lost, both in property and character. I believe all would have gone on well, and we would now have been in possession of Upper Canada, had it not been for the atrocious and disgraceful conduct of Hull. His name is a disgrace to the American character, and I trust he is the only man in the nation who would be capable of doing such an act.

I am very respectfully your ob't servt,
JOHN MILLER,
Col. 19th regt U. S. Infantry.

N. B. Since commencing writing the above I have received orders from Genl Winchester to cause Lieut. Larwill and the troops under his command to be marched to Piqua as soon as possible, where he will join Capt. Cushing of the artillery. I wish you to order him on as soon as practicable. Genl Winchester writes very pressingly. Lieutenant Larwill's troops will be furnished here with clothing. J. M.

Major George Tod, U. States Army, Zanesville, O.

RENDEZVOUS, ZANESVILLE, Oct. 5, 1812.

DEAR SIR—Your communication under date of the 25th ultimo came to hand, to-morrow will be a week. It gave me no small satisfaction to learn from you that the detachment from this, under the command of Capt. Elliott, met your expectations—I mean as to discipline. I would have been glad had its numbers been greater * * * * *

I am, dear sir, very respectfully,
Your ob't. servant,
George Tod, Maj. U. S. A.

Col. John Miller.

FRANKLINTON, Nov. 12, 1812.

SIR: I wish you to send me as much casamere as will make two pair of overhalls. There is superfine blue at Mr. Price's, at four dollars per yard. Capt. Elliott got of it. I wish to have of the same kind and the trimmings, & in so doing, you will oblige.

Your most humble servant,
B. C. HARRISON

P. S. You will have a opportunity of sending it by the post. I expect the troops will march shortly from this place. Genl Harrison arrived here last evening from Delaware. I expected to have returned to Zanesville before I marched, but it was out of my power. I wish you to pay Mr. Burnam for the hire of his horse, three dollars and fifty cents.

B. C. HARRISON.

Major Geo. Tod.

MERCER, PA., Jan. 1st, 1813.

DEAR SIR: * * * &c. I suppose your situation enables you to hear and see all the news. I hope we shall have a different account from Harrison and his brave comrades in arms, than we have had heretofore from other Generals. I am almost ashamed to think of our northern army and acknowledge them as Americans. There is not a day passes but what more or less of the troops from Black Rock passes through this place. They give various accounts. It is difficult to know the real truth, but all agree to fix the blame on Smythe. One thing is certain, that they are much to blame for leaving so much publick property exposed to the British and their savage allies. There must be something "rotten in the state of Denmark." Time will give us the true state of the circumstances. I shall be happy to hear from you occasionally. Accept my warmest wishes for your health and happiness.

Yours, B. PEARSON.

Major George Tod, Chillicothe, Ohio.

EXTRACT FROM GENERAL ORDERS OF 9TH FEB 1813.

"HEADQUARTERS FOOT OF MIAMI RAPIDS.

"A detachment consisting of Captain Langham's Company of the 19th Regiment, U. S. Infantry, & Captain McRea's Volunteers, under the command of Major George Tod."

"This detachment to be under the command of Brigadier General Perkins, who will apply to Headquarters for Orders. The men are to be furnished with one day's rations, exclusive of this day's, *ready cooked.*"

Major Tod requests Captain Langham & Capt. McRae, to have their companies paraded on their respective parade grounds at retreat beat this evening, for the purpose of marching, &c. The orders expressed in the above extract are to be complied with.

GEO. TOD, Major, Com'g the
above named Companies,
Feb. 9th, 1813, in Camp &c.

GOV. MEIGS TO MAJOR TOD.

CHILICOTHE, Feb. 14, 1813.

DEAR MAJOR—Nothing new here—the Legislature on Tuesday last—the 20,000 (one years men law) have passed; M'Arthur, Cass & Findlay alone are exchanged—no others

Give my best regards to Gen. Tupper & Perkins, Col. Rayne and Maj. Whittlesey. Write me every thing by the return of the express. I lament with you the death of Col. J. S. Edward.

God bless you.
R. J. MEIGS.

(Endorsed) "Governor Meigs' letter, Feb. 14, 1813, Rec'd at Fort Meigs."

Western Reserve and Northern Ohio
HISTORICAL SOCIETY.

CLEVELAND, O., NOV., 1873.

NUMBER EIGHTEEN.

WAR CORRESPONDENCE—NORTHERN FRONTIER—1812.
Selection No. 6.

ORDERS AND INSTRUCTIONS TO CALVIN PEASE.

HEAD QUARTERS,
CAMP AT CLEAVELAND,
Aug. 28th, 1812.

CALVIN PEASE, Esq.

Sir: You are hereby ordered & instructed to repair with all convenient speed to the middle or western parts of this state, to ascertain what number of troops are raised, or about to be raised, where stationed & by whom commanded, to gain all possible information respecting the forces of this State & of the United States & of the enemy, to ascertain the best route for a line of communication from this camp to such other camps or posts as shall be established, & confer with the commanding officers of posts upon the means of establishing such line of communication until the commander in Chief shall give orders respecting the same, and transmit to me at my Head Quarters without delay such information as you shall obtain.

You are hereby authorised if necessary to impress any horses necessary for this service & the citizens of this State are requested to afford the said Calvin Pease all necessary assistance; & all Military Officers are requested to give him full credence in the premises.

ELIJAH WADSWORTH,
Majr. Genl. 4th Division Ohio Militia.

GENERAL PERKINS TO COL. WILLIAMS OR MAJOR KREUTZER.

CAMP AT HURON, Sept. 8, 1812.

GENTLEMEN—I wrote you yesterday that no appearance of the enemy had been discovered since our arrival at this station and thinking *that* information may cause you to be less rapid in your movements than you would otherwise have been, I now send Express to you to inform you that the spies sent out yesterday from this camp have returned this morning, with information that the Indians and British are in considerable numbers at Sandusky; that they have burned the public store & Block house, which buildings were on fire when the spies were in sight of them. I am making arrangements to send a force to Sandusky, which will march early to-morrow morning; & as it is possible the enemy may be more than equal to the whole of my detachment, I must beg you to progress with your troops as fast as may be done with safety to yourselves & provisions; but if you should think proper to proceed without your waggons, either a part or the whole of your men, shall be supplied here until your provisions may arrive.

The bearer Mr. Cook will give you such further information on the subject as will be required to enable you to adapt your movements to the importance of the object.

I am gentlemen,
Most respectfully yours.
SIMON PERKINS, Brig Genl.

Presuming you have some direct way of communicating with the Governor, and not knowing myself the chain of communication through your country, I must trust to you to give him such information, as you receive from me and deem of importance to him. S. P.

GENERAL PERKINS TO GENERAL WADSWORTH

HURON, Sept. 10, 1812.

MAJR. GENL. WADSWORTH.

Sir: The bearer Ezekiel Bunkers & his Brother David, Aliens to the United

States, have come out in my detachment expecting that by fighting the Battles of the United States, they might obtain citizenship; but being informed to the contrary they are anxious to return home; & from former acquaintance with them & from information now received by other gentlemen of their acquaintance I am convinced of the truth of their statement: & doubting the propriety of detaining aliens in the army to fight against the government that they have thought proper to flee from, I have granted them a furlough, to go to Head Quarters—& trust you will give them such an order as the nature of their case may merit

I am Sir most respectfully yours
SIMON PERKINS.

GENERAL WADSWORTH TO GENERAL FINDLEY.

HEAD QUARTERS,
CLEAVELAND, Sept. 10, 1812.

General Findley:

SIR: I think it of the utmost importance to the military service of the country that you should proceed to Niagara and communicate to the officers commanding on that station verbally, and I deem it my duty to request you to go there and also to see General Dearborn if practicable, in a short period of time. With my best wishes that your journey may be highly conducive to the safety of your country, I am sir with respect yours,

ELIJAH WADSWORTH,
Maj. Gen. Fourth Division Ohio Militia.

GENERAL WADSWORTH TO GENERAL PERKINS.

(Without date, probably September 10th, 1812, at Cleveland.)

Sir:—This moment I had the misfortune to learn by an express from you, that our brave citizens who are stationed to the westward are in rather a precarious situation. To remedy the evils that appears to surround them I shall forward on from this place all the men that can be fitted for duty immediately—the Detachment under the command of Genl. Beall will be on as soon as possible; likewise all the odd Battalion, a part of which will be mounted on Horseback; these forces united I trust will be sufficient to ensure to us the possession of the Station at Huron—

Respectfully ELIJAH WADSWORTH,
Major General.

EXTRACT FROM A LETTER TO MAJOR GENERAL WADSWORTH.

"My detachment is very considerably depreciating in consequence of sickness, &c. In consequence of arrangements yesterday, I could not send to the Peninsula, but am now about to send 20 men to obtain & bury the dead." Yours,

SIMON PERKINS.
Camp at Huron, Sept. 18, 1812.

GENERAL PERKINS TO GENERAL WADSWORTH, CLEVELAND, O.

CAMP AT HURON, Sept. 11th 1812

SIR—Yours of the 9th is rec'd & although I have no disposition to disrespect orders, yet presuming that you have not been rightly informed of the situation I have selected for my encampment, I have requested Col. Austin the bearer who is well informed in regard to it, to inform you, & any order that is given shall govern me.

I apprehend that you have not had correct information of the strength of my detachment. We have now only about 250 effective men Officers included, & their number fast decreasing by sickness &c, at least 3 or 4 per day, & unless I have soon some addition to my present force I shall be unable to defend a very small number of Block Houses, much less to build new ones. I have no new recruits from this county. Many of the men particularly those of Parkers & Murrays companies remind me of the time of their service being almost out & that they will expect them to be discharged; the time for which many of them volunteered their services was three weeks & they are not by law liable to do military duty. My returns shall be made out & forwarded by the next mail. I am Sir respectlully Your

Most Humble Svt,
SIMON PERKINS,
Brigadier Genl.

GENERAL PERKINS TO GENERAL E. WADSWORTH, CLEVELAND,

CAMP AT HURON, Sept. 12, 1812

SIR: I wrote you yesterday by Col. Austin & by him you will receive full information of my proceedings. I will, however, state to you some of the leading causes that have induced me to pursue the courses that I have from time to time adopted. You will no doubt recollect that when I came here my expectation was to have with me a full Regiment & those well provided. The draft from Jefferson County, and a detachment from Col. Rayens Regiment was to make in addition to those now with me, the Corps, & it was not until the receipt of your order of the 6th inst. which came to hand late on 8th that I was informed of a different course of arrangement. You will no doubt be able to judge whether I can protect this part of the country, with a detachment of about 250 effective men, on the frontier of a powerful & numerous enemy at least 45 or 50 miles in advance of any aid or succour. I have cautiously concealed from my men the number of the force with me, & they have been led to believe that there is 400 that being the No. of which it was said this detachment consisted when we crossed the Cuyahoga. The troops from the south I cannot procure any information from. I have written twice by men from that part of the country who engaged to hand my letter to the officers; I have also sent an express & from all this I have no return.

Returns of the companies have been ordered as by your directions, but I cannot by this mail perfect one to send on; it shall be attended to & forwarded as soon as possible. The Captains have been so much occupyed & their accommodations and conveniences for that duty so imperfect, that I have not been able to procure a return from them all; a return from five companies gives their effective strength—314 with 30 sick—One company I have no return from.

I am, sir, very respectfully yours,

SIMON PERKINS,
Brigadier Genl.

GENERAL WADSWORTH TO GENERAL PERKINS.

HEAD QUARTERS, CLEAVELAND,
September 15th, 1812.

DEAR SIR—Genl. Wadsworth has concluded to send two full companies to your assistance from Col. Rayens Regiment which will set out tomorrow. He earnestly wishes that the property at Sandusky may be brought away if practicable. He would suggest the propriety of sending a force by land to protect the boats. He wishes a Block house built at the place we viewed up the river, to which remove all your stores—& as soon as this shall be complete erect another Block house at the mouth of the River. He will himself repair to the Portage to receive the arms, with the rest of his men & proceed westward. He is in hopes soon to see from his Division 1500 men in service organized in the Regiments, for which purpose he requests you to come to Cleveland at Head Quarters, to receive orders for the raising of your quota; when you will be permitted to return home to arrange your business & prepare for the winter's campaign. The length of time for your absence will be agreed upon here. He is extremely anxious that the Block Houses be immediately erected; not interfering however with securing the property at Sandusky, but without attending to stockading. You will charge Col. Hayes to execute the views of the General in the above particulars—on whom the command will devolve in your absence; trusting that every exertion will be made by him, his Officers & Soldiers for the defence of our coyntry.

The General wishes you to draft in future your furloughs for a definite term of time; or if the men are so far diseased as not to be able to join the troops to give them a discharge. As you now draft them the men will be entitled to draw pay for the term of six months whether they are ordered to rejoin the army or not.

By order of Majr. Genl. WADSWORTH,
ELISHA WHITTLESY, Aid De Camp.

COLONEL EDWARDS TO COLONEL HAYES.

WARREN, Sept. 22 1812.

DR. SIR—I have ten miles west of Sandusky Bay 400 bushels of wheat, which from its situation has probably escaped the general destruction; if it should be prudent to send for it I wish it might be done; and should be glad if you would furnish the necessary guard. My interest & the public are concerned in that quantity of wheat being at this time saved.—it is about eighty rods north of Ramsdales house. Seth Doan of Capt. Murrays company will know where it is—I have no doubt that a sufficient number of men can be readily obtained from Capt. Dulls company for a guard—cannot the men in Capt Bissells company that belong to my regiment, be attached to Capt. Dulls Company. I have no news to communicate; friends are generally well. With my best wishes for your success and the men under your command,

I remain your friend,
JOHN S. EDWARDS.

Col. Richard Hayes.

GENERAL PERKINS TO COLONEL HAYES HURON.

WARREN, TUESDAY EVENING
22nd Sept. 1812

COLONEL HAYES. SIR:—I arrived at the place of date this day about 2 o'clock at noon That you may see how election &c. ripens I send you the papers of this & the last week,

I notice that Mr, Webb (Ed of the *Trump of Fame*) has given an account of the detachment at the Peninsula having been commanded by Majr Austin & fearing that Lieut. Allen would think it possible that I had made to Mr. Webb the communication from which he had recieved his information, I will thank you to present my compliments to him & inform him that that was not the case; but since it has got into the newspapers & the story half told, I will for the next weeks paper prepare the story correctly told with Lieutenant Allen the commandant

Nothing new since I left you more than you will learn by the N. Papers. I expect to return next week, or leave home next week. The sick Moses, got to Cleaveland about as quick as I did. I wrote you from Cleaveland: do let me hear from you by the next mail. My respects to all.

SIMON PERKINS.

MEMORANDUM BY E. WHITTLESEY—GENERAL SIMON PERKINS TO COLONEL RICHADR HAYES.

Mr. Webb having published that the detachment to the Peninsula was commanded by Maj'r Austin, whereas it was commanded by Lieut Allen.

This could not have been the detachment to the Peninsula, to look after Mr. Edwards wheat, as that was commanded by Capt. Cotton & was subsequent to this.

Lieut. Allen I think commanded a detachment to Cunninghams Island & burnt a British vessel. ELISHA WHITTLESY.
June 1st, 1860.

EXTRACTS FROM THE TRUMPS OF FAME

WARREN, Ohio, SEPT. 23, 1812.

"Genl. Wadsworth we are told has removed his Head Quarters from Cleaveland to the Portage between the Cuyahoga & the Tuskarawas branch of the Muskingum after having sent a reenforcement to Genl. Perkins at Huron. The object of this movement we are told is to open a more direct communication between Pittsburgh and Sandusky & to facilitate the transportation of cannon & military stores to the Michigan Territory.'

GENERAL S. PERKINS TO GENERAL WADSWORTH, OLD PORTAGE.

(Sept. 29, 1812, apparently from Cleveland.)

Sir:—This will be handed in by Mr. Leslie who will give you information of the misfortune at the Peninsula. I shall go to Huron as soon as I can get under way the company here; I came here last evening & found Capt. Reed with some as he says bad arms many not fit for use—no powder ball or cartridges, but I have purchased 94 lbs. powder 116 lbs. lead which I am manufacturing into cartridges. I believe I shall be able to procure for each man a flint, but very few if any smare arms. This company has not a cartridge box; could not you send on some immediately. I shall expect that you will send out to Col Hayes by the southern route what succour he can have from you; & it will be important that he be provided for immediately. If a considerable force cannot be immediately sent out I would suggest to you the propriety of a a retreat; you will no no doubt think with me that it is not prudent to keep those few men there to fall gloriously; & as to any relief from the first or second Brigade I feel now as I have told you, that I have not any dependence on them Any further information I must refer you to Mr. Leslie for

I am Sir Yours
SIMON PERKINS

SECOND LETTER OF GENERAL PERKINS TO GENERAL WADSWORTH.

September 29th, 1812.

SIR: Will it not be well to march the men that you do not send across the woods to secure Col. Hayes retreat (if he should be reduced to that necessity) back to Cleaveland. If the enemy learns that there is no force on the lake shore will they not think that we have left it from fear.

I am Sir. yos.
SIMON PERKINS

I shall expect to hear from you as soon as possible.

Genl. Wadsworth Portage.

GENERAL PERKINS TO GENERAL WADSWORTH.

Monday morning Sep 30th 1812.

SIR—The inclosed gives you information of ill fortune at Huron & around here last evening, and find the company now at this place is entirely destitute of every thing but arms & those are as they say much out of repair. Be so good as to forward to the relief of Col. Hayes all the men in your power & I would suggest to you the propriety of recalling the remainder of the troops at Huron unless they can be respectably reinforced. I shall forward with all that can be provided with the needful as soon at possible for them.

I am, sir, yours, SIMON PERKINS.
Genl. Wadsworth.

EXTRACT FROM THE TRUMP OF FAME.

WARREN, OCTOBER 7th, 1812.

To the Commandant at Cleaveland.

SIR—I arrived at camp last evening and find that the engagement on the Peninsula has proved less unfortunate than was at first apprehended—our loss are six killed & ten wounded; the wounded are mostly very slight & none I think mortal.

The names of the killed are James S. Bills, Simon Blackman, Daniel Mingusa Abraham Simons —— Ramsdale, —— Mason. Wounded are Samuel Mann, Moses Eldrige, Jacob French, Samuel B. Tanner John Carlton, John McMahon, Elias Sperry James Jack, a Mr. Lee an inhabitant of this neighborhood &c. Mr Ramsdale also of this vicinity. Knowing the anxiety of the inhabitants at the eastward I detain the messenger no longer than to write the above & am

Sir Yours
SIMON PERKINS

P. S. Our men fought well & the Indians suffered very considerably.

Camp at Avery Huron County October 3d 1812

Western Reserve and Northern Ohio HISTORICAL SOCIETY.

CLEVELAND, O., NOV., 1873.

NUMBER NINETEEN.

BIOGRAPHICAL NOTICES AND CORRESPONDENCE—WAR OF 1812. Selection No. 7.

Biographical Notices.

It will add something to the interest of this correspondence relating to the War of 1812, on this frontier, to have a brief notice of the authors of many of the letters:

MAJOR GENERAL ELIJAH WADSWORTH,

[Commanding Fourth Division Ohio Militia.]

Though born at Hartford, Connecticut, November 4, 1747, he was a resident of Litchfield, in the same State, when the Revolutionary War broke out. He was a Lieutenant in Captain Benjamin Tallmadge's troop of horse, in Colonel Elisha Sheldon's regiment, serving to the end of the war with honor. Like many Revolutionary heroes, he obtained little promotion. Tallmadge's promotion to be Major allowed Wadsworth to be Captain, beyond which he did not rise. Major Andre was placed in his custody soon after his arrest by Williams, Paulding and Van Wert, on the 23d of September, 1780. In 1802 Mr. Wadsworth removed to Canfield, then in Trumbull county, Ohio, where he owned largely of wild lands. In 1804 he was elected by the Ohio Legislature to be Major General of the Fourth Division, embracing the Northeastern part of the State. The promptness, perseverance and patriotism displayed in this command, at the outset of the war of 1812, may be inferred from this correspondence. He was long embarrassed by personal debts, contracted for the Government in raising supplies for the troops. He died at Canfield, on the 30th of December, 1817; where his grave is marked by an appropriate stone.

BRIGADIER GENERAL SIMON PERKINS.

[Commanding 3d Brigade, 4th Division, O. M.]

General Perkins came to Ohio in 1798 as an agent, explorer, and surveyor of lands on the Western Reserve; being then an energetic young man of 27 years. Surveyors, engineers and explorers are the material of which first-class military men are formed. In 1804 he settled at Warren, in Trumbull county, and was appointed postmaster. By General Wadsworth's influence be was commissioned as Brigadier in 1808, our relations with Great Britain having already given premonitions of trouble. When the war occurred, he was at full maturity of mind and body; and having the unlimited confidence of General Wadsworth, was immediately entrusted with the troops and posts at the front. When the term of service of the Ohio volunteers had expired, and their place was filled by the new regiments of the regular army, he was offered a Colonelcy in the United States Infantry. On account of the care of a growing landed estate this was declined, much to the regret of General Harrison and the administration, who were sadly in need of good officers. General Perkins died at Warren on the 19th of November, 1844.

GENERAL JAMES WINCHESTER, U. S. A.

Winchester had been a Lieutenant in the army of the Revolution, from the State of Maryland. Having been a prisoner about two years, he probably had no affection for England, and Englishmen. On the 27th of March, 1812, President Madison appointed him a Brigadier from the State of Tennessee, in the army being then raised in anticipation of war. While in command on the Maumee River, in January, 1813, contrary to Harrison's views, he sent a detachment to the river Raisin or French Town, where is now the city of Monroe, in the State of Michigan. The dreadful results of that mistake are well known, for they have not yet ceased to be a horror in the minds of Americans. He was captured by an Indian, stripped while standing in the snow, and taken to Malden as a prisoner of war. After being exchanged, the command of Fort Defiance, on the Maumee, was given to him; but the Government and the people had lost confidence in his military ability, and in March, 1815, he resigned. He died at Nashville, Tenn., July 27th, 1826.

COLONEL JOHN MILLER, U. S. A.

John Miller, of Steubenville, Ohio, was one of the Brig'er Generals of Militia, and the editor of a newspaper when the prospect of war required an increase of the army. In March, 1812, he was appointed Lieutenant Colonel of the 17th Infantry, of which Samuel Wells, of Kentucky, was Colonel. In July he was promoted to be Colonel of the 19th Infantry. Col. Miller commanded the sortie from Fort Meigs, May 5th, 1813, driving the British from their battery on the southeast of the fort. In February, 1818, he resigned, and returned to his paper, the *Western Herald*, at Steubenville. In 1826 he was appointed Register in a land office in Missouri, was soon elected Governor of that State, and from 1837 to 1843 was in Congress. He died at Florissant, Missouri, March 18 1846.

LIEUTENANT COLONEL GEORGE TOD, U. S. A.

A brief notice of Judge Tod's military service, has been already given in Tract No. 15. He was born at Suffield, Connecticut, of Scotch parentage, December 11th, 1773, and was a graduate of Yale in 1795. He settled at Youngstown, then in Trumbull county, Ohio, in 1800, as a lawyer, and rose rapidly in public life. In 1804 he was elected to the Senate of Ohio, and in 1806 to the Supreme Court of the State. March 12th, 1812, he was appointed a Major in the 19th Infantry, and on the 13th of March, 1814, Lieutenant Colonel of the 17th Regiment. In the sortie of Colonel Miller from Fort Meigs, he acted a prominent and creditable part. He died on the 11th of April, 1841, at the age of 68.

War Correspondence.

CAPTAIN ELLIOTT TO MAJOR TOD.

FORT MEIGS, June 29, 1813.

Major George Tod, 19th Regiment, U S Infantry, Warren, Ohio—

Dear Sir—Yours of the 23d instant I have before me, and hasten to give you the earliest information of the situation of the garrison, and from conjectures the movements contemplated by Genl Harrison, who arrived here on the 26th instant.

On the 20th instant, in company with several officers, visited the Old British Fort in a boat; just as we were pushing off I discovered two armed men approaching in from the bushes, whom upon investigation proved to be one of the prisoners taken by the Indians on the 5th of May, belonging to Col. Dudley's Regt; the other a Canadian who came in company with him from near Detroit, giving us information that Dickinson had arrived at Malden from the North with about four thousand Indians—that the Regulars at Malden were fifteen hundred; that an immediate attack was intended to be made on Fort Meigs. Expresses were immediately dispatched to Genl Harrison, also to Col. Johnson, who was lying at Fort Defiance, with about eight hundred mounted Kentuckians. They arrived here on the 23d inst. The 24th Regt commanded by Col. Anderson, on the 28th. Yesterday Col. Johnson with a detatchment of 150 of his Regt left this for the River Raisin; he is expected back this evening. I am apprehensive he may meet with Indians before he returns. The Genl will leave us immediately on his return for Cleaveland, will take with him Col. Johnsons Regt.

From every information I can obtain, our stay at Fort Meigs will be but short. I presume a co-operation of part of the forces of the Middle and Northwestern army will take place previous to the fall of Malden—much however will depend on the capture of Kingston, having been effected.

The new appointments which have taken place has caused a general resignation of the lieutenants of the 24th regiment, and I am well convinced, the example (though premature) will be followed by the officers of the 17th and 19th regiments, should the Senate confirm many of the appointments which have been lately made.

Our camp is becoming much more healthy. Mitchell is recovering his health. Captain Azaring continues low. Colonel Miller has had a touch of the jaundice, which has reduced him considerably. Captain Langham returned on the 27th to Fort Meigs.

I applied this morning to General Harrison for permission to proceed to Warren for the space of three weeks; he refused granting my request, observing that no officer could obtain furlough at present.

Respectfully yours,

WILSON ELLIOTT.

MAJOR JESSUP TO MAJOR TOD.

CLEAVELAND, CAMP HARRISON,
July 5th, 1813, 7 o'clock, A. M.

SIR—Your letter of the 4th inst is rec'd. Our alarm has entirely subsided. I expect the Gen'l here in the course of two or three hours; Major Ball's Squadron is expected this evening, and part of Col. Johnson's Regiment, with some of the twelve months regulars will join us in two or three days.

Several persons have lately arrived from Detroit—from the information given by them, I am induced to believe the enemy will not act offensively; but will wait our attack at Malden.

Yrs. with much respect,

T S. JESSUP.

Major GEO. TOD, 19th Infantry Warren Ohio

GENERAL HARRISON TO MAJOR TOD.

HEAD QUARTERS, CLEVELAND,
July 6th, 1813.

Dear Sir: It is the General's direction that you forthwith on receipt hereof return to your command at Fort Meigs.

I am respectfully,
Your humble servant,
JOHN O'FALLON,
Aid de Camp.

Major GEO. TOD, U. S. Infantry.

COLONEL MILLER TO MAJOR TOD.

CAMP MEIGS, August 25th, 1813.

Dear Sir: I received yours of the 8th instant and cannot conceive the reason why you should be detained at Camp Senica. I have no field officer to the 19th Regiment, and but four company officers fit for duty, and I have myself been in a very bad state of health, for upwards of two months past, with the jaundice; and I am confident we have as much duty and labor to perform here, to say the least of it, as they have at Camp Senica. You will, therefore, please on receipt of this, to repair to this place as soon as possible, unless forbidden by the express order of Genl Harrison. I wish you before you leave Camp Senica, to collect all the scattering soldiers near that place, belonging to the 19th Regt, and place them under the command of one of its own officers, so that they may join this Regt in a body when necessary.

There is a Lieut. Atchison recruiting at Cleaveland; you will please to order on his recruits to Senica, to join what are there by the first opportunity. No news. I trust we shall soon be off. I am with great respect your obt servt,

JOHN MILLER,
Col. 19th Regt Inft.

MAJ. G. TOD, 19th Regt Inft.

GOVERNOR MEIGS TO MAJOR TOD.

DELAWARE, Sept. 3d, 1813.

My D'r Major—

I regret not to have seen you. I cannot go with you to Canada. The moment I go without the State I cease to have Power or authority. I am deeply impressed with the necessity of confidence—and know it to be the duty of every one to support that confidence in a Comm't. This I have unfortunately done, as regards Genl H.—it was Duty, it was inclination. The uninformed portion of the Public are soonest apt to condemn (what they least understand) military operations.

It was impossible to take the M'a. with me to Canada. They threw down their Implements of Husbandry, and without a change of clothes marched, their corn crops to gather, their small Grain to sow, a long detention would have ruined them.

While I shall continue to give every aid to yr com'r, I must respect myself and the station I occupy—although for the public benefit I would bear more than I could for my own. I hope soon to hear of your embarkation, and victory I hope will await you.

Again and again I regret I could not have seen you—how much could I say—but shall not write.

Your daughter grows lovely, indeed she is a most amiable child. R. J. MEIGS.

COLONEL MILLER TO MAJOR TOD.

CAMP MEIGS, Sept. 12th, 1813.

Dear Sir:—If there is clothing at Camp Seneca or Sandusky for the 19th Regt, I wish you to have all the men belonging to the Regt at Seneca clothed, and all that will be able for the campaign, kept under the command of Ensign Mitchell until they join me. I am informed that there are a number of scattering soldiers of the 19th Regt about Seneca & Sandusky, exclusive of those now with Ensign Mitchell; some driving waggons and some in other Regiments, &c. If you can find any such, you will please to claim them, and attach them to the rest. The brave Capt. Nevung died on the 9th inst., and was buried on the day following. I believe the cause of his death was owing to his over fatiguing himself on his return to this place. He vomited nearly all the way from Camp Seneca, and was taken very bad the same night he arrived here.

Some of our Indians who went in the direction of Brownstown a few days ago, returned this evening, and informs us, that yesterday about 12 o'clock, they saw our fleet, and that of the British engage, and that the engagement continued until midnight. We are in great anxiety here to know the result.

I am with respect & esteem,
Your Obt Servt,
JOHN MILLER,
Col. 19th Infantry.

Major G Tod, 19th Regt Infantry, Camp Seneca.

Express Mails for the Northwestern Army.

CALVIN PEASE TO MAJOR TOD.

LOWER SANDUSKY, Mar. 8th, 1813.

Major Tod, Maumee Rapids:

Sir—I am ordered by the Post-Master General, to run the express mail twice a week from Pittsburgh to the Headquarters of the N. W. Army. For that purpose I have brought on a supply of horses, and intended to have gone to the army, but learning at this place that it was next to impossible to get through at this time, and that Genl Harrison had gone to Cincinnati, I have concluded to return. I wished to have seen Genl Harrison, to get the necessary orders respecting the keeping of the horses and riders, and also to get a route from this place to Headquarters that he would approve of. I have however engaged a young man from Boardman by the name of Abida Ransom. I have no acquaintance with him, but from what information I could obtain I thought it safe to trust him. I am however at liberty to dismiss him at any time, if he does not perform punctually, or if Genl Harrison disapproves of him; he belongs to Capt Walker's company of Trumbull militia, whose approbation I have for his engaging, provided Genl. Harrison approves of it. I am under the necessity of requesting you to obtain from the commanding officer. such orders as are necessary to accomplish the object. I wish to have the horses have an ample allowance of forage, that they may be able to perform. I wish you to urge to Genl Harrison the necessity of establishing a small post at the Portage or Carrying river, with a supply of forage for an express horse to be stationed there. It will be necessary for the safety of the mail, to assist it in passing the river in difficult times, and by having a change of horses at that place. the mail can go with more speed, and less injury to the horses. If the mail carrier is negligent or misbehaves I want to have him displaced by order of the commanding officer or by your order, and another put in his place and information thereof sent to me. Mr. Gideon Granger, P. M. General, has informed me that Mr. James Abbot (late Post Master at Detroit) is appointed agent to establish an express mail from Head Quarters to Chilicothe and Post Master at Head Quarters, and has directed him and me to correspond with each other. If he is in camp I wish you to show him this; perhaps he will pay some attention to it. Whenever Genl. Harrison removes, or is about to remove his Head Quarters, I should be glad to receive the earliest information of it, that I may send on more horses if necessary, that the mail may always go to his Head Quarters, and until I can get such information, I wish the mail to be carried on in some way or other. The times of the arrival and departure of the mail will be as follows:

Leave Washington City every Wednesday and Saturday at 4 P. M, Arrive at Pittsburgh on Saturday and Tuesday at 10 A. M. Returning leave Pittsburgh on Saturday & Tuesday at 2 P. M —arrive at Washington on Tuesday and Friday at 9 A. M. (torn) Pittsburgh on Tuesday & Saturday at 2 P. M. (torn) Detroit on Friday and Tuesday at 5 P. M. Leave Detroit Saturday and Wednesday at 7 (torn) arrive at Pittsburgh on Tuesday and Saturday at 10 A. M. Until the roads become better it will be necessary to give the riders all the time possible. I shall devote the most of my time to the care of this mail and shall probably be at the Head-quarters of the army in two or three months and sooner if necessary. If you will lend me a little assistance in the business at this time you will confer a great favour; I know of no other person in the camp of whom I can freely make the request. I lately heard that your family are well. I wish you to write to me immediately on the receipt of this.

I am with respect
Your friend &c
CALVIN PEASE.

P. S.—By requesting that Genl Harrison should approve of the mail carrier and displace him if necessary, I would not be understood as requesting him to take any trouble. I am not authorised to ask it, but only if he thinks proper to exercise that power.

Western Reserve and Northern Ohio
HISTORICAL SOCIETY.

CLEVELAND, O., FEB'Y, 1874.

NUMBER TWENTY.

DISCOVERY AND OWNERSHIP OF THE NORTHWESTERN TERRITORY, AND SETTLEMENT OF THE WESTERN RESERVE.

An Address delivered at Burton, before the Historical Society of Geauga County, O., Sept. 16, 1873, by Hon. James A. Garfield.

[In furnishing the Geauga County Historical Society with the manuscript of the Address for publication, Mr. Garfield sent the following letter which we give as introductory to the Address.]

WASHINGTON, D. C.,
December 13, 1873.

R. N. FORD, ESQ., COR. SECRETARY:

Dear Sir:—In accordance with the request of many members of the Historical Society of Geauga County, I have written out the substance of my address delivered before that Society on the 16th of Sept. 1873, and enclose it herewith. I have verified most of my references to the history of the discovery, and settlement of this continent, and particularly of the West. It may be a matter of interest to your society, that I name the authorities from which I have drawn my historical data I do this for the further reason that your society, may possibly desire to place in its collections a portion at least of the works to which I refer. I mention the following, as among the chief books I have consulted in the preparation of this address:

"Bancroft's History of the U. S." Vols. I., II., III., IV.

"Annals of the West." James H. Perkins, St. Louis, 1850.

"Notes on the Early Settlement of the Northwestern Territory." Jacob Burnet, N. Y., 1847.

"Historical Collections of Ohio." Henry Howe, Cincinnati, 1847.

"History of the Discovery and Settlement of the Valley of the Mississippi," 2 vols. John W. Monette, N. Y. 1846.

Irving's Conquest of Florida.

Francis Parkman's four histories.

"The Jesuits of North America."

"The Discovery of the Great West."

"The Pioneers of Civilization in the New World."

"The Conspiracy of Pontiac."

"Diplomatic Correspondence." 1776 to 1783, by Jared Sparks.

"Early History of Cleveland, Ohio." Col. Charles Whittlesey, Cleveland, 1867.

"History of the Maumee Valley." H. Knapp, Toledo, 1872.

"Land Laws of Ohio."

I mention last in this connection, what I regard as very important, and what I referred to in my address at Burton, but have omitted in the written text,—the fact that, at the last session of Congress, an appropriation of $10,000 was made to purchase for the Library of Congress a manuscript collection of official reports, now a part of the archives of France, but which have never yet been published. To exhibit the character and value of these documents, I take the liberty of quoting from the *Congressional Globe* a portion of my remarks, made in the House of Representatives on the 18th of Feb., 1873, as follows:

"For more than a century, the French were exploring a great portion of this continent west of the Alleghany Mountains. Under the diretion of their Government, learned men, army officers, men interested in science, were sent out, who made explorations along the great rivers of the Northwest, along our great lakes, and through the Rocky Mountains, long before a man of the Anglo-Saxon race, speaking the English language, had ever trodden any of these wilds. They made reports to the Government at Paris, but, in those days, such reports were buried in the archives of the Government, and were considered secret papers. They have never seen the light. The archivist of the Navy Department of France, Pierre Margry, has had possession of these documents for years, and has with great pains transcribed them. I have received a letter from the greatest of our recent historians, Mr. Francis Parkman, in which he says:

"'I have known about this collection many years, and have several times seen it, and examined it sufficiently to get a clear idea of its contents. Many of the most important documents composing it have been in my hands. I can testify in the strongest terms to its rare value for the history of the West. To the best of my belief, none of these documents which Mr. Margry now proposes to print, have ever been in print before.'"

"Mr. Margry has prepared for publication what will make nine volumes, according to the testimony before the committee. Three volumes relate to the discoveries of La Salle and his companions, Joutel, Tonty, Galinier, and Dollier de Casson; one to La Mothe Cadillac, and the settlement of Detroit; two to discoveries and explorations in the Rocky Mountains, in 1752, by De Niseville and the brothers Veranddiere; one to Fort Du Quesne and Natchitoches; two to the settlement of Louisiana. The volumes will be published by Mr. Margry, under his own direction, if he can be assured of a subscription to a certain number of copies in advance, to be paid for only when the volumes are delivered.

"Now a book of this sort will be little popular in France, as it relates to so distant a country; but, here at home, and especially in the Great Northwest, it will be of vital interest as adding to our knowledge of our ancient history; and we propose, in putting this $10,000 into the hands of the Committee on the Library, that, instead of placing on our shelves a great number of the worthless books that always find their way there, they shall put in this work of inestimable historical value, which cannot be duplicated elsewhere, which cannot be published except by the Government, and which may be lost, and was so near being lost in the late war of the Commune. It seems to me that no wiser or appropriate use could be made of any amount, which we may devote to the Library."

These papers are now being published, and will soon, I hope, be in the hands of students of American history.

Very truly yours.

J. A. GARFIELD.

MR. CHAIRMAN AND FELLOW-CITIZENS: When I accepted the invitation to address you on this interesting occasion, I did not assume that I could contribute anything in the way of original materials for the history of this portion of the Western Reserve. I hoped, however, that I might be able to point out some of the resources from which these materials may be drawn, and to express my interest in the effort you are making to rescue a portion of them from the destroying hand of time.

From the historian's standpoint, our country is peculiarly and exceptionally fortunate. The origin of nearly all great nations, ancient and modern, is shrouded in fable or traditionary legend. The story of the founding of Rome by the wolf-nursed brothers, Romulus and Remus, has long been classed among the myths of history; and the more modern story of Hengist and Horsa leading the Saxons to England, is almost equally legendary. The origin of Paris can never be known. Its foundation was laid long before Gaul had written records. But the settlement, civilization and political institutions of our country, can be traced from their first hour by the clear light of history. It is true that over this continent hangs an impenetrable veil of tradition, mystery and silence. But it is the tradition of races fast passing away; the mystery of a still earlier race, which flourished and perished long before its discovery by the Europeans. The story of the Mound-Builders can never be told. The fate of the Indian Tribes, will soon be a half-forgotten tale. But the history of European civilization and institutions on this continent can be traced with precision and fullness; unless we become forgetful of the past, and neglect to save and perpetuate its precious memorials.

In discussing the scope of historical study in reference to our country, I will call attention to a few general facts concerning its discovery and settlement.

First.—The Romantic Period of Discovery on this Continent.

There can scarcely be found in the realms of romance, anything more fascinating than the records of discovery and adventure, during the two centuries that followed the landing of Columbus on the soil of the New World. The greed for gold; the passion for adventure; the spirit of chivalry; the enthusiasm and fanaticism of religion; all conspired to throw into America the hardest and most daring spirits of Europe, and made the vast wilderness of the New World, the theatre of the most stirring achievements that history has recorded.

Early in the Sixteenth Century, Spain, turning from the conquest of Grenada, and her triumph over the Moors, followed her golden dreams of the New World, with the same spirit that in an earlier day animated her Crusaders. In 1528, Ponce de Leon began his search for the fountain of perpetual youth, the tradition of which he had learned among the natives of the West Indies. He discovered the low lying coasts of Florida, and explored its interior. Instead of the fountain of youth, he found his grave among its everglades

A few years later, De Soto, who had accompanied Pizarro in the conquest of Peru, landed in Florida with a gallant array of knights and nobles, and commenced his explorations through the western wilderness. In 1541, he reached the banks of the Mississippi river, and, crossing it pushed his discoveries westward over the great plains; but, finding neither the gold nor the South Sea of his dreams, he returned to be buried in the waters of the great river he had discovered.

While England was more leisurely exploring the bays and rivers of the Atlantic coast, and searching for gold and peltry, the chevaliers and priests of France were chasing their dreams in the North, searching a passage to China, and the realms of Far Cathay, and telling the mystery of the Cross, to the Indian tribes of the Far West. Coasting northward, her bold navigators discovered the mouth of the St. Lawrence; and, in 1525, Cartier sailed up its broad current to the Rocky heights of Quebec, and to the rapids above Montreal, which were afterwards named La Chine, in derision of the belief that the adventurers were about to find, China.

In 1606, Champlain pushed above the rapids, and discovered the beautiful lake that bears his name. In 1615, Priest La Caron, pushed northward and westward through the wilderness and discovered Lake Huron.

In 1635, the Jesuit Missionaries founded the Mission St. Mary. In 1654, another priest had entered the wilderness of Northern New York, and found the salt springs of Onondaga. In 1659-1660, French traders and priests passed the winter on Lake Superior, and established missions along its shores.

Among the earlier discoverers, no name shines out with more brilliancy than that of the Chevalier La Salle. The story of his explorations can scarcely be equalled in romantic interest by any of the stirring tales of the Crusaders. Born of a proud and wealthy family in the north of France, he was destined for the service of the Church and of the Jesuit Order. But his restless spirit, fired with the love of adventure, broke away from the ecclesiastical restraints, to confront the dangers of the New World, and extend the empire of Louis XIV. From the best evidence accessible, it appears that he was the first white man that saw the Ohio River. At twenty-six years of age, we find him with a small party, near the western extremity of Lake Ontario, boldly entering the domain of the dreaded Iroquois, traveling southward and westward through the wintry wilderness until he reached a branch of the Ohio, probably the Alleghany. He followed it to the main stream, and descended that, until, in the winter of 1669 and 1670, he reached the Falls of the Ohio, near the present site of Louisville. His companions refusing to go further, he returned to Quebec, and prepared for still greater undertakings.

In the meantime the Jesuit missionaries had been pushing their discoveries on the Northern Lake. In 1673, Joliet and Marquette started from Green Bay, dragging their canoes up the rapids of Fox River; crossed Lake Winnebago; found Indian guides to conduct them to the waters of the Wisconsin; descended that stream to the westward, and, on the 16th of June, reached the Mississippi near the spot where now stands the city of Prairie Du Chien. To-morrow will be the two hundredth anniversary of that discovery. One hundred and forty-two years before that time De Soto had seen the same river more than a thousand miles below; but during that interval, it is not known that any white man had looked upon its waters.

Turning southward, these brave priests descended the great river, amid the awful solitudes. The stories of demons and monsters of the wilderness which abounded among the Indian tribes, did not deter them from pushing their discoveries. They continued their journey southward to the mouth of the Arkansas river, telling as best they could the story of the Cross, to the wild tribes along the shores. Returning from the Kaskaskias, and, traveling thence to Lake Michigan reached Green Bay at the end of September, 1673, having on their journey, paddled their canoes more than twenty-five hundred miles. Marquette remained to establish missions among the Indians, and to die three years later, on the western shore of Lake Michigan, while Joliet returned to Quebec to report his discoveries.

In the meantime, Count Frontenac, a noble of France had been made Governor of Canada, and found in La Salle a fit counselor and assistant in his vast schemes of discovery. La Salle was sent to France, to enlist the Court and the Ministers of Louis; and, in 1677-1678, returned to Canada, with full power under Frontenac to carry forward his grand enterprises. He had developed three great purposes: First, To realize the old plan of Champlain, the finding of a pathway to China across the American Continent; Second, To occupy and develop the regions of the Northern Lakes; and, Third, To descend the Mississippi river, and establish a fortified post at its mouth, thus securing an outlet for the trade of the interior and checking the progress of Spain on the Gulf of Mexico.

In pursuance of this plan, we find La Salle and his companions, in January, 1679, dragging their cannon and materials for ship-building around the Falls of Niagara, and laying the keel of a vessel two leagues above the cataract, at the mouth of Cayuga Creek. She was a schooner of forty-five tons burden, and was named "The Griffin." On the 7th of August, 1679, with an armament of five cannon, and a crew and company of thirty-four men, she started on her voyage up Lake Erie, the first sail ever spread over the waters of our Lake. On the fourth day, she entered Detroit river; and, after encountering a terrible storm on Lake Huron, passed the straits and reached Green Bay early in September. A few weeks later, she started back for Niagara laden with furs, and was never heard from.

While awaiting the supplies which the "Griffin" was expected to bring, La Salle explored Lake Michigan to its southern extremity, ascended the Saint Joseph, crossed the portage to the Kankakee, descended the Illinois, and, landing at an Indian village on the site of the present village of Utica, Illinois, celebrated mass on New Year's day, 1680. Before the winter was ended, he became certain that the Griffin was lost. But, undaunted by his disasters, on the 3rd of March, with five companions, he began the incredible feat of making the journey to Quebec on foot, in the dead of winter. This he accomplished. He re-organized his expedition, conquered every difficulty, and, on the 21st December, 1681, with a party of fifty-four Frenchmen and friendly Indians, set out for the present site of Chicago, and, by way of the Illinois River, reached the Mississippi Feb. 6, 1682. He descended its stream, and, on the 9th April of 1682, standing on the shores of the Gulf of Mexico, solemnly proclaimed to his companions and to the wilderness, that in the name of Louis the Great, he took possession of the Great Valley watered by the Mississippi river. He set up a column, and inscribed upon it the arms of France, and named the country Louisania. Upon this act rested the claim of France to the vast region stretching from the Alleghany to the Rocky Mountains, from the Rio Grande and the Gulf to the farthest springs of the Missouri.

I will not follow further the career of the great explorers. Enough has been said to exhibit the spirit and character of their work. I would I were able to inspire the young men of this country, with a desire to read the history of these stirring days of discovery, that opened up to Europe the mysteries of this New World.

As Irving has well said of their work, "It was poetry put into action; it was the knight-errantry of the Old World, carried into the depths of the American Wilderness. The personal adventures; the feats of individual prowess; the picturesque descriptions of steel clad cavaliers, with lance, and helm, and prancing steed, glittering through the wilderness of Florida, Georgia, Alabama, and the prairies of the Far West, would seem to us mere fictions of romance did they not come to us in the matter of fact narratives, of those who were eye witnesses, and who recorded minute memoranda of every incident."

Second—The Struggle for National Dominion.

I next invite your attention to the less stirring but not less important struggle, for the possession of the New World, which succeeded the period of discovery.

At the beginning of the 18th century, North America was claimed mainly by three great powers. Spain held possession of Mexico, and a belt reaching eastward to the Atlantic and northward to the southern line of Georgia, except a portion near the mouth of the Mississippi held by the French. England held from the Spanish line on the south to the Northern Lakes and the Saint Lawrence, and westward to the Alleghanies. France held all north of the lakes and west of the Alleghanies, and southward to the possessions of Spain. Some of the boundary lines were but vaguely defined; others were disputed; but the general outlines were as stated.

Besides the struggle for national possession, the religious element entered largely into the contest. It was a struggle between the Catholic and Protestant faiths. The Protestant colonies of England were enveloped on three sides, by the vigorous and perfectly organized Catholic powers of France and Spain.

Indeed, at an early date, by the Bull of Pope Alexander VI., all America had been given to the Spaniards. But France, with a zeal equal to that of Spain, had entered the lists to contest for the prize. So far as the religious struggle was concerned, the efforts of France and Spain were resisted only by the Protestants of the Atlantic Coast.

The main chain of the Alleghanies was supposed to be impassable until 1714, when Governor Spottswood, of Virginia, led an expedition to discover a pass to the great valley beyond. He found one somewhere near the western boundary of Virginia, and by it descended to the Ohio. On his return, he established the "Transmontane Order," or "Knights of the Golden Horse Shoe" On the sandy plains of Eastern Virginia, horse-shoes were rarely used; but, in climbing the mountains, he had found them necessary; and, on creating his companions knights of this new order, he gave to each a golden horse-shoe, inscribed with the motto :

"*Sic jurat transcendere montes.*"

He represented to the British Ministry the great importance of planting settlements in the western valley; and, with the foresight of a statesman, pointed out the danger of allowing the French the undisputed possession of that rich region.

The progress of England had been slower but more certain than that of her great rival. While the French were establishing trading posts at points widely remote from each other, along the lakes and the Mississippi, and in the wilderness of Ohio Indiana and Illinois, the English were slowly but firmly planting their settlements on the Atlantic slope, and preparing to contest for the rich prize of the Great West. They possessed one great advantage over their French rivals. They had cultivated the friendship of the Iroquois Confederacy, the most powerful combination of Indian tribes known to the New World. That Confederacy held possession of the southern shores of Lakes Ontario and Erie; and their hostility to the French had confined the settlements of that people mainly to the northern shores.

During the first half of the Eighteenth Century, many treaties were made by the English with these confederated tribes, and some valuable grants of land were obtained on the eastern slope of the Mississippi Valley.

About the middle of that century the British Government began to recognize the wisdom of Governor Spottswood, and perceived that an empire was soon to be saved or lost.

In 1748, a company was organized by Thomas Lee, and Lawrence and Augustine Washington, under the name of "The Ohio Company," and received a royal grant of one half million acress of land in the valley of the Ohio. In 1751, a British trading post was established on the Big Miami; but, in the following year, it was destroyed by the French. Many similar efforts of the English colonists were resisted by the French; and, during the years 1751–2–3, it became manifest that a great struggle was imminent, between the French and the English for the possession of the West. The British ministers were too much absorbed in intrigues at home, to appreciate the importance of this contest; and they did but little more than to permit the colonies to protect their rights in the Valley of the Ohio

In 1753, the Ohio Company had opened a road by "Will's Creek" into the western valley, and were preparing to locate their colony. At the same time the French had sent a force to occupy and hold the line of the Ohio. As the Ohio Company was under the especial protection of Virginia, the Governor of that colony determined to send a messenger to the commander of the French forces, and demand the reason for invading the British dominions. For this purpose he selected George Washington, then twenty years of age, who, with six assistants, set out from Williamsburg, Va., in the middle of November, for the waters of the Ohio [illegible]. After a journey of nine days through sleet and snow, he reached the Ohio at the junction of the Alleghany and the Monongahela; and his quick eye seemed to foresee the destiny of the place. "I spent some time," said he, "in viewing the rivers. The land in the fork has the absolute command of both." On this spot Fort Pitt was afterwards built, and, still later, the city of Pittsburg.

As Bancroft has said, "After creating in imagination a fortress and city, his party swam across the Alleghany, wrapped their blankets around them for the night on the northwest bank." Proceeding down the Ohio to Logstown, he held a council with the Shawnees and the Delawares, who promised to secure the aid of the Six Nations in resisting the French. He then proceeded to the French posts at Venango and Fort Le Boeuf, (the latter fifteen miles from Lake Erie,) and warned the commanders that the rights of Virginia must not be invaded. He received for his answer, that the French would seize every Englishman in the Ohio Valley.

Returning to Virginia in January, 1754, he reported to the Governor, and immediate preparations were made by the colonists to maintain their rights in the West, and resist the incursions of the French In this movement originated the first military union among the English colonists.

Although peace existed between France and England, formidable preparations were made by the latter to repel encroachments on the frontier, from Ohio to the Gulf of Saint Lawrence. Braddock was sent to America, and, in 1755, at Alexandria, Va., he planned four expeditions against the French.

It is not necessary to speak in detail of the war that followed. After Braddock's defeat near the forks of the Ohio, which occurred on the 9th of July, 1755, England herself took active measures for prosecuting the war.

On the 25th of November, 1758, Forbes captured Fort DuQuesne, which thus passed into the possession of the English, and was named Fort Pitt, in honor of the great Minister.

In 1759, Quebec was captured by General Wolfe; and the same year Niagara fell into the hands of the English.

In 1760, an English force, under Major Rogers, moved westward from Niagara, to occupy the French posts on the Upper Lakes. They coasted along the south shore of Erie, the first English-speaking people that sailed its waters. Near the mouth of the Grand river they met in council the chiefs of the great warrior Pontiac. A few weeks later, they took possession of Detroit. "Thus," says Mr. Bancroft," was Michigan won by Great Britain, though not for itself. There were those who foresaw that the acquisition of Canada was the prelude of American Independence."

Late in December, Rogers returned to the Maumee; and setting out from the point where Sandusky City now stands, crossed the Huron river to the northern branch of White Woman's river, and, passing thence by the English village of Beaverstown, and up the Ohio, reached Fort Pitt on the 23d of January, 1761, just a month after he left Detroit.

Under the leadership of Pitt, England was finally triumphant in this great struggle; and, by the Treaty of Paris, of February 10th, 1763, she acquired Canada and all the territory east of the Mississippi river, and southward to the Spanish Territory, excepting New Orleans and the island on which it is situated.

During the twelve years which followed the Treaty of Paris, the English colonists were pushing their settlements into the newly- acquired territory; but they encountered the opposition of the Six Nations and their allies, who made fruitless efforts to capture the British posts, Detroit, Niagara and Fort Pitt.

At length, in 1768, Sir William Johnson concluded a treaty at Fort Stanwix, with these tribes, by which all the lands south of the Ohio and the Alleghany were sold to the British; the Indians to remain in undisturbed possession of the territory north and west of those rivers. New companies were organized to occupy the territory thus obtained.

"Among the foremost speculators in Western lands at that time," says the author of 'Annals of the West,' "was George Washington." In 1769, he was one of the signers of a petition to the King for a grant of two and a half millions acres in the West. In 1770, he crossed the mountains and descended the Ohio to the mouth of the Great Kanawha, to locate the ten thousand acres to which he was entitled, for services in the French War.

Virginians planted settlements in Kentucky; and pioneers from all the colonies began to occupy the frontiers, from the Alleghany to the Tennessee.

Third.—The War of the Revolution, and its Relations to the West.

How came the Thirteen Colonies to possess the Valley of the Mississippi? The object of their struggle was independence, and yet, by the Treaty of Peace in 1783, not only was the independence of the Thirteen Colonies conceded, but there was granted to the new Republic, a western territory bounded by the Northern Lakes the Mississippi, and the French and Spanish possessions. How did these hills and valleys become a part of the United States? It is true that, by virtue of royal charters, several of the colonies set up claims extending to the "South Sea". The knowledge which the English possessed of the geography of this country at that time, is illustrated by the fact that Capt. John Smith was commissioned to sail up the Chickahominy, and find a passage to China! But the claims of the colonies were too vague to be of any consequence in determining the boundaries of the two governments. Virginia had indeed extended her settlements into the region south of the Ohio river, and during the Revolution, had annexed that country to the Old Dominion, calling it the County of Kentucky. But, previous to the Revolution, the Colonies had taken no such action in reference in the Territory Northwest of the Ohio.

The cession of that great Territory under the treaty of 1783 was due mainly to the foresight, the courage, and the endurance of one man, who never received from his country any adequate recognition for his great service. That man was George Rogers Clark; and it is worth your while to consider the work he accomplished.—Born in Virginia, he was, in early life, a surveyor, and afterwards served in Lord Dunmore's War. In 1776, he settled in Kentucky, and was, in fact, the founder of that commonwealth.—As the War of the Revolution progressed, he saw that the pioneers west of the Alleghanies were threatened by two formidable dangers: First, by the Indians, many of whom had joined the standard of Great Britian; and, second, by the success of the war itself. For, should the colonies obtain their independence, while the British held possession of the Mississispi Valley, the Alleghanies would be the western boundary of the new Republic, and the pioneers of the West would remain subjects to Great Britain.

Inspired by these views, he made two journeys to Virginia, to represent the case to the authorities of that colony. Failing to impress the House of Burgesses with the importance of warding off these dangers, he appealed to the Governor, Patrick Henry, and received from him authority to enlist seven companies to go to Kentucky subject to his orders, and serve for three months after their arrival in the West. This was a public commission.

Another document, bearing date Williamsburg, Jan. 2, 1778, was a secret commission, which authorized him, in the name of Virginia, to capture the military posts held by the British in the Northwest. Armed with this authority, he proceeded to Pittsburg, where he obtained ammunition, and floated it down the river to Kentucky, succeeded in enlisting seven companies of pioneers, and in the month of June, 1778, commenced his march through the untrodden wilderness to the region of the Illinois. With a daring that is scarcely equaled in the annals of war, he captured the garrisons of Kaskaskia, Saint Vincent and Cahokia, and sent his prisoners to the Governor of Virginia, and by his energy and skill won over the French inhabitants of that region to the American cause.

In October, 1778, the House of Burgesses passed an act declaring that "All the the citizens of the Commonwealth of Virginia, who are already settled there, or shall hereafter be settled on the west side of the Ohio, shall be included in the District of Kentucky, which shall be called Illinois County." In other words, George Rogers Clark conquered the Territory of the Northwest in the name of Virginia, and the flag of the Republic covered it at the close of the war.

In negotiating the Treaty of Peace at Paris, in 1783, the British commissioners insisted on the Ohio river as the northwestern boundary of the United States; and it was found, that the only tenable ground on which the American commissioners relied to sustain our claim to the Lakes and the Mississippi as the boundary, was the fact that George Rogers Clark had conquered the country, and Virginia was in undisputed possession of it at the cessation of hostilities.

In his "Notes on the Early Settlement of the Northwest Territory," Judge Burnet says:—"That fact" (the capture of the British posts "was confirmed and admitted, and was the chief ground on which the British commissioners reluctantly abandoned their claim."

It is a stain upon the honor of our country that such a man, the leader of pioneers who made the first lodgment on the site now accupied by Louisville, who was in fact the founder of the State of Kentucky, and who, by his personal foresight and energy, gave nine great States to the Republic, was allowed to sink under a load of debt incurred for the honor and glory of his country.

In 1799, Judge Burnet rode some ten or twelve miles from Louisville into the country, to visit this veteran hero. He says he was induced to make this visit by the veneration he entertained for Clark's military talents and services.

"He had," says Burnet, "the appearance of a man born to command, and fitted by nature for his destiny. There was a gravity and solemnity in his demeanor, resembling that which so eminently distinguished the venerated father of his country. A person familiar with the lives and character of the military veterans of Rome, in the days of her greatest power, might readily have selected *this remarkable man* as a specimen of the model he had formed of them in his own mind: but he was rapidly falling a victim to his extreme sensibility and to the ingratitude of his native State, under whose banner he had fought bravely, and with great success.

"The time will certainly come when the enlightened and magnanimous citizens of Louisville will remember the debt of gratitude they owe the memory that distinguished man. He was the leader of the pioneers who made the first lodgment on the site now covered by their rich and splendid city. He was its protector during the years of its infancy, and in the period of its greatest danger. Yet the traveler who has read of his achievements, admired his character, and visited the theatre of his brilliant deeds, discovers nothing indicating the place where his remains are deposited, and where he can go and pay a tribute of respect to the memory of the departed and gallant hero.

This eulogy of Judge Burnet is fully warranted by the facts of history. There is preserved in the War Department at Washington, a portrait of Clark, which gives unmistakable evidence of a character of rare grasp and power. No one can look upon that remarkable face without knowing that the original was a man of unusual force,

Fourth—Organization and Settlement of the Western Reserve.

Soon after the close of the Revolution, our Western country was divided into three Territories: the Territory of the Mississippi; the Territory south of the Ohio; and the Territory northwest of the Ohio. For the purposes of this address, I shall consider only the only organization and settlement of the latter.

It would be difficult to find any country so covered with conflicting claims of title as the Territory of the Northwest. Several States, still asserting the validity of their royal charters, set up claims more or less definite to portions of this Territory. First. By royal charter of 1662, confirming a council charter of 1630, Connecticut claimed a strip of land bounded on the east by the Narraganset river, north by Massachusetts, south by Long Island Sound, and extending westward between the parallels of 41 deg and 42 deg. 2' North Latitude, to, the mythical "South Sea." Second. New York, by her charter of 1614, claimed a territory marked by definite boundaries, lying across the boundaries of the Connecticut charter. Third. By the grant to William Penn, in 1664, Pennsylvania claimed a territory overlapping part of the territory of both these colonies. Fourth. The charter of Massachusetts also conflicted with some of the claims above mentioned. Fifth. Virginia claimed the whole of the Northwest Territory by right of conquest, and, in 1779, by an act of her legislature, annexed it as a county. Sixth. Several grants had been made of special tracts to incorporated companies by the different States. And, finally, the whole territory of the Northwest was claimed by the Indians as their own.

The claims of New York, Massachusetts, and part of the claim of Pennsylvania had been settled before the war, by royal commissioners. The others were still unadjusted. It became evident that no satisfactory settlement could be made except by Congress. That body urged the several States to make a cession of the lands they claimed, and thus enable the General Government to open the Northwest for settlement.

On the first of March, 1784, Thomas Jefferson, Samuel Hardy, Arthur Lee and James Monroe, delegates in Congress, executed a deed of cession in the name of Virginia, by which they transferred to the United States the title of Virginia to the Northwest Territory, but reserving to that State one hundred and fifty thousand acres of land which Virginia had promised to George Rogers Clark, and to the officers and soldiers who with him captured the British posts in the West. Also, another tract of land between the Scioto and Little Miami to enable Virginia, to pay her promised bounties to her officers and soldiers of the Revolutionary Army.

On the 27th of October, 1784, a treaty was made at Fort Stanwix, (now Rome, New York) with the Six Nations, by which these tribes ceded to the United State, their vague claims to the lands north and west of the Ohio. On the 31st of January 1785, a treaty was made at Fort McIntosh, (now the town of Beaver, Pa) with the four Western tribes, the

Wyandottes, the Delawares, the Chippewas and the Tawas, by which all their lands in the Northwest Territory were ceded to the United States, except that portion bounded by a line from the mouth of the Cuyahoga up that river to the portage between the Cuyahoga and Tuscarawas; thence down that branch to the mouth of Sandy; thence westwardly to the portage of the Big Miami, which runs into the Ohio; thence along the portage to the Great Miami or Maumee, and down the south east side of the river to its mouth; thence along the shore of Lake Erie to the mouth of the Cuyahoga. The territory thus described was to be forever the exclusive possession of these Indians.

In 1788, a settlement was made at Marietta, and soon after other settlements were begun. But the Indians were dissatisfied, and, by the intrigues of their late allies, the British, a savage and bloody war ensued which delayed for several years the settlement of the State. The campaign of General Harmar in 1790, was only a partial success. In the following year a more formidable force was placed under the command of General St. Clair, who suffered a disastrous and overwhelming defeat on the 4th of November of that year, near the head waters of the Wabash.

It was evident that nothing but a war so decisive as to break the power of the Western tribes,could make the settlement of Ohio possible. There are but few things in the career of George Washington that so strikingly illustrate his sagacity and prudence as the policy he pursued in reference to this subject. He made preparations for organizing an army of five thousand men, appointed Gen. Wayne to the command of a special force, and early in 1792, drafted detailed instructions for giving it special discipline to fit it for Indian warfare. During that and the following year, he exhausted every means to secure the peace of the West by treaties with the tribes.

But agents of England and Spain were busy in intrigues with the Indians in hopes of recovering a portion of the great empire they had lost by the treaty of 1783. So far were the efforts of England carried that a British force was sent to the rapids of the Maumee, where they built a fort, and inspired the Indians with the hope that the British would join them in fighting the forces of the United States.

All efforts to make a peaceable settlement on any other basis than the abandonment on the part of the United States of all territory north of the Ohio having failed, General Wayne proceeded with that wonderful vigor which had made him famous on so many fields of the Revolution, and, on the 20th August, 1794 defeated the Indians and their allies on the banks of the Maumee, and completely broke the power of their confederation.

On the 3d of August 1795, General Wayne concluded at Greenville, a treaty of lasting peace with these tribes, and thus opened the State to settlement. In this treaty, there was reserved to the Indians the same territory west of the Cuyahoga as described in the treaty of Fort McIntosh of 1785.

Fifth.—Settlement of the Western Reserve.

I have now noticed briefly the adjustment of the several claims to the North western Territory, excepting that of Connecticut. It has already been seen that Connecticut claimed a strip westward from the Narragansett river to the Mississippi, between the parallels of 41 degrees and 42 degrees 2 minutes; but that portion of her claim which crossed the terrritory of New York and Pennsylvania, had been extinguished by adjustment. Her claim to the territory west of Pennsylvania was unsettled until September 14th 1786, when she ceded it all to the United States, except that portion lying between the parallels above named, and a line one hundred and twenty miles west of the western line of Pennsylvania and parallel with it. This tract of country was about the size of the present State and was called "New Connecticut."

In May,1792,the Legislature of Connecticut granted to those of her citizens whose property had been burned or otherwise spoliated by the British, during the war of the Revolution, half a million of acres from the west end of the Reserve. These were called "The Fire Lands."

On the 5th of September, 1795, Connecticut executed a deed to John Caldwell, Jonathan Brace and John Morgan, trustees for the Conneticut Land Company, for three million acres of the Reserve, lying west of Pennsylvania, for one million two hundred thousand dollars, or at the rate of forty cents per acre. The State gave only a quit-claim deed, transferring only such title as she possessed, and leaving all the remaining Indian titles to the Reserve, to be extinguished by the purchasers themselves. With the exception of a few hundred acres previously sold, in the neighborhood of the Salt Spring Tract, on the Mahoning, all titles to lands on the Reserve east of "The Fire Lands," rest on this quit-claim deed of Connecticut to the three trustees, who were all living as late as 1836, and joined in making deeds to lands on the Reserve.

On the same day that the trust deed was made, articles of association were signed by the proprietors, providing for the government of the company. The management of its affairs was entrusted to seven directors. They determined to extinguish the Indian title, and survey their land into townships five miles square. Moses Cleaveland, one of the directors, was made General Agent, Augustus Porter Principal Surveyor, and Seth Pease Astronomer and Surveyor. To these were added four assistant surveyors, a commissary, a physician and thirty-seven other employees. This party assembled at Schenectady, N. Y., in the spring of 1796, and prepared for their expedition.

It is interesting to follow them on their way to the Reserve. They ascended the Mohawk river in batteaux, passing through the locks at Little Falls, and, from the present city of Rome, took their boats and stores across into Wood creek. Passing down the stream they crossed the Oneida Lake, down the Oswego to Lake Ontario. Coasting along the lake thence to Niagara, after encountering innumerable hardships, the party reached Buffalo on the 17th of June, where they met "Red Jacket," and the principal chiefs of the Six Nations, and on the 23d of that month, completed a contract with those chiefs, by which they purchased all the rights of those Indians to the lands on the Reserve, for five hundred pounds, New York currency, to be paid in goods, to the Western Indians, and two beef cattle and one hundred gallons of whisky to the Eastern Indians, besides gifts and provisions to all of them.

Setting out from Buffalo on the 27th of June, they coasted along the shore of the lake, some of the party in boats and others marching along the banks.

In the journal of Seth Pease, published in Whittlesey's History of Cleveland, I find the following:

Monday, July 4th, 1796.—We that came by land arrived at the confines of New Connecticut, and gave three cheers precisely at 5 o'clock P. M, We then proceeded to Conneaut, at five hours thirty minutes, our boats got on an hour after; we pitched our tents on the east side."

In the journal of Gen. Cleaveland is the following entry:

"On this Creek, ("Conneaught,") in New Connecticut Land, July 4th, 1796, under Gen. Moses Cleaveland, the surveyors and men sent by the Connecticut Land Company to survey and settle the Connecticut Reserve, and were the first English people who took possession of it. * * We gave three cheers and christened the place Fort Independence; and, after many difficulties, perplexities and hardships were surmounted, and we were on the good and promised land, felt that a just tribute of respect to the day ought to be paid. There were, in all, including women and children, fifty in number. The men, under Captain Tinker, ranged themselves on the beach, and fired a Federal salute of fifteen rounds, and then the sixteenth in honor of New Connecticut. Drank several toasts. * * * Closed with three cheers. Drank several pails of grog. Supped and retired in good order."

Three days afterward General Cleaveland held a council with Paqua, Chief of the Massasaugas, whose village was at Conneaut Creek. The friendship of these Indians was purchased by a few trinkets and twenty-five dollars' worth of whisky.

A cabin was erected on the bank of Conneaut Creek; and, in honor of the commissary of the expedition, was called "Stow Castle." At this time the white inhabitants west of the Genesee river, and along the coasts of the lakes, were as follows: The garrison at Niagara, two families at Lewistown, one at Buffalo, one at Cleveland and one at Sandusky. There were no other families east of Detroit, and with the exexception of a few adventurers at the Salt Springs of the Mahoning, the interior of New Connecticut was an unbroken wilderness.

The work of surveying was commenced at once. One party went southward on the Pennsylvania line to find the 41st parallel, and began the survey; another, under General Cleaveland, coasted along the lake to the mouth of the Cuyahoga, which they reached on the 22nd of July, and there laid the foundation of the chief city of the Reserve. A large portion of the survey was made during that season, and the work was completed in the following year.

By the close of the year 1800, there were thirty-two settlements on the Reserve, though, as yet, no organization of government had been established. But the pioneers were a people who had been trained in the principles and practice of civil order; and these were transplanted to their new home. In New Connecticut, there was but little of that lawlessness which so often characterizes the people of a new country. In many instances, a township organization was completed and their minister chosen before the pioneers left home. Thus they planted the institutions and opinions of Old Conneticut in their new wilderness homes.

There are townships on this Western Reserve which are more thoroughly New England in character and spirit than most of the towns of the New England of today. Cut off as they were from the metropolitan life that has gradually been molding and changing the spirit of New England, they preserved here in the wilderness the characteristics of New England, as it was when they left it at the beginning of the century. This has given to the people of the Western Reserve those strongly marked qualities which have always distinguished them.

For a long time, it was difficult to ascertain the political and legal status of the settlers on the Reserve. The State of Connecticut did not assume jurisdiction over its people, because that State had parted with her claim to the soil.

By a proclamation of Gov. St. Clair, in 1788, Washington county had been organized, having its limits extended westward to the Scioto and northward to the mouth of the Cuyahoga, with Marietta as the county seat. These limits included a portion of the Western Reserve. But the

Connecticut settlers did not consider this a practical government, and most of them doubted its legality.

By the end of the century, seven counties, Washington, Hamilton, Ross, Wayne, Adams, Jefferson and Knox, had been created, but none of them were of any practical service to the settlers on the Reserve. No magistrate had been appointed for that portion of the country, no civil process was established; and no mode existed of making legal conveyances.

But, in the year 1800, the State of Connecticut, by act of her Legislature, transferred to the National Government all her claim to civil jurisdiction. Congress assumed the political control, and the President conveyed by patent the fee of the soil to the Government of the State for the use of the grantees and the parties claiming under them. Whereupon, in pursuance of this authority, on the 22d of September, 1800, Governor St. Clair issued a proclamation establishing the county of Trumbull, to include within its boundaries the "Fire Lands" and adjacent islands, and ordered an election to be held at Warren, its county seat, on the second Tuesday of October. At that election, forty-two votes were cast, of which General Edward Paine received thirty-eight, and was thus elected a member of the Territorial Legislature. All the early deeds on the Reserve are preserved in the records of Trumbull county.

A treaty was held at Fort Industry, on the 4th July, 1805, between the Commissioners of the Connecticut Land Company and the Indians, by which all the lands in the Reserve, west of the Cuyahoga, belonging to the Indians, were ceded to the Connecticut Company.

Geauga was the second county of the Reserve. It was created by an act of the Legislature, December 31st, 1805; and by a subsequent act, its boundaries were made to include the present territory of Cuyahoga county, as far west as the 14th Range.

Portage county was established on the 10th of February, 1807, and, on the 16th of June, 1810, the act establishing Cuyahoga county went into operation. By that act all of Geauga west of the Ninth Range was made a part of Cuyahoga county.

Ashtabula county was established on the 22d of January, 1811.

A considerable number of Indians remained on the Western Reserve until the breaking out of the war of 1812. Most of the Canadian tribes took up arms against the United States in that struggle, and a portion of the Indians of the Western Reserve joined their Canadian brethren. At the close of that war occasional bands of these Indians returned to their old haunts on the Cuyahoga and the Mahoning; but the inhabitants of the Reserve soon made them understand that they were unwelcome visitors, after the part they had taken against us. Thus the war of 1812 substantially cleared the Reserve of its Indian inhabitants.

In this brief survey, I have attempted to indicate the general character of the leading events connected with the discovery and settlement of our country. I cannot, on this occasion, further pursue the history of the settlement and building up of the counties and townships of the Western Reserve. I have already noticed the peculiar character of the people who converted this wilderness into the land of happy homes which we now behold on every hand. But I desire to call the attention of the young men and women who hear me, to the duty they owe to themselves and their ancestors, to study carefully and reverently, the history of the great work which has been accomplished in this New Connecticut.

The pioneers who first broke ground here accomplished a work unlike that which will fall to the lot of any succeeding generation. The hardships they endured, the obstacles they encountered, the life they led, the peculiar qualities they needed in their undertakings, and the traits of character developed by their work, stand alone in our history. The generation that knew these first pioneers is fast passing away. But there are sitting in this audience to-day a few men and women whose memories date back to the early settlement. Here sits a gentlemen near me who is older than the Western Reserve. He remembers a time when the axe of the Connecticut pioneer had never awakened the echoes of the wilderness here. How strange and wonderful a transformation has taken place since he was a child! It is our sacred duty to rescue from oblivion the stirring recollections of such men, and preserve them as memorials of the past, as lessons for our own inspiration, and the instruction of those who shall come after us.

The material for a history of this Reserve are rich and abundant. Its pioneers were not ignorant and thoughtless adventurers, but men of established character, whose opinions on civil and religious liberty had grown with their growth, and become the settled convictions of their maturer years. Both here and in Connecticut, the family records, journals and letters which are preserved in hundreds of families, if brought out and arranged in order, would throw a flood of light on every page of our history. Even the brief notice which informed the citizens of this county that a meeting was to be held here to-day, to organize a Pioneer Society, has called this great audience together; and they have brought with them many rich historical memorials. They have brought old colonial commissions given to early Connecticut soldiers of the Revolution, who became pioneers of the Reserve and whose children are here to-day. They have brought church and other records which date back to the beginning of these settlements. They have shown us implements of industry which the pioneers brought in with them, many of which have been superseded by the superior mechanical contrivances of our time. Some of these implements are symbols of the spirit and character of the pioneers of the Reserve. Here is a broad-axe brought from Connecticut by John Ford, father of the late Governor of Ohio; and we are told that the first work done with this axe, by that sturdy old pioneer, after he had finished a few cabins for the families that came with him, was to hew out the timbers for an Academy—the Burton Academy—to which so many of our older men owe the foundation of their education, and from which sprang the Western Reserve College.

These pioneers knew well that the three great forces which constitute the strength and glory of a free government are, the Family, the School, and the Church. These three they planted here, and they nourished and cherished them with an energy and devotion scarcely equaled in any other quarter of the world. On this height were planted in the wilderness the symbols of this trinity of powers; and here let us hope may be maintained forever the ancient faith of our fathers in the sanctity of the Home, the intelligence of the School and the faithfulness of the Church. Where these three combine in prosperous union, the safety and prosperity of the Nation is assured. The glory of our country can never be dimmed while these three lights are kept shining with an undimmed lustre.

Western Reserve and Northern Ohio

HISTORICAL SOCIETY.

CLEVELAND, O., MAY, 1874.

NUMBER TWENTY-ONE.

SIXTH ANNUAL MEETING—REPORT OF THE PRESIDENT.

The Sixth annual meeting of the Western Reserve and Northern Ohio Historical Society, was held at the Museum in the Savings Bank building, Tuesday evening, May 12, 1874.

REPORT OF THE PRESIDENT.

During the first year after our organization in 1867, this room was not open to the public, and was used principally as a receptacle for donations. Our progress since 1868 has been satisfactory, and much more rapid than is usual in such societies. Mr. Goodman, our late Secretary gave his zealous personal attention to the accumulation of unpublished manuscripts, relating to the West. Through his perseverance in that direction, we have acquired a highly valuable collection of original papers, many of them now ready for the press.

Our general object and purpose is sufficiently set forth in one sentence of the by-laws, viz: "To discover, procure and preserve, whatever relates to the History, Biography, Genealogy, Antiquities and Statistics of the Western Reserve, the State of Ohio, and the Northwest."

Of the books having reference to these subjects, there is not a complete collection in any library in the United States. Our own is already as near complete as any West of the mountains except that of Wisconsin, and is frequently consulted by historical students. Our constitution is simply a section of the charter of the Cleveland Library Association; which is a perpetual institution of which we form a department. The room, for the museum, library, and business of this society, is secured to us by the liberality of the trustees of that institution, and of the Society for Savings.

Constitutions, by-laws and opportunities do not go far towards building up literary societies, unless there is spirit and industry among the members, and funds to meet necessary expenses.

THE FINANCIAL ASPECT.

Until the present year our financial prospects were not promising. The system of annual assessments of members has proved to be wholly insufficient. If it had not been for the financial assistance of a few staunch friends of this institution, our existence would have been short. As I stated last year, the plan of securing life members at $100 each, with no future assessments, was made the prominent feature in lieu of annual memberships, the money to be invested and only the proceeds to be used. Pledges had then been obtained, which were not to be called for until $5,000 was subscribed. If the financial panic of September last had not occurred, this would have been not only secured, but materially increased. This drawback was, however, more than met by the munificent offer of three Cleveland gentlemen, to double that sum as soon as it was collected from single members, and put on interest. This pledge has been kept good, and there is now ten thousand three hundred dollars, ($10,300) in the control of Messrs. Bingham, Bishop and Willey, as legal trustees, invested and to be invested. Though the product of this sum will not be large, it is permanent, and is at least twice as much as we were sure of heretofore from our annual members, a large portion of whom have become life members. About $1.500 more is pledged, payable at some future time, not fixed.

THE MUSEUM.

Although the room has been closed for want of heat, and other reasons nearly one-fourth of the past year, the number of visitors has been about the same as in previous years. Mrs. Milford has improved the time, when the public had not access, in arranging the collections, not only with more system, but, as every one admits, in much better style. She has had a part of the time, the assistance of Miss Seymour, who has displayed a remarkable facility in marking articles with a brush; in place of the paper labels.

Mrs. Milford has also been assiduously engaged making lists of our books, and arranging the cases, so that we are now better able to see what is wanting in order to complete the collection. To classify and catalogue all the articles we have received, is a tedious process requiring time, tact and patience.

PUBLICATIONS,

Since the last annual meeting we have published five tracts, numbered 16 to 20 inclusive.

No. 16—Annual Report, May, 1873, and date of the origin of the State of Ohio.

No. 17—Correspondence—War of 1812—Selection No. 6.

No. 18 -Correspondence—War of 1812—Selection No. 7.

No. 19—Correspondence—War of 1812—Selection No. 8.

No. 20—Historical Address of Hon. J. A. Garfield, September, 1873.

NEWSPAPER FILES BOUND.

Our volumes of bound newspapers—have been very much increased during the year. Including those on deposit, they now number six hundred and forty-five. The *Herald* and *Plain Dealer* of this city, have placed their files with us on deposit, going back to the origin of those papers, the former in 1819, the latter in our files since 1842. Of the *Herald* we now have from 1819 to 1830, with the exception of 1826. The bound files of the *Trump of Fame and Western Reserve Chronicle* from 1811 to 1861 were heretofore donated by Joseph Perkins, Esq. Dr. E. Sterling has placed on deposit, complete volumes of the New York *Herald* during the war of the rebellion. Our miscellaneous volumes, composed of single files of old papers bound according to size, and not yet indexed, embrace many curious, valuable and interesting matters, growing more valuable by the lapse of time. About one hundred volumes of the files of current papers, preserved by the library association, are now being bound for us as a special donation.

SCRAP BOOKS.

Mrs. Milford has spent much time in arranging the clippings from newspapers which have come into our possession. The late General John McCalla, of Washington, a distinguished officer of the war of 1812, sent us some years since a large package of such scraps. Those which our late secretary, Mr. Goodman, had collected, were also donated to the society. From many other sources, this easy form of preserving valuable items, has served to increase our collection until it now fills twenty-four volumes. It is principally historical in its character, and has been indexed with great patience by Mrs. Milford. Those who have not practiced the plan of clipping from transient prints, will be surprised how soon a valuable fund of information on any specialty, may be obtained at a very slight expense of money or time.

ABSTRACT OF HISTORICAL SOCIETIES IN OHIO.

Our Secretary, C. C. Baldwin, Esq., has been engaged during several months in collecting a history, of historical and pioneer associations in Ohio. He has prepared a valuable paper on this subject, arranging the societies by counties, which will form one of our earliest publications and will be appreciated by all local historians.'

COINS.

Articles of general interest and curiosity have come in more rapidly than usual, particularly rare coins. This collection attracts more attention among the young men, than that of any other department. Mr. H. N. Johnson has special charge of this collection, a catalogue of which is being made. There are in American coins and medals, 385; in foreign coins, 513; total in coins and medals, 898.

OLD PAPER CURRENCY.

There are a large number of Revolutionary and Colonial bills, old wild cat currency, shin-plasters, and bills of early banks and others issued before and during the rebellion, both at the North and South They will be arranged as soon as possible and filed in scrap books.

JAPANESE, CHINESE AND INDIAN CURIOSITIES.

W. P. Fogg, Esq , has donated a valuable collection gathered in his "trip around the world," among which are a Japanese table, screen and lady's robe, a bronze vase, fac-similes of boats, curiosities from the pyramids of Egypt, an old copper, a Mosaic cup and saucer over one thousand years old, specimens of the printed language of the Hindoos, Persians and Chinese, old coin and paper money, and many other articles of interest.

RELICS OF THE INDIANS AND MOUND BUILDERS.

One flat glass case has been filled with the stone implements of the Indian and his predecessor the mound builder, not yet catalogued. We have endeavored to separate the relics of each people, but find they run together in a way to indicate that they were closely related. The number of stone ornaments, tools for skinning animals, flint arrow points, lance heads and cutting implements of stone and copper, beads of bone and copper, and other forms, the uses of which are not yet known, is about one thousand. We have tracings on cloth the size of nature of six rock inscriptions in Ohio, that were made by the red man, which are rude symbols, no doubt having a meaning, but do not appear to be continuous records of events. They give very little information of an historical character, but relate principally to personal affairs, messages to friends, or the fancy sketches of idle hours.

OFFICERS OF THE SOCIETY.

President—Charles Whittlesey.
Vice President—J. H. Salisbury and E. Sterling.
Secretary—C. C. Baldwin.
Treasurer—S. Williamson.
Librarian—Mrs. M. Milford.
Legal Trustees—William Bingham, J. P. Bishop, George Willey.

CURATORS ELECTIVE.

Term expires in 1875—C. C. Baldwin, Miss Mary C. Brayton, C. T. Sherman.
Term expires in 1876—Joseph Perkins, Charles Whittlesey, John W. Allen.
Term expires in 1877—J. H. A. Bone, Mrs. George Willey, H. N. Johnson.

PERMANENT CURATORS.

W J Boardman — James Barnett
William Bingham — H M Chapin
B A. Stanard.

RESIDENT LIFE MEMBERS.

Horace Kelly — Amos Townsend
A G Colwell — Silas M Stone
C C Baldwin — W S Chamberlain
L E Holden — Wm S C Otis
H B Tuttle — J H Sargent
A W Fairbanks — H A Harvey
James J Tracy — Leonard Case
Geo Willey — H M Chapin
P H Babcock — Miss L T Guilford
Joseph Perkins — Miss M E Ingersol
Abira Cobb — Miss S L Andrews
Alvah Bradley — Alfred E Buell
S V Harkness — Douglas Perkins
T S Beckwith — Jacob B Perkins
J H Wade — Joseph Perkins, Jr
R P Wade — L Lewis Perkins
Dudley Baldwin — Peter M Hitchcock
Colgate Hoyt — D W Cross
Wm Chisholm — Cleve C Hale
W S Streator — J D Rockefeller
T M Kelley — Mrs Fred Judson
C F Glasser — John Erwin
S L Mather — John W Allen
T P Handy — John Todd
Geo Mygatt — Wm J Gordon
R P Ranney — Charles O Scott
Wm Collins — E P Morgan
O A Childs — N C Baldwin
J P Bishop — J H Salisbury
H. C Blossom — W J Boardman
H P Weddell — Kirtland K Cutter
J H Devereux — H N Johnson
O A Brooks.

LIFE MEMBERS NON-RESIDENTS.

Kent Jarvis, Jr., Massillon, Stark county, O.
Judge Eben Newton, Canfield, Mahoning county, O.
Judge W. G. Lane, Sandusky, O.
Hon. R W. Tayler, Youngstown, O.
Hon. Wm. Henry Smith, Chicago, Ill.
Benson J. Lossing, L. L. D., Dover Plains, N. Y.
General L. V. Bierce, Akron, O.
Theodatus Garlick, M. D., Bedford, O.
Jared P. Kirtland, L. L. D., Rockport, O.
Hon. J. A. Garfield, Hiram, O.
Col. Geo. T. Perkins, Akron, O.
Hon. James Monroe, Oberlin, O.
Total 76.

ANNUAL MEMBERS RESIDENT AND NON-RESIDENT.

Lyman Little — Wm L Cutter
M C Younglove — S C Green
J S Kingsland — Harvey Rice
William Bingham — B A Stanard
B R Beavis — J C Sexton
James Farmer — W C B Richardson
S N Sanford — Jas W Lee
J W Tyler — Benj Harrington
Col C H Carlton, U S A — Chas T Sherman
John N Frazee — David L King, Akron
Chas Bill — A Stone, Jr
James Barnett — L Austin
Miss Mary C Brayton — Jehu Brainerd, Washington, D C
J D Cleveland

PAID IN ADVANCE.

Nathan H. Winslow, Buffalo, to 1882.
C. C. Carlton, Cleveland, to 1878.
Chas. A. Otis, Cleveland, to 1884.

Western Reserve and Northern Ohio HISTORICAL SOCIETY.

CLEVELAND, O., AUGUST, 1874.

NUMBER TWENTY-TWO.

BATTLE OF FRENCH TOWN, 1813—MAJOR CRAIG ON LAKE ERIE, 1782—WHITE MEN AS SCALPERS—GEOGRAPHER GENERAL HUTCHINS.

LETTER FROM REV. THOMAS P. DUDLEY.

LEXINGTON, KY., Oct. 20th, 1870.

A. T. Goodman, Secretary W. R. H. S.

MY DEAR SIR—There is another reminiscence of the War of 1812-15 which may not be uninteresting, if you have not heretofore been advised of it. When the prisoners taken after the battles at French Town, on the River Raisin, reached "New Arch," now called "Niagara" opposite to Fort Niagara on the American side of Niagara river, they were all paroled, officers and men, except General Winchester, Colonel Lewis, and Major Madison who were detained, and sent to Quebec, where they remained in captivity for some eighteen months after our captivity, a part of the time confined in prison. In the spring of 1813 two regiments of Kentucky troops the one commanded by my uncle, Col. Wm. Dudley, the other by Col. Wm. E. Boswell, under the command of Gen. Green Clay, were ordered to reinforce Gen. Harrison at Fort Meigs. Col. Dudley's regiment was ordered to land on the opposite side of the Maumee river, opposite Fort Meigs, and to spike the cannon in a battery, worked by the British and to retreat to the bank of the river, under the guns of Fort Meigs. When Col. Dudley's regiment had succeeded in driving the enemy from the battery and spiking their cannon, his men could not be restrained from the pursuit of the enemy. The result was that Col. Dudley and many of his men were killed; many more taken prisoners, and a few of them retreated to the river, and reached the fort. This was called Dudley's defeat. The following fall Governor Shelby raised a large number of volunteers, and joined Gen. Harrison at Fort Meigs, and after Croghan's victory at Lower Sandusky, and Perry's victory on Lake Erie, pursued the enemy to Detroit and into Canada, following them up the river Thames, where the battle of the Thames was fought, in which Col. R. M. Johnson and others were wounded, and the British army under command of the infamous General Proctor, were captured, Proctor and some of his officers escaping. The officers who were captured at the Thames including Major Muir, (who had released me from Indian captivity at Detroit, and Lieutenants Hale and Watson who had invited me to mess with them while in the Fort at Detroit, during my stay there) were brought to Frankfort, Kentucky, my then residence, as prisoners of war, where they remained several months during a part of which time time they were confined in the penitentiary, in retaliation for the confinement of General Winchester, Colonel Lewis, Major Madison and others in British prisons. When the order came to imprison the British prisoners at Frankfort, I approached Governor Shelby and urged that Major Muir should be allowed the town on parole, as he had shown the spirit of a man and soldier in alleviating the sufferings of the American prisoners taken at Raisin. Major Muir, however, declined accepting the favor, suggesting that it might tend to his prejudice at home. I had the privilege of visiting the British prisoners frequently, while in Frankfort, and was gratified to show them such kindness as was consistent with their circumstances. Allow me to bear testimony to the honorable bearing and soldierly conduct of another British officer. While on the march from Sandwich to "New Arch," now called Niagara, opposite to Fort Niagara on the American side of the river, and on the night previous to our reaching the latter place, I came to a hotel at Eleven Mile Creek, now called St. Catherines, in advance of the officers who had accompanied us, where we found a number of our prisoners who had preceded us on foot. About 8 o'clock two officers, who proved to be Major Merritt of the British dragoons, and his son, Lieut. Merritt, of the same batalion, came up. Major Merritt inquired in a stentorian voice, "Is there not here a Mr. Dudley, a wounded prisoner of war?" Some one replied in the affirmative. Which is he? he said. He was pointed to where I sat, my pulse was greatly quickened, not knowing what misfortune was about to overtake me after so many dangers and so much suffering. He however approached me, and said, Sir, you must go home with me. I replied I can't go. I have suffered much with my wound the past day, and feel like resting very soon. He rejoined, saying, I have a comfortable carryall, and a good span of horses, and only live about two miles from here. I said I do not want to leave my traveling companion, Dr. Overton. He asked which is he. I pointed to him, the Major then said, he must go too.

We assented, and in a very short time we reached his residence, where we found a comfortable fire, and most hospitable family, composed of the Major, his wife, son and grown up daughter, after partaking of an excellent supper, we were seated around the fire, when the Major said to me, "Please give us an account of your two battles on the River Raisin, your capture, the massacre of the prisoners by the Indians, and what subsequently took place." I proceeded to give a detail, pretty much at length, which kept us up until twelve or one o'clock in the morning, when we retired to our lodging room. Early the following morning I reminded the Major of his promise to bring us back early that morning that we might join our officers whom we had left in the rear on the previous evening. I will, said he, on one proviso. Again my heart beat quicker, not knowing what was yet to befall us. I quickly inquired: What is that? and was relieved by the remark, "If your officers will come and dine with me to-day, and you accompany them." I readily assented, when he returned us to the hotel. The Kentucky officers, (prisoners,) soon arrived, and on being introduced to them, he invited them to dine at his house, which invitation they accepted. I left the room to see about the carryall which had brought me there, and found it was about to proceed to Fort George. Maj. Merrit approached me and said, your officers have agreed to dine with me and I claim your promise. I replied, the carryall which brought me here, is about to proceed, and if I do not go in it I shall be deprived of a passage, and I am not in a condition to walk. He quickly rejoined "that shall be no excuse, I will take you to New Arch in my own carryall after dinner." After partaking of a most sumptuous and elegant dinner, we took leave of the hospitable and kind family, and proceeded to New Arch, where I was once more delighted to see the much loved flag of the United States thrown to the breeze on Fort Niagara, on the opposite side of the river, and where I parted with the soldierly and hospitable Major. After my return and the close of the war, I heard from the family, and that they still recollected me. Passing through Canada in the summer of 1855 I inquired for the family and learned that they had all passed away but Sir William Merritt, the projector of the Welland Canal.

How, or by what means Major Merritt had heard of me, and was induced to show so much kindness, I have been unable to learn. If you shall find anything in the foregoing sketch which will interest your society, and be of any service, I shall be gratified. The good book says, "Ingratitude is as the sin of witchcraft." I wish to make this public acknowledgment to the family and friends of those who showed me so much kindness when I so much needed it.

I am, very respectfully, your most obedient,

THOS. P. DUDLEY.

HORACE NYE TO COLONEL ICHABOD NYE, AT MARIETTA.

URBANA, OHIO, Sept. 28, 1812.

DEAR SIR—I have written you before, several times, but have received not a line from Marietta, except from Anselm, since I left that. The articles I sent for were received in good order. General Tupper left this yesterday on a secret expedition; he will command the mounted forces which Harrison intended commanding in person. All mounted, say ten or eleven hundred. Harrison has selected him for the command in preference to the other commanders; it will be a tour of some danger, and will be determined in eight or ten days. I wished to accompany him, but they would not consent. As to the troops at this place, I have the most of the trouble of keeping them in order, which is not small, being quartered in town many of them (for the want of tents), but a full supply will be in this morning from Newport with what we had before. There will likewise be a supply of other articles of camp equipage, but many of the troops are very poorly clad, and no posibility of getting any of account here. Should any person procure a large supply of shoes, socks, thick pantaloons, vests, hunting shirts, coarse shirts, etc., they would find immediate sale for any quantity, at a high price for cash. Shoes and socks particularly, are not to be had If you had a hundred or two on hand, it would nearly pay a man for packing them to this place or further. Peire wished to come here. I wrote to him and expected him here before this, but I have not heard from him. Should he yet be out of business, I think he had better purchase all such articles with anything else that is wanted for clothing and make a load for this place or where ever the Army may be. I could if I were at liberty make money as fast as one could wish, with a small capital—calico shirts would soon be sold. Harrison is now at St. Marys, with the Kentucky troops, which came in last, with some of the first—a party have proceeded down the Miami opposite the lake, as far as Fort Defiance. General Harrison will proceed in a few days to join the Pennsylvania troops, and those from Ohio of Wadsworth's Division, in order to hurry them on, with a large train of Artillery from Pittsburg. General Winchester will have in his advance command those troops West of us, which will be pushed on to the Rapids, from St. Mary's. Those troops at this place, will join them at that place, by Hull's route. The detachment will consist of the Virginia troops now on their march to this place, fifteen hundred strong and about one thousand from this State.

There are besides of Ohio troops now with Harrison 350, exclusive of those mounted for a short time. The whole army when collected will exceed ten thousand men. Provision is only plenty in this part of the State, and those who have furnished for Hull's army as far as the rapids before and are now contractors for Government, say there will be no difficulty in furnishing during the winter, as that will be the best time. The British have but few troops at Detroit, say 50. The Indians have beseiged Fort Harrison, but the accounts from that quarter (as well as from all others) are contradictory, some say they are 1500 strong, but it is not believed. They destroyed all the property within their reach at Fort Wayne, before Harrison came up, but fled immediately on his approach. There were but three men killed at that place, and those were out of the Fort. There have been no depredations of the Indians on this part of the frontier since I came; there were several persons killed on the heads of the Muskingum, and several Indians paid the forfeit. The inhabitants are daily calling for arms from the frontier. There have many been sent. Mr. Gilmore, from Granville, who was with Hull, is now here for arms; he takes one hundred with him for that part of the frontier. There have been several Indian towns destroyed, and all will be that are hostile, within two hundred miles of this betore winter. The Kentucky troops want discipline as well as our own—ours have the name of being the best that has ever been in this part of the country—I mean Militia.

I have written in haste, as Mr. Kinhead, by whom I intend sending this to Chillicothe, starts immediately; there is no post from here to Chillicothe, except by the way of Zanesville.

HORACE NYE.

CLEVELAND IN THE WAR OF THE REVOLUTION.

Isaac Craig, Esq., of Alleghany City, recently addressed a letter to the President of this Society, with the request for assistance in recovering a silver spoon which Mrs. Charles Carpenter found on the beach of the Lake near Rocky River, many years since. The lettering on this spoon was reported to be "I. C.," which Mr. Craig suspected might have stood for the initials of his grandfather, Major Isaac Craig, of the Revolutionary Army. He represented what had not been known here, that Major Craig was ordered to this place toward the close of the war by General Irvine, who was in command at Fort Pitt. The importance of the mouth of the Cuyahoga in a military sense had attracted the attention of the Government. It was suspected that the English, who held Detroit and Lake Erie, were about to establish a post here. A brief biography of Major Craig has been printed by his descendants for private circulation, from which what relates to this daring reconnoissance is given below. Mrs. Carpenter, who now resides at Kelley Island, very promptly sent the spoon to the Historical Room for examination.

An account of the circumstances under which it was found will before long be published. The lettering is not "I. C" but clearly "I. G" which dissipates the hopes of *Mr. Craig*. Probably this spoon is a relic of *Col. Bradstreets'* expedition which met with a disaster in October 1764 on the spot where it was found. Among his officers were Lieut. Coaser and Ensign Camoran, to one of whom the spoon may have belonged.

GEN. IRVINE'S ORDERS TO MAJOR CRAIG.

FORT PITT, Nov. 11th, 1782.

SIR:—I have received intelligence through various channels, that the British have established a post at *Lower Sandusky*, and also information that it is suspected they intend erecting one at either Cuyahoga Creek or Grand River, (Fairport). But as these accounts are not from persons of military knowledge, nor to be fully relied upon in any particular, and I am anxious to have the facts well established; you will therefore proceed with Lieutenant Rose, my aid-de-camp, and six active men, in order to reconnoiter these two places, particular Cuyahoga. As your party is so small, you will use every precaution to avoid being discovered, which service I expect you will be able to perform, as they will probably be relaxed in discipline at this advanced season of the year. When you have reconnoitered these posts (if any) you may try to take a prisoner, provided it can be done without much risque of losing any of your party; which must be guarded against at all events, as it is not your business to come to action. My reasons for allowing you so small a party, being to avoid discovery. I know your zeal will excite you to go lengths, perhaps even beyond your judgment, in order to effect the purposes of your excursion. But, notwithstanding my earnest desire to obtain accurate accounts of the matters mentioned herein, you will please to keep in view that I am extremely solicitous that every man may be brought back safe, and that one man falling into the hands of the enemy may not only ruin your whole present business, but also prevent future discovery.

As it may be necessary for you to detach or separate from Mr. Rose, it will be proper for you to give him a certified copy of this order.

I am, sir, your obedient, humble servant,

WM. IRVINE, B. Genl.

Major Craig.

EXTRACT FROM THE PRIVATELY PRINTED LIFE OF MAJOR ISAAC CRAIG.

"In November, 1782, General Irvine received intelligence that the British had established a military post at Sandusky, and were about to establish one either at Cuyahoga or Grand River; he therefore issued an order to Major Craig, dated November 11th, 1782, to take with him the General's aid, Lieutenant Rose, and six active men, and proceed to Cuyahoga and Grand Rivers, and espcially the former place, to ascertain whether any such attempts were making by the enemy. This order is eloquent in urging Major Craig to be cautious and not to be stimulated by his zeal for the service, to venture too far, and concludes by saying "one man falling into the hands of the enemy, may not only ruin your whole present business, but also prevent future discovery."

The Major, with his party, started on their expedition, on the 13th of November, taking with them one horse, with a supply of provisions; they crossed Big Beaver River at its mouth, and Little Beaver some distance above its mouth, and thence proceeded in a direction south of west, as if bound for the Indian town at the forks of the Muskingum, pursuing that course until night, and then turned directly north, and traveled all night in that direction. This was done to mislead and elude the pursuit of the Indians, who may have followed them. When they arrived, as they supposed, within a days march of the Cuyahoga, they left one man with the extra provisions. It was the intention upon rejoining this man, to have taken a fresh supply of provisions, and then proceed to examine the mouth of the Grand river; one of the points which the enemy was reported to have in view. General Irvine, in his instructions, had treated it as a point of less importance than the Cuyahoga, but yet worthy of attention. The weather proved very unfavorable after the separation; the Major, with his party, was detained beyond the oppointed time, and the soldier with the horse had disappeared, so that when they reached the designated place, weary and half famished, they found no relief, and had before them a journey of more than one hundred miles, through a hostile wilderness. The examination of Grand river had of course to be abandoned, and the party was compelled to hasten back to Fort Pitt. The travel back was laborious and painful, the weather being tempestuous and variable. The party pursued the most direct course homeward. Before they reached the Connequenessing, near about, as Major Craig thought where Old Harmony now stands, the weather became extremely cold, and they found that stream frozen over, but the ice not sufficiently firm to bear the weight of a man. The following expedient was then resorted to as the best the circumstances allowed: A large fire was kindled on the northern bank of the Connequenessing, and when it was burning freely, the party stripped off their clothes; one man took a heavy bludgeon in his hands to break the way while each of the others followed with portions of the clothing, and arms in one hand, and a fire-brand in the other. Upon reaching the southern bank of the stream, these brands were placed together and a brisk fire soon raised, by which the party dressed themselves and then resumed their toilsome march. Upon reaching the Cranberry plains they were delight to find encamped there a hunting party, consisting of Captain Uriah Springer and other officers, and some soldiers from the fort. There, of course, they were welcomed and kindly treated, and arrived at the fort on the evening of the second of December.

"The report of Major Craig was that there was no sign of occupancy at the mouth of the Cuyahoga."

LIEUTENANT ROSE.

"The history of this young officer is somewhat entertaining. He was a Russian nobleman by birth—was engaged in a duel, and had to fly from his native land. He possessed high endowments, and genteel manners, and upon his arrival here, received an appointment as assistant surgeon in the army. General Irvine, who was a physician, perceived that he was a gentleman in his manner, but awkward as a surgeon, and offered him a situation as an aid de camp, which he at once accepted, and discharged its duties with ability and fidelity. After the war he returned to Russia, and many years later Gen. Irvine's son received a letter from him, teeming with expressions of gratitude for the kindness of the General, and signed by "Baron de Rosendolphe." Dr. Irvine, a son of the General, informed me that the Baron was subsequently appointed Field Marshall of the Province of Livonia. Garden, in his "Anecdotes of the Revolution," vol. II., gives a very favorable notice of Lieutenant Rose."

NOTE.—Lieut. Rose was sent by General Irvine, as his representative with the ill-fated expedition of Col. Crawford against the Sandusky villages in June, 1782. He was fortunate enough to escape the clutches of the savages, and to make a good military record. See Butterfield's History of Crawford's expedition.

WHITE MEN AS SCALPERS.

BY COL. CHARLES WHITTLESEY.

The practice of taking human scalps as trophies of war originated with the North American Indians; but there are numerous instances on record in this country where it was adopted by white men. In other countries there have been war customs equally cruel, but with no other people has this special mode of mutilating and insulting the dead ever been practiced. In Central America, among the Aztecs, Toltecs, and Mayas, it was not known, nor among the Peruvians. No people are more ferocious than the primitive inhabitants of Africa and Asia, but I know of no instances where they scalped their dead enemies.

There are many nations making pretentions to civilization, who have been equally savage towards prisoners of war; but have adopted other modes of cruelty, little more refined. Samuel the Judge, and ruler of Israel, hewed the captive Philistine King Agag, in pieces with his own hands. Hector essayed to cut off the head of Patroclus at the risk of his own life.

There are pictorial representations extant in the Etruscan tombs where the Trojan prisoners are being led bound and naked, with ropes around their necks, into the presence of Agamemnon. Their limbs are lacerated and bleeding. Ajax has one by the hair, while Achilles is cutting the throat of another. The Emperor Trajan about the time of Christ treated the Dacians, whom he conquered in a manner equally revolting to us. At the seige of Alesia in Gaul, Vercingetorix and a large number of his soldiers, voluntarily gave themselves up to Julius Cæsar. After exhibiting them in triumph through the camp he made slaves of the men, and put Vercingetorix to death. Still later, when William the Conquerer invaded England, his soldiers disfigured the corpses of Harold's men after the battle of Hastings.

Recently discovered slabs of gypsum at Nineveh with written and hieroglyphical inscriptions now in the British Museum show how prisoners of wai were treated by Sardonapolus and Sennacherib. A scribe took an account of the number of heads of those slain in battle as they were brought to the tent of the victor. The captive leader was beheaded in the presence of his captor. Generals and other officers had their tongues cut out, their hair and beards plucked out, and were cut, beaten, flayed alive and tortured generally very much as North American Indians do. This is done on the day and field of battle, their carcases being left unburied. Tamerlane the Tartar cut off the heads of 90,000 Persians, making a ghastly pile of them at the gates of Bagdad. The North American Indians are therefore not alone in the infliction of mental and bodily torture upon their enemies, though they have a hideous and bloody way of doing it. Before the advent of white people, their knives or cutting implements were made of flint or other hard stone. The edges were rough and saw-like, tearing rather than cutting the flesh. To kill an enemy and not recover his scalp is to an Indian a perpetual disgrace. For this purpose he ceases fighting in the midst of battle. With one hand he seizes the scalp-lock, places his foot on the neck of his foe, whether living or dead, and cuts a circular incision dextrously around the crown of the head. If he cannot then jerk the scalp from the skull, he seizes it with both hands or his teeth, pulls it off instantly, and raises it aloft with a yell of triumph.

I am now to give some instances where white men have perpetrated this bloody practice upon the red.

Before we moralize too closely upon it, we should reflect that war is everywhere a mortal strife, the first object being the most rapid and thorough destruction of our enemies. Indian war is usually more the work of individuals than of organized masses. The red warrior requires some evidence of his success, and none is more covenient or convincing than the scalp of his foe.

Our ancestors who undertook to people North America, did so in defiance of the Indian occupants. Perpetual war was the necessary consequence. If the success of those settlements, and the displacement of the wild tribes, had not been in accordance with the will of God, the feeble white element, surrounded by so numerous a body of savages, must soon have been extirpated. It was necessary for the whites, not only to defend themselves, but to become aggressive; and to succeed in this they must largely adopt the Indians mode of warfare. Skulking through swamps, and thickets, around the new settlements, the red man selected his victim, whom he killed and instantly scalped. With the stealth of a wild animal he came, and fled to his distant wigwam with his trophy. The bold pioneers soon became adepts in this mode of warfare, and as in everything else, their intelligence enabled them to outdo the barbarian. They went out singly or in squads, to hunt their red enemies, as Boone and Kenton did, in after years. Both parties held their lives cheap, and by common usage the scalp was a legitimate trophy.

In this state of affairs, it was a natural and sensible plan, to encourage those who had an inclination for such adventures. Like all other hunts, the scalp was conclusive evidence of success. Besides the bounty which was of small account with these old "Leather Stockings," they relished the exquisite romance of a chase for men, and in addition to this a patriotic pleasure in defending their brethren and their families.

In the colony of Conneticut, according to the "Public Records" for 1706-16, (Hoadley page 167) will be found the following statement. "On account of the continued annoyance of the frontier, particularly in the neighboring county of Hampshire, by skulking parties of our enemy, Indians and French, the "Committee of War" for the county of Hartford, is empowered to employ four or five Englishmen, and "commissionate them" to lead a party of Indian scouts, not exceeding sixty, at the charge of the colony, and supply them with ammunition and provisions.

"The said scouting company shall receive out of the public treasury of this colony, for each Indian scalp of the enemy which they shall bring to said committee, the sum of ten pounds, to be equally shared amongst them."

Governor Dinwiddie, of Virginia, writing to the Board of Trade in December, 1752, says, "the Indians have declared to our traders that the French promised to give them one hundred crowns (about $50) for every white scalp they bring them." This was done by the commandant at Detroit, on the authority of the Governor General of Canada. For George Croghan and James Lowrey, the Pennsylvania traders, they offered a higher price. The Governor of Virginia retaliated by offering a tempting bounty on the scalps of Frenchmen.

Major Rogers, a prominent officer of the French war (journal pages 13 and 14) states that the French on Lake Champlain paid the Indians sixty livres (about $12) for the scalps of Englishmen.

A history of Luzerne county, Pa., recently published by Stewart Pease, Esq., of Wilkesbarre, affirms that Thomas and John Penn, as Governors of the Colony, offered bounties for Delaware scalps, and that Governor Morris in 1756, proclaimed that he would pay $130 for each Indian scalp, and $150 for prisoners. At page 123, he states that the Governor of Canada in the revolutionary war, paid the Senecas of New York for ten hundred and fifty scalps, taken from the heads of Americans on that frontier.

In 1844 I spent an evening with Benjamin Stites, jr., of Madisonville, Ohio, the son of Benjamin Stites, who settled at Columbia, near Cincinnati, in 1788. Benjamin junior was then a boy, but soon grew to be a woodsman and an Indian fighter. Going over the incidents of the pioneer days, he said the settlers of Columbia, agreed to pay ($30) thirty dollars in trade for every Indian scalp. He related an instance of a man who received a mare for a scalp, under this arrangement. The frontier men of those times spoke of "hunting Indians," as they would of hunting wolves, bears, or any other wild animal. I met another old man, who then lived near Covington, on the Kentucky side of the Ohio, who said he had often gone alone up the valley of the Miami on a hunt for scalps. With most of these Indian hunters, the bounty was a minor consideration. The hatred of the red man was a much stronger motive.

William James in 1818 published at London, England, an account of the war of 1812-15, in the United States. He possessed very few of the qualities of an historian, and wrote for the single purpose of injuring the American Government and its army. On page 183, vol. 1, he quotes from what purports to be a newspaper published at Pittsburg, the following advertisement:

"PITTSBURG, May 17th, 1791.

"We, the subscribers, encouraged by a large subscription, do propose to pay ($100) one hundred dollars for every hostile Indian scalp, with both ears, if it be taken between this date and the 15th day of June next, by an inhabitant of Alleghany county.

[Signed] "GEORGE WALLIS,
"ROBERT ELLIOTT,
"WILLIAM AMBERSON,
"ADAMSON TOWNHILL,
"WILLIAM WILKINS, JR.,
"JOHN IRVINE."

I have no means of verifying the accuracy of this quotation.

It is reported that early in the war of 1812, the Parliament House of Toronto, Canada, was ornamented by a scalp placed over the speaker's chair. There is no question but members of the expeditions against the Indians of the Northwest, from 1790 to and including those of the war of 1812, indulged in the practice of scalping.

At the battle of the Thames in October, 1813, not Tecumseh alone' but many of his red warriors, lost their scalp locks, which found their way into Kentucky.

The records of border history, from the days of King Phillip to this hour, are witnesses that each party who engaged in the frontier death struggles, had staked his scalp on the result.

CAPTAIN THOMAS HUTCHINS,

GEOGRAPHER OF THE UNITED STATES, 1778, 1789.

An office was created by the Continental Congress about the middle of the revolution, called the "Geographer of the United States." Its purpose is not now fully understood, but appears at first to have been military. The government and especially the army, needed a bureau of charts and of geographical knowledge, such as all civilized governments have; but of which it was then destitute.

At the opening of the American rebellion Thomas Hutchins of the colony of New Jersey, was a captain in the Sixtieth regiment of foot, which was raised in the colonies, forming one of the battallions known as the "Royal Americans." This regiment constituted part of Col. Bouquet's command in the expeditions of 1763 and 1764, into the Ohio country against the Indians who lived upon the Muskingum river. Hutchins appears to have been a well educated man. Bouquet made him engineer to the expedition, and in pursuance of this duty he surveyed and measured the route day by day, after it moved west of Pittsburg. He was one of those frontier characters who combine fearlessness, intelligence and a love of adventure, of whom there were at that time quite a number in the British army. Hutchins kept a journal of the march, with a map of the route showing the position of each encampment, which was published at Philadelphia in 1765, by the historian of the expedition, the Rev. Wm. Smith, of Philadelphia. While in the Ohio country he conceived the plan of settling it by military colonies, as the best mode of securing peace with the Indians. The scheme was at the same time brilliant and practical.

At the outbreak of the Revolution Captain Hutchins was in London, where he was soon afterwards suspected by the British agents of being in communication with Benjamin Franklin at Paris. He was put in prison, and his fortune, amounting to about $40,000, confiscated. In 1778 he succeeded in reaching Savannah, in Georgia, and was soon after made "Geographer" to the Confederation. There is very little information in regard to his functions until the new government had achieved its independence; and in 1784 acquired title to the western lands. By the ordinance of May 20th, 1785, the geographer is directed to commence the survey of government lands on the north side of the Ohio river where the west line of Pennsylvania should cross the same. An east and west base line was to be run from thence westerly through the territory, which Mr. Hutchins was required to superintend in person, and to take the latitude of certain prominent points; especially the mouths of rivers. Longitude on land was not then attainable, for want of proper instruments.

To that day, the surveys of all countries had been made on a base line determined arbitrarily by roads, rivers, mountains, or coasts. The most simple of all modes, that of north and south and east and west lines, had never entered the minds of mathematicians; or if it had, had never been reduced to practice. The plan provided for in the ordinance of 1785, is no doubt the invention of Mr. Hutchins, which was foreshadowed in his scheme for military settlements, promulgated in 1765.

By this original mode of laying out land, the township lines were to be run in squares, on the true meridian, six miles apart, and at right angles, east and west, parallel to the equator. Within these squares the lots or sections are laid out, also in squares, thirty-six in number, of one mile on a side, each containing 640 acres. All our government lands have been surveyed on that plan, from that day to this. Each section and township throughout this vast space is so marked as to be distinguished from any other. Wherever the corner and witness trees are standing, whoever visits them can at once determine the latitude and longitude of his position, and the distance from each base and meridian line.

Hutchins, as geographer, had power to appoint surveyors, who were first to run the lines of seven ranges of townships, next west of the Pennsylvania line, from the Ohio river to the 41st parallel north latitude. It was accomplished during the years 1786-7, among hostile Indians, who, notwithstanding the land had been ceded to the United States, were wholly opposed to the occupation by white men. Col. Harmar's battallion, stationed on the Ohio and Alleghany rivers, was required to do duty in the woods as a guard with the surveyors. Otherwise the lines could not have been run.

While Hutchins was zealously engaged in this work, having his office at Pittsburg, Pa., he was called away from it by death early in the year 1788. The office of geographer expired with him.

Its duties were for a time transferred to the Treasury Department and eventually the office of "Surveyor General" of the public lands was created. Very little is known of the private history of this modest patriot of the revolution. Probably he left no descendants. The office he held during nearly the entire existence of the Continental Congress was a very important one, requiring a high order of mathematical talent, physical energy and personal courage. As the author of the best system of public surveys now known his name should in some way be made more conspicuous in our annals. Even the place where his remains were interred, has passed into forgetfulness. From his first journey in Ohio with Col. Bouquet, he foresaw and predicted that it would become a populous country. He lived barely long enough to see his favorite scheme of colonization, commenced at Marietta, by the soldiers of the revolution.

WESTERN RESERVE & NORTHERN OHIO

HISTORICAL SOCIETY.

Pamphlets, Memoranda and Scraps,

IN PAMPHLET CASES.

ON DEPOSIT BY CHAS. WHITTLESEY, JANUARY I, 1873.

CASE NO. 1.

GEOLOGICAL.

No.
1. Onward March of the Race, (Winchel.)
2. Metamorphosis of Siredon, (Marsh.)
3. Fossil Horse, Nebraska, (Marsh.)
4. Miocene Vertebrates, (Cope.)
5. Geological Surveys in the United States (Marsh.)
6. Geological Succession, (Winchel.)
7. Classification of Mollusks, (Morse.)
8. Man the Last Term, &c., (Winchel,)
9. Minnesota Geol. Report, (Eames.)
10. Conglomerate Pebbles, (Brainerd.)
11. Rocks of Kansas, (Swallow.)
12. Report on Precious Metals, (Taylor.)
13. Geol. Survey of California, (Whitney's Letter.)
14. Geol. Survey of Michigan, Report on, 1869.
15. Geol. Survey of Ohio, Report on, 1857.
16. Geol. Survey of Ohio, 1869.
17. Geol. Grand Traverse Bay, Michigan, 1866.
18. Geol. Report N. Scotia, 1868, (Hunt.)
19. Glacial action Green Mountains, Vermont, (Hungerford,) 1867.
20. Hairy Elephant restored.

CASE NO. 2.

GEOLOGY—WISCONSIN & MINNESOTA.

1. Outline Report Wisconsin and Michigan, 1850.
2. Wisconsin Survey, 1850, analysis.
3. Menominee River, 1850—1858, Field Notes and Report of progress.
4. Menominee and Montreal Rivers, 1840-41, (D. Houghton.)
5. Minnesota Field Notes, 1848—1864.

CASE NO. 3.

GEOLOGY.

3. Report on Opinike Property, Ashland Co., Wisconsin, 1865, Copper.
4. Report on Marangoin Location, 1865—Magnetic Iron Ore.

No.
5. Penokie Mineral Range, Ashland Co., Wisconsin, 1863.
6. Report on Magnetic Iron Co.'s Land, 1865.
7. Drift Cavities, Wisconsin, 1859, Azoic Rocks, origin of.
8. Dissolution of Ice.
9. Rocks of North Eastern Ohio.
10. Montreal River Lands—Copper, 1865.
11. Tyler's Fork Property—Copper and Lead, 1865.
12. Geology St. Louis River, Minnesota, 1848—1864.
13. Geology Minnesota, 1866.
14. Mineral Resources of the Rocky Mountains, 1863.
15. Ice Movements of the Glacial Era, 1866.
16. Depression of the Sea in the Ice Period, 1869.
17. Occurrence of Iron Ore in Masses, 1867.
18. Water levels, Green Bay, 1858.

CASE NO. 4.

METEOROLOGY, METEORITES, EARTHQUAKES AND FLOODS.

1. Meteors, Meteorites.
2. Climate of Lake Superior, Minnesota and Cleveland.
3. General Meteorology Wisconsin, Lapham's Map.
4. Earthquakes, California and Missouri, Floods, Lake Breezes,
5. Water Spouts.

CASE NO. 5.

GEOLOGY.

1. Minnesota, 1866, (Eames.)
2. Conglomerate Pebbles, (Brainerd,) 1854.
3. Coal, Deep River, North Carolina, (Emmons,) 1859.
4. Michigan Survey, (Winchel,) 1870.
5. Glaciers of the Pyrenees, Montana and Colorada, 1867.
6. New Hampshire Geology, 1869, (Hitchcock.)
7. Kansas, 1869, (Meek and Swallow.)

No.
8. Belmont County, Ohio, 1869, (Welsh.)
9. Cardiff Giant, 1869.
10. New London and Windham Counties, Conn., (Mather,) 1834.
11. Taylor on Gold Mines, United States, 1867.
12. Iron and Steel, United States, (Hewitt,) 1868.

CASE NO. 6.

PRECIOUS METALS, SALT, EMERY, &c.

1. Gold, Vermillion Lake, Minnesota, and elsewhere, (Scraps.)
2. Copper, English and Lake Superior, Copper Creek, (Scraps.)
3. Copper, Lake Superior Outline reports —Ulster County, New York.
4. Silver Lead and Silver, Lake Superior.
5. Lead, Fairview, Illinois—Levan's Cave, Dubuque.
6. Nickel, Wallace Co., Lake Huron.
7. Gold East of Rocky Mountains, Taylor's report, 1867.
8. Salt, Louisianna and elsewhere; Tin, Missouri; Emery, Quicksilver:
9. Mineral Mining Company, Montana Gold Company, Sonora.

CASE NO. 7.

COAL AND IRON.

1. Yellow Creek, Ohio, 1850—Hammondsville, 1866.
2. Cleveland Iron Company, 1860. Iron Business Western Reserve, 1860. Iron making, &c., 1857—1859.
3. Report Penokie Iron, 1865. Report La Pointe Iron Company, 1864—Milwaukee Iron Company, 1864.
4. Coal levels and profiles, Girard and Youngstown, Ohio.
5. Coal levels, Maps and profiles, Lawrence Co., Ohio, 1843-4.
6. Penokie Iron report, 1865, and E. B. Ward's Letter.
7. Origin of Coal, 1857. Mining of Coal, 1851.
8. Stark County, Ohio, 1863. How Coal is mined.
9. Memoranda on Iron making, 1860.

CASE NO. 8.

COAL.

1. Holmes & Coshocton Counties, Ohio, Memoranda 1860 and 1868.
2. Ohio, Pennsylvania, Michigan, Minnesota, Titusville, 1862, Summit Co., Ohio.
3. Brogniart's Coal Plants, 1850, Geological reports, Virginia, 1840. Allegany Coal Felds, 1854.
4. White River Coal, Indiana. Report by Owen.
5. Chester Coal Fields, Illinois, 1868. (Foster.)

CASE NO. 9..

IRON MINES.

1. Lake Superior Iron Co., 1868.
2. Lake Superior Iron Ore & Iron, (Scraps.)
3. Wisconsin & Lake Superior Iron Co., 1860.
4. Mining Laws, Ohio and New York, Surveys and Pre-emptions.
5. Ashland Co. & Lake Superior Iron Ore.
6. Marquette Co.. Michigan.

No.
7. Missouri Iron Mountain. Shepaug Steel Co.
8. Discovery of Iron Ore, Lake Superior.

CASE NO. 10.

MAGNETIC VARIATIONS—GENERAL ELEVATIONS—ASTRONOMY.

1. Magnetic variations, Ohio, Missouri, Illinois, Iowa & United States charts.
2. Elevations—Astronomy—Ohio, Minnesota and General.
3. Elevations—Astronomy, Ohio, Minnesota. Latitude and Longitude.

CASE NO. 11.

ETHNOLOGY.

1. Indians—Ethnology—Mythology—Belmont Co., Ohio, rock inscriptions.
2. American Ethnological Society. Proceedings 1858—1861.
3. Ancient ax marks. American Antiquities.
4. Ancient Mounds, Ohio, relics, plans, descriptions &c.
5. Ancient Works, Cuyahoga Valley.

CASE NO. 12.

MISCELLANY.

1. Railways to Lake Superior, 1853.
2. Climate of Lake Superior, North Western Medical Journal, 1855.
3. Naval Depot, Cleveland, 1865.
4. Military Record, 1864.
5. Major Gladwin & the Indian Girl, 1866.
6. Mound Builders in Ohio, 1865.
7. Combination Tent, 1864.
8. Surveys in Cleveland in 1796.
9. Chamberlain Coal Property, Darlington Pennsylvania, 1864.
10. Report on Pittsburg & Lake Angeline Iron Property, 1866.
11. Northern Pacific Rail Road, Letter to A. C. Stuntz, 1865.
12. Northern Pacific Rail Road. Cleveland Board of Trade, 1867.
13. Catalogue of Minerals, 1862.
14. Petition to Michigan Legislature, 1860.
15. War Letter to Theodore Breck, January, 1861.
16. History of Tallmadge, Ohio, 1842.
17. Chronology of Trees—Weight of Water —Elevation of Lake Superior.
18. Representative Men of Cleveland, 1869.

CASE NO. 13.

RAIL ROADS AND CANALS.

No.
1. Northern Pacific Rail Road, 1869.
2. Union Pacific Rail Road, 1869.
3. Central Pacific Rail Road, 1870.
4. Belgian Rail Roads, 1839.
5. Pennsylvania Central, 1863.
6. Street Rail Roads, (Pittsburg,) 1863.
7. Des Moines, Iowa, 1849, (Curtis.)
8. Water for Locomotives, 1865, (Chandler.)

CASE NO. 14.

RAIL ROAD REPORTS.

1. Cleveland & Pittsburg, 1846—1849—1853
2. Cleveland & Mahoning, 1852—1859—1861 —1862—1863—1864—1867.

No.
3. Galena and Chicago, 1847—1848.
4. Louisville and Charlestown, 1837.
5. Pittsburg and Connellsville, 1847.
6. Buffalo and Missisippi, 1847.
7. Convention, Harrisburg, 1838.
8. Cleveland & Columbus, 1845 & 1846.
9. Cleveland & Wooster, 1868.
10. Wisconsin and Lake Superior, 1853.

CASE NO. 15.

HISTORY AND ANTIQUITIES.

1. Hall's Wyoming Valley.
2. Hall's Monroe County, New York.
3. Hall's Albany County, New York.
4. Hall's Oneida County, New York.
5. Hall's Onondaga County, New York.
6. Hall's Cayuga County, New York.
7. Hall's Erie County, Pennsylvania.
8. Hall's Cuyahoga County, Ohio.
9. Copper Region, (Whittlesey) 1846.
10. Oneota, No. 4, (Schoolcraft.)
11. Jonathan Alder's Captivity.
12. Grinnell Land and Supplement. (P. Force,) 1852.
13. Mounds of the West. (Squier,) 1847.
14. Monuments of the Mississippi Valley. (Squier.) 1847.
15. Egyptian Antiquities. (Abbott,) 1853.

CASE NO. 16.

MISCELLANEOUS AND AGRICULTURAL.

1. Cincinnati Library, 1854.
2. Cincinnati Mechanics' Institute, 1851.
3. State Agricultural Fair, 1851,
4. State Agricultural Report, 1846.
5. Western Reserve Magazine of Agriculture, 1845.
6. Mahoning County Agricultural Society, 1851.
7. Cuyahoga County Agricultural Society, 1851.
8. Discourse on Rail Roads. (Aiken,) 1851.
9. Free Suffrage. (Lyon,) 1865.
10. African Colonization. (Christy,) 1849.
11. Thanksgiving Discourse, Salisbury, Connecticut. (Reid,) 1845.

CASE NO. 17.

MISCELLANEOUS.

1. Nature and the Bible have one Author, (John S. Williams,) 1861.
2. What is Homœopathy? (Wm. Sharp,) 1853.
3. New Gospel of Peace,(Sinclair Tousey,) 4 numbers, 1864.
4. Revelations, a companion to the above, (M. Doolady,) 1865.
5. New Gospel of Peace,(Sinclair Tousey,) Book Second.
6. New Gospel of Peace,(Sinclair Tousey,) Book Third.
7. Report of the Board of Public Works, Madison, Wisconsin, 1849.
8. Speech of Senator Chase at Toledo, 1851.
9. Report on the Organization of Smithsonian Institute, 1847.
10. Chas. Lanman, as a Romancer, (L. H. Hine,) 1847.
11. The First Annual Report of the Am. Museum of Nat. History, 1870.
12. The Tribune Almanac for 1867.
13. Proceedings of the National Convention of Manufacturers, Cleveland. 1867.

No.
14. Annual Report of the Comptroller of the State of California, 1851.
15. Addresses on the death of Hon. James A. Pearce, 1863. The Soldier's Heart at Donelson.
16. Catalogue of Rare American Curiosities in Ohio State Library. Indexes to St. Clair's Papers, 1871.
Catalogue of Manuscripts deposited in the Ohio State Library, 1871.
17. Improvement of the Upper Mississippi River.
18. The American Antiquarian, N. Y., 1870.
19. Catalogue of Flowering Plants in the vicinity of Cincinnati, (Joseph Clark,) 1852.
20. The Missionary Herald, Cincinnati, 1842.

CASE NO. 18.

GEOLOGY AND MINERALS

1. Specimens of William McClure, N. Harmony, 1840.
2. Elevations in Ohio, (Whittlesey,) 1850.
3. Geological Survey of Ohio, 1836, (Hildreth.)
4. Copper Lands, Isle Royal, (Cassells,) 1846.
5. St. Louis Iron Co., 1853.
6. Dauphin Coal Co., Pennsylvania, 1852.
7. Coal and Iron Ore of Pennsylvania, 1839 and 1841, (W. R. Johnson.)
8. Erratic Rocks of North America, (Christy,) 1848.
9. Paleozoic System, (Owen.)
10. Geological Survey of California, (Randall,) 1851.
11. Geology of California, (Tyson and Williamson,) 1850.
12. Murchison's Siluria, (Whitney,) 1855.
13. Carboniferous Rocks of Kentucky, (Owen and Norwood,) 1847.
14. Geology of Kentucky, (Yandell and Shumard,) 1847.
15. Review of New York Reports, (Owen,) 1847.
16. Determination of Minerals, (Egglesston.) 1868.

CASE NO. 19.

GEOLOGY AND MINERALS

1. Mining Magazine, Nos. 1 and 2, 1853.
2. American Geological Meeting, 1844.
3. Megalosaurus, Evansville,(Castleberry,) 1845.
4. Mineral Coal, Origin of, (Whittlesey,) 1845.
5. Northern Mexico, (Wislizenius,) 1848.
6. Lake Superior Mineral Lands, Mich., (Senate,) 1846.
7. How to Collect Minerals, (Smithsonian,) 1844.
8. Ancient Works of Ohio, and Geological Papers, (Locke,) 1843.
9. Ottawa River, Canada, Mineral Products, 1854.
11. Artesian Wells, Paris, 1841.
12. Wellsville Coal and Land Co., 1853.

CASE NO. 20.

MISCELLANEOUS.

1. Whig Almanac, 1843.
2. Idea of Precise Truth, (Azais.)
3. Microscopical Diseases, (Salisbury,) 1867—2 papers.
4. Law of Repulsion. 1853.

No.
5. Niagara Ship Canal, Williams' Report, 1836.
6. General Diseases, (Fitch,) 1845.
7. Discourse at Hudson, O., (St. John,) 1846.
8. National History, Georgia, Texas, (Kennedy,) 1844.
9. Napoleonic Medals, (Garlic,) 1869.
10. American S. S. U., 1845.
11. Discourse on Labor, (Owen,) 1848.
12. National Tax Law, 1848.
13. Muscogee Language, (Brinton,) 1870.
14. Flowering Plants of Ohio, (Newberry,) 1860.
15. Flowering Plants of Wisconsin, (Lapham.)

CASE NO. 21.

EXPLORATIONS AND SCIENTIFIC.

1. Explorations in Minnesota, (Pope.) 1850.
2. Coast Survey, 1850.
3. U. S. Topographical Engineers, 1850.
4. Surveyor General's report, 1845.
5. Michigan and Ohio Boundary reports, 1836.
6. Internal Improvements, Mo., 1847.
7. Military Stations on the Pacific, (Pendleton,) 1842.
8. Mineral Lands of Lake Superior, 1846.
9. Motive Power, Utica, New York, 1845.
10. Water Works of New Haven, 1843.
12. Magnetic Needle, (Loomis,) 1842.
13. Planetary Orbits, (Stockwell,) 1869.
15. England and her Prospects, (Ewing,) 1856.
17. Steamboat, Fairfax against Fulton, 1816.
18. Equations of the Moon, (Stockwell,) 1869.

CASE NO. 22.

CURRENCY & U. P. R. R. REPORTS.

1. U. P. R. R., 1867.
2. U. P. of Kansas, (Copley,) 1867.
3. U. P. R. R., (Col. Simpson.)
4. U. S. Revenue, (Hays,) 1866.
5. National Currency, (J. Sherman,) 1865.
6. " " (Geo. Walker) 1867.
7. Independent Treasury of Ohio, (A. A. Bliss,) 1848.
8. U. S. Currency, (H. S. Carey,) 1865.
9. Taxation of Banks, (J. Sherman,) 1863.

CASE NO. 23.

GEOLOGICAL.

No.
1. Glacial Phenomena—Chronicle, Ann Arbor, 1871. (C. W.)
2. Geological Survey of New Hampshire, 1870-71, (C. H. Hitchcock.)
3. Wisconsin Geological Survey, 1871, (John Murrish.)
4. Vermont Marble, Pittsford, (C. H. Hitchcock,) 1872.
5. Delta of the Mississippi River, (E. G. Hilgard,) 1871.
6. Block Coal of Indiana, (J. W. Foster,) 1871.
7. Chemistry of the Earth, (T. S. Hunt,) 1871.
8. Nipigon Lake, Canada, Geology, (R. Bell,) 1870.
9. Elephant and Mastodon, (Newberry,) 1872.
Archeological Frauds, (Squire.)
10. Marshall Group, Michigan, (Winchel,) 1870.
11. Michigan Geological Survey, (Winchel,) 1870.
12. Marshall Group Fossils, 1870, (Winchel.)
13. Morris Miller, Geology, 1869.
14. Wilcox Coal Tract, East Tennessee, 1871, (E. H. Bradley.)
15. Sandy Creek Coal, Ohio, and Maps, 1870.
16. Missouri Geological Report. 1871, (A. D. Hagar.)

CASE NO. 24.

SCIENTIFIC MISCELLANY.

1. Terrestrial Magnetism, (Richard Owen,) 1871-72.
2. Mississippi River, Physics of, (E. H. Abbott,) 1862.
3. Ohio Drift, Hanover, Ohio, Morris Miller, 1854.
4. Liebig Chemistry, 1841.
5. Missouri Mineral Wealth, (C. D. Wilber,) 1870.
6. Iron and Steel, Paris Exhibition, (A. S. Hewitt,) 1868.
7. Michigan Geological System—Botany and Geology, 1867-8, (A. Winchel.)
8. Kent County, Canada, Geology, (Judge Wells,) 1859.
9. Precious Metals, Gold, (C. D. Wilber,) 1870.
10. Earthquakes, (J. Brainerd,) 1870.
11. Embryology, (L. Agassiz,) 1849.
12. American Association, Salem, 1870.

WESTERN RESERVE & NORTHERN OHIO
HISTORICAL SOCIETY.

Pamphlets, Memoranda and Scraps,

IN PAMPHLET CASES.

Case No. 1.

HISTORICAL SOCIETIES.

No.
1. Chicago Society Constitution, &c.
2. Georgia. Part 1, vol. 3.
3. Wisconsin Address, 1869.
4. Houghton, Mich., 1866.
5. Maryland Report, 1867.
6. Minnesota, (Duplicate,) 1868.
7. Buffalo, 1863.
8. Minnesota Collections, 1860.
9. Wisconsin, (Duplicate,) 1868.
10. Wisconsin, 1855.
11. Wisconsin, 1869.
12. Minnesota, Carver's Centennary, 1869.

Case No. 2.

GENERAL HISTORY, &c.

1. Influence of History, (Chadbourne,) 1868. (Duplicate.)
2. Corn Planter, Sketch of, (Johnson,) 1867.
3. Elliott, Bishop of Georgia, (Cohen,) 1867.
4. Pittsburgh Centennial Celebration, (Loomis,) 1858.
5. Winthrop's Journal, Review of, 1834.
6. Historical Address, (Lewis Cass,) 1863.
7. Leslie Coombs, Sketch of, 1852.
8. Kent Island, Maryland, (Streeter,) 1868.
9. Nine Revolutionary Stories, (Priest.)
10. Connecticut Conventions, 1792—1820.
11. Anti-Masonic Celebration, (W. H. Seward,) 1831.
12. DeWitt Clinton on National Affairs, 1809.

Case No. 3.

EXPLORATIONS, &c.

1. Virginia Physical Survey, 1869.
2. Pacific Railway, 1868.
3. Alabama, Manual of, 1869.
4. Chicago Public Parks, 1869.
5. Sturgeon Bay Canal, Wisconsin, 1869,
6. Minnesota, its Advantages,(Duplicate,) 1869.
7. Nevada, Minerals of, 1867.
8. Red River of Canada, 1868.

Case No. 4.

OHIO LOCAL HISTORY,

No.
1. Pioneer Life at North Bend, (Harrison,) 1867.
2. Licking County Presbyterian Churches, (Duplicate,) 1869.
3. Licking County Welsh Settlement, (Duplicate,) 1869.
4. Licking County Clay Lick Settlement, (Duplicate,) 1869.
5. Oberlin, History of, 1860.
6. Tallmadge Semi-Centennial Celebration, 1869.
7. Toledo War of 1835, (Way,) 1869, (Duplicate)
8. Seneca County, Ohio, Celebration, (Rawson,(1869.
9. Brownhelm, Celebration of Settlement, (Fairchild,) 1867.

Case No.5 .

MISCELLANEOUS.

1. Mammoth Cave, Kentucky.
2. Cincinnati Observatory, 1868.
3. Anti-Bible Movement, Cincinnati, 1869.
4. John Goodman and George F. Train, 1868.
5. Preservation of Wood, 1869.
6. Craycraft to Bishop McIlvaine, Letter, 1868.
7. New Orleans Riots in 1867.
8. National Union Convention, Philadelphia, 1866.
9. Payment of the Public Debt, (Gholson,(1868.
10. Military Commissions, (J. H. James,) 1869.
11. Hartsville, Pennsylvania, Soldiers' Aid Society, 1867.
12. Cow Chase, (Major Andre,) 1780.

Case No. 6.

GENEALOGY.

1. Study of, (Durrie,) 1862.
2. New England Society, (Wilder,) 1869.
3. Scott, of Providence, Rhode Island, (Scott,) 1869.
4. Name of Scott, (Scott,) 1869.

No.
5. New England Society, (Drake,) 1858.
6. Clarke Family, (Clarke,) 1869.
7. Morgan Family, (Morgan,) 1851.
8. Puritan Settlers, Connecticut, (Hinman,) Nos. 5 and 6, 1856.

CASE NO. 7.

BIOGRAPHY.

1. R. M. Briggs, (Harrison,) 1869.
2. Battle of Lake Erie Survivors, (U. M. Parsons,) 1863.
3. C. Beltrami in Italian, 1861.
4. Governor Brough, 1865.
5. Governor Andrew, 1867.
6. Charles M. Crandall, (Hough,) 1868.
7. Matthew Lyon, (White,) 1858.
8. John Delamater, (Goodrich,) 1869.

CASE NO. 8.

PIONEER BIOGRAPHY.

1. Benjamin Tappan — Amzi Atwater — White Indian.
2. James Kingsbury — Lorenzo Carter — Edward Paine — Samuel Gilbert.
3. Simon Perkins — Charles Parker — Calvin Pease — Dr. Metcalf.
4. Ephraim Cutler — J. Delamater — Ely Campbell — John Andrews.
5. Governors of Ohio, (Duplicate): — Reuben Wood — Davd Tod.
6. Heman Oviatt — Nathan Perry — Seneca, an Indian — Lewis Dille — Dr. Long—Alfred Kelley—Q. F. Atkins.
7. Oliver Culver — Leonard Case — Cyrus Prentiss—Zenas Kent — E. Cooke — Lot Sanford.
8. Bronson Family — Cahoon Family.
9. J. S. Clarke—Samuel Dodge.
10. Z. Taylor — E. Mix — James Ward — W. A. Otis—Josiah Harris.
11. H. Manning — M. Deming — J. F. Warner — L, Goodale — F. Wadsworth.
12. Mrs. Julia Long — J. Squire — J. Coit — A. Phelps — P. P. Pease — D. Jarvis — George Hoadley.
13. Robert Kennicott — S. R. Curtis.
14. D. Jones — F. Wadsworth — Joseph Badger — Walworth and Huntington Papers.
15. Dr. T. Garlick.
16. Elisha Norton.

CASE NO. 9.

WESTERN RESERVE AND GENERAL HISTORY.

1. Moravian Missions. First Sunday School.
2. Medina County Celebration, 1857. Put-in Bay Celebration, 1858.
3. Murder of Nicksaw, 1808. Shooting of Diver, 1808. Deerfield, Portage Co., Ohio.
4. Evans' Map, 1755. J. Smith, 1755. Trump of Fame, 1812. Fourth of July at Painesville, 1801.
5. Pioneer Celebration, Cincinnati, 1857-8. Indians, Buffalo Creek.
6. Col. Bouquet's Expedition, 1764.
7. Trumbull and Mahoning Counties, (J. M. Edwards,) 1858.
8. Detroit in Olden Times. Cass Papers.
9. Early Maps of America. St. Mary's, Michigan.
10. Oswego and Onondaga, New York.
11. The Pilgrims and the Puritans.
12. S. C. Aiken's Quarter Century Sermon, 1860.

CASE NO. 10.

HISTORY: CLEVELAND AND WESTERN RESERVE

No.
2. Lorain County — Brownhelm—Penfield —Sheffield.
3. Summit County — Tallmadge, Twinsburg.
4. Portage County (Harmon) — Fairfield County (McCracken.)
5. Cuyahoga County—Early Surveys—Early Courts — Pioneer Celebrations — Huntington and Walworth Papers.
6. Cuyahoga County — Augustus Porter— Alfred Kelley — Rockport — Brecksville.
7. First Presbyterian Church in Cleveland —Manual and Members.
8. Surveys, 1797, A. Atwater. Surveys in 1806, A. Tappan,
9. Western Reserve — Fire Lands. Soldiers of 1812.

CASE NO. 11.

MISCELLANEOUS.

1. Fourth of July Address, Sharon, Conn., 1798, (Smith.)
2. Connecticut Act of Assembly, 1781, relating to the State's quota.
3. Connecticut Act of Assembly, 1781, relating to bounties.
4. Connecticut Act of Assembly, 1765, relating to insolvent debtors.
5. Moses Vindicated. London, 1732. (Underhill.)
6. Geological Survey of Ohio, Report on, March, 1831, (Riddle.)
7 Human Knowledge Classified, (Roswell Park,) 1855.
8. Panic at Nashville, Tennessee, (Terry,) 1862.
9. Bath Street Cases, Cleveland, 1854.
10. Trial of Capt. Frank Gurley, 1864, for the Murder of Gen. McCook, Nashville.
11. Sabbath, Scripture View of, (D. H. Beardsley,) Cleveland, 1864.
12. Social Reform, (McEwen,) Nashville, 1869.
13. Census of the United States. Washington, 1869.
14. National Institute, New York, 1868.
15. Naval Depot, Cleveland, 1864.
16. Reconstruction, (Robert Dale Owen,) 1863.
17. Free Suffrage, (J. B. Lyon,) 1864.
18. Necessity of War, (Goodrich,) 1861.
19. Academy of Natural Sciences, Philadelphia. Report of Trustees. 1868.
20. Pennsylvania Revenue Cases, (McCandless,) 1867.

CASE NO. 12.

HISTORICAL.

1. Battle of Lake Erie Celebration, Sept. 10, 1858.
2. Connecticut Historical Estimate, (Bushnell) 1851.
3. Maumee Valley, (Hosmer,) 1858.
4. Committee of Safety, Hagerstown, Maryland, 1775-7.
5. Mason and Dixon. Cincinnati. (Veech.) 1857.
6. Salisbury, Connecticut, Oct. 1842. (Church.)
7. Cincinnati Astronomical Society, 1843. (Adams.)
8. Suffield Connecticut 150 Anniversary. 1859. (Ruggles.)

No.
9. Beecher Lyman's Trial for Heresy, Cincinnati. 1835.
10. Bayfield. Lake Superior, History of 1858.
11. History of the Pennsylvania troops. Report on. 1866.

CASE NO. 13.

HISTORICAL PAPERS.

1. Moses Cleaveland to Directors Connecticut Land Company. Aug. 17. 1796.
2. Theodore Shephard to Moses Cleveland, Canandaigua, April 1797.
3. Moses Cleaveland and Memoranda of Land Sold. 1796.
4. Moses Cleaveland in account with the Erie Land Company. 1800.
5. Burning of Col. Crawford, near Upper Sandusky, June 11, 1782.
6. Moses Cleaveland's Diary. 1796. Earl of Warwick's deed, 1631.
7. Christopher Cackler's statementof the great Bear Hunt, Streetsboro, Portage County. 1819.
8. Millerism in Cleveland. 1845.
9. Papers of Seth Pease, 1795-1805, from Horace Pease, by F. Kinsman. Oct. 3, 1869.
10. Military papers of Col. Campbell's regiment. Portage county. War of 1812.
11. Memoranda of David Jones. Ohio. 1773.
12. Exports of Cuyahoga County, 1824.
13. Address of L. V. Bierce, Newburgh, Cuyahoga County, Ohio, June 1860.
14. J. N. Wilson. Ancient Mounds of Newark, Ohio. July, 1868.
15. Historical Address of Gen. L. V. Bierce. Bath, Summit county, Ohio, Sept. 10, 1869,
16. Papers of the late Judge P. Hitchcock, from P. M. Hitchcock.
17. Court House of Champion, Geauga County, 1809. Subscription to build.
18. Rebel correspondence captured at Wytheville, Virginia, Dec. 18, 1864.
19. John Harmon's History of Campbell's Regiment, Portage county. War of 1812.

CASE NO. 14.

HISTORICAL MISCELLANEOUS.

1. Historical Address of Woolsey Wells, Lorain county, Ohio.
2. Pioneer Celebration, Newburg, June 1860.
3. Specimens of the Great Seals of Ohio.
4. Pioneer Celebration and Ancient Mounds, Licking county, Ohio.
5. Pioneer Celebration at Newburgh, Oct. 1858.
6. Execution and Trial of Lewis Davis, Cleveland, Feb. 4, 1869.
7. Records of a Court at Warwick county Virginia, May 1859.
8. Mound Builders of Newark, by Isaac Smucker.
9. Organization of Young Men's Literary Society, Cleveland, 1869.

MAPS & ILLUSTRATIONS, IN BINDING.

A general Atlas of the World, very full as to Europe, containing with illustrations 95 sheets folio, bound, of date 1701 to 1720, by John Bapiste Homan Nuremberg, Deposited by Breno Nicolais, Cleveland.
Map of "Carolana and the River Meschacebe," by Daniel Coxe, 1727.
British North America, with the French and Spanish settlements adjacent, by Henry Popple, London, 1732.
"Possessions Anglaise et Francaise," by I. Rotter, Amsterdam, 1752.
"British and French Dominions in North America," eight large sheets, bound by John Mitchel, Amsterdam, 1755. Presented by Rev. E. A. Dalrymple, Secretary Maryland Historical Society,
"Middle British Colonies in America," by Lewis Evans, with Pownall's topographical descriptions, London and Philadelphia, 1775; same second edition, with descriptions by Evans, Philadelphia, 1760. Printed by B. Franklin and D. Hall.
"Atlas of British Colonies in North America," including admiralty surveys, twenty-five large sheets, by William Fadden, London, 1777.
Charts and illustrations of Captain Cook's voyages around the world, 1772 to 1780, thick volume folio, on depositby C. C. Baldwin, Esq.
Large bound volume of manuscriptmaps, from the papers of the Connecticut Land Company, 1796-7.
General Atlas of the World: Dublin, 1800. Presented by Hon. S. Williamson.
General Atlas, by Matthew Cary & Son, Philadelphia, 1818. Presented by J. P. Kirtland, LL. D.
Maps of Northern boundary, Commission of 1820. Presented by the late M.B. Scott, Esq.
Pyramids of the Nile, illustrated.
Catherwood's Antiquities of Central America, illustrations.
Chronological Chart of the World.
Battles in Mexico, illustrated.
Trajans Column, and the war in Dacia, about A. D. 100, &c., illustrated.

MOUNTED MAPS.

No.
1. United States, by the National Observatory, 1862. Duplicate.
2. Middle States, by Johnson, 1856.
3. Ohio, by Walling, 1861.

OHIO COUNTY MAPS.

4. Lorain, by Geil, 1859.
5. Geauga and Lake, by Matthews. 1857. Duplicate.
6. Trumbull, by Brown and Matthews.
7. Summit, by Paul, 1856. Duplicate.
8. Holmes, by Walling, 1861.
9. Coshocton, by Becker.
10. Cuyahoga, by Matthews, 1858. Duplicate.
11. Ashtabula, by Baker, 1856.
12. Fairfield, by Towson, 1848.
13. Muskingum, by Bennett.
14. Belmont, by Charlesworth, 1855.
15. Ohio, by John F. Mansfield. 1806.
16. Ohio, by Hough and Bourne, 1814.
17. Ohio, by, John Kilbourne, 1822.
18. Ohio, by Howard, 1828.
19. Ohio, by Adams and Eggleston, 1848.
20. Western Reserve, by Reed and Rollo, 1842.
21. Pennsylvania, by Howell, 1792.
22. Railroad Map of the United States, 1870.
23. United States, 1853.
24. Berghaus' Chart of the World. Gotha. 1871.

MAPS, MISCELLANEOUS.

City of Washington. (John Brannan.) 1828.
Lloyd's New Military Map of the Southern and Border States. New York. 1864.
Western Reserve, 1826. (Wm. Sumner.)
New Military Map of Middle Europe.
Sebastopol, Crimea, and the Black Sea, 1854. (Jocelyn.)

Town 2, Range 10, (Tallmadge,) as surveyed by S. E. Ensign, 1806.
Amos Spafford's Map of Cleveland, 1796. (Copy.)
Western District of Upper Canada.
Plan of New Market, Mouth of Grand river, Ohio, 1804.
Cleveland and its environs, 1835. (A. Merchant.) Duplicate.
Firelands, 1808. (Almon Ruggles.) Duplicates.
Plan of the Road leading from the foot of the Rapids of the Miami of Lake Erie to the Western Boundary of the Connecticut Western Reserve, 1823.
Map of the Country bordering the Buffalo and Mississippi Railroad. (G. R. Baldwin.) 1846.
Kansas, 1870, (Mills and Smith.)
St. Louis and Vicinity, (Urban and Fisher.) 1854.
Township No. 16, 17th Range.
Ohio, 1833. (Justin Carpenter.)
Fac simile of a map made by the Jesuit Missionaries, 1670-1. Paris. 1672. Triplicates.
Village of Eagle Harbor. Houghon, Mich. 1851.
Norfolk, Va., and Vicinity.
Ohio, 1812.
Boston, 1862. (L. Prang & Co.)
Map of the country within Five Hundred Miles of Cairo, Ill., 1861. (G. W. Colton.)
Map of Wilmington, N. C. showing the position of the blockading fleet, war of the Rebellion.
Map of Mackinaw City (B. C. Phillips.) 1857.
Map of the Straits of Mackinaw, 1857. (B. C. Phillips.)
Map illustrating the Canada Pacific, and Northern Pacific and other proposed Railroads connecting at Mackinaw City.
Large Map of Pennsylvania on Cloth, by R. Howell, 1792.
Vermont. Triplicates. (Jewett and Chandler) 1870
Ohio in 1833.
New York City, by Perris, 1850-1.
City of Paris and its Fortifications. (From N. C. Winslow.)
Survey of Wellsville and Fairport Railroad, by White, 1836.
Hutchins' Map of the Ohio Territory. 1763.
Jesuits Map of Lake Superior, 1672.
Champlain's Map of New France or Canada, 1632.
Manuscript map of the west end of Lake Erie, apparently for the use of the army in 1813, from the papers of John Walworth.
Lake Survey Charts, complete.
Coast Survey of the United States, complete.

Case No. 15.

MAPS DEPOSITED BY CHAS. WHITTLESEY. LAND OFFICE.

No.
1. Louisiana, Arkansas.
2. Florida, Mississippi, Alabama.
3. Iowa.
4. Missouri.
5. Dacotah, Kansas, Colorado, Nebraska.
6. Washington, Oregon, Montana, Idaho.
7. New Mexico, Texas, Arizona.
8. Illinois.
9. Indiana.
10. California, 1861.

Case No. 16.

RAILROADS, CANALS AND CITIES.

1. St. Croix and Lake Superior Railroad.
2. Harrisburg and Pittsburgh, 1839.

No.
3. Green Bay and Ontonagon.
4. Des Moines Canal, Iowa City Survey.
5. Lake Michigan to Lake Superior, 1855.
6. Washington City and Capitol.
7. New York.
8. Madison, Wisconsin.
9. Vicinity of St. Louis, Missouri.

Case No. 17.

MAPS OF THE STATES.

1. Kentucky, 1862.
2. Tennessee, 1862.
3. West Virginia, 1862.
4. United States Military Map, 1863.
5. Virginia, Maryland, and East Tennessee, 1861.
6. Virginia, 1862.
7. East Virginia, 1862. Duplicate.
8. South Virginia and Washington City, 1862.
9. United States Land Office Map, 1866.

Case No. 18.

1. United States, (Colton,) 1861.
2. Red River and Lake Superior Wagon Roads, (Russell,) 1868.
3. Elevations from Independence, Missouri, to the Rio Grande.
4. North America, (Gilpin,) 1861.
5. Northern Boundary of the U. States, Maine, 1839.
6. Province of New York, 1779.
7. Tehuantepec Railroad Survey, 1848.
8. Fremont's Expeditions, 1840 and 1845.

Case No. 19.

1. Europe, (Colton.)
2. Nicaragua, 1856.
3. New Haven Water Works, 1856.
4. Europe, 1851.
5. Lombardy and Venice, 1859.
6. North Polar Regions, 1852.
7. Seat of War in the U. States, 1860.

Case No. 20.

1. Lake Superior, (Chapman,) 1857, and Land Office Map.
2. Lake Superior Geological Map, 1850.
3. Copper Locations, Point Keweenaw, 1846, '51 and '54.
4. Plans of Mines: North American, Cliff, Phœnix and Lac La Belle.
5. Mining Locations, Point Keweenaw, 1846.
6. Marquette, Escanaba and Menominee Regions.
7. Isle Royal and its Harbors.
8. Point Keweenaw, 1856 and 1860.

Case No. 21.

1. Marquette County and vicinity.
2. Point Keweenaw Mining Locations and Towns.
3. Marquette and Menominee Rivers, (Hurlbut,) 1856.
4. Matchegummi Lake and Keweenaw Bay, (Banfield,) 1856.
5. Upper Peninsula, (Farmer,) 1847.
6. Coal Fields of Michigan, Grand Traverse Bay, (Winchell.)

Case No. 22.

1. Geological Report and Profile, (Foster and Whitney,) 1849.
2. Lake Superior, 1845-6.
3. St. Mary's Canal Company Lands.
4. Sectional Map, by Chapman, 1857.
5. Porcupine Mountains, Ontonagon and Montreal River—4 Maps.
6. Portage Lake and Ontonagon, 1851.

WESTERN RESERVE & NORTHERN OHIO
HISTORICAL SOCIETY.

Pamphlets, Memoranda and Scraps,

IN PAMPHLET CASES.

CASE NO. 1.

HISTORICAL SOCIETIES.

No.
1. Chicago Society Constitution, &c.
2. Georgia. Part 1, vol. 3.
3. Wisconsin Address, 1869.
4. Houghton, Mich., 1866.
5. Maryland Report, 1867.
6. Minnesota, (Duplicate,) 1868.
7. Buffalo, 1863.
8. Minnesota Collections, 1860.
9. Wisconsin, (Duplicate,) 1868.
10. Wisconsin, 1855.
11. Wisconsin, 1869.
12. Minnesota, Carver's Centennary, 1869.

CASE NO. 2.

GENERAL HISTORY, &c.

1. Influence of History, (Chadbourne,) 1868. (Duplicate.)
2. Corn Planter, Sketch of, (Johnson,) 1867.
3. Elliott, Bishop of Georgia, (Cohen,) 1867.
4. Pittsburgh Centennial Celebration, (Loomis,) 1858.
5. Winthrop's Journal, Review of, 1834.
6. Historical Address, (Lewis Cass,) 1863.
7. Leslie Coombs, Sketch of, 1852.
8. Kent Island, Maryland, (Streeter,) 1868.
9. Nine Revolutionary Stories, (Priest.)
10. Connecticut Conventions, 1792—1820.
11. Anti-Masonic Celebration, (W. H. Seward,) 1831.
12. DeWitt Clinton on National Affairs, 1809.

CASE NO. 3.

EXPLORATIONS, &c.

1. Virginia Physical Survey, 1869.
2. Pacific Railway, 1868.
3. Alabama, Manual of, 1869.
4. Chicago Public Parks, 1869.
5. Sturgeon Bay Canal, Wisconsin, 1869,
6. Minnesota, its Advantages, (Duplicate,) 1869.
7. Nevada, Minerals of, 1867.
8. Red River of Canada, 1868.

CASE NO. 4.

OHIO LOCAL HISTORY,

No.
1. Pioneer Life at North Bend, (Harrison,) 1867.
2. Licking County Presbyterian Churches, (Duplicate,) 1869.
3. Licking County Welsh Settlement, (Duplicate,) 1869.
4. Licking County Clay Lick Settlement, (Duplicate,) 1869.
5. Oberlin, History of, 1860.
6. Tallmadge Semi-Centennial Celebration, 1869.
7. Toledo War of 1835, (Way,) 1869, (Duplicate.)
8. Seneca County, Ohio, Celebration, (Rawson,(1869.
9. Brownhelm, Celebration of Settlement, (Fairchild,) 1867.

CASE NO.5 .

MISCELLANEOUS.

1. Mammoth Cave, Kentucky.
2. Cincinnati Observatory, 1868.
3. Anti-Bible Movement, Cincinnati, 1869.
4. John Goodman and George F. Train, 1868.
5. Preservation of Wood, 1869.
6. Craycraft to Bishop McIlvaine, Letter, 1868.
7. New Orleans Riots in 1867.
8. National Union Convention, Philadelphia, 1866.
9. Payment of the Public Debt, (Gholson,(1868.
10. Military Commissions, (J. H. James,) 1869.
11. Hartsville, Pennsylvania, Soldiers' Aid Society, 1867.
12. Cow Chase, (Major Andre,) 1780.

CASE NO. 6.

GENEALOGY.

1. Study of, (Durrie,) 1862.
2. New England Society, (Wilder,) 1869.
3. Scott, of Providence, Rhode Island, (Scott,) 1869.
4. Name of Scott, (Scott,) 1869.

No.
5. New England Society, (Drake,) 1858.
6. Clarke Family, (Clarke,) 1869.
7. Morgan Family, (Morgan,) 1851.
8. Puritan Settlers, Connecticut, (Hinman,) Nos. 5 and 6, 1856.

CASE NO. 7.

BIOGRAPHY.

1. R. M. Briggs, (Harrison,) 1869.
2. Battle of Lake Erie Survivors, (U. M. Parsons,) 1863.
3. C. Beltrami in Italian, 1861.
4. Governor Brough, 1865.
5. Governor Andrew, 1867.
6. Charles M. Crandall, (Hough,) 1868.
7. Matthew Lyon, (White,) 1858.
8. John Delamater, (Goodrich,) 1869.

CASE NO. 8.

PIONEER BIOGRAPHY.

1. Benjamin Tappan — Amzi Atwater — White Indian.
2. James Kingsbury — Lorenzo Carter — Edward Paine — Samuel Gilbert.
3. Simon Perkins — Charles Parker — Calvin Pease — Dr. Metcalf.
4. Ephraim Cutler — J. Delamater — Ely Campbell — John Andrews.
5. Governors of Ohio, (Duplicate): — Reuben Wood — Davd Tod.
6. Heman Oviatt — Nathan Perry — Seneca, an Indian — Lewis Dille — Dr. Long—Alfred Kelley—Q. F. Atkins.
7. Oliver Culver — Leonard Case — Cyrus Prentiss—Zenas Kent — E. Cooke — Lot Sanford.
8. Bronson Family — Cahoon Family.
9. J. S. Clarke—Samuel Dodge.
10. Z. Taylor — E. Mix — James Ward — W. A. Otis—Josiah Harris.
11. H. Manning — M. Deming — J. F. Warner — L. Goodale — F. Wadsworth.
12. Mrs. Julia Long — J. Squire — J. Coit — A. Phelps — P. P. Pease — D. Jarvis — George Hoadley.
13. Robert Kennicott — S. R. Curtis.
14. D. Jones — F. Wadsworth — Joseph Badger — Walworth and Huntington Papers.
15. Dr. T. Garlick.
16. Elisha Norton.

CASE NO. 9.

WESTERN RESERVE AND GENERAL HISTORY.

1. Moravian Missions. First Sunday School.
2. Medina County Celebration, 1857. Put-in Bay Celebration, 1858.
3. Murder of Nicksaw, 1808. Shooting of Diver, 1808. Deerfield, Portage Co., Ohio.
4. Evans' Map, 1755. J. Smith, 1755. Trump of Fame, 1812. Fourth of July at Painesville, 1801.
5. Pioneer Celebration, Cincinnati, 1857-8. Indians, Buffalo Creek.
6. Col. Bouquet's Expedition, 1764.
7. Trumbull and Mahoning Counties, (J. M. Edwards,) 1858.
8. Detroit in Olden Times. Cass Papers.
9. Early Maps of America. St. Mary's, Michigan.
10. Oswego and Onondaga, New York.
11. The Pilgrims and the Puritans.
12. S. C. Aiken's Quarter Century Sermon, 1860.

CASE NO. 10.

HISTORY: CLEVELAND AND WESTERN RESERVE

No.
2. Lorain County — Brownhelm—Penfield —Sheffield.
3. Summit County — Tallmadge, Twinsburg.
4. Portage County (Harmon) — Fairfield County (McCracken.)
5. Cuyahoga County—Early Surveys—Early Courts — Pioneer Celebrations — Huntington and Walworth Papers.
6. Cuyahoga County — Augustus Porter— Alfred Kelley — Rockport — Brecksville.
7. First Presbyterian Church in Cleveland —Manual and Members.
8. Surveys, 1797, A. Atwater. Surveys in 1806, A. Tappan,
9. Western Reserve — Fire Lands. Soldiers of 1812.

CASE NO. 11.

MISCELLANEOUS.

1. Fourth of July Address, Sharon, Conn., 1798, (Smith.)
2. Connecticut Act of Assembly, 1781, relating to the State's quota.
3. Connecticut Act of Assembly, 1781, relating to bounties.
4. Connecticut Act of Assembly, 1765, relating to insolvent debtors.
5. Moses Vindicated. London, 1732. (Underhill.)
6. Geological Survey of Ohio, Report on, March, 1831, (Riddle.)
7 Human Knowledge Classified, (Roswell Park,) 1855.
8. Panic at Nashville, Tennessee, (Terry,) 1862.
9. Bath Street Cases, Cleveland, 1854.
10. Trial of Capt. Frank Gurley, 1864, for the Murder of Gen. McCook, Nashville.
11. Sabbath, Scripture View of, (D. H. Beardsley,) Cleveland, 1864.
12. Social Reform, (McEwen,) Nashville, 1869.
13. Census of the United States. Washington, 1869.
14. National Institute, New York, 1868.
15. Naval Depot, Cleveland, 1864.
16. Reconstruction, (Robert Dale Owen,) 1863.
17. Free Suffrage, (J. B. Lyon,) 1864.
18. Necessity of War, (Goodrich,) 1861.
19. Academy of Natural Sciences, Philadelphia. Report of Trustees. 1868.
20. Pennsylvania Revenue Cases, (McCandless,) 1867.

CASE NO. 12.

HISTORICAL.

1. Battle of Lake Erie Celebration, Sept. 10, 1858.
2. Connecticut Historical Estimate, (Bushnell) 1851.
3. Maumee Valley, (Hosmer,) 1858.
4. Committee of Safety, Hagerstown, Maryland, 1775-7.
5. Mason and Dixon. Cincinnati. (Veech.) 1857.
6. Salisbury, Connecticut, Oct. 1842. (Church.)
7. Cincinnati Astronomical Society, 1843. (Adams.)
8. Suffield Connecticut 150 Anniversary. 1859. (Ruggles.)

No.
9. Beecher Lyman's Trial for Heresy, Cincinnati. 1835.
10. Bayfield. Lake Superior, History of 1858.
11. History of the Pennsylvania troops. Report on. 1866.

CASE NO. 13.

HISTORICAL PAPERS.

1. Moses Cleaveland to Directors Connecticut Land Company. Aug. 17. 1796.
2. Theodore Shephard to Moses Cleveland, Canandaigua, April 1797.
3. Moses Cleaveland and Memoranda of Land Sold. 1796.
4. Moses Cleaveland in account with the Erie Land Company. 1800.
5. Burning of Col. Crawford, near Upper Sandusky, June 11, 1782.
6. Moses Cleaveland's Diary. 1796. Earl of Warwick's deed, 1631.
7. Christopher Cackler's statementof the great Bear Hunt, Streetsboro, Portage County. 1819.
8. Millerism in Cleveland. 1845.
9. Papers of Seth Pease, 1795-1805, from Horace Pease, by F. Kinsman. Oct. 3, 1869.
10. Military papers of Col. Campbell's regiment. Portage county. War of 1812.
11. Memoranda of David Jones. Ohio. 1773.
12. Exports of Cuyahoga County, 1824.
13. Address of L. V. Bierce, Newburgh, Cuyahoga County, Ohio, June 1860.
14. J. N. Wilson. Ancient Mounds of Newark, Ohio. July, 1868.
15. Historical Address of Gen. L. V. Bierce. Bath, Summit county, Ohio, Sept. 10, 1869,
16. Papers of the late Judge P. Hitchcock, from P. M. Hitchcock.
17. Court House of Champion, Geauga County, 1809. Subscription to build.
18. Rebel correspondence captured at Wytheville, Virginia, Dec. 18, 1864.
19. John Harmon's History of Campbell's Regiment, Portage county. War of 1812.

CASE NO. 14.

HISTORICAL MISCELLANEOUS.

1. Historical Address of Woolsey Wells, Lorain county, Ohio.
2' Pioneer Celebration, Newburg, June 1860.
3. Specimens of the Great Seals of Ohio.
4. Pioneer Celebration and Ancient Mounds, Licking county, Ohio.
5. Pioneer Celebration at Newburgh, Oct. 1858.
6. Execution and Trial of Lewis Davis, Cleveland, Feb. 4, 1869.
7. Records of a Court at Warwick county Virginia, May 1859.
8. Mound Builders of Newark, by Isaac Smucker.
9. Organization of Young Men's Literary Society, Cleveland, 1869.

MAPS & ILLUSTRATIONS, IN BINDING.

A general Atlas of the World, very full as to Europe, containing with illustrations 95 sheets folio, bound, of date 1701 to 1720, by John Bapiste Homan Nuremberg, Deposited by Breno Nicolais, Cleveland.
Map of "Carolana and the River Meschacebe," by Daniel Coxe, 1727.
British North America, with the French and Spanish settlements adjacent, by Henry Popple, London, 1732.
"Possessions Anglaise et Francaise," by F. Rotter, Amsterdam, 1752.
"British and French Dominions in North America," eight large sheets, bound by John Mitchel, Amsterdam, 1755. Presented by Rev. E. A. Dalrymple, Secretary Maryland Historical Society,
"Middle British Colonies in America," by Lewis Evans, with Pownall's topographical descriptions, London and Philadelphia, 1775; same second edition, with descriptions by Evans, Philadelphia, 1760. Printed by B. Franklin and D. Hall.
"Atlas of British Colonies in North America," including admiralty surveys, twenty-five large sheets, by William Fadden, London, 1777.
Charts and illustrations of Captain Cook's voyages around the world, 1772 to 1780, thick volume folio, on depositby C. C. Baldwin, Esq.
Large bound volume of manuscriptmaps, from the papers of the Connecticut Land Company, 1796-7.
General Atlas of the World: Dublin, 1800. Presented by Hon. S. Williamson.
General Atlas, by Matthew Cary & Son, Philadelphia, 1818. Presented by J. P. Kirtland, LL. D.
Maps of Northern boundary, Commission of 1820. Presented by the late M.B. Scott, Esq.
Pyramids of the Nile, illustrated.
Catherwood's Antiquities of Central America, illustrations.
Chronological Chart of the World.
Battles in Mexico, illustrated.
Trajans Column, and the war in Dacia, about A. D. 100, &c., illustrated.

MOUNTED MAPS.

No.
1. United States, by the National Observatory, 1862. Duplicate.
2. Middle States, by Johnson, 1856.
3. Ohio, by Walling, 1861.

OHIO COUNTY MAPS.

4. Lorain, by Geil, 1859.
5. Geauga and Lake, by Matthews. 1857. Duplicate.
6. Trumbull, by Brown and Matthews.
7. Summit, by Paul, 1856. Duplicate.
8. Holmes, by Walling, 1861.
9. Coshocton, by Becker.
10. Cuyahoga, by Matthews, 1858. Duplicate.
11. Ashtabula, by Baker, 1856.
12. Fairfield, by Towson, 1848.
13. Muskingum, by Bennett.
14. Belmont, by Charlesworth, 1855.
15. Ohio, by John F. Mansfield. 1806.
16. Ohio, by Hough and Bourne, 1814.
17. Ohio, by, John Kilbourne, 1822.
18. Ohio, by Howard, 1828.
19. Ohio, by Adams and Eggleston, 1848.
20. Western Reserve, by Reed and Rollo. 1842.
21. Pennsylvania, by Howell, 1792.
22. Railroad Map of the United States, 1870.
23. United States, 1853.
24. Berghaus' Chart of the World. Gotha. 1871.

MAPS, MISCELLANEOUS.

City of Washington. (John Brannan.) 1828.
Lloyd's New Military Map of the Southern and Border States. New York. 1864.
Western Reserve, 1826. (Wm. Sumner.)
New Military Map of Middle Europe.
Sebastopol, Crimea, and the Black Sea, 1854. (Jocelyn.)

Town 2, Range 10, (Tallmadge,) as surveyed by S. E. Ensign, 1806.
Amos Spafford's Map of Cleveland, 1796. (Copy.)
Western District of Upper Canada.
Plan of New Market, Mouth of Grand river, Ohio, 1804.
Cleveland and its environs, 1835. (A. Merchant.) Duplicate.
Firelands, 1808. (Almon Ruggles.) Duplicates.
Plan of the Road leading from the foot of the Rapids of the Miami of Lake Erie to the Western Boundary of the Connecticut Western Reserve, 1823.
Map of the Country bordering the Buffalo and Mississippi Railroad. (G. R. Baldwin.) 1846.
Kansas, 1870, (Mills and Smith.)
St. Louis and Vicinity, (Urban and Fisher.) 1854.
Township No. 16, 17th Range.
Ohio, 1833. (Justin Carpenter.)
Fac simile of a map made by the Jesuit Missionaries, 1670-1. Paris. 1672. Triplicates.
Village of Eagle Harbor. Houghon, Mich. 1851.
Norfolk, Va., and Vicinity.
Ohio, 1812.
Boston, 1862. (L. Prang & Co.)
Map of the country within Five Hundred Miles of Cairo, Ill., 1861. (G. W. Colton.)
Map of Wilmington, N. C. showing the position of the blockading fleet, war of the Rebellion.
Map of Mackinaw City (B. C. Phillips.) 1857. Map of the Straits of Mackinaw, 1857. (B. C. Phillips.)
Map illustrating the Canada Pacific, and Northern Pacific and other proposed Railroads connecting at Mackinaw City.
Large Map of Pennsylvania on Cloth, by R. Howell, 1792.
Vermont. Triplicates. (Jewett and Chandler.) 1870
Ohio in 1833.
New York City, by Perris, 1850-1.
City of Paris and its Fortifications. (From N. C. Winslow.)
Survey of Wellsville and Fairport Railroad, by White, 1836.
Hutchins' Map of the Ohio Territory. 1763.
Jesuits Map of Lake Superior, 1672.
Champlain's Map of New France or Canada, 1632.
Manuscript map of the west end of Lake Erie, apparently for the use of the army in 1813, from the papers of John Walworth.
Lake Survey Charts, complete.
Coast Survey of the United States, complete.

CASE NO. 15.

MAPS DEPOSITED BY CHAS. WHITTLESEY. LAND OFFICE.

No.
1. Louisiana, Arkansas.
2. Florida, Mississippi, Alabama.
3. Iowa.
4. Missouri.
5. Dacotah, Kansas, Colorado, Nebraska.
6. Washington, Oregon, Montana, Idaho.
7. New Mexico, Texas, Arizona.
8. Illinois.
9. Indiana.
10. California, 1861.

CASE NO. 16.

RAILROADS, CANALS AND CITIES.

1. St. Croix and Lake Superior Railroad.
2. Harrisburg and Pittsburgh, 1839.

No.
3. Green Bay and Ontonagon.
4. Des Moines Canal, Iowa City Survey.
5. Lake Michigan to Lake Superior, 1855.
6. Washington City and Capitol.
7. New York.
8. Madison, Wisconsin.
9. Vicinity of St. Louis, Missouri.

CASE NO. 17.

MAPS OF THE STATES.

1. Kentucky, 1862.
2. Tennessee, 1862.
3. West Virginia, 1862.
4. United States Military Map, 1863.
5. Virginia, Maryland, and East Tennessee, 1861.
6. Virginia, 1862.
7. East Virginia, 1862. Duplicate.
8. South Virginia and Washington City, 1862.
9. United States Land Office Map, 1866.

CASE NO. 18.

1. United States, (Colton,) 1861.
2. Red River and Lake Superior Wagon Roads, (Russell,) 1868.
3. Elevations from Independence, Missouri, to the Rio Grande.
4. North America, (Gilpin,) 1861.
5. Northern Boundary of the U. States, Maine, 1839.
6. Province of New York, 1779.
7. Tehuantepec Railroad Survey, 1848.
8. Fremont's Expeditions, 1840 and 1845.

CASE NO. 19.

1. Europe, (Colton.)
2. Nicaragua, 1856.
3. New Haven Water Works, 1856.
4. Europe, 1851.
5. Lombardy and Venice, 1859.
6. North Polar Regions, 1852.
7. Seat of War in the U. States, 1860.

CASE NO. 20.

1. Lake Superior, (Chapman,) 1857, and Land Office Map.
2. Lake Superior Geological Map, 1850.
3. Copper Locations, Point Keweenaw, 1846, '51 and '54.
4. Plans of Mines: North American, Cliff, Phœnix and Lac La Belle.
5. Mining Locations, Point Keweenaw, 1846.
6. Marquette, Escanaba and Menominee Regions.
7. Isle Royal and its Harbors.
8. Point Keweenaw, 1856 and 1860.

CASE NO. 21.

1. Marquette County and vicinity.
2. Point Keweenaw Mining Locations and Towns.
3. Marquette and Menominee Rivers, (Hurlbut,) 1856.
4. Matchegummi Lake and Keweenaw Bay, (Banfield,) 1856.
5. Upper Peninsula, (Farmer,) 1847.
6. Coal Fields of Michigan, Grand Traverse Bay, (Winchell.)

CASE NO. 22.

1 Geological Report and Profile, (Foster and Whitney,) 1849.
2. Lake Superior, 1845-6.
3. St. Mary's Canal Company Lands.
4. Sectional Map, by Chapman, 1857.
5. Porcupine Mountains, Ontonagon and Montreal River—4 Maps.
6. Portage Lake and Ontonagon, 1851.

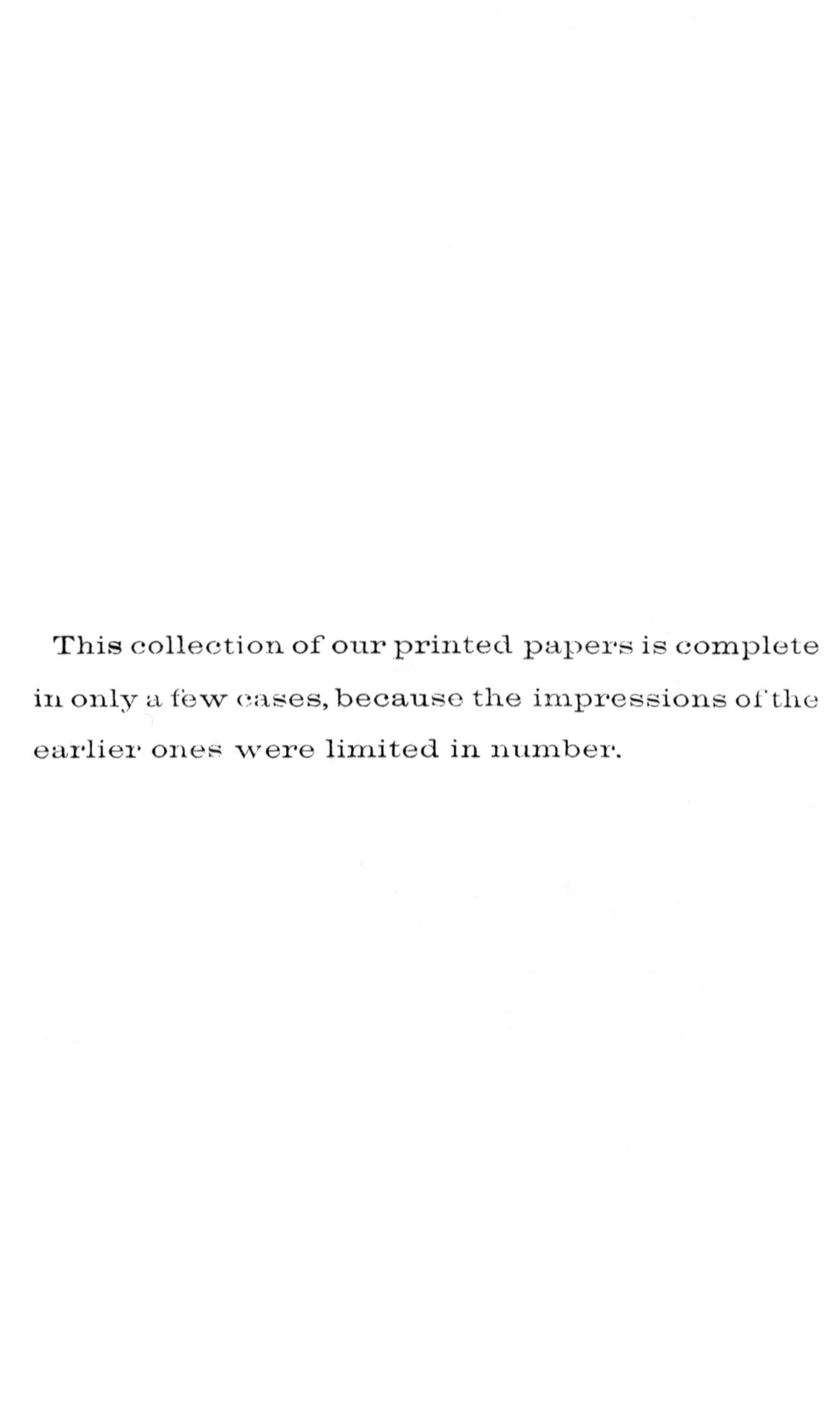

This collection of our printed papers is complete in only a few cases, because the impressions of the earlier ones were limited in number.

Western Reserve and Northern Ohio

HISTORICAL SOCIETY,

CLEVELAND, OHIO.

No. Twenty-Three—October, 1874.

RELICS OF THE MOUND BUILDERS.

BY C. C. BALDWIN, SECRETARY.

In July, 1874, the Secretary of the Western Reserve and Northern Ohio Historical Society brought with him from Memphis, Tennessee, a very valuable addition to the collection of relics now in the Society's museum belonging to that mysterious race, the Mound Builders.

They are the generous gift of Colonel L. J. Du Pre, editor of the Memphis *Appeal*, a gentleman whose contributions in print and in manuscript concerning the first known inhabitants of our country are of absorbing interest.

With one exception the mounds from which these articles were taken are located on Mississippi River, about sixty miles below Memphis.

Among them is a skull in good preservation, showing at its base the marks of pressure against a board or other hard substance, producing a flat depression. The skull is said to have been taken from the bottom of a mound about forty or fifty miles below Memphis.

Among the contents of the mounds of this vicinity was a black baked basin, shaped much like a tin wash-basin, which contained a skull lying within it face upward. The material of the basin is similar to that of the black vessels hereinafter described, and the skull (now in Memphis) is in a state of preservation similar to that donated to the society. Both skulls are of uncommon thickness and strength.

The donation contains numerous specimens of pottery. Some of them are of brown clay baked and retaining its color, some of them are black throughout as if made of river mud. They are all mixed with pounded shells in the manner common with the Mound Builders except No. 14. None of this pottery is glazed, although some of it is very smoothly and handsomely made and some pieces have a hard outside finish that appears something like glazing.

No. 1 is a vase of handsome form, painted red and of smooth, hard surface, nine inches in diameter, six and a half inches high to the shoulder. The mouth or spout is broken away, but may be guessed to have been like number three.

No. 2 is a soft, black porous vessel, not far from round, about eight and one-half inches in diameter, five and three-fourths inches high to the spout, which is one and three-fourths inches wide, and of which about that length remains. This vessel was probably a water cooler, to which use it was by shape and structure well adapted.

No. 3 is a vase of smooth, hard surface—striped in three colors, red, white and brown, about the size and shape of number one. There remains, however, the spout or top of the vase, striped, five inches long in diameter, at the lower end one and five-eights inches, at the upper end one-half inch aperture. The spout stood upon the top of the vase, and the whole resembled in shape some of the Peruvian vases, used for holding fluids, and closed with a round stone used as a cork.

This and number one are too smooth, sharp and regular in outline to have been formed with the hand. They were very likely moulded, and very nicely too, as the joints do not show. The inside shows the plain marks of fingers pressing the fine brown clay against the moulds. The shells are pounded much finer in this and number one than in the others.

No. 4 is an unbroken pot, five inches in diameter and five high, with a curved mouth two inches in diameter. It is made of brown, hard baked clay, color stained by fire, and of close texture.

No 5 was found with the skull already mentioned, and is a black vase six inches in diameter four and one half high, with a mouth two and three fourths inches across. The outline of this vase is quite sharp and graceful, showing good taste and skill. The material is hard. This and No. 4 both look as if they might have been used in cooking, although differing much in form, color and material.

No. 6 is four and a half inches in diameter, by four high and two across the mouth. It is of rough pottery and very nearly whole.

No. 7 is a rare bit of pottery, black in material and color, well baked, pear shaped, with a round unprojecting mouth near the top. This vase is not whole. It shows that it was much thicker above the mouth with a protuberance, which perhaps had a hole through it for the purpose of suspending it to the side of the room or cabin.

Among the vases found in the locality of this, were some with small perforated ears, intended for suspension, by passing a thong through them.

A view of the inside of the cabin of a Mojave family, found in Lieut. Ive's report upon the Colorado river, well illustrates this custom.

The diameter of this vase is four and one half inches, total height remaining, six inches, of which half an inch is above the upper side of the mouth.

The officers of the society do not remember to have seen figured any vessel of similiar shape to this, and it may be considered almost or quite unique.

No. 8 is five and one-third inches in diameter, three inches high, and three and three-fourths inches across the mouth. It is shaped like a small basin, with contracted mouth. It has marks of fire and is of brown clay.

No. 9 is four and one-third inches in diameter, three and one-half inches high by two and one-half inches diameter across a low mouth. It is rough baked clay, with marks of fire.

No. 10 is a small basin six and one-fourth inches in diameter, narrowing at the top to five and one-fourth inches, two and three-fourths high, black in color, and the upper part ornamented with diagonal marks. This is a kind of ornamentation very common in the pottery of the Mound Builders and Indians, but the only ornamentation of that kind in the collection we are now describing.

No. 11 is a very small vase, brown clay color, a little over two inches in diameter and two high, one and one-half across the inside of the mouth.

No. 12 is very much like No. 11, a little larger, and mouth gone.

No. 13 is the ornamental handle of a scoop or dipper, with a part of the vessel attached. It is painted red. The handle represents the head and beak of a bird, much like those ornaments not uncommon in Peruvian and Mound Builder ceramic ware. The handle is a very convenient one, the thumb resting nicely on the crest.

No. 14 is a graceful vase, almost perfect, of thick but brittle ware, painted red, with a long, narrow neck—looking as if it might have held some perfume or precious liquid. Its diameter is three inches; height five inches, of which two is neck; the diameter of the neck is one inch. This vase is the only one which has no pounded shells mixed with it.

None of the vessels have any feet. Indeed, vessels with feet are exceedingly uncommon among relics of the mounds. There are, however, three hollow feet which evidently belonged to some vessel shaped apparently like our old-fashioned iron pots. These feet are of some size, being three and three-fourths inches high, and two inches in diameter. The bottoms imitate the cat-like feet and toes of some animal, joining usefulness and an artistic imitation of some object in natural history—an art in which the Mound Builders excelled.

In this collection is also a skinning knife made of polished quartz, streaked white and red; an instrument for dressing skins, of slate colored quartz rock, also polished very smooth. Also an implement of quartz, three inches long and one wide, with a blunt edge on each end.

There is yet to be described a very interesting relic, it is a round stone of reddish quartz, three and three quarter inches in diameter, one and one-eighth inches in thickness, nicely worked with a a depression pecked on one side for the thumb. The edge is straight from side to side of the stone, but beveled. The use of this stone is unmistakable. It was rolled along the ground in one of their games, which came down to some of the Indian tribes within the time of history. It was played by two players at a time, each of whom had a pole. One rolled the stone, which from its beveled edge must continually turn toward the right. As soon as the stone started the two players threw their poles and the one whose pole lay nearest to the stone when it stopped was the victor, and had the right to roll the stone the next time. Such is the mode of playing described by Du Pratz in his History of Louisiana, published in 1758.

Adair's book, published in 1775, describes the game as played among the Cherokees.

"The warriors have another favorite game called chungke. They have a square piece of ground well cleaned. Only one or two on a side play at this ancient game. They have a stone about two fingers broad at the edge, and two spans round; each party has a pole about eight feet long, smooth and tapering at each end, the points flat." Adair then gives the method of playing, substantially as above, and adds: "In this manner the players will keep running most part of the day at half speed, under the violent heat of the sun staking their silver ornaments, nose, finger and ear rings, their breast, arm and wrist plates, and their wearing apparel." All the American Indians. says Adair, are much addicted to this game, which to us appears to be a task of stupid drudgery; it seems, however, to be of early origin when their forefathers used diversions as simple as their manners. The hurling stones they use at present were from time immemorial, rubbed smooth on the rocks and with prodigious labor; they are kept with the strictest religious care from one generation to another, and are exempted from being buried with the dead. They belong to the town where they are used and are carefully preserved."

If public property they would rarely be buried with the dead. They are however sometimes found in mounds, and Mr. C. C. Jones, in his excellent books on the Antiquities of Georgia, relates the finding of a fine one in a mound at a depth of thirty feet.

There are in Arkansas and perhaps in other States along the Mississippi river prepared grounds, sometimes with sun-baked brick. These places are called by those living in the vicinity threshing-floors. Is it not probable that they were chungke yards?

The aborigines had little grain to thresh, all our ordinary grains being of European origin.

The game seems to have been of general and great interest, where says Captain Romans, "They bet high." Here you may see a savage come and bring all his skins stake them and lose them, next his pipe, his beads, trinkets and ornaments; at last his blanket and other garments, and even all their arms and after all it is not uncommon for them to go home, borrow a gun, and shoot themselves.

Catlin says that the Mandans used sometimes to stake their liberty upon the issue of this game.

Adair says the Cherokees had a piece of ground carefully prepared and kept for this game near their council house, or as he calls it "State House."

Mr. Jones says the traces left in Georgia of such grounds show a careful preparation and are parallelograms in shape slightly elevated from sixty to ninety feet in length and about half as wide.

Captain Romans describes the ground as being an alley about two hundred feet in length where a smooth clay ground "is laid which when dry is very hard."

May not some of the mysterious and carefully prepared grounds of the mound builders within the State of Ohio, have been public yards for the playing of this game.

It is curious that the Mandans whom Catlin found west of the Missour River and whose traditions pointed to the Ohio River had the same name for this game, as had the Creeks.

Col. Du Pre also presented to the society several photographs, two of a skull taken from one of the mounds, the others representing various objects of curious interest.

CAMPAIGN OF 1813 ON THE OHIO FRONTIER.

SORTIE AT FORT MEIGS, MAY 1813.

ADDRESS OF THOMAS CHRISTIAN, A VOLUNTEER IN COL. DUDLEY'S REGIMENT.

LEXINGTON, KY., JUNE 20, '70.

To A. T. Goodman Esq., Sec't W. R. H. Society:

DEAR SIR:—This simple narrative was prepared for the old soldiers who met at Paris yesterday, but I think it worth preserving, and therefore enclose it to you. I have no doubt of its accuracy, for the writer is a very respectable farmer, and I *witnessed* the principal events myself. In the battle of 5th May, '13, under Dudley, I was a (*boy*) Captain, commanded two spy companies and a few friendly Indians in advance, was badly wounded, taken prisoner, forced to run the Indian gauntlet, and saved by Tecumseh as stated. Yours, truly, LESLIE COMBS.

Fellow-soldiers and fellow-sufferers in a short but bloody war, long since passed but ever to be remembered, it would afford me more pleasure to be with you to-day, or upon any other occasion when assembled, than I dare attempt to describe; but great as that pleasure would be of seeing you face to face and conversing with you, old age and feeble health deny to me its enjoyment. And were it not for the kindness of our ever-generous friend, fellow-soldier and fellow-sufferer, General Leslie Combs, I would not even enjoy this second best of pleasures. Being thus remembered by you, giving you my best wishes for this life's enjoyments, and most fervent prayers for your eternal happiness in the great, unbounded and eternal camping-grounds, where peace ever reigns and Jesus commands, where no savage *war-whoop* excites the passions of strife, where no uplifted tomahawk or scalping-knife intimidates or arouses, where there is no surrendering to a relentless foe, or running the gauntlet or submitting to savage massacre, but where instead is heard the voice of eternal love and praise, and we are led, willing captives, into salvation's impregnable fortress. But let me be brief; we are all *old* now and easily fatigued, and our object is to entertain one another, with as little tax upon time and patience as possible. And as our generous fellow-soldier, Gen. Combs, has persuaded me that a short narrative of the little service I rendered our country in 1813 would not be unpleasant to you, considering the impossibility of my being with you in person, I have consented to give it in as brief method as I can master. But in attempting to do so strange indeed are my feelings, fellow-soldiers, as I about-face to review the past. I again hear the tap of the drum that sounded in the little village of Athens, Fayette county, for volunteers in the winter of 1813, just upon the excitement of Winchester's defeat. I again hear the voice of my Captain, Archibald Morrison, and see the faces of my fellow-volunteers as they fall in line. Salutations are being received upon every side and the din of innumerable familiar voices are heard; alas! only in the imagination, for those voices were long since hushed and those faces we will see no more this side of the grave. My father's "Good-bye, my boy," my mother's blessings and tears, all pass in review before me now. Soon my loose warm jeans roundabout seems to be my most protecting friend, as our rendezvous at Lexington has been far in the rear, and we are upon a forced march across the swampy marshes of Ohio, rendered almost impassable by incessant spring rains, to the relief of General Harrison at Fort Meigs. One shower after another, and each one seemingly colder than its predecessor, is pelting us day and night. Upon brush-piles cut for the occasion, we are compelled to sleep to keep above water. Our brave, kind-hearted and generous Colonel Dudley is busy encouraging his men and aided by the other officers doing all that can be done to lessen our sufferings; but continual wading in water is beginning to tell and the skin is peeling from our weary legs, from the knee down; the well-clothed and well-protected camp followers, with their wagons of luxuries and drinkables, are extorting more and more as we leave civilization farther behind, and now a drink of their cider-oil is out of reach of two-thirds the command, and they have lost their popularity with both men and officers; consequently another fatiguing day's march, with the prospect of another night, twin-sister to the rest, plays havoc with the hucksters; the cider-oil wagons are upset, barrels are being rolled hither and thither. No orders to that effect have been issued, and without any one seemingly to know who were doing these things or why they were being done, *presto* the drinkables have disappeared and every soldier in camp suddenly forgets his fatigue and becomes Lieutenant General commanding innumerable hosts of invincible veterans. Commands of officers in the heat of terrible battle are heard in every direction, innumerable game cocks are loudly crowing and all manner of songs are singing, concord and discord all around. This last jollification of our little command. Oh! how soon after was hushed forever on earth the joyful voices of almost every messmate and friend I *there* had, and *then* so gay. But a very few nights after, amid darkness and pelting rain, we are cautiously and as rapid as practicable descending the Maumee, to surprise Proctor, whip the Indians, raise the siege, and relieve Fort Meigs, but ere we reach the Fort many of my companions' guns are full of water, as the pouring from their muzzles plainly indicates when they are brought from a perpendicular to a horizontal position, preparatory to the bloody action soon to commence. Some faint signs of coming day and many indications of the immediate presence of onr savage foe, left no doubt in the mind of any one just then of a terrible conflict just commencing. The morning of the memorable 5th of May was dawning. Officers and men were hurrying from boats, and the quick flashes and the keen reports of many guns pronounced the battle commenced. Many were being wounded around me. My captain, Archibald Morrison, had formed in good marching order and was under way when the brave Captain John Morrison was shot through the head, both eye-balls bursting clean from their sockets. Dying, but undaunted, he orders his men forward to a post of honor, where they could do their country good service, and not waste their precious time with a dying man. Officers and men then bounded forward, soon dispersing the besiegers and capturing the guns we were ordered to capture. And now flushed with victory, and maddened by the sight of fallen, bleeding and dying comrades our brave Colonel Dudley and men could not resist the desire of following the retreating enemy and wreaking vengeance upon them for the loss of near relatives and friends. So without taking time to roll the captured guns into the river after them, we went, and had it not been for the dense forest and undergrowth we would have made short work of them. But, alas! that aid to the enemy was death for us. They formed an ambush, and securely hid from view, had every advantage. Our futile attempts to dislodge them gave that portion of the enemy upon the opposite side of the river ample time to cross over in our rear, completely hemming us in upon every side. Our case was then hopeless. Our ranks scattered, our brave Colonel slain, and most of the other officers mortally wounded, seems sufficient to have unnerved the bravest hero, but even then many heroic deeds of personal valor were enacted and I still occasionally heard the loud, shrill game cock crowing of one brave spirit who seemed determined to die game and cheer his comrades to the last. What became of him who knows? Louder and louder, nearer and nearer came the savage yells of the bloodthirsty foe from every quarter and fainter grew the resistance offered by our thinned and dispirited ranks, until bursting forth in our very midst, the deafening, demoniac yells drowned all other sounds save the coarse, broad command, "*ground* your arms, surrender," pronounced by British officers banishing all hope of successful resistance. Captured, brave Dudley is defeated and we are prisoners in savage hands, were the thoughts that then rushed to my mind, causing me to forget upon the instant to throw down my arms; but just then that same broad command, this time to me personally, "Damn your eyes, ground your arms, or you will be slain," brought me hastily to my senses. Down went gun, off came knapsack, &c., to hastily disappear beneath the mud and water, then ankle deep where

I stood, and with my full weight I aided their exit from further service, pressing them as deeply into the mud as possible; then stepping towards where the prisoners were being collected, the first man I met with whom I was acquainted was old Mr. Bradburn, but he could give me no information as to the whereabouts of any of our messmates, as I was then the only acquaintance he had met since the surrender. The sad fact was that but few of our particular mess were left to meet again upon earth, and soon, very soon, even his blood and brains were destined to bespatter me and others, as the enraged savages tomahawked him in our midst. Now too late, we saw the error of surrendering to such a foe, and every soldier keenly felt the difference between dying in the heat of battle, contending for right, and the cold-blooded massacre that now plainly awaited him. For the few British who were with the Indians had no power to control them, being in almost as bad a situation as ourselves, the savages threatening to exterminate them if they offered any resistance to their inhuman desire to butcher the 'prisoners, and did kill one of them in my presence for begging the life of one prisoner, who had thrown himself under his protection. Consequently the British aided by some of the Indians hurried us on as rapidly as they could down the river to an old deserted fort where they assured us that we could and should be protected. But the bloody tomahawk was busy along the whole route, leaving behind us a path of blood and scalped comrades. Matters growing worse and worse at every step, the savages becoming more and more enraged and bloodthirsty as we neared the fort, shortly before reaching which I was halted by some Indians and a sprightly stripling of some sixteen summers hastily proceeded to search my pockets; feeling much resentment, I suppose I must have exhibited some, for instantly two paint be-daubed warriors, with uplifted tomahawks made a rush towards me, and would, perhaps, have instantly buried them deep in my brain, but just then their attention was arrested by the glittering appearance of a brass inkstand the young savage had extracted from my pocket, where in marching it had rubbed to a glittering brightness equal to gold. The few silver dollars I had left soon shared the same fate of the inkstand, and amid the forward pressure I soon passed out of sight of my Indian boy and his captured goods which it seemed put him and his companions wild with delight. But getting rid of them could afford no joy or feeling of relief; for lifting my eyes, there stood a few hundred yards off the old deserted fort, with thick lines of savages extending from either side of its entrance to the very spot where I stood, clubbing and tomahawking all they could of the terror-stricken prisoners as they made their wild, panic-race for its entrance, where they foolishly hoped to find protection and safety. Each one as he reached the head of the savage lines comprehended at a glance the nature of his situation. To hesitate was instant death, and without further orders each made his individual dash for life through the yelling savage lines with superhuman speed and agility. Many who were knocked down gained the entrance upon all-fours with astonishing speed. The prisoner in front of me received a deep gash in the shoulder as he ran, but succeeded in entering the fort. And now it was my time. The way was slippery with human blood and blocked in places by the slain. No time for thought or preparation. The loose, warm jean roundabout which I before mentioned and which had done me so much good service through the long, cold, wet marches, was buttoned to the throat, and with a strength and speed that astonished me I made a bolt, but ere I had reached the prized entry, I felt a sudden jerk at the back of my head, saw a button strike the ground some feet in front, my arms were forciby jerked back, and the precious gift of my dear old mother was lost forever, without my having time to say, good-bye, dear old friend roundabout. A few more bounds landed me in the fort, or rather slaughter-pen; and here we seemed to be in, if possible, a worse situation than ever; for the savages rudely shoved the British sentinels aside, and with unearthly yells poured in upon us, killing and scalping as fast as their own crowded ranks would admit, while we, like terror-stricken sheep hemmed in by dogs, or a parcel of hogs in a butcher's pen, were piled one upon another in one corner Those at the bottom were being smothered, while those upon the top were being drenched with blood and brains. Just then, suddenly as the lightning's flash, the yelling ceased, the uplifted war clubs descended harmlessly by the side of the now shamed warriors, and above the groans of the dying, and the prayers of the living, is heard the brave Tecumseh putting a stop to the massacre, shaming his warriors for behaving like squaws. The few now left are saved from death, but the little band or remnant of the once proud regiment of 800 brave Kentuckians are still destined to undergo much suffering for nakedness, cold, hunger and death still waited upon and thinned their ranks; and the exposure while being taken prisoners down the Maumee to the lakes or place of exchange, proved too great for almost all of us, and many perished from it before reaching home, while the most of us were a long time in recovering. The cold was intense upon the water in open boats, and for three days and nights we had nothing to eat save a mess of horse-beef that we much relished and wished for more. At the mouth of Huron river we were turned loose without sufficient clothing to keep us warm, without money, and nothing to eat save one ration sent to us by General Harrison. He would have done more for us, but it was out of his power. From that point we had to find our way home as best we could through an almost friendless country, traveling a very circuitous route to avoid falling in the hands of Indians, each little party of friends taking a different way, agreeing to assist one another, for there were many sick, and some of the sick had to accompany each party. Our little party homeward bound was composed of Robert Simpson, Daniel Carter, George Sherwin and Joseph Franklin. On account of my sickness we had to travel very slowly; in fact, all of us were unable to stand much fatigue. I was so weak much of the time that it was impossible for me to get up, but when lifted upon my feet could manage to walk for several hours by occasionally leaning against something to rest, living much of the time upon slippery elm bark, and begging our way as we slowly advanced towards the Ohio river. We were sometimes refused anything to eat, but as we neared the river we fared better and the sick got occasional chances to ride. Meeting a chance to ride a led horse belonging to a gentleman who was coming several miles in the direction of the river put me so far in advance of my friends that they never overhauled me again before reaching home. After this I found other opportunities of getting short rides which soon brought me to the banks of the river opposite Maysville then called Limestone. Here a gentleman let me stay all night and finding an opportunity of crossing to the opposite bank early next morning, I met with a strange coincidence, for just as I landed upon the Kentucky shore, I saw my father standing near the water's edge, and looking intently up the stream at a boat descending. He had just arrived and something persuaded him that I was near, perhaps in the boat. So intent was his gaze that he did not see me until I spoke. We were astonished at the strange meeting, both having arrived upon the spot almost simultaneously. I soon arrived home amid the welcoming of many friends, and in much improved health, but so lean that all declared that I had grown at least two inches taller. The girls treated me to cakes and strawberries, the young men introduced me to their sweethearts, and the old gave me much praise, so I got along swimmingly for a few months, when serious notions of returning upon the war path disturbed my dreams for a few weeks. Finding my services were not needed I joyfully gave up the idea, went resolutely to work, and with God's aid have succeeded in making a good provision for my family, and I trust *peace* with my Maker.

Fellow-soldiers, reiterating with most fervent prayer my greatest desire that God's choicest blessings may descend upon each of you, I bid you a most affectionate good-bye. We may meet again upon earth, but probably our next meeting will be "beyond the river resting in the shade." Good-bye.

THOMAS CHRISTIAN.

Western Reserve and Northern Ohio HISTORICAL SOCIETY,

CLEVELAND, OHIO.

No. Twenty-Four—October, 1874.

RECENT DONATIONS BY W. P. FOGG, ESQ.,

WITH HIS DESCRIPTION AND REMARKS.

The following is a list of the articles donated by W. P. Fogg, of Cleveland, to the Museum of the Western Reserve and Northern Ohio Historical Society. He has appended to this list a paper relative to several of these articles which will be found of great interest.

LIST OF DONATIONS.

Large brick from the ruins of Babylon, stamped with *name* and *titles* of *Nebuchadnezzar* in cuneiform characters.

Large brick from Nineveh, stamped with cuneiform characters.

"Black basaltic polished stone like a pestle or grinder, with cuneiform transcription in Persian, Median, and Babylonian, of Darius the great, about 500 B. C." See description by *Prof. George Smith*, Director of Department of Assyrian Antiquities in British Museum.

Small cylinder of black basalt with figures and characters engraven upon it, found among the mounds of Babylon.

Piece of glazed tile from the Mosque of Omar, built on the site of Solomon's Temple at Jerusalem.

Piece of brick from the Arch of Ctesiphon. This celebrated Arch is 106 feet high, by about 100 feet in breadth. It is situated upon the banks of the Tigris. about 15 miles below Bagdad; and is all that remains of a great city, once the capital of the Parthian Empire.

Four alabaster tear bottles; one large earthern vase; three small ones; fragments of alabaster, and earthen images; earthen pottery and lamps; earthen bowl, the inside covered with Persian writing. All found among the ruins.

Coral from the Red Sea.

Egyptian lady's veil.

Embroidered tobacco pouch. Persian.

Fort at Allahabad, India, painted on Ivory

A newspaper printed at Bagdad in Turkish and Arabic.

Letters of Introduction, written in Persian and Arabic.

A coin struck at Tarsus, by a Satrap of the King of Persia, 450 B. C.

Gold piece; Byzantine Empire 5th Century.

Silver piece; Byzantine Empire, 6th Century.

Six bronze coins from Babylon.

One Turkish Mudjidi, gold.

One Turkish Cumrais, copper.

Turkish Piastres, one copper, two silver.

Turkish "Righ" Piastre, silver.

Persian Keran, silver.

The "Cuneiform," or "Arrow-head," Inscriptions of Assyria.

The word *cuneiform* is derived from the Latin *cuneus*—a wedge—and in this style of letter are all the monumental records of the ancient empires of Assyria, Babylonia and Persia. The accidental discovery of the famous Rosetta Stone, (now in the British Museum) furnished the key to decipher the hieroglyphics of Ancient Egypt, by means of which a flood of light has been thrown upon the history and civilization of the Pharaohs. The patience and perseverance of Rawlinson, Layard, and others have rescued the Cuneiform from a "dead language" to one full of life and interest to the antiquary and the student of ancient history.

Pliny declares that it is to the Assyrians we owe the invention of letters; and it would seem probable that simple perpendicular and horizontal lines, of which the *Cuneiform* is composed, preceded the rounded or cursive forms, being better suited to letters carved by a primitive people on stone tablets, or the smoothed faces of rocks. The great antiquity of carving documents on stone is shown by the Bible. The Divine commands were first given to mankind on stone tablets, and in early ages this was considered the most appropriate and durable method of perpetuating records. The cuneiform inscriptions on most of the monuments of Assyria and Persia were formed with great neatness and care. The letters were evidently cut with sharp implements of iron or copper, and on the seals, gems, and small cylinders of stone the characters were so elaborately made and so accurately minute that only an instrument of the most delicate construction could have produced them. It is said that no implements or tools of iron or steel, but only those of copper have been discovered among the ruins of ancient Egypt. But the cutting tools of the Egyptians, as well as of the early Asiatic nations, were not of pure copper, nor were they of *bronze*, according to the modern acceptation of that term They were made of copper with an alloy of about 5 per cent of tin which gave them the requisite hardness for use.

We know little of the civilization of the Assyrians except what can be gathered from the casual notices scattered through the works of the Greeks. It is evident that they attained a high degree of culture at a very remote period. The testimony of the Bible and the monuments of the Egyptians, on which the conquests of that people over the Asiatic nations are recorded, lead to this conclusion. There is a great variation in the dates assigned by savans to the earlier monuments of Egypt, but very few ascribe them to an epoch later than that of the foundation of Nineveh, about 2,000 years B. C. It is probable that the Assyrians at that time shared in the arts and sciences which had already reached so high a degree of perfection in Egypt. They copied nature more carefully, and gave more scope to taste and invention than their Egyptian rivals, who were restricted by certain prejudices and superstitions to a conventional style, from which it was not lawful to depart.

The exact date of the destruction of Nineveh, the proud Capital of the Eastern world, by Cyaxares, King of the Medes and Persians, as fixed by the concurrent testimony of Scripture and Herodotus, was about 608 years B. C. It did not occur before the death of Josiah, King of Judah B. C. 609, because a King of Assyria is mentioned at that time; and Zephaniah in a prophecy delivered in the reign of Josiah predicts the destruction of Nineveh as a future event. But the prophecy of Jeremiah, written in the first year of the captivity of the Jews, B. C. 605, enumerates all the Kings of the north, far and wide, and all the Kingdoms of the world, and among these Nineveh is not named. The statement of Herodotus that in the year 608 B. C. Cyaxares conquered Assyria to revenge his father's death is remarkably consistent with the accounts of Scripture. The destruction of Nineveh was so complete that when Xenophon passed over the remains of that city in his retreat some centuries later with the ten thousand Greeks, its very name had been forgotten, and he describes it as a vast uninhabited city. called Narissa, anciently inhabited by the Medes. Lucian speaks of it as so completely laid waste, that not an inhabitant or scarcely a vestige remained of the magnificent palaces, once the dwelling place of the Assyrian Monarchs.

The earliest records of the Assyrians, like those of most ancient nations, were probably monumental, and these are all in the arrow-head, or cuneiform character. There are three dialects or forms of these letters—the Assyrian or Babylonian, the Median, and the Persian, and to one of these may be referred all the cuneiform inscriptions that are known to exist. The Babylo-Assyrian alphabet contains about 300 letters, while the Persian cuneiform has but 40. The former is supposed to be of much more ancient date, as in this dialect are all the inscriptions found in Nimroud and Nineveh, belonging to a period preceding the Persian domination.

The element of all the characters in the three different dialects of the cuneiform is *the wedge*; and they differ only in the combination of wedges to form the letters. In many of the records of the Persian monarchs the three dialects occur in parallel columns, representing three languages.

The most remarkable inscription in this trilingual cuneiform character is that on the sacred rocks at a place called Behistun, ("God's Place") on the western frontiers of Persia. Here Darius, "the great King," inscribed his conquests and the most important events of his reign. Until within a few years this immense tablet has been a wonder and a puzzle to the most learned antiquaries, and to the few European travelers who have visited these remote regions. The labor of deciphering an unknown character, probably representing an extinct dialect, if not an extinct language, must be very great. To Major Rawlinson, whose ingenuity and perserverance have given an accurate translation of the inscription at Behistun, we are indebted for this valuable addition to the written records of the ancient world.

Here upon the main road between Assyria and Persia, the rocks rise abruptly from the plain to the height of nearly 1700 feet. The inscription covers several hundred square feet. It is unrivalled in extent, beauty of execution and correctness, especially the Persian, which is said to be superior to any engraving of the kind, even that on the tomb of Darius, near Persopolis, the ancient capital of Persia. It is about 300 feet above the base of the rock, and its inaccessibility has preserved it from the iconoclastic fury of the Mohammetans. It is probable that after the inscription was completed the rock beneath was cut away, so that the whole immense face is nearly vertical. The rock is limestone, and a coat of silicious varnish is yet visible on the tablet, which was designed to protect it from the atmosphere.

Darius begins by proclaiming his genealogy and titles, tracing his descent from Adam. He then enumerates the provinces of his empire, which in extent would seem to entitle him to the name of "the great King." After these follow the great events of his reign, the reform of the national faith, his victories over the rebels in Assyria and Babylon, and the suppression of insurrections in other parts of his vast empire. He also, engraves his thanksgiving to Ormuzd on this sacred spot, and in many particulars this record corroborates the Mosaic accounts as well as the writings of Herodotus.

There is one peculiarity of all cuneiform writing, that it reads from left to right; while the ancient languages composed of rounded forms of letters (the Arabic, Hebrew and Persian), read, like the Chinese, from right to left. They are stamped or engraved, according to the nature of the material, on all the ruins of the great cities of Assyria and Babylonia—on the bricks of all the public buildings, on the walls of temples, palaces and other edifices, on stone slabs and bas-reliefs, on vases, gems, seals and small cylinders, some being so minute as to require a microscope to decipher them. For thousands of years these inscriptions were an unknown tongue. An attempt to do justice to the wonders which the key to the cuneiform inscriptions has unlocked would occupy volumes. I can only hope in this article to call attention to a subject on which very little is known to the mass of our people. This is an age of scientific research—and while our savans are opening new fields of knowledge, it seems eminently proper that they should recover from the remote past, whatever of value is already recorded upon tables of stone.

THE BRICKS FROM BABYLON AND NINEVEH.

Upon the brick brought by the writer from Babylon is the standard inscription of Nebuchadnezzar. It gives his name and titles, describes the wonders of the great city, and invokes the gods to grant duration to the temples and other great edifices which he had built. The inscriptions on the Babylonian bricks are uniformly enclosed in a small square, and are formed with considerable care and nicety. They appear to have been impressed with a stamp upon which the entire inscription, not isolated letters, was cut in relief. This art, so nearly approaching the modern invention of printing, is proved to have been known to the Egyptians and Chinese at a very remote period. The Pharaohs stamped their names on bricks, the stamps used being of wood, and several are preserved in European collections. But all the impressions on Egyptian bricks, unlike those of Assyria, are in relief.

The Babylonian bricks are of uniform size, about 15 inches square by 3 inches thick. They are made of a very tenacious clay mixed with chopped straw, and burnt hard in a kiln. They were always laid face downward in a cement of bitumen so hard as to make it almost impossible to remove one entire.

The brick from Nineveh is also rectangular, but somewhat thicker than the Babylonian. The inscriptions on these Assyrian bricks appear to have been made in single cuneiform letters, and sometimes the workmen may have been careless in stamping them. On this specimen the parallel columns are somewhat irregular, but the impressions are quite distinct. I am unable to give a literal translation of the inscription, but presume it is of the same general character as on the one from Babylon, giving the name and titles of the monarch reigning at Nineveh, perhaps, 3,000 years ago.

Among other antiques from Babylon which I was fortunate enough to secure is a small black cylinder of very hard stone with an exceedingly fine grain. It is an inch long by about 3-8 in diameter, and was picked up in the sand among the mounds of the ancient city. The surface of the cylinder is completely covered with an inscription in minute cuneiform letters very finely cut. A copy is given below, the letters being considerably magnified.

For the translation I am indebted to the kindness of Prof. George Smith, of the British Museum.

"*The seal, or amulet, of a man named Kizirtu, son of the woman Satumani, belonging to the family of Ishtar and Nana.*"

THE BLACK STONE FROM BABYLON, which can be seen at the rooms of the Historical Society, is perhaps the most curious and interesting relic that I was able to bring away. It is about four inches in height, of a slightly pyramidal form, and weighs four pounds. The texture of the stone is very hard and fine, and it appears to have once been completely covered with an inscription, very delicately cut, but now almost obliterated. When in London, on my return from the East, I submitted this *antique* to Prof. Smith, who is the director of the Assyrian department in the British Museum, and at his request I left it with him for several days. He gave it a very careful inspection and study, and I append his statement in regard to it.

Note of GEORGE SMITH, director in the Assyrian department of the British Museum, London, Oct. 1, 1874, to Mr. Fogg:

"This black stone with cuneiform transcription in Persian, Median and Babylonian, is of the age of Darius, the great King, about B. C. 500.

"GEORGE SMITH."

Beyond the facts that the inscription is in three dialects of *cuneiform* letters, (Assyrian, Median and Persian,) and of the time of Darius, about 500 years B. C., he would venture no opinion as to its original use or design. It is evidently much worn, perhaps by the hand, as an implement of culinary use, or it may have been an utensil devoted to sacred purposes in a temple. The laws of the Medes and Persians may have once been engraved upon this stone, but the laws and the inscription have alike faded from the knowledge of mankind. I can only testify to its authenticity as a relic of ancient Babylon. W. P. F.

Western Reserve and Northern Ohio

HISTORICAL SOCIETY.

CLEVELAND, O., APRIL, 1875.

NUMBER TWENTY-FIVE.

EARLY MAPS OF OHIO AND THE WEST.

BY C. C. BALDWIN, SECRETARY.

It seems strange that America was not sooner known. The world is lately convinced that it has been discovered time and again. There were navigators who took journeys much longer than to America; they circumnavigated Africa, and there was a large trade with the East, including India, China, and Japan.

In the voyages of Columbus and many after, that route to China and Japan was sought which is only just completed by the Pacific Railroad.

The course of nearly all settlement and discovery has been by sea, lake or river; and the first investigation of the West, was made by following up the St. Lawrence. It took long to do this.

The early history of the St. Lawrence is handsomely illustrated by numerous maps in the new volume published by the Maine Historical Society, assisted by the State of Maine. No more interesting publication could be made than a collection of later maps showing to the eye at a glance; the progress of discovery, until the colonies came under the complete domination of the English.

The first consciousness that there was a vast interior, appears in a map by

JUAN DE LA COSA, DATED 1500.

He was a companion of Columbus, and celebrated for his after voyages. The lower part of the United States seems pretty correct. Newfoundland appears as part of the main land; there is nothing that appears like a trace of the St. Lawrence; there appear small lakes in the interior, which from their situation would seem to show that some Indian had told Cosa or his informant that there were lakes in a vast background.

The following maps however, show no consciousness of any such bodies of water.

PEDRO REINEL IN 1505,

a Portugese pilot of great fame, made a map wherein Greenland, Hudson's Strait, and for the first time, the entrance of the Gulf of St Lawrence, are laid down with some approach to accuracy, and it would be impossible to mistake his chart for the western coast of Asia.

The learned Geographers however, represented the matter quite differently.

PTOLEMY'S GEOGRAPHY OF 1508,

represents an open sea between South America and the Cuban Islands extending clear to Asia. Above the Cuban Islands, we again find a clear passage by water to that continent, and the navigator sailing in the direction of Lake Erie would first reach Bengal, with Thibet behind it; while from the latitude of the St. Lawrence extending northward, he would find Gog and Magog.

The learned

JOHANN SCHONER, IN 1520

lays down Newfoundland with a broad sea between that and "Terra de Cuba," which Mr. Kohl supposes to be an exaggeration of the Gulf of St. Lawrence. West of Canada, is a great open sea, through which is easy access to the fabled "deserts" of Asia and the Island of Zipangi, (Japan) close behind the "Terra de Cuba." The "Terra de Cuba," ends at latitude 50 with the words "ulterius incognita," which adjective might extend on this map in any direction from "ulterius" and certainly include all the great lakes.

Other nations prosecuted discoveries on the northern coast of America, and followed the fisheries with zeal, but the French were destined to follow up the river whose source was long to remain in obscurity.

Yet Cartier, who entered the northern mouth of the Gulf in 1534, after cruises in the Gulf alone, did not know that the St. Lawrence was only a river, but returned to France to get a new outfit to pursue the sea channel, a passage to the west. The prospect of the western passage was alluring, and the next season on the 10th of August, the day of St. Lawrence, he entered a little bay named by him from the day.

The Indians told him that it was a river called "Hochelaga," and at "Canada," very narrow, and that further on (probably rapids) only small boats could pass. He still looked for a passage to Asia, and finding the beautiful Saguenay, to be very deep, thought it a passage to a northern sea.

He turned however, and ascending the St. Lawrence to "Hochelaga" made the first tour around the mountain and saw the Lachine rapids near by, impeding further navigation, and called the mountain Mount Royal.

The Indians reported to Cartier that there were three large lakes, and a sea of fresh water without end. The great Francis of France, and Cartier supposed this discovery one of the northwestern part of Asia, and for 60 years discovery was not carried substantially, beyond the limit of Cartier in 1535, though the whole region was from that time called

"NOUVELLE FRANCE,"

for 60 years a name, then for 160 a reality. The name however, appears on the coast on some maps before Cartier's discovery; as on that in

PTOLEMY OF 1530

"Francesca," and in 1550 in the Italian map of Gastaldi with a river running clear around it and with the St. Lawrence running from the northwest.

Many Geographers seem, during the earlier part of the 16th century, to have considered the country as not Asia, though they generally made North America quite narrow, often with a great bay covering all Canada. Witness the Ptolemy of 1530; other maps of about that period of which that of Ruscelli in 1544 is most specific; that of Agnere in 1536 most accurate in the real distance from Asia.

MICHAEL LOK,

born in Leyden represents in 1582 a broad river, or great bay, on which were Saguenay and Hochelaga, with the "Mare de Verra Zana" dividing the continent of North America almost in two, and coming to the Mountains in New England.

The French maps from the time of Cartier, until the conquest of Canada by the English in 1760, continued generally to be far superior to those of any other nation.

One in 1543 is quite accurate, and represents the Ottawa and the St. Lawrence proper, and excels in accuracy, a fine English one of 1544.

A map of

DIEGO HOMEN, A PORTUGESE,

in 1558, is remarkable for laying down what in shape resembles Lake Ontario and Lake Erie, but only accidentally so, the upper of them is Lake St. Peter in the St. Lawrence below Hochelaga.

The broad sea is just beyond and parallel to the St. Lawrence. A broad river flows to the southwest, in position something like some of the affluents of the Mississippi; but no doubt a mistaken representation of the Hudson, as described to Cartier by the Indians.

In the Library of the Historical Society, is an early atlas, published in Venice in 1572, of the Islands of the world, entitled "L'Isole Piu Famose del Mondo descritte da Thomaso Porcacchi da Castiglione," engraved by Girolamo Porra, a Paduan.

On page 157, appears a plan of the city of Mexico.

Page 161 contains a map of the Islands and lands of the "Holy Cross" or "New World," followed by a description.

The sea to the north is all open. The straits of Anian, much better represent Behrings, than the after maps for very many years.

A large lake appears, with a river flowing south. It lies with "Ochelaga," site of Montreal, on the north and between Labrador on the northeast, Canada west, and "La Nova Franza" south of west. "Larcadia" lies to the southwest of the lake and river, What was the lake and river? Hudson's River with Lake Champlain, or more likely the St. Lawrence with some faint idea of great waters beyond.

Japan lies in mid-ocean.

There follow maps of the West India Islands.

The map of

1569 BY G. MERCATOR,

drawn upon the projection named from the author, represents the St. Lawrence as a long, narrow river, draining all the Upper Mississippi Valley. It is remarkable for first laying down with some accuracy, the Alleghanies. connecting however in a chain with the mountains of New England.

The name Appalachian, afterwards applied to the whole Alleghanies, appears on what would be the west of South Carolina. as "Apalachen."

Nearly 600 miles above the St, Lawrence, and nearly as wide, is the eastern end of a sea of fresh water "dulcium aquarum," of the extent of which the inhabitants of Canada, drawing their information from the Indians of Saguenay, are ignorant.

In subsequent Mercator maps, this lake was omitted, probably because careful Geographers did not like to take it upon Indian report.

On the atlas of Hondius, based on Mercator edition 1633, (American Geographical Society) all the lakes are omitted.

In the latter part of the 16th century, lived a celebrated Geographer named Ortelius, of whose atlases there were several editions, all now scarce. The edition of 1573 is in the Library of the Am. Geog. Soc.

North America, curiously appears more accurate in detail, than as a whole; looking as if parts of it were drawn on different scales and then placed together.

The continent is much too wide.

There are several rivers flowing into the Gulf of Mexico, difficult to identify.

As in Mercator, a range of mountains runs paralel with the Gulf, making the rivers flowing south short, and throwing the vast interior of North America drained by the Mississippi, into the valley of the St, Lawrence, which is separated by a range of mountains from the stream "Tiguas Rio" flowing into the "Mar Vermeio" or Red sea, being the Gulf of California.

Hudson's Bay is a strait running from Ocean to Ocean.

The name Nova Francia—New France—appears to be the name given to the country drained by the St. Lawrence, until it came under the dominion of the English. although Charlevoix in his history, says it was first bestowed by Samuel de Champlain in1609.

Mr. Shea in his valuable edition and tranlation of Charlevoix says, the name is first known upon the Copper Globe of Ulphius in 1542; and appears next in Cartier 1545 who speaks ofHochelaga and Canada, otherwise called byus New France, showing the name to have been somewhat common.

Mr. Parkman says the name was first used, after the return in 1524 of Verrezano to France.

Ortellius in the map described, omits Lake Huron, though in the much less accurate map from Hakluyt, (ed. 1587) it reappears.

In the last map the country lying north of the St. Lawrence is called "Bacalaos," a word meaning codfish, intending Newfoundland.

For many years however, after the discoveries of Cartier little or no progress was made in the interior geography of the parts of America drained by the St. Lawrence and Mississippi.

France was too much absorbed in wars, religious and other, to prosecute discovery. First came the war with Charles V. in 1552. In 1562 the first Huguenot war, in 1572 the Massacre of St. Bartholomew, and a constant state of tumult until the Edict of Nantes in 1598, when France began to rest.

In 1603 two tiny vessels, one of 12 and one of 15 tons, sailed up the St. Lawrence. The expedition was commanded by De Chastes, but his companion was Champlain; a man whose energy and achievements in the discovery and settlement of the great unknown wilderness, entitled him to the appellation of

"THE FATHER OF NEW FRANCE."

The expedition sailed up as far as Montreal. Champlain tried to pass the rapids above but failed, and the Indians made rude plans of the river above, which were so indefinite that Niagara was understood to be a rapid only.

The French, like all nations making early dicoveries, had keen eyes for commercial growth. Champlain had, before the expedition of 1603, urged the plan for a canal across the Isthmus of Darien,—renewed in our own day. In 1608, he again sailed up the St. Lawrence, himself in command of a vessel, to make a settlement upon the Saint Lawrence and a search for the inland passage to the East Indies.

They commenced the city of Quebec in 1608. In 1609, Champlain in behalf of an Indian party from the Ottawa River, met in battle the Iroquois upon the western border of the lake that has ever since borne his name.

He published a wood-cut of the battle,—found in his works,—where it looks easier for him to knock over the Iroquois with the but-end of his gun than to shoot them, such is the defiance of perspective. He also published a map in which this lake appears. The eastern end of Lake Ontario is seen for the first time as Lac St. Louis. The map is generally in the French language but is somewhat amusing in using names and remarks in other languages in a manner that shows the author was not as good a linguist as traveller. It is common in the old maps to find on the same sheet, names in French, Dutch, English, Latin and other tongues. In this map Hudson's Bay reaches far down, near the St. Lawrence, with a note at the bottom, "The bay wher hudson did wente."

It's position with the Saguenay would make us think that the "Mer Douce" of

Mercator was here merged with Hudson's Bay.

In 1609, after his fight with the Iroquois Nicholas de Vignan, offered to return with the Indian allies and winter with them. He was not seen again for some months, and in 1612 appeared in Paris, telling large stories about his passing up the Ottawa, crossing a great lake, finding a great river flowing north, descending it and finding a shipwrecked English vessel.

In 1613, Champlain retraced the route with him, but up the Ottawa Vignan became a convicted liar. He had remained on the river with the Indians, and his travels were imaginary. Champlain returned discouraged; but in 1615, made a second excursion up the Ottawa reaching Lake Huron, that immense body of water from the borders of which had come his guides and hosts.

Champlain on his return, crossed the lower end of Lake Ontario, advanced to the westward, and near one of the lakes of middle New York again met the Iroquois.

He was not as successful as before, owing to the want of steady courage in his allies, the Hurons, who wished to wait for a war party of 500 men from the tribe from which Lake Erie took its name.

His intrepid interpreter

ETIENNE BRULÉ,

visited this tribe to hasten the reinforcements. He descended a river, evidently the Susquehanna to the salt water, returned, was captured by the Iroquois, and returned to the French in 1618. The Eries inhabited a country reaching south of the lake of that name.

His story appears in Champlain's narrative of his voyage in 1618; but is omitted in the condensed edition of 1632, which is the one a reprint of which is in the library of the Historical Society, with copies of the original maps.

It is said, that in 1621 Champlain had an interview with the Iroquois and drew topographical maps of their country and the circumjacent places, " so that since that time the territory of these Indians, is seen in the maps to be comprehended within that of New France."* thus beginning that geographical aggression which after led to the use of much ink, and shedding of much blood.

IN 1632, CHAMPLAIN

made the first attempt to map out the Great Lakes. The map and a description of it in French, appear in his works. A copy of it with a description if it in English, together with a portion of his description of his expeditions of 1609 and 1615 is in the 3rd volume of the "Documentary History of New York"—by Dr. O'Callaghan.

The map is indeed interesting: Lake Ontario runs northeast, and Niagara is a "very high waterfall" descending which, various sorts of fish become dizzy.

Lake Erie, unnamed, is little but a very wide irregular river leading from Mer Douce (Lake Huron) to Lac St. Louis, (Ontario). One would infer that it was doubtful if Brulé really stood on its banks, though he visited the people living there. The direction of Lake Erie is a little south of east. The Peninsula between Lake Ontario, Erie, and Huron, is a mere tongue of land, the outlet of Lake Huron being near its western end and the lake being large, and stretching from east to west some 650 miles.

The effect of the whole is to leave it very doubtful what knowledge, if any Champlain had of Lake Erie.

There empties into Lake Huron from the west, "Grand Lac," supposed to be Lake Superior, by a sault of which he gives such a description as to well identify Sault St. Mary. From the north there empties by the river "des Puans" another smaller lake, where, says our author, "there is a mine of red copper," and in the Lake is placed an island where there had been seen a mine of copper.

This description makes one think of Lake Superior and Isle Royale, yet the direction and shape of the larger, represents Superior best.

He knew these lakes, as appears by his explanation, from the reports of the Indians and rightly making two lakes has divided the characteristics of the one, between the two.

Champlain places the "Puants" among the upper lakes, who belonged after, and apparently at that time, around Lake Michigan, and Green Bay which was long called "Bay des Puans."

Champlain died in 1635, and was buried in Quebec; and with him died the energy of discovery that seemed to have been born in his coming.

After his death, New France suffered much from Indian wars, in great degree the legacy of Champlain, and resulting from his interference between the Iroquois and their enemies. The Jesuits and the traders lived among the Indians.

In after years they labored upon Lake Huron and Michigan, and explored Lake Superior until they prefixed to their relation of 1671 (Jesuit Relations' reprint, Quebec 1858 Hist. Soc.) a map of Lake Superior excelling in accuracy that of any of the lakes then published.

This map has also been reprinted in Foster and Whitney's Geological Report of

* Memoir of 1699 on the Encroachments of the English, N. Y. Col. Documents.

Lake Superior, in Bancroft's United States, Vol. 3, and Monettes Mississippi Vol. 1.

But the Geographers seemed to learn very slowly of the labors of Champlain.

PETER HEYLIN—(ENGLISH) 1600—1662,

in his Cosmographie, London 1626 says: A chain of mountains below latitude 40, separates all the streams into the Gulf of Mexico, from the territory north.

He separates America into Mexicana and Peruana; and just about in the vacant position of the Lakes appears the name "America Mexicana."

Lower California long before joined to the continent, is now, with the superior learning of later geographers become a huge island, with the "Mare Vermiglio" (Red Sea) flowing between it and the main land The west coast, which in former times had reached far to the west, runs north, and in latitude 60 is a dim outline of Behrings Straits, which were in after maps as "Anian" brought nearer and nearer to the immense island of California.

Our au.hor speaks modestly of the "Streits of Anian,if such streits there be." He elsewhere places in the northwest corner of America the supposed kingdom of Anian whence the name of the strait "thought by some to part America from Asia, the very being of such a kingdom and of such streits being much suspected," the river Canada (St.Lawrence) "hath its fountain in the un discouvered parts of this Northern Tract sometimes enlarged into great lakes, and presently reduced to a narrower channel." His map notices none of the great lakes and leaves it doubtful whether the author meant more than the occasional widening of the St. Lawrence proper. The English feeling is shown in the statement that the French are "shut up in a few weak forts on the North of the Canada."

He places Canada or Nova Francia north of the river, and Virginia is liberally bounded "on the North, Canada; on the South, Florida; on the East, Mare del Noort; the western boundaries not known."

A large river flows into the Gulf of Mexico, located much like the Mississippi.

It is called the "Canaveral," a name given in after maps to the river flowing into Mobile Bay, (to wit: Senex Atlas, 1722). De Soto had found the lower Mississippi in 1542, and its character no doubt transferred to the Mobile river. In most of the early maps a long line of coast between Mobile and Mexico was omitted. The "Canaveral" connects in its branches with the San Spirito, as if there were some inkling of the great western branches of the Mississippi. The "San Spirito" was the early name for the Mississippi after De Soto's discovery,

HEYLIN'S MAP AND BOOK OF 1652,

are similar to the edition of 1626, this "learned" man having learned nothing in the meantime.

A French map of 1656 published by N. Sanson d' Abbeville, an industrious and famous Royal Geographer of France, gives parts of Lake Superior and Michigan. This map (Harvard College Library) is referred to by that too little known writer the late Rev. J. H. Perkins, in N. Am Review Jany. 1839, and he suggests the publication of a copy of that and several other maps.

In a map of Sanson's dated 1669 in his Atlas (Am. Geog. Soc.,) "Lac. Erie" is not far out of shape, and Lakes Huron, Michigan and Superior appear, the last not being defined, towards the west.

This map represents California as an island.

On a map of Gerard Valk and Peter Schenk of Amsterdam, in the Hist. Soc., no date, but prior to 1708, it is also laid down as an island, with the careful statement that by former Geographers it has always been made a part of the continent, and so taken by Dutch from Spanish maps; but now known to be an island &c &c.

This error became general, long before 1700 and as late as 1767 an edition of Lord Anson's Voyage Round the World (in possession of H. C. Gaylord Esq.) makes the same blunder, giving the fancied island the same square end towards the north it generally received.

A MAP OF 1658, JOHN JANSSON,

of Amsterdam, taken from his Atlas of 1658, represents the lakes on a very small scale, inaccurately; the Niagara River is longer than either of the lakes, and Superior and Huron are supposed to be disconnect- from the others, and empty separately into the St. Lawrence.

California is a peninsula and America stretches to the west, as in the earlier maps.

Meanwhile the progress of discovery was steady, though slow. The Jesuits were pursuing their missions. I have already referred to their map of Lake Superior, with parts of Huron and Michigan, in 1670 and 1671. It is minutely and nicely laid down—Lake Neepigon is more accurately laid down than it has been in the maps of our own time, until since the Canadian survey some 40 years ago. Isle Royale (Minong) is down but once, while after maps often had it down twice, probably because it can be seen from the north side of the lake and also from the long peninsula running from the south far into the lake.

The Indians talked much of the great river to the west, and the reverend fathers occasionally mentioned it, Father Allouez in 1666, conjecturing that it empties into the Sea by Virginia and calling it the "Messipi."

It was generally thought, however, that it emptied into the Gulf of California or the Gulf of Mexico; and that the discovery would give the French the knowledge and possession of the Southern or Western Sea.

In the Relation accompanying the map last described, Father Dablon speaks of the great river called the "Missisipi which can have its mouth only in the Florida Sea."

He seems to have appreciated its size, saying it seems to encircle all our lakes, and emptying into the Red Sea (Gulf of California) or that of Florida.

In 1673, the good fathers on Lake Superior planned its discovery. Marquette was of the party and the only one whose narrative of the expedition is preserved.

His map is published in Shea's "Discovery and Exploration of the Mississippi," in facsimile, from the original preserved in Montreal accompanied with a translation of his Journal.

The map gives all of Lake Superior or "de Tracy," but the extreme north; the west shore of "Lac des Illinois" (Michigan) and the River "de la Conception" (Mississippi) by the Wisconsin by which river he entered, past the "Pekittanoui" or Missouri and the "Wabonkigon" (Ohio) to a village called Akansea. The travellers returned by the Illinois which is also laid down on the map. One can also recognize the early forms of many familiar names.

A map published in this same year, and to be found in Blome's Brittania, London, seems almost the complement of that last described. It is said to be designed by "Mousieur Sanson, Geographer to the French king, and revised into English, and illustrated by Richard Blome, by his Majesties especial Command."

The relative positions of Lakes Erie and Huron, are much improved from former maps, and the peninsula between them much better given. The direction of the shores of Lake Erie (not named) are given more correctly than in most after maps until the present century, The whole lake is sunk too far to the south. Only the eastern end of Superior is given, and quite incorrectly.

Lake Michigan proper is ignored, there appearing; Green Bay as "Lack of Puans" reaching far west but not completed. There are the usual ranges of mountains dividing the rest of the continent from the lower Mississippi Valley, the river appears without name, and emptying into the Bay of "Spirito Santo."

The Glacial Sea a branch of Hudson's Bay, is not far nothwest of Lake Superior. The west coast of America is given only a little above the blunt northern end of the Island of California.

Our Author thinks that there is some likelihood it may be discovered that Lake Superior "disburthens itself into the sea by two or more different courses, one towards us, which is that of Canada, another towards west and above California, the third towards the north and into the Christian Sea; and that the mouth of this may show us the way we have so long sought, to go to the East Indies by the West."

Christian Sea, is another name for Hudson's Bay, which no doubt was supposed to open freely by the "Glacicke Sea" already mentioned, to the west.

Sanson was no donbt much indebted to maps, still in manuscript, of which what is now known is contained in the appendix to Mr. Parkman's Discovery of the Great West; an appendix very valuable upon the subject matter we are now pursuing.

THE MAP OF GALINEE 1670,

gives the Upper St. Lawrence, Lake Ontario, River Niagara, North Shore of Lake Erie, Detroit River, and the East and North Shores of Lake Huron, with considerable accuracy. He claimed to have visited these shores.

About 1672, another map was made supposed to be by La Salle.

All the great lakes, says Mr. Parkman, are laid down with considerable accuracy

Opposite the site of Chicago is the statement in effect that by a portage of a thousand paces one can go to the River Colbert (Mississippi), and thence to the Gulf of Mexico.

The whole length of the Ohio River is laid down, with the name it now bears; so called by the Iroquois, on account of its beauty, which the Sieur de la Salle descended·

It is a pity these two maps are yet unpublished. The Mississippi must have been laid down from a fortunate guess, as La Salle himself was yet some years after to trace its course.

In 1669 or 1670, he had entered within a few miles of Lake Erie, a branch of the Ohio; and descended as far as Louisville. In 1670, he embarked on Lake Erie, sailed through Huron passed through into Green Bay, and by that, into the main body of Lake Michigan.

Did he sail along the hitherto unexplored south shore of Lake Erie, and was that the origin of the improved map?

But very little was known of these journeys. La Salle was so eminent as an explorer that his is one of four portraits of discoverers in the Capitol at Washington.

He spent wealth, years, and wonderful energy in his travels. The Jesuit Annual Relations are our general authority for early Canadian history. He had ceased to belong to their order, and is never mentioned in these accounts.

There are published no journals of his earlier travels. Others attempted in the accounts of his adventures, most widely circulated after his death, to steal his glory and vilify him. He was finally murdered by his own men.

There are however, in existence in France many docnments, papers and maps of these times yet unpublished. Mr. Pierre Margry, of Paris, is especially noted for his knowledge of them. No one can investigate these early times without indebtedness to him. These valuable documents are soon to be given to the world, by Mr, Margry with the especial request and at the expense of the United States. I will state in this connection that this plan of publication orginated with the Historical Society at Cleveland.

O. H. Marshall Esq., of our neighboring-city of Buffalo, has recently visited Mr Margry, and the result, is a very interesting address delivered before the Buffalo Historical Society, which tell us in substance that:

In 1669, La Salle, with Gallinee and another, was among the Senecas wishing to explore the Ohio and Mississippi, and after a present of "two coats, four kettles, six hatchets, and some glass beads," declared they had come "to see the people called by them 'Toagenha' living on the River Ohio," and desired a captive of that nation as a guide.

They inquired about the route, and were told it required six days journey by land, of twelve leagues each. "This induced us to believe that we could not possibly reach it in that way, as we would hardly be able to carry for so long a journey our necessary provisions, much less our baggage. But they told us at the same time that in going to find it by the way of Lake Erie in canoes, we would have only a three days portage before arriving at that river, reaching it at a point much nearer the people we were seeking, than to go by Sonnontonouan."

If they were to go by portage from the westerly end of Lake Erie, the "Toagenha" were probably well down the Ohio, and were no doubt the Shawnees.

They finally got two guides, one of whom —a Shawnee— fell to La Salle. The party went to the head of Lake Ontario, crossed to the Grand River, of Lake Erie, and there La Salle left them. They prosecuted a journey along the north shore, and by a roundabout way, back to Montreal. It was from this excursion, that Gallinee made his map.

Where was La Salle during the next three years? Perhaps Mr. Margry's papers will tell us more fully. He was exploring, it is thought, during a portion of the time, the Ohio, and some of its branches. It is even thought by some, that he reached the Missis sippi, which he called "Colbert," after the Prime Minister of Louis XIV.

Mr. Margry, in a letter addressed to Col. Whittlesey, President of the Historical Society, after expressing in the kindest manner his thanks, for the influence exerted here in behalf of his project, communicates the following extract from an unpublished letter of La Salle; (no date) which translated reads:

"The river which you see marked on my map, of the southern coast of this Lake (Erie), and towards the extremity, called by the Iroquois, "Tiotontaenon" is without doubt the passage into the Ohio, or Olighira Sipon, as it is called in Iroquois, or in Ottawa "The Beautiful River." The distance from one to the other is considerable, and the communication more difficult; but within a days journey from its mouth at Lake Erie, (washing as it flows a beautiful country,) and at a musket shot from its banks there is a little lake from which flows a stream, three or four fathoms (toises) wide at the outlet from the lake one fathom (toise) in depth. It soon changes however, into a river by the junction of a number of other streams, which after a course of a hundred leagues, without rapids, receives another small river that comes from near the Miamis, and five or six others quite as large, and flowing with greater rapidity along the declivity of a mountain and discharging into the Illinois (Ohio?) two leagues below a village and from thence into the River Colbert. It is called Ouabachi or Aramouni."

The original of this letter, was sent to Mr. Parkman, who kindly returned it with the following note.

JAMAICA PLAINS, Mass., 9 Sept., 1872.

"DEAR SIR: With regard to the extract from La Salle's letter, one or two points, are worth attention. It looks like an account made from hearsay. On the map described on pp. 406, 7 of "Discovery of Great West," the Maumee river is clearly laid down, with a portage direct to the Ohio, which is brought close to Lake Erie. This map is clearly anterior to 1680. On the map of Franquelin, 1684, made after data furnished by La Salle, the Maumee is also laid down, with a branch of the Wabash, designated as

R. Agonasake, closely approaching it. Now I have little doubt that "la riviére que vous avez vue marquée dans ma carte," is the Maumee, the natural route "pour aller à la riviére Ohio ou Oléghin (Alleghany) Sipon."

"The distance to the portage at Fort Wayne is certainly far more than "une, journée," but accuracy is scarcely to be expected. After crossing the portage, La Salle speaks of a stream "qui se change bientôt en riviére par la jonction de quantité de semblables (et) qui aprés le cours de plus de 100 lieues sans rapides reçoit une autre petite riviére qui vient de proche celle des Miamis." Such a "petite riviére" is laid down on Franquelin's map.

It flows into the Wabash, and answers to the Tippecanoe. The "riviere des Miamis," on Franquelin's and the other contemporary maps, is the St. Joseph of Lake Michigan. La Salle goes on to say that the main river in question, called by him "Ouabache or Aramoni," "constant le long au penchant d'une montagne, se va descharger dans celle des Illinois deux lieues an dessous du village, et de là dans le fleuve Colbert" (Mississippi.)

"He begins with professing to indicate the way to the Ohio, but ends with bringing the traveller not to the Ohio, but to the Illinois. I can see no other explanation of the passage, than that of a slip of the pen on La Salle's part, (or that of some copyist,) writing Illinois for Ohio. I can think of no other way of making the passage intelligable. This solution derives some support, from the circumstance that on Franquelin's map an Indian village Taarsila, is laid down a little above the mouth of the Wabash (Ouabache.) La Salle, you remember, says, that the mouth of his river is "two leagues below the village."

"The river is called by him "Aramoni ou Ouabache." He speaks a few years later, of another Aramoni, identical with the Big Vermillion, a branch of the Illinois. One of the branches of the Wabash, is also now called "Big Vermillion," and the name Vermillion is given to the county of Indiana, where this branch joins the main stream. The coincidence is worth remarking. Vermillion is mentiond in La Salle's time, as among the chief articles of Indian trade, and possibly Aramoni may be the Illinois or Miami name for it.

Yours very truly

F. Parkman.

It is, as is seen, very difficult from the brief description, to trace La Salle's route.

A common passage, in after years, was by the Maumee into the Wabash, by a portage at Fort Wayne. In fact the Ohio and Wabash were frequeutly confounded. This portage was much easier than those farther east.

La Salle's portage may have been by some branch of the Maumee into some small lake, not easily found at this day.

No doubt, M. Margry's maps and books will help us to locate more accurately this description of a journey through a portion of Ohio into the river that is its southern boundary.

La Salle in August 1679, launched into the Niagara river, above the falls, the first sail vessel navigating the lakes, called the Griffin. His plan was to sail through Lake Michigan, build another vessel on the Illinois, and follow down the Mississippi. Shea has suggested, that he had better have built a vessel on the Alleghany, and sailed down the Ohio; but he may have anticipated interruption in building his vessel and the portage was too long. He wished to build at Niagara a fort, but the Senecas would not allow it. He sailed to Green Bay. His vessel was wreck-on her return, his men deserted. He began on the Kankakee a branch of the Illinois, the erection of Fort Broken Heart. "Crevecoeur"

He sent Father Hennepin to explore the Illinois to the Mississippi, who in 1680, explored the Mississippi north, as far as the falls named by him in honor of St. Anthony of Padua. Hennepin returned to France, and in 1683 published "Description de la Louisiane," with a map, of which more presently.

La Salle entered the Mississippi, February 6th, 1682, with three canoes. He followed its course and on the 9th of April 1682 entered the Sea. He returned up the stream.

The next year he sailed from France, to reach the mouth of the river by sea, having sent Tonty down the stream to meet him. They were never to meet again. La Salle passed the mouth, and after great disheartenings was killed by his own men, on a branch of the Trinity River, in Texas.

Tonty returned disappointed, and his letter left with an Indian chief for La Salle, was delivered, fourteen years after to Iberville.

Joutel, a fellow-townsman of La Salle, was his companion in his last unfortunate expedition, and its historian. His journal, with a map, was published in Paris in 1713, and an English edition of 1714, is in the Historical Room.

An account, however, by Father Douay, was also published in 1697, by Le Clercq, which was suppressed. Hennepin learned something of the narrative, and in 1697, published "Nouvelle Decouverte d'un tres grand Pays situé dans l'Amerique," containing his former work and other matter. He has stamped himself as a wonderful liar, claiming to have himself, descended to the mouth of the Mississippi in 1680, with such circumstances as would of themselves show his tale impossible; and habitually, making larger the stories of his first book. This was published in Utrecht, with a new map Hennepin having retired from France, and in 1798, an edition still enlarged, was published in London, with the same map; both dedicated to William, king of England. It so happened that Hennepin's books received a wide circulation, and for a long time the expeditions of La Salle were known mostly through them. Hennepin did a good deal to debase the geographical accuracy of the maps of North America.

His two maps correspond with his change of claims. His first shows the upper part of the Mississippi, having in the lower part a dotted line as a guess into the Gulf of Mexico. The other is carried to the Gulf, much abridged in length, but with the characteristic curves, islands, and cut-offs. The upper Mississippi is much alike in the two maps, though in the last Lake Superior is more correctly shaped, and Lake Michigan less sprawling.

The river Seignalay becomes the Illinois, and Fort des Miamis and the river it was on, now St. Joseph, is moved from the east and correct side of Lake Michigan to the west, The portage is marked alike in both.

Lake Erie reaches down in the first, to latitude 34, like a well filled round sack with its bottom to the south, and its south shore is wonderfully inaccurate to follow so closely other maps based upon La Salle's. In the second Lake Erie is hardly mended, reaching like a narrow bag to latitude 37. A range of hills is below it, and from its source nearly to its mouth the "Hohio" flows west. The Missouri appears as the "Otenta," reaching far from the west, and as in Marquette's map the name the river now bears appears among the people upon its banks. The Ohio is in another place called the "Ouye," and below it are the mountains "Apalache."

The Falls of Niagara, called in the first map the Grand Fall—and said in his first book to be 500 feet high—have grown in the second map to be more than 600.

Lake de Conty, or Erie, of the first map, is in the second Lake Erie, or "du Chat," the ancient Eries having been otherwise called Nation of the Cat.

The tribe themselves Erieckronois (Erie Nation) are well along the lake·

Several rivers appear; but the whole lake and country included in Ohio are so incorrectly given that there is no place for a river to flow correctly or be identified.

The Sioux appear where they were first heard of. They were feared in the West much as the Iroquois in the East; and continued to inhabit much the same place where they made war as late as 1865, two hundred years after they are first heard of.

The map in Joutel's "Journal of La Salle's Last Voyage," London, 1714, is little more than a sketch. The lower part bears marks of actual observation, though the the Mississippi is not as correctly given in its course as in Hennepin's even. It is called Mississippi, or Colbert, with a note that in the year 1712 "it changed its name and is called St. Louis."

The Missouri appears by that name. The river "Ullinois or Seignely" is too far east. A branch, the "Ramany," reaches below the west end of Lake "Eria," the direction and position of which is more correct than in Hennepin's, but it has square ends. The river "Douo or Abacha"' (Ohio or Wabash), is far too small and too far south.

M. Joutel returned along the Illinois. On the 19th of August, 1687, he passed the "River called Houabache" (Ohio), "said to come from the country of the Iroquois towards New England." He thought it a very fine river, extraordinarily clear, and its current gentle.

His Indians "offered up to it by way of sacrifice some tobacco and beef steaks, which they fixed on forks, and left them on the bank to be disposed of as the river thought fit."

If Hennepin had a rival in literary fame, it was the

BARON LA HONTAN,

whose maps were as mendacious as the other's books. His travels, published at The Hague in 1705, have only a small map of the lake region, where Lake Ontario is not far from round, and Lake Erie has a very square, broad end towards the east.

He reports to have traveled up a large river, emptying into the Mississippi about where St. Paul now stands. After travelling up this river for eighty days, he returned, having found many and civilized tribes of Indians, and being informed that the river continued its course from the west until with a short portage connection was made with another large river, flowing westward and emptying into the salt sea.

His river was called according to some people the "Dead River," because of its slow current, while others called it the "Long River."

He has a large map on a smaller and wider scale in the edition published at the Hague in 1715.

Lake Superior is not badly-shaped though it turns too much to the northwest.

Lake Illinois has more nearly its proper shape than on most contemporary maps, though its south part is carried too far west.

The passages to the Mississippi by the head of Lake Superior by the Wisconsin river, and by the Saint Joseph and Illinois, are all well marked.

The "Ouabach" does not show its origin.

This literary imposture seems more remarkable than Hennepin's. The latter seems to have been moved by malice toward La Salle, and vanity for himself to claim discoveries of real objects though with a strong exaggeration in describing them. He doubtless expected his claims to be successful.

La Hontan apparently drew purely upon his imagination in falsehoods which must necessarily be detected. The account of Long river is contained in a letter purporting to have been written in 1689 in Michilimacinac.

As the Indians told Nicholas de Vignan tales of western waters, and the missionaries of the Mississippi, the "Great Water," so they may have told La Hontan stories either not well understood or perhaps purposely misleading, as Indians have always been wont to do. The Baron was in his day considered a man of respectability abroad, and was afterwards Governor of New Foundland. His book ends with a conjugation of the verb to love, in the Indian tongue. The upper end of his river was singularly enough a salt lake, in latitude 45, and supposed to be far over towards the west coast, and the furthest Indians he saw, knew the Spaniards. One might think he had ascended the Missouri and the Platte, and been told of the Salt Lake and the Spaniards beyond, except that he carefully tells that after returning from the Long River he descended the Mississippi and then ascended the Missouri. The Baron's Dead River and Salt Lake had life enough to creep into the maps of many highly respectable geographers. One

ENGLISH GEOGRAPHER, HERMAN MOLL,

several of whose maps are in the Historical Room, evidently believed in him fully. The lakes appear much larger than in La Hontan's maps, but all in the same peculiar forms as in La Hontan; while the "Long River" and the Salt Lake are all laid down with express reference to our imaginative traveler.

Moll's dated maps range from 1711 to 1720. The Ohio is called the Sault River; the Wabash the Oubach or St. Jerome; the name Oubach in one instance covering the lower Ohio.

In the map of 1711, the Upper Ohio is called Ochio, and takes its origin in Oniasont Lake (Chautauqua).

The map of 1720 makes the Wabash rise in this lake. It flows along parallel with Lake "Irrie or Chat," and not fifty miles south of it.

In fact, a correct knowedge of the Ohio was yet far off, and for many years it was yet to be represented nearly parallel to the lake, and too near it. Where white men travelled through the present State of Ohio at all, they took portage on the rivers at the west part of the State, the portages being much easier, and the travel safer for the French.

A map of Peter Schenck, Amsterdam, 1708, makes the river Auabach, otherwise called Ohio or Belle River, with a portage from the Maumee. This map is evidently taken from the French, and is superior in general knowledge to others of the same map maker of date apparently not long previous.

JOHN HOMANS

was a celebrated geographer of about this date, of Nuremberg, and it seems singular that a town so inland should have been so famous in geography as Homans and his heirs, and others made it. His large atlas, in four thick folio volumes, is in the library of the American Geographical Society. A general map of North America is in the room of our own Historical Society. It is a photograph taken by Mr. E. Decker, of our city, from the original owned by him. La Hontan's River and Lake are down, but Lake Erie is more like Hennepin's, reaching far to the South. Lake Superior has a long arm to the West. Maps on a larger scale in the grand atlas represent the lakes better. The rivers Wabash and Ohio are one. John Senex, F. R. S., (English), in 1710, gives a better representation of the lakes. He makes the Wabash, Oho or Belle River, all the same. He has the Long River down, and the lake beyond it. He gives a brief account of its discovery, but with a suspicion of the truth, says: "Unless the Baron La Hontan has invented these things, which is hard to resolve, he being the only person that has traveled into those vast countries."

In the room of the Historical Society is the General Atlas of the World of

JOHN SENEX, LONDON, 1721,

a huge folio volume.

A map of 1719 is quite inaccurate. Lake "Erius, or Felis als Cadaraqua," looks like a flight of steps, such are its sinuosities. The west end has so narrow a strait into the rest of the lake that it seems almost a separate lake.

The Felians (Cats, or Eries,) appear in large letters, while the tribe then really holding the country modestly appears in small pica as the "Sinneks," on a small stream. Oneida Lake empties into Lake Erie by a river named "Onydas."

The Ohio is laid down very imperfectly, with only the name—Sabsqungs—to that branch, the Ohio above the Wabash. Neither

Ohio or the Wabash rise as far east as the west of Lake Erie.

A map of Louisiana and the Mississippi, inscribed to William Law, however, is quite full and satisfactory, and up to the learning of the times. It is plainly based upon the maps of the French geographer De L'Isle.

The Ohio, or Belle, rises well up as it should. After the union with the Wabash, it is called the "Ouabache, or St. Jerome." Lake Sandouske appears by that name with the islands.

"Chicagou" appears with houses meant for Indian huts, but looking as if our neighbor, settled so late and grown so fast, was then something of a town.

La Hontan's river does not appear, though he is not unfrequently quoted in the text.

"Louisiana," or what the French call "West Canada," and the Spaniards "Florida," includes all the West.

The Mississippi scheme was then in full favor.

Our author says the French King gave a grant of this country to M. Crozat, 14th September, 1712, N. S.; the River Mississippi being then called St. Louis, and the country, Louisiana, and the country *now* given to the "United French East and West India Companies," "the shares of whose stock by the management of Mr. Law, a Scotch gentleman, rose in 1719 to 1200 per cent., by which many people in France and elsewhere got vast estates."

He describes all the lakes except Erie, and not badly.

He places south of the Ohio River by his map, "a desert 160 leagues in compass, where the Illinois hunt 'cows,'" meaning buffaloes.

The time was now approaching when the geography of our interior was to be more thoroughly studied. The French had long completed their chain of occupation through the lakes and the Mississippi, and were gradually establishing other posts further to the east.

The English had taken the Iroquois under their nominal protection.

The next map I shall mention is in a

"DESCRIPTION OF CAROLANA," LONDON, 1727,

by Daniel Coxe. Our author is careful to state in the first line of his book that "Carolana and Carolina are two distinct though bordering provinces, the east of Carolana joining to the west of Carolina," and the title of the book indicates that Carolana is but another name for the Spanish Florida and French Louisana, claimed to be English property and granted by Charles 1st to Sir Robert Heath and then belonging to persons holding under his title.

The Ohio in this map makes from its source "back of New York," a much more proper curve in its course than any of the maps we have mentioned, instead of the general direction near Lake Erie. The "Ouabachee" has its source about the middle of Lake Erie and close to it, and joins with the Ohio in a lake twenty miles long and ten miles above the Mississippi.

Mr. Coxe was a believer in what he calls the "faithful and judicious history of the Baron La Hontan." The Long River and the great interior lake, appear on his map, and the long journey, the civilized nations, the great ships and well built houses in his book.

The Long River he calls otherwise the Mitchagona, and the Moingana (Des Moines), (a river suggested by other early geographers as being the "Long River" itself,) takes a diagonal from it to the Mississippi.

He thinks that if ever it comes to be settled, there will be easy communication with the Pacific by a branch of the Great Yellow River across a range of hills little north of New Mexico to a river flowing into a great lake.

The Yellowstone really has its source very near the Lewis; but it is doubtful if this fact was then known. Coxe suggests that the lake is the same as the Baron's.

A geographer very celebrated in his time, was

WILLIAM DE L'ISLE, ROYAL GEOGRAPHER

to the French King. He was born in in 1675 died in Paris in 1726; and is considered the most learned geographer of France. He produced a large number of excellent maps, having wonderful industry, and was the authority for map makers of all other countries.

He seems to have worked modestly, and at his death was preparing a new map of America which he hoped to be much better than those he had made already.

Governor Burnett of New York, in his memoir to the Lords of Trade governing the English colonies, Nov, 26 1720, (V. N. Y. Col. Doc. 577) complains that De L'Isle in his map of 1718, makes encroachments on the King's territories from his map of 1703 complaining that "All Canada is taken in fifty leagues all along the edge of Pensilvania and New York more than in the former map."

It is instructive to see how often De L'Isle's maps are mentioned in the Colonial dispatches, and how many plans even of the English territories taken from them, were sent to England.

Gov. Colden, who was excellent authority, in his memoir on the Fur Trade, Nov. 18 1724 (V. Col. Doc. p. 726) refers to this encroachment of the maps, and speaks of the French as being indefatigable in discoveries and commerce with (Indian) nations of which the English know nothing but what they see in French maps and books. In another place he describes the map of 1718 as being the best he had seen. As late as 1755 we find Palairet describing a new chart drawn by Mr. Buache from the memoirs of M. de L'Isle, and published in 1750.

The maps of De L'Isle in the Historical Room are, one from Covens' and Mortier's atlas, published at Amsterdam in 1722; and a fac-simile of one with no date, but evidently late in De L'Isle's life, found in the Hist. Collections of Louisiana, by B. F. French, part 2, 1850.

The very maps discussed by the colonists in their complaints, would be of great interest.

The lakes in the two maps above named, are much alike, and approaching accuracy; Ontario is somewhat round and Erie too round at the west end.

On both maps the Ohio flows too near the Lake. The last only extends east to the half of Lake Erie. The first shows the Ouabache, otherwise called the Ohio or Belle River, rising in the Oniasonke Lake, brought down nearly to the northern boundary of Maryland.

The colony of New York has very narrow limits by the colored lines, the French territory being bounded by Lake Champlain, a line from its south end striking New Jersey and then following the bounds of New Jersey to the northern line of Pennsylvania which turns south long before it reaches lake Erie.

On this map appears La Hontan's Salt Lake and Long River called here the "Moingona."

In the other map, which is a better one, the lake and Long river are left out, and the Moingona appears with the alias "Des Moines." The Wabash and Ohio are better, the Ohio being a branch of the Ouabache or St Jerome. In neither of these maps is the course of the Ohio as correctly defined as in Coxe's map.

Coxe's travels were in the southern part of our country, and there is nothing in his books to show how he arrived at this knowledge of the Ohio. The course he gives it does not seem the work of chance.

I suspect that Coxe was after all considerably indebted to De L'Isle.

South of the Ohio appears the same desert "where the Illinis hunt cattle."

The location of tribes, forts, and mines, is quite full. In fact, most of the early map makers had a quick eye for promise of mineral wealth.

The last map shows the St. Peter or Mini Sota rising in a lake of some size. Not far off is a smaller lake, with an outlet to the north, as if to lend color to Mr. Perkins' surmise that La Hontan's river may have been the St. Peter widened with its waters set back, and rising near Red River, flowing through Lake Winnepeg and Nelson River into Hudson's Bay a salt sea, supposed on report to be the desired route to the East. (N. A. Review, Jany., 1839 writings of J.H. Perkins Vol. 2 p 167.)

The English were now giving much attention to the interior of America.

In 1701, the Iroquois made a deed to the King of Great Britian, speciously claimed by the English to convey the right of sovereignty to that monarch.

In 1726, Governor Burnett sends to the Board of Trade, a deed dated Sept. 14 of that year, from three of the Five Nations, confirming the deed of 1701 and and also claimed to grant land said to extend from the Cuyahoga River east. (V Col. Rec. 800) This deed is recorded in Albany, and the Governor sent to England two maps with the places named marked in red ink.

The English maps, however, were yet based on the French and not with the best of judgment.

There lies before me an atlas of "America Septentrionalis" (North) by Henry Popple, published in London in 1733, and now in the Historical Room.

These maps were undertaken with the approbation of the Lords of Trade, using all the maps, charts, and observations that could be found; and especially the authentic records and actual surveys transmitted by the governors of the British Plantations. They are certified to strongly as more accurate than any extant by "ye Learned Dr. Edm Halley" of Oxford, and F. R. S. The engraver has bestowed much labor upon them, but the progress is backwards. Lake Ontario or Frontenac forms two well shaped steps toward the northeast. Lake Erie is long and runs due east and west; Lake Huron is much too short north and south; Lake Illinois is drawn too short; Lake Superior is drawn too far north with a great square bay below its whole east half.

Our old acquaintance the Long River, reappears as Moingona. The Hohio, is as usual, near the lake with a branch from the south from the Chautauqua Lake there not named.

A consciousness, slightly intelligent, appears of the bays and rivers flowing north into Lake Erie and 'I Sandoski.' The Miami and Muskingum, not named, appear as branches of the Ohio; the Miami having appeared much larger and named previously in the maps of De L'Isle.

The scale on which the larger maps are drawn is very satisfactory; and the various portages showing routes of travel are laid down with care.

Chicagou appears with its houses and its river of that name with Fort Miamis or Ouamis, which was really located on the St. Joseph on the east side of Lake Michigan, there called Illinois.

On the west side of the lake appears the "Melleky" River, (Milwuakee?)

A map by Emanuel Bowen, of the European settlements in America 1774. is of interest as being published with the book of that name, of which Edmund Burke was the principal author. It is too small to be valuable.

Behrings Straits appear in latitude 45, as the "supposed Str. of Annian."

FATHER CHARLEVOIX,

a French Jesuit of sense and ability published in 1744 a History of New France in six volumes, illusrated by maps and plans of great value. This is the edition in the Historical Room. The work has been translated within a few years, with copious and very able notes by Dr. John G. Shea, a gentleman well known to scholars by his many services to the learning of ancient America and to a wider public by his occasional publications, and as the author of all the articles on Indian matters in the new American Cyclopedia.

This edition is in the city library. It is to be regretted that it does not secure a larger audience by being published in less expensive, and more compact form.

The work contains an excellent introductory bibliographical notice by Charlevoix of the geograpical and historical works used by him.

Charlevoix was born in 1682, and died 1761. He was sent as missionary to Canada, and his journal in the form of letters of his journey through Canada, the country of the Illinois, and down the Mississipi, covers 1720 to 1722.

The map in his Journal is too small to compare in value with those in his History.

Vol. 1 of that work contains a general map reaching nearly to the north of Lake Huron; and Vol 5, a map of the great lakes. In general accuracy they are a great advance on former maps. The author modestly attributes this in great degree to N. Bellin, engraver of the department of Marine and the charts and plans accumulated there.

Lake Ontario is still too round, Lake Erie with a broad round end east, and the middle of the lake lowest rounding easily towards each end. Lake Michigan lies too much towards the southeast, and Lake Superior is too broad.

Isle Royal still appears twice; once under that name, and again as I. Philippeaux or I. Minong, the name given to it by Champlain.

Charlevoix speaks of the mines of Lake Superior as having been re-discovered in his time after being forgotten for 70 years.

La Hontan's river is dropped not again to appear, and a note on the map says that the sources of the Moingona are not known.

Chicagou has become a "Port"

Among the affluents of the Illinois appears the river "des Iroquois," a fact alleged afterwards as illustrating the extent of the occupation of that tribe.

The river "Ouabache ou St. Jerome" takes its rise in lakes near the Maumee much reduced in size reminding one of La Salle's letter before quoted

The Maumee is called Miamis.

The present Miami and the Scioto both rise very near the lake with each a portage. The first is called the Chionouské, the second the Chiagués.

The mastodon had apparently been found, for near the falls of the Ohio is a note that here were found in 1729 the bones of an elephant.

The upper branches of the "Oyo ou La Belle" are liberally represented; and along them and the Ohio appear Indian Villages. The ancient Eries, "who were destroyed by the Iroquois," are fairly located between the lake and the river.

The source of the Ohio is carried east and opposite the end of Lake Erie.

On the one map a branch from the north flows from the Chautauqua Lake called Lake Niatacnon, the stream from it Little Kannavagon, flows into Great Kanavagen, becoming in Evans' map 1755, Canavagy Creek, and still called Conewango Creek; on the other map this becomes the portage and Lake of Kanavangon.

River "au Beufs" (Buffalo River) starts from a lake near Erie, and represents French Creek.

On this as on previous maps is a marked bay with two small rivers which I have no doubt is an exaggeration of the curve of the Lake at Cleveland.

In the west end of Lake Erie are Rattlesnake Islands, "des Serpens Sonnettes."

I have said early in these papers that the south shore of Lake Erie was the last part of the Lake region to become known, a fact illustrated by our author's notes along it—"all this shore is nearly unknown."

That the English had begun to work over the mountains, appears in the English posts and names on the Cherokee river and its branches, now the Tennessee.

Charlevoix left Niagara to go by the north shore of Lake Erie, May 21, 1721. He says the course by the south shore was much more agreeable, but longer by half. His scription of Lake Erie is in the second volume of his Journal.

I may be pardoned for mentioning that my copy published in London, 1761, has in it the autograph and arms of Sir. Wm. Johnson. Born in Ireland, he settled in central New York, in 1746 was made a war chief of the Iroquois; in 1755 a baronet of Great Britain, in 1756 "Colonel, Agent and sole Superintendent of all the affairs of the Six Nations and other northern Indians." His life was for some time before his death half the history of New York. He died jnst as the Revolution commenced, and his children and hereditary influence carried the Iroquois against us in that contest. He negotiated the treaties under which the British claimed the country of the Ohio.

The arms are supported on each side by Indians with bows and arrows, surmounted by flags, spear, and tomahawk. The crest is an uplifted hand with an arrow. The motto is "Deo Regique Debeo." I owe duty to God and the King. The coat of arms caused me first to suspect the book once his.

1755, the year of Braddock's defeat, was a fruitful year for maps.

In 1748, the Ohio company had been formed with the design to settle beyond the Alleghanies or "Endless mountains" as named time and again in the maps.

In 1750, Gist their surveyor traveled down the Ohio.

Early in the year 1753, the English learned that the French had crossed Lake Erie, fortified Presque Isle, (now Erie) and settled upon the branches of the upper Ohio.

WASHINGTON

was sent to see them. His journal commencing Oct. 31st, 1753, was published in London, 1754, accompanied by a map the author of which does not appear.

It is evidently based upon that of Charlevoix but with additions.

Lake Erie has at its east end more its proper course. At Presque Isle appears a French fort with a portage fifteen miles to another on "Beef River or French Creek."

The Mahoning River appears as Great Beaver Creek, the name Beaver now existing in the lower river and eastern branch.

Two streams appear, one called Yellow Creek, between that and the Muskingum, called with its branch to the north (Tuscarawas River), White Woman's Creek. Tuskaroras is a village upon the east branch. Muskingum, and White Woman's Town, are two villages at the junction.

Farther southwest we find the Hokhoking (Hocking), with a village of the name upon it.

The "Sikader" River (Scioto) is well defined. Then the Little Miami without name, the "Great Miyamis" with name, both quite incorrectly, with an English post "Pikkavalinna" (Pickawillany) upon the Great Miami.

From a small stream at the east end of Lake Erie to the Miamis, entering at the other end, no stream appears on the south shore of Lake Erie.

A criticism appears, that the space between the "Alligany Mountains and the Mississippi is too great in the French maps." I do not see that in this or in the French maps the space differs materially from the fact.

In 1755 was published at London "The History of the Five Indian Nations" by C. Colden, Surveyor General of New York. Although the book is valuable and in 1750 Governor Burnett supposed Colden "to know the geography of this country better than any other person," the map in the second volume of this work is of little value, and carries one back in Ohio to the old mistakes.

There are in the rooms of the Historical Society, two maps dated 1755, designed especially to show the dispute between Great Britain and France

One published by R. and J. Ottens, Amsterdam, is in a reprint of Mitchell's atlas of that date published at Amsterdam by Covens and Mortier, and presented by Rev. E. A. Dalrymple the, Secretary of the Maryland Historical Society, to our own.

The other is engraved by Thomas Kitchen and sold in London, but even the title is French. These maps, as well as one in the Historical Rooms published at Amsterdam 1752 were, I am satisfied, the 14th of the Atlas Methodique of J. Palairet "agent of their High Mightinesses the States General of the United Province &c., and described in his "Concise Description" for the better explaining of the map, London 1755.

The territory marked disputed, is bounded north by the Lower St. Lawrence, the Ottawa, a line north of Lake Huron and turning south to the Lake near its west end, thence by Lake Huron, Michigan, and the Illinois River, to and down the Mississippi River; Thence along the Gulf to Pensacola Bay, thence irregularly north stretching towards the east, and west, again north through the middle of Tennessee, thence south of and nearly parallel to the Ohio and about seventy miles distant nearly to its source, thence about thirty or forty miles west of present Buffalo to Lake Ontario, thence along its south shore and in a line with it to the head of Lake Champlain and nearly to the Connecticut River thence up to opposite the outlet of Lake Champlain, thence nearly east to the sea.

In these maps the bay which I have spoken of as in other maps intended for the depression in Lake Erie at Cleveland, is called

Canahogue Bay, and a settlement upon the east side of the river Gwahoga.

At "Sanduske" is a French fort.

LEWIS EVANS

was an American geographer and surveyor, born about 1700, and died June, 1756. His home was in Pennsylvania, and he was much employed there and elsewhere.

He published a map of the Middle Colonies in 1755, with an analysis. The map itself is an epitome of history and geography. It was engraved by Jas. Turner and printed by B. Franklin and D. Hall in Philadelphia It was dedicated to Governor Pownall, who in 1776 published a folio (also in the Historical Room) with an enlarged analysis but the same map, in which the Governor stood stoutly by his deceased friend against other maps pirated or other.

The advance in local knowledge in this map is large.

The Cherage River marked "deep," lies in such a position that it must be the Conneaut. Between that and the Cuyahoga is a small stream called the Elk, which may be either the Grand or Chagrin-

The Cayahoga is laid down with local but not accurate knowledge; it is said to be muddy and pretty gentle. Up stream on the east are the "Tawas." Opposite is a French House with a Mingo town just above it. It rises in a pond with a portage of one mile to a branch of the Muskingum.

The next river west is the "Guahadahuri," not far from the Sandusky River, and seemingly too far west to be the Black although the name sounds a little like the "Canasadohara," the name given to the Black by James Smith, prisoner in the country just south of Lake Erie in 1755.

The Sandusky River has Wiandot on the east, Fort Sandusky on the west; above them is a round lake, the river flowing directly north. The inference would be that the lake was intended for the bay, and the village and fort were situated respectively on the south and north side of the narrower part of the bay.

Above the lake on the east is "Junandat" built 1754, and a Wyandot village.

A portage of four miles leads to the Scioto, and one of ten to the Miami.

Lake Erie is too square at its ends, and too near east and west.

This map is partly reproduced and described in Col. Whittlesey's History of Cleveland.

The land between the Cuyahoga and Conneaut Rivers is "level rich land intermixed with swamps and ponds."

The Beaver has two branches; the east interlocks with the "Cherage" and "French Creek," the other (Mahoning) westward with Muskingum and Cuyahoga; on this, flowing nearly due east, are many salt springs about thirty miles above the forks." Mr. Evans thinks the swamps and ponds prevent a good portage to the Cuyahoga, "but will no doubt in future ages be fit to open a canal between the waters of Ohio and Lake Erie."

Cuyahoga is "muddy and middling swift" but nowhere obstructed with Falls or Rifts. As this has fine land, and extended meadows, lofty timber oak and mulberry fitted for ship-building, walnut, chesnut, and poplar for domestic services, and furnishes the shortest and best portage between Ohio and Lake Erie, and its mouth is sufficient to receive good sloops from the Lake, it will in time become a place of consequence."

The Muskingum has coals, white clay and free-stone, marked on the map. Whetstone, freestone, coal, salt, and petroleum are marked in such a way as to show an intelligent examination by his informants, for Mr. Evans says his knowledge of the Ohio country was from traders and others.

Opposite Wheeling Creek are antique sculptures.

The map has many trails and portages with distances marked, which are not noticed here as that may be the subject of a future paper.

Opposite Sandusky are laid down three islands stretching at regular distances across the lake, where the Indians cross from Canada to trade.

A map which was repeatedly printed, much used and long authority, was Mitchell's.

JOHN MITCHELL, M. D. F. R. S.,

came to Virginia early in the 18th century, as a botanist. He lived long in America, and died in England in 1768.

His large and elaborate map has a certificate from John Pownall, Secretary of the Board of Trade and brother of Governor Thomas, that it was undertaken at his request, composed from drafts, charts and actual surveys, transmitted from the different colonies by the governors thereof. This certificate is dated July 1 1755.

The various editions of the map generally have no date but this. It continued to be much thought of, and was used by the Commissioners in making the treaty of peace in 1783 by which our country became a nation. The copy thus used was not long since presented by the English Government to Hon. Chas. Francis Adams who gave it to the American Geographical Society; and it hangs as a principal ornament in its lecture room in New York City.

There are three copies of Mitchell's map in

the Historical room, one published in London and the other two in Holland.

A copy of Mitchell's map belonging to Mr. Barras of E. B. Hale and Co., seems, as far as I can judge, to be of the edition used at the treaty.

The governors no doubt had given a good deal of pains to make accurate returns.

Governor Moore of New York, in 1766 writes to the Earl of Dartmouth "I must knowledge to your lordship that upon mentioning a map I cannot help being under some kind of terror from the remembrance of what I suffered in the last attempt of this kind; the breach which was then made in my small fortune is by no means repaid."

Many places were laid down from observations. William Smith, the early historian of New York, declared it to be "the only authentic one extant at the time;" and it certainly appears to be a great advance upon previous attempts. It is nearly as full in comments as Evans' covering much more territory. The whole map is more artistic and less stiff than Evans'. That part of it covering Ohio is sometimes more accurate than Evans', and sometimes less so.

No river is named between Presque Isle and present Cleveland. The Conneaut has not its proper curve from the east to the north. Then two smaller rivers, likely the Grand and Chagrin; then the Gwahago River with Gwahoga, an Iroquois town thirty miles from its mouth between its branches. The river empties into "Canahogue Bay, middle of the Lake."

It is forty miles by trail from the Cuyahoga to the Sandusky River; and the country between called Canahogue, is the seat of war, the mart of trade and chief hunting grounds of the Six Nations on the lakes and the Ohio.

Plenty of salt ponds appear about thirty to forty miles south of the Lake.

Sandusky Bay not named, is the bottom of the lake; the river is named "Blanc" (White). Junandat appears as a town named Ayonanton, between a branch to the east and lake of considerable size called Otsanderket, which seems like a repetition of Sandusky Bay although it is made the source of a principal and eastern branch of the Muskingum or Elk River. These names occur in a letter dated Aug. 10, 1751, from Marquis de la Jonquiére to Governor Clinton which says that three Englishmen were arrested at Ayonontout, the place selected in 1747 by Nicolas, the rebel Huron Chief, as his stronghold near the little lake of Otsanderket (VI N.Y. Col. Doc. p. 733). This is supposed by the editor of the Col. Doc., to be the same place with Junandat which post was built in 1754.

The Ohio River has an alias of "Splawacipiki;" but the first name has maintained its ground.

The Scioto is also called the "Chianotho."

Evans' knowledge of Ohio from the reports of the traders and agents traveling over the mountains and into that country, was more practical and reliable than that from the officials of New york.

The general form of Lake Erie is the best in Mitchell.

The Maumee is best in his map.

There are English factories in Ohio.

The territory claimed by the English is bounded by the western and northern limits of Palairet; and it is claimed that since the year 1672, when the Iroquois overcame the Shawnees they were in possession, and granted their rights to the English in 1701, renewed in 1726 and 1744.

The bounds of the province of Pennsylvania include most of central New York State reaching as far north as Niagara River, as far east as sixty miles west of the Hudson, and including a corner of Canada. The map is of great value for locating Indian tribes.

The river Melliki appears again with Miskonakimina at its mouth.

A map of Louisiana, 1757 by M. Le Page Du Pratz and accompanying his Histoire de la Louisiane, Paris 1758, is far behind the times. Even the Dead River is raised again and called the Grand. Lake Erie has its old form of a flight of steps. He is fully up with the times in pushing the "Montes Apalaches" pretty well east, and making them everywhere the English boundary.

A map of date 1758, by Captain Pouchot, is sent by him from Montreal, April 14, to Marshal a Belle Isle. The English frontier he lays down "from their best maps." His map is in his "Memoirs on the Last War," and in volume X, N. Y. Col. Doc., p. 694.

The Ohio country shows that he had seen Evans' map, though his own is not on the whole as accurate.

The Cuyahoga is the Gayouge; the Scioto, the Soniobato. From West Virginia the Petroleum River flows into the Ohio. The shape of Lake Ontario in this map is an improvement on the maps then current which generally made it too round, with too small an extension at the west.

Captain Pouchot speaks of the detail of Lake Erie as entirely unknown, and perhaps as navigable for large vessels as Lake Ontario, X. N. Y. Col. Doc. p. 694.

While the British and French were nominally at peace, the quarrel went on about the Ohio; and the French declined to give up their posts connecting from Presque Isle with Fort Du Quesne and down the Ohio. Braddock's ill-fated expedition set out to break the line by force.

James Smith, who had for some time been

a prisoner moving around Northern Ohio, was now with his captors at Fort Pitt. Braddock's army was spied every day; and an Indian showed Smith their close line of march, and anticipated the battle, by saying the Indians would surround them, take trees and "shoot um all one pigeon." (Ind. Captivities. p. 183).

Braddock's defeat was July 8, 1755. The war dragged until Pitt was placed at the head of the English ministry in 1757. In 1758 it was pushed with vigor, and the French disheartened elsewhere, abandoned Fort Du Quesne, November 25. The French meant to attempt its recapture in 1759; but Canada was vigorously attacked, and September 18, 1759, Quebec was surrendered to the English.

September 8, 1760, all Canada was surrendered; the title to be as should be determined at the Treaty of Peace, and in America the strife with France was ended.

In November 1762, a Treaty was agreed to and ratified in February 1763. By this the bounds between the English and French possessions were fixed at the Mississippi River, from its source by one of its eastern branches to the sea.

But the western Indians had been wi h the French, and it was vastly easier for the French in 1760 to surrender their posts than for the English to take actual possession.

Sept. 12, 1760, Major Rogers was ordered to proceed to the western posts. About the first of November he left Presque Isle with his command, to continue along the south coast of Lake Erie. Nov. 7 they reached the river called by Rogers the Chogage. Here he met a party of Indians from Detroit.

That the Chogage was not the Cuyahoga, as has been supposed, seems very satisfactorily established by Col. Whittlesey in his History of Cleveland. Was it not the Conneaut, called in 1755 on Evans' map and in 1776 in Pownall's description, the Cherage?

That the Cherage was the Conneaut appears from its position on Evans' map and from the statement, that with French Creek (emptying at Erie) it interlaced with the east branch of Beaver Creek.

The supposition that the Chogage was Grand River, carries the conclusion that the river called by the Indians, the Elk River, was the Cuyahoga; but the Elk is placed by all, east of the Cuyahoga, and the last was the best known and surest to be laid down, of all the rivers from the south of Lake Erie except the Maumee, and by names not far different from the present. It, was as we have seen, noted for its easy portage.

The distances cannot be very certain on any mode of settling the question, but distances in the West in those times were very uncertain.

Rogers makes the Elk fifty miles east of Sandusky, which, if it is east of the Cuyahoga is too little. Yet all the maps place the Elk east of the Cuyahoga, and Rogers in his Concise Account of North America, p. 198, makes the Cuyahoga about forty miles east of Sandusky.

Major Rogers found Pontiac, the able Indian chief of the west, a haughty man, and most of the western Indians dissatisfied. He took possession of Detroit and other posts; but in the Spring of 1763, Pontiac captured most of the posts in the West.

The encroachments of the English had been watched with a jealous eye. One chief had stated the English and French claims and aptly asked "Where lie the Indians' lands?"

Even the Five Nations wavered. They could not understand that the English owned their soil, and it required all the influence and address of Sir William Johnson to keep them from joining the Western Confederacy.

It was plainly necessary for the English to be careful.

A military proclamation was issued in 1762, by Col. Henry Bouquet from Fort Pitt, reserving the land west of the mountains as hunting grounds for the Indians.

The English at home laid out the governments and the Gentleman's Magazine, October 1763, Vol. 33, p. 476, contains a map of them laid down agreeably to the Royal Proclamation of Oct. 7, 1763. The western bounds are the Alleghanies. The lands west are marked, "Lands reserved for the Indians," and the proclamation strictly forbids settlement beyond, or any extension of the old colonies beyond the heads of the rivers falling into the Atlantic,

The Annual Register for 1763, contains the map, proclamation, and comments; giving as the main reason, the fear of alarming the Indians.

The English made two expeditions along the coast of Lake Erie which met with mishaps.

November 7, Major Wilkins, going to the relief of Detroit, was wrecked at Point aux Pins.

This place appears in Mitchell's map of 1755, in Charlevoix of 1744, and Pownall's of 1777, toward the west end of the north shore, and in other maps the name still adheres. Long Point also on that shore, was mentioned in the narrative of the expedition. (See Whittlesey's History of Cleveland, and Hist. Soc. Tract No. 13.)

In 1764, the British government sent two expeditions into the Ohio country; the one commanded by

COL. JOHN BRADSTEET

was, it seems, to go along the southern shore and strike into the Scioto country.

His expedition was unsatisfactory. He was unable to go to the Scioto country; and a letter from one of its officers, intimates that it was from such geographical ignorance as expected boats to sail where there was only dry ground. The real difficulty, was the incapacity of the commander, who allowed the Indians to deceive him, and when undeceived showed no efficiency.

On his return, on the night of October 19 and 20, 1764, a sudden storm overtook him at Rocky River; twenty-five of his boats were destroyed, and much suffering ensued. Many relics of this disaster have been found, most of which are in the room of the Historical Society, and have been described in a careful paper by Dr. J. P. Kirtland in Whittlesey's History of Cleveland.

All that can be found, giving an account of the disaster appears in the paper referred to, and in Tracts thirteen and fourteen of the Historical Society.

There is no doubt of the locality of the disaster.

In May 1765, the schooner Victory was sent to take up the cannon, left by Col. Bradstreet near the "Riviere aux Roches," which is the first use of this name I have noticed, and it is in the French language. The New York Mercury of November 26, 1764, says the night was very dark, and little else could be saved than small quantities of provision.

The army then proceeded to "Grand" River (first appearance I know of that name) where they had another storm. The poor Colonel met with still another on Lake Ontario, and lost effects, "but happily no lives." He was much blamed for his conduct. His own report is not to be found. An officer named Mante published a brief account of the expedition, and said no lives were lost. In the immediate vicinity of the relics, were found in a mound some dozen bodies, with metalic buttons and other evidences that they were whites. Loskiel, in his History of Indian Missions, translation, London 1794, locates this disaster, and says many lives were lost, and in this he is followed by Morse, the American Geographer in 1798. These rocks were in old times quite a terror in navigation by boats and the Indians offered tobacco to appease them.

HENRY BOUQUET'S EXPEDITION OF 1764

into the Ohio country, was a great success. The account of it, published the next year with maps, and reprinted in 1868 in the Ohio Historical Series of Robert Clarke & Co., of Cincinnati, has a map of Capt. Thomas Hutchins, who accompanied it. The map is very much more accurate than any preceeding one, having been laid down from careful observation. Several trails are laid down and carefully described. Mahoning town is on the river now of that name, and 104 miles from Fort Pitt. Thence it is forty-two to the Cuyahoga River, and thence ten miles to Ottawa town on the Cuyahoga.

The course of the Mahoning is very well observed. The Cuyahoga has quite its proper course. Cuyahoga Town is where it turns north from east, and Ottawa Town about fifteen or twenty miles from the Lake.

Sandusky Bay, called Lake, is for the first time in proper shape. Sandusky Fort is on the south side, and Wyandot Town, called "Junandat" in the text, is just south of it. "Junqueindundah" is a town about twenty miles west of it, and upon Sandusky River. The Huron River is called "Bald Eagle Creek," and is sixty yards wide. Between it and Mohicon Johnstown are the remains of a fort built by the Ottawas. The Mineame (Maumee) has also more nearly than usual its proper course. There are unnamed small streams besides, flowing from the south into Lake Erie but not to be identified.

In short, the map does decided credit to the patriotic Captain Hutchins. At the Revolution he was in London. In 1778 he was suspected of correspondence with Franklin and escaped to America. Here he was made geographer of the United States. He organized our system of land surveys, but died in 1788. A sketch of him will be found in Historical Tract No. 22.

In 1778, his Topographical Description was published "for the author" in London. It was mostly from Evans', and would tell the enemy little they could not already know. It refers to his map, which is not in the Historical Room though the book is.

I have referred to the proclamation of 1763. The English were, however, pressing westward. Many capitalists, among them Washington, were thinking that western lands would be valuable, and in 1768 at Fort Stanwix, Sir. Wm. Johnsou made a treaty by which the boundary of the Indian Lands was fixed as follows: commencing on the Ohio at the mouth of the Cherokee, (Tennessee) thence up the Ohio and Alleghany to Kittanning, thence across to the Susquehanna, placing a great share of New York State to the Indians. How much, appears in a map dated 1771, made by Guy Johnson, to be found in the 4th Volume of N. Y. Col. History, p. 1090. Yet it was considered that the Indians had made large concessions.

The hard feeling engendered among the Indians, by the aggression of settlers and traders, made them ready to side against the colonies, during the war for independence.

So little geoghaphical progress was made during the war, that, as we have seen, the map of 1755, was the basis of the treaty of 1783.

A map in some respects showing a curious mixture of knowledge, and the want of it, is

CAPTAIN CARVER'S,

published in London, in 1781, to illustrate his travels on the Upper Mississippi in 1766 and 1767. The general map is on a small scale, but carefully studied. The large one has many details of Lake Superior, and the country west of it. The general map has the west coast, wherein appears Vancouver's Island not named, while the great Western Sea within shows it was not fully explored, and the Straits of "Anian," remind us of the early times when Behring's was confounded with the sea around Vancouver's Island.

Of the maps and books of Revolutionary times, in the library of the Hist. Soc., "The North American and the West Indian Gazetteer," London, 1778, 2d ed., is quite celebrated as a bibliographical curiosity for its account of Bristol, Rhode Island.

Bristol is a county and town in New England, "having a commodious harbor at the entrance of which lies Rhode Island." "The capital is remarkable for the King of Spain's having a palace in it, and being killed there, and also for Crown, the poet, begging it of Charles 2d."

The maps in this 12mo. are very fair for their size.

A map printed in London, 1777, for Robt. Sayer and John Bennett, compiled from Mr. D'Anville's maps, corrected from the original materials of Governor Pownall, gives the relative position and form of lakes and rivers quite accurately, more so than Mitchell's though on a small scale.

All the lakes seem quite natural. The Ohio and its branches from the north are not far enough east, but quite good in form. The draughtsman gives our antipodes credit for some knowledge of the continent. He lays down on the west coast between Lat. 50 and 55 "Fou Sang of the Chinese."

But a map of 1779, "laid down from the latest surveys," and corrected in like manner, goes back to the errors of Evans' in the forms of Lake Erie and Michigan. It is not nearly as accurate as D'Anville's, and is reduced from Evans' and Mitchell's.

THE AMERICAN ATLAS OF THOMAS JEFFREYS

published in London, during, and after the Revolutionary war is not uncommon.

One purchased by the writer in Glasgow, Scotland, is on deposit in the Historical Rooms "Composed from numerous surveys, by Major Holland, Lewis Evans, William Scull, Henry Monson, Lieut. Ross, J. Cook, Michael Lane, Joseph Gilbert, Gardner, Hillock, &c., &c.; engraved on forty-nine copper plates.

The original date was 1776, but by a pasted slip is 1794, and some changes appear.

The Index for maps 5 and 6, describes the map above of 1779, laid down according to the treaty of 1763. The plate is the same, but for the text of the treaty of 1763, passing so much territory from France to England, is substituted a new treaty of 1783 with the "people of the United States."

A map of the United States of 1790, has in colors its flag, but its Lake Erie has gone back a hundred years to the old flight of steps.

"A map of the United States, by Samuel Dunn," improved from Captain Carver, is a good, but small map.

There is also in the Historical Room a large atlas of

FADEN'S.

The first map, "The British Colonies in North America, engraved by Wm. Faden 1777, is a very fair abridgment of Mitchell's.

Two maps of Pennsylvania show a very little of Ohio; one of them has the Hokhoking River or the Long-necked Bottle, too far east. The war did not call for maps of Ohio; but the "Rebel works at Boston," Philadelphia, and Independence Hall, are well represented.

Not long after the treaty of peace, the western country again attracted attention.

In 1787, was formed the North-west Territory.

Anticipating its value,

JOHN FITCH,

of steamboat memory, spent considerable time in surveys, within the bounds of Ohio and Kentucky. He had previously traveled the country as a prisoner among the Indians.

In 1785, he made a map of the "North-western country" based upon Hutchins' and Morrow's maps, but containing original and accurate information. He prepared the copper plate and engraved it himself, and took his impressions in a cider press. He was then living in Bucks County, Pennsylvania, and engaged in inventions using steam. The map was sold at six shilling a copy to raise money to pursue his experiments upon steamboats.

This map I have never seen. It is partially described in Col. Whittlesey's life of Fitch, in Spark's Am. Biography, 2nd Series, Vol. 6. The positions of the main rivers and great lakes are remarkably accurate. On its face are engraved sentences, as was the fashion at that day, which showed his clos knowledge of the country; as—"The lands on this Lake (Erie) are generally thin and swampy, but will make good pasture and meadow lands."

"This country (Illinois) has once been settled by a people more expert in war than the present. Regular fortifications, and some of these incredibly large, are to be found; also many graves or towers, like pyramids of earth."

Fitch's own projected land company was not a success; but other companies were formed, which surveyed and settled the lands west of the Alleghanies.

A valuable atlas presented to the Historical Society, by Mr. Geo. W. Howe of Cleveland, while these papers are being printed, is

"THE UNIVERSAL ATLAS;" LONDON 1796

being a complete collection of the most approved maps extant, corrected with the greatest care, and augmented from the last edition of D'Anville and Robert with many improvements by Major James Rennel and other eminent geographers; engraved on 100 plates in 66 maps, by Thomas Kitchen Senior and others, in one large folio volume.

Plates 56 and 57, are a fine map of North and South America, where the United States are laid down according to the proclamation of peace signed at Versailles Jan. 20, 1783, compiled from Mr. D'Anville's maps with corrections in the British provinces from Governor Pownall's materials.

The Lakes are much more correct than in the English maps. The French maps generally, gave more correctly the position of the lakes, but not so much in detail the country.

Map 58 is our old friend, originally published with the text of the "last treaty" of 1763, republished with the text of the treaty of 1783.

Map No. 63 "of the Middle Dominions belonging to the United States of America," is a very satisfactory map upon a large scale. It is quite distinct from either Evans or Mitchell. The south shore of Lake Erie takes a serpentine direction south of west. Oxhurene Bay is just east of the Cherage River and is quite large.

The Elk Creek seems to correspond with the Grand River though quite inaccurate.

The map follows Evans and Mitchell in making the portage from the Cuyahoga to the Muskingum, one mile instead of eight as it should be. Rocky River is small and unnamed. Black River is large and unnamed. Beaver Creek is as it should be, small, and is unnamed. The Guahadahuyi answers to the Vermillion. The Huron appears as Bald Eagle Creek. Sandusky Bay and River (the last is named) are quite proper.

The whole of Ohio shows the author's information to have been accurate and extensive for the times.

It was not until the surveys of the Connecticut Land Company, that the northern coast of Ohio was known The travelers and gazetteers to be sure gave some knowledge.

There is in the library of the Historical Society, a

MANUSCRIPT MAP BY JOHN HECKEWELDER,

the Moravian Missionary, made Jan. 12, 1796. It is from the papers of General Moses Cleaveland of the Connecticut Land Company, and presented to the Society by his daughter, Mrs. Morgan of Norwich, Connecticut. It extends from Presque Isle to the Huron River. Coneought Creek is just west of the Pennsylvania line, and just within that State, "grant of 2500 Acres of Land to the Moravians."

Up the Mahoning, called Big Beaver Creek, is the "Path from Pittsburg to the Salt Spring, Mahoning old Town, Gajahaga."

The path passes near "Salt Spring," "Mahoning old T.," and a "great deer lick," goes west to "Cajahoga, Sandusky, and Detroit," striking the "Cajahoga R.," some distance above the falls; there the path divides, one goes north-west through a "swamp which will make good meadows," to "Moravian Ind. Town in 1786," located on the east of the Cuyahoga just above a little stream rising from three little lakes or ponds. This was "Pilgerruh" (Pilgrim's rest) where the poor Moravians and their Indian converts after the bloody massacre at Gnadenhutten, hoped to find *rest*, but where they were permitted to sojourn only a few months; then going to Black River to locate some five miles from its mouth, and without locating there compelled to settle near Sandusky. Pilgerruh is supposed to have been near the northern line of Independence in this county.

The second path crosses the river just above the falls, running west to "Cuyahaga old Town" on the west side of the river where it turns north; thence, one path leads west to Lower Sandusky, the other north on the west side the Cuyahoga to the mouth, thence close around the shore west. The old river bed appears as a "fine duck pond," a description which settlers not the oldest can verify.

A small stream enters the Cuyahoga from the west, which is—"so far navigable with sloops."

The Cuyahoga and the Muskingum appear as the line between the Indians and the United States.

An Indian path runs "along the Lake" west.

The character of the shore is shown by

"Perpendicular Rocky Bank" marked between the rivers Cuyahoga and Black.

The Rocky, Black, and Vermilion, are marked, but not named.

The Huron River receives more attention and on the east, some miles from the mouth, is an "Old Moravian Indian Town."

Heckewelder himself lived in this little village on the Cuyahoga, and I cannot without emotion look at this memento of men so pious, selfdenying and long suffering, as the Moravians: men who took constantly their lives in their hands, and were only driven from one place to brave death in another, all for the love of Christ and their fellowmen..

The location of the division between the trail down the Cuyahoga River and to Sandusky, is fixed by a letter in Whittlesey's History from Colonel James Hillman.

In May 1786, he took the Indian trail for Sandusky until he arrived "at the 'Standing Stone' on the Cuyahoga a litle below the mouth of Break-neck Creek, where the village of Franklin is now." There he took a trail "direct to Tinker's Creek where was a little town built by Heckewelder and Zeisberger with a number of Moravian Indians. They were Moravian preachers."

The township surveys made by the Land Company, gave for the first time a definite knowledge of the Reserve.

There are in the Historical rooms, several maps of great interest in this connection.

A MANUSCRIPT MAP 1797, BY SETH PEASE,

donated by his nephew Horace Pease, Esq., of Dayton, showing the variation of the compass.

A manuscript map of the Connecticut Western Reserve from actual survey by Seth Pease, (from the Walworth papers) was evidently prepared for publication. Conneought Creek, Ashtabula Creek, Grand River, Chagrine River, and the Cayahoga are there all properly laid down, together with the trails from the Big Beaver, and Indian paths.

The Reserve west of the Cuyahoga is unsurveyed and subject to Indian claims; and less accurately appear the rivers Rocky, Renihua, Vermillion and Huron. This map was engraved the same year and printed at New Haven.

A map of the Connecticut Land Company's lands west of the River Cuyahoga, with no date but supposed to be 1806, gives the rivers Rocky, Black, Beaver Creek, Vermillion; names ever since used. Numerous local trails appear which would be of considerable interest to the local historian.

An engraved map, probably ot date 1808 by Seth Pease and Abraham Tappan, has the rivers west of the Cuyahoga well laid down in the following order; Rocky, Black, Vermillion, River la Chappel, Old Woman's Creek, Huron River and Pipe Creek.

An excellent map of this period was the foreign one of Arrowsmith, a celebrated map maker of London. It is not in our library. A fine French map based on it by P. F. Tordieu, engraver, 1802, gives the following names to the rivers, beginning at the east—Connieaught, Ashtabula not named, Grand, Biche, Shaguin, Boche, (meaning no doubt, Roche,) Cuyahoga, Elsabaca, (Rocky) Renesbona (Black), Grus (Beaver Creek) Vermillion, Huron, Portage, and Miami du Lac. This map belongs to Mr. George W. Ford of New York City, to whose courtesy I am indebted for its examination.

The gazetteers of those days furnished little information of the North-west Territory.

The map of

JOSEPH SCOTT, PHILADELPHIA, 1795,

is after the Mitchell of 1755, but less accurate.

The text states the boundaries of the treaty of Greenville, 1795, by which the Indians granted all east from the mouth of the Cuyahoga, up the river by the Portage, to the Tuscarawas branch of the Muskingum, thence down it to a crossing place above Fort Laurens, thence to a branch of the Great Miami near which stood 'Lorrimer's Store" thence westerly to Fort Recovery on a branch of the Wabash, thence South West to the Ohio River opposite the Kentucky River.

The map of the Northern part of the United States in the "American Gazetteer" of

JEDEDIAH MORSE, D. D. BOSTON, 1797,

reprinted London, 1798 is a very creditable outline, showing greater correctness in form and information.

New Connecticut appears as well as the Greenville line, and the additional reserved lands for the forts in various places.

The Cuyahoga has the name "Cayuga," and Morse in his text calls it the Cayahoga or Cayuga sometimes called the Great (Grand) River: a statement taken by him from Loskiel's Missions. Mr. J. W. Taylor in his excellent History of Ohio, thinks the names of the Cuyahoga and Geauga Rivers both are from the occupation of their banks by a band of the Cayugas, one of the five Nations.

Mr. William M. Darlington of Pittsburgh, in his notes to Smith's Narrative, derives it from the Mohawk word for river—Ka-ih-ogh-ha.

The generally erroneous notions as to the south shore of Lake Erie, led to some pracical business results in the history of our land titles.

When the State of Connecticut proposed

to sell its "Western Reserve" there was more than one party of gentlemen prepared to bid for it.

The result was a compromise between Oliver Phelps and his associates, afterwards known as the "Connecticut Land Company," and John Livingston and his associates, afterwards called the

"EXCESS COMPANY."

The Excess Company agreed to withdraw all propositions made by them for purchase and to assist their competitors. The Excess Company was to be entitled to the excess over 3,000,000 acres of land, to be released to them and paid for by them at the *pro rata* price of the whole land, and were to be to that extent tenants in common with the Connecticut Land Company. This agreement, a copy of which is in the library of the Historical Society, is dated 12th August, 1795.

The 13th of May 1796, the individuals of the Excess Company conveyed all their title to John Morgan, John Caldwell, and Jonathan Brace, the same trustees who acted for the Land Company, by conveyance quite similar to that of the Land Company, to them. It was provided, however that the joint report of the surveyors then acting in the examination of the new territory should be final as to the quantity of land to be held in common by the Excess Company.

The report of the surveyors was made 28th January, 1797, and it was found that the Land Company had less than 3,000,000 acres, and the Excess Company nothing. General Hull, afterwards so unfortunate in the war of 1812, was a principal stock holder in this company, and the common geographical error of a hundred years nearly ruined him.

The

NAMES OF THE LAKES

seemed to be determined in spite of effort, and are generally Indian names. The first discoverer of Ontario called it "St. Louis:" The early French called it "Frontenac," after the Governor, who was not unwilling to be complimented, but it was afterwards "Ontario or Frontenac." The English, as they first claimed dominion, called it "Katarakui or Ontario" (Washington's Journal). Mitchell, "Ontario or Catarakui;" and Pownall, the same: but the name Ontario was always used.

Huron was named from the unfortunate tribe on its shores when it was first discovered, "des Hurons", of the Hurons. From Homans, 1706, and De L'Isle, 1722, it received the alias of "Michigan;" Hennepin in 1698, and Coxe in 1721, called it "Huron or Karegnondi;" Washington's Journal in 1754, "Ouatoghi or Hurons." No one of the lakes so uniformly received the same name.

Lake Michigan persistently called at first "Illinois," was called "Michigan" in 1719 by Senex, in 1744 by Charlevoix, and it continued generally after this to have that name.

Superior, called by Champlain its first topographer, "Grand Lac" was named by the Jesuits in their wonderful map "Tracy" or "Superior." Called by the English Senex in 1719 and Coxe in 1721, as an alias, after the "Nadoussians" (Sioux) on its shore it uniformly had from the time of the Jesuit map its present name, with occasionally in early maps the name of Tracy.

Lake Erie received its name from the Eries on its bank, and uniformly had that name. The tribe was otherwise called the Cat nation, whence the lake had sometimes the alias of "the Cat," "Felis," "Du Chat." Senex in 1719 called it also "Cadaraqua" the name sometimes given to Ontario. Washington's Journal, Mitchell, and Pownall called it also Okswego.

The Ohio River for many years was confounded with the Wabash, and called either name. The lower Ohio in early discoveries was called "Wabonquigon;" Hennepin called it "Hohio;" La Hontan, "Ouabach;" Joutel, "Douo or Abacha."

The English made their acquaintance with this river from its upper end, and were more inclined to extend the name Alleghany down the river.

Evans in 1755 calls it "Ohio or Alleghany or La Belle, and Palaw Thépiki by the Shawenese. Mitchell calls it "Ohio or Splawcipiki."

The Muskingum was called almost uniformly by that name, sometimes Elk. Mr. Harris in his Tour into the Territory North West of the Alleghanies (1805) says, it is an Indian word meaning The Elk's Eye. This name is given by Mitchell to one of its branches.

Mr. Howe (Hist. Coll. of Ohio, 594), says it is a Delaware word meaning a town on the river side.

The Walhonding was often called "White Woman's Creek," because a captive white woman lived on it among the Indians.

The Killbuck was named from a Delaware chief.

The Mohican was called Mohican Johns, from Mohican Johns Town formerly upon its banks, no doubt from an Indian of that tribe.

The Hocking was the Hock Hocking, a word meaning,—says Mr. Howe—bottle in Delaware; and one map has an alias to it "or long-necked Bottle."

The name of the Scioto was uniform. In Mitchell's it was "Scioto or Chianotto," apparently the same name.

The Maumee was originally the river of

the Miamis (Indians;) and often called in the books "Miami du Lac" to distinguish it from the Miami flowing into the Ohio. The contraction to Maumee was very convenient to distinguish it.

The name "Sandouski" appears upon Homan's map, 1707, to the bay. The word is said to be Wyand, and meaning "water" or water within water.

Maps in Possession of the Western Reserve and Northern Ohio Historical Society Including the Lake Region of North America to 1800 Inclusive.

1400 to 1582—Documentary History of the State of Maine, Vol. 1, containing a History of the Discovery of Maine, by J. G. Kohl, Portland, 1869, containing 31 maps.

1529. Mappemundi Hieronimus de Verrezano, reduced copies. Journal of the Am. Geog. Soc. 1872.

Very early, but no date or place of publication.

La Florida (including the Mississippi). Hieron.

Nova Hispania.

Peruvianae Auriferae Regionis Typus.

1572—L'Isole Piu Famose del Mondo, by Thomas Porcacchi da Castiglione--Venice.

1626—Cosmographie of Peter Heylin, book 4, part 2—(America) London.

1609—Oeuvres de Champlain, reprint Quebec, 1870. Map of Lake Champlain, including east end of Lake Ontario.

1633—Some work—fac-simile in Vol. 6 of Map of the Lakes. Description in French; also Vol. 3rd Documentary History of New York, by Dr. O'Callaghan. Description in English.

1633—Tracing from Hondius' Atlas, based upon Mercator; original in Am. Geog. Soc.

1638—At, or before this date.

Insulae Americanae, Wm. Blaeu, Amsterdam.

Virginia by the same. Amsterdam.

After 1631. Several Sea Charts by John Keulen, Amsterdam.

Northern Part of North America.

Gulf of Mexico.

North and South America.

Also an early Dutch chart of N. and S. America, with the sea currents,—no date.

1652. Heylin's Cosmographie. London. Deposit by Mr. Charles Scott.

1657—8. America noviter delineata, by John Janson, from his "Novus Atlas," Amsterdam.

Three tracings from the atlas; original in Am. Geog. Soc.

Nova Hispania et Nova Galicia.

1665—Cosmographie Blavianae, John Blaeu, Amsterdam. Tracing of general map of North America; original in Am. Geog. Soc.

1670—71. Jesuit maps, with Relation of those years. Reprint of Jesuit Relations, 1870, Montreal. Foster & Whitney's Lake Superior, Part 2. Bancroft's United States, Vol. 3. Monnette's Mississippi Valley, Vol. 1.

1673. Marquette's map. Fac-simile from the original in Montreal, in Shea's Discovery of the Mississippi.

1673 "Blome's Brittannia," map designed by Sanson, London.

1680. Two maps from the "English Atlas" London, Tracings. Original in Am. Geog. Soc.

1681. Map published with Marquette's Journal, by Thevenot. Copy in Bancroft's History of the United States Volume 3, p. 160.

1683. Louis Hennepin, in his "Description de la Louisana" &c Paris 1688.

1696. Tracing from Atlas of Vanderbest, Amsterdam—original in Am. Geog. Soc.

1697. Louis Hennepin, in his Decouverte dans L'Amerique, Utrecht; also in "Hennepin's Discovery of America," London 1698.

"A map of a Large Country Newly Discovered in the Northern America."

1705. La Hontan, Memoires de L'Amerique Septentrionale, Vols. 1 and 2.

1706. Tracing from Homan's Atlas, Nuremberg—original in Am. Geog. Soc.

1708. (Prior to). North America, Gerard Valk, and Peter Schenk, Amsterdam.

1708. Tracing from Atlas N. Visscher, Amsterdam.—orig. in Am. Geog. Soc.

1708 America, Peter Schenk, Amsterdam. Mexico, Florida, and Mississippi, same.

Tracing from Atlas of same—original in Am. Geog. Soc.

No date, but about (1708), two tracings from F. Dewitt's Atlas. Amsterdam. Original in Am. Geog. Soc.

1710. John Homan's, Nuremberg. Photograph from his atlas.

1710. North America, John Senex, F.R.S., London.

1713. Journal of Last Voyage of La Salle, by Joutel, London, 1714.

1715. Nouveaux Voyages &c., La Hontan. The Hague.

1715. Map of Dominions of Great Britain, Herman Moll.

South Sea Company's Trade. (no date). North America (no date).

From H. Moll's Atlas: 4 small maps with no dates.

West Indies, Mexico, and New Spain.

America.

Florida, or Louisiana.

Louisiana, Mississippi, Canada, and New France.

1720. Parts of North America claimed by France. H. Moll.

1721. General Atlas of the World, with text. Thick folio. John Senex, London.

1722. Description of the English Possessions, Danl. Coxe, London 1727; St. Louis 1840.

1722. Map by William de L'Isle, Royal Geographer to French King, from Covens' and Mortier's Atlas. Amsterdam.

1722. "Historie de L'Amerique Septentrionale." La Poterie, Vol. 2. Paris.

1726 or prior. Louisane et Cours du Mississippi, without date. Wm. de L'Isle. Fac-simile in Hist. Coll. of Louisiana, by B. F. French, Part 2, 1850. Philadelphia.

1733. British North America, with the French and Spanish Settlements Adjacent. Henry Popple, London, 1 Vol. folio.

1744; Carte de la Louisane &c. by N. Bellin Histoire de la Nouvelle France by Charlevoix Vol. 1.

Amerique Septentrionale by N. Bellen Vol. 5 of same work.

1747. North America, Emanuel Bowen, in "European Settlements in America," by Edmund Burke.

1752. Possessions Anglaise e Francaise, I. Ritter, Amsterdam.

1754. Map of the western parts of the Colony of Virginia as far as the Mississippi, with Washington's Journal, London, 1754. Reprint New York, 1865.

1755. History of the Five Nations, Colden London.

1755. Carte des Possessions Angloises and Francoises du Continent de L'Amerique Septentrionale; inserted in Sener Atlas 1721. Engraved by Thomas Kitchen. This and a similar map printed in Amsterdam, inserted in Mitchell's Atlas, 1755, are described in "A Concise Description of the English and French Possessions in N. America &c. by J. Palareti London, 1755.

1755. A general map of the Middle British Colonies in America, by Louis Evans, accompanied by an analysis of the map by Louis Evans, Philadelphia, 1755, 1 Vol.4 to.

1755. A map of the British and French Dominions in North America &c., by Jno Mitchell, D.F., with improvements. Printed for I Covens and C. Mortier, Amsterdam. 1 Vol. large folio.

1755. A map of the British Colonies in North America. Inscribed to the Earl of Halifax and the other Lords Commissioners for Trade and Plantations, by Jno. Mitchell. Pub. Feb. 1755, for Jeffreys and Faden, London. Thomas Kitchen engraver.

1758. Map of Capt. Pouchot X. N. Y. Colonial Documents.

1761. Part of North America in Journal of a Voyage to North America by Charlevoix, London.

1763. Annual Register, London.

1763. Gentleman's Magazine, Vol. 33 p. 476.

1764. A map of the country on the Ohio and Muskingum Rivers by Thos. Hutchins Hist. Account of Bouquet's Expedition against the Ohio Indians, Phil. 1765 Reprint Cincinnati 1868. Also Parkman's Conspiracy of Pontiac, Boston 1868. Pioneer History by S. O. Hildreth Cincinnatti 1848.

1768. Map corrected and improved from Evans' by Guy Johnson, VIII N. Y. Col. Documents. Annexed to Report to Board of Trade.

1771. map of the country of the Six Nations proper, by Guy Johnson, IV Doc. Hist. of N. Y.

1774. Complete History of the Late War, Dublin.

1775. History of the American Indians, James Adair, London.

1776. A Topographical Description of such parts of North America as are contained in the annexed map (Lewis Evans) of the Middle British Colonies in North America, by T. Pownall, late Governor &c., London.

1777. A new map of the whole continent of America with the European Possessions as settled at the Treaty of Peace 1763; compiled from Mr. Danville's maps, and corrected in the several parts belonging to Great Britain, from the original materials of Governor Pownall. M. P., with the text of the treaty, London.

1777. Atlas of British Colonies in North America, by Wm. Faden, London, very large folio volume.

1778. A new map of North America. Travels through the interior parts of North America in the years 1766, 1767 and 1768, by J. Carver, London, 1781.

1778. The North American and West Indian Gazetteer, 2d ed. London.

1778. A Topographical Description of Virginia &c., comprehending the Rivers Ohio, Kenhawa, Scioto, &c.; by Thomas Hutchins, London. No map.

1779. A new and correct map of North America, divided according to the last Treaty of Peace concluded at Paris, Feb. 10 1763; laid down according to the latest surveys and corrected from the original materials of Governor Pownall.

1780. Impartial History of the War in America, by J. Carver, London 1771. Reprint New York, 1838.

1786. North America with the West Indies, by Saml. Dunn, London.

New map of the United States of North America &c. by Saml. Dunn, improved from the surveys of Captain Carver, London.

1788. History of Independence of United States, Wm Gordon, D. D., London.

1789. Travels through the Interior Part of America, by an Officer. London.

1790. Manuscript map of the Battles fought around the Forks of the Maumee River (now Fort Wayne Indiana) Oct. 1790, by Capt Jonathan Heart, 1st. Regt. U. S. Infantry.

1793. Topographical Description by Geo. Imlay, London.

1793. The American Universal Geography by Jedidiah Morse, A. M., Boston.

1794. The American Atlas, or a Geographical Description of the whole Continent of America, by the late Mr. Thomas Jeffreys, Geographer to the King, and others. London.

1794. History of the Missions of the United Brethren among the Indians in North America, by Loskiel, London.

1795. The United States Gazeteer, by Joseph Scott, Phil.

1796. Manuscript map of the Connecticut Western Reserve, made by Rev. John Heckewelder, Jan. 12.

1796. A new Universal Atlas, a complete collection of the most approved maps extant, corrected and augmented from the last edition of Danville and Robert, by Major James Rennel and other eminent Geographers; engraved by Thos. Kitchen, Senr and others. Thick folio. London.

1797. Manuscript map of Western Reserve, showing variation of compass, by Seth Pease. Manuscript map of Western Reserve that part east of the Cuyahoga being laid down from actual survey, by Seth Pease.

The same engraved. New Haven Ct.

1798. American Gazetteer, by Jedidiah Morse, D. D., 1797, Boston. 1798 London.

1800. Atlas, published by J. Stockdale, London.

1804. Map of the State of Ohio, by Rufus Putnam, Surveyor General of the United States in Journal of a Tour into the Territory N. W. of the Alleghany mountains by T. M. Harris, Boston, 1805.

1806. A manuscript map of the Ct. Land Company's Land west of the Cuyahoga, no date, but supposed 1806.

1806. Map of the Ssate of Ohio taken from the returns in the office of the Treasurer General by John F. Mansfield, Oct. 7. Philadelphia.

This is presumed to be the first engraved map of Ohio after its organization as a State.

1808. An engraved map of the Western Reserve, by Seth Pease and Abraham Tappan.

LATE MAPS DESIGNED TO SHOW EARLY GEOGRAPHY.

Aboriginal America East of the Mississippi, Vol. 3, Bancroft's History of United States p. 240. Boston, 1846.

1655. Location of Indian Tribes around Lakes Ontario, Erie, and Georgian Bay. Jesuits in North America, Francis Parkman. Boston, 1867.

1655. Map of the French, English, Dutch, Swedish, and Spanish Possessions or claims, Bancroft's History of the United States Vol. 2 p. 296, Boston 1855.

1745. Map of the French, English, and Spanish Possessions in North America. Hist. of Discovery &c., of Mississippi, by John W. Monette M. D., New York, 1846.

1763. Forts and Settlements in America. Conspiracy of Pontiac, by Francis Parkman, Boston, 1868.

1750 to 1780. Historical Map of the State of Ohio, showing the location of Ancient Earth works, and the country occupied by the principal Indian Tribes between 1750 and 1780, with their principal trails and war paths, by Col. Charles Whittlesey, Cleveland, 1872; published in Walling and Gray's New Topographical Atlas of Ohio, Philadelphia, 1872, and reprinted and published with a Topograpical and Historical Sketch, also by Col. Whittlesey, by O. W. Gray Philadelphia, 1872.

Historical and Chronological Map of the Territory of the United States, Northwest of the River Ohio, by John B. Dillon, and in his History of Indiana. Indianopolis, 1859.

Western Reserve and Northern Ohio

HISTORICAL SOCIETY.

CLEVELAND, O., JUNE, 1875.

NUMBER TWENTY-SIX.

SEVENTH ANNUAL MEETING, MAY 11, 1875.

The seventh annual meeting of this society was held at its rooms in the Savings Bank Building, Tuesday evening, May 11th, 1875:

The Secretary made the following

REPORT.

The past year has been in some respects a quiet one.

We commenced three years ago the raising of an endowment by the system of life memberships. At the annual meeting, a year ago, we were able to report $10,300. We are not able to report any increase, although a sum considerably larger could be used with great profit to the society and the public. $800 is a small sum with which to pay the ordinary expenses of such an enterprise.

The depression in financial circles has been such that the society should be content to hold its own.

Besides the ordinary addition to

THE MUSEUM

we should mention especially a collection of Babylonian and other antiques made by Wm. P. Fogg, Esq., in his recent trip around the world. A more full account of them is given in our Historical Tract No. 24.

Mr. Fogg's book, soon to be published, will be looked for with much interest.

Last July, Col. L. J. DuPre, of Memphis, Tennessee, presented a collection of vases and other curiosities, taken from the mounds on the Mississippi river near Memphis. This was a very handsome addition to the Museum of mementoes of a race whose relics are rare in Northern Ohio. They are described in tract No. 23, and some of them are described and engraved in an article by the accomplished donor in Harpers' Magazine for February, 1875.

The style of these vases compare favorably with those in the Fogg collection brought from the valley of the Euphrates.

THE VATICAN AND NAPOLEON MEDALS

are the liberal gift of a number of gentlemen. The Vatican are one hundred and seventy-six in number, and are exact copies in plaster of ancient cameos of emperors, warriors, philosophers and other celebrities The originals are in the Vatican at Rome.

The others, eighty-two, obverse and reverse, one hundred and sixty-four in all, form a complete set of casts of the Napoleon medallions.

These medals were collected with much pains by Dr. Theodatus Garlick, and were furnished by him to the Society at much less than their first cost.

A graceful gift made us by Dr. Garlick is a

BUST OF DR. JARED P. KIRTLAND.

It represents Dr. Kirtland as he appeared twenty-five years ago, the original cast having been taken then. It is said by those who knew the subject at that time to be a very faithful likeness. The bust is a labor of love, the work of Dr. Garlick's own hands.

An addition of considerable value to the

MANUSCRIPTS AND AUTOGRAPHS

of the society is contained in the papers of the late secretary, Mr. Goodman. He had an especial fondness for and remarkable talent in the pursuit of such property.

The manuscript collections of the

HISTORICAL SOCIETY OF ASHTABULA COUNTY,

have long been known to be of great value. The Society was one of the earliest in the State, being in active operation so early as 1841. We are happy to say that the gentlemen having charge of this valuable property have placed it in the rooms of our society. A more particular description of it will appear at a proper time.

SANITARY COMMISSION.

The voluminous books and papers of the Northwestern Branch of the Sanitary Commission are placed among our archives in a beautiful walnut case, indexed and labelled for future reference. This was done by the commission under the care of Mrs. Maynard, its secretary, and the work was completed during the past year.

BINDING.

During the past year there have been bound 175 volumes of newspapers, at the expense of a friend of the society.

About the time of our last annual meeting, Dr. John Ludlow, of Springfield, Clarke county, O., gave the society a scrap book containing a series of articles about the early settlement of Springfield, published by him in a local paper.

It was a thoughtful act easily done, preserving valuable matter where it is generally accessible, which might otherwise, in a few years be lost.

I mention it especially for the example. Editors, writers, or other gentlemen, in different counties, might easily furnish us much valuable history.

INDEXING AND CATALOGUEING.

The property of an institution like ours needs to be carefully and systematically indexed and catalogued, to show its value.

It is to be regretted that we cannot have more help in the field. Miss Seymour, our librarian, seems well adapted to the systematic care of such a room, and to take a hearty interest, above a money interest, in the welfare of the society. Her time is much occupied afternoons in the care of visitors. She has considerable copying to do for the society, and her forenoons are not sufficient for such work as needs doing.

President Whittlesey and Miss Seymour have done a great service in arranging in boxes and indexing manuscripts, and Miss Seymour is with courage and not much time endeavoring to make a catalogue of the library.

THE AUTOGRAPHS

of the society are many, and one of the board, Mr. Johnson, has kindly consented to give such time as he can to the arrangement of them.

His patient care during the past year has well arranged our very respectable coin collection, which, by the way, attracts much attention from our visitors.

EARLY MAPS.

Considerable attention has been given during the past year to the early maps of Ohio and the West, and the society has of its own and on deposit quite a large collection. A good many of them are described in tract No. 25.

THE PUBLICATIONS OF THE YEAR

have not been numerous. Nearly every thing that touches the public will affect such a society as ours. Even the Tilton-Beecher case has, by filling the newspaper columns to overflowing, crowded out our tracts.

Those of the year have been:

No. 21. Sixth annual meeting, May 1874. Report of President Whittlesey.

No. 22. Battle of Frenchtown, by Rev. Thomas P. Dudley. Major Isaac Craig on Lake Erie, 1782. White men as scalpers. Thomas Hutchins, Geographer General, United States, 1779, 1788, the last three articles being by Colonel Whittlesey.

No. 23. Relics of the Mound Builders, by the Secretary. Campaign of 1813 on the Ohio frontier. An address by Thomas Christian, communicated by Hon. Leslie Combs, of Kentucky.

No. 24. Recent donations by Mr. Fogg with his descriptions and remarks.

No. 25. Early maps of Ohio and the West, by the Secretary.

VISITORS.

The number of visitors registered is about 2,000, an increase of about one-fourth over the previous year.

DECEASE OF LIBRARIAN AND MEMBERS.

It is with feelings of great respect and affection that I speak of Mrs. Milford, for several years our librarian. She died on the 24th day of September last.

Judge John Barr, one of our original members, died on the 24th day of January, 1875.

We have also lost during the year by death Henry R. Mygatt, of Oxford, New York, a corresponding member.

Brief biographies accompany this reort.

C. C. BALDWIN, Secretary.

OBITUARY NOTICES.

Mrs. Miranda Milford, late Librarian.

In 1871 Mrs. Milford was appointed custodian of the museum, including books, maps, manuscripts, and relics, under the name of librarian. She continued in this position until her death, on the 26th of September, 1874.

The salary we had been able to pay her was so small that her services were substantially a donation to the public; but the occupation was one for which she was so thoroughly fitted, that it was to her a source of pleasure if not of profit.

Her love of order manifested itself at once in bringing our large collections into something like systematic arrangement; a labor that only those who were frequent visitors at the room will appreciate.

Having a special fondness for antiquities, she spent much more time here than was required of her. This pleasant room with, what were to her, pleasant surroundings, afforded an unfailing resource to one to whom health and most of the usual attractions of life were wanting.

She enjoyed the visits of young children to the Museum, to whom she became an instructress, exhibiting and explaining to them the many curious objects in our cases. They will never forget the interesting ideas acquired from her at this place.

With our limited number of shelves and cases for exhibition, it required not only patience to arrange such heterogeneous materials, but an artistic skill to give them an attractive appearance. This important work, and that of a general catalogue, was finished only in part, when she was called away.

Mrs. Milford *ne* McKay, was born in Caledonia, Livingston county, New York, March 12th, 1810; and was therefore sixty-four years of age at her death.

She was married in 1830, to the late Wm. Milford, Esq., of this city, who died in 1854. They settled at Cleveland in 1835, their home being socially, one of the most hospitable and attractive of those days.

Mr. Milford was a native of Ireland, naturalized about the time of their marriage, who became an active business man, and an enterprising character in regard to the public interests of our growing city. Since his death her health and pecuniary circumstances have been such as would have crushed, or at least greatly depressed, an ordinary character. But with an inquisitive mind, coupled with a resolute will and active personal habits, she maintained a cheerful spirit at all times.

In this community her friends were numerous, and her attachment to them was true and strong. She had besides a firm Christian faith, being a consistent member of Trinity Church from a very early period.

Judge John Barr, the First Honorary Member of this Society.

The father of Judge Barr was the Rev. Thomas Barr, one of the early settlers in Liberty, Trumbull county, Ohio, where he pursued the trade of a carpenter.

Under the influence of the Rev. Mr. Hughes, of Darlington, Pa., he was converted soon after the birth of John, and became a student in the Academy at Darlington.

He joined the Presbyterian Church with a view to become a minister, as soon as his education would permit of it. Being filled with the enthusiasm of an evangelist, he made such progress that he was soon licensed to preach.

Judge Barr was born at Liberty, in 1804. In 1810 his farther was settled at Euclid, Cuyahoga county, over the congregation of that place. Since that time to his death, Judge Barr was a resident of this county or city. From his early manhood he has taken a lively and practical interest in the local history of the Western Reserve. No one has done more to found, or to encourage pioneer associations. His personal recollections, embracing a period of sixty years, were remarkably clear and full. About 1825 he was made deputy sheriff of this county by the late James S. Clarke, who was a neighbor and a friend of the family. He occupied this position under the late Edward Baldwin, the successor of Mr. Clarke, and in 1830 was himself elected sheriff, to succeed Mr. Baldwin. During his time as sheriff he was obliged to make arrests of very desperate characters, who were carrying on a systematic course of counterfeiting in the valley of the Cuyahoga. One of them was captured in the streets of Columbus, by drawing a bag over his head. After serving two terms of two years each, he declined the office for the purpose of joining the law firm of Silliman & Stetson.

The office of Silliman, Stetson & Barr, was on the corner of Superior street and the Square, in Rouse's two-story frame building; represented in Parker's painting of 1839.

Cleveland had at this time begun to feel the impulses of a commercial city. All the members of this firm took a lively and practical interestin public affairs.

Mr. Silliman was the father-in-law of Stetson, and a brother-in-law to General Cass. Mr. Silliman died, the health of Mr. Stetson failed and the firm was broken up.

Judge Barr had a mild and courteous manner, rendering him popular with the masses. The reverses of 1837, especially his close financial relations with his enterprising friends the late James S. Clarke and Judge J. W. Willey, greatly impaired his fortune. These difficulties, to which was added impaired health, seemed to require of him a return to office.

He was first elected Judge of the Police Court, and resigned that office to become Clerk of the Court of Common Pleas.

In historical matters he had the lively interest of a native born actor in the early settlements.

For some years prior to 1845 he used his leisure time in putting on paper the tales of the pioneers with whom he came in contact during long service as sheriff or under-sheriff. An epitome of these memoranda, supplemented by his personal memories, relating especially to Cleveland, was published in the National Magazine at New York in 1845.

A much fuller statement of the pioneer times was given by him in the lectures before the Cleveland Lyceum in 1846. Free extracts from these lectures, the MSS. of which are in our collection, are to be found in the "Early History of Cleveland," published in 1867. These lectures and publications excited so much attention that he was able to bring into existence a County Pioneer Society, with branches in each township, which continued until the war of the rebellion occurred in 1861. He made an effort to resume it after the war, but so many of the early settlers had passed out of time that he did not succeed.

Most of his papers and memoranda are now in the possession of this society.

His death occurred suddenly while sitting in his chair on the 24th of January, 1875, being then seventy-one years of age. For many years, owing to a personal injury, he had ceased to take an active part in business or in public affairs. His mind and memory were unimpaired, but he had postponed making the record of his life, and its interesting associations too long. Very little of it can now be recovered.

Henry R. Mygatt.

Henry R. Mygatt, LL. D., of Oxford, Chenango county, New York, was a corresponding member of our society. He made us valuable contributions, and we had reason to think that he contemplated others of still greater interest.

He was born at Oxford in 1810, graduated at Union College in 1830, studied law with James Clapp, of Oxford, a man of high repute. He commenced practice in 1833, and labored most assiduously in a very extensive business until within a couple of years ago. The reports of of the highest courts of New York and of the

United States bear ample proofs of his professional ability.

His pursuit of the right, when a fact was in question or a legal principle involved, was untiring and defeat in the lower courts seemed only to nerve him to still higher efforts in the appellate ones.

The reputation he acquired and the rewards he received were fairly won. Industry, integrity and good judgment were the basis of his success. But better than this he was a man unexceptionable in private life, of great benevolence, confided in and beloved by all. He was a religious man, an ardent Episcopalian, but not a bigot and ready to help, munificently, any enterprise favorable to religion without reference to sect. He was a Christian gentleman. He died March 31st, 1875.

OFFICERS OF THE SOCIETY.

President—Charles Whittlesey.

Vice Presidents—J. H. Salisbury and E. Sterling.

Secretary—C. C. Baldwin.

Treasurer—S. Williamson.

Librarian—Miss C. M. Seymour.

Legal Trustees—William Bingham, J. P. Bishop, George Willey.

CURATORS ELECTIVE.

Term expires in 1876—Joseph Perkins, Charles Whittlesey, John W. Allen.

Term expires in 1877—J. H. A. Bone, Mrs. George Willey, H. N. Johnson.

Term expires in 1878—C. C. Baldwin, Mrs. Alleyne Maynard, C. T. Sherman.

PERMANENT CURATORS.

W. J. Boardman, James Barnett,
William Bingham, H. M. Chapin,
B. A. Stanard.

RESIDENT LIFE MEMBERS.

Horace Kelly, A. G. Colwell, C. C. Baldwin, L. E. Holden, H. B. Tuttle, A. W. Fairbanks, James J. Tracy, Geo. Willey, P. H. Babcock, Joseph Perkins, Abira Cobb, Alvah Bradley, S. V. Harkness, T. S. Beckwith, J. H. Wade, R. P. Wade, Dudley Baldwin, Colgate Hoyt, Wm. Chisholm, W. S. Streator, T. M. Kelley, Amos Townsend, Silas M. Stone, W. S. Chamberlain, Wm. S. C. Otis, J. H. Sargent, H. A. Harvey, Leonard Case, H. M. Chapin, Miss L. T. Guilford, Miss M. E. Ingersol, Miss S. L. Andrews, Alfred E. Buell, Douglas Perkins, Jacob B. Perkins, Jos. Perkins, Jr., L. Lewis Perkins, Peter M. Hitchcock, D. W. Cross, Cleve C. Hale, J. D. Rockefeller, Mrs. Fred Judson, C. F. Glasser, S. L. Mather, T. P. Handy, George Mygatt, R. P. Ranney, William Collins, O. A. Childs, J. P. Bishop, H. C. Blossom, H. P. Weddell, J. H. Devereaux, S. C. Baldwin, John Erwin, John W. Allen, John Todd, William J. Gordon, Charles O. Scott, E. P. Morgan, N. C. Baldwin, J. H. Salisbury, W. J. Boardman, Kirtland K. Cutter, H. N. Johnson, O. A. Brooks, W. P. Fogg.

LIFE MEMBERS NON-RESIDENTS.

Kent Jarvis, Jr., Massillon, Stark county, Ohio.

Judge Eben Newton, Canfield, Mahoning county, Ohio.

Judge W. G. Lane, Sandusky, Ohio.

Hon. R. W. Tayler, Youngstown, Ohio.

Hon. Wm. Henry Smith, Chicago, Illinois.

Benson J. Lossing, LL. D., Dover Plains, New York.

General L. V. Bierce, Akron, Ohio.

Theodatus Garlick, M. D., Bedford, Ohio.

Jared P. Kirtland, LL. D., Rockport, Ohio.

Hon. J. A. Garfield, Hiram, Ohio.

Col. George T. Perkins, Akron, Ohio.

Hon. James Monroe, Oberlin, Ohio.

Hon. O. H. Marshall, Buffalo, New York.

Wm. M. Darlington, Pittsburg, Pa.

Dr. Franklin B Hough, Lowville, Lewis county, New York.

M. M. Jones, Utica, New York.

L. C. Draper, Madison, Wisconsin.

J. D. Baldwin, Worcester, Mass.

I. A. Lapham, LL. D., Milwaukee, Wisconsin.

ANNUAL MEMBERS RESIDENT AND NON RESIDENT.

Lyman Little, M. C. Younglove, J. S. Kingsland, William Bingham, B. R. Beavis, W. C. B. Richardson, J. W. Tyler, Col. C. H. Carlton, U. S. A., A. Stone, Jr., L. Austin, Wm. L. Cutter, S. C. Green, Harvey Rice, B. A. Stanard, J. C. Saxton, Jas. W. Lee, Benj. Harrington, Chas. T. Sherman, John N. Frazee, James Barnett, Miss Mary C. Brayton, J. D. Cleveland.

Nathan H. Winslow, Buffalo, to 1882.

C. C. Carlton, Cleveland, 1878.

Chas. A. Otis, Cleveland, to 1884.

E. N. Winslow, G. G. Norris, Mrs. J. McDermott, J. Ireland, Dr. Henry Parker, Berea, O., C. J. Comstock, J. M. Jones, Elijah Bingham.

Western Reserve and Northern Ohio

HISTORICAL SOCIETY.

CLEVELAND, O., JULY, 1875.

NUMBER TWENTY-SEVEN.

NOTICE OF HISTORICAL AND PIONEER SOCIETIES IN OHIO.

By C. C. BALDWIN, Secretary.

For the purpose of preparing as full an account as possible of all associations in Ohio of an historical character, whether local or general, our Secretary in the fall of 1873, gave a wide circulation to the following note:

SIR: Will you be good enough to inform me, as soon as practicable, whether there is or has been an Historical or Pioneer Society in your town or county, and if so, when it was formed, its name or style, and who are or were its managers, what papers, books, relics or records are in existence and in whose custody? If there has been none, state that fact in your reply.

Yours, very truly,
C. C. BALDWIN,
Secretary W. R. & N. O. His. Socy.

In case no response was made by the officers of societies or when it was presumed none were in existence, recourse was had to the County Auditors, to Postmasters and other public men of the counties. The following list and notices is made up from replies to the circulars and from all other accessible sources of information.

The spirit of historical research has never been a prominent characteristic of Ohio. In Wisconsin, Minnesota and Iowa—States which were organized after Ohio had been so long in existence that its history began to be lost—the Legislatures have by an annual appropriation, given their historical societies the means which are necessary to every enterprise of the kind.

In 1851 an effort was made to induce the Legislature to assist in the publication of a selection of documents, relating to events prior to 1803, when the State government was organized. But the first and only money appropriated for historical purposes in this State was for the purchase of the St. Clair papers, in 1870, which are now in the State Library, which was procured through the exertions of this Society, with the hearty assistance of Governor Hayes.

STATE HISTORICAL SOCIETY.

On the first of February 1822, several prominent public men who were at Columbus secured the passage of an act to incorporate the "Historical Society of Ohio." The first meeting was to be held in Columbus, September 1822. In an address delivered before the Firelands Historical Society, June 1858, the late Hon. Elisha Whittlesey, stated that he went to Columbus "to participate in the proceedings of the society," that "Jeremiah Morrow, Duncan McArthur, "and many more worthy and distinguished pioneers were there, who assembled "in the evening, and a very interesting and "delightful conversation took place, about "the early settlements of different sections "of the State. Towards twelve o'clock, "he suggested to Governor Morrow that "it was well to call the meeting to order "and organize. The Governor concurred "but immediately reunited in conversation "with others, and somewhere between 2 "o'clock, and daylight, those who remained "in the room at that time separated without "an organization of the society."

The men of that day did not sufficiently value the record of their own deeds. The charter for this society is to be found in the local laws of the session of 1821-2, p. 47.

HISTORICAL AND PHILOSOPHICAL SOCIETY OF OHIO.

On the 11th day of February 1831 another act was passed by the Legislature, the first section of which provided that, Benjamin Tappen, and twenty-nine other persons, from various counties of the State, named in the act, with such other persons as might from time to time, become members, should be "a body corporate, and politic, by the name of the Historical and Philosophical Society of Ohio," with the usual provision as to the powers of corporations, it being carefully "Provided, moreover, that the funds of said corporation, shall not be used and appropriated to the purpose of *banking*." Among the corporators was Jared P. Kirtland, of Trumbull county, now of Cuyahoga county, gratefully remembered in the name of our sister society. "The Kirtland Society of Natural History," of Cleveland.

This society was organized, its by-laws being passed 31st December 1831, and the following officers elected:

President, Benjamin Tappen.

Vice Presidents, Ebenezer Lane, Rev. Wm. Preston.

Cor. Secretary, Alfred Kelly.

Rec. Secretary, P. B. Wilcox.

Treasurer, John W. Campbell.

Curators, Gustavus Swan, Edward King, S. P. Hildreth, B. G. Leonard, J. P. Kirtland.

An account of the succeeding officers will be found in "A Sketch of the Historical Societies of Ohio," made by James H. Perkins and G William Kendall, in 1849, a committee of the society, published in 1850, with the annual discourse delivered by Wm. D. Gallagher.

This society published in 1838, at Columbus, one volume printed by Cutler & Pilsbury, an octavo, of 111 pages, containing various addresses made before it, and other historical articles.

The President, Mr. Tappen, in the first annual address, alluded to the brief history of the first "Ohio Historical Society," and the purpose in the new society to collect material for the natural as well as the civil history of the State. The society, however, has always been strictly historical.

In 1839, part 2d of volume one of its transactions 1 vol. 8 vo. pp. 334, was published, a book of great value, containing Burnett's letters on the North West, since republished separately, and other valuable addresses and essays, one of them "On the Aborigines of the valley of the Ohio," by President Harrison.

Other addresses were separately published, among which was one delivered in 1841, by Col. Charles Whittlesey, relating to Lord Dunmore's expedition of 1774

The next meeting was held in 1844, and the next, which was in December, 1848, was adjourned to be held in the city of Cincinnati in February, 1849, when the members of the "Cincinnati Historical Society" were elected members, and a donation of the property of that society was accepted.

The object of this measure was to transfer the society from the capital to Cincinnati. Up to that time it had neither museum, library or funds. During most of the time annual addresses had been delivered at Columbus, during the session of the Legislature —some of which are of great value.

The officers of the society at its new quarters in 1849 were: President, Wm. D. Gallagher: Vice Presidents, James H. Perkins, Edward D. Mansfield, Charles Whittlesey. and the usual other officers including five Curators.

The society, to quote the report of 1849, now had a library of respectable size (4,000 volumes) and some very rare and valuable historical material, consisting of books, maps, charts, and sketches. A very valuable work entitled "Pioneer History," being an account of the first examination of the Ohio valley, and the early settlement of the Northwest Territory, by S. P. Hildreth, 8-vo. pp. 528, Cincinnati, H. W. Derby & Co, was published in 1848, under the superintendence of the Society, as the first volume of its new transactions. It was delivered in sheets to the Society, and issued by it in 1849; as appears from a Cincinnati paper of the time.

With it was given to the society, the manuscript of "Biographical and Historical memories of the early pioneers, settlers of Ohio, with narratives of incidents, &c." by the same author. This was published in 1852, with an appendix containing the journal of Col. R. J. Meigs, by H. W. Derby & Co., Cincinnati, 1 vol. 8-vo. pp. 539 under the auspices of the Ohio Historical Society.

The society flourished for a few years and finally became dormant. Its books and pamphlets were deposited in the Public Library of Cincinnati, and shared its fortune and misfortune until the society was re-organized on the 7th of December. 1868, and reclaimed its own room, the books then numbering about eight hundred, the pamphlets sixteen hundred.

The officers since that time have been:

Presidents — Robert Buchanan, 1868–9; Gen. M. F. Force, since December, 1869.

Vice Presidents—George Graham, Stanley Matthews, 1868–9; George Graham, S. E. Wright, 1869–'70; S. E. Wright, W. H. Muzzey, since December, 1870.

Corresponding Secretaries—Gen. M. F. Force, 1868–9; L. E. Mills, 1869–'72; Hon. R. B. Hayes, 1872–3; Robert Clarke, 1873–4.

Recording Secretaries — Julius Dexter, 1868–9; Horatio Wood, 1869–'74.

Librarians—John M. Newton, 1868–9; Julius Dexter, 1869–'74.

Part 1st, volume 1st, of the Society's publications, issued in 1838, had become very scarce, only three copies being known, none of which were in the library of the Society itself. In 1872 it was republished by the Society, and in 1873 the Society published, through Robert Clarke, in Cincinnati, a very handsome, large octavo volume, pp. 160, containing "Journal and Letters of Col. John May, of Boston, relating to two journeys to the Ohio country in 1788 and '89," accompanied by a biographical sketch and notes. This volume is offered by the Society, as the commencement of a new series.

The Society has in its varied fortunes been of great value to the State, and has in its publications preserved much that would now be lost were it not for its efforts. Its indirect influence upon individuals, and their contributions to the history of our State has been not less valuable. It has now an endowment of $8,650, including furniture, 4,645 books, and 13,066 pamphlets, and a small museum of relics of Indians and Mound Builders.

FIRELANDS HISTORICAL SOCIETY.

The next society, extending over more than one county, was "Firelands Historical Society," organized at Norwalk, Huron county, the 20th May, 1857.

Its objects are stated in its constitution to be "to collect and preserve in proper form the facts constituting the full history of the "Fire Lands," also to obtain and preserve an authentic and general statement of their resources and productions of all kinds." At the second meeting, 17th June, 1857, the following officers were elected:

President—Platt Benedict.

Five Vice Presidents.

Treasurer—Charles A. Preston.

Recording Secretary—Phillip N. Schuyler.

Corresponding Secretaries—F. D. Parish, G. T. Stewart.

Committees were appointed for each township of the Firelands.

The society commenced at once the publication of the "Fireland's Pioneer," and has collected and published in that form a large quantity of valuable addresses, township history, personal reminiscences, and other interesting matter.

The public interest in this society and its meetings has been greater than any other of this State. In 1861 it had had fourteen quarterly general assemblies, without missing one. It has collected a museum of relics and other articles of historic and antiquarian value in its hall at Norwalk. Mr Benedict continued to be its President until 25th October, 1866, when he died, aged 91 years, 7 months and 7 days. He was succeeded by Z. Phillips. In 1838 the Corresponding Secretaries were D. H. Pease and P. N. Schuyler. From 1869 to 1875 the Corresponding Secretaries were Hon. F. D. Parish, Sandusky; P. N. Schuyler, Norwalk. The Recording Secretary, 1875, is C. E. Carrington, of Norwalk.

The last publication is volume eleven, October, 1874, edited by Hon. G. T. Stewart, of Norwalk.

W. R. AND N. O. HISTORICAL SOCIETY.

The Western Reserve and Northern Ohio Historical Society has its rooms at Cleveland, Cuyahoga county. It was planned in 1866, but no public steps were taken for its organization until the 11th of April, 1867, when several gentlemen met in the rooms of the Library Association, and the society was organized 28th of May, 1867. Its officers first elected were:

President—Col. Chas. Whittlesey.

Vice President—M. B. Scott.

Secretary—J. C. Buell.

Treasurer—A. K. Spencer.

Curators for one year, J. C. Buell and H. A. Smith; for two years, C. C. Baldwin, M B. Scott; for three years, Joseph Perkins and Charles Whittlesey.

Mr. Buell never acted as Secretary, and upon his resignation C. C. Baldwin was elected to the place until the 19th of October, 1868, when he resigned, and A. T. Goodman was elected.

Under an arrangement with the Cleveland "Society for Savings" and the Cleveland Library Association, the Historical Society has the perpetual use, at a low rent, of the third floor of a stone fire-proof building, erected by the Society for Savings, fronting the Public Square, near the Postoffice.

The objects of the Society are "to discover, procure, and preserve whatever relates to the history, biography, genealogy, antiquities, and statistics of the Western Reserve, State of Ohio, and the Northwest." Its purposes include everything relating to western history. It has been very successful for its age and has accumulated a very valuable property. It had at its annual meeting, 12th of May, 1874, 2,424 bound volumes, 3,385 pamphlets, 645 bound volumes of newspapers, 1,552 maps. It has also a large number of manuscripts, many of them of great value, and a fine collection of relics of the Mound Builders and Indians, relics of Bradstreet's expedition of 1764, Japanese and other curiosities. It has also a collection of copies of ancient rock inscriptions, made by painting the artificial chiselings on the rock and pressing a cloth into them. Its library includes the most valuable and expensive books upon archæology, including Lord Kingsborough's Antiquities of Mexico.

In June, 1869, the Society made the first movement in the matter of the purchase of the papers of General Arthur St. Clair, the first Governor of the Northwestern Territory, by furnishing the funds to send its Secretary, the late Alfred T. Goodman, to examine those papers then in Kansas.

It has now (1875) a fair representation of the stone implements of the primitive races in Ohio and the West. Also some vases, pottery and copper tools of the Mound Builders, with relics from the valley of the Euphrates recently donated by W. P. Fogg, Esq., of this city, copies of the Vatican and Napoleon medals, and a good beginning on a collection of coins, and autographs. Our maps of the West of early date are certainly worthy the attention of geographers. Our endowment fund is about $10,000.

COUNTY AND TOWN SOCIETIES.

Adams county—None, (Dec. 25, 1873.)

Allen county—None, (Oct. 23, 1873.)

Ashland county—None, (Oct. 13, 1873.) The history of the county has been written by H. S. Knapp, entitled a History of the Pioneer and Modern Times of Ashland County, Ohio. Philadelphia: 1863. 1 vol. 8 mo., pp. 550. Another by Geo. W. Hill, M. D., is now publishing in the "Ashland Press," which is also expected to be put in book form.

Ashtabula county, Jefferson, county seat.—The Historical Society of Ashtabula county, Ohio, one of the earlies in the State, was in active operation as early as 1841, and Mr. Howe in his "Historical Collections," p. 37, acknowledges his obligation to it. It made a large and very valuable collection of manuscripts and some relics. The cabinet is at Jefferson, and a portion of the papers have been published recently in the Geneva Times, by Warren P. Spencer, the editor, who in 1853-4, was the last secretary of the society. Mr. Platt R. Spencer, celebrated as a penman, was for a long time secretary of the society, and the society owe him much for copying, collecting and arranging manuscript. The society is now dormant. Its remaining manuscripts, still of great value, were, in July, 1874, in charge of Hon. J. A. Giddings, Wm. C. Howells, J. A. Howells, W. P. Spencer, and H. R. Gaylord. These gentlemen at that time placed them in care of the Western Reserve and Northern Ohio Historical Society in its fire-proof room in Cleveland.

Athens county, Athens, county seat.—The "Athens County Pioneer Association," was organized 26th of December, 1868, and has held regular meetings till this time (October 1873.) The officers in October, 1873, were John Ballard, President; A. B. Waller, Secretary. It has a collection of biographies, early history, and books. The history of the county has been written by Charles M. Walker and published in a handsome octavo volume, pp. 600, by Robert Clarke & Co., Cincinnati, Ohio, 1869.

Auglaize—None, (Oct. 14th, 1873.)

Belmont—Never any, (Dec. 15th, 1873.) Sketches of church history have bean published in pamphlets, by Rev. R. Alexander, of St. Clairsville, and Rev. Dr. Crawford, of Moorfield.

Brown County—None, (Jan., 1874.)

Butler County, Hamilton, county seat—A Pioneer Association was formed in this county about 1869. The officers are John M. Milliken, Fergus Anderson, Dr. Falconer and H. S. Earheart. The society has no extensive collections. The biographies of the most prominent pioneers have been written by the late James McBride, of Hamilton, and published by Robert Clark & Co., of Cincinnati, Ohio. "Pioneer Biographies, by James McBride; Vol. I., 8vo., pp. 352, in 1869; Vol. II., 8vo., pp. 288, 1870."

Carrol County—None, (Jan., 1874.)

Champaign county, Urbana, county seat—"The Western Pioneer Association," formed in 1870, composed of old settlers of Champaign and Logan counties, Sept. 7, 1871, met at Bellefontaine. A committee was appointed to collect, arrange and prepare the material for a pioneer history of these counties; Committee, Dr. B. S. Brown, Dr. Thomas Cowgill and Joshua Antrim. The work is being published as "Antrim's History," ($3 per vol., 400 to 500 pp.) Mr. Antrim's address is East Liberty, Logan Co., O.

The society has records, relics, &c., in the custody of its secretary, T. S. McFarland, of Concord, Champaign county. President, J. M. Glover, of West Liberty, Ohio.

Clark county, Springfield—"The Clark County Pioneer Society" was organized on the 7th of June, 1870, and had monthly meetings for two years, but has ceased to meet regularly; A. Bassett, President; John Ludlow, Vice President; James S. Austin, Treasurer. It has no property. Papers have been published by members of the society, furnishing sketches of Springfield and Clarke county from 1796 to 1828. This society is called in vol. 9 of the Fireland Pioneer, "The Mad River Valley Pioneer and Historical Association." The address delivered at its organization, 2d of May, 1870, is contained in that volume. It has held no meeting for some years. (1874.)

Clermont county, Batavia, April 3d, 1874. —Has never had a society. Some years ago

R. W. Clarke, Esq., commenced a history the county, which was interrupted by his death about 1872.

Clinton county—None, October 27th, 1873.

Columbiana county—The Columbiana Pioneer Association and Historical Society was organized in 1870. It holds annual meetings in September with a dinner and celebration.

President—H. H. Gregg, New Lisbon.

Vice President—W. D. Hinkle, Salem.

Secretary—P. C. Young, New Lisbon.

Treasurer—John Frost, New Lisbon.

Has published several old newspaper records; biographies, &c.

Coshocton county—Never any, (Oct. 1st, 1873.)

Crawford county—A society called the "Crawford County Pioneer Society" was attempted some years ago. Its existence was so ephemeral that it did nothing whatever. (Oct. 13, 1873.)

Cuyahoga County, Cleveland—The "Historical Society of Cuyahoga County," was founded in 1857, and the organization was completed 15th February 1858. The officers were: President, Leonard Case, with a Vice President in every town in the county; John Barr, Secretary; a committee was appointed for each township to preserve the local history; of which committee the Vice President for that township, was the chairman. A grand picnic was held at Newburg, 20th October, 1858, at which it is estimated five thousand persons were present. Hon. R. P. Spalding, of Cleveland, delivered the address. The celebration was very successful. The 13th June, 1860, a second celebration was held in the same town, which was in every way as successful as the first. Col. Charles Whittlesey, of Cleveland, delivered the address. The Rebellion broke up the association. An attempt was made to revive it in 1870, which utterly failed. The papers of the society are in the possession of the Western Reserve & Northern Ohio Historical Society. The local history of most of the towns was presented to the society and published in the Cleveland papers.

Darke county, Greenville—"Darke County Pioneer Association" organized 4th July 1871.

President—John S. Hiller.

Secretary– D. M. Stephenson.

Corresponding Secretary—H. K. McConnell, Judge John Wharry.

No collections beyond a few articles of local value (May 13th, 1874.)

Defiance county, no society (Oct. 13th, 1873)—H. S. Knapp has recently published "A History of the Maumee Valley," at the Blade Office, Toledo, which includes this county.

Delaware county—There is a pioneer society in this county organized July 1870.

President—E C. Vining.

Secretary—James McCoy.

The society has collected no relics or papers of especial value.

Erie county—No society, Oct. 1873.

Fairfield county—None, May 17th, 1874.

Fayette county—Has a Pioneer Society, which collects relics, facts, books, &c.

Adam Glaze, President, Washington C. H. I have failed to learn more (Dec. 16, 1873.)

Franklin county, Columbus—"The Pioneer Association of Franklin County," was organized June 2d, 1866. Officers in 1873:

J. E. St. Clair, President.

Col. G. S. Innis, Secretary.

Have records of proceedings and a number of historical sketches.

The history of Franklin county has been written by William F. Martin, in an 8 vo. volume, pp 450, published 1858, at Columbus, O. A history of Columbus, by Jacob H. Strider, 1 vol. 8 vo., pp 584, 1873, Columbus.

Fulton county—None (Oct. 13th, 1873.)

Gallia county—None (Oct. 23d, 1873.)

Geauga county—The Historical Society of this county was formed 16th September, 1873.

It meets annually at Burton, on 10th of September, and at other times on call.

Its President is Hon. Lester Taylor, of Chardon.

Vice Presidents—One for each township.

Secretary—S. Clapp, Huntsburg.

Corresponding Secretary—R. N. Ford, Burton. And a Board of Managers.

Its object is to collect the history of the pioneers and relics.

General J. A. Garfield delivered an able address on the discovery and ownership of the Northwestern Territory and settlement of the Western Reserve, which has been published in the county and other papers, also by this Society in pamphlet form.

The history of many of the townships has been written by General Pierce, and published in the newspapers.

Greene county—None, (Oct. 13th, 1873.)

Guernsey county—None, (Oct. 15th, 1873.)

Hamilton county—"The Cincinnati Historical Society" was organized in August, 1844. Its officers were then:

President—Rev. James H. Perkins.

Vice Presidents—John P. Foote, Wm. D. Gallagher.

Recording Secretary—E. P. Norton.

Treasurer—R. Buchanan.

Librarian—A. Randall.

It published in 1845 No. 1 of its annuals, containing its constitution, a circular, and an address by D. K. Este.

In 1847, Dr. Hildreth presented to it the manuscript of his "Pioneer History." In 1848 its President, Vice Presidents and Secretary were the same as those of the Ohio Historical and Philosophical Society for 1849. The members then voted to donate their property to the other, the members of this society having been elected members of the other. See account of the Ohio Historical and Philosophical Society herein.

"The Cincinnati Pioneer Association" was organized 23d November 1856, its members all persons who resided in Ohio, on or before July 4,1812, which time is since extended to July 1815. Its officers in 1873 were:

Pres. Hon. David K. Este.

Vice President, Nicholas Gorham.

Cor. Sec., Jeremiah M. Clark.

Rec. Sec., John D. Caldwell.

Its proceedings appear in "the Cincinnati Pioneer." published from time to time by its Recording Secretary. Its last celebration which has attracted my notice was held April 7, 1874.

Hancock county—None (Oct. 14, 1873.)

Harrison county—None (Oct. 21, 1873.)

Hardin county—Kenton.

The Hardin county Pioneer Association, was organized 9th June 1868.

Judge Hugh Stetson, President.

A. W. Newman, M. D. Secretary. Its members are all citizens immigrating prior to January 1840. Meetings second Saturday of June annually. Has books, records, and sketches of pioneer life.

Henry county—None (Oct. 10, 1873.)

Highland county—None (Dec. 16, 1873.)

Hocking county—None (Dec. 20, 1873.)

Holmes county—None.

Huron County, Norwalk—"The Historical and Geological Society of Norwalk Seminary was organized in 1842, to collect facts and incidents, relative to the early history of Ohio."

President—Rev. A. Wilson.

Secretary—H. Dwight.

It made a collection of geological specimens, but nothing historical. It lived but a short time.

For the "Fireland's Pioneer Association," which has its headquarters at Norwalk, see the account of general societies at the beginning of this paper.

Jackson County—None, (Dec. 24th, 1873.)

Jefferson County—None. There was at Steubenville for a time a society called "The Triangle," composed of three ministers, three doctors, and three lawyers, who met weekly to investigate literary, scientific, and historical questions. It had no collections, but kept a record.

Knox County—None. "The History of Knox County," from 1778 to 1862, inclusive, has been written by A. Banning Norton, of Mount Vernon, Ohio. 8vo., pp. 424.; Columbus, O.

Lake County—None. (Oct. 11, 1873.)

Lawrence county—None (October 10th, 1873.)

Licking county—Newark.—The Licking County Pioneer, Historical and Antiquarian Society organized May 1867. From the annual report made July 4th, 1873 and published in the Newark American of 11th July, 1873, it appears that the society has a library of 148 volumes, 127 pamphlets, and hundreds of newspapers and newspaper slips. Also numerous manuscripts, and a collection of relics of the mound builders, Indians, Revolutionary times and pioneers in great variety. The society has published eight pamphlets, devoted to the history of the county, and 107 pioneer papers, describing the works of the mound builders, the county Indian history, sketches of the the early settlers and pioneer history. It has been conducted with zeal and efficiency, and has in its possession the material for a systematic, particular, and full history of the county.

It seems exceedingly desirable that the society should publish in book form the substance of their papers. Pamphlets and and newspaper slips are riches that soon take wings and fly away. An account of the history of the county cannot but interest the entire State. An account of the works of the mound builders in that county which are so celebrated, would interest the world.

Enough appears in the report of the Secretary to show that the book would be one of romantic interest.

During the year ending 4th of July, 1873, the society lost by death Hon. Wm. Stanberry and Dr. J. N. Wilson, President and Vice President of the society from 1867 to the time of their deaths.

The officers elected 4th of July, 1873, for the ensuing year were:

President—P. N. O'Barron.

Vice Presidents—T. J. Anderson, M. M. Munson, Daniel Torry.

Corresponding Secretary—C. B. Giffin.

Recording Secretary—Isaac Smucker.

Treasurer—Enoch Wilson.

Chaplain—Rev. C. Springer.

Logan county—There is a pioneer society for this and Champaign county jointly, a more full account of which will be found under Champaign county. Its President, J. M. Glover, resides at West Liberty, in Logan county.

Lorain county—In 1857 a Pioneer Association was formed, which in the fall of 1859, had a large meeting and an address.

It had an annual address on the 4th of July of each year, until 1861, when the war stopped it. The meetings were large and interesting, and addresses good. The late Dr. Betts of Brownhelm was President.

The address of 1860 by Gen. L. V. Bierce is published in Fireland's Pioneer for 1861.

Lucas county, Toledo—The "Toledo Historical and Geographical Society" was organized June 13th, 1871. It has a small library, and some relics. Officers Oct. 10th,'73.

President—E. H Fitch.

Vice President—H. M. Bacon.

Treasurer—Dr. J. T. Woods.

The President was Secretary pro tem.

Madison county—None, (Oct. 14th, 1873.))

Mahoning county—None, (Dec. 6th, 1873.)

The Hon. Elisha Whittiesey and Hon. Frederick Wadsworth, both now deceased, prepared two manuscript volumes of the local history and biography of this County.

Marion county—None, (Oct. 17th, 1873.)

Medina county—None.

"The Pioneer History of Medina county," appears in a 12-mo vol. pp. 221, published in Medina in 1861, by the author, N. B. Northrop, of that place.

Meigs County—None, (Oct. 14th, 1873.)

Mercer County—None, (Oct. 24th, 1873,) but some talk of organizing one.

Miami County—None, (Oct. 21st, 1873.)

Monroe County—None, (Oct 15th, 1873.)

Montgomery County, Dayton—"The Montgomery County Pioneer Association," was organized November, 1867. George B. Holt, now deceased, was its President. Its President in October, 1873, was Henry L. Brown. It has no collection of books or papers except such records as are usual in such societies. It was visited by the Cincinnati Pioneers in September, 1873. The very interesting addresses are to be found in "Cincinnati Pioneer," No. 2, published by John D. Caldwell, Secretary of the Cincinnati Society.

Morgan County—None, (Dec. 18, 1873.)

Morrow County—None, (Nov. 3d, 1873.)

Muskingum County—None, (Oct.20th,'73.)

Noble County—None, (Oct. 26th, 1873.)

Ottawa County—None. (Oct. 15th, 1873.)

Paulding County—None,'(Oct. 15th, 1873.)

Perry County—None, (1873.)

Pickaway County, Circleville—The "Pickaway County Historical and Pioneer Association" was formed January, 1873.

President—Dr Wayne Griswold, deceased.

Secretary—Alfred Williams.

It has no library or relics. There was published at Circleville in 1873, a very interesting and pertinent address delivered by its secretary. 8 mo. 14 pp.

The objects of the society are stated to be: 1st. The collection of material for the historian. 2d. The promotion of social intercourse among the pioneers of the county.

Pike county—None, (April 9, 1874.

Portage county—None, Oct. 18, 1873.

General L. V. Bierce, of Akron, has written the history of all the townships of the county which has been published in the county papers.

Preble county—The Pioneer Association of Preble county was formed about 1868, and many sketches and reminiscences were collected.

President—Henry Kerling.

Secretary—Jesse B. Stephens.

The president, secretary, and many old settlers died, and the society ceased to exist.

A. Haines, Sr., of Eaton, has written an outline sketch of the early courts,of the early settlers of the township, of mound builders, &c., published in the county papers.

Putnam county—None, (Dec. 16, 1873.)

Richland county, Mansfield—"Richland County Historical Society," organized 21st October, 1869.

President—Alexander C. Welch.

A Vice President for each township.

Recorder—Henry C. Hedges.

Secretary—General R. Brinkerhoff.

The society has no general collection. General Brinkerhoff has published from time to time in the county papers sketches of its history, which should be published in more permanent form.

Ross county, Chillicothe—The Logan Historical Society was formed 28th of July, 1841.

President—Felix Renick.

Secretary—John S. Williams.

In 1849, Messrs. James H. Perkins and George Kendall state that an attempt was then being made to revive the society. It seems to have been unsuccessful. The existence of the society led to the following well known and valuable publication: The American Pioneer, a monthly periodical devoted to the objects of the Logan Historical Society, edited and published by John S. Williams. It commenced January, 1842, the last number, closing the second volume, was issued October, 1843.

"The Pioneer History of Ross County, Ohio," is a collection of township and biographical sketches of Isaac J. Finley and Rufus Putnam. 1 vol., 8vo., pp. 148. Cincinnati. 1871.

Sandusky county—Preliminary steps, but 13th Dec. 1873 organization not perfected, says Rev. E. Bushnell, &c.

Gov. R. B. Hayes, Fremont 13th Dec. 1873,expects the society to organize in June.

Have preserved various addresses and newspaper articles.

Scioto county—"The Pioneer Association of the State of Ohio," was organized 24th April 1873.

President, Eli Glover,

Secretary, Thomas S. Hall.

Treasurer, Col. R. Kinney.

No papers except a muster roll, 1809 to 1812, in the hands of the President.

Seneca county, Tiffin—"Seneca county Pioneer and Historical Society," Officers in 1870:

President, Dr. Henry Kuhn.

Sec. and Biographer, W. Lang.

Treasurer, Lyman White.

Some account of the society will be found in Knapp's History of the Maumee valley, pp. 493 to 497.

"The History of Seneca county," by Consul W. Butterfield, now of Bucyrus, Ohio, 1875 of Madison, Wisconsin, was published in Sandusky in 1848, in a 12 mo. volume pp. 252. The author of that book has written "Crawford's Campaign against Sandusky, in 1782," 1 mo. 8 vo. pp. 403, published 1873 by Robert Clarke & Co., at Cincinnati.

Shelby county—None.

Stark county—None.

Summit county—None for the county.

An annual Pioneer picnic is held 10th September of each year, in Bath township, including pioneers of adjoining towns in Summit and Medina counties.

The Tallmadge Historical Society, in the township of that name, is collecting a very complete history of the township; was organized 24th March 1858, and the following officers were chosen:

President—Amos Seward.

Vice President—Sidney Edgarton.

Recording Secretary—L. C. Walton.

Corresponding Secretary—Andrew Fenn

Treasurer—L V. Bierce, Jr.

Executive Committee—J. O. Wolcutt and C. C. Bronson.

The society has 235 pages of records and a large amount of historical matter. Some of their proceedings have been published in newspapers and the semi-centennial proceedings of June, 1857, in pamphlet form. The history of the county has been published by General L. V. Bierce, of Akron, 1 vol., 12 mo., pp 157; and the history of Tallmadge, by Colonel Charles Whittlesey, 1842.

Trumbull County—None (1874.)

Tuscarawas county—None (Oct. 23, 1873.)

Union county—None (Dec, 13, 1873), but says my informant, the Rev. W. G. March, of Marysville,—"much needed."

Van Vert County—none 28th October, 1873. One was attempted 4th July, 1872, but the organization was not completed. It is contemplated to form one.

Vinton County—none (December 17th, 73)

Warren County—none (December 15th, 1873.)

Washington County—Marietta.—The Marietta Historical Association was formed 24th November, 1841, "expecting," says Hon. D. K. Lete in his address before referred to, "a hope to do its share in the preparation of Western History." The officers according to to the Cincinnati report, were:

President—Ephraim Cutler.

Vice President—Arius Nye.

Corresponding Secretary—Caleb Emerson.

Recording Secretary—Arius S. Nye.

Curators—William R. Putnam, John Mills, A. T. Nye.

It made collections embracing 150 volumes, some volumes of old newspapers, and manuscripts. It was apparently expected to make some publications, but the society long ago disbanded, and its collections are scattered.

"The Pioneer Association of Washington county, Ohio," was organized 22d February, 1869—Objects, social intercourse, personal narratives, and any other information valuable to the history of the county or State.

At the annual meeting 7th April, 1874, the following officers were elected:

President—Wm. R Putnam, (grandson of Gen. Rufus Putnam.)

Vice President—E. S. McIntosh.

Secretary—Wm. F. Curtis.

Corresponding Secretary—A. T. Nye, with a treasurer and an executive committee.

Wayne county, Wooster—The Wooster Historical Society was organized at the Court House, in a citizens meeting Nov. 19th, 1875, and the following were elected:

President—Constant Lake.

Vice President—John McClellan.

Treasurer—S. R. Bonewitz.

Recording Secretary—Benjamin Eason.

Corresponding Secretary—Thomas Woodland, with an executive committee and an historian, Benjamin Douglass.

Its specific purpose is to collect all suitable material for, and publish in a book form a complete history of the county. Its collections are, in February, 1874, about complete, and the manuscript is nearly ready for the publisher.

Benjamin Eason (February 1874) the recording secretary, gives me the foregoing information.

Williams county—There was an old settlers association formed in 1860 or 1861. The war coming on the association was dropped.

Wood county—None.

Wyandot county—None.

Western Reserve and Northern Ohio HISTORICAL SOCIETY.

CLEVELAND, O., OCTOBER, 1875.

NUMBER TWENTY-EIGHT.

WAR OF 1812 CORRESPONDENCE—SELECTION NO. 8.

GENERAL HULL TO CAPTAIN CAMPBELL.

SANDWICH, Upper Canada, }
July 15, 1812. }

SIR: Immediately on the receipt of this letter you will march your company, with that of Captain Roland, to Detroit. When you arrive at the foot of the Rapids you will relieve the officer commanding the blockhouse there and his party, by placing one subaltern, two sergeants, two corporals and sixteen privates at that post, who will be supplied with provisions by the contractor's agent at the foot of the Rapids, and must report to me from time to time. An equal proportion of this relief will be furnished from each of your companies, according to their strength.

I am your ob't serv't,
W. HULL, B. Gen.

Captain CAMPBELL.

CAPITULATION OF GENERAL HULL.

[From the papers of the late Col. Wm. Rayen, of Youngstown, Ohio.]

This document has been often published, but to many of the present generation it will be new. Those of that period who survive will, on reading it, bring back the memory of the anguish it carried to every log cabin of the frontier. It caused a general storm of indignation against Hull throughout the United States. Subsequent evidence and a court of inquiry did not much improve the General's case, except to relieve him from the charge of treason.

HEADQUARTERS AT DETROIT, AUG. 16, 1812.
GENERAL ORDERS.

It is with pain and anxiety that Brigadier General Hull announces to the Northwestern Army, that he has been compelled from a view of duty, to agree to the following articles of capitulation:

CAMP AT DETROIT, 16 AUG. 1812.

Capitulation for the surrender of Fort Detroit, entered into between Major-General Brock, commanding His Brittanick Majesty's forces on the one part, and Brigadier General Hull, commanding the Northwestern Army of the United States on the other part.

Art. 1. Fort Detroit with all the troops, regular as well as militia, will be immediately delivered up to the British forces under command of Major-General Brock, and will be considered as prisoners of war with the exception of such of the militia of the Michigan Territory, who have not joined the army.

Art. 2. All public stores, arms, and all public documents, including every thing else of a public nature, will be immediately given up.

Art. 3. Private persons and property of every description will be respected.

Art. 4. His excellency, Brigadier-General Hull, having expressed a desire that a detachment from the State of Ohio on its way to join the army, as well as one sent from Fort Detroit under the command of Colonel McArthur, should be included in the above capitulation. It is accordingly agreed to. It is to be understood that such part of the Ohio militia as have not joined the army will be permitted to return to their homes, on condition that they will not serve during the war. Their arms, however, will be delivered up, it belonging to the public.

ART. 5. The garrison will march out at twelve o'clock this day, and the British forces will take immediate possession of the fort.

J. M. DONALD,
Lieut. Col. Mil. A. D. C.
J. B. G. GREGG,
Maj. A. D. C.

Approved—W. HULL, Brig. Gen'l Commanding the N. W. Army.

JAMES MILLER,
Lieut. Col. 5th U. S. Infantry.
E. BRUSH,
Col. 1st Reg. Michigan Militia.

Approved—ISAAC BROCK, Major General.

The army this day, at twelve o'clock will march out of the East Gate, where they will stack their arms, and will then be subject to the articles of capitulation.

W. HULL, Brig. General.

ELIJAH HANKS TO EPRHRAIM ROOT, SECRETARY OF THE LAND COMPANY,

DEAR FRIEND: I have a moment's opportunity to write a line to you to let you know something of our present situation in this country. You have been informed that our frontiers are invaded by the British and Indians, and that part of our militia are gone out to Huron in order to keep the savages from approaching any nearer; and your son James was with our army. A number of our men were on a scout and discovered a party of Indians; they did not discover our scout; who returned to our main body. A number, to the amount of one hundred, were sent immediately to attack the savages, but their number was too great; they killed and wounded the greatest part of our men.

Among those that were killed was your son;* he, with a number more, ran into a small hut in order to have a better chance to attack their enemy, but the savages soon surrounded the hut and massacred the whole, which took place the 27th of September last. This may not be correct, but I received my information from the express last evening, which came direct from the army.

Sir, it appears as if it was determined that our thin settlements should defend the whole of our western frontiers when the militia of the Eastern states can be at home in order to defend themselves, when there is no enemy perhaps within five hundred miles of them, except what are among themselves. It is very surprising to me to see how this war has been carried on.

May the Lord deliver us from Burrs, Hulls, and savages.

I must close for I expect the mail every moment.

I expected to have seen you before this time but I wish to hear from you by letter.

Sir, since the above I have had further information concerning the battle your son was in. Although the death of your son will strike the most tender cords of your heart, yet you may have this to say in your mournful hours that he fought manfully for his country; for when every man had left the ground that was able, except James, he was seen to kill a number of the savages, for he was surrounded. It was thought by those that made their escape that he killed more than twenty, for every jump he made, he killed an Indian with his bayonet. I believe it to be a mistake that he got into a log hut.

Two of my young men are out there and I do not know but they have shared the same fate.

This country has been in a state of alarm ever since Hull sold his army In haste,

ELIJAH HANKS.

MADISON, Geauga Co., O., Oct. 1, 1812.

MAJOR GEORGE TOD TO GEN. MILLER.

This paper is apparently a copy, the address and the signature wanting.

"RECRUITING RENDEZVOUS,
ZANESVILLE, O., July, 29, 1812.

Sir:—By my weekly report ending with the 20th inst and herewith transmitted, it may appear as if those names were all the officers in the district, engaged in the recruiting service. To explain this I beg leave to remark that in this district there are only officers for two companies of infantry, and one first lieutenant in the artillery. Lieutenant Samuel P. Booker, of Capt. Elliott's company, has been recruiting under my immediate orders * * has Lieutenant Joseph H. Larwill and Lieutenant Timothy E. Donelson; the other Lieutenant and Ensign are recruiting under their respective Capt's to whom they were ordered to report themselves.

Some of the officers recruiting, have been more successful than others. To what cause to ascribe this different measure of success, I know not. Your orders of July 8th have been received. The officers are all at their posts, and as far as my knowledge extends are vigilant in the discharge of their duty.

We hope shortly to be able to give you a better account of ourselves; strict and constant attention is paid to drill service, and

*This is an error—James Root died recently at Hartford, Conn. He made a brave defense, but was not hurt.

our efforts are not without success. I have the vanity to believe that in point of discipline the troops here will match any within your command. Two of the rooms in the barracks, (there are four in all), I have caused to be fitted up with comfortable palliasses, each large enough for two men.

Very early in the month of August correct and ample returns for the present month shall be made.

The Governor of this State has had the goodness to leave me some arms for the use of the soldiers, which have been deposited here for the use of the militia. It is not certain when these arms must be returned, and, as many of the men have become considerable proficients in some parts of the "soldier's drill," permit me again, sir, to * * at the propriety of having a few arms at * * furnished us.

In my account for contingent expenses it may be that powder was purchased for a salute, &c. The reasons which led me to incur that expense, were the * * leaving. Governor Meigs gave me notice that he would be in town in a few hours, that war had been declared. R—— suggested the propriety of firing a few guns. I thought the occasion demanded a salute and of course ordered it to be given. I mention these things that my motives in incurring that expense to the U. S. may be understood.

Report says that a part of General Hull's army has had a brush with an enemy in Canada and repulsed them.

CAPTAIN WILSON ELLIOTT TO MAJOR TOD.

FORT MEIGS, Aug. 17, 1813.

Major GEORGE TOD—Dear Sir: I received yours of the 15th inst., which to the best of my recollection is but your second since leaving the place; however, I will not be positive; probably I might have received one during my indisposition, which I assure you was extremely violent. At a particular stage of the disease I was fully impressed with the opinion of Corporal Trim, that I should have gone hence, but my faithful Dr. Torney swore pretty much in the style of Uncle Toby, that I should appear before the walls of Malden, the idea seemed to stimulate and invigorate the system; I continued to mend, and flatter myself in a few weeks of having my health perfectly restored.

A few days since the drill service was commenced with considerable ambition, fearful that we should be surpassed by the new recruits at Seneca, but, alas! scarcely one order is issued until there is another countermanding it. I am informed that by to-day's mail orders have been received from General Harrison to circumscribe the Fort so as to be large enough to contain about three or four hundred men, consequently every man not mounting guard will be on fatigue, until the whole is completed, when I presume we shall bid adieu to Fort Meigs, a period anxiously looked for by every officer and soldier in the garrison. What in the name of God is the matter with our district paymaster? The troops are complaining loudly for their pay.

I feel anxious to visit Warren previous to our setting out for Malden. I have business of importance that ought to be adjusted; but I am fearful I shall be unable to accomplish the object of obtaining a furlough, only for three weeks. If you have any weight with General Harrison I would feel myself under peculiar obligation would you interest yourself for me. You can mention my convalescent state, and the fact is I shall not be fit for duty for that period.

We have no news to communicate. Captain Cushing is lying very ill, and indeed I think his case very doubtful.

I am sincerely yours, &c.,

WILSON ELLIOTT.

Major GEORGE TOD, Camp Lower Seneca, Sandusky.

MAJOR TOD TO GENERAL HARRISON.

SACKET'S HARBOUR, Dec. 23d, 1813.

DEAR SIR: Whatever relates to the accommodation of your troops at this station is progressing with as much rapidity as could have been looked for. In a few days officers and men will be comfortably situated in barracks; the detachments under my command are tolerably so now.

I have delayed the drill until we can all be assembled in barrack quarters; then it shall be commenced in earnest and prosecuted with diligence and zeal. Knowing, sir, that I have a family, and that family has claims on a small portion of my personal attention, you cannot but feel sensible, that a short visit to them during the winter, on their part, is fervently hoped for, and on my part most earnestly desired. No consideration has supported them in my absence but my assurance that I should occasionally cheer them by my presence at their fireside.

I entered the service of my country with the determination to continue in it so long as my services are felt beneficial, but whenever from that service I can be spared, then the claims of my family become importunate, and pressingly so. I am not aware that my continuance here through the winter can be deemed necessary. If it had been I should not have troubled you with this application. I feel no disposition to be excused from any necessary duty, and as long as I may form a unit in the army, I never wish to be.

Should it comport, General, with your views of military propriety, that I might leave this on a visit to "wife, children and friends" immediately after my monthly returns for January next shall have been forwarded or sooner, I here very respectfully request of you a furlough. I wish that my return to duty should anticipate Spring operations.

Colonel Miller left this for Washington the 19th inst,, and has given us reason to look for his rejoining his command in February next—between my departure, therefore, and his return not much time can intervene.

If granting my request promises to injure me in my character as a soldier, I beg, sir, you will deny me. To a continuance here, should prefer being ordered to the New England States, on the recruiting service, for the winter; and would most cheerfully enter on that command, because there is some prospect of rendering essential service to our army.

Have written to my friend Creighton, in Congress from Ohio, on that subject. Should the plan suggested to him meet with too little patronage in Washington for its success, it would be gratifying to my feelings to be permitted to perform my proposed visit. Let me hope, sir, to receive an answer.

I am, my D'r Gen'l, most respectfully your friend and ob't serv't, GEORGE TOD,
Major 19th Inft'y.

Maj'r Gen'l WM. HARRISON.

Western Reserve and Northern Ohio HISTORICAL SOCIETY.

CLEVELAND, O., DECEMBER, 1875.

NUMBER TWENTY-NINE.

Tradition of Brady, the Indian Hunter—Letter of General L. V. Bierce to Judge John Barr—Letter of Hon. F. Wadsworth to Seth Day, Esq.

Captain Brady's escape from the Indians during the war of the Revolution, by jumping the Cuyahoga river at Kent, is a feat well chronicled in border history. Those who examine the place at this time declare it to be impossible, and place the accounts of it among the excusable fictions of the Indian wars. Such persons should take into consideration the changes that have been wrought by bridges and mill-dams, and by the construction of the Pennsylvania and Ohio Canal, since the days of Brady. In its natural state the river ran for about a mile in what was an impassable gulf, even in low water. From a point below the cotton mill, nearly up to the old glass works of 1825, or the upper village, it rushed through a straight, narrow channel, with natural walls of rock twenty to thirty feet high, fringed with overhanging trees. In many places the breadth was not much greater than the depth. When the river was in a flood the water was very deep, coursing swiftly through the dark chasm, with resistless power, made more sombre by its chocolate color. This chasm was produced by the wearing action of the water upon the rocks during incomprehensible periods of time. In the lower part of the present village, there must have been in the early ages a cataract twenty or thirty feet high over the edge of the conglomerate. Particle by particle it has been carried away, the channel receding up stream, until it let off the water from a natural basin above the old village, through a cut merely wide enough for the discharge of a full river. A short distance above the present bridge at Main street, there was left standing a natural column of rock in the middle of the channel, with a dwarf pine on the top, known as the "Standing Stone." It was nearly round, its surface nearly on the level with the banks, and not quite as large around as a hay-stack. The waters surging by it, slowly wore away its base; but it was still strong and firm when the Pennsylvania and Ohio Canal was constructed. The engineers made slack water of this portion of the gorge, by means of a dam and locks. They demolished the "Standing Stone," and cut down the craggy edges of the east bank for a tow path. This accounts for the apparent impossibility of a man jumping the Cuyahoga at this point.

In the earliest history, this place, the "Standing Stone," a name suggested by the natural monument which I have described, was well known as the crossing place of an ancient Indian trail, leading from the Ohio river at the mouth of Beaver, up that stream and up the Mahoning river, over the Summit, a short distance south of Ravenna, down the Breakneck creek, to a ford over a ripple in the upper village. From there the Indian road had two main branches. One led north, directly to the Cuyahoga, at the mouth of Tinker's Creek; the other continued through Stow near the centre, past Cuyahoga Falls, to the "Old Portage," three miles north of Akron. Here the great trail, or "carrying place," from the Tuscarawas came to the Cuyahoga river from the south, and from thence there was free navigation for canoes to the lake at Cleveland. These were well beaten paths used by Indians and traders, on foot and with ponies, visible long after the settlement of the country in places, where the forest had not been cut away. The first road from the western part of Portage county to Ravenna, crossed at the upper ford, near where the red man had his crossing; but eventually a more direct route became necessary, and a bridge was built near the spot of "Brady's leap," because here it was most narrow. Before the bridge there was a crossing for foot passengers, on a tree felled across the chasm. On the eastern bank, the shelving rock just above the bridge had fallen, forming a pile of rough stones with bushes growing out of the crevices. The stringers of the first bridge were said to be twenty-seven feet long.

With these explanations, the impossibility of the leap is wholly removed. A stout man, stimulated by an unlifted tomahawk in the hands of a savage, or the still more horrid expectation of death torture by fire, would quickly take the risk. He is reputed to have sprung from the edge of the west bank, twenty-five feet above the water, and descending as he went, to have landed on the broken stones on the east side near the water level. By the help of bushes and roots he scrambled out of the gorge and reached "Brady Lake," before his red foes overtook him.

The letters of Gen. Bierce and Mr. Wadsworth explain the principal incidents of this, the most exciting foot race yet chronicled in Northern Ohio. C. W.

GENERAL BIERCE'S LETTER.

Judge Barr, Cleveland:

The numerous traditions respecting "Brady's Leap" across the Cuyahoga river, and many other "hair breadth escapes" and adventures of that old frontiersman grow more and more vague and conflicting, with lapse of time.

Even those which have been published at various times in the newspapers and elsewhere, do not agree with each other, nor with the most reliable oral tradition. The following, the origin of which is explained, has been kindly furnished me by F. Wadsworth, Esq. It is unnecessary to say that Mr. Wadsworth has faithfully given what he learned by his own investigation, and it seems probable, that his sources of information are as worthy of confidence as any that have been accessible since the death of the actor himself. Mr. Day, to whom the letter is addressed, settled in Ohio, I believe, in 1800; Mr. Wadsworth in 1802. Yours, respectfully, L. V. BIERCE.

MR. WADSWORTH'S LETTER.

AKRON, Feb. 26. 1856.

Seth Day, Esq.:

MY DEAR SIR—During the two very pleasant days we spent together last week in going to and from Pittsburg, among other topics of conversation, was the first settlement of Ohio; for both you and myself were residents of Ohio whilst it was yet a part of the Northwestern Territory. Amongst other things, you said you had been applied to by some gentleman, (from Philadelphia, perhaps,) that he had once called on you at Ravenna, to get, if possible, some history of Brady's expedition into the Indian country, particularly his much talked of leap across the Cuyahoga river. You said that on inquiry amongst the oldest settlers in Franklin township, in your county, where the leap was said to have been made, you could learn nothing satisfactory about it. I promised you on my return home I would relate to you all that I knew or had heard upon the subject, and now I sit down to do it. I will certainly relate to you nothing but what I have heard, and nothing but what from circumstances which took place, I believe to be substantially correct. Do with this communication what you please. If you think it of sufficient interest to send it to the gentleman who applied to you for information, you will of course do so. If not destroy it, for I have received ample remuneration for the few hours I devoted to the subject, by its bringing fresh to my recollection circumstances which had transpired more than half a century ago.

I find there is some little confusion in my recollection of the cause given me for Brady's deadly hostility to the Indians; but in substance what I give you is correct. Permit me to say that this is the first time I ever thought of placing these transactions on paper.

In the year 1802 I went to Pittsburg and resided there three or four years. Brady (I believe his christian name was Samuel) died a number of years before (six or eight years, if I am not mistaken,) but from his very noted character as an Indian hunter, he was much talked about, and I soon became very much interested in his history, and became acquainted with a man by the name of John Sumerall, who had for a long time resided in Pittsburg. He was an intelligent, observing man, and had been an intimate friend of Brady. He described Brady as not being uncommonly large, but as a powerful strong man; kind hearted, but an uncompromising and deadly enemy to the Indians. He gave this in substance, as the reason for Brady's undying hostility to the whole Indian race: When Brady was quite a youth he lived with some of his father's connections, an uncle perhaps, somewhere in Pennsylvania. The Indians made an incursion on the settlement and killed almost the whole of the families where he resided. He escaped by some means, and then swore eternal enmity to the whole Indian race. During his whole after life he never forgot his oath. I believe none of the family were taken prisoners excepting a boy, who had been taken when quite an infant into the family and adopted as a son. His name was Simon Girty, and as he was not found with the others that were killed, he was supposed to have been carried off by the Indians, which afterwards proved to be correct.

I have listened with intense interest to Sumerall's relations of the incidents attending on Brady's excursions into the Indian country, and of his desperate and deadly fights with the Indians. When there was open war between the whites and the Indians, Brady would sometimes bring in Indian prisoners, but in times of peace he always killed them. He was arrested and tried two or three times in Western Pennsylvania for killing Indians in times of peace, and although the proof was positive against him, he was always permitted to escape without severe punishment.

Sumerall gave me the history of a number of fights which Brady had with the Indians, on what is now called Brady's Run and Brady Hill, in the western part of Pennsylvania, in Beaver county. But from the length of time which has elapsed, I cannot call the circumstances with sufficient distinctness to my recollection to relate them. He also related to me the circumstances attending a number of fights he had, in what is now Portage county, Ohio. There is a small lake in the township of Franklin, Portage county, O., which still retains the name of Brady's Lake. Sumerall gave me many of the particular transactions of a battle Brady had with the Indians immediately on the south side of that lake. He had collected a force of some twenty men to go with him on an expedition against the Indians in the Sandusky country. He appears not to have proceeded on this expedition with his usual caution and secresy, for the Indians by some means obtained information of his movements, and, with a much superior force, waylaid him at Brady's Lake, and cut off his almost entire force. If I mistake not, Sumerall informed me that the whole party were killed, with the exception of Brady and one other person.

A number of years after I left Pittsburg, I went to reside at Ravenna, Portage county, Ohio, and with a number of others, I went and examined at Brady's Lake, for the place where the action had been fought, and found the place to be precisely where Sumerall had described it to be, immediately on the south side of the lake. By scraping the leaves and loose earth away, we found many human bones scattered over an acre or two of ground. We took to Ravenna a number of skull bones, as well as many other human bones. A basket hilted sword was found; the blade had rusted off, so that it was only six or eight inches long. I left the sword with Jonathan Sloane, Esq., at Ravenna, with a promise that it should be kept safe. A few years afterwards, on inquiring of Mr. Sloane, the sword could not be found.

I did suppose you were with us when we made the examination, but you inform me you was not. You recollect seeing the sword at Mr. Sloane's.

The lake was named partly from this fight, and from Brady's having at another time secreted himself from the Indians in it. I will give you the history of this transaction as related to me by Sumerall. I cannot pretend to give the dates, although in every transaction related to me by Sumerall, he gave the year in which they took place.

Brady started from Pittsburg or its neighborhood with a small force with him, not more than three or four. He preferred always to go alone, or to have but one or two with him, although at times he was persuaded to have a much larger force. He started on a scout toward the Sandusky villages, and had arrived in their neighborhood, when he was discovered by a party of ten or twelve Indians, and after a sharp fight he was taken prisoner. Those that were with him were killed, and five or six of the Indians. Brady was taken to the Sandusky villages; and as he was, and had been for years, the most noted and feared white man, there was great rejoicing amongst the Indians at the capture of Brady, and great preparations and parade were made for torturing him. Runners were sent to all the neighboring Indians, with the news that Brady was a prisoner and every Indian that got the news was there on the day set for his execution. A very large body of Indians, old and young, were collected together. Brady said that when he was first taken to Sandusky, there was something in one of the chiefs which struck him very forcibly. He soon became satisfied that he had somewhere seen him before. And after close observation and examination, he became satisfied that this person was Simon Girty, the boy who was brought up with him as a brother. He took the first opportunity he could get, to say to him that he knew him as Simon Girty. He told him who he was, and related transactions that took place when they were boys, that he could not possibly have forgotten for some time. Girty refused to know him, or even to understand a word of English; but at last he owned himself as Simon Girty. He was at this time a noted chief amongst the Indians, and was noted as being the most savage amongst the savages. Another tradition of Girty, was that Brady and he were young together, and intimate acquaintances and associations; that Girty was at one time a leader in the excursions against the Indians, but for some reason he left the whites, joined with and became a celebrated and savage chief amongst the Indians. Brady plead with Girty at first to assist him to escape: that he could do it without the fear of detection; that from their early associations and friendship he was bound to do it. He used and urged by every reason and argument he could think of to induce him to do so, but without effect. Girty would have but little conversation with him, and refused to assist him in the least. As the time for Brady's execution drew nigh he begged of Girty to furnish him with the means to take his own life, and escape the tortures preparing for him, but all without effect. The time for his execution arrived; the fires were lighted, and the excitement among the Indians became intense. Their pow-wows had commenced, and the circle around him was drawing closer, and he began sensibly to feel the effects of the fire. The withes which confined his arms and legs were getting loose by the effects of the fire, and he soon found he could at any time free himself from them. He watched his opportunity, when in the excitement of the scene, a fine looking squaw, a squaw of one of the chiefs, ventured a little too near him for her own safety, and entirely within his reach. He, by one powerful exertion, cleared himself from everything by which he had been confined, caught the squaw by the head and shoulders and threw her on the top of the burning pile, and in the confusion that followed made his escape. And Brady said when he was twenty rods ahead he had no fears for the result. He felt the bad effects of having been confined for a number of days, but as he said, not knowing what might happen, he had used every means in his power to keep his blood in circulation during his confinement. During the excitement of getting the squaw out of the fire, Brady was enabled to get a considerable distance ahead. The Indians, however, were soon in hot pursuit after him, and a number of times came very near catching him, before he arrived at the Cuyahoga river, a distance of more than one hundred miles from the Sandusky villages. When he arrived near the Cuyahoga river, in Franklin, Portage county, Ohio, (now Kent,) he found the Indians were getting very near to him. He had intended to have crossed the Cuyahoga at a very noted place, known as the Standing Stone, on the Indian trail from Sandusky to the Salt Springs, a few miles south of Warren, in Trumbull county, Ohio. The Standing Stone is about a mile above the present village of Franklin, but he found the Indians would head him, and get there before he could. He then steered his course down the river, intending to cross it below the present village of Franklin, where the bed of the river was wide, and the water shallow, but soon found his pursuers had headed him there, too; and they were already on the bank of the river both above and below him, and when he got to the river, he found himself at the narrow gorge, in the now village of Franklin, and the Indians close on his track behind him. He had not a moment to spare, and, as it was life or death with him, he made the famous Brady's leap across the Cuyahoga river. The river, as you well know, at that place is, or was, very narrow. It used to be for some distance, from twenty-five to forty feet wide It is, I should suspose, from the surface of the rock to the water, some twenty feet; and the water is, I have been told, from twenty to thirty feet deep.

Many years ago, being in that neighborhood, I went with a man who lived in Franklin, by the name of Haymaker, to examine and satisfy myself, if I could, where Brady had jumped across the Cuyahoga. Mr. Haymaker was formerly from the neighborhood of Pittsburg. He had been personally acquainted with Brady, and had heard him tell the story, which agreed well with what Sumerall had told me. We measured the river where we supposed the leap was made, and found it between twenty-four and twenty-six feet; my present impression is that it was a few inches less than than twenty-five feet. There were bushes and evergreens growing out of the fissures in the rock on each side of the stream. He jumped from the west to east side; the banks on each side of the steam were nearly of the same height, the flat rock on the west side descending a very little from the west to the east. He caught the bushes on the bank and fell some three or four or five feet before he recovered, and got out; by this time the Indians were within a few rods of the river, and when they saw him on the opposite bank of the river they set up a terrible yell; but none of them attempted to follow in jumping the river. Three or four of the Indians fired at him, and wounded him slightly in the leg. Very soon Brady found that the Indians had crossed the river at the Standing Stone, in hot pursuit; and when he arrived at the small lake (Brady's Lake), about a mile east of the Cuyahoga river, he found the Indians were gaining on him, and as the wound in his leg was troubling him a little, he must either secrete himself in the lake or be again taken prisoner. He went into the lake, and secreted himself under water, amongst the lily pads, or pond lilies. He found a hollow weed which he could breathe through, with his head under the water. This was in the fore part of the day, and he remained in the lake until the next morning. He heard the Indians about the lake all day and until late at night.

The Indians followed him no farther, but said afterwards that they had no doubt but when they shot at him across the river, they had mortally wounded him, and that he had gone into the lake and sunk, as they had tracked him into the lake but could find no tracks out.

In the fall of the year 1805, I went from Pittsburg to Kentucky. Mr. Sumerall, the man referred to above, was going to Cincinnati with some boats, and I embraced the favorable opportunity of going with him. We were eight or ten days in going from Pittsburg to Limestone, or Maysville, in Kentucky, where I left him. It was during this trip that I heard from him the history of Brady's exploits, more in detail than I had ever heard before. A very short distance below Wheeling, Virginia, Mr. Sumerall pointed to the remains of a log cabin, on the Ohio side of the river, the roof had fallen in but the body of the cabin was still standing. He said that in the last Indian war Brady brought to that house five Indian prisoners. Brady when he started on the expedition to d his friends at Wheeling that he was on an Indian expedition, and should bring in prisoners instead of scalps. He was gone from Wheeling some two or three weeks, and returned with five prisoners; an Indian and his squaw, a boy eight or ten years old, a girl five or six, and a papoose. Sumerall gave a long and very circumstantial history of this expedition, which I cannot pretend to do. Brady would suffer no one to go with him. Sumerall pointed the direction Brady went, a little north of west from Wheeling. He went to two Indian villages represented as being situated on the west and northwest side of an alder swamp. He arrived there in the night and secreted himself in the swamp, and remained there the whole of the next day. He saw where the family of five, mentioned above, in the evening went into a cabin which was a small distance from the other cabins in the village. In the night when all was still about twelve or one o'clock, he went to the cabin, broke open the door, and told them he was Brady; that if they made the least noise he would kill every one of them. The Indians knew enough of Brady, to know that he would do as he said. He told them if they would go peaceably he would take them without injury to Wheeling. He pinioned the Indian and squaw safely; made the squaw carry the papoose, and drove them all before him. Brady traveled with his prisoners only in the night. He had selected his places to stay during the day, some fifteen or twenty miles apart. He was pursued as he expected to be. He had selected his places to stay during the day, at places he could reach by traveling either up or down in a stream of water, a mile or two, so that his pursuers could not possibly track him. Sumerall described the location of the villages, the swamp in front of them; the location of the cabin from which Brady took his prisoners so accurately that five or six years afterwards I was traveling through the the State of Ohio, in going from Mansfield, in Richland county, to Wooster, in Wayne county, (there were no white inhabitants between Mansfield and Wooster,) and I had not until then heard of the Indian villages of Green and Jeromes Towns; yet when I came to those villages, Sumerall's description of them was so correct that I knew them at once, and I could not have given a more correct description of them than I had received second hand from Brady five or six years before.

Brady, as I had before stated, had a number of fights with the Indians on Brady's Hill and Brady's Run, in Western Pennsylvania. I cannot recollect any of them with sufficient distinctness to pretend to relate them. I, however, recollect the conclusion of one of them, which, as far as fighting was concerned, ended on Brady's Hill. He started from Pittsburg with three or four with him on an expedition towards the Sandusky villages, killed a number of Indians; but on their way back were overtaken by the Indians all killed or taken prisoners with the exception of Brady. He succeeded in getting back as far as Brady's Hill, not wounded, but almost dead with fatigue. Sometime before he arrived there he had discovered by some means that the Indians were still in pursuit of him. He was so much fatigued that he knew well if he could not by some means get the advantage of his pursuers he must be overtaken by them before he could get back to the settlement. And he fell on a plan which proved successful. He selected his place, a tree blown down, of sufficient height to sit comfortably upon. He went carefully back in his tracks for, say, half a mile, then turned about and again went in his old tracks to the fallen tree, making his tracks quite plain. He then selected his place for concealment within a good rifle shot distance from the fallen tree, being very careful to make no marks from it to his place of concealment. He said that he expected when the Indians arrived at the end of his tracks, they would stop for consultation, and would seat themselves on the fallen tree, which proved to be correct. After he had been secreted two or three hours, three Indians came up in hot pursuit. They closely examined for the continuation of his tracks, but not finding them they seated themselves on the fallen tree, as he had expected they would. He had selected his place for concealment, so that he could rake the body of the tree with his rifle, which he did most effectually. The whole three fell when he fired; one was shot dead, and the other two severely wounded. He clubbed his rifle, knocked one in the head, and tomahawked the other, took the three scalps, and then proceeded slowly but safely to Pittsburg.

The present generation cannot probably realize the satisfaction and real enjoyment that many of the old pioneers and hunters (of what used to be called the Western country) took in hunting and killing Indians, in the early settlement of this country. I became well acquainted with many of them, and particularly so with Adam Poe, who was quite noted for his fight with, and killing the celebrated Indian chief Big Foot. I have often heard him relate the circumstances attending that transaction, or fight; the pursuit of the Indians, his overtaking Big Foot on the banks of the Ohio river, and his finally killing him in the river. He appeared to regret, more than for any other thing that took place, that Big Foot sunk before he could take off his scalp. He has often showed me the scars of the wounds he received, being shot entirely through the body. He was also severely wounded in other places, by the scalping knife of Big Foot. His relation to me of the transaction did not materially differ from the account you have seen published. Mr. Poe was a very old man when I was first acquainted with him, but he would become very much excited and animated when relating his old hunting stories. I recollect well the last time I saw him, at the close of a long evening's conversation, when he had told me many of his old hunting stories, he put his hand on my shoulder and said: "Mr Wadsworth, no man ever took more satisfaction in hunting deer, bear, wolves, and buffalo than I have, but the greatest enjoyment I ever took in hunting was in hunting Indians." Yours truly,

FRED'K WADSWORTH.

WESTERN RESERVE

AND

NORTHERN OHIO

Historical Society

No. 30.

March, 1876.

EARLY SETTLEMENT OF

WARREN, TRUMBULL CO., OHIO.

BY THE LATE

LEONARD CASE.

CLEVELAND:
FAIRBANKS, BENEDICT & CO., PRINTERS, HERALD OFFICE.
1876.

EARLY SETTLEMENT OF TRUMBULL COUNTY, OHIO.

BY THE LATE LEONARD CASE, OF CLEVELAND.

The writer of the following notes on the history of Trumbull county, was, on the 10th of April, 1800, a lad thirteen years and nine months old. On that day, he left Fallowfield township, Washington county, Pennsylvania, for the Western Reserve. Passed by land to Beavertown, detained there three days; passed on crossed the territorial line south-east of Poland, 17th; and arrived at Mahoning, near the afterward village of Warren, 19th, 4 P. M. He believes on that day there were not more than 20,000 inhabitants (exclusive of French settlements on the Mississippi, Detroit and Mackinaw,) on the old North-west Territory, notwithstanding the census of 1800 gives 45,065.

The usual incidents attended the journey until crossing the south line, on 41° N. L. From there to Yellow Creek, in Poland, was a very muddy road called "The Swamp." In Poland, a settlement was begun, Judge Turhand Kirtland and family living on the east side, and Jonathan Fowler and wife, a sister of the Judge, keeping a tavern on the west side. From thence our way was through woods to where was a family by the name of Stevens, who had been there three years or more. The wife's name was Hannah. With her, our family had been acquainted. She said she had been there three years, without seeing the face of a white woman. There our party and cattle stayed over night. Next morning, we passed up the west side of the river, (for want of means to cross it,) to James Hillman's, and then through woods, on the old road made by the Connecticut

Land Company, to the Salt Spring. There were some settlers, Jos. McMahon among the rest, engaged in making salt. From there we passed (through woods,) to the cabin and clearing of Benjamin Davison, on the north half of Lot No. 42, in Warren, town 4, range 4; then on one-quarter of a mile to a path that turned east to the Fusselman place, on the south half of Lot No. 35, and then to the residence of Richard Storer, arriving there about 4 o'clock, P. M., on the 18th day of April, 1800.

After our passage through woods and mud, the leeks on the Indian Field on Mahoning Bottom made a most beautiful appearance.

SETTLERS.

As near as the writer can recollect, the settlers then were, in and about Warren,

EPHRAIM QUINBY,	WILLIAM CROOKS,
RICHARD STORER,	JONATHAN CHURCH,
FRANCES CARLTON,	JOSHUA CHURCH,
WILLIAM FENTON,	EDWARD JONES.

In Howland,

JOHN H. ADGATE.

They camethere in 1799 and in the following winter.

Their families were,

MRS. QUINBY, Nancy, Samuel and Abrilla.

MRS. STORER, two sons and a daughter.

JOHN CARLTON, William, Margaret and Peter.

MRS. FENTON and two children.

MRS. JONES and one child.

MRS. ADGATE, Sally, Belinda, Caroline, John H., Nancy, Charles, Ulysses, James and one or two more.

CALEB JONES, wife and child.

In May, 1801, GEORGE LOVELACE settled on the north half of Lot No. 27.

On and soon after the 18th of April, 1800, there arrived from Pennsylvania,

MESHACH CASE and MAGDALEN his wife, Elizabeth, Leonard, (the writer of this,) Catharine, Mary Reuben and Sarah.

HENRY LANE, SEN. and wife, John, Asa, Benjamin, Catherine and Ann.

HENRY LANE, JR., and his wife ELSIE.

CHARLES DAILEY and wife, JENNY and several children.

ISAAC DAILEY & wife EFFIE, and several children.

JOHN DAILEY, wife and child.

Soon after these, came,

BENJAMIN DAVISON and wife, George, Liberty, Polly, Prudence, Ann, Samuel, William, Walter, James, Betsey and Benjamin

to their cabin erected by the old gentleman in the fall of 1799.

In June, 1800, there arrived, by the south route,

JOHN LEAVITT, Esq. and family.

EBENEZER SHELDON and family.

Sheldon and family passed on to Aurora.

Leavitt and family tarried in Warren, his family:

MRS. SILENCE LEAVITT, Will'm, John, jr., Cynthia, Sally, Henry F., Abiah, Humphrey and some hired men, Elam & Eli Blair, (twin brothers.)

About the same time there came

PHINEAS LEFFINGWELL & wife.

John H. Adgate and family were already on their farm in the south-west corner of Howland, (1600 acres, being 160 chains N. & S. and 100 chains wide,) and had commenced improvements in 1799. Besides the family before mentioned, they had with them some help and old BENONI OCKUM, an Indian of the Stockbridge tribe. They had resided there during the winter of 1799, 1800. A pleasant family.

In 1799, Benjamin Davison, Esq. purchased the north half of Lots 41 & 42 Warren. The old gentleman had erected a cabin on the old road to Beavertown, on Lot 42, about 40 rods west from the present buildings. In May 1800, the family commenced their labors for a crop.*

*Wolves and bears committed depredations almost continually upon the cattle and hogs, and other smaller vermin upon the domestic fowls. The wolves would

PREACHING.

In June, 1800, HENRY SPEERS, a preacher of the Baptist order, from our former neighborhood in Washington county, Pa., and an old acquaintance, visited the settlers at Warren. Short notice was given, and he preached a sermon in the forenoon in the shade of the trees along the road south of the Mahoning, about 60 rods from the house of Henry Lane, Sr. Perhaps 50 persons assembled. They gave him a very respectful attention. This was the first sermon preached in Warren which has come to the knowledge of the writer.

In the fall of 1800, Rev. Joseph Badger came, by order of the Missionary Society in Connecticut. and for some time preached to us occasionally in the private houses of the settlers.

Either in the fall of 1801, or early in 1802, Rev. Thomas G. Jones, of the Baptist order, who resided on the Shenango east of Brookfield, was engaged for every other Sabbath at Warren. He it is believed, was the first preacher engaged regularly at Warren. He continued until after 1806. Among the members of his society were Isaac Dailey and wife, Samuel Burnett and wife and Will Jackman and wife.

In the meantime, the Presbyterians were supplied with occasional preachers; however, besides the Rev. Mr. Badger, the

approach even within two rods of the cabin, seize a pig, run off with it and eat it, and as soon as the flock became still again, would return again and seize another in like manner; pursuing their depredations to such an extent as to render it difficult to raise anything. The wolves would likewise seize and destroy the weaker cattle. In winter, when quite hungry, they were bold and would come among the settlers' cabins. The writer recollects one night in February, 1801, when the weather had been stormy—the wind then blowing a severe gale—when the wolves attacked the cattle on the Bottoms, on Lots 35 & 42 in Warren. The cattle gathered together in large numbers; the oxen and stronger ones endeavoring to defend the weaker ones. They ran, bellowing, from one place to another and the wolves, trying to seize their prey, howled fearfully. In the morning, it was evident, that the oxen had pitched at the wolves, burying their horns up to their sculls in the mud and earth. Several of the weaker cattle were found badly bitten.

The bears preyed more upon the larger hogs; frequently carrying off alive some weighing as much as 150 pounds, though they preferred smaller ones.

The foxes and other vermin so preyed upon the domestic fowls, that for some years it was difficult to keep any. That wolves prey upon sheep is usual wherever they exist in the same vicinity; but they were so bad about Trumbull, in its early settlement, that the settlers were unable to protect the sheep from the ravages of the wolves, for six or seven years.

writer does not recall their names. In about 1808, the Rev. Mr. Dawes was regularly engaged. Among the Presbyterians, were Benjamin Davison and Anna his wife, Thos. Pryor and Elizabeth his wife, Elsie Lane, —— Lane, and John Leavitt and wife.

FOURTH OF JULY.

In 1800 there was a 4th of July celebration at the place of Mr. Quinby. They were much at a loss for musical instruments.—Elam and Eli Blair, the twin young men who came with John Leavitt, Esq.—one a drummer and the other a fifer—surmounted the difficulty. One found a large, strong, stem-elder and soon made a fife. The other cut down a hollow pepperidge tree and with only a hand-axe and jack plane made a drum-cylinder. With the skin of a fawn, killed for him by William Crooks, he made heads for the drum and for the cords used a pair of new plow-lines belonging to M. Case. They discoursed most patriotic music. Of course, all had guns. So, the usual amount of patriotism was demonstrated in proper style by music and the burning of gunpowder. John Leavitt, Esq. played the militia captain. A good dinner was had in a bowery. Toasts were duly given and honored with the needful amount of stimulus. All went off merrily.

Quite a number of the guests were from abroad, among whom were John Young, Calvin Austin and some others from Youngstown; Gen. Edward Paine and Judge Eliphalet Austin from the lake shore, and other gentlemen from other places.

OLD MERRYMAN.

When the first settlers came, they found in the land —— Merryman, a perfect patriarch of a hunter, of some 60 winters. He had for years been lord of the soil: his "right" there was "none to dispute." But after the white men came—like the natives—there was no place for him. Whence he originally came, or whither he finally went, or how he was descended, the writer hath no knowledge.

FLOUR MILLS.

The first grist-mill, for custom grinding, was on Mill creek in Boardman. It was started (as currently stated) in the last of Nov., 1799, and was the first mill erected on the Reserve, unless the mill erected by W. W. Williams at Newburg had priority.*

It answered a tolerably good purpose for the people about Warren,† until Henry Lane, jr., and Charles Dailey put their mill in operation in 1802. They commenced building their dam across the Mahoning in 1800; but the winter flood destroyed their work. They then exerted themselves to have their mill going in 1801, and the neighbors assisted, but they did not succeed until the Spring of 1802.

* P. S. MARCH 29, 1862. Saw Allen Gaylord, Esq. of Newburg village, who says he came with David Hudson, Will Wheeler Williams, etc., in the spring of the year 1800, removing with their families to the Reserve. He joined them in the State of New York, at or near Irondquoit, and came with them to Cleveland. Williams stopped at Cleveland. Gaylord went with Hudson to the township of Hudson. Gaylord was well acquainted with them in Connecticut. They were both out in 1799, when Hudson surveyed Hudson and Williams erected the mills on Mill creek, on Lot No. 464, front of now Newburg village. Williams had caused the mill to be started before leaving the Reserve with Hudson in the fall of 1799. They arrived in Con't. in November of 1799, and consequently the mill must have been set agoing in October. The mill was in operation when Gaylord arrived in the spring of 1800. He has known it ever since.

He was informed that Williams was furnished with the materials for building the mill, besides the donation of the lot of land No. 464. The deed of this lot was made by Trustees Conn. Land Co. April 4, 1804, to Samuel Huntington, Recorded in Trum. Nov. 21, 1804, G. p. 45. This mill in Newburg must have been the first started. Mr. Gaylord says the rock where the stones were quarried he has seen, not long since, near by.

The writer has seen in the accounts of Directors of Conn. Land Co. viz.

"1800, April, advanced W. W. Williams to erect mill at Cleveland, 255.83
23 pairs of shoes delivered W. W. Williams 23.00"

The 100 acre lot No. 464 deeded to S. Huntington, is said to have been part of the consideration for the mill,

† In February 1801, Benj'n. Davison, Esq. the father of the family on the north half of Lot 42, Warren, his son Samuel, a lad about 16 or 17, and Ebenezer Earle (brother of John Earle of Howland) a bachelor about 30, agreed to take a sled load of wheat and corn to the mill on Mill creek in Boardman.

The sled had a new wood rack with two yoke of oxen. There was snow, but rather thin sledding. These three with the team started pretty early in the day for the mill, twelve miles distant. Soon after they started it grew warmer and began to thaw. It was after dark before they got their grain ground, but knowing that the road (the road which the Connecticut Land Co. caused to be opened from Poland, by the Salt Springs, Warren and to Painesville) would soon break,

The stones were placed in a saw-mill, the bed-stone on the sawing platform. Spur-wheels were placed on the flutter-wheel of the saw-mill, one on the lower end of an upright shaft and geared together. The running stone was placed on the upper end of the shaft, and with a hoop and appurtenances, ground tolerably well ; but each customer had to bolt his own flour.

It was said that the builder had a favorable contract for a piece of land, on the conditions that he should have a saw-mill and grist-mill running by the first of December, 1799. He found the time growing short and resorted to the above device in order to comply with the letter of his conditions.

MERCHANTS.

The first supply of merchandise which the writer recollects was under the control of James E. Caldwell who, with an assistant, about once in two weeks poled a canoe up the Mahoning—in 1801. When he came in sight of a settler he blew a horn, and those who wanted goods resorted to the canoe for a supply.

Either in the fall of 1801, or early in 1802, George Lovelace opened a small shop in Warren, on the east side of Main street and some rods north of South street.

About the same time, Boyle Erwin set up his nephew, Robert Erwin, with a small assortment of goods in a building nearly opposite Holliday's tavern-stand (lately Walter King's place.)*

and likewise the ice over the Big Meander, they started for home in the night. They had not gone far before the ice over the mud-holes began to give way. Old Mr. Davison went forward to pilot the boys along the muddy places, particularly where the brush and logs were turned out and piled up like winrows. He would frequently break through. Then he would call to the boys, "Turn out, boys, turn out!" "a bad place here." When they came to the Meander it had risen so as to be above their sled beams. In order to save their load from the wet, they placed chains crosswise at the top of their rack, laid poles, crosswise with the chains, on them and piled their bags upon the poles. At a little more than half way across, the weight crushed down the rack. They and their load together found the water. It was up to their knees. However, they drove on. It was about four o'clock in the morning when we heard them half a mile off. Soon after, they reached my father's—the first house after leaving the Salt Springs—not much the worse, after they got dry. The water did not penetrate into the mea bags much. This was the first trip to mill by the two families of Case and Davison. Previous to that time the hand-mill had been brought into requisition.

*August 1.—1860, I saw a notice of the death of Boyle Erwin, near Pittsburgh, a few days since, aged 88 years. He closed Robert's affairs at Warren in 1807.

In 1820 or 1803, Zebina Weatherby and James Reed started a rather larger store, (on the site lately occupied by Leicester King,) and for several years did a considerable business, selling merchandise and driving cattle.*

MAILS.

The first post route established to Warren was from Pittsburgh to Warren, upon application to the P. M. G., from Elijah Wadsworth, of Canfield, by letter of 30th April, 1801. It was not carried into effect before 24th October, 1801.†

General Wadsworth was well acquainted with Gideon Granger, the P. M. G., who (Mr. G.) had also a large interest on the Reserve.

The appointment of Simon Perkins bears date October 24th, 1801. Eleazar Gilson was first engaged as mail-carrier. Gilson probably carried a short time.

The first mail delivered at Warren was October 30, 1801. It seems probable, however, that the mail carrying was not very regular until July, 1802. A letter post-marked at Chillicothe, January 19, 1802, from Hon. George Tod to Col. Samuel Huntington, at Warren, has a note on it requesting Mr. Perkins to procure the letter to be forwarded to Col. Huntington. Major Perkins had a post-office at Youngstown February 10, 1802. Hon. George Tod says in a letter, of that date, to S. Huntington that a letter had lain in that office some time. Elisha Tracy also speaks of it May 15th, 1802. Thus it appears that strict regularity was wanting as late as May 15th, 1802.

Mr. Gilson, soon after his contract to carry the mail, appointed Joseph McInrue as his deputy mail carrier. The writer saw McInrue on the route some two miles southerly from Warren,

*Weatherbee died September 1811 or '12. Reed left for parts unknown in 1815.

†THE ROUTE.—From Pittsburgh, on the south side of the Ohio river, to the mouth of the Beaver, say 27 miles; over to Ft. McIntosh, John Coulter, Postmaster; back to the south side of the Ohio and to Georgetown, 12 miles, John Beaver, P. M. there; direct to Canfield, on the Reserve, 27 miles, Capt. Elijah Wadsworth, P. M. there; then to Youngstown, 8 miles, Calvin Pease, P. M. there; thence to Warren, 12 miles, to the termination of the route, Simon Perkins, P. M. there; ——— and return once a week.

with the mail matter tied up in his pocket-handkerchief along with the key for the Warren office, and understood that he had delivered others on the route. The Warren key had attached to it a label of wood on which was the date of its first delivery at Warren—July, 1802—plainly marked. This key was in the office of General Perkins in 1806 and several years after, wherever the office was kept, until 1816, when the writer left Warren. The General kept the office at his boarding house, the tavern of John Leavitt, Esq., and [follows copy,] with some aid until 1804—a part of 1805 was kept by the Clerk of the Court, George Phelps, on the lot *after* owned by Leicester King. Then at the log office of the General, fall 1805—all 1806. Early in 1807 by George Parsons at the Calvin Austiu place—and then on the Jackman lot, Liberty street—until the new court house was finished. Then by Samuel Quinby, for a time, and then, as the writer has been informed, by Samuel Chesney for several years.

GOVERNMENT.

The history of the Western Reserve of Connecticut is among the various items of evidence which go to show that a majority of the members of Congress believed that all the waste and western lands belonged to the United States, as a nation, after allowing to the chartered colonies a reasonable territory as occupied by each; and that Congress never did, nor would admit that the claiming colonies, had title to any more lands than had been occupied and used by each to a reasonable extent, until an actual adjustment took place. It was so with the Reserve.

WASHINGTON COUNTY.

After the organization of the N. W. Territory in 1788, the Governor, St. Clair, included the Western Reserve east of the Cuyahoga in Washington county, which was bounded: Beginning on the Pennsylvania line, at its crossing of the Ohio river and by it to Lake Erie; along the southern shore to the Cuyahoga; up it to the Portage; to the Tuscarawas; down that stream to the crossing above Fort Lawrence; then westerly to the Big Miami; south, etc.; to the beginning. (See III Chase, 2,096.)

2

WAYNE COUNTY, MICHIGAN.

In 1796, Wayne county,* Michigan, included west of the Cuyahoga, etc., to the head waters west of Lake Michigan, which drained the country into it; north—to Lakes Superior, Huron and Erie—and the territorial line. (III Ch., 2,096.)

JEFFERSON COUNTY.

Established July 29, 1797, included all of the Reserve east of the Cuyahoga. (III Ch., 2,096.)

TRUMBULL COUNTY.

In the years 1799 and 1800, an arrangement took place between the United States and Connecticut and its purchasers of the Reserve, and deeds were passed May 30, 1800, whereby Connecticut ceded to the United states the political jurisdiction, and Congress confirmed to Connecticut the title of the land, for the benefit of its purchasers. This transaction first gave the assent of Congress to the title of Connecticut.

*Howe, in his book, page 518, makes a material mistake in relation to Wayne county, by connecting the Wayne county established by Governor St. Clair, Aug. 15, 1796, with the present Wayne county in Ohio. The Wayne county established by Governor St. Clair was bounded as stated by Howe; but all that part of it north of the north boundary of Ohio was cut off by organizing Ohio and remained Wayne county in Michigan. All the records, doings, archives, etc., remained in Wayne county, Michigan, in Detroit, and are there still—in 1860. That part of the old Wayne county remaining in Ohio, so much as was included in the Western Reserve, was included in Trumbull county, established July 10, 1800. It is very uncertain what county or counties had jurisdiction over the residue, until, under the State authority, counties were erected covering it. The *present* county of Wayne is composed of part of the territory of the old county. It was established February 13, 1808, and embraced the land south of the Western Reserve, north of Wayne's Treaty, or U. S. Military District lines, west of 10th range, east of 16th range; was attached to Stark until organized March 10, 1812 The territory included in the first Wayne, cut off by Ohio south and west of Western Reserve was disposed of after the State was organized. *In March, 1803, the Legislature erected:*

COLUMBIANA COUNTY—And took from Jefferson county near the Muskingum—but little.

MONTGOMERY COUNTY—Extending on the west and north to the lines of the State.

GREENE COUNTY—East of Montgomery, north to the State line, and east to a line near the Scioto and Sandusky.

The land east of that remaining of the territory of the old Wayne county, east of about Sandusky river, to the west of the Reserve, and south of it as far as Tuscarawas, seems not to have been included in any county until 1820, excepting what was included in Richland, Wayne and Stark, south of the Reserve. (See Chase III from 2,098 to 2,106.)

On the 10th of July, 1800, Governor St. Clair erected the whole of the Reserve into Trumbull county, bounded: South by 41° north latitude, and west 120 miles west from Pennsylvania; north by latitude 42° 2′, and east by Pennsylvania. (III Ch., 2,097,) and forthwith appointed officers and organized it with the county seat at Warren.

The first court was held August 25th, 1800, at 4 o'clock, P. M., between the corn-cribs of E. Quinby, on Main street, fronting the Brooks' House, just south of Liberty street. These cribs had regular clapboard cabin roofs—not as Lane says, covered with boards.

After this the southeast towns became more thickly inhabited, and the inhabitants in that quarter wished the county seat removed to Youngstown. A hewn-log jail, which had been erected on the northwest part of the Square, was burned on the 28th* of February, 1804, and thereupon exertions were seriously made to have the county seat removed to Youngstown.

GEAUGA COUNTY

Was set off December 31, 1805, including towns† No. 8, west to west of line of range No. 5; then south to the north line of town 5; then west to the Cuyahoga. Geauga was organized March 1, 1806.

ASHTABULA AND PORTAGE COUNTIES

Were erected February 10, 1808, and the towns No. 8 included in Ashtabula. (III Ch., 2,105.) The towns No. 8 were set back to Trumbull county on the 20th of February, 1809. (III Ch., 2,110.)

"TOWNS NUMBER EIGHT."

The inhabitants of the townships No. 8, as far west as to include the 5th range, complained that, during the struggle and contest about the county seat betweeen Warren and

*The date of the burning of the log-jail was found in a letter from Calvin Pease to Samuel Huntington.

†These "towns No. 8" were a bone of contention, and were several times set back and forth to Trumbull and Ashtabula. Judge Solomon Griswold said they had no privileges in either county, and were sued in all.

Youngstown, from 1804 to 1809, they had no privileges in either of the adjoining counties, and were sued in all of them. However that might have been, the struggle was severe.

The southeasterly part being the most densely inhabited, generally carried the election of a representative favorable to the Youngstown interest, until in 1809, as mentioned below. The Warren people were therefore compelled to appoint and support "lobby members" to attend to their interests at Chillicothe, which was no little bill of expense, besides the vexation.*

STRIFE FOR COUNTY SEAT.

Until the year 1809 aliens were permitted to vote at elections. There were many such in the southeast part of Trumbull, and with their aid elections were carried. It was found after the election in 1809, that the representative and commissioner favorable to Youngstown were elected, but if the votes of aliens should be thrown out, the representative, Thomas G. Jones, and commissioner favorable to Warren would be elected. The election was contested.

In the September previous, the writer, then a little over 23 years of age, had been elected a Justice of the Peace. His commission hardly dry, he and William Chidester, of Canfield, were selected as the Justices to take the testimony; the first day in Hubbard, next in Youngstown and last in Poland. The aliens were mostly Irishmen and were greatly excited; 1st. because they considered the proceeding as striking at their liberties; and 2d, as a party measure. Daniel Shehy made a flaming speech at Hubbard an hour and a half long. The Justices had to force him to silence.

Homer Hine was for the respondents;

J. S. Edwards for the contestants.

Many of those summoned to give testimony refused to testify, until about to be arrested and sent to jail—then they agreed to

*In the struggle about county seats E. Root, John Kinsman and others wanted a county seat on the east line of the Reserve. Elias Tracy wanted it on the corners of Morgan, Rome, Lenox and New Lyme, or all New Lyme, No. 9, 3d range—his town.

and did give their testimony. About one hundred depositions were taken.

The next day, in Youngstown, about the same course was attempted by the witnesses, but the Justices compelled the business to proceed, and took something more than another hundred depositions.

The next day after, at Poland, the same course was again attempted; but the Justices put Shehy under keepers during the day and progressed with their business. They had a very boisterous time of it.

They took in all some four hundred depositions, which, upon trial turned the election in favor of Warren.

A contract was soon after entered into for the building of a Court-House and Jail. This ended the contest about the county seat. It was extremely bitter while it lasted—some five years—whole townships giving their vote on one side or the other without a dissenting vote.

REMINISCENCES OF BENJAMIN LANE.

WARREN IN 1799—THE FIRST SETTLERS.

[EXTRACT FROM A WARREN NEWSPAPER.]—(DATE NOT KNOWN.)

"For the following reminiscences of the first settlement in this county, we are indebted to Mr. Benjamin Lane, who still resides on the same spot which his father bought in the year 1799, and who lived in the first house built in this county—as bounded at present.

The first white man who purchased land in this township, for actual settlement, was the late Hon. Ephraim Quinby, (Note 1) who bought the land on both sides of the river, on which this town now stands, and also the land still owned, and occupied by his son, Hon. Samuel Quinby.

Mr. Quinby arrived here, early in the spring of 1799, probably in the latter part of March, accompanied by Mr. William Fenton and wife, and William Carlton, and his sister Peggy Carlton.—(Note 2.)

The first house built in the township stood on the south side of the river, and on the east side of the road, just opposite Mr. Lane's present residence.

This log-house was built by Mr. John Young, (the proprietor of Youngstown, Mahoning Co.) in the spring of the year 1798.

He then owned the land where Youngstown now stands, but owned no land in this township, and he came here to raise corn, there being about twenty acres of land (once owned by the late Judge Freeman) which had been cleared by the Indians, probably very many years before, as the stumps of trees had all rotted out.

There were also some sixty acres on the south side of the river which had been cleared, part of which now belongs to the Fusselman farm, and part to Mr. Benjamin Lane's home farm.

Several other pieces of the Mahoning bottom land in this vicinity, between this place and the Salt Springs, had been cleared amounting in all, to several hundred acres. Mr. Young planted some seventeen or eighteen acres of the land on this side of the river, in corn, occupying the house afore-mentioned, until the crop was gathered, stored it in the house until snow fell in the winter, when he hauled it to Youngstown.

Mr. Henry Lane purchased two hundred and fifteen acres, fifty-five acres of which, lay on the north side of the river, and now belongs to Mr. Charles Smith. The balance, one hundred and sixty acres on the south side of the river, belongs to Mr. Benjamin Lane, and upon which he has lived since the first purchase.

The first house built within the corporate limits of Warren, and the second in the township, was built in the spring of 1799, by Hon. Ephraim Quinby, and stood upon the west side of Main street, on, or near where the post-office now stands. The next house built, was also by Mr. Quinby, in the fall of 1799 ; and was on the corner of Main and South streets, near where the C. & M. R. R. Depot now stands. This was of logs, partially hewn. One room, about ten feet square, was used as a jail for several years. (Note 3.)

The hewed log-house which still stands on the east side of the road, opposite Mr. Lane's house, was built in the summer of the year 1800, and adjoined the house first built. In April 1799, Mr. Henry Lane, accompanied by his son John, and Mr. Edward Jones, came ; Mr. Henry Lane purchased his land, then returned to Washington Co., Pa., his son John, and Mr. Jones remained here, and planted corn, (about five acres,) on the bottom land which now forms a part of Mr. Benjamin Lane's home-farm.

The corn land was not fenced in, because there were no animals except deer, to disturb it, and they troubled it but little.

In October of the same year, Mr. Henry Lane returned, and this time his son Benjamin came with him.

Mr. Lane brought one hundred small apple trees, tied in two bundles, and strapped on the horse, Benjamin Lane (then a boy of fourteen years) riding the horse, and sitting between the bundles of apple trees. These trees were immediately planted, and some of them are still living, thrifty bearing trees.

About the 10th of December, Mr. Lane and his two sons returned to Pennsylvania, leaving Mr. Jones and his wife in the house.

The next April, Mr. Lane returned with his family, consisting of his wife, the two sons before mentioned, and another (Asa) and two daughters, Catherine (now Mrs. John Tait, who still lives in Lordstown,) and Anne, who married Samuel Phillips, and died some eight years since, in Austintown, Mahoning Co. Mr. Asa Lane returned to Pennsylvania about the year 1820, and died there.

Before the return of Mr. Lane, in the spring of 1800, Mr. Jones had built a house on the farm, now owned by Mr. Isaac Daily, on the west side of the river, and removed there with his wife.

There was born of Mrs. Jones, in February, 1800, the first white child in this county. This was a girl, who married with William Dutchin, about the year 1820, and died some twenty years since. Mrs. Jones, the mother, is still living in Austintown, Mahoning Co. (Note 4.)

In the summer of the same year, 1799, Captain John Leavitt and Ebenezer King, (who with Ebenezer Sheldon, first bought this township from the Connecticut Land Company) came, and brought with them Mr. Wil'm Crooks, with his wife. (Note 5.)

Messrs King. and Leavitt returned to Connecticut in the fall Crooks and wife remaining.

Before their return, they built a log-house, cleared some eighteen acres of land, and sowed it with wheat, on what is now called the Murburger farm, two miles west of this place.

This wheat was the first raised in the county, our informant being one of the reapers; in July 1800.

In June, 1800, Mr. Leavitt (called Esquire John) returned with his family, consisting of his wife, four sons, and three daughters.

All of these are now dead, except one of the sons, Hon. Humphrey Leavitt, of Steubenville, O.

During the year 1800, about twenty families came in, and settled in this township; built houses, and made clearings. One, Mr. John Adgate with his family, settled in Howland, where his grand-son, Mr. Adgate, now lives. Salt was very scarce, very difficult to get, and sold for $16 per bushel. At the Salt Springs, in Weathersfield, in July 1800, Joseph McMahon and two other men were engaged in making salt.

The Indians were numerous in the vicinity at that time, and some fifteen or twenty of them who had been at Youngtown and purchased some whiskey, came to the Salt Springs with their squaws and pappooses, and had a drunken spree, in which McMahon and the two white men joined. In the course of the spree, they got into a row, and the Indians drove the white men off.

The whites came to this place, and the next day returned, accompanied by eight or ten other men, among whom were Mr. Ephraim Quinby, Messrs. Benjamin, John, and Asa Lane, John Bently, Richard Story, and Jonathan Church, and others armed with rifles. When they reached Salt Springs, they found the Indians encamped there. McMahon went up to the chief, whose name was Tuscarawa George, a man of immense size (who boasted that he had killed 112 white men,) and spoke to him in the Indian language. The Indian sprang to his feet, seized his tomahawk which stuck in a tree at his side, and struck at Mr. McMahon, who dodged the blow, at the same time presenting his rifle, fired and killed the Indian.

At the same time, Story also fired, killing another Indian, called Spotted John; the bullet passing through the body of John, breaking the arm of one pappoose, the leg of another, which was in the arms of a squaw, and just touching the neck of the squaw, and raising a blister.

The whites in this vicinity, were greatly alarmed, for fear the Indians would make reprisals, and for about two weeks, they all barricaded themselves within Mr. Quinby's house every night, but they were not attacked.

The day after the affray, Mr. McMahon was arrested, taken to Pittsburg, and confined in Jail for some weeks, until some time in August, when he was brought back to Youngstown, tried, and acquitted on the ground of self-defence. McMahon immediately left this part of the country, with his family, and returned to his former home in Pennsylvania.

Story left before he could be taken, and was not afterward arrested." (Note 6.)

NOTES BY LEONARD CASE, Sen.

On Benjamin Lane's statements above quoted, in relation to matters that happened about the year 1800, made from memory only; as he had never taken notes in writing, they are of course subject to many allowances. He does not mean to contradict any other person, but merely to state matters as they remain in his recollection. His statements from hearsay, are generally from the relation of some one or more, who were present at the time stated.

Note 1. Richard Storer was the neighbor of Ephraim Quinby, in Washington co. Pa. for several years before 1799.

They came together to the Reserve in the fall of 1798, and purchased land. Quinby, the whole of lot 28 in Warren, and perhaps more; Storer, the south half of lot 35 (the Fusselman place.) In the Spring of 1799, they came to their respective places, bringing hands with them, and each commenced improvements, and putting in crops, corn, &c.

In April, Storer erected his cabin where the Fusselman buildings are. Quinby had a small building on the bank at the Mill-dam, a little way northwest from the residence of Judge Austin.

Will Fenton and wife, &c. lived in it. He built the house part of the log house and Jail (Jeremiah Brooks occupied the same after 1807.) Adjoining the same, were the hewn logs of a house, raised and covered in 1799, and finished in the spring of 1800. John Shaffer, carpenter.

Soon after April 1799, Henry Lane Sr., his son John, and step-son Edward Jones, and Meshach Case went to view the country. Lane purchased their home farm ; and left his son John, with Jones, to raise corn.

On that farm, was the cabin spoken of in Lane's statement.

M. Case returned without purchasing then ; but he came out again in August, and purchased the south half of lot 42, 198 acres ; cleared some two acres, and erected a cabin—nothing more than a shell and cover—and returned to his home in Washington Co. Pa., in the last days of September.

Note 2. When Quinby returned in the spring of 1799, there came out with him the Carlton's, viz. : Francis the father ; sons, William, John and Peter, a boy ; and daughter Margaret.

He purchased from Quinby, a part of lot 28—afterwards owned by General Perkins,

Note 3. In the winter following 1799, E. Quinby removed Mrs. Quinby, Nancy, Samuel, Abrilla, and perhaps William.

Storer had removed Mrs. Storer and three children not long before—it was after the fall of 1799.

Mrs Stevens had two children born, near the crossing of the river, below Youngstown, before April, 1800. She said she had resided there three years, before seeing the face of a white woman.

Note 4 *Query:* Why did not Benjamin Lane state that about the time his father removed out in the spring of 1800, the family of M. Case came along the same road? and that next came Henry Lane, Jr., and his wife Elsie, Charles Daily and wife and family, Isaac Daily and wife and family, and John Daily, wife and child—all from the same neighborhood!

Note 5. It is hardly necessary to correct the statement about the pur chase of land by Eb. King and John Leavitt, in 1799. King and Leavitt were members of the Connecticut Land Company, and were the original owners of land, in common in drafts Nos. 8, 9, 10, and 11, made in 1798. These drafts were made on $51,612.92 stock, which drew 78,497 acres of land, among which was the township of Warren. Leavitt and King had their lands by partition deeds, out of the land drawn. (See Trumbull County Records and Drafts of Connecticut Land Co., Recorder's Office, Warren, Book D., 114, 136, 123—1801, April, etc.)

Note 6. About the killing of the Indians at the Salt Springs in the latter part (about the 30th, Sunday was the 27th) of July, 1800, the writer hesitates to say much, as he has seen several accounts of that transaction, which differ materially from each other, as well as from the account given by Benjamin Lane.

But as the writer saw part, and heard more from those who were present, he will give a short statement of the transaction as he recollects it.

Jos. McMahon and wife, and perhaps three children, had been about

Warren in 1797 and 1798, and perhaps earlier, among the Indians, and but little if any better than they. In 1799 he had erected a small house near the southwest corner post of Howland, at the south end of the Goose Pond, which he left in the spring of 1800, and went to the Salt Springs.

He had taken about four acres of bottom land from Storer, at the south end of the bottom, to raise corn, and in the spring of 1800 planted it.

In July, a party of Indians encamped about sixty rods up the Salt Spring run ravine, at an old camping ground. The ravine was thick with brush. The camp ground was open, except some large trees.

The Indians got whiskey, and had a general drunken revel, in which McMahon and some other whites joined. The whiskey of the Indians having been exhausted, the whites were not satisfied, but sent to Quinby's at Warren, and obtained a small further supply.

The Indians suspected this, but the whites denied it, and would not let the Indians have any.

On, say Tuesday, McMahon left, and went to Storer's to tend his corn. Soon after he had left, the Indians began to tease his wife—wanted her to serve as squaw—and finally threatened to kill her and her children.

On Thursday the wife, taking one child in her arms, and leading the others, went to Storer's, where her husband was, stayed over night, and he went back with her and the children in the morning. (The writer, after much reflection, is in some doubt whether Mrs. McMahon stayed that night at Storer's, or whether he for some cause had started for home at the Springs, and met his wife on the road—an old road long since abandoned—near south line of Lot No. 41. At all events, they, McMahon and his wife, were at the Springs next forenoon, had a conversation with the Indians, and supposed the difficulties all settled satisfactorily at that time. At least such was the statement at the time, as well by others present as by McMahon and his wife. Joseph and John Filles were present, who afterwards stayed at my father's cabin three days immediately after the killing of the Indians.) He had a talk with the Indians of the camp, and apparently settled the matter.

They agreed to be peaceable, and he returned to tend his corn at Storer's. Soon after he had left, the Indians began again to threaten the woman and children, and it was said, an Indian struck one of the children with the handle of his tomahawk.

Matters went from bad to worse, until on Saturday afternoon, the wife again took the children, and started for Storer's. She met her husband on the way, a short distance from Storer's, opposite my father's farm. They returned to Storer's, and remained there Saturday night, telling over and nursing their grievances.

On Sunday morning, the 27th, McMahon went up along the river, among the settlers, told over his side of the story, and begged for aid to go with him, and make a permanent settlement of the difficulty.

Most of the young and middle-aged men whom he met went with him. He got together about thirteen men and two boys. (Among them were Henry Lane, Jr., Ephraim Quinby, John Lane, Asa Lane, Richard Storer, Will Carleton, William Fenton, Charles Dailey, John Bentley, Jonathan Church, Benjamin Lane, McMahon, of course, and others whom I do not recollect. The two lads were Thomas Fenton and Peter Carlton, about ten or eleven years old, perhaps older.)

In those days it was customary for every man to carry his gun, and the party had each a gun, except the boys.

The writer saw the company passing his father's house, about ten o'clock, on their way to the Springs. As the story was related at the time, they passed along in a jovial manner, engaged in miscellaneous conversation, until they reached the run at the Salt Springs, below the camp.

There Mr. Quinby, who in those times was generally looked up to as a kind of leader, called a halt. It was agreed that he should go up to the camp, and see what the difficulty was, and return and let them know. The others all stopped. He passed on to the camp. There the Indians lay lolling about. Among them were Captain George, a Tuscarawa, who spoke English, and John Winslow, a Seneca, called "Spotted John," because he was part white.

He inquired of Captain George, what was the difficulty between him and McMahon, and his family. George answered: "Oh, Joe damn fool! The Indians don't want to hurt him or his family. They (the whites) drank up all the Indian's whisky, and then wouldn't let the Indians have any of theirs. They were a little mad, but don't care any more about it. They (Mr. McMahon and family) may come back and live as long as they like; the Indians won't hurt them." Mr. Quinby returned to his comrades, expecting to find them where he had left them.

But, in the meantime, they had sauntered up the path in the ravine, along the run, and when Mr. Quinby met them, were just emerging from the ravine and coming up the bank.

On meeting Quinby, all halted, except McMahon. He strode on and the boys followed him. As he passed, Quinby said, "Stop, Joe," but he did not heed it.

The others listened to the relation by Quinby, of what had passed at the camp between him and the Indians.

In the meantime they had risen from the ravine into plain open view of the camp, some twelve or fifteen rods distant, with only an occasional larger tree between them; and while Quinby was relating what the Indians had said, Joe McMahon and the two boys had got to the camp.

Captain George was sitting on the root of rather a large tree, leaning his body against the body of the tree, when McMahon approached him. The other Indians, some five or six, and several squaws and papooses, were lolling around the camp.

McMahon said to George—" Are you for peace or war? Yesterday you had your men, now I have got mine." A tomahawk was sticking in the body of the tree, immediately above the head of George. He sprang to his feet, seized the tomahawk, and was in the act of swinging it, as if to sink it into Joe's head, when Joe, being too near to shoot, jumping backward, brought his rifle to bear, and instantly shot George in the breast. The blood spirted nearly to McMahon. McMahon cried out, " Shoot! shoot! " to the men standing in open view, without anything to screen them.

At the same instant the Indians jumped up, caught their rifles, treed, and aimed at the whites. Of course the whites brought their rifles to bear, Storer among the rest. Several of their guns were snapped, but missed fire. The morning had been drizzling with rain and the guns were damp. Storer saw John Winslow, (Spotted John,) aiming, as he supposed, at him, and without further reflection, threw his rifle into position, (it was an excellent rifle and always in good order,) and fired.

At the same moment, Winslow's squaw was endeavoring to screen herself and papooses behind the same tree with Winslow, and was directly behind him.

Winslow's hips were all of him that was exposed. Storer's ball passed through them, and passing on, broke a boy's arm, passed under the cords of the neck of his girl, and grazed the throat of his squaw.

The two boys, Fenton and Carleton, who were forward with McMahon, seeing him shoot George, fled for home. The sound of the second gun added to their speed.

They ran without halting, three and a half miles to Davison's, and reached there so overdone that for sometime they were unable to tell what had happened. They could only say "shoot," and then stop for breath. At the camp, after the shooting, of course all was confusion, among the whites, as well as the Indians.

The whites left the scene of action at rather a quick pace.

The writer saw the party on their return between one and two o'clock, P. M. The Indians, it was said, dug slight holes, covered the dead with dirt and leaves, and all, except the squaw with her wounded children, fled for the woods, expecting the whites would be after and murder them. They took a path to Newton Falls, and there encamped.

They were afraid to hunt. The wounded squaw took her two wounded children in her arms, and started for the place of James Hillman, an old Indian trader who lived near Youngstown—a distance of nine miles—where she arrived, it was estimated, in an hour and a half.

None of the whites who went with McMahon had any expectation of serious difficulty.

Some of them said, afterwards, that they thought while going there, they discovered evil intentions in McMahon. Others thought differently.

The men who went with him went as peacemakers, and had no thought of violence to the Indians.

There was not attached to them any blame, or even want of discretion. As evidence of the opinions of those acquainted with the affair at the time, Quinby was elected a member of the first General Assembly under the Constitution, in March, 1803; Henry Lane, Jr., has since been a member of the General Assembly several times, and many others of that party have held stations of trust and confidence. There was no moral turpitude attached to any one else than McMahon.

The party, as was stated, returned in some haste to the settlement. Soon afterwards, they put McMahon under arrest.

He was placed under guard, and taken to Pittsburgh, as the nearest place where a prisoner could be kept.

Some of the inhabitants, who had not been engaged in the transaction, thought that Storer ought to be arrested also. The gathering was at his house, on what is now the Fusselman place.

He quietly observed what was going on around him. He concluded from what he saw and heard, that he too might perhaps be arrested and put on trial, and on reflection, believing that would be inconvenient he, about four o'clock in the afternoon, walked into his cabin, put on his hat, took down his rifle from its place on the hooks, and quietly walked off before them all, saying he must go to look for his cows, and went west to the woods. (His reflections were, as I afterwards heard him say—at that time we had no organized government on the Reserve. The jurisdiction had been ceded to the United States, but this was not known then among ordinary people at Warren—Storer said he knew he had done nothing criminal. He had gone to the Salt Springs with the intent, only and entirely, of settling a difficulty. He suddenly found himself in imminent and instant danger of being shot, without any possible means of escape. He had shot to save his own life. If he submited to be taken and tried, he had no knowledge of what law he was to be tried by, or by whom he was to be tried. Under these circumstances he deemed himself justified, in protecting his own life, by absenting himself from the power of those who sought to call him to account for the deed.) No one molested him, or tried in any way to hinder him; it was probably best, and that most present knew, for although a very quiet and civil man, of as good moral character as any other, he was an efficient man in whatever he undertook to do.

This I saw, and I am the more particular because I have seen a different account of the transaction.

From that time all was confusion in the neighborhood. The whites, supposing that the Indians would be upon them for vengeance, gathered in squads for safety. They mostly met at Quinby's. All kept guard and lookout.

On Monday Mrs. Storer mounted her two horses with her three children, and what goods and clothing she could carry, and started for her former home, in Washington county, Pa., alone, except that Mr. Asahel Mills of Nelson, who was on his way to Beavertown, accompanied her as far as the latter place. The rest of her property was left to such care as a few friendly neighbors could give to it.

The report of the affray had spread like wildfire, and by three or four o'clock of the same day, it had brought Hillman, John Young—afterwards Judge—and some others to Warren.

Hillman, the Indian trader, had long been acquainted with Indians, and all were anxious for his advice and assistance.

They prevailed upon Hillman to follow the Indians, and make some arrangement with them.

A day or two afterwards, in company with, I believe, Mr. David Randall, he took with him the wounded boy, and followed the trail of the Indians through the woods to their camp. They had been so much frightened that they dared not hunt, and when Hillman came in sight they fled to the woods, and even with the aid of the boy he found it difficult to induce the Indians to return to their camp. They, however, did return, and Hillman made with them a temporary arrangement, upon which the whites returned to their houses, and the Indians to their hunting.

Afterwards the United States officers made some final arrangement, with the particulars of which the writer is not acquainted.

At the time of that quarrel, the ordinary inhabitants were not aware of the existence of any organized government upon the Reserve.

The United States had claimed political jurisdiction, and had included a part of the Reserve, as far west as the Cuyahoga river, first in Washington county, in 1788, and afterwards in Jefferson county.

In 1796, Wayne County, Michigan, was extended over all of the Reserve, west of the Cuyahoga.

But until May 30, 1800, the Reserve was claimed as a part of the State of

Connecticut, although that State had neglected to extend its laws over it. In 1792–1800, laws were passed by Connecticut, authorizing the cession of the political Jurisdiction to the United States, and Congress passed a law authorizing the President to convey to Connecticut for the benefit of its grantees, a title to the soil.

On the 30th May, 1800, deeds were exchanged. On the 10th July, 1800, Governor St. Clair erected Trumbull county, and soon afterwards organized it and appointed officers.

Until that time, the common citizens on the Reserve had supposed themselves without any legally organized government.

. . . James Hillman was appointed Sheriff, and John Young, presiding Judge of the County Court of Quarter Sessions.

Several Justices of the quorum were also appointed. and on the 25th of August, court was held, between E. Quinby's corn-cribs, where there is now a street before the house of Quinby—the Jer-Brooks residences.

Early in the September following, by order of Governor St. Clair, a court was held at Youngstown, by Judges of the General Court.

Return J. Meigs and the Governor in person, but not as a Judge, attended.

A jury was summoned by Sheriff and—law or no law, jurisdiction or not—Joseph McMahon was put upon his trial.

George Tod and some other lawyers were for the people. John S. Ed wards, and Benjamin Tappen, of the Territory, and Steel Sample, of Pittsburgh, were for McMahon. The most of the facts which have been stated were given in evidence. After a full and fair trial the jury found McMahon not guilty of murder—for which he was indicted.

So far as appeared in evidence, all was brawl and talk, until George caught his tomahawk with the evident intention of burying it in the brains of McMahon.

The writer has heard that verdict rather severely criticised, but he has no doubt that it was in accordance with the law as generally applied to murder—the evidence being as there given. Moreover, those jurors would have compared favorably with jurors selected to try like cases at the present day.

Joseph and John Filles, two young men, who were at the Salt Springs during the fracas, some three days afterwards stayed at the house of the father of the writer. They both made a statement to us, which was never given in evidence, which would have been material to show George's motives; it was this: During the drunken scrape, George several times said that he had killed *nineteen* white men, and he wanted to kill one more to make an even number. But the Filles left for the Ohio, and were not at McMahon's trial.

GENERAL REVIEW OF TITLE.

ORIGIN OF TITLE.

There are several questions of interest, which might have arisen in the trial of McMahon and Storer, if they had been put upon trial, from the uncertainty of who or what political power had the real title to the Connecticut Western Reserve, or whether any law was in force upon it, at that time.

It is admitted by all, that Great Britain in 1664 owned the land between latitudes 41° N. and 42° 2′ N,, and that Charles Second granted a territory, between those lines westward throughout the precinct from sea to sea, to the colonists of Connecticut, and claimed the title to it.

Between that time and 1763, the French king claimed the same land west of the Alleghany mountains.

Wars ensued. Great Britain was successful, and, by treaty in 1763, obtained a cession of all west to the Mississippi. Connecticut still continued her claim. In the treaty of peace, in 1783, Great Britain ceded to the United States all her possessions west to the Mississippi.

Many of the States forming the confederation in the United States claimed all the lands westerly of the settlements, as belonging to the United States by conquest, for a fund to pay the war debts, etc. The colonies having charters, claimed to the extent of their boundaries, and unless France really had title which she ceded to Great Britain in 1763, the colonies had good title under their charters, which was doubtful if France had title which she ceded to Great Britain, and upon which the crown could make title by conquest against its prior grants. However this might have been, Congress admitted the claims of the charter-colonies, and appealed to them for liberal grants for the benefit of the whole. New York responded and made a release of most of her western lands, March 1, 1781; Virginia, March 1, 1784; Massachusetts, 178–, and finally Connecticut executed her release of all her lands in her charter, lying west of a line parallel with the Pennsylvania line, and one hundred and twenty miles west from it, September 13, 1786—reserving what lay east of it, which constitutes the Connecticut Western Reserve, nearly three and a half millions of acres. Five hundred thousand acres of the west end of the Reserve, she appropriated to pay sufferers by fire, in the Revolutionary war, by act of her Legislature in the year 1792, and sold the residue to a company, September 5, 1795, which company surveyed the same, east of Cuyahoga, in 1796–7, and divided it and made actual settlement, sales, etc.

In the meantime, Arthur St. Clair, Governor of the territory north-west of the Ohio river, established a territorial government in 1788, and established counties.

Washington county extended up the Ohio from Scioto to Pennsylvania; then with Pennsylvania to Lake Erie, and with it to Cuyahoga; up it to the Tuscarawas, west to Scioto, and to the first beginning. A regular government was established, laws were enacted. In April, 1800, Congress passed a law authorizing the President to release all the United States claim to the right of soil to Connecticut for the use of its purchasers, if Connecticut would release all its claim of jurisdiction to the United States. The Legislature of Connecticut, the same winter, passed a law authorizing its Governor to release the said jurisdiction. Deeds of cession were executed according to these acts, and mutually exchanged the 30th May, 1800.

It seems pretty clear that Connecticut owned the Reserve land; at least that she owned and was in possession of the political jurisdiction up to May 30, 1800, but had always declined extending her laws over it.

The Territory had passed various laws for the government of the Territory; but could those laws have any operation on the Reserve while Connecticut held the jurisdiction?

It is believed not, nor afterwards until the law-making power should, by express legislation, have extended those laws over the territory of the Reserve.

Such is the usual custom of the United States when Congress purchases a territory. The laws of the United States are extended over it by express legislation, or new laws are made for the new government. The laws in force in the Northwestern Territory were made without the concurrence of any person on the Reserve, and they were never extended over the Reserve by any express legislation.

The Superior Court of the Territory—Return J. Meigs and Joseph Gilman, judges—on the application of George Tod, Calvin Pease, Samuel Huntington, John S. Edwards and Benjamin Tappan to be admitted as lawyers, at Marietta, in October, 1800, decided that the Reserve had been part of Connecticut until the deeds in May were exchanged, and admitted them without further inquiry.

Then by what right, or by what law did the court at Youngstown, in September, 1800, try Joseph McMahon for killing the Indian at the Salt Springs in the last of July, 1800?

FIRST DEED FROM THE STATE, FEBRUARY, 1788, SALT SPRING TRACT, TRUMBULL COUNTY.

THE STATE OF CONNECTICUT,
TO
SAMUEL H. PARSONS.

The State of Connecticut, one of the United States of America, to all to whom these presents shall come, greeting:

WHEREAS, The State of Connecticut in General Court assembled, by their several acts passed on the second Thursday of October, one thousand seven hundred and eighty-six, and on the second Thursday of May, one thousand seven hundred and eighty-seven, did resolve, direct, and order that the land belonging to said State, from the completion of the latitude forty-one, to the latitude forty-two degrees and two minutes north, and between Pennsylvania and a line drawn from the mouth of the Cuyahoga river, where the same falls into Lake Erie, and up the stream of said river to the Portage path; and thence by the Portage way to the head of the Muskingum river; and thence by a straight line to the Tuscarawas, at the south-east corner of the Indian Reserve, and so southerly to the latitude of forty-one degrees north, should be sold; and did appoint, authorize, and empower Benjamin Huntington, John Chester, and Thaddeus Burr, Esquires, a committee to sell said land—townships of six miles square, or in part of townships—and,

Whereas said State in general court assembled, did resolve and order, that whenever a purchaser or purchasers should procure a certificate from any one of said committee, that he or they have purchased and paid for any part of said lands, it shall be the duty of the Governor of said State of Connecticut, to execute a patent of such lands so purchased to the purchaser, or purchasers thereof.

And, whereas, Benjamin Huntington, Esquire, one of said committee, hath, pursuant to said resolves, certified to the Governor of said State of Connecticut, that Samuel Holden Parsons, of Middletown, in the county of Middlesex, and State of Connecticut, Esquire, hath purchased of said committee and paid to him, said Benjamin Huntington the full amount thereof, a certain tract of land parcel of the lands ordered to be sold as aforesaid. And said Samuel Holden Parsons, Esquire, now moving for a patent and full confirmation of said land as purchased as aforesaid, now KNOW YE, That we, the State of Connecticut, in pursuance of the several acts, resolves and orders of the General Assembly before in these presents referred to—Do, by these presents, fully, freely, and absolutely GIVE, GRANT, RATIFY AND CONFIRM to the said Samuel Holden Parsons, Esquire, the lands within the following boundaries, viz: Beginning at the north-east corner of the first Township, in the third Range of townships ordered to be sold as aforesaid; thence running northerly in the west line of the second Range of said lands to latitude forty-one degrees and twelve minutes north; thence west three miles; thence southerly parallel to the west line of Pennsylvania two miles and one-half; thence west three miles to the west line of said third range; thence southerly parallel to the west line of Pennsylvania to the north line of the first Township in said third Range; thence east to the first boundary.

Said lands, before described, being the lands certified by said Benjamin Huntington, Esquire, to be purchased and paid for by said Samuel Holden Parsons, Esquire, and lying within the third Range of townships ordered to be sold as aforesaid. To have and to hold all the said granted and described premises, with the privileges and appurtenances thereof, unto him, the said Samuel Holden Parsons, his heirs and assigns, forever, as a clear and absolute estate in fee-simple, excepting the lands which are reserved to be sequestered for the use of the ministry and schools, agreeably to the acts and resolves of Assembly, before mentioned.

In witness whereof, the said State of Connecticut have caused these presents to be signed by the Governor and Secretary, and the seal of the said State to be hereunto affixed. Dated at Hartford, this tenth day of February, Anno Domini one thousand seven hundred and eighty-eight.

[Seal.] SAMUEL HUNTINGTON, *Governor.*
GEORGE WYLLIS, *Secretary.*

The lands mentioned in the within patent, as sequestered for the use of the ministry and schools, and reserved and excepted out of this patent, are one thousand acres only; the remaining part of the lands within the boundaries of this patent being paid for by the patentee.

Certified this tenth day of February, one thousand, seven hundred and eighty-eight.

BENJAMIN HUNTINGTON, *Committee.*

October 19, 1789.

A true record. Attest. ALBERT ENOCH PARSONS, *Register.*

THE STATE OF OHIO, } ss.
WASHINGTON COUNTY. }

The foregoing is a true copy of the original record as recorded in volume number one, at pages twenty-three and twenty-four. In witness of which, I hereto subscribe my name officially.

WILLIAM B. MASON,
Recorder, W. Co., Ohio.

June 30, 1858.

SALT SPRING TRACT—ORIGINAL OWNERS.

GRANTOR.	GRANTEE.	PAGE.	REMARKS.	DATE OF DEED.
Parsons, Sam'l H..				
1,240	Eliph Dyer	1	1,240 acres of within tract,	Mar. 10, 1788
340	Eliph Dyer	2	340 "	Mar. 10, 1788
1,111	Isaac Cowles	3	1,111 "	Feb. 21, 1788
1,722	Oliver Ellsworth	4	1,722 "	Mar. 10, 1788
4,413	Oliver Ellsworth	5	⅛ part of 4,000 acres	Feb. 10, 1788
1,111	David Bull	6	1,111 acres of Conn. tract	Feb. 21, 1788
1,320	Timothy Hosmer	7	1,320 "	Feb. 21, 1788
900	Jonathan Hart	8	900 "	Feb. 21, 1788
3,331	William Judd	9	687 "	Mar. 28, 1788
	William Judd	10	6-13 of the unsold land	Feb. 21, 1788
555	Gad Wadsworth	11	555 acres of Conn. tract	Feb. 21, 1788
1,111	Noadiah Hooker	12	1,111 "	Feb. 21, 1788
1,111	Will Wadsworth	13	1,111 "	Feb. 21, 1788
500	Elijah Wadsworth	14	500 "	Feb. 21, 1788
1,111	Solomon Whiting, Jr.	15	1,111 "	Feb. 21, 1788
555	Amos Porter	16	555 "	Feb. 21, 1788
395	Will Hillhouse	17	395 "	Feb. 21, 1788
5,338	Enoch Parsons	21	All his right and title to Conn. lands including Salt Spring,	Aug. 4, 1789
13,082				
	Matthew Carr	24	8 acre lot	July 5, 1789
	Richard Butler	25	¼ of 4,000 acres and ¼ of Salt Spring,	Nov. 5, 1788
	Richard Butler	35	Article of Agreement for making Salt	Jan. 14, 1789
	Richard Butler	39	⅛ of 4,000 acres that I reserved of Conn. lands	Nov. 5, 1788
	Matthew Carr	44	8 acre lot, mouth of Muskingum,	July 15, 1788
	Moses Cleveland	F 156	1,817 acres.	
	Joshua Stow	H 396	1,726 acres.	

In those marked thus —, a reservation of 4,000 acres around the Salt Spring is made.

GENERAL SAMUEL H. PARSONS.

Judge Parsons, named in the above deed, seems to have been an active, enterprising man, who had early examined the western country. He is mentioned in Hildreth's History, pp. 190 to 209; Burnet's Notes, p. 40.

He writes a letter December 20, 1785, to some persons, making inquiries about the country, saying he had been one hundred and fifty miles westerly of the Miami.

He was one of a committee to frame a treaty with the Shawnee Indians, and concluded it on the north bank of the Ohio at the Miami, Jan. 31, 1786. (See vol. of U. S. treaties.) He was one of the Ohio Company, formed by Manasseh Cutler, Rufus Putnam, etc., in 1786–7, and was one of its directors. He was one of the first judges of the general court under the territory, and was active in organizing the territory.

Connecticut did not release her claim to western lands, lying one hundred and twenty miles west of Pennsylvania, until September 13, 1786.

The Legislature, at its session in October, 1786, made provision for selling her Reserve lands east of Cuyahoga, and, as appears by the above deed, Parsons soon afterwards purchased of Connecticut about 25,000 acres of the Reserve lands.

When the writer first came to the Reserve, in April, 1800, it was the current report that Judge Parsons and his assignees, had made salt there ten or fifteen years.

The remains of foundations of cabins, of stone furnaces to hold salt-kettles, fragments of kettles for boiling salt, decayed timber and stumps, several acres of land run over and partly cleared—clearly indicated that the white man had several years before 1800, made settlement at those springs.

It is probable that Parsons was drowned on Beaver Falls, the the latter part of the year 1789, as he was re-elected or appointed a judge of the General Court, under the Constitution of the United States, August 4, 1789, and in the spring of 1790, Rufus Putnam was in his place as his successor. (Burnet, p. 40.)

The writer has just (1861, July 18,) seen a journal of the doings of the "Cincinnati," held at Philadelphia, Pa., May 4, 1794, in which it is stated that General Samuel Holden Parsons was drowned in Beaver Creek, Pa., in N. W. T., November 17, 1789, in attempting to pass the Falls in a canoe, one man only with him.

Born, May 14, 1737.

Western Reserve and Northern Ohio
HISTORICAL SOCIETY.

ANNUAL MEETING, MAY, 1876.

TRACT THIRTY-ONE.

The eighth annual meeting of the Western Reserve and Northern Ohio Historical Society was held at the rooms, Tuesday evening, May 9th, 1876.

THE ANNUAL REPORT

was made by the secretary as follows:

The general object and purpose of the society is "to discover, procure, and preserve "whatever relates to the History, Biography, "Genealogy, Antiquities and Statistics of "the Western Reserve, the State of Ohio, "and the North-west."

Its purposes are general to the State and we are glad to believe that its usefulness in this respect is recognized. A large share of the visitors and of the contributions to its museum come from other counties than Cuyahoga.

THE HISTORY

of Ohio will receive during the present year much more than usual attention. The secretary has addressed to the editors of each of the 537 newspapers of the State a request that all articles of a local or general historical interest be sent to the society. It is not to be supposed that the collection will be by any means complete, but it will no doubt be of large value. Contributions are received every day. There will be formed during the year numbers of local historical or pioneer societies. A circular has been prepared by the State Archæological Society at Columbus, containing a form of constitution suggested for such societies. One clause requires the officers of such societies to send to this society and its sister at Cincinnati a copy of all its publications, book, pamphlet or newspaper. It is believed that the placing of such matter with this society will be a decided benefit to each local society.

GENEALOGY

is beginning to attract considerable attention in this part of the country. It may not be generally understood that most people of the State, if they try, can trace their lineage to the early settlers of this continent. It must be done, however, before many years, or it will not be done at all. Records were generally well kept, down to a time after the Revolution, but not long after. The New England Historic Genealogical Society may almost be said to have created this science, if such it may be called. But the taste for it is rapidly increasing, and many inquiries are made of the society upon such matters. There is not in the State of Ohio a respectable public library upon that subject. Shall there not be such a library in our rooms? A public spirited friend, (Mr. Peter Thatcher), has kindly offered to place in our rooms the only complete set in the city, of the New England Historic Genealogical Register, thirty octavo volumes, and the society has, also, besides the works of Mr. Savage, and others, a growing collection of genealogies and local histories.

THE MUSEUM

has had a steady increase during the year. A comparison of it with any west of the Alleghanies will make it respected. There is need of new cases for the proper display of the too crowded objects of interest.

The number of visitors increases rapidly. Those enrolled were for the quarter ending

1 July, 1875	403
1 October, 1875	524
1 January, 1876	851
1 April, 1876	1,143
	2,921

Mr. Johnson, who has charge of the

COINS,

reports that the coins, medals, and tokens numbered in 1873, about 500. On the first of May, 1876, there were 1641. By sales and exchanges, many of the poor and worthless of 1873 are replaced by better. In 1875 there were added 287, and since the first of January, 1876, 276.

The additions of this year cannot be displayed for want of show cases. Special cases should be made of different pattern from those used for general display. There is a growing interest in numismatics, and the collection, though not a large one, is no unimportant feature of the museum.

THE PUBLICATIONS

of the year have been as follows:

No. 26, June 1875.—Seventh Annual Meeting, May 1875.

No. 27, July 1875.—Notice of Historical and Pioneer Societies in Ohio, by C. C. Baldwin.

No. 28, October 1875.—War of 1812. Selection No. 8, of correspondence.

No. 29, December 1875.—Traditions of Brady the Indian Hunter, by President Whittlesey, with letters attached, from Gen. L. V. Bierce and Hon. Frederick Wadsworth.

No. 30, March 1876.—Early settlement of Trumbull County, Ohio; General Review of Title -both by the late Leonard Case.

LIBRARY AND CATALOGUE.

Miss Dockstader is working as steadily as her other engagements will permit on what will be a very complete catalogue of the library.

The books are necessarily in some confusion while the titles are being taken, but it is expected that they will be ere long newly and systematically arranged and perfectly accessible.

THE MARGRY PAPERS.

This society, in 1872, originated a petition to Congress, asking for the purchase of a large collection of papers relating to French discoveries in North America.

The collection was made by M. Pierre Margry, of Paris, the correspondence embracing that of La Salle, and other explorers, from 1670 to 1750

Nearly all the historical societies of the United States, and most of the prominent historians, joined with us in this effort

General Garfield and Mr. Monroe, members of Congress from Northern Ohio, supported our plan with zeal, and, so far as we know, all the members from this State voted for the appropriation. Those from the New England States, and from the Gulf States, in both Houses, also gave it their support.

The sum of $10,000 was placed in the hands of the Joint Library Committee of Congress, and a contract for six printed volumes was made with Mr. Margry. There are to be 500 copies of each delivered to the Library Committee as soon as practicable.

Yesterday a letter was received by our president from Mr. Margry dated Paris, April 19th, in which he says: "Our first volume, having for its title, 'Voyages of the French upon the Great Lakes, and Discoveries of the Ohio and Mississippi,' will soon appear. Since you, with Mr. Parkman and Mr. Marshall, are the promoters of this publication, it is right that a copy be sent you with a portrait of La Salle." * * * *

"I regret not having been able to acknowledge your society on the cover of my book, as it would give me great pleasure as an act of gratitude towards you; but the contract is so drawn that I am in doubt about the fate of the work until the sixth volume is reached."

"I wish in this work to give the savans of your continent an opportunity to examine with care the localities visited by the Cavalier La Salle. For a Frenchman, even with the charts, this is surrounded with great difficulties.

If I was a younger man I should very much like see all those countries. But it is necessary to limit myself to seeking out papers in France, as I have done since 1842. My collection is unique: among which are documents necessary to America, and which it will be for Americans who are conversant with the country, to interpret."

From the imperfect portions of LaSalle's correspondence, maps, and reports it appears that he passed from Lake Erie to the Ohio river, about ten years before he discovered the Mississippi; but as yet it is not practicable to determine the route he followed. He certainly ascended a river emptying into the westerly part of Lake Erie, and, crossing a short portage, descended a large river leading to the Ohio.

He reached the falls of that river but was deserted by his men and forced to return to the St. Lawrence apparently alone."

We hope the publications of Mr. Margry will solve the mysteries that now envelop the movements of LaSalle in the territory of Ohio.

FINANCES.

The balance in the hands of the Treasurer (Mr Williamson) at his report last year was ....$	107 00
The income during the year last past has been, from endowment.......	678 34
Annual membership and subscription....	281 00
	$1,066 34
The disbursements for all purposes have been.....	969 04
Balance. ... .$	97 30

Of which $59.56 is in the hands of the Treasurer personally and the balance in working committees.

The rooms have been, before the last year, heated by steam, but it has been found that this in severe weather interfered with the comfort of the rooms below, and the Society for Savings declined to longer furnish us. It was at one time contemplated to close the rooms during the severer winter weather, but a large stove was procured of the best modern construction, and the room has been heated by that very easily and comfortably. The discount made by the Society for Savings on account of heat with a discount upon the rent of the additional room back of our main room will make an annual saving of from $50 to $100 over our previous expenses, in this behalf. On the first of October last, Miss Seymour, our librarian removed from the city. A tribute of thanks is due for her faithful service. Miss Dockstader has filled the place since with efficient energy.

MEMBERSHIP.

The number of life members is 85, of annual members 68.

The progress of the society has been great for its age. I may add that its friends have expended much labor and considerable money in its behalf. It should have a much larger annual membership than it receives. The Buffalo Historical Society reported in 1875, an annual membership of 345. Their terms require a preliminary fee of $5, in addition to the annual fee required by that society and our own.

Why should not we receive like support? A little money goes a great ways when the only salary is $240, to the librarian. There are many advantageous uses to which an increase might be put. The publication of a substantial volume would help much. We have abundant valuable material. A single year of such support as the Buffalo society receives would enable us to do this

The Buffalo society have found club meetings at residences of members to be of much interest. Their meetings are similar to those held by our own society in its early days. The experiment is perhaps worth repeating here.

I report with sorrow the death of one of our earliest life members Mr. T. Sterling Beckwith of this city, who died 28th March 1876, and of Increase A. Lapham of Milwaukee who died in September 1875.

Brief biographies are appended.

Respectfully,

C. C. BALDWIN, Secretary.

The following resolution, offered by Dan P. Eells, Esq., was adopted:

RESOLVED, That there shall be created in this society an order of members to be called Patrons. Any person may, by vote of the curators, be constituted a patron when his aggregate cash payments for the use of the society shall have amounted to the sum of five hundred dollars.

The following resolution, offered by H. N Johnson, Esq., was also adopted:

RESOLVED, That the curators be requested to consider the question of charging an admission fee to the museum and library to persons not members and not entitled to admission as donors, the curators to act in the matter as they may deem best.

The following resolution, offered by Hon. J. P. Bishop, was also adopted:

RESOLVED, That the thanks of the society be given to its officers for the efficient manner in which they have performed their duties.

Obituaries.

THOMAS STERLING BECKWITH

was born in Lyme, Conn , 11th January, 1821. He was son of Frederick A. and Jerusha (Sill) Beckwith, and of a family settled in Lyme two hundred years ago.

When aged 14, he commenced clerking in Jefferson county, New York. In 1839, aged 18, he came to Cleveland and commenced as a clerk at the spot on Superior street, where he afterwards was so prominent a merchant.

When aged 24, he became partner in the dry goods business with the late P. M. Weddell, Dudley Baldwin and W. E. Beckwick, his brother. This firm the two Beckwiths succeeded, and, with changes, did an extensive business, and the firm finally became Beckwith, Sterling & Co. In 1854, he sold out of this firm and opened the first store in Cleveland for the exclusive sale of carpets, in which Mr. F. A. Sterling, of his late firm, became again connected with him, and the firm—again Beckwith, Sterling & Co.—continued in that name until the death of its senior partner.

Mr. Beckwith was a very successful merchant, and the firm was so conspicuous in the trade of Cleveland that it may be said to almost have historic interest. He was also a leader in several manufacturing enterprises, which have contributed to the prosperity of our city. He was a quiet gentleman, of pleasant manners, firm, steady and correct in his judgment.

Mr. Beckwith was more than a mere business man. He was a kind, public spirited citizen and Christian gentleman. He was among the earliest of our life members, and was a person of whom this would be expected with confidence, for the sake of the good to be done. He was active in benevolent and religious enterprise, for many years member and a deacon in the Second Presbyterian church; active in the Bethel Sunday-school and for a number of years superintendent.

He married, in 1849, Miss Sarah Oliphant, of Grandville, New York, and leaves a family.

He died the 28th of March, 1876.

INCREASE ALLEN LAPHAM, LL. D.,

also a life member of our society, was born in Palmyra, N. Y., March 7, 1811. In August, 1826, his father secured him a place on the Miami Canal, under Byron Kilbourn, then Assistant Engineer. In 1827 he was employed on the canal around the falls of the Ohio. That year—only sixteen years old—he wrote his first scientific paper on the canal and the geology of the vicinity. It was published in the American Journal of Science and Art, and highly commended by Professor Silliman. He was afterwards employed on the Ohio Canal, and published in 1832 an article on the Geology of Ohio. In 1833 he was living at Columbus, as Secretary of the State Board of Canal Commissioners. He was an ardent student of science, and an active member and officer of the Ohio Historical and Philosophical Society. He was active in encouraging the first geological survey of this State.

In 1836 he settled in Milwaukee. He became early a trusted and eminent citizen. He continued also to be a close observer and student. In 1838 he commenced a series of publications about the natural history and other history of Wisconsin, the bare catalogue of which would exceed the limits which can be given in this notice.

In his botanical investigation, studies of forests, winds and waters, he was always in the front rank of men eminent over the world for their achievements. His most elaborate work was his "Antiquities of Wisconsin," an illustrated quarto volume upon the effigy mounds of the west, published by the Smithsonian Institute in 1855. It is recognized by archæologists all over the world as *the* work upon the subject. One of his last labors was the preparation of a series of bas relief models of some of these mounds for the Centennial Exposition.

He was a thoughtful observer of atmospheric phenomena. In 1858, he appealed to steamboat owners to take measures to learn of approaching storms. He afterwards addressed Capt. E. B. Ward, of Detroit, assuring him that a knowledge of approaching storms could be obtained, in many cases, at least twelve hours in advance. At length Chicago gentlemen resolved that the matter should be tested, and a joint stock company with $100,000 capital was preparing to do the work which the Government now does so efficiently. But, meanwhile, Dr. Lapham's personal agency procured the act of Congress which led to the Weather Bureau. He was for a while Chief Geologist of Wisconsin, until ousted by a political change. He was authority in anything relating to the State he lived in, and when asked what were his studies, replied, "I am studying Wisconsin," and he studied it with little thought of personal emolument to himself, ever busy with something of use to all. He received the degree of LL.D. from Amherst College in 1860. He was a quiet, modest gentleman, simple in his tastes and habits, generous, scrupulously honest in business and science, gentle and cheerful. The 14th of September, 1875, he finished a paper upon the capacity for fish production of Oconomonoc and other small lakes of Wisconsin and pushed out upon the lake named for an hour's rest.

His body was found in the bottom of the boat, having died of heart disease without a struggle and alone.

LIST OF OFFICERS AND MEMBERS.

President—Charles Whittlesey.

Vice Presidents—J. H. Salisbury and E. Sterling.

Secretary—C. C. Baldwin.

Treasurer—S. Williamson.

Librarian—Miss E. S. Dockstader.

Legal Trustees—William Bingham, J. P. Bishop, George Willey.

CURATORS ELECTIVE.

Term expires in 1877—J. H. A. Bone, Mrs. George Willey, H. N. Johnson.

Term expires in 1878—C. C. Baldwin, Mrs. Alleyne Maynard, C. T. Sherman.

Term expires in 1879—Joseph Perkins, Charles Whittlesey, John W. Allen.

PERMANENT CURATORS.

W. J. Boardman, James Barnett,
William Bingham, H. M. Chapin,
B. A. Stanard.

LIFE MEMBERS.

John W. Allen,
Miss Sarah L. Andrews,
P. H. Babcock,
C. C. Baldwin,
Colgate Hoyt,
Miss M. E. Ingersoll,
H. N. Johnson,
Mrs. F. Judson,
Dudley Baldwin,
John D. Baldwin,
N. C. Baldwin,
S. C. Baldwin,
T. S. Beckwith,*
L. V. Bierce,
J. P. Bishop,
H. C. Blossom,
Wm. J. Boardman,
A. Bradley,
O. A. Brooks,
A. E. Buell,
Leonard Case,
W. S. Chamberlain,
H. M. Chapin,
O. A. Childs,
Ahira Cobb,
Wm. Collins,
A. G. Colwell,
D. W. Cross,
Wm. Chisholm,
Wm. M. Darlington,
J. H. Devereux,
L. C. Draper,
John Erwin,
M. F. Force,
A. W. Fairbanks,
Wm. P. Fogg,
J. A. Garfield,
Theodatus Garlick,
W. J. Gordon,
Miss L. T. Guilford,
C. F. Glaser,
T. P. Handy,
S. V. Harkness,
H. A. Harvey,
C. C. Hale,
L. E. Holden,
Franklin B. Hough,
Kent Jarvis, Jr.,
M. M. Jones,
T. M. Kelley,
Horace Keller,
Jared P. Kirtland,
W. G. Lane,
I. A. Lapham,*
Benson J. Lossing,
O. H. Marshall,
S. L. Mather,
James Monroe,
E. P. Morgan,
George Mygatt,
Eben Newton,
W. S. C. Otis,
Douglas Perkins,
George G. Perkins,
Jacob B. Perkins,
Joseph Perkins,
Joseph Perkins, Jr.,
L. Lewis Perkins,
F. W. Putnam,
Rufus P. Ranney,
J. D. Rockefeller,
J. H. Salisbury,
John H. Sargent,
C. O. Scott,
W. H. Smith,
Silas M. Stone,
W. S. Streator,
R. W. Tayler,
John Tod,
Amos Townsend,
J. J. Tracy,
H. B. Tuttle,
J. P. Wade,
R. P. Wade,
H. P. Weddell,
George Willey.

ANNUAL MEMBERS.

G. E. Armstrong,
Linus Austin,
E. I. Baldwin,
Jas Barnett,
W. H. Barras,
C. H. Bill,
Wm. Bingham,
Sam Briggs,
H. W. Boardman,
E. H. Bohm,
S. Burke,
George P. Burwell,
C. C. Carlton,
S. Chamberlain,
E. D. Childs,
J. D. Cleveland,
B. J. Cobb,
B. S. Cogswell,
J. Colwell,
C. J. Comstock,
S. H. Curtiss,
W. L. Cutter,
Wm. Edwards,
D. P. Eells,
Alfred Eyears,
L. W. Ford,
J. Newton Frazee,
S. C. Greene,
S. O. Griswold,
N. H. Hand,
G. C. F. Hayne,
G. E. Herrick,
James M. Hoyt,
Hopson Hurd,
Henry R. Hatch,
J. E. Ingersoll,
Joseph Ireland,
W. S. Jones,
Thomas Kilpatrick,
J. S. Kingsland,
James W. Lee,
Lyman Little,
Frank Lynch,
F. A. Marble,
Mrs. Alleyne Maynard,
L. McBride,
Mrs. J. McDermott,
G. G. Norris,
Charles A. Otis,
Dr. Henry Parker,
F. W. Pelton,
W. H. Price,
H. C. Ranney,
W. C. B. Richardson,
Harvey Rice,
E. C. Rouse,
George A. Stanley,
C. T. Sherman,
J. Clinton Saxton,
W. P. Southworth,
Amasa Stone, Jr.,
E. Sterling,
William Taylor,
V. C. Taylor,
G. A. Tisdale,
J. W. Tyler,
S. E. Williamson,
E. N. Winslow.
N. H. Winslow.

*Deceased.

Western Reserve and Northern Ohio
HISTORICAL SOCIETY.

No. 32—JUNE, 1876.

WESTERN RESERVE—ORIGIN OF TITLE.

BY COL. CHAS. WHITTLESEY.

Many of the papers of the Connecticut Land Company were procured by this society with funds furnished by the Commissioners of the county of Cuyahoga.

In addition to the ordinary sources of historical information, I have thus been able to consult portions of the Land Company's records.

These papers are by no means complete, and the early laws of this State, not providing for an official record of the surveys and other proceedings of the Land Company, it is now impossible to determine fully what was done by it, in 1796-7.

Among these documents is a printed copy of a full and clear Report on the subject of title to the Western Reserve, made by John Marshall, afterward Chief Justice of the United States Supreme Court, to the House of Representatives, March 21st, 1800.

This contains a detailed statement of the early grants to the Virginia and New England Companies, carried along to the proposed release of the right of soil in the Western Reserve, then pending in Congress.

This valuable paper, may be found at page 94, vol. 16, American State Papers, Public Lands, vol. 1. This society has also a copy of the argument of the late Hon. Samuel F. Vinton, of Ohio, before the General Court of Virginia, in the case of Peter M. Garner and others, December 1845, whom he was employed by the State of Ohio to defend.

Garner et al. were captured by the authorities of Virginia on the Ohio shore, between high and low water, charged with abducting slaves, and convicted in the State courts on this charge.

The defense rested mainly on the claim that Virginia had no jurisdiction, having never held title to the bed of the Ohio river. The pamphlet is now so rare that it should be reprinted. For a legal argument its style is unusually interesting, the diction clear, and the investigation exhaustive. Mr. Vinton exhibits the acuteness of a good lawyer, the broad perceptions of a statesman, and the eloquence of a practiced historian.

GRANTS AND CONVEYANCES, AFFECTING TITLES ON THE WESTERN RESERVE.

April 10, 1606.—Charter of Virginia, 34 deg. to 45 deg. N. latitude in two colonies, under the names of the London, and the Plymouth companies.

May 23,1609.—Second charter of Virginia, 400 miles on the coast with Point Comfort at the middle.

March 12, 1611-12.—Third charter of Virginia, including certain islands, from the 30th deg. to 41 deg. N. latitude.

Nov. 3, 1620.—N. England, or the Plymouth Company chartered, 40 deg. to 48 deg. N. latitude.

May 13, 1625.—These charters having been adjudged forfeit, Charles I., by proclamation, makes Virginia a royal colony without charters.

March 4, 1627.—The council of the Plymouth Company, conveyed to Sir Henry Roswell and others the country called Massachusetts.

March 4, 1629.—The above grant confirmed by Charles I., and a charter given.

March 19, 1632.—The Earl of Warwick, president of Plymouth Council, conveyed Connecticut to Lords Sayand Seal, and others.

June 7, 1635.—The Council of Connecticut surrendered their charter.

April 23, 1662.—Charles II. granted a charter to the Colony of Connecticut.

March 12, 1664.—Charles II. granted to the Duke of York from the Connecticut to the Delaware rivers, and other lands on the St. Croix river in Maine, conflicting with Connecticut, this difficulty settled by Royal Commission Nov. 30, 1664

March 4, 1681,– Grant of Pennsylvania to William Penn.

Nov. 15, 1783.—Governor Trumbull, of Connecticut, issued a proclamation warning all persons away from the lands west of Pennsylvania, between latitude 41 deg. and 42 deg. 2 min. north.

Second Thursday of Oct., 1786.—The Legislature of Connecticut offer that part of the Reserve, east of the Cuyahoga for sale at 50 cents an acre.

Feb. 10, 1788.—State of Connecticut to Sam'l Holden Parsons, deed of the Salt Spring tract under the above resolution—covering about 24,000 acres. Printed in our No. 31.

Nov. 10, 1792.—By resolution of the Legislature of Connecticut, 500,000 acres of land from the west end of the Reserve was released to her citizens, who suffered by the conflagrations of the enemy during the Revolution.

Sept. 2, 1795.—Deeds of the State of Connecticut to the negotiators of the Land Co., thirty-five (35) in number.

Sept. 5, 1795.—Deed of the negotiators to the members of the Land Company. (Original in the Museum of this Society.)

Sept. 5, 1795.—Deed of trust by the members of the Land Company to John Morgan, Jonathan Brace, and John Caldwell, from whom deeds were made to the owners and purchasers. (Original in this Society.)

Sept. 5, 1795.—Members of the Connecticut Land Company, in trust, to John Morgan, John Caldwell, and Jonathan Brace, for the benefit of the Excess Company, all lands on the Reserve over 3,500,000 acres, (Original in this Society.)

May 30, 1800.—United States deed to the State of Connecticut, a release of all claims to the soil of the Western Reserve.

Besides the above deeds and grants there were several written agreements in reference to the supposed "Excess," some of which are in possession of this society. The proceedings connected with the purchase of 1795 are marked by great circumspection. Several of the deeds and contracts are on parchment, written in a large, plain hand, ponderous in form, and prolix in composition.

John Livingston was a competitor with the Land Company for the purchase of the Western Reserve. He assigned to William, afterwards General, Hull, of Newtown, Massachusetts. Hull agreed to withdraw his bid if the Land Company would release to him the *excess* over 3,000,000 of acres, supposed to be about half a million, besides the Fire Lands. Relating to this arrangement, the following papers are among the archives of the Western Reserve Historical Society:

First—A contract dated September 5th, 1795, reciting the contract assigned by Livingston.

Second—An agreement signed by Wm. Hull and Moses Cleaveland, agent of the Land Company, April 9th, 1796.

Third—A bond of Gen. Hull, in relation to the expenses of survey, May 2d, 1796.

There are also among the documents of this society the following papers from among those secured at Hartford:

First—The articles of association adopted September 5th, 1795.

Second—Plan of partition agreed upon in April, 1796.

Third—A report of the Senate Committee on Western Lands, February 17th, 1799, which is substantially the same as the one made by John Marshall in the House of Representatives, March 21st, 1800, published in the American Archives.

The Spanish King laid claim to America on the basis of discovery, and a grant from the successor of St. Peter. This functionary, as the vicegerent of God on earth, affected the proprietorship of vacant parts of the earth, but neither Protestant England or Catholic France paid much attention to the grants of his Holiness. Actual or constructive possession, under the law of nations, was regarded as necessary to a good title by such civilized nations, as had not been favored by the Pope. Constructive possession, was extended over the entire valleys of rivers, the mouths of which were in actual occupancy by a recognized power. When the French established themselves at Quebec, on the St. Lawrence, and at New Orleans, on the Mississippi, they secured in this way a recognized claim to a vast country, the multitude of whose streams discharged their united volume into tide waters at these places.

In 1497 the Cabots, following the impulses of Columbus, examined the Atlantic coast from Cape Fear to Newfoundland, and made discoveries which laid the foundation of the English claims on this continent. Raleigh's attempted settlement in North Carolina in 1582, and the power of England, confined the Spaniards to regions more to the south, which went by the general name of Florida.

On the 22d of August, 1606, two companies were chartered in England, under the name of North and South Virginia, in order to secure actual possession of the shores which the Cabots had explored, or at least had seen from their ships. A settlement was made in North Virginia, at the Kennebec or Snake river in Maine, and in South Virginia at Jamestown, on the James river, in 1607.

The "London Company," to whom South Virginia was granted, extended from Cape Fear to the Potomac. North Virginia was conveyed to the "Plymouth Company," covering the Atlantic coast from Newfoundland to the Hudson, their limits on the west being very indefinite.

A new arrangement of the vacant territory was made in 1609. In this grant the London Company received "all those lands, countries, and territories lying and being in that part of America, called Virginia, from the point of land called Cape or Point Comfort, all along the sea coast to the southward 200 miles, and all that space and circuit of land from the sea coast of the precinct aforesaid, up into the land throughout from sea to sea, west and northwest."

By such ambiguous terms the Colony of Virginia was described, until after the compromises following the American Revolution.

On the south the boundary was an east and west line, corresponding to a parallel of latitude at about 34 degrees south; on the north by an oblique line starting near Cape May, running north 45 deg. west; across the east end of Lake Erie through lakes Huron and Superior, to the Arctic Sea, near the mouth of the Mackenzie river.

Under this grant Virginia claimed Western Pennsylvania, Ohio, and all the Northwest Territory. The Plymouth Company under the new arrangement was bounded by parallels of latitude from about 40 deg. to 48 deg. north. Its settlement on the Kennebec had failed. In 1620, (Nov. 3d,) while the "Pilgrim Fathers" were seeking a home in the New World, the Plymouth Company received a fresh charter, with varied corporate powers. Their territory was forever to be called "New England." King James gave it gratuitously to several of his favorites, saying, "The principal effect which we can desire or expect of this action, is the conversion or reduction of the people in those parts to the true worship of God and Christian religion."

In 1630 the Plymouth Company, of which Robert, Earl of Warwick, was president, conveyed to him what is known as Connecticut, and on the 19th of March, 1632, he conveyed, by the same boundaries, to Viscount Say and Seal (or Sele) and to Lord Brook by a deed, an unofficial transcript of which is here inserted:

DEED OF ROBERT, EARL OF WARWICK—MARCH 19, 1632.

To all people unto whom this present writing shall come, Robert, Earl of Warwick, sendeth greeting, in our Lord God everlasting;

KNOW YE—that the said Robert, Earl of Warwick, for divers good causes and considerations him thereunto moving, hath given, granted, bargained, sold, enfeoffed, aliened, and confirmed, and by these presents doth give, grant, bargain, sell, enfeoff, alien, and confirm, unto Right Honorable William, Viscount Say and Seal, the Right Honorable Robert, Lord Brook, the Right Honorable Lord Rich, and the Honorable Charles Fienner, Esq., Sir Nathaniel Rich, Knt., Sir Richard Saltonstall, Richard Knightly, Esq., John Pym, Esq., John Hampden, Esq., John Humphrey, Herbert Pellam their heirs and assigns and their associates forever, all that part of New England in America which lies and extends itself from a river there called Narragansett river, the space of forty leagues upon a straight line near the sea shore towards the southwest, west and by south, or as the coast lieth towards Virginia accounting three English miles to the league, and also all and singular the lands and hereditaments whatsoever lying and being within the lands aforesaid north and south in latitude and breadth and length and longitude of and within all the breadth aforesaid throughout the main lands there from the Western Ocean to the South Sea, and all lands and grounds, place and places, soil and woods, grounds, havens, ports, creeks and rivers, waters, fishings, and hereditaments whatsoever lying within the said space, and every part and parcel thereof.

And also all islands lying in America aforesaid in the said seas, or either of them, on the western or eastern coasts or parts of the said tracts of land by these presents mentioned, to be given, granted, bargained, sold, enfeoffed, aliened, and confirmed, also all mines and minerals, as well Royal mines of gold and silver as other mines and minerals whatsoever in the said lands and premises or any part thereof, and also the several rivers within the said limits by what name or names soever called or known, and all jurisdiction, rights, Royalties, liberties, freedoms, immunities, powers, privileges, franchises, pre-eminences and commodities whatsoever which the said Robert, Earl of Warwick, now hath or had, or might use, exercise, or enjoy, in or within any part or parcel thereof, excepting and reserving to his Majesty, his heirs and successors, the fifth part of all gold and silver ore that shall be found within the said premises or any part or parcel thereof. To have and to hold the said part of New England in America which lies and extends and is abutted as aforesaid: and the said several rivers and every part and parcel thereof and all the said islands, rivers, ports, havens, waters, fishings, mines, minerals, jurisdictions, powers, franchises, Royalties, liberties, privileges, commodities, hereditaments and premises whatsoever, with the appurtenances unto the said William, Viscount

Say and Seal, Robert, Lord Brook, Robert, Lord Rich, Charles Fienner, Sir Nathaniel Rich, Sir Richard Saltonstall, Richard Knightly, John Pym, John Hampden, John Humphrey, and Herbert Pellam, their heirs and assigns and their associates forevermore. In witness thereof the said Robert, Earl of Warwick, hath set his hand and seal this nineteenth day of March, in the seventh year of the reign of our Sovereign Lord Charles, by the Grace of God King of England, Scotland, France, and Irefand, Defender of the Faith, &c.

Anno Domini 1632.

Signed, sealed and delivered in the presence of
WALTER WILLIAMS, } ROBERT WARWICK.
THOMAS HAWSON. } [A Seal.]

In the course of time it was decided that the south line of this ambiguous grant should be on the forty-first (41st) parallel north, and the north line, forty-two degrees two minutes (42 deg. 2 min.), corresponding with south line of Massachusetts. In the mountains of Pennsylvania, near Hornellsville and thence to the southeast, Connecticut and Virginia came in direct contact by the oblique line running northwest from Cape May. While the Crown was modifying the grant to Virginia in 1609, Hendrik Hudson, in the name of the "Dutch West India Company," sailed past the island of Manhattan up into the country, as far as the "Overslaugh." Another claimant on the part of Holland, and a corporation the rival of the West India Company of Britain, was thus brought into the case.

In 1613-14, the Dutch established posts at New York, and at Albany, claiming from the Delaware to the Connecticut river, under the name of "New Netherlands." No Englishman was then living in New England.

The result of this unexpected occupation was, that the province of New York eventually interposed, between the present New England, and the extreme western part of her grant. Thus the confusion of lines and conflicts of jurisdiction multiplied, and continued until A. D. 1800.

On the north and west, there existed another disturbing element, no less formidable than France, a first class rival power

An abortive attempt at actual settlement was made by the French at Quebec in 1603, before Jamestown, or the Kennebec. The next year after 1607, Quebec became a permanent settlement. From thence, the French pushed westward to Lake Huron in 1614; to the Ohio in 1670; to the Mississippi in 1673, and thence to its mouth, April 9th, 1682.

This introduced more new questions on colonial boundaries. When the English and French governments were discussing the terms of the treaty of Aix-la-Chapelle, in 1748, they labored long to settle upon a western boundary for the British colonies.

There was then a line of French forts and trading posts, entirely surrounding the English settlements. At the ocean, there was one on the Bay of Fundy, another on the Connecticut river below Long Falls, called Fort Cohassett; on Lake Champlain, Crown Point; Forts Niagara and Oswego, on Lake Ontario; Forts Erie and Presque Isle, (at Erie, Pa.,) on Lake Erie; Fort Le Beuf, on the head waters of French creek; Fort Venango, on the Alleghany, at Franklin, Pa.; and Fort Du Quesne, at the forks of the Ohio.

The French negotiators insisted upon the Alleghany mountains as their boundary, as far north as the Susquehanna river, thence to Fort Cohassett on the Connecticut, and to the Kennebec river in Maine.

England admitted the line of the Alleghany mountains from the sources of the Appalachicola river as far north as the forks of the Ohio, thence up the Alleghany river to the lakes and the St. Lawrence, though she held claims through the Iroquois, to territory west of this line; (New York Colonial Documents—Palairet's Description, p. 59). Had either of these propositions been accepted, Ohio would have formed no part of New England, or of Virginia.

The two nations soon became involved in a war in the new world, on this very subject, and when in 1760 England was victorious, she immediately prohibited all settlements west of the Alleghanies.

This severe and unpopular proceeding, was based upon the theory that her title beyond the heads of the Atlantic rivers was defective, until the date of the conquest from France; and therefore all previous grants were restricted by the French boundary. Great Britain, in order to conciliate the Indians, decided to give up the valley of the Ohio to the barbarians, and to guarantee them against intrusion.

But the Virginians paid little attention to the proclamation of 1760. Many of them had been through the country as traders, prisoners, or soldiers. They had seen the surprising luxuriance of its soil, and had enjoyed the moderate climate which characterizes this region. They held large numbers of warrants, which the Colony had issued to her troops engaged in the late French war. As to the Indian, they neither feared him or cared for his rights. Squatter-sovereignty was triumphant, even over British authority, until after the Revolution; when Great Britain lost all power in the West. In this way the colonies, when the war of 1775 broke out, extended their limits to the westward without restraint.

About a century before this time the Province of New York, had been thrust in among the old grants in the following manner:

In 1664 Charles II., of England, paying no attention to the Royal grants of 1624, ceded to his brother James, Duke of York, the country known as "New Netherlands," then occupied by the Dutch. New Netherlands purported to extend along the coast from the Delaware, to the Connecticut rivers. To this prospective Province, the King gave the name of New York, and sent an English fleet to conquer it. When the Dutch war terminated in 1674 and possession was secured, a new patent was issued to the Duke of York, who set up a government under it. A copy of this grant may be seen in vol. 3, p. 235, New York Colonial History.

Like the other old deeds and patents, the boundary is so indefinite, that it led to disputes which were not settled for an hundred years. New York claimed an indefinite expansion westward even into the valley of the Ohio. In the grants to the Penns the colony of Pennsylvania was intended to be definite on the west, but this intention was not so clearly expressed as to preclude controversy. The expressions used might mean a straight line in longitude five (5) degrees west of the Delaware river or a crooked line of the figure of the river, as laid down on the early maps, bringing the Pennsylvania line nearly to the Cuyahoga river. Without any authority or right whatever, Indian traders from Pennsylvania, spread themselves beyond every part of this line over the entire State of Ohio.

Virginia interposed by force to limit Pennsylvania on the west, and was making good her possession, when the Revolution turned the attention of the Colonies, from their local quarrels to their common oppressions by the Crown. As the Revolution ended in a new government, the present line between Ohio and Pennsylvania was agreed upon as a compromise, in accordance with the patriotic temper of the times. Thomas Hutchins, John Ewing, and Andrew Ellicott began the survey in 1785. In 1786 it was completed by Andrew Porter and Alexander McClean. [See American Archives, Vols. 10 and 11.]

This line being settled, the State of Connecticut passed resolutions, providing for the sale of lands on the Western Reserve.

The first lands disposed of by the State were sold under the recommendation of Captain Jonathan Heart, of Harmar's battalion of United States troops. The journal and many letters of Captain Heart are in the archives of this society. He had been an officer in the Revolutionary army of the Connecticut Line. When appointed a captain of the Connecticut quota under Lieut. Colonel Harmar, he was a citizen of Berlin, near Hartford. His company was raised, and commenced its march for Fort Pitt in September, 1785. In 1787 he was ordered up the Allegheny river, to build a fort at the mouth of French creek, where were the remains of the old French Fort Venango.

During the summer he had command of the troops which were detailed as a guard to the surveyors under Thomas Hutchins, on the surveys of the seven Ranges next south of the Reserve. He was killed at St. Clair's defeat in November, 1791. His journal and letters show, that in 1788 he made an exploration by way of the Big Beaver river up the Mahoning, across to the Cuyahoga at the old portage, near Akron, and thence down the river to its mouth. Here he located a quarter of a township on the east side, where the city of Cleveland was laid out ten years later. By his representations, General Parsons and a number of his friends in the east, formed a company, or partnership, to purchase lands on the Reserve, east of the Cuyahoga, under the terms of the resolutions of 1786. In her negotiations with the United States, Connecticut was more tenacious of her claims west of Pennsylvania, because she had lost the Susquehanna claim around Wyoming, under an arbitration provided for by the Confederate Congress in 1783.

Though somewhat out of place, I introduce here extracts from Heart's letters, which, taken in connection with the statements of Mr. Case, explain the doings of the first Land Company. The death of General Parsons put an end to further operations.

FORT PITT, Dec. 25, 1789.

Major William Judd, Farmington, Conn.:

DEAR SIR: The papers have no doubt before this announced the death of your most respectable friend, General Parsons. He left me at the Salt Springs (Weathersfield, Trumbull co., Ohio), to return to Fort Pitt, and meet me at Conneaut, on Lake Erie.

As he was in commission for negotiating a purchase of the Western Reserve, and as his papers are lost, and he had often consulted with me on the subject, I enclose you the copy of a letter to him, which he was pleased to consider of importance.

You well know our worthy friend, and however some might retort and say he had his views, I am able to declare that he was using every exertion to bring about an extinguishment of the Indian claims.

By agreement with him, I have made the necessary minutes for laying down the outlines of the Connecticut Reserve, and as he is no more, I cannot through his hands, obtain the expected compensation.

It is almost three months since I have seen Mrs. Heart, who is at the Muskingum, having been during that time in the woods, and returned here two days ago, and leave for Muskingum to-morrow. Major Wyllys passed here a few days before I arrived.

Dec. 26.—P. S. As it rains I cannot go till to-morrow. Many promising prospects to the proprietors of the Springs, are lost by the death of our friend. You know I am not interested in the Springs, though I am in the lands. I believe I will transmit you the map of the Reserve, and trust its fate with the full assurance that you will do the best in your power for my interest. I have not time to write brother Jack, or other brothers.

FORT HARMAR, Jan. 6, 1790.

DEAR SIR: The death of General Parsons, who went with me as far as the salt springs, and left me with a design to return to Fort Pitt, make some arrangements and meet me at Conneaut, has made great derangements in the Connecticut Reserve, and in the Ohio Company, as well as in his family affairs. It is a great misfortune to the State, as it will be difficult for another Commissioner to take up the arrangements, where he left them. As his papers are lost, many of his designs will not be found. Much will depend on the appointment of his successor, and I wish you may obtain it. It is extraordinary that Gen. Parsons, a few days before he left me, was particularly communicative. His conduct indicated a full expectation that he should not put a finishing stroke to the business. He appeared to wish to communicate the general system to me, but the business I was particularly attending to, and the expectation of finding him on Lake Erie, prevented my entering so fully in every point into his views as I wish I had done.

I am told that $2,000 has been appropriated for surveying the lands, and that $1,000 is already expended, but I am confident there is not a survey made, and no minutes from which a map of the tract can be made except mine.

FORT HARMAR, Jan'y 12, 1790.

SIR: I have but just returned from a most fatiguing march up the waters of the Beaver, across to the head waters of the Cuyahoga, and down that river to the lake. From thence we went along Lake Erie to Conneaut, to Fort Franklin, (mouth of French Creek, Pa.,) down the Alleghany and down the Ohio to this place. In this march that severe and ever to be lamented misfortune, the death of General Parsons, happened. I am this moment again embarking for a like expedition down the Ohio, and have scarcely time to write. I have mentioned the importance of having a proper person appointed surveyor of the Connecticut claim.

FALLS OF THE OHIO, Jan'y 27, 1790.

I wrote you from Fort Pitt, and also from the Muskingum, but have been so constantly driven from one post to another that I have not had time to arrange my thoughts. We left Muskingum, (Fort Harmar,) about Nov. 20; went up the waters of the Beaver, across to the Cuyahoga, down it and around to the Pennsylvania line; from there went across to the waters of the Alleghany to Fort Pitt, and thence to this place, which is 620 miles from Fort Pitt. I am waiting here a few days to proceed with Major Doughty down the Ohio. The officer who forwards this goes to-morrow morning. I have not had time to lay down the surveys of the Connecticut Reserve, or plats of the valuable tracts I located in accordance with the agreement between Oliver Wolcott and General Parsons. General Parsons had not time to transact the business himself, and I was to locate one-fourth of a township on the Cuyahoga in the first and second township from the Lake. I have located a tract at the mouth of the Cuyahoga, beginning at a point on the bank of Lake Erie, four miles east of low water mark, where the Cuyahoga enters the lake, thence south until a line drawn due west to the Cuyahoga at low water and down it to the lake, and along the lake to the point of beginning, shall contain said quantity of one-quarter of a township, and will transmit a plat as soon as possible. I have also located a tract in the second township, if the mouth of the Cuyahoga should be disposed of. Have also located eight other tracts at least equal if not better than the mouth of the Cuyahoga, but the situation of that induces me to recommend it. If he hesitates in complying with the agreement I should advise my friends to make the purchase. It embraces a fine tract and a beautiful situation for a town. The line may be extended further east and south to contain more land. The other tracts are valuable for the richness of the soil.

With respect to the salt springs, they are worth working, and I should advise a settlement of a few families there. I do not know how your bargain stands. You and General Butler are I think proprietors, and General Parsons. Whether his papers are in such a situation that he may not be cheated out of it, I am in doubt.

I am so much pleased with the country that I would gladly turn the whole of my property that way, and become one of a company, provided the lands are granted in such a manner that a man can know where the tracts are he purchases. I expect next spring to take another march into the same country. JONATHAN HEART.

Extracts from the pamphlets of Chief Justice Marshall and of Mr. Vinton, which lie at the foundation of the history of our titles, may be given hereafter.

Western Reserve and Northern Ohio HISTORICAL SOCIETY.

No. 33—NOVEMBER, 1876.

ARCHÆOLOGICAL FRAUDS.

BY COL. CHAS. WHITTLESEY.

Since the publication of our paper No. 9, in February, 1872, on the subject of inscriptions on stone, purporting to be ancient, and to represent alphabetical characters of the era of the mound builders, other such stones have made their appearance. The supply appears to be fully equal to the demand. When the Arab laborers in the excavations at Jerusalem ascertain what relics the explorers want, it is not long before they make their appearance. In England, there was, not long since, a manufacturer of ancient flint arrow points, some of them purporting to be of the era of the glacial drift. The workmen in the gravel pits of Abbeville, and above there in the valley of the Somme, to Amiens, have been accused of fabricating relics to match those of Boucher-de-Perthes, found in the diluvium.

In the United States during the past half century, archæologists have felt an intense interest in the question, whether the mound builders had a written language. Of course, anything resembling letters, purporting to come from an ancient mound, excited universal attention, and imitators soon made their appearance. I propose to notice more fully than heretofore, the efforts of this genus to solve the question of an ancient alphabet in North America.

I do not imagine that exposure will put an end to their operations, so long as there are persons disposed to encourage them. Archæology has now passed from the field of mystery and conjecture, to that of observed facts, constituting a science. However it may be with exuberant theorists, thorough students do not wish to be deceived. They are not prepared to receive suspicious relics merely because they are wonderful, or sustain their own predilections. A recent occurrence abroad, has given both a ludicrous and a serious aspect, to the matter of spurious inscriptions here. In 1847, nearly thirty years since, E. George Squier, the leading archæologist of the United States, after a critical examination of the Grave Creek stone, pronounced it to be a modern fabrication.

Professor Daniel Wilson, whose reputation is well established in Europe and America, came to the same conclusion. In 1859, Dr. E. H Davis, of Ohio. a life-long student of our relics, sustained the views of Mr. Squier. All these opinions have been widely published in the United States. The archæologists of Europe interested in American antiquities, held a Congress at Nancy, in France, in July, 1875. A dissertation upon this stone was received and published in their proceedings. The writer seems to have convinced the Congress that the inscription is genuine, and was made in letters of the ancient Canaanites, to which reference is made below. At the same meeting a copy of another stone, purporting to have been exhumed from a mound in Licking county, Ohio, was presented and published, but was received with great doubt by the Congress.

On this the characters are partly Hebrew, very imperfectly reproduced, and in part a resemblance to some forms of Syriac and Armenian.

I now give a list of all the engraved stones in the United States which I have seen, or of which there are copies accessible to me, for which there have been advocates in favor of their genuineness, and of their linguistic value.

First—From the Grave Creek mound, of which there will be found below six copies, all different and all purporting to be facsimiles.

Second—Characters engraved upon a quartz ax, sketched by Dr. G. J. Farish for Professor Wilson, who regards them as genuine. Discovered by Dr. Farish near the ocean beach, at Yarmouth Bay, Nova Scotia. (Not engraved.)

Third—A grooved stone ax or maul, first described by the late Dr. John Evans, of Pemberton, New Jersey, reproduced by Dr. Wilson in his "Prehistoric Man," page 412. Engravings of this tool and its inscriptions are given below.

Fourth—The "Holy Stone" of David Wyrick, purporting to have been exhumed by him from the central depression of an ancient circle of earth, near Newark, Licking, county, Ohio, June 28th, 1860, now universally regarded as spurious. On this the characters are Hebrew, of the twelfth century, and are easily read. (Not reproduced here).

Fifth—An epitome of the Ten Commandments in the same Hebrew, with an effigy of Moses; taken by Mr. Wyrick from the base of the great stone mound near Jacktown, Licking county, O., in November, 1860. (Spurious, like No. 4, and not reproduced).

Sixth—A stone similar in shape to the Holy Stone, represented to have been taken from a mound in Licking county, O., by David M. Johnson, of Coshocton, O., in 1867, delivered to N. Roe Bradner, M. D., of Philadelphia, and endorsed by the late Dr. Samuel Barlow. (Not reproduced here).

This purports to have been found in a human skull, taken from the same mound as the Ten Commandments.

Seventh—A grooved stone ax, or maul, sent me in 1874 from Butler county, Ohio, about the size of the Pemberton ax, covered with English letters so rude and fresh as to deceive no one versed in antiquities. The purport of this inscription is that in 1689 Captain H. Argill passed there, and secreted two hundred bags of gold near a spring. (Not engraved.)

Eighth—A stone purporting to have been plowed up on the eastern shore of Grand Traverse Bay, Michigan. An imperfect cast of this stone is among the collections of the State of Michigan at the Centennial Exhibition. The original is in the cabinet of the Kent County Institute, Grand Rapids. Michigan; from which by the kindness of M. L. Coffinbury, Esq., one of the Curators, I have obtained a photograph.

An engraving of this copy will be found below. It is imperfectly executed, probably with a knife, and evidently of recent make, in which Greek, Bardic, and fictitious letters are jumbled together without order.

Ninth—In 1875, a stone maul was discovered in an ancient mine pit near Lake Desor, Isle Royal, Lake Superior, on which were cut several lines that were at first regarded as letters.

The Hon. S. W. Hill, of Marshalville, Mich., who superintended the excavations, has given me a description of this stone and its surroundings, with a drawing which I give in its proper place.

It is evident there was here no attempt at an alphabet. I plac it in this list merely as a matter of interest to archæologists, and with a view to present every ancient thing, which has even a remote resemblance to engraved characters.

COPY OF THE GRAVE CREEK STONE—NO. 1. BY CAPTAIN EASTMAN, UNITED STATES ARMY.

Captain Seth Eastman was a graduate and teacher of drawing at West Point. He was an accomplished draughtsman and painter detailed by the War Department to furnish the illustrations for "Schoolcraft's Indian Tribes," published by the Government. This copy was made in his official capacity, with the stone before him, and therefore takes the first rank as authority. There are between the lines, twenty-two characters, but one is repeated three times and another twice, leaving only twenty. The figure below, if it has any significance, is undoubtedly pictorial.

COPY NO. 2—FROM THE AMERICAN PIONEER, MAY, 1843.

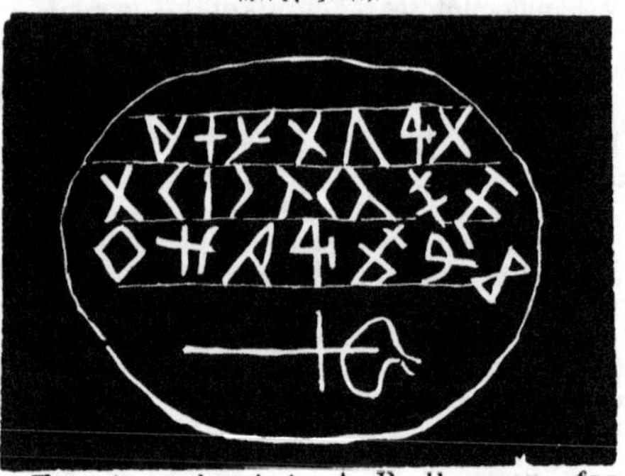

This is a sketch by A. B. Boreman for

John S. Williams, editor of the Pioneer. The sixth and seventh characters from the left in the second line are apparently so joined as to represent one.

In that case the number of letters is (19) nineteen. The second letter from the left in the third line is so different from Captain Eastman's that no person would give them the same interpretation.

COPY NO. 3—USED BY MONSIEUR JOMARD AT PARIS, 1843.

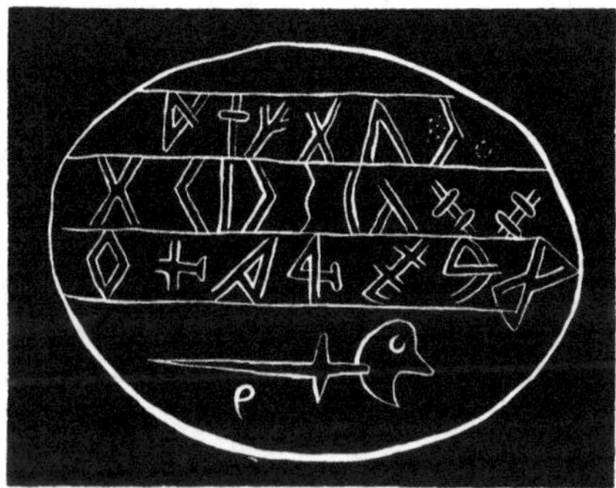

From this copy M. Jomard considered the letters to be Lybian, a language derived from the Phonecian. At the right of the upper line, one is omitted, and another bears no resemblance to the original. The fifth character of the second line is equally defective and objectionable. The second, fifth and sixth of the lower line are little better. In the rude profile of a human face beneath, an eye has been introduced, and the slender cross lines attached to it have assumed the proportions of a dagger or sword. For the linguist or ethnologist this copy is entirely worthless.

COPY NO. 4—SENT TO PROFESSOR RAFN, COPENHAGEN, 1843.

This is so imperfect and has so many additions, that it is little better than a burlesque upon the original. No one will be surprised that the learned Danish antiquarian could find in it no resemblance to the Runic, with which he was thoroughly familiar.

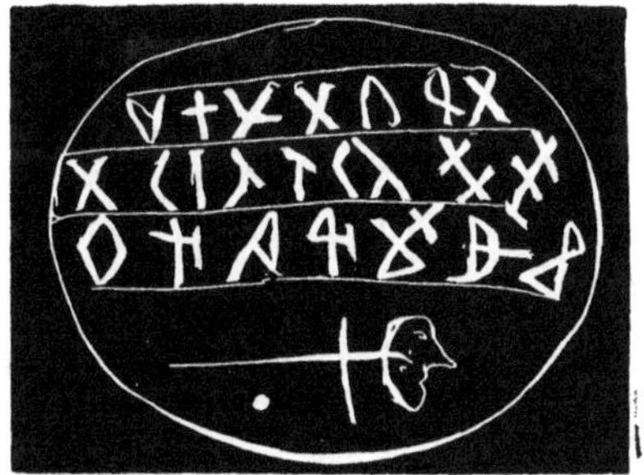

COPY NO. 5.—PROFESSOR DANIEL WILSON'S PRE-HISTORIC MAN, PAGE 409.

This purports to be from an impression of the stone in wax. The differences from Captain Eastman's are similar to those of the American Pioneer, No. 2. Something like an eye, a compressed mouth, and a pointed nose, give it an aspect materially different from either Nos. 1 or 2.—number of separate characters (19) nineteen. Professor Wilson is not a believer in the genuineness of the inscription.

GRAVE CREEK STONE—NO. 6.

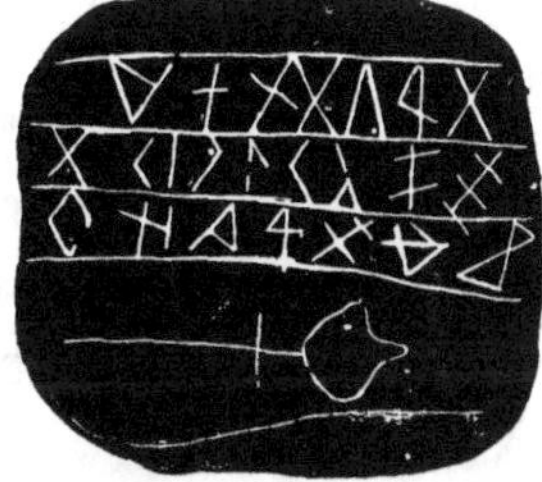

The above is the copy used by Monsieur Levy Bing, at the Congress of Nancy (Compte Rendu Tome 1, p. 218).

In the upper line letters 3 and 4, numbering from the left, are joined together, in a manner not seen in any of the other copies.

In the second line, letters 6 and 7 are separated, which in the original are joined.

No. 2 of the third line is so much distorted that it cannot be regarded as a copy, and No. 6 is little more accurate.

The horizontal line below the cross is a fabrication, introduced here for the first time.

The number of single characters, not counting repetitions, is nineteen.

Mons. Bing states that "after different combinations of the twenty-three letters I obtain the following result, that is, eight (8) Canaanite words, having complete sense;

forming a phrase which corresponds admirably with the symbol below the inscription."

"This symbol is a naked sword horizontally directed toward an arc, and supported upon the human head imperfectly designed, which reposes upon two long arms."

"This must represent the idea of Sovereignty and Conquest."

In Roman characters, M. Bing's twenty-three Canaanite letters represent only nine, which he marshals into the eight words as follows: AT—TTGD—TTL—NGT—LGA—HDQ—AQQ. The translation of which is "What thou sayest, thou dost impose it, thou shinest in impetuous elan, and rapid chamois;" "but in better French:" "Thy orders are laws, thou shinest in thy impetuous elan, and rapid as the chamois." Monsieur Bing then adds: "I not only sustain but justify the authenticity of the twenty-three Canaanite or Phonecian letters, composing the eight words of the Grave Creek inscription." Nothing can be more positive.

In a note on page 224 he adds: "This inscription must be of the third or second century before Christ, and the work of a Phonecian, having resided in Greece a long time; where the Phonecians themselves were accustomed to write their own language from left to right."

M. Bing is the author of a Canaanite Dictionary, in French, to which he has devoted a large portion of his life. He regards the old Hebrew as derived from the language of ancient Canaan. Nearly all writers who have discussed this relic, find some resemblance in it to the Phonecian.

In 1857, Monsieur Maurice Schwab made the first effort as a translator of this legend, in the Review Archæologique, for February of that year. His rendering is as follows: "The Chief of Emigration who reached these places (or this island), has fixed these statutes forever."

M. Schwab was followed by M. Oppert, according to whom it reads thus: "The grave of one who was assassinated here. May God to revenge him strike his murderer, cutting off the hand of his existence." This may not in the closing line be correctly translated from the French, but I have endeavored to make it literal, at the expense of sense and grammar.

Mr. Schoolcraft was a believer in the genuineness of the inscription, relying upon the statements of Mr. Tomlinson the owner, and of Dr. Clemens, of Wheeling, both made in 1838. Mr. Schoolcraft gives the following analysis of what he regards as twenty-two separate characters on this stone: There are in Greek, 4; Etruscan, 4; North Runic, 5; ancient Gaelic, 6; Old Erse, 7; Phonecian, 10; Old British, 16. These languages have letters in common. There are characters which are found in March's Icelandic grammar, and also several which Dr. Platt, in his history of Staffordshire, England, has shown to be on the ancient British "stick books."

This was the mode of making records on square sticks of wood, in the days of the Druids. Their written or sculptured language was a modified Celtic, of which there are specimens, discovered in Wales. Three of the Grave Creek characters, have been thought to form part of the inscription on Dighton Rock, Rhode Island, and three in the Norse Runic at Kingitorsoak, in Greenland, bearing date A. D. 1032. No one in this country has ventured upon a translation of any of the various copies now before the public.

Mr. Schoolcraft, who accepted the engraving as ancient, and therefore genuine, was inclined to regard it as having some connection with the emigration of Madoc from Wales, in the 12th century, A. D. Monsieur Goppert's translation, to a limited extent, harmonizes with this theory. The age of trees growing upon the mound, indicated the 12th century, as the period of its abandonment by the mound builders. It is evident, however, they had been in occupation many centuries before that time. If Madoc's fleet, and his followers, reached America, and the valley of the Ohio, they found a numerous population already occupying the valley of the Mississippi. Though few in number, and soon absorbed or destroyed by the native race, they could not have forgotten their language, or their mode of making records, by "stick books." But admitting such speculations to have some value, they bring no help to the theory that the mound builders had a written language. If they had, they were in possession of abundant means to perpetuate it. In their mounds there are numerous plates and articles of copper, shell and polished slate, on which they would certainly have engraved letters, if they had them. Their language, both oral and written, must have been in use over large tracts of country, and if put in the form of words, they must have been similar, in all the region extending from the Gulf of Mexico to Lake Superior.

The Hon. E. George Squier was the first to call in question the authenticity of this notorious stone, which he did in the second volume of the Transactions of the American Ethnological Society. His reasons in general are, that it being conceded not to be pictorial or hieroglyptical, it belongs to some of the ancient and numerous alphabets of which the Phonecian is the early type. Therefore the mound builders had a written language, or this inscription is of European origin.

The latter is within the scope of a possibility. Some sturdy Celt may have crossed the ocean and found his way to the Ohio and become a chief, over whose remains they raised a sepulchral mound. But the first question is whether it is authentic. Dr. Clemens, in his first account of the opening of the mound, makes no mention of ,this stone. The object of the opening was gain to the proprietor. The owner may himself have been imposed upon. It has no analogy to other inscriptions in North America, purporting to be ancient. Such are the principal difficulties that occurred to Mr. Squier.

On the other side, in addition to the statements of Mr. Tomlinson and Dr. Clemens, I have a letter from Mr. J. E. Wharton, now of Portsmouth, O., dated May 20th, 1876, in which he states that he was present in 1838 while the mound was being opened. The substance of his letter is that he saw Messrs. Clemens and Tomlinson at the time, and they were in the adit, which was being driven at the base of the mound.

After several wheelbarrow-loads of earth had been brought from the vault at the center, in which were bones, beads, mica pipes, etc., among them a small oval stone was discovered, a little more than an inch by an inch and one-half across, on which were three rows of Phonecian letters, but some are partial Runic, and he concludes by saying: "I know there could have been no deception."

Mr. Tomlinson, in a letter to the American Pioneer, received in May, 1843, states that it came from the upper vault about two (2) feet from a skeleton

None of these gentlemen profess to have seen the stone imbedded in the undisturbed earth of the mound. It was first seen by them on the barrows of shoveled earth, as the workmen brought them out along the adit.

No one questions the sincerity of their belief that it is of the age of the mound itself, but none of them state, or can state, that he saw the stone in its place. Both myself and the late Israel Dille, of Newark, O., saw the first of Wyrick's "Holy Stones" in his hands, at the place where he said he uncovered it, within an hour after he said it was found, and while it was still partially encrusted with earth. It was seen the same afternoon by the Rev. Mr. McCarthy, who read the incription, and by a number of other citizens of Newark, including the late Dr. J. N. Wilson, all of whom then believed it to be ancient, and have so stated. They conceived Wyrick to be incapable of such a fraud. But when his second find occurred in November of the same year, embracing the ten commandments written in the same character, they began to be suspicious. Dr. Nichols, who was present, charged him with deception at the time. After his death proofs were found, showing that all the incriptions were made by him with great labor from an old Hebrew Bible in his possession. Since that time a party in the same region has confessed to the fabrication of more inscribed stones, which may account for the appearance of those which came into the possession of Messrs. Barlow and Bradner.

If the Grave Creek find was free from suspicion as to its integrity, it has undergone so many mutations from transcribers and translators, that its value to ethnologists is gone. Before it can be used for scientific purposes, by those who confide in its genuineness they must establish its authenticity. It will not be sufficient for them to assume this, and call upon those who dissent to prove the contrary. The best authorities in the United States have condemned it during many years. The preponderances of proof as well as of probabilities are decidedly against it.

FAC-SIMILE OF ANOTHER ENGRAVED STONE PURPORTING TO BE FROM THE GRAVE CREEK MOUND.

On this there is but one figure that approaches the form of a letter, as represented on the larger stone from the same mound. It is inserted with a view to present in this paper everything within my reach that bears upon the subject of ancient alphabetical characters.

THE NEW JERSEY STONE AX ACCORDING TO WILSON—ONE-THIRD OF NATURE.

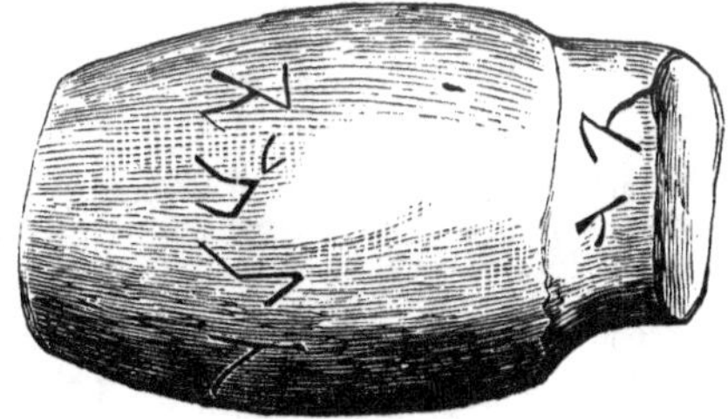

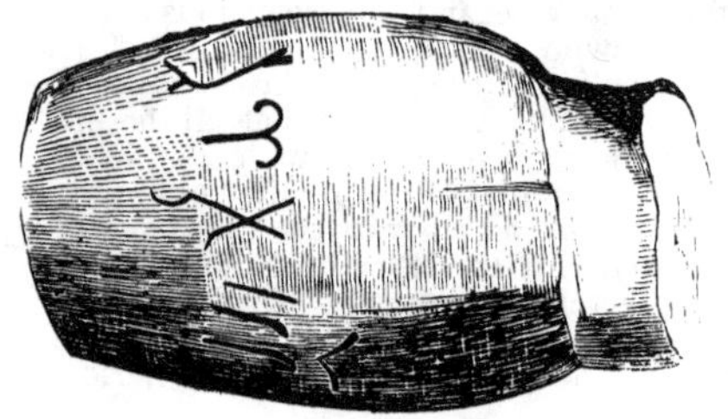

These characters are cut in the groove and on the blade, as represented above. They are neither Runic, Scandinavian, nor Anglo-Saxon. It was first described by Dr. John Evans, of Pemberton, N. J., near where it was found, prior to 1859. Dr. E. H. Davis who saw the stone, does not regard the inscription as ancient. The characters had been retouched before he saw them.

The characters inserted below are of the size of nature.

CHARACTERS ON THE PEMBERTON AX—SIZE OF NATURE.

No one competent to judge of the antiquity of these figures saw the stones until after they were injured, by recent scraping and cutting. The most singular feature of the characters, lies in a remote resemblance to those on the Moabite stone. The right hand one in the upper group, if bottom end upward, might represent the K of the Northmen. Those parallel lines at the extreme right of the blade, are common in the pictorial inscriptions of the red men. They may be seen on the "Turkey Foot" rock at the Maumee rapids; on the Newark inscriptions copied by Dr. Salisbury, and on the stone maul from Isle Royal, described by Mr. Hill.

STONE MAUL FROM ISLE ROYAL ⅓ LINEAR.

In the fall of 1874, Mr. Hill was engaged in clearing out an ancient mine-pit near Lake Desor, on Isle Royal, of Lake Superior. Among the stone mauls, which are always found in the works of the ancient copper miners of Lake Superior, was one on which were marks, which at first view were thought to resemble letters.

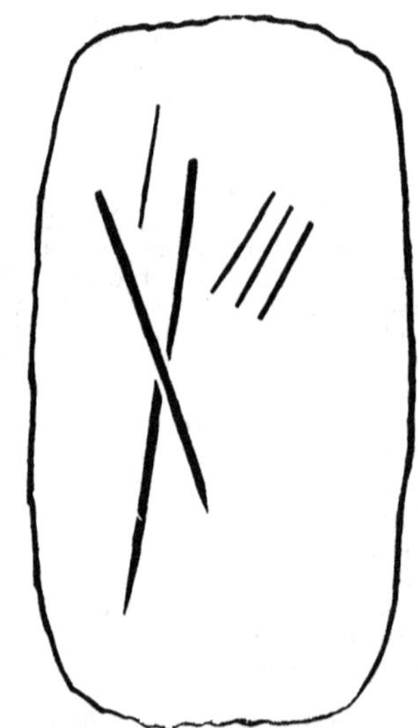

Its weight is four pounds, length seven inches, and its mineral composition is a tough hard variety of trap, known on Lake Superior as "greenstone."

Mr. Hill states that he took it from a depth of twelve feet below the surface. It is bruised at both ends by use, but is without a groove around the middle, such as are found on most of the mauls of these ancient miners. They may have held the grooveless ones in the hand, or may have fastened them in a wooden handle. Many others were found in this pit. Trees of the usual size grow over the works, which are of the era of the mounds. The markings on this maul have no significance as alphabetical characters.

FAC SIMILE OF THE STONE FROM GRAND TRAVERSE BAY, MICH.

This cut is inserted as a prevention against its being made the basis of dissertations at home and abroad.

The stone is sand rock, half an inch thick, with both faces flat, and the edges the result of natural cleavage. In texture it is of medium grain, rather gritty, and not very hard. The color is pale reddish brown, inclined to gray, owing to the presence of oxide of iron. Under a magnifier the engraving appears fresh and recent, as though it had been done with a knife, in the hands of one who is far from an expert. The arrangement of the supposed signs or letters is confused and the characters lack individuality. It is not easy to determine which was intended to be the upper side.

Looking over the evidence as it now stands, it may be safely affirmed, as it was twenty years since by Mr. Glidden, that when the Spaniards overran America there was not in the United States, nor had there been, any written or engraved alphabets in use. Nothing has as yet been discovered that is in advance of the usual pictorial or hieroglyphic mode of making records. The ancient Aztec characters found by Humboldt engraved upon an ax of jade, or chalcedony, in Mexico, were not letters but symbols. These are found in various degrees of perfection all over North America, even among the lowest and rudest people.

A mere collection of letters from various languages is not an alphabet. Words cannot be formed or ideas communicated in that way. When a people adopt the alphabetical signs of another they adopt the general style of the characters, and more often the characters in detail. Such signs had already an arrangement into syllables and words which had a known significance. A jumble of letters from a variety of nations bears internal evidence, that the author did not have an intelligent meaning to convey to others, and did not comprehend the languages from which the letters were selected.

In the case of the Grave Creek stone the various and contradictory attempts to extract a meaning from it, show that it belongs to no rational record of events, and is therefore not yet brought within the scope of historical inscriptions.

Western Reserve and Northern Ohio HISTORICAL SOCIETY.

TRACT No. 34—NOVEMBER, 1876.

THE MARGRY PAPERS.

VOLUME ONE.

By C. C. BALDWIN.

Western Reserve and Northern Ohio
HISTORICAL SOCIETY.

TRACT No. 34—NOVEMBER, 1876.

THE MARGRY PAPERS.

VOLUME ONE.

BY C. C. BALDWIN.

Découvertes et Établissements des Francais dans l'Ouest et dans le Sud de l'Amérique, Septentrionale, 1614-1754.

Mémoires et Documents Originaux recueillis et publiés par Pierre Margry, Première partie, 1614-1684. Paris, 1875.

The great West was, until a comparatively late period, under the dominion of France. Frenchmen made the first discoveries. Many years ago they made settlements, traded, and occupied the country until, with the capture of Quebec in 1760, all the Western posts were surrendered to Great Britain. It is then to France that we must look for its early history. It is only within a few years that extensive researches have been made in that country. The State of New York expended a very large sum to publish in eleven immense quarto volumes documents of especial interest in that State. For the history of New England, New Jersey, and Louisiana other investigations have been made. A quiet gentleman of Paris, M. Pierre Margry, long connected with the Department of the Marine, has devoted many years to gathering what would illustrate the foreign history of France, especially in America. He has already rendered this country great service in the investigations already referred to. His manuscripts, yet unpublished, were carefully collected from all parts of France and are unique. The knowledge of these treasures could not but make their publication much desired. Were it not for the "Boston fire" this would have been done by private hands, but that conflagration destroying such hopes, Congress came to the rescue and appropriated a sum, not too large, in the purchase of copies to encourage the publication of such portions as relate to our own country.

This plan of publication originated with the Historical Society at Cleveland and was warmly seconded by Mr. Parkman and by other societies and historical scholars throughout the country.

The first of the nine volumes is indeed full of interest. The materials for the early French history in this country are in some respects very full and in others very scanty. The Jesuits were powerful in the New World and their Relations were regularly transmitted to the mother country. But the Jesuits were not all the colony nor were all the discoveries made under their auspices, though they apparently desired that it should be so. La Salle was the first discoverer of the Ohio, the first to trace the Mississippi to the sea. The French rested their claim to the great West mainly upon these facts, and to-day his portrait adorns the Capitol at Washington as one of the four great discoverers of America. But he is hardly mentioned in these Relations. M. Margry has done more than any other to recover the history of La Salle. The handsome volume before us is ornamented with his portrait as he appeared in his younger days, with long curls and the dress of a man of the world. There is, however, a determination in the face and a restless, dreamy look to the eyes as if the portrait was not an unlikely one for the man who, in spite of the opposition of all, could penetrate alone vast countries, could give his fortune to discovery, and persist with such force of will that he should be slain by his own men in a pathless wilderness, thousands of miles from even the settlements of his own countrymen in the Western world.

The earlier papers in the volume relate to the Recollets—the "first missionaries of the West and South, in North America." They were professedly poor and plain. They hastened to the new land and established a convent at Quebec and posts at other places. The Jesuits came over after, partly on their invitation, and in the end very decidedly turned them out of Canada. The second, and larger paper, is a memoir desiring relief for them from the obstacles placed in their way by the Jesuits, and the Government of Canada controlled by that order. There seems to have been danger that in a few years there would not be a Recollet in Canada. This strife between the religious sects deserves a paper of its own. The Jesuits, at first, certainly very devout and self-sacrificing men, and sometimes martyrs, were too devoted to the success of their order, and the Colonial Government was hampered by them. The Government at home opposed them secretly and not openly. Recollets were meant to be encouraged to offset them The Count de Frontenac in his letters wrote earnestly against them in cipher, praising them in other parts of the same letter which might fall under their eyes. In a later paper from him in this volume are presented his views with much earnestness and in plain French. He sketches their power and possessions, their hostility to the Recollets, and accuses them of a want of fidelity to the King. "This general animosity against all the most faithful servants of the King shows well enough their designs." "They would not allow the Recollets," says he, "to hear confession or administer sacrament." He had charged them in a previous letter with caring more for beavers than for souls. "They had opposed," says Frontenac, "the sale of brandy to the Indians, without which the fur trade could not be successful and now even opposed the sale of wine, to place a new yoke on the people." It was common knowledge that they took directly or indirectly the management of everything, and used for that purpose a powerful espionage. They did not teach the Indians French lest they should become friends of the civil power. A vocabulary for Indian use defined equal "the Black Robe (Jesuit priest) is equal to Onontio (Indian name for the Governor of Canada)." They told other savages that they were the masters of Onontio. And in truth they do not seem in saying that to have very violently stretched the truth

Two papers present a lively picture of the commercial strife with the Dutch for the trade of the Indians. The Iroquois had killed the beaver south of the lakes and were getting them from the North and Northwest and selling them at Albany and at better prices than the French had paid. The whole volume shows the projects for extension of Western and Southern trade by the unknow river Ohio and the unknown river Miss sippi, even to the "Mer Vermeio," Gulf California, and in other directions. Su were the motives held forth to the King f such expeditions as were made by La Sall though La Salle himself seems to have bee actuated by an innate love of adventure ar discovery such as very few men have ev had.

Page 170, Lake Erie is mentioned in 16 as called by the savages "Techaronkion."

Temperance men will find in the volum an interesting discussion concerning tl sale of brandy to the Indians, and the view of various persons are presented much i the manner of witnesses in a Congression commission, with the usual diversity of opi ion.

There appear the "Details of the voyag of Louis Jolliet," who visited in 1673 th Mississippi, having departed from Quebec b order of Frontenac to discover the Sout Sea. His map is mentioned, which we hop M. Margry will publish.

The interest of the volume centers in L Salle. Although in a very early day he dis covered the Ohio, but little has been known or in fact is now, of the particulars. I pur posely omit discussion of this journey. I this volume appears much history of L Salle, his plans, expenses, draft upon his family and friends, how he built upon Lake Ontari and planned to build upon Lake Erie anc further west; how he built on the Niagara river, on the river St. Joseph in the southwest part of Michigan, and away within the wilds of Illinois, among the tribe of that name, the fourth fort, Crevecoeur. An interesting memoir is that of a friend of the Abbe de Gallinée relating, from the information of La Salle himself, the particulars of his journey with the Abbe, including accounts of the Indian tribes and their manners. In 1669 Gallinée, Dollier, and La Salle left Montreal to seek the Ohio known by report. They turned toward its source, but the Iroquois dissuaded the two priests from the journey, much to the dissatisfaction of La Salle, and the party turned to the north of Lake Erie. The report of Abbe Gallinée of this journey is also in this volume. From it we extract but a single word, Paouitikoungraentaouak, the Algonkin name for the Chippeways. The feelings of La Salle were with the Recollets. They were first; the Jesuits came after (says the memoir), and the Recollets gave them half their house. The Jesuits shortly got the other half and the Recollets had hard work to get it back. The Jesuits were established in Quebec, "where they are absolute masters" L'Evesque (the Governor) was their creature and would do nothing without them. La Salle complains that the Jesuits sought to control trade. One Indian said that "when the Black Robes were among us we worshipped God, but when there were no more beavers we see them no more." The Jesuits disliked La Salle very much. Frontenac in this volume (page 323) says "their design, as it appeared in the end, was to set a trap whichever path I took, or to derange everything, to place the country in disorder from which they would not hesitate to profit, and to ruin M. de la Salle." "He has become the object of their envy and aversion." This enmity was no doubt much prompted by their pious zeal. They had made discoveries. Their map of Lake Superior of 1671 was almost wonderful. They were searching for the Mississippi, and their schemes of power, wealth, and dominion, for their order in the great valley of North America, may have been as grand and magnificent as those of La Salle for his King.

The paper lets us into such lively views of the times as are not given in ordinary history, and we see how, after all, love of gain, love of power, and jealousy of others influenced history in such solitudes as would seem to be free from such disturbing elements if any freedom could be found.

The most valuable paper of the volume is called a "Relation of the Discoveries and Travels of Sir de la Salle, Lord and Governor of Fort Frontenac, beyond the great lakes of New France, made by order of M. Colbert, 1679–80–81." It is a narrative covering 150 pages of the events of those years, and probably the official report made after the return of La Salle to Montreal. In 1677 La Salle was in France. He was already famous and of influence. His scheme was vast. He wanted to penetrate to the great valley of our continent and lay there the foundation of powerful colonies "in a country temperate in climate, rich and fertile, and capable of a grand commerce." Such hold of the continent would be taken that, at the next war with Spain, France could oust her in North America. In the commencement of 1679 he built the Griffin, the first vessel navigating Lake Erie, meeting some opposition from the Iroquois, but less because that nation was at war beyond Lake Erie. The early part of the story is well known from other sources, but the narrative of La Salle's travels after he left Fort Crevecoeur and parted with the expedition to the North has never been told so completely as here. We wish we could present the whole paper to our English readers, but we cannot follow in detail the straight, business-like story of adventure, travel, description of countries and Indian nations, contests, diplomacy, discouragements and perseverance. The Iroquois traveled from their homes in New York all through the West, and it was dangerous to take sides or not to. They were then fighting the Illinois and the Miamis. First living south of Lake Ontario, the best armed and most warlike tribe in America, they defeated and exterminated (says our memoir) all their neighbors. They bore their arms to the Gulf of St. Lawrence, to the North Sea, in Florida, and even beyond the river Mississippi. They have (says the writer) in thirty years destroyed over 600,000 lives, and made desert most of the country round the great lakes.

La Salle had expected the Griffin with supplies for his journey down the river. He never saw the vessel again. She was lost, he believed by treachery, and he must return for succor. Early in 1680 he reached St. Joseph. He found two men whom he had sent around the lake, but they did not find the Griffin. Arrived at length at Niagara, he found he had also lost a ship with supplies from France. He reached Montreal, May 6th, 1680 His creditors had siezed his property and his resources seemed entirely wasted. On his return to Frontenac he learned by letter from Tonty that his men left at Crevecoeur had deserted after destroying the fort, carrying away what property they could and destroying the balance. They destroyed Fort St. Joseph and also seized La Salle's property at Niagara. He was not disheartened. He started to succor Tonty and save if he could the vessel building on the Illinois with which he meant to descend to the sea. November 4th, 1680, he reached the mouth of the St. Joseph. The Iroquois had fought the Illinois, and as he approached Crevecoeur there were only scenes of death and devastation. When he reached that post he found it silent; the planks of his vessel were there and on one of them was written, "Nous sommes tous savages ce 19 A—, 1680"—we are all savages. Was it prophetic that he had named the fort Crevecoeur (Broken Heart). The romantic interest of the relation is here at its height, but La Salle does not stop to dwell upon the picture. His first thought was, did the A mean Aout or Avril, August or April. He wished to find the faithful Tonty. Tonty's fate appears partly in this relation and partly in his subsequent memoir in this volume. Not the Jesuits alone regarded La Salle with jealousy. The Iroquois were not without reason fearful that the Western tribes would be armed against them with fire-arms and other assistance, and that a great trade in the West would draw from their own profits with the Dutch and English. While Tonty was absent the desertion had taken place. After he returned he was captured by the Iroquois.

In May, 1681, after unsuccessful search and hard labors, building up Indian succors and strength, La Salle left the fort on the St. Joseph for Michilimackinac, where he found Tonty and Father Membré. They returned to Frontenac, and this paper is the relation to that time.

Of his new, wonderful resurrection of recourses and eventual success we do not speak, although a new and brief relation of it from information of his brother is also in this volume.

The resolute will and wonderful power of La Salle appear nowhere so strongly as in the narrative we have quoted. There seems almost a direct triumph of will over every opposition, of mind over matter. This is the fullest, most explicit and valuable account of this series of expeditions. By whom was it committed to writing? Evidently by some one fully informed and from notes made day by day, with dates as in a diary. This, as well as the expedition of 1682, wherein he descended the Mississippi, were made under the commission of 1678, wherein the King was graciously pleased to permit La Salle to discover these new lands provided he did it at his own expense. The official report of the last expedition was made by Father Zenobe Membré, a Recollet. See La Salle's memoir to Seignelay, in Falconer's Mississippi and Oregon, which leaves it almost doubtful whether La Salle did not mean to say that Membré wrote the official report of all his expeditions under the leave of 1678. Membré was with La Salle in the first one, and it seems probable that he drew this report. It ends with the embarkation of La Salle on Lake Ontario for Montreal, the last of August, 1681, and then adds the hope that the end of the year 1682 will find the discovery of the mouth of the Mississippi made.

Some parts of the report relating to those parts of the journey where Hennepin was present bear a striking resemblance to his first book, published in 1684. I translate, for instance, from page 440. The two reports are word for word the same, except where differences are marked, this report as 1, and Hennepin as 2.

"The Sieur de La Salle could not build a barque at Fort de Frontenac because of a portage of two leagues at the great fall of Niagara, without which one could sail in a large vessel to Fort Frontenac to the bottom of Lake (Illinois, 1) (Dauphin, 2) by the lakes which are with reason called fresh water seas. The great river of St. Lawrence takes its origin from several great lakes, among which are five of an extraordinary size, and which are badly laid down in the printed maps. These lakes are (1. Lake Superior, the Lake of the Illinois, the Lake of the Hurons, the Lake Erie, the Lake Frontenac); (2, the first Lake de Condé, or Tracy, second, Lake Dauphin or of the Illinois, the third, Lake of Orleans or of the Hurons, fourth, Lake de Conty or Erie, and fifth, Lake Ontario named de Frontenac.) They are all of fresh water and very good to drink, abounding in fish and surrounded by fertile lands. With the exception of the first, navigation is easy in summer even for large vessels, but difficult in winter because of the strong winds which blow there." I might continue the parallel at some length. The account of Hennepin's journey among the Sioux bears a similar verbal similarity. On page 478 of this volume appears the beginning of that part translated by Mr. Shea in his Discovery of the Mississippi, and continuing for four or five pages Hennepin, however, calls the Mississippi "Colbert." By very far the larger part of the report bears no resemblance to Hennepin. Hennepin was not above copying the report had he wished to do so for his book. Much of his second book was copied from the suppressed Le Clercq. Still I cannot but think that those parts of the paper which have much resemblance to Hennepin bear his mark. His egotism and desire for prominence are apparent.

"The Father Louis Hennepin offered himself to make this journey" (to the Sioux,) "to commence acquaintance with nations among whom he had thought he would go soon to establish himself in preaching the faith."

Page 440. The carpenters are said to have been sent to Niagara under the charge of La Motte and Father Louis Hennepin. In other accounts it is said La Motte had charge.

Page 444. The carpenters would have been frightened away by the Senecas if La Salle and Father Louis had not taken pains to reassure them. There are examples of the vanity characteristic of Hennepin's book quickly noticed by anyone who has read Mr. Shea's excellent bibliographical sketch of that work. The differences are suggestive. In Hennepin the account is occasionally enlarged by introduction of other matter as it by afterthought. The forms of the names of the lakes bear the stamp of the wilderness Superior, of the Illinois, of the Hurons. Erie, in Hennepin called in compliment to Frenchmen, de Conde or Tracy, Dauphin, d'Orleans, de Conty.

Hennepin's own name is in this paper

Henpin, while La Salle in his letters calls him Hempin. Henpin was not unlikely the original, euphonised by speech into Hempin and by himself to the more musical Hennepin.

At the time this relation was made Hennepin had returned from his captivity, and he probably furnished his report in writing, used by his brother Recollet in a friendly spirit. He very likely met La Salle himself, who writes, in August, to a friend in France, that Hennepin was about to go to France; that he would not hesitate to exaggerate; "it is his character," and he speaks "nearer what he wishes than what he does." I doubt not the report of Hennepin was quite cut short in this paper; in fact, it so appears.

Following this relation is the recital from Nicholas de la Salle of the discovery of the mouth of our great river, in 1682, and the return to Quebec. Next is a general relation of the enterprises of La Salle from 1678 to 1683 made by Tonty, whose nickname, "Main de fer,"—hand of iron—reminds one of the knights of old while his heart was as stout and trusty as his hand—a real hand of iron, by the way, found by more than one Indian to give a very heavy blow. Tonty was successively commander at Niagara, Crevecoeur and Fort St. Louis, and descended the Mississippi with LaSalle. The contents of these 600 pages cannot be made known in a review. Their value consists mainly in the more complete variety and perfect knowledge which they give of these great enterprises of which we had some previous knowledge. Their apparent value increases by comparison with less authentic and particular accounts. LaSalle is by all means the most prominent figure in interior discovery. We have indicated how vast his plans. His life was romantic, his death tragic. In later times claims to large territories were made under his discoveries. The French claimed under that right even the Ohio and the forts at Pittsburg and Erie, wrested from them by the English. Still later the population, French by extraction, leaned to the United States in the Revolutionary war and made easy such occupation and control as gave the United States the Northwest Territory. In still later times, when our Northwestern boundary was disputed, La Salle's doings were discussed as if on them turned the fate of vast territory.

We say then that we feel under great obligation to M. Margry who, with patriotic care, has collected and preserved much valuable matter; and we were before this publication much indebted for the liberal use of his treasures he has permitted to Americans. While it has given the public a foretaste of his riches, it has stimulated that patriotic zeal which makes the student of history desire access to the original authorities, so that he can see for himself the original and life-like records of the times. The English reader cannot better estimate the value of this volume than to see how often in the Discovery of the Great West these unpublished treasures have been to Mr. Parkman his best and frequently his only guide. The early maps which accompany these and other relations have not been yet published. We hope M. Margry may be able to furnish them. Some of the early manuscript maps are vastly in advance of those published. On seeing them, one has a profound respect for the discoverers, somewhat, it must be confessed, at the expense of the early geographers.

Some of the best and clearest evidences of what was done and known, arise from the maps.

Western Reserve and Northern Ohio

HISTORICAL SOCIETY.

TRACT THIRTY-FIVE—DECEMBER 1876.

A CENTENNIAL LAW SUIT.

BY C. C. BALDWIN.

During the present year the Supreme Court of the United States has rendered a judgment for about $50,000 on a claim which originated nearly one hundred years ago.

The facts of the case well illustrate the history of western dominion and are interesting in the patriotism and long suffering of its hero.

At the breaking out of the Revolutionary war the colony of Virginia claimed jurisdiction of Kentucky and the country northwest of the Ohio. The border settlers had had much trouble with the Indians. This had quieted, but the British contemplated such arming and use of their savage allies as threatened the destruction of all settlers west of the mountains. Major (afterwards General) George Rogers Clark lived in Kentucky and was the most able and eminent of the early heroes of the West. In 1776, he visited Virginia to meet the Legislature He was too late, but he got the powder he wanted of the Governor (Patrick Henry) and the Executive Council. This was brought to Kentucky by way of Pittsburgh The next two years were full of border depredations. Clark saw that the western British forts must be captured, and in January, 1778, he was instructed by his State to attack Kaskaskia, in the southwestern part of what is now the State of Illinois.

He captured Kaskaskia, Cahokia and Vincennes. These were old French towns surrendered with Quebec to the British in 1760. They were, by the way, in "Illinois county," Virginia, that State having provided that all its citizens who were or should be settled "on the western side of the Ohio" should be included in a distinct county, which shall be called Illinois county. St. Louis, at that time, was an old town governed by Spain.

The hero of our law suit, Col. Francis Vigo, was a Spanish merchant there, who had a hearty sympathy with the Americans, and visited Clark at Kaskaskia

Col. Clark had received a communication from Capt. Helms, whom he had left in command at Vincennes, stating that he was destitute Clark could not send supplies, but he requested Vigo to go and procure them of the French inhabitants there, to whom he was well-known. In the meantime Vincennes had been recaptured by the British and Indians, so that Vigo was taken prisoner. Though a Spanish subject, he was suspected of having too warm an interest in the American cause, and was told he might depart on condition he would not do anything during the war injurious to the British. He finally pledged himself to do nothing on his way to St. Louis. He kept his promise sacredly, but immediately left St. Louis for Kaskaskia and gave Col. Clark full information of Vincennes.

The French inhabitants of that place might be expected to favor the expedition. In fact the inhabitants of Kaskaskia had themselves raised the American flag. But Clark was needy. The statement of facts in the case shows that "the soldiers were in a state of almost entire destitution, being without clothing or means of subsistance" They had the colonial money of Virginia. But the French had a very healthy dislike of an unconvertible currency, and would not take it. Clark would perhaps have been helpless, but Vigo cashed his drafts on the agent of Virginia at New Orleans. Vigo seems to have felt a very hearty sympathy with America, and to have thoroughly committed himself and his fortune to the issue. He advanced some $12,000, in those days a large sum. The draft, which was the basis of the suit, was dated December 4th, 1778, and was for $8,716 40.

On the 5th of February following Clark, with one hundred and seventy men, started for Vincennes I cannot follow the details of the campaign, called in the opinion of the Supreme Court, one of the most romantic of the West down to this day.

No statement of the sufferings of these hardy men could be more effective than the simple daily record of the officers. We make but few extracts:

18th (February 1779) "spent day and night in the water to no purpose, for there was not one foot of dry land to be found"

19th.—"Col. Clark sent two men in the canoe down to meet the batteau with orders to come on day and night, that being our last hope, and we starving, many of the men much cast down, particularly the volunteers. No provision of any sort now two days."

20th.—"Camp very quiet, but hungry. Some almost in despair. Made canoes."

21st.—"Army over, but no dry land. Rain all this day, no provisions."

22d.—"Col. Clark encourages his men, which gave them great spirits. Marched on in the water. Those that were weak and famished from so much fatigue went in the canoes. We came one league further to some sugar camps, where we stayed all night Heard the evening and morning guns from the fort. No provisions yet. Lord help us."

Next day they waded over Horse Shoe Plain, about four miles long, all covered with water breast high, when they caught a man hunting ducks. Governor Hamilton, commander at St. Vincents, had offered rewards for American scalps, and Clark was not disposed to grant many "honors."

He sent a letter by the duck-hunter to the inhabitants, desiring them to remain in their houses, as he was determined to take the post that night Those that "are friends to the King will instantly repair to the fort and join the Hair Buyer General and fight like men." Clark's little army occupied the town that night, and there was some fighting.

Next morning he "ordered" Hamilton to surrender in terms so expressive of the intense feeling engendered by the Indian atrocities that I reproduce it:

"SIR: In order to save yourself from the impending storm that now threatens you I order you immediately to surrender yourself with all your garrison, stores, etc., etc. For if I am obliged to storm you may depend on such treatment as is justly due to a murderer. Beware of destroying stores of any kind, or any papers or letters that are in your possession, for, by Heavens, if you do, there shall be no mercy shown you."

After further engagement Hamilton proposed a truce, which was declined and he surrendered at once.

The immense consequences of this brief campaign, with few men and small means, are not easily realized It gave the Americans possession of the main posts in the west, south of Detroit. When peace was made in 1783 with Great Britain, that nation desired the Ohio as a boundary, and many Americans would have favored such a concession, but the United States was in actual possession of the territory, and continued so.

But our hero, Colonel Vigo, waits with his draft upon New Orleans. It was not paid, and at the close of the war constituted a claim against the State of Virginia.

The Congress of the Confederation, September 6th, 1780, considered it "advisable to press upon those States which can remove the embarrassments repecting the Western country a liberal surrender of a portion of their territorial claims, since they cannot be possessed entire without endangering the stability of the general Confederacy," and it was "earnestly recommended to those States who have claims to the Western country to pass such laws, and give their delegates in Congress such powers as may effectually remove the only obstacle to a final ratification of the articles of Confederation."

On the 20th of October, 1783, Virginia passed an act authorizing a conveyance, which was made on the 1st of March, 1784, by Thomas Jefferson, Samuel Hardy, Arthur Lee and James Monroe, then delegates from that State. One of the conditions was "that the necessary and reasonable expenses incurred by this State in subduing British posts or maintaining forts and garrisons within and for the defense, or in acquiring any part of the territory so ceded or relinquished, shall be fully reimbursed by the United States."

Several acts were passed in reference to claims, but no claims were to be allowed which had not been allowed by Virginia prior to the 24th of September, 1788.

Colonel Vigo's claim does not appear to have been presented to Virginia prior to that date, nor to the United States within the not long time fixed for presentation. He lived clear upon the frontier and perhaps did not know the need of it.

In one of the papers in the case, General Gratiot relates that his father, having claims against Virginia, went to New Orleans, thence to Havana, thence to North Carolina and Richmond as being safer than a more direct journey. He was engaged two or three years in getting his pay, and but for strong friends must have been a ruined man. He received but little money, negroes and tobacco at a high price, and a quantity of land esteemed not worth looking after. On returning to the Illinois country, Gratiot's report caused the other creditors to lose heart.

The western commissioners, in 1783, by their views, would not make claims very valuable. It was their opinion that bills drawn on the treasury of Virginia ought to be paid off according to the Illinois scale of depreciation, by which they were estimated at a small per cent.

In Clark's accounts in evidence, he credits in January, 1778, $1,143, 1·5 for £1,200, Virginia currency; in May 1779, $4,000, for £9,400 Virginia currency.

Vigo's bills were included in Clark's accounts, and a round allowance was made by the United States to Virginia of half a million dollars.

Colonel Francis Vigo was born in Mondovi, in the kingdom of Sardinia, in 1747. At an early age he enlisted in a Spanish regiment and accompanied it to New Orleans There he left the army and engaged in the Indian trade, settling a few years after in St. Louis. He is said to have been there connected in business with the Governor of Upper Lousiana. So essential was his help to Clark that Judge Law in his History of Vincennes, says the whole credit of the conquest belonged to two men, Gen. George Rogers Clark and Colonel Francis Vigo.

Besides the losses already mentioned, Vigo had taken Clark's depreciated currency, which became valueless. Vigo settled in Vincennes, much crippled by his patriotic efforts, and continued there to see the forest he had rescued grow into a great country.

He continued comparatively poor. He seems to have led a pure, patriotic life and been much respected for his integrity, good character, and sense. The original papers on file in the suit, says the attorney for the claimants, show that he possessed the esteem and confidence of General Knox, the then Secretary of War, General Anthony Wayne, and General Harrison, and that he subsequently performed valuable services to this country. As late as 1811, General Clark wrote him in the warmest terms of friendship and favorable mention is made of the services he rendered to his adopted country by Judge Marshal in his Life of Washington, (vol. 3, p 566), and by General Clark himself in his letter to Thomas Jefferson, (Jefferson's works, vol. 1, p 453). Judge Burnett, in his notes on the Northwestern Territory, says Vigo voluntarily surrendered his property for the support of the regiment.

At the hearing was produced a letter of General Harrison, who says in 1834 he had known him thirty-nine years, and for thirteen years, while Governor of Indiana, lived in the same town with him and on terms of the most intimate friendship. He declared Vigo "utterly incapable of misrepresentation, however great his interest," and that he was confident there "were more respectable persons in Indiana who would become the guarantors of his integrity than could be induced to for any other person." "His whole life, as long as his circumstances were prosperous, was spent in acts of kindness, and benevolence to individuals and his public spirit and attachment to the institutions of our country were proverbial."

Vigo continued to reside in Indiana until his death at Terre Haute, March 22, 1836.

His claim was, from time to time, presented to Congress. Judge Burnett himself had it in charge for a while. Seven times the House Committee reported in favor of it, and twice bills for its payment passed that House. In the Senate bills were reported providing for its payment.

Finally, in 1872 an act passed both Houses referring it to the Court of Claims, in which court Archibald McKee and others, as his heirs, commenced their proceeding upon the claim. In 1873 the court found in their favor. The United States took the case to the Supreme Court, which in May, 1876, decided in favor of the claimants for the original amount, with interest from 1778 at five per cent. per annum, the interest, at that rate, being several times the principal.

I am indebted to D. W. Middleton, Esq., Clerk of the Supreme Court, and to W. Penn Clarke, Esq., counsel for the plaintiffs, for the copies of arguments, facts and testimony in the case.

Western Reserve and Northern Ohio HISTORICAL SOCIETY.

TRACT No. 36—JANUARY, 1877.

Memoranda and Notes by the late Alfred T. Goodman.

Among the papers of our late secretary are many unfinished articles on various historical and biographical subjects. They all bear the marks of his capacity in gathering materials of this kind, and, incomplete as they are, possess too much value to be lost. With so much industry and a memory that seemed to retain everything that he read, had his life been spared there is no part of our local and personal history which he would not in process of time have made perfect in all its details. We shall publish occasionally from these fragments, a portion of which are presented here:

First—The bison or buffalo on the Ohio.

Second—Statements of General George Sanderson, Lancaster, O., April, 1870. War of 1812.

Third—Major Amos Stoddard, killed at Fort Meigs.

Fourth—General Harrison at Cleveland, O., 1812.

On the Bison and Buffalo in Ohio.

FORT HARMAR, Nov. 9, 1789.

General Harmar to General Thomas Mifflin, writes that he is about to move to Fort Washington, opposite mouth of Licking, and in describing the neighborhood says that buffalo are in abundance.

FORT WASHINGTON, Feb. 25, 1790.

Harmar to Jonathan Williams, Philadelphia, (extract)—"Buffalo, venison, turkeys, fish, of uncommon size (when the season arrives), we have in the greatest abundance."

FORT WASHINGTON, March 1, 1790.

Harmar to Daniel Clymer, of Reading, Pa., inviting him to visit the West, says—"We can afford you buffalo and venison in abundance."

Denny's Journal, October 4th, 1787—"Passed over a great deal of poor land, particularly near the Great Lick, (presumed to be in Indiana) which is not far distant from the road. When within a few miles of the Lick our hunters had leave to go ahead. Presently we heard the report of both their guns, and in a few minutes five buffaloes made their appearance, bearing furiously toward the head of the column. When within fifty paces the men in front were permitted to fire. This turned the heads of the animals; they passed along and received the fire of the whole line. Those only were shot down near the rear, where they approached within twenty paces."

Bison were found by James Smith in Southern Ohio in 1750. 1746—Seen by General Croghan near Lake Erie. 1772—Rev. D. Jones found them on the Scioto and at the mouth of the Great Guyandotte. M. de Vandreuil, in a memoir on Canada, 1687—"Buffaloes abound on the south shore of Lake Erie, but not on the north."

Ninety leagues up the Miami river at a place called La Glaise, (Defiance, O.) buffaloes are always found. They were observed "to wallow in the mud and eat the dirt."

Charlevoix writing in 1721, under date of June 1st, at Long Point on Lake Erie, says "I know that on the south side of the lake there are vast herds of wild cattle."

1787, March 27th. "Some of the hunters brought into the fort a buffalo that was eighteen hands high and weighed one thousand pounds." Journal Sergeant John Bruck, Fort Harmar.

The same year a company from Fort Harmar left for Vincennes, on their return to the Falls of Ohio. Under date of October 4th, Sergeant Bruck says: "On our march to-day we came across five buffaloes. They tried to force a passage through our column. The General ordered the men to fire on them; three were killed and the others wounded."

In a letter of Thomas Morehead, of Zanesville, Ohio, dated February 13th, 1863, he says: "Captain James Ross, who has resided here fifty-five years, says that Ebenezer and James Ryan often talked with him of having killed buffaloes on the branch of Will's creek, which still is called "Buffalo Fork," twenty miles east of Zanesville."

Dr. S. P. Hildreth, of Marietta, O., in a letter dated February 25th, 1863, says: "I came to Marietta in 1806, and have seen many of the old inhabitants who have killed them (buffaloes) and eaten their flesh. Near the vicinity of Salt Springs their paths or roads were very distinct and plain after I came to Ohio, and to this day, on the hills there are large patches of ground, destitute of bushes and trees, where they used to congregate to stamp off the flies, digging the surface into deep hollows, called "Buffalo Stamps."

Albert Gallatin, when a young man surveying in West Pennsylvania and Virginia, observed buffaloes. He says: "In my time, 1784–5, they (buffaloes) were abundant on the south side of the Ohio, joining the great and little Kanawha. I have during eight months lived principally on their flesh."

As he describes the buffalo "tracks" or roads leading from the buffalo pasture-ground in Ohio to the Onondaga Lake, a distance of over 200 miles.

Filson mentions the buffalo as an inhabitant of Kentucky in 1784.

HARMAR TO KNOX.

Nov. 24, 1787.

"We arrived on the 7th of October at the rapids of the Ohio. The distance from Fort Vincennes is about 130 miles. We saw no Indians or signs of Indians. We had an action with five buffaloes, who would have run through the column had they not been prevented by the men facing and firing a volley at them. They killed three of them."

HARMAR TO MICHAEL HILLEGAS, N. Y.

FORT HARMAR, April 30, 1789.

DEAR SIR: I had the pleasure of receiving your letter by Captain Bradford, and now send you some more of the buffalo wool of a superior quality to the former. In the months of February and March is the time the wool is in proper season. I am apprehensive what was at first sent will not answer your purpose. But few buffalo are killed in the vicinity of Muskingum. * * * *

I am, &c., JOS. HARMAR.

The last buffalo were killed in Ohio at Jackson county, in 1802, by a man who was living in 1838. Their paths or roads were then visible on the waters of Salt creek.

Statement of General George Sanderson, of Lancaster, O.

APRIL, 1870.

I was born at Carlisle, Cumberland county, Pa., January 10th, 1789, and removed to Kentucky with my parents in 1797. In 1800 we came to Ohio, and settled at Lancaster.

DEATH OF TECUMSEH.

At the battle of the Thames I commanded a company of Ohio Volunteers raised in Fairfield county. My command numbered 142 men. I remember Tecumseh. I saw him a number of times previous to the war. He was a man of huge frame, powerfully built, and was about six feet two inches in height. I saw his body on the Thames field before it was cold. Whether Colonel Johnson killed him or not I cannot say. During the battle all was smoke, noise, and confusion. Indeed, I never heard anyone speak of Colonel Johnson's having killed Tecumseh until years afterward.

Johnson was a brave man and was badly wounded in the battle in a very painful part —his knuckles, and also, I think, in his body. He was carried past me in a litter. In the evening I was appointed by Harrison to guard the prisoners with my company. The location was near a swamp. There is no doubt about the fact the Kentuckians skinned Tecumseh's body. *I saw them in the act.* They would cut strips about a half a foot in length and an inch and a half wide, which would stretch like gum-elastic. I saw a piece two inches long, which, when dry, could be stretched nearly a foot in length. That it was Tecumseh's body which was skinned there can be no question. I knew him, and the Indian prisoners under my charge continually pointed to his body, which lay close by, and uttered the most bewailing cries at his loss. By noon the day after the battle the body could hardly be recognized, it had been so thoroughly skinned. My men covered it with brush and logs, and it was probably eaten by wolves. Although the officers did not like the conduct of the Kentuckians, they dare not interfere. The troops from that State were infuriated at the massacre at the River Raisin, and their battle cry was, "Remember the massacre of the River Raisin." It was with difficulty that the Indian prisoners could be guarded, so general was the disposition of the Kentuckians to massacre them.

HULL'S SURRENDER.

In 1812 I raised a company in Fairfield county and formed a part of the regiment of Colonel Lewis Cass. Was surrendered at Detroit by General Hull. My opinion of General Hull's conduct, formed at the time, was —and events since have not changed it—that

Hull was an imbecile, not a traitor or a coward, but an imbecile, caused by drunkenness. He was an ardent drinker. On the day before the surrender, his son, Captain Abraham F. Hull, came among my men in a beastly state of drunkenness.

The British had erected fortifications across the river, which kept up a continuous fire upon us. Hull should never have allowed the enemy to construct those works.

On the day of the surrender I saw Hull frequently. His face about his mouth and chin was covered with tobacco juice, and I thought, in common with other officers, that the General was under the influence of liquor. He was surrounded with a military family, the members of which were fond of high times, wines and liquors. After his surrender, and before the enemy had entered, many officers begged Colonel James Findlay to take command of the American forces and resist the enemy, but he declined to take command. Colonel James Miller was also requested to take command, but he was unwilling to assume the responsibility, saying, "Matters have gone too far, but had Hull signified to me his intention of surrendering I would have assumed command and defended the fort to the last." Miller would have done so, too.

After the surrender General Isaac Brock, the British commander, came into the fort. We were ordered to the parade ground, and there piled up our muskets, swords, pistols, knives, cartridge boxes, etc. A heavy guard was placed over us, and we were then sent to the "citadel," where we were kept until released on parole. Hull and the regular officers were sent to Quebec. Brock was a heavily built man, about six feet three inches in height, broad shoulders, large hips, and was lame, walking with a cane. One of his eyes, the left one I think, was closed, and he was withal the ugliest officer I ever saw. He wore a scarlet uniform, with a sash wrapped tight around his waist.

When he came to my company, he said to me, "If your men attempt to escape, or to complain of their treatment, I cannot be answerable for the consequences, but if they remain quiet and orderly, will shortly be released and no harm shall befall them."

All the officers of our army who conversed with Brock; spoke of him as a very gallant and agreeable gentleman, who had seen much service in India and in the East.

Colonel George Paull, who commanded the Twenty-seventh United States Infantry, was a lawyer, and resided at St. Clairsville, O. I think he was born about the year 1775, in Pennsylvania. His father, of the same name, was a major of Pennsylvania Militia in Harmar's campaign. Colonel Paull was a man of small frame, light complexion, and did not enjoy good health while in the service. He was rather unpopular with the men, but was a gallant soldier, and fearless in the discharge of duty.

He died many years ago at St. Clairsville.

CHARLES T. SHERMAN.

Judge Sherman was a man of genial temperament, kind, social and agreeable, very popular with members of the bar. He was a lawyer of fine talent. In 1810 he came to Lancaster from Connecticut, and in 1811 returned for his wife and child. I have heard it stated that Mrs. Sherman carried her infant son from Connecticut to Ohio, (now Judge Charles T. Sherman, of Cleveland) on a pillow in front of her on horseback. Judge Sherman had been revenue collector for the Fairfield district, and became a poor man through the negligence, carelessness, and fraud of his deputies. He had the respect of citizens of every range of politics, and when elected Judge of the Supreme Court received every vote in the State House of Representatives. I revere his memory.

April 16, 1870. GEORGE SANDERSON.

MAJOR AMOS STODDARD, KILLED AT FORT MEIGS IN MAY, 1813.

Born in Woodbury, Conn., 1759, son of Anthony Stoddard, of Woodbury, and grandson of Rev. Anthony Stoddard, of Woodbury. Entered the Revolutionary army, 1779; served till 1783, when he settled at Boston, Mass., as Clerk of the Supreme Court. Studied law with Theophilus Parsons, admitted, and settled as a barrister at Hallowell, Me., in 1791. In 1799 appointed captain of artillery, promoted to major, June 7th, 1807; served in Louisiana as Military Governor of that Territory after the purchase from France. He was a man of ability. Early in the war of 1812 he was appointed by Harrison Chief of Artillery, Northwestern Army. At Fort Meigs, May 11th, 1813, he was wounded by a shell, which produced lockjaw. Author of "Political Crisis" and Sketches of Louisiana.

It is reported that by his own request his body was buried in one of the bastions. As yet the place of burial has not been identified.

His dirk, an elegant weapon, which he carried at Fort Meigs, is in possession of the Western Reserve Historical Society, Cleveland, O.

A brother resided in Boardman, Trumbull

county, O., and a nephew recently in East Cleveland.

NOTE —Anthony Stoddard died at Boston, March 15th, 1687, aged 70.

Solomon Stoddard (son of above), born in Boston, 1643, died February 11th, 1729, aged 85.

Anthony Stoddard (son of Solomon), born 1678, died September 6th, 1760, aged 82.

Cleveland, War of 1812.

On the 8th of July, 1813, General Harrison, leaving General Clay in command of Fort Meigs, proceeded to Lower Sandusky and Cleveland to make arrangements for the security of those places. The people residing at Cleveland, numbering but fifty souls, had become alarmed for the safety of their little settlement. Proctor had under his command thousands of ruthless savages, headed by Tecumseh, who never lost an opportunity to use the tomahawk and scalping knife.

Settlers in the vicinity of Sandusky and along the southwest shore of the lake had fallen victims to the atrocious mode of warfare adopted by Proctor and the uncivilized Indians who followed him. It was therefore natural that the inhabitants of Cleveland should feel some alarm. There was no blockhouse or other fortifications of consequence at this place. The apparent necessity for some defenses induced the people to call on Harrison for aid. That indefatigable commander, always looking to the comfort and safety of those in the region of his command, responded to the call of the citizens at once, and having arrived in the village he proceeded to adopt measures for its its defense. A stockade was erected at the foot of Ontario street, on the bank of the lake, made of pickets, reinforced in the interior with bags filled with sand, which made the place one of some strength, and though it would not have withstood the attack of a very large force, yet it answered the purpose in some measure, and produced a feeling of security. This was called Fort Huntington, in honor of our second Governor. The stockade was provided with two pieces of artillery and garrisoned by regulars under the command of Major Thomas L. Jessup, who afterward attained distinguished reputation in Virginia and in Florida, and became a Major General. Harrison, during his stay in Cleveland, or until about the 7th of July, encamped his men along the lake at the foot of Seneca street.

The General occupied a tent there, as also did such honored patriots as Lewis Cass, then a Brigadier General in the United States service; Col. Samuel Wells, Seventeenth U. S. Infantry; Col. Thomas D. Owings, Twenty-eighth U. S. Infantry; Col. George Paull, Seventeenth U. S. Infantry; J. C. Bartlett, Colonel and Quarter Master General of the army; James V. Ball, commanding Ball's heroic cavalry; Robert Morrison, Lieutenant Colonel, U. S. Army; Major George Tod, of the Nineteenth U. S. Infantry (father of ex-Governor Tod); Major William Trigg, Twenty-eighth U. S. Infantry; Major James Smiley; Major Richard Graham; Major L. Hukill, Assistant Inspector General; Major E. D. Wood, of the U. S. Engineer Corps, afterward slain at the sortie from Fort Erie, and Major George Croghan, the defender of Fort Stevenson.

> "How sleep the brave
> Who sink to rest,
> Forever by their country blest."

Of these illustrious men who once breathed, as it were, in our presence, not one survives. The last on that roll of heroes was General Cass, who died in 1866, "full of years and full of honors."

It was while at Cleveland that General Harrison received information from Colonel Richard M. Johnson, who had been ordered to join him at Cleveland with his regiment of mounted Kentuckians, that his horses were giving way, and asking permission to return to Kentucky and recruit. This request was granted, though it took one of the best regiments from Harrison's command.

The importance of Cleveland as an army depot was at once seen by the commanding General. During his visit he made arrangements for receiving supplies from the War Department by way of Cleveland.

www.ingramcontent.com/pod-product-compliance
Lightning Source LLC
LaVergne TN
LVHW010134110826
845151LV00002B/349

* 9 7 8 1 4 2 5 5 3 9 7 9 5 *